UNDERSTANDING AND MANAGING DIVERSITY

READINGS, CASES, AND EXERCISES

Carol P. Harvey
Assumption College

M. June Allard
Assumption College
Worcester State University, Professor Emerita

PEARSON

Boston   Columbus   Indianapolis   New York   San Francisco   Upper Saddle River
Amsterdam   Cape Town   Dubai   London   York St John   Milan   Munich   Paris   Montreal   Toronto
Delhi   Mexico City   São Paulo   Seoul   Singapore   Taipei   Tokyo

The fifth edition is dedicated to Molly

Editorial Director: Sally Yagan
Editor in Chief: Eric Svendsen
Acquisitions Editor: Brian Mickelson
Director of Editorial Services: Ashley Santora
Director of Marketing: Patrice Lumumba Jones
Senior Marketing Manager: Nikki Jones
Marketing Assistant: Ian Gold
Senior Managing Editor: Judy Leale
Supervisor: Lynn Savino
Production Project Manager: Debbie Ryan

Art Director: Jayne Conte
Cover Designer: Jodi Notowitz
Lead Media Project Manager: Lisa Rinaldi
Full-Service Project Management: Revathi Viswanathan/PreMediaGlobal
Composition: PreMediaGlobal
Printer/Binder: Courier Companies, Inc.
Cover Printer: Courier Companies, Inc.
Text Font: 10/12 Minion

If you purchased this book within the United States or Canada you should be aware that it has been imported without the approval of the Publisher or the Author.

Credits and acknowledgments borrowed from other sources and reproduced, with permission, in this textbook appear on appropriate page within text.

10 9 8 7 6 5 4 3 2 1

PEARSON   ISBN 10:   0-13-284770-1
                                    ISBN 13: 978-0-13-284770-4

CONTENTS

Diversity on the Web Assignment

Points of Law

w Writing Assignment

*Integrative Materials

🏛 Diversity on the Web Assignment

🖳 Points of Law

𝒘 Writing Assignment

*Integrative Materials

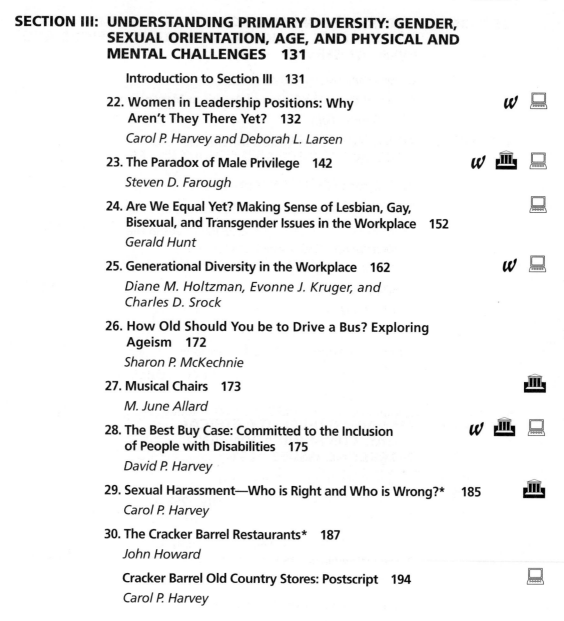
Diversity on the Web Assignment

Points of Law

W Writing Assignment

*Integrative Materials

🏛   Diversity on the Web Assignment

💻   Points of Law

W   Writing Assignment

*Integrative Materials

🏛 Diversity on the Web Assignment

💻 Points of Law

w Writing Assignment

*Integrative Materials

PREFACE

In terms of diversity, much has changed since the fourth edition of *Understanding and Managing Diversity: Readings, Cases and Exercises* was published. There is an African American president in the White House, the U.S. government has ended the "Don't Ask, Don't Tell" policy for gays in the military, there are three women on the Supreme Court, and there were female candidates for the presidency and the vice-presidency in the last national election.

However, progressive these events may seem, they do not tell the whole story about changing stereotypes, prejudice, and workplace policies and practices. We have prepared this fifth edition with this question as the theme: **How can organizations change to meet the challenges of diverse stakeholders: employees, customers, suppliers, and communities?**

NEW IN THE FIFTH EDITION

In response to suggestions from our reviewers, feedback from instructors, and our own classroom experiences, we have incorporated the following content and pedagogical innovations to improve the students' learning experiences:

- The content has been substantially changed and updated to reflect changing diversity issues in today's workplace. The fifth edition features *eighteen* new and *fifteen* revised articles/ cases/exercises.
- We have reorganized the text into six sections, each of which ends with integrative learning experiences: cases, exercises, and broad discussion questions that are designed to help students synthesize their learning across the topics.

    Section I—Understanding who you are and how it affects your perceptions and stereotypes of those with whom you interact. This section ends with an example of an organization that has utilized diversity to its business advantage (Pitney Bowes).

    Sections II and III—Understanding how members of specific social identity groups experience the workplace in terms of primary diversity. These sections conclude with cases that provide examples of an organization that has changed its approach to diversity management as a result of a major civil rights lawsuit (Coca-Cola) and one that has not made such progress (Cracker Barrel).

    Section IV—Understanding how the secondary and more changeable aspects of diversity can impact individuals and organizations. The integrative case provides an example of how an organization struggled with a hiring decision and discrimination involving multiple social identities, age (in terms of youth), and weight, neither of which are protected under current federal civil rights legislation (Fairfax Memorial).

    Section V—Understanding the ethical, legal, and economic challenges that diversity brings to organizations. This section closes with an exercise reviewing legal considerations and a case that demonstrates how poor diversity management and failure to change can result in legal challenges and lost marketing opportunities (UBS).

    Section VI—Understanding how organizations can change through initiatives such as improved corporate leadership, active employee resource groups, effective social responsibility/ philanthropy efforts, supplier diversity, and training programs. Both the diversity awards article and diversity audit assignment provide students with an opportunity to learn how the change loop is completed through external evaluation and feedback. The text closes with a case that demonstrates what happens when an organization lacks effective management and programs (Air Force Academy).

- New and timely diversity topics have been added, including racial identity, work-life balance, military veterans, diversity leadership, corporate philanthropy, workplace communication, marketing to diverse consumers, training and diversity awards.
- A Best Practices feature that provides examples of successful innovations that are intended to stimulate creative thinking about managing diversity.
- New cases such as UBS and Best Buy join revised cases such as Coca-Cola, Cracker Barrel, Fairfax, and the Air Force Academy. *Additional cases can be found in the Instructor's Manual available online to faculty.*
- New exercises on attribution, age, intercultural communication, sexual harassment, and legal issues have been added.
- Expansion of existing pedagogical features include: Points of Law expanded from seven to thirteen; Diversity on the Web from twenty-eight to thirty-one, and Writing Assignments from eight to twenty-two.
- Substantial revisions of existing discussion questions that require higher-order critical thinking skills.

FOCUS OF THE FIFTH EDITION

This text was written to meet the needs of students and instructors in college- and graduate-level diversity courses. In terms of content, this edition is focused on changing diversity management policies and practices, primarily in North American organizations. Although space limitations prevent us from broadening this to be as inclusive as we would like of an international workplace, we have tried to include some of the aspects of our global economy that cross over by incorporating topics such as immigration, call centers, and Canadian employment law.

Our approach is unique in that we consider diversity as a complex issue, crossing into many disciplines and requiring a wide range of expertise. So, we have once again utilized a diversity of authors and experts: experienced interdisciplinary instructors (from business, psychology, economics, theology, law, politics, history, etc.) as well as practitioners (diversity trainers and corporate managers, etc.). Although somewhat constrained by the difficulties of obtaining permissions for electronic duplication for the eBook, we are still able to feature seminal articles by noted authors such as Horace Miner, R. Roosevelt Thomas, Jr., Peggy McIntosh, Thomas Sowell, Amitai Etzioni, and Jeswald W. Salacuse.

Although this book was written primarily as a business text, we are well aware that it is used in many non-business-related diversity classes because of its interdisciplinary approach and the diversity of the authors. Consequently, the variety and scope of the material in it was carefully designed and written for usage both in business and non-business courses.

The Association to Advance Collegiate Schools of Business (AACSB)

The AACSB accreditation standards cite cultural diversity among employees and customers as one of the four major challenges to business education and require that accredited institutions integrate diversity education into business programs in a manner consistent with their missions. Because of the flexibility of the readings and cases and exercises in this text, instructors can easily design their courses around their needs. Sample syllabi are available in the online Instructor's Manual to make such adaptations easier for faculty.

FACULTY RESOURCES

Instructor Resource Center

At http://www.pearsonhighered.com/educator, instructors can access a variety of print, media, and presentation resources available with this text in downloadable, digital format.

Once you register, you will not have additional forms to fill out, or multiple usernames and passwords to remember to access new titles and/or editions. As a registered faculty member, you can log in directly to download resource files, and receive immediate access and instructions for installing course management content to your campus server.

Our dedicated technical support team is ready to assist instructors with questions about the media supplements that accompany this text. Visit http://247pearsoned.custhelp.com for answers to frequently asked questions and toll-free user support phone numbers.

To download the supplements available with this book, please visit http://www.pearsonhighered. com/educator. The following supplements are available for download to adopting instructors:

- *Instructor's Manual*   This resource features over 500 pages of information that will make teaching about diversity easier and more productive. To plan your course, there are subject matrices, outlines, sample syllabi, summaries, answers to discussion questions, extra cases, teaching tips, a test bank, assessment materials, and a guide to using films in diversity classes. This manual is available for download from http://www.pearsonhighered.com/educator.
- *PowerPoints*   The PowerPoints that accompany this text feature basic outlines and key points from each chapter, and are available for download from http://www.pearsonhighered. com/educator.

ACKNOWLEDGMENTS

Producing this text requires a diversity of talents. We are most grateful to our contributors whose expertise makes this text possible; to Assumption College staff, particularly Lynn Cooke, Carmella Murphy, Maria Alicata, Philip Waterman, and Kelly Jo Woodside whose technical, clerical, and research skills were so willingly given; to our reviewers Donita Whitney-Bammerlin of Kansas State University, Robert DelCampo of The University of New Mexico, Sheryl Hurner of American River College, Dyan Pease of Sacramento City College, and Ellen J. Mullen of Iowa State University, and to the staff at Prentice Hall who make all of this happen: Eric Svendsen, Editor-in-Chief; Ashley Santora, Director of Editorial Services; Brian Mickelson, Acquisitions Editor; and Carter Anderson, Editorial Assistant. We would like to extend *very* special thank yous to Meg O'Rourke and Ashley Santora, our editorial project managers, whose support and assistance was invaluable to the completion of this text.

ABOUT THE AUTHORS

Carol P. Harvey, EdD is a Professor and former Chair of the Business Studies Department at Assumption College. Her doctorate is from the University of Massachusetts in Teaching and Learning in Higher Education with a specialization in Organizational Behavior. She has an MBA and Certificate of Advanced Studies from Northeastern University and a MA in Psychology.

Formerly employed as a manager at the Xerox Corporation, her research interests include implementing diversity initiatives in organizations and improving critical thinking skills in higher education. She has taught courses such as Managing Diversity, International Communication, Organizational Behavior, Organizational Change, Training and Development, Marketing and Small Business Management on the undergraduate and graduate levels. She has served as an evaluator on six NEASC college accreditation teams.

Professor Harvey received the ALANA faculty award for 2011at Assumption College and she is the co-recipient of the 2004 Roethlisberger Memorial Award from the Organizational Behavior Teaching Society for the best article from the *Journal of Management Education*, "Critical Thinking in the Management Classroom: Bloom's Taxonomy as a Learning Tool" and the 2002 recipient of the Volunteer of the Year Award from the Center for Women in Enterprise (charvey@assumption.edu or coolidgeroad@verizon.net).

M. June Allard is *Professor Emerita* from Worcester State University where she served as Chair of the Psychology and the Social and Behavioral Science departments. She holds a PhD from Michigan State University in Social Psychology with a specialization in cross-cultural research. She is the recipient of nine national fellowships, numerous Distinguished Service and Outstanding Teaching awards, and is listed in a number of national and international directories of scientists and women leaders.

Dr. Allard has conducted program reviews and evaluations for over thirty years and is a recognized expert in this field. She currently maintains a consulting practice, designing and conducting research and program evaluations. Formerly employed as a senior scientist in the Research and Development industry in Washington, DC, she has directed a wide range of projects on government contracts in industry as well as in university research institutes. She has been a site visitor for the New England Association of Schools and Colleges for collegiate accreditation and on the Accreditation Visiting Committee for the American Psychological Association (APA) as well as a member of the APA Department Consulting Service. Dr. Allard designs program assessment and teaches Research and Evaluation in the School Counseling gradute program at Asumption College (jallard1833@yahoo.com).

INTRODUCTION TO UNDERSTANDING AND MANAGING DIVERSITY

GOALS

- To understand why diversity management requires organizational change
- To present common definitions of terms and theoretical frameworks which provide a foundation for this text
- To explain how diversity can become a competitive advantage in today's marketplace

Welcome to the fifth edition of *Understanding and Managing Diversity: Readings Cases and Exercises.* Because workplace diversity is now accepted as a fact of organizational life, there is a corresponding need to learn how to capitalize on its advantages and to minimize its complexities. On a daily basis, workers still struggle with prejudice, sexual harassment, and discrimination. Organizations still get sued over civil rights violations, overlook opportunities to benefit from their diverse workforces and boards, and fail to see the marketing potential of diverse consumers. While many organizations have tried to adapt their policies and practices to the more female, less white, more open about religion, and sexual orientation, and multi-generational workforce, the transition is not easy and corporate leadership is often lacking. As a result, organizations are facing new challenges and the need for change. Consequently, *the theme for this edition is understanding diversity and managing the organizational change process for today's workplace.* (See Figure I.1.)

Since the last edition was published, there are additional forces pushing for the *unfreezing of* traditional ways of managing diversity: more acknowledgment of different dimensions of diversity, new legislation, a movement to value differences, growing opportunities to serve new global and domestic markets, and an awareness that diversity if valued and managed well can produce more motivated employees and a competitive advantage to the bottom line, that is, the business case for diversity.

At the same time, there is a growing realization that this *change* effort will happen only with solid diversity leadership both on the corporate and employee network group levels, assessment of diversity efforts, and effective training that changes individual attitudes and organizational cultures in terms of differences. The *refreezing* that results produces new ways of working, new policies and programs, community outreach to diverse populations, and assessment that leads to further strategic changes. Throughout this text, we have provided examples of "Best Practices," that is, changes that have worked for specific organizations. However, as the R. Roosevelt Thomas article points out, these initiatives will not necessarily work for every organization but are intended only to demonstrate the creative solutions that some organizations have implemented.

UNDERSTANDING WORKFORCE DIVERSITY

We have been writing diversity textbooks since 1995 and we have seen the definition of diversity evolve and broaden from a micro individual level of differences to the macro level that includes both internal and external stakeholders. Initially, diversity was defined by the dimensions protected under **Title VII of the Civil Rights Act of 1964** (race, color, national origin, religion, and sex). As more legislation protecting specific groups such as people with disabilities and older workers was passed, more categories were added. However, these definitions excluded many differences and did not account for either the individual saliency of a dimension to a particular person's identity or to the complexities of having multiple identities such as being a Black gay man. Some organizations use this approach to define diversity. For example, Ernst & Young, the consulting services giant, defines diversity not just "by race and gender; it encompasses the whole human experience—age, culture, education, personality, skills, and life experiences" (Ernst & Young, 2019, p. i).

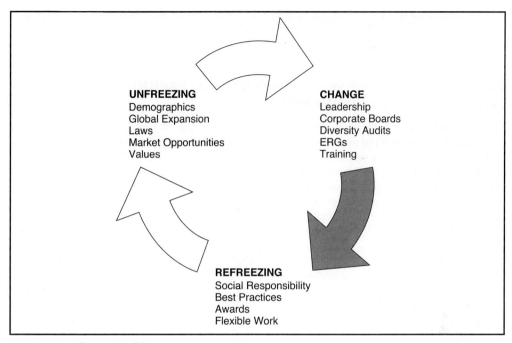

FIGURE I-1   Change Model

The concerns of a definition that lists differences is that it implies that all members of a group have similar needs; it may feel exclusionary to some people, particularly white men, and that it positions diversity more as an individual or social identity issue but not as an organizational imperative for change.

> Using another perspective, AT&T's chief diversity officer, Cindy Brinkley, provides a strategic definition that considers diversity in terms of its potential as a competitive market advantage, that is, the business case for diversity.
>
> It's really a recognition that achieving sustainable growth requires that we always remember: the markets and customers we serve are diverse . . . our ownership is diverse . . . and our workforce is diverse. So being inclusive of a wide range of perspectives makes us more competitive and more likely to be a provider of choice, employer of choice and a preferred business partner." (Cindy Brinkley, 2010)

Sodexho, #1 on the 2010 *DiversityInc* Top 50 Companies for Diversity list, defines diversity more in terms of a broad stakeholder model by focusing on inclusion and extending organizational diversity to include the external stakeholders.

> At Sodexho, we believe that diversity and inclusion is a business imperative and ethical and social responsibility are grounded in our core values of team spirit and the spirit of service and progress. In our continuing effort to attain an inclusive organization, we embrace, leverage and respect the diversity of our workforce, our clientele and the communities in which we work and serve. (Sodexousa.com)

> We prefer a broad definition that is inclusive of many newly recognized types of difference but also recognizes the need for organizations to change the way they manage their people and structure work as well as how they interact with their external environments (suppliers, customers, and communities). For this text we

define ***diversity*** as both the ways that people differ that may affect their workplace experiences in terms of performance, motivation, communication, and inclusion and the need for organizational strategies that address the diversity of the changing external environment such as customers, suppliers, and the community.

UNDERSTANDING OURSELVES AND OTHERS: PREJUDICE, STEREOTYPES, DISCRIMINATION

Until we examine our own knowledge, attitudes and beliefs, it is difficult, if not impossible, to appreciate others' differences. Section I of the text sets the stage for this process. Begin by understanding that the life experiences of others may be very different from your own. Bringing diverse workers into an organization is seldom a seamless transition. Some may have experienced considerable **prejudice**, that is, a preconceived evaluative *attitude* based on their social group memberships. Prejudices can come from many sources including our socialization as children, the media, our peers, and so on. For example, as McNickles points out in her article, there is documented research that job applicants with African American sounding names are less apt to be called in for a job interview than equally qualified candidates with traditional Anglo-American names.

Although prejudices can be positive, neutral, or negative, and conscious or unconscious, it is the negative and unconscious ones that most often lead to the **stereotypes**, that is, generalized beliefs that all members of a group possess the same characteristics that are the most problematic in the workforce. For example, an interviewer may find herself thinking more positively about young job applicants than older ones with more experience simply because she assumes that all of the younger ones will have a superior understanding of technology.

Like prejudice, stereotypes are learned rather than innate and can be positive or neutral, as well as negative. However, negative stereotypes are "more likely in groups with unbalanced representation of subgroups, i.e., when there is a minority" (Chen & DiTomaso, 1996). The psychologist, Gordon Allport wrote that, "The human mind must think with the aid of categories, . . . (which are) the basis for normal prejudgment. We cannot possibly avoid this process. Orderly living depends on it" (p. 20, 1954).

Gregory Sawin (1991) uses complexity-identity theory to clarify the influence of stereotypes on our thinking by referring to them as "mental maps." He writes that the accuracy of our perceptions and judgments depends on the quality and quantity of the direct experience we have with people who represent a category, that is, a social identity group. The more we have experienced what he calls "the territory," the more able we are to know that those within that category are not all alike and may exhibit a wide range of behaviors. This should improve the accuracy of our "map" of these individuals.

While stereotypes are mental processes, they can lead to **discrimination**, which is a *behavior* that occurs when members of a social identity group are treated unfairly or unequally, because of their group memberships. Negative stereotypes can be particularly problematic in the workforce because they may influence important decisions (i.e., become the basis for discriminatory actions) in hiring, promotions performance appraisals, and so on. If we acknowledge our prejudices, and realize that stereotypes do not apply to all members of a particular group, it can help us to avoid conscious or unconscious discriminatory actions. If we deny our prejudices, and fail to recognize our stereotypes, we are more apt to discriminate.

UNDERSTANDING SOCIAL GROUP MEMBERSHIPS

As much as we may like to believe that "all people are created equal" in reality, our group memberships often do affect our personal and professional lives. Marilyn Loden (1996) provides a framework by dividing these dimensions of memberships into two interlocking categories: **primary** that are more permanent, less changeable, and usually more central to one's self-perception and **secondary**, those differences that are more changeable and less visible. It is important to remember that people have multiple social identities and that this model does not account for individual saliency. For example, to a working mother, her status as a parent, (secondary) may be more relevant to her performance, decisions, career motivation, and so on, than her gender (primary).

Loden's Dimensions of Diversity	
Primary Dimensions	**Secondary Dimensions**
Age	Geographic Location
Gender	Military and Work Experience
Mental/Physical abilities	Family Status
Race	Income, Religion
Ethnic Heritage	First Language, Education
Sexual Orientation	Organizational Role and Level Communication and Work Styles
Adapted from Loden, M. (1996). *Implementing Diversity*. (New York: McGraw-Hill).	

Sections II and III of this text cover the primary dimensions and Section IV addresses the secondary characteristics of diversity.

MANAGING DIVERSITY AND ORGANIZATIONAL CHANGE

While many of the forces pushing organizations to adapt to diversity are external and not controllable, organizational culture, strategy, policies, and procedures can be managed. The following three frameworks will help you to analyze Sections V and VI, managing diversity and change in organizations.

The first is Schein's levels of culture (see the following box).

Levels of Organizational Culture	
Surface Level Artifacts (visible)	Includes organizational structures, processes, dress, rituals, physical layout, etc.
Values (espoused and operational)	Espoused values are what the what the organization *says* it values in terms, of strategies philosophies, etc., not necessarily what it *does*. What it does are the operational values.
Basic Underlying Assumptions	Real source of values and behavior; Philosophies that are sometimes unconscious and difficult to change
Adapted from Schein, E. (1997). *Organizational Culture and Leadership*. (San Francisco: Jossey-Bass), pp. 16–27.	

According to Schein, in order to understand an organizational culture, one needs to assess its artifacts (who has power, how the work is structured, what policies and rituals are in place, etc.). However, these are difficult to interpret until you know if the espoused (what they say they do) and operational (what they really do) values coincide. Further analysis should lead to understanding the underlying assumptions which determine if and how an organization will deal with diversity.

A second approach is to analyze where an organization is starting this change process by applying Thomas and Ely's three-stage paradigm model. The first stage is the *discrimination and fairness paradigm*, that is, where an organization is focused on avoiding lawsuits through recruitment and retention of diverse employees who are expected to assimilate into the dominant group. The second is the *access and legitimacy paradigm,* where diversity is considered as a competitive advantage in terms of understanding changing customer markets. The third, where diversity really works best, is the *learning and effectiveness paradigm,* which occurs when an organization has internalized diversity as part of its mission, connects the needs of diverse workers to the way that work is done, and makes workers feel valued and included. Thomas and Ely suggest that the most effective way to build a business case is to link diversity to the specific needs and mission of an organization, such as optimizing market opportunities, developing creative solutions to problems, and decreasing the turnover of talented diverse employees. Then, make a plan to achieve these goals and track and measure these long-term results both quantitatively and qualitatively, and adjust as necessary, that is, the diversity change model in action.

A third useful approach is to think about organizational diversity in terms of achieving a change called by Miller & Katz, an **inclusion breakthrough.** This is breaking out of the diversity-in-a-box model by changing the culture to one that not only values and supports the individual but also unleashes the power of diversity to change the organization and operationalize diversity as a competitive advantage. (See Diversity on the Web.) As you proceed through the text, you will be expected to apply all three of these models to the cases that are assigned.

A student once asked one of the authors, what can one person do to change workplace diversity? We hope that after you complete this course, you will understand her answer, "everything." We have provided the basic information on individual, group, and organizational diversity. The rest is up to you.

Bibliography

Allport, G. (1954). *The nature of prejudice.* Reading, MA: Addison-Wesley.

Brinkley, C. (2010). Media inquiry from A T & T corporate communications.

December 16, 2010.

Ernst & Young. (2010). Is your campus environment inclusive? Retrieved on December 14, 2010, from www.ey.com.

Chen,C., & DiTomaso, N. (1996). Performance appraisal and demographic diversity:

Issues regarding appraisals, appraisers and appraising. In *Managing Diversity: Human Resource Strategies for Transforming the Workplace,* E. Kossek & S Lobel (Eds.), Blackwell Business: Cambridge MA.

Loden, M. (1996). *Implementing diversity.* Chicago: Business One Irwin. p. 16.

Miller, F.A., & Katz, J. H. (2002). The inclusion breakthrough: Unleashing the real power of diversity. San Francisco: Berrett-Koehler.

Sawin, G. (1991). How stereotypes influence opinions about individuals. *Et Cetra,* vol. 48, 2, Summer, 210–212.

Schein, E. (1997). *Organizational culture and leadership.* SanFrancisco: Jossey-Bass.

Sodexho.us.com. Retrieved December 16, 2010.

Thomas, D. A., & Ely, R.J. (1996). Making differences matter: A new paradigm for managing diversity. *Harvard Business Review,* September–October.

Diversity on the Web

Go to www.bkconnection.com and search for "The Inclusion Breakthrough: Unleashing the Real Power of Diversity" by Fredrick Miller and Judith Katz. Read the excerpt provided. The main premise here is that diversity without inclusion does not work. What are the barriers that prevent an organization from building an inclusive culture and what are the costs of not having one?

1

Understanding Individual Perspectives of Diversity

In this section, students will

- Examine their individual knowledge and perspectives about diversity.
- Have an opportunity to think about the emotional issues involved in learning about workplace diversity.
- Learn why effective diversity management initiatives have to be specific to the culture, leadership, and mission of an organization.
- Have an opportunity to integrate learning through case analysis and exploring diversity in an organization.

Section I opens with an evaluation of your basic knowledge about diversity (Aurelio & Laib; Gorski) and provides the opportunity for introspection and honest discussion about prejudices, stereotypes, attributions, and privileges (Allard; Miner; Bowman; McIntosh). The Dunlap reading presents theories of racial development and discusses the challenges of taking a diversity course. Differences often bring out conflicts that can be positive if well managed. However, if differences are ignored, the conflict usually escalates (Parker).

This section closes by introducing the reader to an explanation of what is really meant by "best practices" for diversity management (Thomas) and an example of how diversity is well managed at Pitney Bowes (Harvey). Lastly, there is an opportunity for students to evaluate diversity at their college, university, or workplace (Harvey).

DIVERSITY!

Jeanne M. Aurelio
Bridgewater State University

Christopher Laib
University of Massachusetts, Dartmouth

GOALS

- To enable students to test their knowledge of some aspects of diversity in an engaging way
- To learn about diversity and its wide-ranging subject matter
- To become acquainted with fellow students

Most Americans in the workforce experience people who are very different from themselves on a daily basis. Those differences certainly include temperament and personality, but also culture, gender, ethnicity, religion, sexual orientation, ability, age, and size differences. Much is known about the kinds of differences people possess, yet far too much knowledge is available for any single person to know all about diversity. What is needed is openness to differences, and the understanding that everyone's behavior is partially influenced by their diversity profiles. In the interest of being able to work with others (and they with us), we must continually strive both to educate ourselves on what is known about how and why people are different, and to keep an open mind.

PURPOSE

The purpose of the game **Diversity!** is to provide knowledge about many areas of diversity, plus some information about the U.S. laws regarding these differences. Because the game is played in teams, it will also enable students to get to know one another.

HOW TO PLAY

1. Choose teams of 4–5 people or more. One team will randomly be chosen to select the first question category and level.

2. All teams will debate their answers internally and one team member will raise a hand or use their assigned team noisemaker when the team is ready. The instructor will call on the first team to respond. If their answer is correct, they will receive the number of points indicated and choose the next question category and level. If their answer is incorrect, the instructor will call upon the second quickest team to respond, and so on.

3. In the event that no team answers the question correctly, the instructor will give the correct response. The team that chose last still has control of the board and should choose the next question. Scores will be recorded and the winning team announced at the end of one or two rounds, depending upon the time available. As the class responds to various questions, make note of those you would like to discuss at the conclusion of the game.

Questions on the game board cover five levels of difficulty. Here are some practice questions at various levels. (Answers appear below in Figure 1-1.)

1. *Level 2:* In 1983, this astronaut became the first American woman in space.
2. *Level 3:* This is the number of languages known to be spoken in the world.
3. *Level 4:* In cultures that embrace this religion, men may have multiple wives while women must remain monogamous.

DISCUSSION QUESTIONS

After one or two rounds of **Diversity!** the class should focus upon the following questions intended to stimulate interest and learning.

1. Which of the **Diversity!** questions would you like to discuss further?

2. What did you learn as a result of this game that you did not know prior to it?

3. In what areas did you notice that you and/or class members were particularly knowledgeable? In what areas did you lack knowledge?

4. What is your reaction to this experience?

5. How do you think this experience ties in with the purpose of your course?

Jeanne M. Aurelio, DBA, is a Professor of Management at Bridgewater State University. She has consulted with numerous corporations and federal agencies on topics including organizational performance, diversity, managerial effectiveness, and performance counseling. Contact her at jaurelio@bridgew.edu.

Christopher Laib is the Assistant Director of the University of Massachusetts Dartmouth Student Activities, Involvement & Leadership Office. He has worked in higher education administration for over fifteen years, presenting training sessions dealing with diversity, ethics, and organization/team development. Contact him at claib@umassd.edu.

Instructor: To access the DIVERSITY! game, see the online Instructor Manual under DIVERSITY!

1. Sally Ride   2. 6,800   3. Islam

FIGURE 1-1   **Answers to Practice Questions**

Understanding Attribution Theory by Using Visual Literacy

Carol P. Harvey
Assumption College

When Miriam went into the Vice-President's office, she slammed the door behind her. Two co-workers witnessed this behavior and began to speculate why she did this. Her best friend Jennifer hoped that Miriam was filing a sexual harassment complaint about the off color jokes that that creepy Sean has been telling the women in the office. Jennifer admitted that although she didn't have the courage to turn Sean in, it was about time somebody complained and you could always count on Miriam to take a leadership role. Dean, who often conflicted with Miriam over key accounts, thought that she was angry about her recent performance appraisal and the small raises that due to the recession the company was giving all managers this year. To him this was another example of Miriam's emotional and selfish behavior in the office when things didn't go her way. He also said that behavior reminded him of why he believed that women were not suitable for management positions.

Attempting to explain why someone does something is called making an **attribution.** Quite simply, we instantaneously: 1) see someone do something 2) judge the intention of the other person and 3) draw conclusions about the cause of the action based upon our own thoughts, prejudices and biases. In the case above, these co-workers are providing different reasons for Miriam's behavior. Notice that her friend's perception of Miriam's behavior is that it was externally caused by a coworker's actions, i.e., an external attribution. In contrast, Dean made an internal attribution, i.e., he attributed the reason for Miriam's behavior to personality characteristics and extends his attribution to a stereotype about all women. It is common to make external attributions about people we consider like us, and more likable, i.e., in group members and internal attributions about people we consider unlike us and less likable, i.e., out group members.

Although neither person *really* knows the cause of Miriam's behavior at this point, that doesn't stop the unconscious attribution process.

Attribution is a very complex theory but according to Kelly's highly researched theory of causal attribution, people classify behaviors into two categories of causality: internal causes which the individual can control like being honest or having a hard work ethic or external causes which an individual has no control over such as another coworker or the economy (1972).

If we learn that other people act like this one (consensus is high), this person behaves in the same manner at other times (consistency is high) and that the same person does not act in the same manner in other situations (distinctiveness is high), we are likely to conclude that this person's behavior stemmed from external causes. In contrast, imagine learning that other people do not act like this one (consensus is low), this person behaves in the same manner at other times (consistency is high) and that this person acts in the same manner in other situations (distinctiveness is low). In this case, we would conclude that this person's behavior stemmed from *internal* causes.

(GREENBURG, 2010, pp. 77–78)

It is important to remember that we make our attributions based on our perceptions which are subjective judgments and not necessarily factual. Psychologists tell us that people make judgments about other people in the first seven to seventeen seconds that they interact with a stranger. When we are trying to decide why someone did something and we don't know that person, there is a tendency to attribute causality to our perceptions about that person's social group identities, i.e., to rely on our stereotypes of that group as Dean did of women managers in the case. Our perceptions are influenced by three factors: our values, attitudes, motivators, and past experiences; the physical setting in which the interaction occurs and the characteristics of the person we are perceiving.

Although the attribution process is quite complex, three factors determine if we attribute causality to internal or external factors: distinctiveness, consensus and consistency.

Distinctiveness   Does the situation represent usual or unusual behavior? In this case, Jennifer perceives Miriam's behavior as unusual (high distinctiveness) but Dean perceives it as another example of Miriam being selfish and emotional at work (low distinctiveness).

Consensus   Do most people act in the same way that the person we are observing is acting? Jennifer felt that others had complained yet no action was taken. So Miriam's anger was justified (high consensus). However, according to Dean most male managers would not behave this way (low consensus).

Consistency   Is this an isolated incident or is it consistent over time? To Jennifer Miriam is a good performer, who often stands up for what is right (high consistency). To Dean, Miriam always behaves emotionally when things don't go her way, etc. (high consistency).

> Low consensus + high consistency + low distinctiveness = Internal attribution
>
> High consensus + high consistency + high distinctiveness = External attribution

So, in applying attribution theory to this case, Jennifer concludes that Miriam's behavior was caused by external factors (a coworker's behavior over which she has no control) while Dean concludes that Miriam's behavior was caused by internal factors (her selfishness and emotionalism), and sees her behavior as representative of women in general. This provides an example of another aspect of attribution theory, **fundamental attribution error** which is the tendency to attribute others' actions to internal causes or traits while ignoring possible external causes, such as the real one: somebody had keyed her new car in the company parking lot and she was angry!

LEARNING ABOUT ATTRIBUTION THEORY THROUGH VISUAL LITERACY

Visual literacy is defined as "interpreting, analyzing, evaluating meaning and judging" through some visual media. (Christopherson, 1993, p. 170) Pictures can be a powerful tool for understanding because they draw on our own cultural experiences (Thomas, Place & Hillyard, 2008) to help us understand attribution. The following exercise will enable you to apply this theory through a visual literacy experience.

BEFORE CLASS

1. Go to one of the following photography websites. Select a photo that interests you. Enlarge it and print it out. (www.images.search.yahoo.com & images.google.com and search for "diversity in the workplace")
2. Observe the photograph carefully. Really look and think about what it implies to you. There is no right or wrong answer, just your perceptions.
3. Write a one page description of what you saw in this photograph—What is happening here? Describe the characters and the situation. Why are they behaving this way?

IN CLASS

1. Form groups of two to three students. Each student will read his essay. There should be *no* comments or conversation at this point. As each students reads, the other members of the group should write down the answers to the following questions for *each* essay:
   a. How distinctive were the behaviors described? Does anything in this essay suggest that this behavior applies to other situations besides this particular one?
      Yes—Characters in photo would behave the same way in other situations = low distinction
      No—Characters in photo would behave differently in other situations = high distinction
   b. Is the behavior described in the photo something that happens frequently, i.e., is it consistent?
      Yes—Characters often behave the same way = high consistency
      No—Characters do not often behave the same way = low consistency
   c. Does the essay imply that that other people would behave in the same way as the characters in the photos, i.e., is there consensus?
      Yes = high consensus
      No = low consensus
   d. Was the behavior pictured in the photo attributed to internal or external causes?
2. After all essays have been read, the group members should share their observations with the author in the same order as the essays were read.
3. As a group what has this exercise taught you about the accuracy of your own attributions? Plan to share this answer with the class.

Bibliography

Christopher, J. T. (1996). The growing need for visual literacy at the university. *Visual Quest: Journeys Toward Visual Literacy*, edited by R. E. Griffin, J. M. Hunter, and W. J. Gibbs. International Visual Literacy Conference Proceedings: Cheyenne, WY, 169–175.

Greenburg, J. (2011). *Behavior in organizations.* Upper Saddle River: N.J.: Pearson Prentice Hall.

Kelly, H.H. (1972) *Casual scemata and the attribution process.* New York: General Learning Press.

Spencer, D. (2008). The attribution process: A study of three major theorists. Retrieved from psychenergy.com/doryArticles/attribution.html on November 2, 2010.

Thomas, E., Place, N. & Hillyard, C. (2008). Students and teachers learning to see. *College Teaching,* 56, 1, pp. 23–27.

Special thanks to Janine Dewitt, Carolyn Oxenford and Marcia Dursi from Marymount University. Their presentation on visual literacy at the 2010, Improving University Teaching Conference inspired this exercise.

I AM . . .

M. June Allard

Assumption College
Worcester State University, Professor Emerita

Instructions

1. Think about how you would describe yourself to someone you have never met. On each line below, write a single-word description.

I AM a(an)

_____   _____

_____   _____

_____   _____

_____   _____

_____   _____

_____   _____

_____   _____

_____   _____

2. Place a star by the three most important descriptors.

DIVERSITY AWARENESS QUIZ

Paul C. Gorski
George Mason University

Please circle the correct answer to each question.

1. According to the National Center for Educational Statistics, what is the percentage of U.S. schools with no teachers of color on staff?
   a. 0%
   b. 20%
   c. 40%
   d. 60%

2. According to a study by the American Association of Physicians for Human Rights, what percentage of physicians report witnessing a colleague giving reduced care or refusing care to lesbian, gay, or bisexual patients?
   a. 12%
   b. 32%
   c. 52%
   d. 72%

3. Compared with their U.S. born peers, how likely are immigrant men in the U.S. ages 18–39, to be in jail or prison, according to a 2008 report from the Immigration Policy Center?
   a. 15 times more likely
   b. 5 times more likely
   c. Equally likely
   d. 5 times less likely

4. According to the U.S. Census bureau, the median annual income for U.S. white men, 25 years or older, who have earned graduate degrees, is $80,000. What are the median annual incomes for Latina and Native American women, age 25 or older who have earned graduate degrees?
   a. $80,000 & $80,000 respectively
   b. $70,000 and $68,000 respectively
   c. $60,000 and $62,000 respectively
   d. $50,000 and $40,000 respectively

5. What percentage of gay, lesbian, bisexual and transgender high school students report that their teachers "never" or "rarely" respond to homophobic remarks made by other students, according to a national study by GLSEN?
   a. 15.1%
   b. 37.8%
   c. 3.63.2%
   d. 84.5%*

6. Based on a 2007 report from the Economic Policy Institute, the *annual* earnings of the average full-time U.S. worker is roughly equal to:
   a. The *hourly* earnings of the average CEO in the U.S.
   b. The *daily* earnings of the average CEO in the U.S.
   c. The *weekly* earnings of the average CEO in the U.S.
   d. The *monthly* earnings of the average CEO in the U.S.

7. A Princeton Study of elite universities in the U.S. found that legacy applicants—people usually white and wealthy, with a parent or grandparent who attended the institution—are far more privileged by the legacy status than applicants of color are by affirmative action policies. The study determined that legacy status was roughly equivalent to how much of a boost to the applicant's SAT score?
   a. 20 points
   b. 90 points
   c. 160 points
   d. 220 points

8. In 1978 corporate CEOs in the United States earned, on average, 35 times more than the average worker. Today, they earn _____ times more than the average worker.
   a. 35
   b. 150
   c. 240
   d. 300

9. Which of the following variables most closely predicts how high someone will score on the SAT test?
   a. Race
   b. Religion
   c. Family income
   d. Parents academic achievement

10. According to the U.S. Census Bureau, how much more likely are African Americans and Latino mortgage applicants to be turned down for a loan, even after controlling for employment, financial, and neighborhood factors?
    a. 15%
    b. 30%
    c. 45%
    d. 60%

---

*Used with permission from Paul C. Gorski and EdChange.org.

11. According to a Catalyst study, what percentage of Fortune 500 CEOs are women?
    a. 50%
    b. 22.4%
    c. 8.3%
    d. 1.2%

12. How many people in the U.S. live in poverty according to the U.S. Census Bureau?
    a. 1 million
    b. 12 million
    c. 37 million
    d. 120 million

Paul Gorski is an Assistant Professor at George Mason University's New Century College where he teaches courses on class, poverty, educational equity, and environmental justice. He created, and continues to maintain, the Multicultural Pavilion, a Web site focused on multicultural education.

Thriving in a Multicultural Classroom

Michelle R. Dunlap
Connecticut College

GOALS

- To assist students of all backgrounds in preparing for the emotional work that can be involved when engaged in a multicultural curriculum
- To familiarize students with the concepts of racial identity development and white privilege, and to brief them on how these concepts may play a role in their multicultural learning experience

INITIAL CHALLENGES

Walking into a classroom to learn about multicultural or diversity issues can be like walking into a minefield (Williams, Dunlap, McCandies, 1999). You may be apprehensive with good reason. Likewise, professors may be anxious and fearful of discussing issues of racism, sexism, cultural differences, and oppression, and they may exhibit their discomfort through verbal and non-verbal communication (or lack of) communication (Ladson-Billings, 1996). Some may argue that there is no obligation to help you feel more emotionally comfortable when dealing cross-culturally or when talking about racism and other forms of oppression—it's a tough world out there and many people have to deal with cross-cultural discomforts on a daily basis. Some students and teachers do not mind the anxiety and stress that often comes along with talking about these issues, but many still do and for them, this article provides four steps/strategies that may help prepare them for the multicultural learning process.

Step 1: **Considering the Emotions Involved in the Diversity Learning Process**   Often when we think of participating in a multiculturalism curriculum, we think of it as an *intellectual* endeavor. However, it also is an *emotional* endeavor, and emotions are often overlooked by participants in the diversity learning process. Students may experience a wide range of emotions and feelings such as anxiety, confusion, anger, relief, validation, and guilt (Davi, Dunlap, & Green, 2007 & 2008; Tatum, 1992; Williams et al., 1999). Overlooking the emotions involved in experiencing a multicultural curricula can make the process even more difficult, or can even hinder the diversity learning process altogether. Students often resist multicultural courses because of anxiety, fear, anger, and guilt (Tatum, 1992; Williams et al., 1999).

It is healthy for faculty to create a time or space within a multicultural course for grappling with the emotional components of the course so that students will not shut-down and remain silent throughout the semester. Ladson-Billings (1996) strongly urges educators to create a space wherein, and methods by which, all participants can feel emotionally empowered to speak concerning their fear, anger, confusion, disagreement, etc. while engaged in a multicultural learning. Not all educators feel empowered enough or are well versed enough with diversity to do that. Nonetheless, that does not decrease the importance or need for students to be prepared.

Beverly Tatum (1992) uses a developmental model for understanding the emotional stages that students may be in as they grapple with a multicultural curriculum. She relates students' attitudes concerning multicultural and diversity issues and ties these to their beliefs in a meritocracy. She proposes that those who are in early stages of racial identity development have not yet internalized the shared experience or awareness of white privilege, discrimination, prejudice, etc., and the ability of these experiences to impact a person's status (in spite of how hard-working, smart, etc. one may be).

When students brainstorm with one another about the emotions that they associate with discussions of race, gender, oppression, and multiculturalism, the list they produce is a long one with emotions that vary from the very overwhelming and/or negative to the relieving and/or positive (Davi et al., 2007 & 2008; Williams et al., 1999).

Thus, being in a situation where issues of oppression, differences, multiculturalism, etc. are going to be the topic of the day may pose a formidable challenge both to the students and facilitators of the multicultural and diversity-learning processes. Given the volatility that can accompany such discussions, students may find it helpful to develop a set of their own collective rules for safe communication in class. When encouraged to do this, students usually begin by sharing their need for respectful communication, confidentiality, etc., but they may also deal with questions of expected political correctness, and use of racial epithets (Williams et al., 1999). Addressing the multicultural learning process as an emotional process in itself can provide some relief for students who may be experiencing a variety of emotions (Davi et al., 2007 & 2008; Ladson-Billings, 1996; Williams et al., 1999). Without understanding the process, students may exclusively attribute any negative emotions to the instructor, their fellow students, the curriculum, etc., and not to the emotional process itself. When students have an opportunity to deal with emotions upfront in the classroom, it can help them to attribute some of their discomfort to the challenging *process* of communicating with relative strangers about an often difficult, emotion-laden topic.

Step 2: Becoming Familiar with the Concept of Racial Identity Development   Racial Identity Development and its stages are concepts that most students find extremely helpful as they enter into a multicultural curriculum. **Racial identity development** is the degree to which a person feels at one with, or connected with, the experiences of a racial group (Helms, 1990b). This connectedness, or lack of connectedness, can impact how students in a mixed-race classroom view their fellow classmates and the curriculum (Tatum, 1992). One of the most widely used resources for helping students prepare for a multicultural curriculum in the last two decades has been Beverly Tatum's (1992) article, *Talking about Race: The Application of Racial Identity Development Theory in the Classroom* (currently available at ets.mnsu.edu/darbook/ ethn201/race.pdf.). In this classic article, Tatum makes a practical application of racial identity theories. She not only addresses diversity as an emotional issue, but also presents two classic racial identity models (Helms, 1990a; Cross, Parham, & Helms, 1991) to help individuals understand how they may respond when confronted with discussions of diversity and multiculturalism by using Cross *et al.* (1991) model of Black Racial Identity Development and Helms' (1990a) model of White Racial Identity Development.

EXHIBIT 1   Comparison of Racial Identity Development Models

Identity Models

	I. Helms	II. Cross *et al.*	III. Atkinson *et al.*
Stages	**White Racial Identity**	**Black Racial Identity**	**Racial/Cultural Identity**
1	Contact	Pre-encounter	Conformity
2	Disintegration	Encounter	Dissonance
3	Reintegration	Immersion/Emersion	Resistance-Emersion
4	Pseudo-Independence	Internalization	Introspection
5	Immersion/Emersion	Internalization-Commitment	Integrative Awareness
6	Autonomy	——	——

The work of Helms and Cross *et al.* proposes that, based on their own experiences, people developmentally progress through various levels or stages of maturity with respect to understanding and internalizing the shared exposure to and reality of racism and oppression that has existed in our society.

As outlined in Dunlap (in press), the Helms (1990a) White Racial Identity model consists of six stages: Contact, Disintegration, Reintegration, Pseudo-Independence, Immersion/Emersion, and Autonomy (see Exhibit 2). In contrast, the Cross et al. (1991) Black Racial Identity model consists of five stages: Pre-encounter, Encounter, Immersion/Emersion, Internalization, and Internalization-Commitment (see Exhibit 3). A third alternative, the more racially inclusive, the Atkinson, Morten, & Sue (1989).

EXHIBIT 2   White Racial Identity Development (Helms)

	Definitions of Stages of White Racial Identity Development; Summarized by Richard (1996)
Contact	"Person is oblivious to own racial characteristics ('color-blind') and pretends others have none, is naïve, and shows 'accidental' insensitivity."
Disintegration	"Person consciously acknowledges own White identity and experiences race-related moral dilemmas from the perspective of an unfairly advantaged group."
Reintegration	"Person resolves racial moral dilemmas by trying to reestablish a status quo in which whites are superior and entitled to privilege and Blacks are inferior and entitled to disadvantage."
Pseudo-Independent	"Person has an intellectualized awareness of own race and societal racial issues. 'Intelligent non-Whites' are the best ones to understand and explain racism."
Immersion/Emersion	"Person honestly appraises what it means to be White in this society."
Autonomy	"Person adopts a positive, realistic White identity, interacts with others from a humanistic orientation, and fights oppression."

EXHIBIT 3 Black Racial Identity Development (Cross *et al.*)	
	Definitions of Stages of Black Racial Identity Development; Summarized by Richard (1996) and Vandiver et al. (2001)
Pre-Encounter	"Person denigrates black culture, idealizes White culture, and denies personal significance of race or racism."
Encounter	"Person questions self and others about racial issues. Stage terminates with a decision to restructure one's racial identity."
Immersion/Emersion	"Phase 1—Person shows extreme anger, idealizes everything Black, and denigrates and avoid everything White. Phase 2—Person actively redefines *self* according to Black and African historical perspectives."
Internalization	"Person adopts positive realistic Black identity, interacts with others from a humanistic orientation, and fights oppression."
Internalization-Commitment	". . . racial identity development that is based in involvement and activism . . . evidenced in regular involvement in diverse organizations."

Model, Racial/Cultural Identity (see Exhibit 4) consists of five stages: Conformity, Dissonance, Resistance/Emersion, Introspection, and Integrative Awareness. In the Conformity stage, African Americans and other minorities may not question racist practices and policies, may deny that such discriminatory practices exist, or may accept them as the status quo. For those a little more advanced in these stages, i.e., dissonance, they may feel confused and may begin to intellectually grapple with the systems of oppression that are becoming more obvious to them. Beyond

EXHIBIT 4 Minority Identity Development Model (Atkinson *et al.*)	
	Definition of Stages of Racial/Cultural Identity Development; Summarized by Merrell (2003)
Conformity	"Depreciating attitude toward self and others of same minority group: discriminatory attitude toward other minority groups; appreciating attitude toward dominant group."
Dissonance	"Conflict between appreciating and depreciating attitudes toward self, others of same minority group, other minority groups, and dominant group."
Resistance/Emersion	"Appreciating attitude toward self and others of same minority group; conflict between empathetic and culturocentric feelings toward other minority groups; depreciating attitude toward dominant group."
Introspection	"Concern with basis of self-appreciation and unequivocal nature of appreciation toward others of same minority group; concern with culture-centric views toward members of other minority groups; concern with basis of depreciation of dominant group."
Integrative Awareness	"Appreciating attitudes toward self, others of same minority group, and other minority groups; selective appreciation for dominant group."

that stage, in dissonance/emersion, African Americans may resist the status quo and begin to immerse themselves into their own culture and history which is a very energy consuming process. At the more advanced stage of Introspection, minorities may become more introspective as they try to understand the complications of the socially constructed systems of racial oppression and the limitations in fighting it. Finally, in the Integrative Awareness stage, they may find themselves choosing their battles more strategically, garnering their resources and alliances and expending their energies carefully while working to raise awareness among their social spheres (see Exhibit 4).

European Americans in the early stages of racial identity development may assume the systems of racial advantage that they live to be natural or the norm, and therefore may conform to the *status quo* unconsciously or without much question (see Exhibit 2). Likewise, especially if they are experiencing diversity for the first time, they may not understand the sensitivity and passion of students of color concerning these issues (McIntosh, 1989; Tatum, 1992). Once they begin to learn that inequities and oppressions exist, European-Americans may experience intellectual dissonance, which eventually will take them to one of two paths: either they will resist the status quo, or they will further immerse themselves in it. Although either can lead to further introspection and learning, one may be more positive than the other.

Tatum then takes Black and White student comments, and fits them into either the Helms or Cross *et al.* models, so that the students' feelings, intellectual engagement, etc. can be understood within the context of a larger developmental framework and process. Again, this then helps students who read her article to depersonalize some of their own discomfort with a multicultural curriculum and put their emotional and intellectual stretching and growth into a larger framework of developmental progression. For example, a white student who asks during a child development course group discussion, "Why are we talking about race and culture in a child development class?" arguably may be in the Contact stage of Helm's model, wherein he or she has not yet grasped the role that race, culture, ethnicity, gender, and oppression may play, even today, in a person of color's environment and developmental experiences.

When students are aware that racial identity development models and stages exist, such knowledge can help provide a context for comments that they hear one another make during a course—comments about which they may not relate nor understand initially. So, when they hear these kinds of questions and comments, they can try to predict where within the racial identity developmental process their peers may be, and can hear their comments and questions as existing within a dynamic process rather than as an unchanging static state. Based on these models, students can anticipate that a fellow student who is naïve about racism and other forms of oppression is likely at the beginning of a journey of growth that over time, will take him to a different stage of racial identity. Your peers may grow and move beyond the stage(s) by way of class discussions.

Familiarity with these models may also assist you when your course instructors appear to be at racial identity development stages different from your own, or that do not match what the curriculum may need or call for. Thus, you should read Tatum's classic article before starting a multicultural course, and should attempt to consider both your early and current experiences with race and racism. You also should ponder where in the models you find yourself (that is, at which stages would you place yourself and why). This task can challenge you to attempt to both reflect on and to talk about much avoided topics such as racism, sexism, etc., and can allow you to become adequately familiar with the models so that you can use them to understand your own and your peers' developmental progression(s).

Step 3: Considering an Alternate Model That May Be Useful for Exploring Racial Identity Development Some of you may find that you do not easily fit into the currently available models of Racial Identity Development. Some of the models are not applicable to your racial background and experiences. For example, Hispanic students may find the Helms (1990a) and Cross *et al.* (1991) models do not specifically apply to them. Likewise, students who have been marginalized in ways other than race, e.g., LBGTQ (lesbian, gay, bisexual, transgender and questioning) students, may not find such models applicable to their experiences of oppression. While there are models that have been developed to try to address the diversity of racial identity backgrounds, no general model has been developed that may be able to address all categories of marginalization and oppression, be it racial, gender, sexual orientation, religion, etc.

One alternative proposed here involves considering the Helms (1990), Cross *et al.* (1991), and Atkinson *et al.* (1989) Racial Identity Development models, and contemplate the possible commonalities or parallels in their progressive stages. For example, they all involve an initial naïvety or lack of experience, then a grappling or dissonance experience, and eventually integration and resolving of new learning or to use other interdisciplinary theories. Considering the Helms, Cross *et al.* and Atkinson *et al.* models together, a similar progression can be argued for the path that people may take when trying to come to terms with and acknowledge the role that racism and other forms of oppression still play within our society. To accept that inequities, injustice, prejudice, racism, sexism, heterosexism, xenophobia, etc. still exist within the new millennium may require a cognitive shaking-up or dissonant grappling for those who previously have not been aware of the relevancy of these issues.

Another option is to apply the Elizabeth Kubler-Ross Model of Death and Dying (see Exhibit 5) in which dying patients come to terms with the shock and trauma of an impending death by progressing through five stages: denial, anger, bargaining, depression, and acceptance.

EXHIBIT 5 **Stages of Death and Dying**

	Definitions of Stages of Kubler-Ross (1969/1997) Model of Death and Dying; Summarized by Funeral Guide South Africa
Denial	"Shock, disbelief and confusion. 'This isn't happening to me.' A conscious or subconscious refusal to accept the reality of the situation."
Anger	"People can be angry at themselves, and/or with others, especially those close to them . . . [and the] grieving person [can] lash out in anger."
Bargaining	"Traditionally the bargaining stage . . . can involve attempting to bargain [or cognitively grapple] with whatever God the person believes in. 'I promise I'll be a better person if . . .,' or 'Please just let me live until . . .'"
Depression	"This phase varies from person to person involving sadness, regret, fear, numbness, fatigue, [retreat], etc. It shows that the person has at least begun to accept the reality."
Acceptance	"Some emotional detachment and objectivity begins to surface. 'I'm ready, I don't want to struggle anymore.' People dying can enter this stage a long time before the people they leave behind. For those grieving the loss of a loved one, this can be a time where they begin to re-enter a more 'normal' social life and are ready to start moving forwards."

Some students, regardless of their ethnic or racial background naïvely may be in *denial* concerning racism and the role of racism in people's lives today. Others may progress to the *anger* stage where they are now fully aware of these inequities and are upset that such injustice still exists. Yet others may experience a period where they have discovered that injustices can be so prevalent that they find themselves confused or alternatively they may try to fight each one alone and may grapple with how to prioritize their concerns, choose their battles, and rally resources and support (*bargaining*). Others may experience a period of sadness and *depression* concerning the state of race relations, racism, and other oppressions in our environments. Yet others may have reached a point of greater mastery of accepting that not every battle can be fought and won, but that among the battles that they do select, they can resist and rally strategically, resourcefully and hopefully effectively (*acceptance*). This alternative model may be helpful to you if you feel that none of the current models apply to your particular experience, or your particular category of social oppression or privilege.

EXHIBIT 6   **Proposed Aligning of Stages of Kubler-Ross's Model to Explain Student's Experiences in Multicultural Environments and/or Curriculum**

Helms (1990a & b) Model of White Racial Identity Development; Tatum (1992)	Cross et al. (1991) Black Racial Identity Development; Tatum (1992)	Atkinson et al. (1989) Racial/Cultural Identity Development	Kubler-Ross (1969/1997) Model of Death and Dying	Proposed common processes as applied to a Multicultural Classroom and/or Curriculum
Contact	Pre-Encounter	Conformity	Denial	Individuals may assume the systems of advantage to be natural, and may not question them. Also individuals may be unaware of or confused by opposing views. Thus, some students may be in *denial* concerning racism and the role of systems of oppression in people's lives today.
Disintegration/Reintegration	Encounter (and also includes Phase 1 or "Immersion" of the next BRI stage as well)	Resistance/Emersion	Anger	Individuals may become more aware that there are issues of unfairness, disparity, and/or oppression, and may experience upset and angst that such injustice still exists.
Pseudo-Independent	Immersion/Emersion	Dissonance	Bargaining	Individuals spend time and cognitive and/or emotional energy analyzing new information and experiences provided in a multicultural curriculum and/or diverse environment. Students may grapple with how to prioritize their concerns, choose their battles, and rally resources and support.

Immersion/ Emersion	Internalization	Introspection	Depression	An individual may to one extent or another attempt to conserve cognitive and emotional energy by retreating for a time to reflect on what they are learning. Students also may experience a period of disillusionment and sadness concerning the state of race relations, racism, and other oppressions in our environments.
Autonomy	Internalization- Commitment	Integrative Awareness	Acceptance	Individuals develop greater maturity, awareness, understanding, and ability to critically analyze a multicultural curriculum, choose battles, rally resources, raise issues, engage in activism, and increases skills to negotiate and facilitate positive change. Among the battles selected, individuals may resist and rally more strategically and resourcefully than in earlier stages.

Step 4: Understanding the Concept of White Privilege   Both Black and White students, especially in the early stages of racial identity development can benefit from a greater awareness of the concept of white privilege. **White privileges** are norms or actions that are so common that many do not notice them although they may systematically put or keep European Americans in a position of relative advantage (socially, economically, etc.) in comparison to others in our society (McIntosh, 1989). In McIntosh's classic work, "White Privilege and Male Privilege . . ." (in this text), she provides dozens of examples of white privilege that often are unnoticed by European Americans because of the norm or prevalence of such privileges in comparison to the minority experience (e.g., most European Americans are able to go into a store to shop without it being assumed that they may steal, etc.).

Other authors also have spoken to such advantage in addressing the related systemic and daily burden experienced by minorities because of the continuing significance of racism and other forms of oppression in our society (e.g., Feagin, 1998 & 2006). McIntosh's article can be helpful to most students of all backgrounds in that it opens up discussion of systematic and structural hindrances, advantages, etc., and allows those in the early stages of racial identity development to have an opportunity to grapple with these issues. Students who are thinking about and coming to terms with white privilege for the first time may also benefit from additional resources and supports offered through organizations such as Teaching Tolerance (www.teachingtolerance.org) and Understanding Prejudice (www.understandingprejudice.org).

Engaging in these steps may assist you in your emotional preparation for the multicultural curriculum and learning process. Considering the emotions that can be involved, familiarizing oneself with racial identity development and other theories that may be applicable, understanding the concept of white privilege, and seeking resources and supports may all assist in your adjusting successfully in a multicultural curriculum and this course. Proactively preparing oneself for the internal challenges that can come with a multicultural curriculum hopefully may help to more effectively facilitate student learning.

DISCUSSION QUESTIONS

1. What was one of your earliest experiences concerning race?
   a. Describe the experience, how you felt, and how the experience was handled.
   b. If you could rewrite that experience, how would you change it and/or how it was handled?

2. Think of three different ages or points in your life, for example, ages 6, 12, and 18.
   a. What racial identity development stage would you say you were in for each of these stages and why?
   b. What factors can you think of that may have impacted any changes in your racial identity development stages from one age to another?
   c. How do you feel that each of these stages could have been better supported by the caregivers, educators, peers, or colleagues around you?

3. If you could rewrite your first experience with race, racism, or oppression, and how it was handled by the adults or others in a position of authority:
   a. Would you change it? If so, in what ways would you change it?
   b. How would you better facilitate the learning and/or support among those involved or impacted at the time?

4. What does racial identity development have to do with (emotional) death and dying?

5. Create a list of all of the emotions that you can recall from the moment you began reading on this topic and/or working with the discussion questions. What is the significance of those emotions in terms of your own development and learning about a multicultural curriculum?

Writing Assignment

Read and reflect on Tatum's 1992 article on racial identity development. (See bibliography).

1. Describe in 2–3 pages, your initial reactions to the work of Tatum and her students.

2. Using one of the models provided in this chapter, prepare a statement describing your racial identity development and stage(s) up to this point in your life.

3. Include a description of any key person(s) or event(s) that have been instrumental in your racial identity development thus far.

References

Atkinson, D.R., Morten, G. & Sue, D.W. (1989), A minority identity development model. In D.R. Atkinson, G. Morten, & D.W. Sue (Eds), *Counseling American Minorities* (pp. 35–52), Dubuque, IA: William C. Brown.

Cross, W.E. Jr., Parham, T.A., Helms, J.E. (1991). The stages of black racial identity development: Nigrescence Models. In R. Jones (Ed.) *Black Psychology* (3rd Edition), pp. 319–338. San Francisco: Cobb and Henry.

Davi, A., Dunlap, M. & Green, A. (2007), Exploring difference in the service-earning classroom: Three teachers write about anger, sexuality, and justice." *Reflections: Writing, Service-Learning, and Community Literacy,* 6(1), 41–66.

Davi, A., Dunlap, M., Green, A. (2008), Feminist ways of seeing: Preparing students for service-learning. In K. Dugger (Ed.) *Handbook on Service Learning in Women's Studies and the Disciplines.* Baltimore, MD: Institute for Teaching and Research on Women, 14–25.

Dunlap, M. (In Press). Cross-cultural community engagement, Elizabeth Kubler-Ross's model of death and dying, and racial identity development, In. H. Fitzgerald (Ed.), *Going Places.*

Feagin, J. (1998). The continuing significance of race: Antiblack discrimination in public places. In J. Feagin (Ed.), *The New Urban Paradigm: Critical Perspectives on the City.* Lanham, MD: Rowman & Littlefield Publishers.

Feagin, J. (2006). *Systemic Racism: A Theory of Oppression.* NY: Routledge Press.

Funeral Guide South Africa (website). http:// funeralguide.co.za/coping-with-grief/the-5-stages-of-grief.html

Helms, J. E. (Ed.) (1990a). *Black and White Racial Identity: Theory, Research and Practice.* Westport, CT: Greenwood Press.

Helms, J. E. (Ed.) (1990b). *Training Manual for Diagnosing Racial Identity in Social Interactions.* Topeka, KS: Content Communications. Westport, CT: Greenwood Press.

Kubler-Ross, E. (1969/1997). *On Death and Dying.* NY: Simon & Schuster/Scribner.

Ladson-Billings, G. (1996). Silences as weapons: Challenges of a Black professor teaching White students. *Theory into Practice*, 35 (2), 79–85.

McIntosh, P. (1989). White privilege: Unpacking the invisible knapsack. *Peace and Freedom*, July/August.

Merrell, K. (2003). *Behavioral, Social, and Emotional Assessment of Children and Adolescents*, Mahwah, NJ: Lawrence Erlbaum Associates, pp. 394–396.

Richard, H. (1996). Filmed in Black and White: Teaching the concept of Racial Identity at a predominantly White university. *Teaching of Psychology*, 23 (3), 159–161.

Tatum, B. (1992). Talking about race: The application of racial identity development theory in the classroom. *Harvard Educational Review,* Vol. 62 (1), 1–24.

Vandiver, B., Fhagen-Smith, P., Cokley, K., Cross, W., & Worrel, F. (2001). Cross's Negrescence Model: From theory to scale to theory. *Journal of Multicultural Counseling and Development*, 29 (3), 174–200.

Williams, M., Dunlap, M. & McCandies, T. (1999), Keeping it real: Three Black women educators discuss how we deal with student resistance to multicultural inclusion in the curriculum. *Transformations: The New Jersey Project Journal for Curriculum Transformation and Scholarship*, 10 (2), 11–22.

Michelle R. Dunlap is a Professor at Connecticut College. Most recently, she co-edited African Americans & Community Engagement in Higher Education (2009).

BODY RITUAL AMONG THE NACIREMA

Horace Miner

GOALS

- To better understand the role that culture plays in the development of stereotypes and prejudices
- To see one's culture from a different perspective

The anthropologist has become so familiar with the diversity of ways in which different peoples behave in similar situations that he is not apt to be surprised by even the most exotic customs. In fact, if all of the logically possible combinations of behavior have not been found somewhere in the world, he is apt to suspect that they must be present in some yet undescribed tribe. This point has, in fact, been expressed with respect to clan organization by Murdock (1948:71). In this light, the magical beliefs and practices of the Nacirema present such unusual aspects that it seems desirable to describe them as an example of the extremes to which human behavior can go.

Professor Linton first brought the ritual of the Nacirema to the attention of anthropologists twenty years ago (1936:326), but the culture of this people is still very poorly understood. They are a North American group living in the territory between the Canadian Cree, the Yaqui and Tarahumare of Mexico, and the Carib and Arawak of the Antilles. Little is known of their origin, although tradition states that they came from the east. According to Nacirema mythology, their nation was originated by a culture hero, Notgnihsaw, who is otherwise known for two great feats of strength—the throwing of a piece of wampum across the river Pa-To-Mac and the chopping down of a cherry tree in which the Spirit of Truth resided.

Nacirema culture is characterized by a highly developed market economy which has evolved in a rich natural habitat. While much of the people's time is devoted to economic pursuits, a large part of the fruits of these labors and a considerable portion of the day are spent in ritual activity. The focus of this activity is the human body, the appearance and health of which loom as a dominant concern in the ethos of the people. While such concern is certainly not unusual, its ceremonial aspects and associated philosophy are unique.

The fundamental belief underlying the whole system appears to be that the human body is ugly and that its natural tendency is to debility and disease. Incarcerated in such a body, man's only hope is to avert these characteristics through the use of the powerful influences of ritual and ceremony. Every household has one or more shrines devoted to this purpose. The more powerful individuals in the society have several shrines in their houses and, in fact, the opulence of a house is often referred to in terms of the number of such ritual centers it possesses. Most houses are of wattle and daub construction, but the shrine rooms of the wealthy are walled with stone. Poorer families imitate the rich by applying pottery plaques to their shrine walls.

*From the *American Anthropologist*, volume 58, #1, 1956, pp. 18–21.

While each family has at least one shrine, the rituals associated with it are not family cere-monies but are private and secret. The rites are normally only discussed with children, and then only during the period when they are being initiated into these mysteries. I was able, however, to establish sufficient rapport with the natives to examine these shrines and to have the rituals described to me.

The focal point of the shrine is a box or chest, which is built into the wall. In this chest are kept the many charms and magical potions without which no native believes he could live.

These preparations are secured from a variety of specialized practitioners. The most pow-erful of these are the medicine men, whose assistance must be rewarded with substantial gifts. However, the medicine men do not provide the curative potions for their clients, but decide what the ingredients should be and then write them down in an ancient and secret language. This writ-ing is understood only by the medicine men and by the herbalists who, for another gift, provide the required charm.

The charm is not disposed of after it has served its purpose, but is placed in the charm-box of the household shrine. As these magical materials are specific for certain ills, and the real or imagined maladies of the people are many, the charm-box is usually full to overflowing. The magical packets are so numerous that the people forget what their purposes were and fear to use them again. While the natives are very vague on this point, we can only assume that the idea in retaining all the old magical materials is that their presence in the charm-box, before which the body rituals are conducted, will in some way protect the worshipper.

Beneath the charm-box is a small font. Each day every member of the family, in succession, enters the shrine room, bows his head before the charm-box, mingles different sorts of holy waters in the font, and proceeds with a brief ritual of ablution. The holy waters are secured from the Water Temple of the community, where the priests conduct elaborate ceremonies to make the liquid ritually pure.

In the hierarchy of magical practitioners, and below the medicine men in prestige, are spe-cialists whose designation is best translated "holy-mouth-men." The Nacirema have an almost pathological horror of and fascination with the mouth, the condition of which is believed to have a supernatural influence on all social relationships. Were it not for the rituals of the mouth, they believe that their teeth would fall out, their gums bleed, their jaws shrink, their friends desert them, and their lovers reject them. They also believe that a strong relationship exists between oral and moral characteristics. For example, there is a ritual ablution of the mouth for children which is supposed to improve their moral fiber.

The daily body ritual performed by everyone includes a mouth-rite. Despite the fact that these people are so punctilious about care of the mouth, this rite involves a practice which strikes the uninitiated stranger as revolting. It was reported to me that the ritual consists of inserting a magic bundle of hog hairs into the mouth, along with certain magical powder, and then moving the bundle in a highly formalized series of gestures.

In addition to the private mouth-rite, the people seek out the holy-mouth-man once or twice a year. These practitioners have an impressive set of paraphernalia, consisting of a variety of augers, awls, probes, and prods. The use of these objects in the exorcism of the evils of the mouth involves almost unbelievable ritual torture of the client. The holy-mouth-man opens the client's mouth and, using the above mentioned tools, enlarges any holes, which may have been created in the teeth. Magical materials are put into these holes. If there are no naturally occurring holes in the teeth, large sections of one or more teeth are gouged out so that the supernatural substance can be applied. In the client's view, the purpose of the ministrations is to arrest decay and to draw friends. The extremely sacred and traditional character of the rite is evident in the fact that the natives return to the holy-mouth-man, despite the fact that their teeth continue to decay.

It is to be hoped that, when a thorough study of the Nacirema is made, there will be careful inquiry into the personality structure of these people. One has but to watch the gleam in the eye of a holy-mouth-man, as he jabs an awl into an exposed nerve, to suspect that a certain amount of sadism is involved. If this can be established, a very interesting pattern emerges, for most of the population shows definite masochistic tendencies. It was to these that Professor Linton referred in discussing a distinctive part of the daily body ritual which was performed only by men. This part of the rite involves scraping and lacerating the surface of the face with a sharp instrument. Special women's rites are performed only four times during each lunar month, but what they lack in frequency is made up for in barbarity. As part of this ceremony, women bake their heads in small ovens for about an hour. The theoretically interesting point is that what seems to be a preponderantly masochistic people have developed sadistic specialists.

The medicine men have an imposing temple, or latipso, in every community of any size. The more elaborate ceremonies required to treat very sick patients can only be performed at this temple. These ceremonies involve not only the thaumaturge but a permanent group of vestal maidens who move sedately about the temple chambers in distinctive costume and headdress.

The latipso ceremonies are so harsh that it is phenomenal that a fair proportion of the really sick natives who enter the temple ever recover. Small children whose indoctrination is still incomplete have been known to resist attempts to take them to the temple because "that is where you go to die." Despite this fact, sick adults are not only willing but eager to undergo the protracted ritual purification, if they can afford to do so. No matter how ill the supplicant or how grave the emergency, the guardians of many temples will not admit a client if he cannot give a rich gift to the custodian. Even after one has gained admission and survived the ceremonies, the guardians will not permit the neophyte to leave until he makes still another gift.

The supplicant entering the temple is first stripped of all his or her clothes. In everyday life the Nacirema avoids exposure of his body and its natural functions. Bathing and excretory acts are performed only in the secrecy of the household shrine, where they are ritualized as part of the body-rites. Psychological shock results from the fact that body secrecy is suddenly lost upon entry into the latipso. This sort of ceremonial treatment is necessitated by the fact that the excreta are used by a diviner to ascertain the course and nature of the client's sickness. Female clients, on the other hand, find their naked bodies are subjected to the scrutiny, manipulation, and prodding of the medicine men.

Few supplicants in the temple are well enough to do anything but lie on their hard beds. The daily ceremonies, like the rites of the holy-mouth-men, involve discomfort and torture. With ritual precision, the vestals awaken their miserable charges each dawn and roll them about on their beds of pain while performing ablutions, in the formal movements of which the maidens are highly trained. At other times they insert magic wands in the supplicant's mouth or force him to eat substances which are supposed to be healing. From time to time the medicine men come to their clients and jab magically treated needles into their flesh. The fact that these ceremonies may not cure, and may even kill the neophyte, in no way decreases the people's faith in the medicine men.

There remains one other kind of practitioner, known as a "listener." This witch-doctor has the power to exorcise the devils that lodge in the heads of people who have been bewitched. The Nacirema believe that parents bewitched their own children. Mothers are particularly suspected of putting a curse on children while teaching them the secret body rituals. The counter-magic of the witch-doctor is unusual in its lack of ritual. The patient simply tells the "listener" all his troubles and fears, beginning with the earliest difficulties he can remember. The memory displayed by the Nacirema in these exorcism sessions is truly remarkable. It is not uncommon for the patient to bemoan the rejection he felt upon being weaned as a babe, and a few individuals even see their troubles going back to the traumatic effects of their own birth.

In conclusion, mention must be made of certain practices which have their base in native esthetics but which depend upon the pervasive aversion to the natural body and its functions. There are ritual fasts to make fat people thin and ceremonial feasts to make thin people fat. Still other rites are used to make women's breasts larger if they are small, and smaller if they are large. General dissatisfaction with breast shape is symbolized in the fact that the ideal form is virtually outside the range of human variation. A few women afflicted with almost inhuman hypermammary development are so idolized that they make a handsome living by simply going from village to village and permitting the natives to stare at them for a fee.

Reference has already been made to the fact that excretory functions are ritualized, routinized, and relegated to secrecy. Natural reproduction functions are similarly distorted. Intercourse is taboo as a topic and secluded as an act. Efforts are made to avoid pregnancy by the use of magical materials or by limiting intercourse to certain phases of the moon. Conception is actually very infrequent. When pregnant, women dress so as to hide their condition. Parturition takes place in secret, without friends or relatives to assist, and the majority of women do not nurse their infants.

Our review of the ritual life of the Nacirema has certainly shown them to be a magic-ridden people. It is hard to understand how they have managed to exist so long under the burdens which they have imposed upon themselves. But even such exotic customs as these take on real meaning when they are viewed with the insight provided by Malinowski when he wrote (1948:70).

> Looking from far and above, from our high places of safety in developed civilization, it is easy to see all the crudity and irrelevance of magic. But without its power and guidance, early man could not have advanced to the higher stages of civilization.

Bibliography

Linton, Ralph. (1936). The study of man. New York: D. Appleton-Century Co.

Malinowski, B. (1948). Magic science and religion. Glencoe, IL: The Free Press.

Murdock, G. P. (1948). Social structure. New York: The MacMillan Company.

DISCUSSION QUESTIONS

1. What general message do you think the author was trying to convey in his description of this culture?

2. What stereotypes could you have about the Nacireman culture and its people if this reading were your only source of information?

3. The many strange and interesting rituals observed by Miner lead him to conclude that the Nacirema have a strong underlying belief about the human body. What is this belief?

4. Assume that you are carrying on the work of Miner and study the Nacireman culture as it exists now in the 21st century.
   a. What additional body-related activities could you observe in their culture today?
   b. Is Miner's observation about the preoccupation with body and health still valid today? Explain.

    c. Is Miner's observation about the underlying belief about the human body still valid today? Explain.

5. Describe as Miner might have, two or more of the body-related activities you listed for question 4(a).

6. How does Miner's article relate to modern business in terms of

    a. outsourcing

    b. international business negotiations

    c. marketing to growing ethnic populations?

7. On a scale from 1 to 10 (10 being very important) how would you rate the appearance and body rituals observed by Miner and by yourself in terms of their importance

    a. to personal life? Explain your rating.

    b. to the business world? Explain your rating.

8. Other facets of this culture also yield many rituals today. There is, for example, WIKI, a ritual that appears to involve belief in magic. Student Naciremans trade information with each other in this ritual. They believe that when they read a WIKI, whatever it says, is indeed fact. Somehow, WIKIs magically hold all-knowing truths. How might this ritual relate to prejudice and stereotypes?

9. Vast numbers of individual Naciremans also conduct a Ritual of Networking using magic boxes to weave social "webs." They exchange pictures of themselves and much personal information with strangers on their webs. "Participants" of the Networking ritual seem to constantly check their webs and respond to them. They walk around webbing; they eat with their boxes and check their webs during meals. The magic boxes are always nearby even when Naciremans are in their shrines devoted to health and appearance ceremonies. It is said that some even sleep with their boxes. This appears to be very ego-centered activity. What does this say about how people in this culture relate to each other?

10. Nacireman market economy also has rituals. Among these is the Business-Hiring ritual. In this ritual, business chiefs check the social webs of those desiring to join their tribes before hiring (sometimes even before interviewing) a position-seeker. Business chiefs do not appear to favor position-seekers who have social webs that indicate values and beliefs different from their own. This is not a secret. It is actually a very curious thing: Large numbers of Naciremans insist upon conducting the social web ritual even though they know that business chiefs may very well disapprove. Business chiefs appear to belong to a different group within this society.

    a. When a "participant" is both employment-seeking and networking at the same time, hiring rituals assume great importance. How might the Ritual of the Social Networking help or hurt a position-seeker?

    b. How do these clashing rituals reflect the values of the position-seekers and the business chiefs?

11. Participants in the modern Nacireman market economy sometimes create relationships that only exist electronically. They create groups, called "Virtual Teams" whose members never meet each other in person. Considering the rituals of Networking, WIKI and Virtual Teams, what stereotypes might strangers have about Nacireman culture if these three rituals were their only source of information?

Diversity on the Web

NACIREMA EXTENDED

You are a member of a team of anthropologists studying a large and rather diverse group of people. These people have a primitive information and communication system called "Internet" that will provide you with a first glimpse of their culture. To begin examining this culture, the team decides to scan "Internet" for information on their rituals.

1. Read the "Body Ritual Among the Nacirema" article in this text.
2. Using the Web sites listed at the bottom of this box as a starting point, investigate (scan) Internet for descriptions of one ritual. Be complete in your investigation, searching for symbolism and note how the ritual relates to a holiday or event. What does the ritual celebrate? Are there special roles in the event? Who participates?
3. Using a style similar to Miner's, record your perceptions of one of the events from the list that follows. A sample description, "Observation of the Cultural Event Called Halloween," appears on the next page.
4. Based *solely* on the information in your report, what kinds of stereotypes of American culture could result from these observations?

College Graduation Ceremonies
- http://brownielocks.com/graduation_ceremony.html
- http://www.wrightwood.com/college.htm
- http://timesofindia.indiatimes.com/Delhi_times/An_underwater_degree_ceremony/articleshow/22050.cms

National Political Conventions
- http://people.howstuffworks.com/political-convention.htm
- http://wikipedia.org/wiki/united_states_presidential_nominating_convention
- http://en.wikiedia.org/wiki/political_convention

Saint Patrick's Day Parade	http://www.saintpatricksdayparade.com
Mardi Gras Parade	http://www.holidays.net/mardigras/parades.htm
Thanksgiving Parade	http://www.nyctourist.com/macys_menu.htm
Easter Parade	http://www.ny.com/holiday/easter
Rose Parade	http://www.tournamentofroses.com/aboutus/officialPhotos.asp

Adapted from "Nacirema Extended" by M. J. Allard from C. P. Harvey & M. J. Allard: *Understanding and Managing Diversity* 3rd ed. Prentice Hall, 2005.

SAMPLE DESCRIPTION

Observation of Cultural Event Called Halloween

Halloween is a very strange custom. It doesn't appear to be a holiday; it is more like an event—an event characterized by at least two rituals and many symbols. There seem to be no special roles for males, females, or elders. The chief rituals appear to be the 1) Ritual of the Pumpkins and 2) Ritual of the Begging.

Ritual of the Pumpkins

The pumpkin vegetable, which apparently is eaten at other times of the year, is not eaten at this event. Instead, the people paint strange faces on pumpkins or carve faces on empty pumpkin shells. Lighted candles are placed inside the carved pumpkins. Decorated pumpkins appear in windows facing outdoors or on display outside of homes.

Ritual of the Begging

This is a special ritual for children. On Halloween night, children dress up in costumes that frequently represent mythical characters—ghosts, witches, monsters, ghouls, cartoon characters. They wear masks to hide their identities. After dark the children go begging from house to house, calling out "trick or treat." People then open their doors and give candy to the children. Sometimes the children play pranks on the people.

Symbols

Among the prominent symbols of Halloween are ghosts, skeletons, spiders, witches, black cats, graveyards, and monsters, all of which seem to be very frightening, gory, ugly, or sinister in character. Not only are these symbols displayed in the costumes the children wear, but many houses are adorned on the outside with displays of them, particularly witches and ghosts.

Sometimes people visit "haunted houses" (eerie houses where frightening creatures lurk in dark corners to scare people). Sometimes, too, people attend social events called Halloween parties where they play strange games such as dunking their heads in buckets of water while trying to catch an apple in their teeth.

These events are sometimes for adults and sometimes for children.

Increasing Multicultural Understanding: Uncovering Stereotypes

John R. Bowman
University of North Carolina at Pembroke

INSTRUCTIONS PRIOR TO CLASS

1. Turn to the Uncovering Stereotypes Worksheet: (Worksheet A).
2. Follow your instructor's directions for completing the blank category boxes that reflect different special populations.
3. **Instructions for working individually:**
   - Complete the **First Thought/Judgment** column by writing your first thought about or judgment of each category. Refer to the example given on Worksheet A.
   - Rate each thought/judgment as positive (+), negative (−), or neutral (0) and enter these ratings in the **Rating** column.
   - Complete the **Sources** column by indicating the source of your judgment for each category.

Instructions for Working as a Group in Class:
   - Turn to the Uncovering Stereotypes Group Summary Sheet: (Worksheet B).
   - Five categories (Family, Media, Experience, Work Experience, Friends) have already been listed on the summary sheet. Add additional categories (derived from your group discussions) to the sheet.
   - Take a quick count of the number of positive, negative, and neutral thoughts/judgments made by your group for each of the Source Categories and enter totals on the last line.
   - As a class, discuss which sources lead to positive, which to negative, and which to neutral judgments.
   - Discuss the implications of having negative or positive stereotypes/judgments from different perspectives; for example, among workers, between managers and workers, and at the corporate level.

WORKSHEET A: UNCOVERING STEREOTYPES			
Category	**First Thought/Judgment**	**Rating***	**Sources**
Working Mother	Neglects children, busy, tired	–, 0, 0	Own experience, movies
Southerner			
Physically-challenged Job Applicant			
Smoker			
Hispanic			
Muslim Female			
Gay Female President of the U.S.			

*(+) = positive
 (–) = negative
 (0) = neutral

WORKSHEET B: UNCOVERING STEREOTYPES GROUP SUMMARY SHEET			
Source Categories	**Positive (+) Thoughts/Judgments**	**Negative (−) Thoughts/Judgments**	**Neutral (0) Thoughts/Judgments**
Family			
Media			
Experience			
Work Experience			
Friends			
Other			
Total			

WHITE PRIVILEGE AND MALE PRIVILEGE: A PERSONAL ACCOUNT OF COMING TO SEE CORRESPONDENCES THROUGH WORK IN WOMEN'S STUDIES

Peggy McIntosh
Wellesley College

Through work to bring materials and perspectives from Women's Studies into the rest of the curriculum, I have often noticed men's unwillingness to grant that they are over privileged in the curriculum, even though they may grant that women are disadvantaged. Denials which amount to taboos surround the subject of advantages which men gain from women's disadvantages. These denials protect male privilege from being fully recognized, acknowledged, lessened, or ended.

Thinking through unacknowledged male privilege as a phenomenon with a life of its own, I realized that since hierarchies in our society are interlocking, there was most likely a phenomenon of white privilege which was similarly denied and protected, but alive and real in its effects. As a white person, I realized I had been taught about racism as something which puts others at a disadvantage, but had been taught not to see one of its corollary aspects, white privilege, which puts me at an advantage.

I think whites are carefully taught not to recognize white privilege, as males are taught not to recognize male privilege. So I have begun in an untutored way to ask what it is like to have white privilege. This paper is a partial record of my personal observations, and not a scholarly analysis. It is based on my daily experiences within my particular circumstances.

I have come to see white privilege as an invisible package of unearned assets which I can count on cashing in each day, but about which I was "meant" to remain oblivious. White privilege is like an invisible weightless knapsack of special provisions, assurances, tools, maps, guides, codebooks, passports, visas, clothes, compass, emergency gear, and blank checks.

Since I have had trouble facing white privilege, and describing its results in my life, I saw parallels here with men's reluctance to acknowledge male privilege. Only rarely will a man go beyond acknowledging that women are disadvantaged to acknowledging that men have unearned advantage, or that unearned privilege has not been good for men's development as human beings, or for society's development, or that privilege systems might ever be challenged and *changed*.

I will review here several types or layers of denial which I see at work protecting, and preventing awareness about, entrenched male privilege. Then I will draw parallels, from my own experience, with the denials which veil the facts of white privilege. Finally, I will list 46 ordinary and daily ways in which I experience having white privilege, within my life situation and its particular social and political frameworks.

Writing this paper has been difficult, despite warm receptions for the talks on which it is based.[1] For describing white privilege makes one newly accountable. As we in Women's Studies work to reveal male privilege and ask men to give up some of their power, so one who writes about having white privilege must ask, "Having described it, what will I do to lessen or end it?"

The denial of men's over-privileged state takes many forms in discussions of curriculum-change work. Some claim that men must be central in the curriculum because they have done most of what is important or distinctive in life or in civilization. Some recognize sexism in the curriculum but deny that it makes male students seem unduly important in life. Others agree that certain *individual* thinkers are blindly male-oriented but deny that there is any systemic tendency in disciplinary frameworks or epistemology to over-empower men as a group. Those men who do grant that male privilege takes institutionalized and embedded forms are still likely to deny that male hegemony has opened doors for them personally. Virtually all men deny that male over-reward alone can explain men's centrality in all the inner sanctums of our most powerful institutions. Moreover, those few who will acknowledge that male privilege systems have over-empowered them usually end up doubting that we could dismantle these privilege systems. They may say they will work to improve women's status, in the society or in the university, but they can't or won't support the idea of lessening men's. In curricular terms, this is the point at which they say that they regret they cannot use any of the interesting new scholarship on women because the syllabus is full. When the talk turns to giving men less cultural room, even the most fair-minded of the men I know will tend to reflect, or fall back on, conservative assumptions about the inevitability of present gender relations and distributions of power, calling on precedent or sociobiology and psychobiology to demonstrate that male domination is natural and follows inevitably from evolutionary pressures. Others resort to arguments from "experience" or religion or social responsibility or wishing and dreaming.

After I realized, through faculty development work in Women's Studies, the extent to which men work from a base of unacknowledged privilege, I understood that much of their oppressiveness was unconscious. Then I remembered the frequent charges from women of color that white women whom they encounter are oppressive. I began to understand why we are justly seen as oppressive, even when we don't see ourselves that way. At the very least, obliviousness of one's privileged state can make a person or group irritating to be with. I began to count the ways in which I enjoy unearned skin privilege and have been conditioned into oblivion about its existence, unable to see that it put me "ahead" in any way, or put my people ahead, over-rewarding us and yet also paradoxically damaging us, or that it could or should be changed.

My schooling gave me no training in seeing myself as an oppressor, as an unfairly advantaged person, or as a participant in a damaged culture. I was taught to see myself as an individual whose moral state depended on her individual moral will. At school, we were not taught about slavery in any depth; we were not taught to see slaveholders as damaged people. Slaves were seen as the only group at risk of being dehumanized. My schooling followed the pattern which Elizabeth Minnich has pointed out: Whites are taught to think of their lives as morally neutral, normative, and average, and also ideal, so that when we work to benefit others, this is seen as work which will allow "them" to be more like "us." I think many of us know how obnoxious this attitude can be in men.

After frustration with men who would not recognize male privilege, I decided to try to work on myself at least by identifying some of the daily effects of white privilege in my life. It is crude work, at this stage, but I will give here a list of special circumstances and conditions I experience which I did not earn but which I have been made to feel are mine by birth, by citizenship, and by virtue of being a conscientious law-abiding "normal" person of good will. I have chosen those conditions which I think in my case *attach somewhat more to skin-color privilege* than to class, religion, ethnic status, or geographical location, though of course all these other factors are intricately intertwined. As far as I can see, my Afro-American co-workers, friends, and acquaintances with whom I come into daily or frequent contact in this particular time, place, and line of work cannot count on most of these conditions.

1. I can if I wish arrange to be in the company of people of my race most of the time.
2. I can avoid spending time with people whom I was trained to mistrust and who have learned to mistrust my kind or me.
3. If I should need to move, I can be pretty sure of renting or purchasing housing in an area which I can afford and in which I would want to live.
4. I can be pretty sure that my neighbors in such a location will be neutral or pleasant to me.
5. I can go shopping alone most of the time, pretty well assured that I will not be followed or harassed.
6. I can turn on the television or open to the front page of the paper and see people of my race widely represented.
7. When I am told about our national heritage or about "civilization," I am shown that people of my color made it what it is.
8. I can be sure that my children will be given curricular materials that testify to the existence of their race.
9. If I want to, I can be pretty sure of finding a publisher for this piece on white privilege.
10. I can be pretty sure of having my voice heard in a group in which I am the only member of my race.
11. I can be casual about whether or not to listen to another woman's voice in a group in which she is the only member of her race.
12. I can go into a music shop and count on finding the music of my race represented, into a supermarket and find the staple foods which fit with my cultural traditions, into a hairdresser's shop and find someone who can cut my hair.
13. Whether I use checks, credit cards, or cash, I can count on my skin color not to work against the appearance of financial reliability.
14. I can arrange to protect my children most of the time from people who might not like them.
15. I do not have to educate my children to be aware of systemic racism for their own daily physical protection.
16. I can be pretty sure that my children's teachers and employers will tolerate them if they fit school and workplace norms; my chief worries about them do not concern others' attitudes toward their race.
17. I can talk with my mouth full and not have people put this down to my color.
18. I can swear, or dress in second-hand clothes, or not answer letters, without having people attribute these choices to the bad morals, the poverty, or the illiteracy of my race.
19. I can speak in public to a powerful male group without putting my race on trial.
20. I can do well in a challenging situation without being called a credit to my race.
21. I am never asked to speak for all the people of my racial group.

22. I can remain oblivious of the language and customs of persons of color who constitute the world's majority without feeling in my culture any penalty for such oblivion.
23. I can criticize our government and talk about how much I fear its policies and behavior without being seen as a cultural outsider.
24. I can be pretty sure that if I ask to talk to "the person in charge," I will be facing a person of my race.
25. If a traffic cop pulls me over or if the IRS audits my tax return, I can be sure I haven't been singled out because of my race.
26. I can easily buy posters, postcards, picture books, greeting cards, dolls, toys, and children's magazines featuring people of my race.
27. I can go home from most meetings of organizations I belong to feeling somewhat tied in, rather than isolated, out-of-place, outnumbered, unheard, held at a distance, or feared.
28. I can be pretty sure that an argument with a colleague of another race is more likely to jeopardize her chances for advancement than to jeopardize mine.
29. I can be pretty sure that if I argue for the promotion of a person of another race, or a program centering on race, this is not likely to cost me heavily within my present setting, even if my colleagues disagree with me.
30. If I declare there is a racial issue at hand, or there isn't a racial issue at hand, my race will lend me more credibility for either position than a person of color will have.
31. I can choose to ignore developments in minority writing and minority activist programs, or disparage them, or learn from them, but in any case, I can find ways to be more or less protected from negative consequences of any of these choices.
32. My culture gives me little fear about ignoring the perspectives and powers of people of other races.
33. I am not made acutely aware that my shape, bearing, or body odor will be taken as a reflection of my race.
34. I can worry about racism without being seen as self-interested or self-seeking.
35. I can take a job with an affirmative action employer without having my coworkers on the job suspect that I got it because of my race.
36. If my day, week, or year is going badly, I need not ask of each negative episode or situation whether it has racial overtones.
37. I can be pretty sure of finding people who would be willing to talk with me and advise me about my next steps, professionally.
38. I can think over many options, social, political, imaginative, or professional, without asking whether a person of my race would be accepted or allowed to do what I want to do.
39. I can be late to a meeting without having the lateness reflect on my race.
40. I can choose public accommodation without fearing that people of my race cannot get in or will be mistreated in the places I have chosen.
41. I can be sure that if I need legal or medical help, my race will not work against me.
42. I can arrange my activities so that I will never have to experience feelings of rejection owing to my race.
43. If I have low credibility as a leader I can be sure that my race is not the problem.
44. I can easily find academic courses and institutions which give attention only to people of my race.
45. I can expect figurative language and imagery in all of the arts to testify to experiences of my race.
46. I can choose blemish cover or bandages in "flesh" color and have them more or less match my skin.

I repeatedly forgot each of the realizations on this list until I wrote it down. For me, white privilege has turned out to be an elusive and fugitive subject. The pressure to avoid it is great, for in facing it I must give up the myth of meritocracy. If these things are true, this is not such a free country; one's life is not what one makes it; many doors open for certain people through no virtues of their own. These perceptions mean also that my moral condition is not what I had been led to believe. The appearance of being a good citizen rather than a troublemaker comes in large part from having all sorts of doors open automatically because of my color.

A further paralysis of nerve comes from literary silence protecting privilege. My clearest memories of finding such analysis are in Lillian Smith's unparalleled *Killers of the Dream* and Margaret Andersen's review of Karen and Mamie Fields' *Lemon Swamp.* Smith, for example, wrote about walking toward black children on the street and knowing they would step into the gutter; Andersen contrasted the pleasure which she, as a white child, took on summer driving trips to the south with Karen Fields' memories of driving in a closed car stocked with all necessities lest, in stopping, her black family should suffer "insult, or worse." Adreinne Rich also recognizes and writes about daily experiences of privilege, but in my observation, white women's writing in this area is far more often on systemic racism than on our daily lives as light-skinned women.[2]

In unpacking this invisible knapsack of white privilege, I have listed conditions of daily experience which I once took for granted, as neutral, normal, and universally available to everybody, just as I once thought of a male-focused curriculum as the neutral or accurate account which can speak for all. Nor did I think any of these perquisites as bad for the holder. I now think that we need a more finely differentiated taxonomy of privilege, for some of these varieties are only what one would want for everyone in a just society, and others give license to be ignorant, oblivious, arrogant, and destructive. Before proposing some more finely-tuned categorization, I will make some observations about the general effects of these conditions on my life and expectations.

In this potpourri of examples, some privileges make me feel at home in the world. Others allow me to escape penalties or dangers which others suffer. Through some, I escape fear, anxiety, or a sense of not being welcome or not being real. Some keep me from having to hide, to be in disguise, to feel sick or crazy, to negotiate each transaction from the position of being an outsider or, within my group, a person who is suspected of having too close links with a dominant culture. Most keep me from having to be angry.

I see a pattern running through the matrix of white privilege, a pattern of assumptions which were passed on to me as a white person. There was one main piece of cultural turf; it was my own turf, and I was among those who could control the turf. I could measure up to the cultural standards and take advantage of the many options I saw around me to make what the culture would call a success of my life. *My skin color was an asset for any move I was educated to want to make.* I could think of myself as "belonging" in major ways, and of making social systems work for me. I could freely disparage, fear, neglect, or be oblivious to anything outside of the dominant cultural forms. Being of the main culture, I could also criticize it fairly freely. My life was reflected back to me frequently enough so that I felt, with regard to my race, if not to my sex, like one of the real people.

Whether through the curriculum or in the newspaper, the television, the economic system, or the general look of people in the streets, we received daily signals and indications that my people counted, and that others *either didn't exist or must be trying not very successfully, to be like people of my race.* We were given cultural permission not to hear voices of people of other races, or a tepid cultural tolerance for hearing or acting on such voices. I was also raised not to suffer seriously from anything which darker-skinned people might say about my group, "protected," though perhaps I should more accurately say *prohibited*, through the habits of my economic class and social group, from living in racially mixed groups or being reflective about interactions between people of differing races.

In proportion as my racial group was being made confident, comfortable, and oblivious, other groups were likely being made unconfident, uncomfortable, and alienated. Whiteness protected me from many kinds of hostility, distress, and violence, which I was being subtly trained to visit in turn upon people of color.

For this reason, the word *privilege* now seems to me misleading. Its connotations are too positive to fit the conditions and behaviors which "privilege systems" produce. We usually think of privilege as being a favored state, whether earned, or conferred by birth or luck. School graduates are reminded they are privileged and urged to use their (enviable) assets well. The word *privilege* carries the connotation of being something everyone must want. Yet some of the conditions I have described here work to systemically over-empower certain groups. Such privilege simply *confers dominance,* gives permission to control, because of one's race or sex. The kind of privilege which gives license to some people to be, at best, thoughtless and, and, at worst, murderous should not continue to be referred to as a desirable attribute. Such "privilege" may be widely desired without being in any way beneficial to the whole society.

Moreover, though "privilege" may confer power, it does not confer moral strength. Those who do not depend on conferred dominance have traits and qualities which may never develop in those who do. Just as Women's Studies courses indicate that women survive their political circumstances to lead lives which hold the human race together, so "underprivileged" people of color who are the world's majority have survived their oppression and lived survivor's lives from which the white global minority can and must learn. In some groups, those dominated have actually become strong through *not* having all of these unearned advantages, and this gives them a great deal to teach the others. Members of the so-called privileged groups can seem foolish, ridiculous, infantile, or dangerous by contrast.

I want, then, to distinguish between earned strength and unearned power conferred systemically. Power from unearned privilege can look like strength when it is in fact permission to escape or to dominate. But not all of the privileges on my list are inevitably damaging. Some, like the expectation that neighbors will be decent to you, or that your race will not count against you in court, should be the norm in a just society and should be considered as the entitlement of everyone. Others, like the privilege not to listen to less powerful people, distort the humanity of the holders as well as the ignored groups. Still others, like finding one's staple foods everywhere, may be a function of being a member of a numerical majority in the population. Others have to do with not having to labor under pervasive negative stereotyping and mythology.

We might at least start by distinguishing between positive advantages which we can work to spread, to the point where they are not advantages at all but simply part of the normal civic and social fabric, and negative types of advantage which unless rejected will always reinforce our present hierarchies. For example, the positive "privilege" of belonging, the feeling that one belongs within the human circle, as Native Americans say, fosters development and should not be seen as privilege for a few. It is, let us say, an entitlement which none of us should have to earn; ideally it is an *unearned entitlement.* At present, since only a few have it, it is an *unearned advantage* for them. The negative "privilege" which gave me cultural permission not to take darker-skinned others seriously can be seen as arbitrarily conferred dominance and should not be desirable for anyone. This paper results from a process of coming to see that some of the power which I originally saw as attendant on being a human being in the United States consisted in *unearned advantage* and *conferred dominance,* as well as other kinds of special circumstance not universally taken for granted.

In writing this paper I have also realized that white identity and status (as well as class identity and status) give me considerable power to choose whether to broach this subject and its trouble. I can pretty well decide whether to disappear and avoid and not listen and escape the dislike I may engender in other people through this essay, or interrupt, take over, dominate, preach, direct, criticize, or control to some extent what goes on in reaction to it. Being white, I am given considerable power to escape many kinds of danger or penalty as well as to choose which risks I want to take.

There is an analogy here, once again, with Women's Studies. Our male colleagues do not have a great deal to lose in supporting Women's Studies, but they do decide whether to commit themselves to more equitable distributions of power. They will probably feel few penalties whatever choice they make; they do not seem, in any obvious short-term sense, the ones at risk, though they and we are all at risk because of the behaviors which have been rewarded in them.

Through Women's Studies work I have met very few men who are truly distressed about systemic, unearned male advantage and conferred dominance. And so one question for me and others like me is whether we will be like them, or whether we will get truly distressed, even outraged, about unearned race advantage and conferred dominance and if so, what we will do to lessen them. In any case, we need to do more work in identifying how they actually affect our daily lives. We need more down-to-earth writing by people about these taboo subjects. We need more understanding of the ways in which white "privilege" damages white people, for these are not the same ways in which it damages the victimized. Skewed white psyches are an inseparable part of the picture, though I do not want to confuse the kinds of damage done to the holders of special assets and to those who suffer the deficits. Many, perhaps most, of our white students in the United States think that racism doesn't affect them because they are not people of color; they do not see "whiteness" as a racial identity. Many men likewise think that Women's Studies does not bear on their own existences because they are not female; they do not see themselves as having gendered identities. Insisting on the universal *effects* of "privilege" systems, then, becomes one of our chief tasks, and being more explicit about the *particular* effects in particular contexts is another. Men need to join us in this work.

In addition, since race and sex are not the only advantaging systems at work, we need to similarly examine the daily experience of having age advantage, or ethnic advantage, or physical ability, or advantage related to nationality, religion, or sexual orientation. Professor Marnie Evans suggested to me that in many ways the list I made also applies directly to heterosexual privilege. This is a still more taboo subject than race privilege: the daily ways in which heterosexual privilege makes married persons comfortable or powerful, providing supports, assets, approvals, and rewards to those who live or expect to live in heterosexual pairs. Unpacking that content is still more difficult, owing to the deeper embeddedness of heterosexual advantage and dominance, and stricter taboos surrounding these.

But to start such an analysis I would put this observation from my own experience: The fact that I live under the same roof with a man triggers all kinds of societal assumptions about my worth, politics, life, and values, and triggers a host of unearned advantages and powers. After recasting many elements from the original list I would add further observations like these:

1. My children do not have to answer questions about why I live with my partner (my husband).
2. I have no difficulty finding neighborhoods where people approve of our household.

3. My children are given texts and classes which implicitly support our kind of family unit, and do not turn them against my choice of domestic partnership.
4. I can travel alone or with my husband without expecting embarrassment or hostility in those who deal with us.
5. Most people I meet will see my marital arrangements as an asset to my life or as a favorable comment on my likability, my competence, or my mental health.
6. I can talk about the social events of a weekend without fearing most listener's reactions.
7. I will feel welcomed and "normal" in the usual walks of public life, institutional, and social.
8. In many contexts, I am seen as "all right" in daily work on women because I do not live chiefly with women.

Difficulties and dangers surrounding the task of finding parallels are many. Since racism, sexism, and heterosexism are not the same, the advantaging associated with them should not be seen as the same. In addition, it is hard to disentangle aspects of unearned advantage which rests more on social class, economic class, race, religion, sex, and ethnic identity than on other factors. Still, all of the oppressions are interlocking, as the Combahee River Collective statement of 1977 continues to remind us eloquently.[3]

One factor seems clear about all of the interlocking oppressions. They take both active forms which we can see and embedded forms which as a member of the dominant group one is taught not to see. In my class and place, I did not see myself as racist because I was taught to recognize racism only in individual acts of meanness by members of my group, never in invisible systems conferring unsought racial dominance on my group from birth. Likewise, we are taught to think that sexism or heterosexism is carried on only through individual acts of discrimination, meanness, or cruelty toward women, gays, and lesbians, rather than in invisible systems conferring unsought dominance on certain groups. Disapproving of the systems won't be enough to change them. I was taught to think that racism could end if white individuals changed their attitudes; many men think sexism can be ended by individual changes in daily behavior toward women. But a man's sex provides advantage for him whether or not he approves of the way in which dominance has been conferred on his group. A "white" skin in the United States opens many doors for whites whether or not we approve of the way dominance had been conferred on us. Individual acts can palliate, but cannot end, these problems. To redesign social systems we need first to acknowledge their colossal unseen dimensions. The silences and denials surrounding privilege are the key political tools here. They keep thinking about equality or equity incomplete, protecting unearned advantage and conferred dominance by making these taboo subjects. Most talk by whites about equal opportunity seems to me now to be about equal opportunity to try to get in to a position of dominance while denying that *systems* of dominance exist.

It seems to me that obliviousness about white advantage, like obliviousness about male advantage, is kept strongly inculturated in the United States so as to maintain the myth of meritocracy, the myth that democratic choice is equally available to all. Keeping most people unaware that freedom of confident action is there for just a small number of people props up those in power, and serves to keep power in the hands of the same groups that have most of it already. Though systemic change takes many decades, there are pressing questions for me and I imagine for some others like me if we raise our daily consciousness on the perquisites of being light-skinned. What will we do with such knowledge? As we know from watching men, it is an open question whether we will choose to use unearned advantage to weaken hidden systems of advantage, and whether we will use any of our arbitrarily-awarded power to try to reconstruct power systems on a broader base.

DISCUSSION QUESTIONS

1. What does the author mean by the concept of "white privilege"?

2. Reread the author's list of 46 examples of white privilege. Select the five examples that seem the most significant in helping you to understand that white people are privileged. Explain your selections.

3. In addition to white privilege, the author also cites examples of heterosexual privilege. In a similar manner, develop a list of privileges that the able bodied enjoy that the physically challenged do not experience.

4. Most of us have experienced privilege in some form. Describe an example from your experience.

5. How does this article help you to understand the oppression that members of other groups may experience?

Notes

1. This paper was presented at the Virginia Women's Studies Association conference in Richmond in April 1986 and the American Educational Research Association conference in Boston in October 1986 and discussed with two groups of participants in the Dodge Seminars for Secondary School Teachers in New York and Boston in the spring of 1987.

2. Andersen, Margaret, "Race and the Social Science Curriculum: A Teaching and Learning Discussion." *Radical Teacher,* November 1984, pp. 17–20; Smith, Lillian. 1949. *Killers of the Dream.* New York: W.W. Norton.

3. "A Black Feminist Statement." The Combahee River Collective. In Hull, Scott, and Smith (eds.). *All the Women Are White, All the Blacks Are Men. But Some of Us Are Brave: Black Women's Studies.* The Feminist Press, 1982, pp. 13–22.

Diversity on the Web

Peggy McIntosh writes about the notion of racial, gender, and straight privilege and makes it clear that most people are unaware of their privileges. Watch "The Miniature Earth" video at:

www.miniature-earth.com

What does this short video teach you about your educational and social class privileges?

What are the global and future implications of the data presented in the video?

THE EMOTIONAL CONNECTION OF DISTINGUISHING DIFFERENCES AND CONFLICT

Carole G. Parker

GOALS

- To understand how emotions can escalate into conflicts
- To learn when it is appropriate to avoid and repress differences
- To be aware of the dangers of avoidance and repression in terms of the business case for diversity

In recent years, diversity in organizations has been an exciting, stimulating, frustrating, and intriguing topic. Some organizations continue to struggle for diversity whereas others have a fully integrated diverse workforce. The challenge to increase and manage diversity continues to be critical to organizational goals, particularly as more organizations, large and small, transact business internationally. Some organizations work to appreciate diversity and value differences, whereas others continue to discount differences and diversity. Smart managers today realize the importance of balance in work groups. Attempts to incorporate differences in age, gender, race, culture, sexual preference, and styles of being in their organizations to capitalize on the incredible potential diversity offers are occurring. Managing differences requires energy, commitment, tolerance, and finally, appreciation among all parties involved. Differences among people are not inherently good or bad; there is no one "right" way to deal with differences. Learning to manage and ultimately appreciate differences requires learning, emotional growth, and stretching the boundaries of all participants. Although differences can be challenging, they also lead to very important benefits, both to individuals, groups and organizations.

HOW DIFFERENCES ARE OFTEN MANAGED

What action and factors must be uppermost in selecting the most appropriate approach to addressing differences? Often avoidance or repression is used to manage differences. The avoidance of differences often takes the form of associating with individuals of similar backgrounds, experiences, beliefs, and values. This strategy enables an environment of mutual support and predictability. Those who are adverse to risk or challenges are apt to select this strategy. Another avoidance strategy is to separate individuals who create sparks between each other. Although this strategy may reduce tension, it minimizes the opportunity for individuals and the organization to learn and grow.

The repression of differences occurs when an individual or organization refuses to allow disagreements to emerge. Top management often influences the culture by stressing conformity, which naturally affects diversity. Statements by managers such as: "We must work on this project in a professional and collegial manner," or "By working together cooperatively, we will succeed during these difficult times," create the boundaries for behavior limited to cooperation, collaboration, and loyalty and limit the opportunity for challenging assumptions, testing new ideas, and strategies for success. Repression is quite costly. Resistances develop that have both organizational and individual consequences. Blocking strong feelings and repressing differences may result in desensitization and loss of productivity. When individual differences come together, managers exert control to reduce conflict.

Both appropriate times and dangers are associated with the use of avoidance and repression in managing differences. Teams or work groups faced with tight deadlines may want to limit the number and type of ideas generated. Avoidance may be an appropriate interim strategy for dealing with differences by enabling an individual to learn more about a person or situation before advancing a stance. The challenge to management is to decide when it is most appropriate to use these approaches. The skill level of the manager, rather than an overt choice, may also influence the decision. Avoidance can lead to groupthink, which occurs when everyone in a group agrees with everyone else, even though there are differences among group members. Groupthink is the result of not challenging ideas, opinions, values, or beliefs. Individuals may not believe it is safe (concerns about advancing or retaining one's job) to challenge, particularly if management does not model this behavior.

Still another danger in avoiding differences is overcompatibility. When overcompatibility exists in an organization, it may be due to a strong need for support, reassurance, or security or a need to eliminate perceived threats. In an organization, this can severely hamper the development of new ideas, productivity, growth, and development. Avoidance and repression of differences are not viable solutions. When differences are present, they must be expressed and worked through. If not, unnecessary conflict will result.

POSITIVE ASPECTS OF DIFFERENCES

- Differences are opportunities. The old adage "Two heads are better than one" has merit. When combining multiple perspectives, one gains a richer set of experiences, and the variability of these often leads to a more creative approach than could be achieved independently.
- Differences are tests to the strength of a position. One needs to be sure all the perspectives, opinions, and perceptions enhance the final product.

A healthy interaction among differences (gender, age, race, culture, etc.) could address the preceding concerns. Two factors influence the treatment of differences: first, the needs, wants and goals of the individual; and second, the value placed on the relationship. People are often motivated by the desire to meet their needs and satisfy their wants and desires. The stronger the motivation, the greater the likelihood of addressing differences. Furthermore, when the persons involved are important to each other, or valued, the tendency to manage the difference increases to preserve the relationship. The reverse is likely when there is no value in the relationship. Once these factors are assessed, it becomes necessary to recognize behavior and attitudes that *will* be helpful in managing the differences.

Differences are not problems to be solved; they are dilemmas to be managed. Successful managers of difference reduce their judgments and accept the difference as legitimate. Clear boundaries between self and others, a willingness and interest in being influenced, and an awareness of choice with the ability to make choices are also helpful. Using strong language such as *ought to, cannot, necessary, impossible, requirement,* or *mandate* will diminish success.

Differences are experienced from contact with others who are dissimilar. A range of life experiences and success in interpersonal relationships support the ability to deal with differences. Individuals who have traveled nationally and internationally or who have had unusual experiences beyond the normal scope of their daily activities tend to develop an appreciation for differences, even though at the time of initial contact there may have been challenges, fear, and longing for what is familiar. Managing differences is not an individual process; it is interactive among individuals. When only one individual is attempting to deal with the difference, the result is coping behavior. Dealing with differences evokes emotion. A range of emotions for human interaction that leads to awareness of differences is necessary. These emotions can lead to conflict but conflict is *not* a prerequisite to managing differences. Differences evoke emotions, ranging from small or minor to large and major. An inverted triangle graphically shows the escalating intensity in each level of emotion as differences are encountered (see Figure 1.2).

This model is based on the assumption that difficulties will likely result from contact with differences. The first level involves an awareness of the difference. Here the parties are exploring and learning about each other—what is similar, what is not, what is discomforting; the second level may result. One becomes uncomfortable with boundaries being pushed while values or beliefs are challenged. When the differences appear to be greater than the similarities, annoyance occurs. The parties are not able to appreciate how their differences may be beneficial to each other. Irritation, on the next level, may result from continued exploration, possibly through a dialectic process. Tension is heightening as more contact occurs; there is possibly an overlay of fear. The boundaries of self are threatened (What will happen to me if I continue with this encounter?), and frustration leading to open disagreement develops.

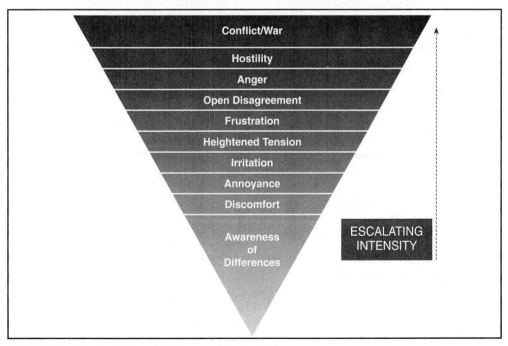

FIGURE 1-2 The Escalation of Differences into Conflict

Anger, often a protective strategy, shifts the emotions to the next level, and hostility erupts while the dispute solidifies. Each party has a firm stance reflecting their position. The final level is conflict or war, where each party works hard to repress, neutralize or destroy the other. In Figure 1, we suggest that an individual, group, organization, or society may, depending on the situation, traverse through each of these emotional levels when encountering differences. The process is not necessarily a linear one. Emotions run deep on various issues and could erupt immediately from awareness to hostility or anger or any other step on the triangle. In fact, awareness can lead to avoidance, tolerance, or appreciation.

Recent history lends itself to application to the triangle. In 1993, terrorists, who had different values and beliefs than most Americans, bombed the New York City World Trade Center. The explosion caused six deaths, 1,042 injuries, and nearly $600 million in damages. Americans were shocked, and then President Clinton declared that every effort should be taken to bring those responsible to justice. Swift actions lead to the prosecution and conviction of four of seven coconspirators. Yet, the American public, although outraged and frightened by the experience, only demonstrated minimal awareness that there were dramatic differences between the U.S. foreign policy and those on the receiving end of the policy. Not until seven years later, with the attacks on the World Trade Center, along with the Pentagon, did awareness shift to outrage, anger, hostility, and ultimately conflict/war.

During the aftermath of the events of September 11, 2001, when thousands of people from many countries met their peril in the attack on the World Trade Center, the United States unified against all who would harm her. In many instances, those who disagreed with the policy to go to war against those responsible for this terrorist act were afraid to speak out. It was considered anti-American to express different opinions about how to handle terrorist activity focused on the United States. Such behavior is an example of groupthink, mentioned earlier in this chapter. The government is particularly susceptible to groupthink where patriotism must be at the highest, yet evidence of dissent tends to make its way to the media, newsprint, or television. Still, individuals may be reluctant to speak candidly against the actions of government policy.

Conflict, at the top of the triangle, may result or emerge from differences. There are many definitions of conflict. Listed here are typical examples of definitions:

1. Conflict exists when two or more parties want the same thing or their wants are incompatible in some way.
2. Conflict must involve emotionality; it is a disturbing emotion within ourselves and may involve feelings of anger and frustration.
3. The higher the stakes, the greater the conflict; one must *care* to have conflict.
4. Conflict can be internal: within oneself, a group, or between groups. Conflict involves competition of wants and viewpoints.
5. Conflict can be enjoyable.

It is important to distinguish conflict from difference. Difference and conflict are both important and necessary ingredients in human interaction and, if valued, can lead to opportunity, creativity, and appreciation. Difference is a component of diversity, which is a constant in our environment. Managers and the workforce are grappling with this constant and learning that appreciating or valuing differences opens the door to new and creative ways of addressing organizational challenges. For example, when a group of salaried and union personnel from the automotive industry were invited to identify adjectives they associate with conflict, most of the language was highly charged, emotional, and violent (see Table 1). The autoworkers pointed out that differences can lead to conflict and cited examples including the inability to motivate

Table 1.1 Distinguishing Difference and Conflict	
Conflict	**Difference**
Anger	Opinions
War	Ideas
Teansion	Options
Kill	Methods
Hostility	Skills
Shouting	Race
	Gender
	Jobs
	Age
	Interpretation
	Values
	Environment

employees to complete their assigned jobs, poor communication, pressures concerning time, inequity in work assignments, differences of opinions, and methods for getting work done. They further pointed out how important it is for people to listen to each other and pay attention to the difference, incorporating the difference in the process of solving a problem or completing a task, not just engaging in conflict because of the difference.

It was believed that when a diverse team worked together, there was greater creativity and innovation, a sense of connectedness, more risk taking, less boredom, higher productivity, and greater cooperation. On the other hand, the mismanagement of differences or engaging in conflictual behavior in the organization would most likely lead to higher stress, individual withdrawal, limited learning, less risk taking, overcompatibility, interpersonal tension, and decreased communication.

THE EMOTIONAL CONNECTION

Emotional intelligence is one key to developing the ability to manage and appreciate differences. Emotional intelligence involves at least five elements: awareness of self, the ability to recognize personal emotions when they are occurring; managing self, which involves awareness of and engaging in emotions that are appropriate to a situation; self-motivation, putting emotional energy into action for a useful person and controlling emotions when necessary; awareness of emotions in others, which involves empathy and demonstrating caring when appropriate; and finally, managing interpersonal relationships, which involves dealing with both self and others in social, professional and personal interactions (Goleman, 1995). Emotional intelligence, then, is the ability to be aware of, name, and manage individual experience of emotions. The triangle in Figure 1 illustrates the escalating intensity of emotions when differences are mismanaged or misunderstood and develop into conflict. Managers must recognize that it is the diversity in styles of interacting and the particular way a person or group makes meaning of their experience that creates the experience of difference. Difference enables choice and opportunity as much as it may create tension and insecurity; this also enables the organization to achieve its objectives. Differences provide opportunities to develop our emotional intelligence. According to Cherniss and Goleman (2001), managers and workers who develop their emotional intelligence may be able to improve their effectiveness at work and potential for advancement. In addition, personal relationships will also improve and strengthen when an individual develops emotional intelligence.

The family unit is an excellent and readily accessible unit for exploring and experimenting with emotional intelligence. Our home life is often a place where we must manage differences with significant consequences for either harmony or unrest. One answer to understanding the emotional impact of encountering differences at home or in the work environment may come with knowledge of three major transitions occurring in contemporary society. Fritz Capra (1982) suggests that a paradigm shift in the thoughts, perceptions, and values that form a particular view of reality is essential if the world is to survive. This is a pattern or paradigm shift involving moving from certainty to uncertainty, closed to open systems, truth to no truth, and a realization of multiple realities coexisting in a complex society. Recognition and mastery of this paradigm shift may prove to be a motivation for developing the emotional skills necessary for valuing diversity and managing differences.

Historically, it has not been acceptable for professionals to exhibit emotions in the workplace; with the introduction of emotional intelligence, there is more acceptance of the whole person and the resulting complexity. When managing diversity or differences, one has at least four options for guiding behavior: avoidance, conflict, tolerance, and appreciation. Avoidance provides an opportunity to learn more about the difference before declaring a stance. In this sense, avoidance as a strategy for managing differences may facilitate new learning and greater opportunity for future interaction of a productive nature. On the other hand, avoidance may be a survival strategy between different status levels within the organization. Clearly, a manager may tell a subordinate to "sit down and just be quiet." Under these circumstances, the worker could jeopardize their position with the organization if they chose to noncompliance.

Tolerance as a strategy may be influenced by status within the organization. Managers generally have the power and authority to get their viewpoints adopted. Nonmangers often must compromise or tolerate the views of their managers, even when they feel the freedom to express an opposing viewpoint. Oftentimes, adopting tolerance is necessary because it allows for the expression of differences; however, when there is an imbalance of power, the options for influence are limited. The upside of tolerance is an individual's opportunity to express a point of view that is active involvement rather than passive participation in an event. Conflict as a strategy may also serve some purpose. Conflict involves direct and active resistance to another and may involve judgments of good, bad, right, or wrong. Often conflict occurs more openly among managers, who have higher status and more latitude than subordinates in resisting a point of view or directives of each other and top management. Finally, appreciation of differences or diversity demonstrates a high degree of personal development and growth at the individual level. The process of appreciation involves a collaborative interaction among various parties with differences. When differences are appreciated, there are usually organizational norms that support the freedom of expression without fear of reprisal. With the ability to discuss differences openly, using a dialectical process, parties are often able to employ multiple strategies, resulting ultimately in appreciation. Appreciation results from applying the skills of emotional intelligence mentioned earlier.

Developing healthy ways to acknowledge and respond to diversity (differences) and the emotions evoked increases our ability to not only manage ourselves but also to manage others in workplace and personal settings. Employing a combination of strategies such as conflict, avoidance, tolerance, and appreciation may demonstrate the capacity of an individual to manage differences and value diversity.

DISCUSSION QUESTIONS

1. How can one distinguish difference from conflict?

2. What are some of the dangers of avoiding and repressing differences?

3. Think of an experience that you had in an organization or social setting involving avoidance or repression of differences. What was the outcome? How did you feel about the outcome?

4. What are some positive aspects of difference anad what roles do emotions play in our ability to manage differences?

5. How can you develop the skills needed to increase your emotional intelligence?

Bibliography

Cherniss, C., & Goleman, D. (2001). *The emotionally intelligent workplace*. San Francisco: Jossey-Bass.

Capra, F. (1982). *The turning point*. New York: Bantam.

Goleman, D. (1995). *Emotional intelligence*. New York: Bantam.

Diversity on the Web

Research the history of a major class action lawsuit such as Bell South, Texaco, Denny's, Georgia Power, Wal-Mart, etc. Develop a time line of the events that led to these lawsuits.

Do the events listed on the time line indicate escalating conflict as illustrated by Parker's triangle?

What actions or interventions could have been taken to prevent these conflicts from escalating into costly lawsuits?

Carole G. Parker, PhD, is a retired associate professor of Management from Seaton Hill University. She has served on the staff of the Gestalt Institute of Cleveland.

THE BEST OF THE BEST

R. Roosevelt Thomas, Jr.

GOALS

- To understand what is really meant by a "best practice" initiative in terms of diversity management
- To raise awareness of how complicated it is to develop effective and creative diversity policies and programs
- To provide guidelines for developing suitable "best practices" for an organization

WHAT EXACTLY DOES "BEST PRACTICE" MEAN WITH REGARD TO DIVERSITY STRATEGY?

Diversity practitioners—whether launching a diversity thrust or building on existing efforts—frequently seek out best practices data. But is this approach to developing a diversity management strategy effective? Several reasons exist for treading carefully with best practices.

First, the notion of best practices presumes that a solution exists. However for embryonic, emerging field like diversity management, solutions may not yet be developed, so best practices at best would represent steps toward a desired resolution.

Second, best practices may represent the best at a given point in time, but not necessarily where you hope to be ultimately. This can occur when best practices are developed against progress to date, rather than on the basis of ultimate success.

Third, best practices can generate dysfunctional discussions about apples and oranges, especially in a young field like diversity where consensus is not present regarding basic concepts, definitions and aspirations. Care must be taken to assume the best practices relate to your organization's diversity context.

Fourth, best practices in one setting may not work in another. Organizations can have vastly different cultures. An empowerment set of best practices, for example, might not fit in a rigid, hierarchal culture. Here, more would be required.

Fifth, best practices do not necessarily mean that progress exists. I was present when one organization announced it had received a best practices award. The immediate, incredulous responses from employees were, "How? For what? In relation to what?" Stated differently, utilization of best practices does not necessarily translate into best results.

Sixth, the implementation of best practices can lead to complacency: Now that we have adopted best practices, what else is there to do?

---

*Reprinted with permission from *Diversity Executive*, July/August 2050 p. 50.

In spite of these challenges, a best practices approach to strategy can offer four critical benefits:

1. Minimize the need to start strategizing from scratch.
2. Enhance credibility with external and internal constituencies.
3. Benchmark opportunities against other organizations.
4. Offer a foundation on which to build.

While best practices can be a basis for the development of diversity, executives should keep in mind that in a developing field like diversity, best practices do not negate the need for pioneering and creativity, and best practices are not the only source of ideas for strategy. Chief diversity officers considering best practices should do the following.

1. *Specify their operational context.* They then will have a framework to assess the appropriateness of any best practices they discover. Specifically, CDO's should seek clarity regardinsg their diversity definitions, concepts, frameworks and aspirations. As they consider best practices, practitioners should compare their operational context with those of the best practices they uncover.
2. *Identify the assumptions and motives undergirding your organization's diversity work.* Sometimes CDO's are not aware of these undergirding factors; they are only are that "the CEO wants to do this."

   In one corporation where the decision had been made to launch a diversity thrust, everyone cited the CEO's supports as the driving force, but few knew what his motivation or goals were. Will the motivation sustain the work needed?
3. *Identify action options.* CDO's should not use best practices as their vehicle to discover the field. On their own, they should map out the field's alternatives and then search for best practices that are appropriate within their organizational context. This pre-identification of options can be invaluable to explore and assess best practices.
4. *Develop a pioneering mindset and spirit.* A pioneering attitude reinforces the notion that best practices are only one input that can be supportive of strategizing.

These preparation guidelines reflect my view that CDO's should do their homework before considering the adoption of best practices. Further, I place considerable importance on the need for pioneering creativity.

Accordingly, it might be more appropriate to refer to best practices as pioneering practices and to refer to organizations that are best in class as pioneers. This nomenclature would more aptly capture the evolving nature and spirit of the field and minimize the likelihood of premature stagnation and complacency.

DISCUSSION QUESTIONS

1. How does this article make developing a "best practice" for diversity initiative simpler to do and how does it also make it more complicated?

2. From what you have learned so far in this class, why does the author's statement about best practices generating "dysfunctional discussions" make sense?

3. Why do you think that it is important to "enhance credibility with external and internal stakeholders" to implement a diversity management strategy effectively?

4. What does the author suggest about the validity of diversity awards?

THE PITNEY BOWES CASE: A LEGACY OF DIVERSITY MANAGEMENT

Carol P. Harvey
Assumption College

GOALS

- To provide an example of an organization that has been successful at linking diversity initiatives to its business strategy planning processes
- To illustrate the importance of corporate leadership support for successful diversity management
- To show the impact of organizational values on programs and policies
- To demonstrate that diversity can be a competitive advantage

On July 2, 2004, Pitney Bowes' CEO Michael Critelli said,

> Diversity is a part of our DNA at Pitney Bowes. We view diversity as a competitive imperative that helps drive innovation, deliver customer value, reach new markets and serve businesses of all sizes in over 130 countries worldwide. We also recognize that our future success is closely tied with our ability to attract, develop and retain top talent and our inclusive culture will help us regardless of race, gender or ethnicity (Critelli, 2001).

In April 1942, Pitney Bowes' CEO Walter Wheeler, said,

> There has never been any management policy in Pitney Bowes, which would preclude any individual qualified to do a job from obtaining it. Human nature being what it is, however, I have no doubt but what prejudices on the part of individuals already employed may have prevented some applicant from obtaining employment with us. It is the responsibility of the Personnel Department to see that these personal prejudices do not prevent the employment of qualified people regardless of race, color or religion (Cahn, 1961, p. 204).

As the opening quotations illustrate, Pitney Bowes, the world's leading provider of integrated mail and document systems and services solutions is an example of a corporation with a long tradition of diversity management. Pitney Bowes' business success is built on a culture that values innovation, change, and growth—and diversity is an integral part of that culture. Managers are held accountable for diversity, recruiters form partnerships with community organizations that help bring the most talented minority interns and workers into the organization, the company has an award-winning diversity supplier program and diversity is incorporated into the strategic planning process.

EARLY COMPANY HISTORY

To improve the efficiency of the U.S. post office, prevent stamp thefts, and simplify the business mailing process, Arthur H. Pitney patented the first practical postage meter in the United States in 1901. Although somewhat successful with his invention, the growth of his business, the American Postage Meter Company, was complicated because the post office would not approve its use for first class mail. In the meantime, the Universal Stamping Machine Company, under the leadership of its founder, Walter H. Bowes, was renting stamp-canceling machines to U.S. post offices. Rather than continue to compete with each other, the two men recognized their complementary talents of marketing (Bowes) and technology (Pitney) and merged into the Pitney Bowes Postage Meter Company in 1920. In the same year, Congress and the U.S. Post Office approved the postage meter for first class mail (Critelli, 2000).

In the 1920s and 1930s, Pitney Bowes, located in Stamford Ct, benefited from decreased government regulations on metered mail and achieved much of its growth through technological inventions that solved specific customer mailing problems. Even in these early years, Pitney Bowes was progressive in its treatment of employees. Rather than lay off employees during the depression, the corporation cut wages by 10 percent and eliminated stockholder dividends. Efforts to unionize the employees were unsuccessful due to the company's generous benefits programs (Pedersen, 2002).

A TRADITION OF DIVERSITY LEADERSHIP: THREE CEOs

Understanding diversity at Pitney Bowes today requires an historical examination of leadership and organizational culture. In 1937, Walter H. Wheeler Jr., who is credited with the origins of Pitney Bowes diversity initiatives, became company president. Wheeler, the stepson of Bowes, was educated at Worcester Academy "where the headmaster, Daniel Webster Abercrombie, had his own form of democracy where all the boys were treated equally at least in class, in the dining hall, assemblies, student government, etc." (Frank Callahan, 2007). This school was "one of the earliest schools to accept students regardless of race or nationality . . . It was here that Walter was first introduced to certain principles of democracy that were to have dramatic applications years later" (Cahn, p. 76).

To understand how innovative Wheeler's diversity values and policies were at this time, it is necessary to understand the historical context. In the 1940s there was no national Civil Rights legislation in the United States. It was perfectly legal to refuse to hire, promote or to fire someone because of his/her race, ethnicity, gender, religion, etc. In some parts of the country, Blacks still drank from separate water fountains, rode in the back of the bus and attended separate public schools. Women were relegated to applying only for jobs that were advertised in newspapers as "help wanted female." These positions consisted mainly of low-paying clerical and retail jobs and for the highly educated women, mostly limited to helping professions like teaching, social work, and nursing. Anti-Semitism was rampant. In fact, Wheeler once resigned from a local yacht club because of their policy to deny membership to Jews.

There are many examples of Wheeler's infusion of his personal values into the corporate culture and management policies of Pitney Bowes. Predating the Civil Rights Act by twenty years, he directed his managers to hire the same percentage of "colored workers" and "Hebrews" as were living in the Stamford area (Cahn, 1961, p. 204). He walked out of a New Orleans hotel when management refused to register a Black Pitney Bowes employee. During World War II, like many

U.S. manufacturing plants, Pitney Bowes suspended production of its own products to manufacture replacement parts for planes, guns, etc. However, at Wheeler's direction unlike many U.S. corporations, after the war Pitney Bowes retained the women and racial minorities who had been hired to replace the white male workers deployed overseas.

Wheeler also recognized that just hiring diverse workers was not enough. The corporation also had to make an effort to integrate them into the organization. Open communication and honesty have long been a crucial element of the diversity initiatives at Pitney Bowes. In 1946 Pitney Bowes hired its first African American office employee, Gladys Robinson. Although she was selected on the basis of her interviews and aptitude test (i.e., fully qualified), she was also prepared by management for any negative comments that she might receive from co-workers. Management discussed her hiring with the employees in her department before her arrival. This preparation of both employee and co-workers resulted in a friendly welcome from her new co-workers and became a standard procedure for new workers for some time. Mrs. Robinson said that she

> Detected an attempt on the part of my fellow employees to reassure me that I was wanted. After about six months I noticed the self-consciousness on the part of my fellow employees was beginning to wane. I was merely accepted as another worker and this suited me just fine . . . By now, however, most people have become accustomed to the fact that Negroes are employed in most every department in the company (Cahn, 1961, p. 207).

When anti-trust legislation threatened Pitney Bowes in the late 1950s, the corporation embarked on a strategy of diversification into copiers, leasing equipment, retail supply chain products, etc. However, Chairman Wheeler stated that his company's dominance in the postage meter industry was not due to anti-competitive business practices but to positive employee relations that resulted in productive workers, lower costs, and innovative products (Pederson, 2002, pp. 296–7).

In the late 1980s George Harvey became the CEO at Pitney Bowes and took Wheeler's value of inclusiveness to the level of a business imperative. He recognized that "those who have previously been denied opportunity are often better performers who are more committed to excellence when they are given a chance" (Critelli, 2001, p. 19). His diversity focus was to see that all employees had the opportunity to advance their careers and become part of the leadership team, not just because it was the right thing to do but also because it would enable the company to remain competitive by recruiting and promoting the most talented workers.

According to Sheryl Battles, long-time employee and now Vice-President of Corporate Communication, Harvey once looked out at a room full of managers and said that too many of them looked just like him and that was going to change. When women were hired away from traditional low-paying jobs into the sales force where they could earn commissions and bonuses, they started to outperform the men. Harvey was quoted as saying "if this is what diversity does for business results, I want more diversity" (Battles, interview 6/16/06).

Along with the twenty-first century challenges of continued growth in a slow economy, increased competition, and the threat of terrorism through the mail, the current CEO and Chairman, Michael J. Critelli, continues the legacy of diversity leadership. Currently serving his second term as Chairman of the Board of the National Urban League, the country's largest and oldest African-American organization, Critelli sees three dimensions to diversity management today at Pitney Bowes: becoming the employer of choice for a diversified workforce; understanding the challenges of global diversity; and implementing supplier diversity programs that create jobs for women and minority entrepreneurs (Bean, 2003, p. 54). Currently, women comprise 25 percent of the CEO's direct reports and 40 percent of the sales force.

Twenty percent of the companies' officers and managers are people of color. Worldwide 40 percent of the corporation's 33,000 employees are people of color. In 2000 Pitney Bowes purchased $47.5 million dollars worth of goods and services from women and minority-owned businesses (Business Wire, 2001).

PITNEY BOWES TODAY

Although this corporation was built on the success of manufacturing, leasing, and repairing postage meter equipment, Pitney Bowes, like all other U.S. manufactures, is facing new challenges. In response to globalization, Pitney Bowes is now doing business in 130 countries and has over 34,000 employees worldwide. International operations account for 17 percent of their total revenue. With the shift from a manufacturing to a service economy, Pitney Bowes has retrained its workers to move from a manufacturing to an assembly model of production. In addition, the corporation has broadened its mission to focus on "integrated mail and document management" or "mailstream" services such as package tracking and logistical transportation software.

Rather than be threatened by the impact of technology such as the Internet and mobile phones on decreasing volumes of traditional mail, Pitney Bowes considers these as business opportunities. Pitney Bowes provides customized U.S. postage stamps available on Zazzle.com and has formed a partnership with eBay to provide web-based postage applications. Based on a system of longitude and latitude, T-Mobile uses Pitney Bowes' GeoTAX software to apply the correct federal state and municipal taxes to 20 million customer bills each month. In 2005, the company continued to grow through innovative services and acquisitions with nearly 25 percent of Pitney Bowes' $5.4 billion revenue coming from companies that they acquired since 2001 (Pitney Bowes, 2005). Standard & Poor's recently rated Pitney Bowes stock, as a "buy" with an expectation that gross margins will soon hit 55 percent (Marcial, 2006).

DIVERSITY INITIATIVES: USING A HUMAN CAPITAL APPROACH

Considering employees as human capital means that an organization realizes the economic value of its employees and their role in achieving profits, innovation, productivity, and long-term growth. Because being inclusive offers an organization a wider selection of talented people, it is a key element in the implementation of a business strategy based on the human capital approach. However, having diverse employees—i.e., the "numbers"—is not enough. Diverse employees can only become a competitive advantage if an organization capitalizes on the variety of perspectives and viewpoints of its employees in a supportive and cooperative culture (Kochan, et. al, 2003).

RECRUITMENT

At Pitney Bowes, the key human resource functions of selection/recruiting, evaluating performance, training, benefits, etc., reflect the systemic nature of diversity as an organizational value. In order to have access to the best and the brightest diverse employee pool, the corporation uses a multi-level approach that includes advertising in publications targeted to the diverse community, forming external partnerships and alliances with organizations that represent a diverse talent pool, and sponsoring diversity-related events and causes. Some of these partnerships include Inroads (for interns), the National Urban League, the U.S. Hispanic Chamber of Commerce, Women's Business Enterprise National Council, National Society of Hispanic MBAs, National Black MBA Association, The Association of Latino Professionals in Finance and Accounting, The Connecticut Asian Pacific American Bar Association, Society of Women Engineers, National

Society of Black Engineers, etc. Recently, Pitney Bowes' Literary and Education Fund donated $50,000 to the National Action Council for Minorities in Engineering Inc. (NACME) to develop a community college recruitment program that would help prepare African American, Native American, and Latinos for careers in math, engineering, and science (Pitney Bowes, 2006).

These relationships give Pitney Bowes a positive image in diverse communities and result in a more diverse but qualified pool of directors and job applicants. Currently, 25 percent of the Board of Directors are female or racial minorities. As of April 19, 2004, Pitney Bowes had a workforce comprised of 26 percent African Americans, 10 percent Latino and 5 percent Asian Americans (Torsone, 2006).

EVALUATION OF DIVERSITY MANAGEMENT

Diversity management plays a key role in the evaluation process and is included as one of the criteria for each business unit president and his/her managers' performance appraisals. In 1992 the Diversity Task Force (DTF) was established to develop a mission statement and implementation plan for accountability for diversity within the organization. A year later the DTF proposed a diversity strategic planning process that is still in place today. Each business unit develops a strategic plan based on corporate goals. These plans address: communications and training, employee development and work/life balance, business diversity, and community relations.

Within each unit there is a Diversity Leadership Council made up of employees who meet frequently to ensure that these goals are met. Achievement of these goals is taken into consideration when determining executive compensation (Pitney Bowes, 2006). Susan Johnson, VP of Strategic Talent Management and Diversity Leadership, said that this process turns something "soft and mushy into something measurable" and "the planning process becomes part of the fabric of diversity" (Johnson, 2006).

WORKPLACE BENEFITS

Even the benefit program at Pitney Bowes reflects the intersection of sound business practice with a focus on the preventing illness and recognizing that employees are individuals with different needs. Great Expectations is a program available to employees and spouses that provides prenatal care, risk assessment, and monitoring to prevent high-risk pregnancies. Employees with chronic conditions like diabetes or high blood pressure are offered on-site medical care and free prescriptions to encourage them to manage their illnesses. Employees who attend healthcare seminars can reduce their out of pocket healthcare costs and premiums. The Choice Time Program allows non-exempt employees to bank time off (flex days, etc.) to use for unplanned absences (Torsone, 2006).

RECOGNITION FOR DIVERSITY

Although Pitney Bowes has received numerous awards from external organizations and publications for its diversity efforts (see Exhibit 7), the corporation also rewards employees who demonstrate excellence in diversity through the annual PRISM award. Any individual employee or team can be nominated for the crystal trophy, cash award, and lunch with the CEO and senior management. Recently, this award was given for a program that employs people with disabilities in the outsourced mailrooms that Pitney Bowes manages in other companies (Torsone, 2006). In the fall the Sheldon, Connecticut, campus hosts a family day, called a Diversity Festival that is open to all local employees. The event features entertainment, exhibits, and food from a variety of cultures.

EXHIBIT 7   **Recent Diversity Awards Received by Pitney Bowes**
Business Ethics magazine's **100 Best Corporate Citizen's List**
National Society of Hispanic MBA's **Corporate Partner of the Year**
DiversityInc. Ranked **#1 on Top 10 Companies for Diversity List**
Fortune magazine's **Best Companies for Minorities List**
Working Woman's magazine's **Top 25 Public Companies for Executive Women**
Hispanic magazine's **Top 25 Vendor Programs for Latinos**

ORGANIZATIONAL COMMUNICATION

At Pitney Bowes, the management/employee communication process also is rooted in a tradition of systemic inclusiveness. In the 1940s Wheeler felt that he should be as accountable to his employees as he was to his shareholders. So, he began a series of *Job Holders* meetings based on his philosophy that everyone has something valuable to contribute to Pitney Bowes. At these meetings managers explained the state of the business and then answered employees' questions in a two-way dialogue. Today, since the corporation has expanded and become less centralized to Stamford, Connecticut, these meetings take the form of *Town Hall* forums. Each of the direct reports to the CEO travels around the country to present an overview of the business and then responds to employee comments and questions in an open forum format.

When 9/11 and the anthrax mail crises occurred, Pitney Bowes stayed in constant contact with its employees through its voice mail system. The effectiveness of this communication evolved into *Power Talk*, a weekly voice mail from the Chairman or one of his direct reports that is broadcast over the voice mail system. These brief messages cover topics that impact employees such as postal reform, announcement of company awards, company strategies, etc. This practice ensures that employees hear company news first hand rather than depending on the media or informal networks (Battles, 2006).

It is clear that diversity is integrated into the systems and management practices at Pitney Bowes. Because diversity has a long history at the corporation and because there has been continual support at the corporate and Board levels, currently, Pitney Bowes provides an example of a corporation that has used diversity to its competitive advantage. However, as the company continues to grow, particularly by acquisition and global expansion, maintaining diversity as a value will be the challenge of the future.

DISCUSSION QUESTIONS

1. Given Pitney Bowes' growth and globalization strategies, analyze the forces for and against maintaining an organizational culture that supports diversity as a business imperative.

2. Provide specific examples of ways that Pitney Bowes has aligned diversity goals with a market-driven approach to meeting customer needs.

3. At Pitney Bowes, diversity in addition to being an ethical imperative, is a business imperative. How does diversity create competitive advantages for this corporation?

4. Into which of Thomas and Ely's three paradigms does Pitney Bowes fit? Which of their eight preconditions for "making the paradigm shift" apply to Pitney Bowes?

Bibliography

Battles, S. (2006). Interview, June 16.

Battles, S. (1999). Pitney Bowes creates guide for Latina business women. *Business Wire*, November 23.

Bean, L. (2003). Pitney Bowes' CEO Michael Critelli: this change agent understands the value of diversity. *DiversityInc*. October-November, 50–54.

Business Wire Inc. (2001). Pitney Bowes creates web link to expand opportunities for minority and women suppliers: diversity 2000 partners to launch Pitney Bowes Information. February 15.

Cahn, W. (1961). *The story of Pitney-Bowes*. New York: Harper and Brothers.

Callahan, F. (2007) Worcester Academy. e-mail received July 1, 2007.

Critelli, M.J. (2001). *Pitney Bowes, Inc. from mail to messaging: the leading provider of informed mail and messaging management*. Address to the Newcomen Society.

Johnson, S. (2006) interview, June 14.

Kochan, T., Ely, R., Jackson, S., Joshi, A., Jehn, J., Leonard, J., Levine, D., and Thomas, D. (2003). The effects of diversity on business performance: Report of the diversity research network. *Human Resource Management*, 42, #1, 3–22.

Marcial, G. (2006). For Pitney Bowes, a stamp of approval. *Business Week*, 3988, June 12.

Pedersen, J.P. (ed). (2002). Pitney Bowes. *International Directory of Company Histories*, St. James Press: Farmington Hills MI., 47, 295–299.

Pitney Bowes. (2006). Retrieved from Web site pb.com on June 6, 2006.

Pitney Bowes. (2005). Annual report. Stamford, CT.

Tessler, C. (2004). Fortune magazine ranks Pitney Bowes one of America's 50 best companies for minorities. *Fortune Magazine*. July 2, 2004 (11A).

Torsonne, J.G. (2006). Pitney Bowes 2006 annual corporate social responsibility report. Retrieved from pb.com/esearch/uijsp2006annualreport on May 3, 2011

Diversity on the Web

The last sentence of the Pitney Bowes case mentions that the corporation's commitment to diversity could be affected by its growth and global strategies. An additional threat would be hiring a new CEO who does not value diversity as a strategic value. Although the current CEO, Murray Martin, continues the diversity legacy at Pitney Bowes, what has happened in terms of the organization's efforts to maintain an inclusive and diverse culture during a time of internal and external change? How has Pitney Bowes adapted to becoming more of a global business while maintaining diversity as a core value?

To answer these questions, go to the Web site below. Reading this document affirms that diversity and inclusion are still important in the Pitney Bowes culture. Evaluate the 2009 report in terms of

   a. The organization's efforts to maintain an inclusive and diverse culture during a time of internal and external change and
   b. Pitney Bowes' adaptation to becoming more of a global business while maintaining diversity as a core value.
   c. What have they done and why has it worked?

pb.com (Search for the "2009 CR report")

EXPLORING DIVERSITY IN YOUR ORGANIZATION

Carol P. Harvey
Assumption College

A good beginning to a course in diversity is to analyze how diversity or lack of diversity could impact an organization with which you are quite familiar. Your instructor can assign either Option A, exploring diversity on a college campus, or Option B, examining an organization where you are or have been recently employed.

INSTRUCTIONS

Option A—Exploring Diversity on Your College Campus

1. *Organizational Leadership.* Using the catalog, Web page, or other resources, research your college to determine who has the power to make important decisions in the organization. How diverse is this college in terms of its board of trustees and senior staff such as vice presidents, provosts, deans, and above?

2. *Faculty.* Using the catalog, Web page, or other resources, research your college's faculty to determine how diverse they are. Contrast the effects of having a more homogeneous faculty and a more heterogeneous faculty in terms of: (a) your learning experiences, (b) your advising/mentoring experiences, or (c) any other aspects of your college life such as athletics, extracurricular activities, and so on.

3. *Student Body.* Compare the student body to the organizational leadership and faculty. In most cases, the students are younger and less educated but are there other obvious differences such as race, gender, or ethnicity?

   How does the student body compare with the community in which the college is located? (Check www.census.gov.) If there are major differences, how can these be an advantage or a disadvantage to your college experience? Explain your answer.

4. If your college is diverse in terms of leadership, faculty, and/or students, how does diversity contribute to your learning experience and/or personal development? If your college isn't diverse, how does the lack of diversity impact your learning experience and/or personal development?

Option B—Exploring Diversity in Your Work Organization

1. *Organizational Leadership.* Using the organizational chart, Web page, or other resources, research your company to determine who has the power to make important decisions. How diverse is this organization in terms of its board of directors and senior managers such as vice presidents, area managers, and above? *(Note: Their criteria for defining diversity may be related to the location and the mission of your company. For example, if you are working in a racially diverse city, you may find more African Americans. If you are working in fashion retail, you may find more women in leadership positions.)*

2. *Lower-level and/or hourly workers.* How does the diversity of the board and management of your organization compare to the composition of the various levels of your organization? What types of issues does this raise? Provide specific examples.

3. *Customers.* If your organization works with consumers and clients, how do your target markets compare with the management and staff of your organization in terms of diversity?

4. In the future, how could diversity or lack of diversity impact your career and/or the ability of the organization to meet customer/client needs?

Integrative Questions for Section 1

1. What did you learn about workplace diversity from this section that you did not know before you began this course? What are the implications of what you selected for organizations in the future?

2. What did you learn about yourself from this section that you did not know before you began this course? Why is this important to your future in the workplace?

3. Considering these readings and exercises, what are the obstacles/challenges for a) individuals and b) organizations to respond to the need to change to meet the challenge of diversity?

4. Why would some of the "best practices" from the Pitney Bowes case not necessarily work in another organization? Be specific in your answer.

5. Why would some of the "best practices" from the Pitney Bowes case not necessarily work in the organization you used for the "Exploring Diversity . . ." exercise? Be specific in your answer.

6. What is/are the common theme(s) between the Bowman exercise and the Miner article?

7. Have you ever done volunteer work or taken a community service learning class? If so, how has this helped you to learn about diversity? Provide an example from that experienced-based learning that relates to something from this section of the text.

2

Understanding Primary Aspects of Diversity: Race and Ethnicity

In this section, students will

- Learn how cultures have changed and adapted throughout history.
- Explore the issue of racism in American society.
- Consider the current status of Hispanics, Asians, and immigrants in America.
- Examine the intercultural negotiation process.
- Analyze a case that demonstrates why organizations lose lawsuits.
- Experience what it is like to be different from others.

The primary dimensions of diversity are considered to be those social group memberships that are fixed and usually very central to one's self-identity like race, ethnicity, age, gender, mental and physical abilities, and sexual orientation. In Section II we begin by examining the first two: race and ethnicity. First, we explore the inter-relationship between cultures and examine how cultures change and evolve (Sowell). The next three readings address the three major racial/ethnic groups in the United States: African Americans (McNickles), Asians (Meadows), and Hispanics (Etzioni). This leads to an examination of current immigration trends and issues (Allard) and a framework (Salacuse) that can be applied to negotiations among cultural groups (Harvey). Section II closes with a case that illustrates how corporations can manage differences poorly (Harvey) and an exercise that provides an opportunity to see what it feels like when you are a minority in some significant way (Harvey).

A World View of Cultural Diversity

Thomas Sowell

GOALS

- To understand the process of cultural evolution and change
- To learn how other cultures influence Western traditions
- To become aware of the interdependence of global cultures

Diversity has become one of the most often used words of our time—and a word almost never defined. Diversity is invoked in discussions of everything from employment policy to curriculum reform and from entertainment to politics. Nor is the word merely a description of the long-known fact that the American population is made up of people from many countries, many races, and many cultural backgrounds. All this was well known long before the word *diversity* became an insistent part of our vocabulary, an invocation, an imperative, or a bludgeon in ideological conflicts.

The very motto of the country, *E. Pluribus Unum,* recognizes the diversity of the American people. For generations, this diversity has been celebrated, whether in comedies like *Abie's Irish Rose* (the famous play featuring a Jewish boy and an Irish girl) or in patriotic speeches on the Fourth of July. Yet one senses something very different in today's crusades for "diversity"; certainly not a patriotic celebration of America and often a sweeping criticism of the United States, or even a condemnation of Western civilization as a whole.

At the very least, we need to separate the issue of the general importance of cultural diversity—not only in the United States but in the world at large—from the more specific, more parochial, and more ideological agendas that have become associated with this word in recent years. I would like to talk about the worldwide importance of cultural diversity over centuries of human history before returning to the narrower issues of our time.

The entire history of the human race, the rise of man from the caves, has been marked by transfers of cultural advances from one group to another and from one civilization to another. Paper and printing, for example, are today vital parts of Western civilization, but they originated in China centuries before they made their way to Europe. So did the magnetic compass, which made possible the great ages of exploration that put the Western hemisphere in touch with the rest of mankind. Mathematical concepts likewise migrated from one culture to another: Trigonometry from ancient Egypt, and the whole numbering system now used throughout the world originated among the Hindus of India, though Europeans called this system *Arabic numerals* because it was the Arabs who were the intermediaries through which these numbers reached medieval Europe. Indeed, much of

Article reprinted by permission of Springer and Transaction Publications from *Society*, Volume 29, No. 1, 1991, pp. 37–44, "A World View of Cultural Diversity," by Thomas Sowell. With kind permission from Springer Science and Business Media.

the philosophy of ancient Greece first reached Western Europe in Arabic translations, which were then retranslated into Latin or into the vernacular languages of the West Europeans.

Much that became part of the culture of Western civilization originated outside that civilization, often in the Middle East or Asia. The game of chess came from India, gunpowder from China, and various mathematical concepts from the Islamic world, for example. The conquest of Spain by Moslems in the eighth century A.D. made Spain a center for the diffusion into Western Europe of the more advanced knowledge of the Mediterranean world and of the Orient in astronomy, medicine, optics, and geometry.

The later rise of Western Europe to world preeminence in science and technology built upon these foundations, and then the science and technology of European civilization began to spread around the world, not only to European offshoot societies such as the United States or Australia, but also to non-European cultures, of which Japan is perhaps the most striking example.

The historic sharing of cultural advances, until they became the common inheritance of the human race, implied much more than cultural diversity. It implied that some cultural features were not only different from others but better than others. The very fact that people—all people, whether Europeans, Africans, Asians, or others—have repeatedly chosen to abandon some feature of their own culture in order to replace it with something from another culture implies that the replacement served their purposes more effectively. Arabic numerals are not simply different from Roman numerals, they are better than Roman numerals. This is shown by their replacing Roman numerals in many countries whose own cultures derived from Rome, as well as in other countries whose respective numbering systems were likewise superseded by so-called Arabic numerals.

It is virtually inconceivable today that the distances in astronomy or the complexities of higher mathematics should be expressed in Roman numerals. Merely to express the year of the declaration of American independence as MDCCLXXVI requires more than twice as many Roman numerals as Arabic numerals. Moreover, Roman numerals offer more opportunities for errors, as the same digit may be either added or subtracted, depending on its place in sequence. Roman numerals are good for numbering kings or Super Bowls, but they cannot match the efficiency of Arabic numerals in most mathematical operations—and that is, after all, why we have numbers at all. Cultural features do not exist merely as badges of identity to which we have some emotional attachment. They exist to meet the necessities and to forward the purposes of human life. When they are surpassed by features of other cultures, they tend to fall by the wayside or to survive only as marginal curiosities like Roman numerals today.

Not only concepts, information, products, and technologies transfer from one culture to another. The natural produce of the earth does the same. Malaysia is the world's leading grower of rubber trees—but those trees are indigenous to Brazil. Most of rice grown in Africa today originated in Asia, and its tobacco originated in the Western hemisphere. Even a great wheat-exporting nation like Argentina once imported wheat, which was not an indigenous crop to that country. Cultural diversity, viewed internationally and historically, is not a static picture of differentness but a dynamic picture of competition in which what serves human purposes more effectively survives while what does not tends to decline or disappear.

Manuscript scrolls once preserved the precious records, knowledge, and thought of European or Middle Eastern cultures. But once paper and printing from China became known in these cultures, books were clearly far faster and cheaper to produce and drove scrolls virtually into extinction. Books were not simply different from scrolls; they were better than scrolls. The point that some cultural features are better than others must be insisted on today because so many among the intelligentsia either evade or deny this plain reality. The intelligentsia often use words like *perceptions* and *values* as they argue in effect that it is all a matter of how you choose to look at it.

They may have a point in such things as music, art, and literature from different cultures, but there are many human purposes common to peoples of all cultures. They want to live rather than die, for example. When Europeans first ventured into the arid interior of Australia, they often died of thirst or hunger in a land where the Australian aborigines had no trouble finding food or water, within that particular setting, at least, the aboriginal culture enabled people to do what both the aborigines and Europeans wanted to do—survive. A given culture may not be superior for all things in all settings, much less remain superior over time, but particular cultural features may nevertheless be clearly better for some purposes—not just different.

Why is there any such argument in the first place? Perhaps it is because we are still living in the long, grim shadow of the Nazi Holocaust and are, therefore, understandably reluctant to label anything or anyone "superior" or "inferior." But we do not need to. We need only recognize that particular products, skills, technologies, agricultural crops, or intellectual concepts accomplish particular purposes better than their alternatives. It is not necessary to rank one whole culture over another in all things, much less to claim that they remain in that same ranking throughout history. They do not.

Clearly, cultural leadership in various fields has changed hands many times. China was far in advance of any country in Europe in a large number of fields for at least a thousand years and, as late as the sixteenth century, had the highest standard of living in the world. Equally clearly, China today is one of the poorer nations of the world and is having great difficulty trying to catch up to the technological level of Japan and the West, with no real hope of regaining its former world preeminence in the foreseeable future.

Similar rises and falls of nations and empires have been common over long stretches of human history—for example, the rise and fall of the Roman Empire, the "golden age" of medieval Spain and its decline to the level of one of the poorest nations in Europe today, the centuries-long triumphs of the Ottoman Empire intellectually as well as on the battlefields of Europe and the Middle East, and then its long decline to become known as "the sick man of Europe." Yet, while cultural leadership has changed hands many times, that leadership had been real at given times, and much of what was achieved in the process has contributed enormously to our well-being and opportunities today. Cultural competition is not a zero-sum game. It is what advances the human race.

If nations and civilizations differ in their effectiveness in different fields of endeavor, so do social groups. Here is especially strong resistance to accepting the reality of different levels and kinds of skills, interests, habits, and orientations among different groups of people. One academic writer, for example, said that nineteenth-century Jewish immigrants to the United States were fortunate to arrive just as the garment industry in New York began to develop. I could not help thinking that Hank Aaron was similarly fortunate that he often came to bat just as a home run was due to be hit. It might be possible to believe that these Jewish immigrants just happened to be in the right place at the right time if you restricted yourself to their history in the United States. But, again taking a world view, we find Jews prominent, often predominant, and usually prospering, in the apparel industry in medieval Spain, in the Ottoman Empire, in the Russian Empire, in Argentina, in Australia, and in Brazil. How surprised should we be to find them predominant in the same industry in America?

Other groups have excelled in other special occupations and industries. Indeed, virtually every group excels at something. Germans, for example, have been prominent as pioneers in the piano industry. American piano brands like Steinway and Knabe, not to mention the Wurlitzer organ, are signs of the long prominence of Germans in this industry, where they produced the first pianos in Colonial America. Germans also pioneered in piano-building in Czarist Russia, Australia, France, and England. Chinese immigrants have, at one period of history or another, run more than half the grocery stores in Kingston, Jamaica, and Panama City and conducted more than half of all retail trade in Malaysia, the Philippines, Vietnam, and Cambodia. Other groups have dominated the retail trade in other parts of the world—the Gujaratis from India in East Africa and in Fiji or the Lebanese in parts of West Africa, for example.

Nothing has been more common than for particular groups—often a minority—to dominate particular occupations or industries. Seldom do they have any ability to keep out others and certainly not to keep out the majority population. They are simply better at the particular skills required in that occupation or industry. Sometimes we can see why. When Italians have made wine in Italy for centuries, it is hardly surprising that they should become prominent among winemakers in Argentina and in California's Napa Valley. Similarly, when Germans in Germany have been for centuries renowned for their beermaking, how surprised should we be that in Argentina they became as prominent among brewers as Italians among winemakers? How surprised should we be that beermaking, in the United States arose where there were concentrations of German immigrants in Milwaukee and St. Louis, for example? Or that the leading beer producers to this day have German names like Anheuser-Busch or Coors, among many other German names?

Just as cultural leadership in a particular field is not permanent for nations or civilizations, neither is it permanent for given racial, ethnic, or religious groups. By the time the Jews were expelled from Spain in 1492, Europe had overtaken the Islamic world in medical science, so that Jewish physicians who sought refuge in the Ottoman Empire found themselves in great demand in that Moslem country. By the early sixteenth century, the sultan of the Ottoman Empire had on his palace medical staff 42 Jewish physicians and 21 Moslem physicians.

With the passage of time, however, the source of the Jews' advantage—their knowledge of Western medicine—eroded as successive generations of Ottoman Jews lost contact with the West and its further progress. Christian minorities within the Ottoman Empire began to replace the Jews, not only in medicine but also in international trade and even in the theater, once dominated by Jews. The difference was that these Christian minorities—notably Greeks and Armenians—maintained their ties in Christian Europe and often sent their sons there to be educated. It was not race or ethnicity as such that was crucial but maintaining contacts with the ongoing progress of Western civilization. By contrast, the Ottoman Jews became a declining people in a declining empire. Many, if not most, were Sephardic Jews from Spain, once the elite of the world Jewry. But by the time the state of Israel was formed in the twentieth century, those Sephardic Jews who had settled for centuries in the Islamic world now lagged painfully behind the Ashkenazic Jews of the Western world—notably in income and education. To get some idea what a historic reversal that has been in the relative positions of Sephardic Jews and Ashkenazic Jews, one need only note that Sephardic Jews in colonial America sometimes disinherited their own children for marrying Ashkenazic Jews.

Why do some groups, subgroups, nations, or whole civilizations excel in some particular fields rather than others? All too often, the answer to this question must be: Nobody really knows. It is an unanswered question largely because it is an unasked question. There is an uphill struggle merely to get acceptance of the fact that large differences exist among peoples, not just in specific skills in the narrow sense (computer science, basketball, or brewing beer) but more fundamentally in different interests, orientations, and values that determine which particular skills they seek to develop and with what degree of success. Merely to suggest that these internal cultural factors play a significant role in various economic, educational, or social outcomes is to invite charges of "blaming the victim." It is much more widely acceptable to blame surrounding social conditions or institutional policies.

But if we look at cultural diversity internationally and historically, there is a more basic question than whether blame is the real issue. Surely, no human being should be blamed for the way his culture evolved for centuries before he was born. Blame has nothing to do with it. Another explanation that has had varying amounts of acceptance at different times and places is the biological or genetic theory of differences among peoples. I have argued against this theory in many places but will not take the time to go into these lengthy arguments here. A world view of cultural differences over the centuries undermines the genetic theory as well. Europeans and Chinese, for example, are clearly genetically different. Equally clearly, China was a more advanced civilization than Europe in many ways, scientific, technological, and organizational, for at least a thousand years. Yet over the past few centuries, Europe has moved ahead of China in many of these same ways. If those cultural differences were due to genes, how could these two races have changed positions so radically from one epoch in history to another?

All explanations of differences between groups can be broken down into heredity and environment. Yet a world view of the history of cultural diversity seems, on the surface at least, to deny both. One reason for this is that we have thought of environment too narrowly, as the immediate surrounding circumstances or differing institutional policies toward different groups. Environment in that narrow sense may explain some group differences, but the histories of many groups completely contradict that particular version of environment as an explanation. Let us take just two examples out of many that are available.

Jewish immigrants from Eastern Europe and Italian immigrants from southern Italy began arriving in the United States in large numbers at about the same time in the late nineteenth century, and their large-scale immigration also ended at the same time, when restrictive immigration laws were passed in the 1920s. The two groups arrived here in virtually the same economic condition—namely, destitute. They often lived in the same neighborhoods and their children attended the same schools, sitting side by side in the same classrooms. Their environments, in the narrow sense in which the term is commonly used, were virtually identical. Yet their social histories in the United States have been very different.

Over the generations, both groups rose, but they rose at different rates, through different means, and in a very different mixture of occupations and industries. Even wealthy Jews and wealthy Italians tended to become rich in different sectors of the economy. The California wine industry, for example, is full of Italian names like Mondavi, Gallo, and Rossi, but the only prominent Jewish winemaker, Manishewitz, makes an entirely different kind of wine, and no one would compare Jewish winemakers with Italian winemakers in the United States. When we look at Jews and Italians in the very different environmental setting of Argentina, we see the same general pattern of differences between them. The same is true if we look at the differences between Jews and Italians in Australia, or Canada, or Western Europe.

Jews are not Italians and Italians are not Jews. Anyone familiar with their very different histories over many centuries should not be surprised. Their fate in America was not determined solely by their surrounding social conditions in America or by how they were treated by American society. They were different before they got on the boats to cross the ocean, and those differences crossed the ocean with them.

We can take it a step further. Even Ashkenazic Jews, those originating in Eastern Europe, have had significantly different economic and social histories from those originating in Germanic Central Europe, including Austria as well as Germany itself. These differences have persisted among their descendents not only in New York and Chicago but as far away as Melbourne and Sydney. In Australia, Jews from Eastern Europe have tended to cluster in and around Melbourne, while Germanic Jews have settled in and around Sydney. They even have a saying among themselves that Melbourne is a cold city with warm Jews while Sydney is a warm city with cold Jews.

A second and very different example of persistent cultural differences involves immigrants from Japan. As everyone knows, many Japanese-Americans were interned during the Second World War. What is less well known is that there is and has been an even larger Japanese population in Brazil than in the United States. These Japanese, incidentally, own approximately three-quarters as much land in Brazil as there is in Japan. (The Japanese almost certainly own more agricultural land in Brazil than in Japan.) In any event, very few Japanese in Brazil were interned during the Second World War. Moreover, the Japanese in Brazil were never subjected to the discrimination suffered by Japanese-Americans in the decades before the Second World War.

Yet, during the war, Japanese-Americans overwhelmingly remained loyal to the United States and Japanese-American soldiers won more than their share of medals in combat. But in Brazil, the Japanese were overwhelmingly and even fanatically loyal to Japan. You cannot explain the difference by anything in the environment of the United States or the environment of Brazil. But if you know something about the history of those Japanese who settled in these two countries, you know that they were culturally different in Japan before they ever got on the boats to take them across the Pacific Ocean and they were still different decades later. These two groups of immigrants left Japan during very different periods in the cultural evolution of Japan itself. A modern Japanese scholar has said: "If you want to see Japan of the Meiji era, go to the United States. If you want to see Japan of the Taisho era, go to Brazil." The Meiji era was a more cosmopolitan, pro-American era; the Taisho era was one of fanatical Japanese nationalism.

If the narrow concept of environment fails to explain many profound differences between groups and subgroups, it likewise fails to explain many very large differences in the economic and social performances of nations and civilizations. An eighteenth-century writer in Chile described that country's many natural advantages in climate, soil, and natural resources and then asked in complete bewilderment why it was such a poverty-stricken country. The same question could be asked of many countries today.

Conversely, we could ask why Japan and Switzerland are so prosperous when they are both almost totally lacking in natural resources. Both are rich in what economists call "human capital"—the skills of their people. No doubt there is a long and complicated history behind the different skill levels of different peoples and nations. The point here is that the immediate environment—whether social or geographic—is only part of the story.

Geography may well have a significant role in the history of peoples, but perhaps not simply by presenting them with more or less natural resources. Geography shapes or limits peoples' opportunities for cultural interaction and the mutual development that comes out of this. Small, isolated islands in the sea have seldom been sources of new scientific advances of technological breakthroughs, regardless of where such islands were located and regardless of the race of people on these islands. There are islands on land as well. Where soil, fertile enough to support human life, exists only in isolated patches, widely separated, there tend to be isolate cultures (often with different languages or dialects) in a culturally fragmented region. Isolated highlands often produce insular cultures, lagging in many ways behind the cultures of the lowlanders of the same race—whether we are talking about medieval Scotland, colonial Ceylon, or the contemporary montagnards of Vietnam.

With geographical environments as with social environments, we are talking about long-run effects not simply the effects, of immediate surroundings. When Scottish highlanders, for example, immigrated to North Carolina in colonial times, they had a very different history from that of Scottish lowlanders who settled in North Carolina. For one thing, the lowlanders spoke English while the highlanders spoke Gaelic on into the nineteenth century. Obviously, speaking only Gaelic in an English-speaking country affects a group's whole economic and social progress.

Geographical conditions vary as radically in terms of how well they facilitate or impede large-scale cultural interactions as they do in their distribution of natural resources. We are not even close to being able to explain how all these geographical influences have operated throughout history. This too is an unanswered question largely because it is an unasked question, and it is an unasked question because many are seeking answers in terms of immediate social environment or are vehemently insistent that they have already found the answer in those terms.

How radically do geographic environments differ, not just in terms of tropical versus arctic climates, but also in the very configuration of the land and how this helps or hinders large-scale interactions among peoples? Consider one statistic: Africa is more than twice the size of Europe, and yet Africa has a shorter coastline than Europe. This seems almost impossible. But the reason is that Europe's coastline is far more convoluted, with many harbors and inlets being formed all around the continent. Much of the coastline of Africa is smooth, which is to say, lacking in the harbors that make large-scale maritime trade possible by sheltering the ships at anchor from the rough waters of the open sea.

Waterways of all sorts have played a major role in the evolution of cultures and nations around the world. Harbors on the sea are not the only waterways. Rivers are also very important. Virtually every major city on earth is located either on a river or a harbor. Whether it is such great harbors as those in Sydney, Singapore, or San Francisco; or London on the Thames, Paris on the Seine, or numerous other European cities on the Danube—waterways have been the lifeblood of urban centers for centuries. Only very recently has man-made, self-powered transportation, like automobiles and airplanes, made it possible to produce an exception to the rule like Los Angeles. (There is a Los Angeles River, but you do not have to be Moses to walk across it in the summertime.) New York has both a long and deep river and a huge sheltered harbor.

None of these geographical features in themselves create a great city or develop an urban culture. Human beings do that. But geography sets the limits within which people can operate and in some places it sets those limits much wider than in others. Returning to our comparison of the continents of Europe and Africa, we find that they differ as radically in rivers as they do in harbors. There are entire nations in Africa without a single navigable river—Libya and South Africa, for example.

"Navigable" is the crucial word. Some African rivers are navigable only during the rainy season. Some are navigable only between numerous cataracts and waterfalls. Even the Zaire River, which is longer than any river in North America and carries a larger volume of water, has too many waterfalls too close to the ocean for it to become a major artery of international commerce. Such commerce is facilitated in Europe not only by numerous navigable rivers but also by the fact that no spot on the continent, outside of Russia, is more than 500 miles from the sea. Many places in Africa are more than 500 miles from the sea, including the entire nation of Uganda.

Against this background, how surprised should we be to find that Europe is the most urbanized of all inhabited continents and Africa the least urbanized? Urbanization is not the be-all and end-all of life, but certainly an urban culture is bound to differ substantially from non-urban cultures, and the skills peculiar to an urban culture are far more likely to be found among groups from an urban civilization. Conversely, an interesting history could be written about the failures of urbanized groups in agricultural settlements.

Looking within Africa, the influence of geography seems equally clear. The most famous ancient civilization on the continent arose within a few miles on either side of Africa's longest navigable river, the Nile, and even today the two largest cities on the continent, Cairo and Alexandria, are on that river. The great West African kingdoms in the region served by the Niger River and the long-flourishing East African economy based around the great natural harbor on the island of Zanzibar are further evidences of the role of geography. Again, geography is not all-determining—the economy of Zanzibar has been ruined by government policy in recent decades—but nevertheless, geography is an important long-run influence on the shaping of cultures as well as in narrow economic terms.

What are the implications of a world view of cultural diversity on the narrower issues being debated under that label in the United States today? Although "diversity" is used in so many different ways in so many different contexts that it seems to mean all things to all people, there are a few themes that appear again and again. One of these broad themes is that diversity implies organized efforts at the preservation of cultural differences, perhaps governmental efforts, perhaps government subsidies to various programs run by the advocates of diversity.

This approach raises questions as to what the purpose of culture is. If what is important about cultures is that they are emotionally symbolic, and if differentness is cherished for the sake of differentness, then this particular version of cultural diversity might make some sense. But cultures exist even in isolated societies where there are no other cultures around—where there is no one else and nothing else from which to be different. Cultures exist to serve the vital, practical requirements of human life—to structure a society so as to perpetuate the species, to pass on the hard-earned knowledge and experience of generations past and centuries past to the young and inexperienced in order to spare the next generation the costly and dangerous process of learning everything all over again from scratch through trial and error—including fatal errors. Cultures exist so that people can know how to get food and put a roof over their head, how to cure the sick, how to cope with the death of loved ones, and how to get along with the living. Cultures are not bumper stickers. They are living, changing ways of doing all the things that have to be done in life.

Every culture discards over time the things that no longer do the job or which do not do the job as well as things borrowed from other cultures. Each individual does this, consciously or not, on a day-to-day basis. Languages take words from other languages, so that Spanish as spoken in Spain includes words taken from Arabic, and Spanish as spoken in Argentina has Italian words taken from the large Italian immigrant population there. People eat Kentucky Fried Chicken in Singapore and stay in Hilton Hotels in Cairo. This is not what some of the advocates of diversity have in mind. They seem to want to preserve cultures in their purity, almost like butterflies preserved in amber. Decisions about change, if any, seem to be regarded as collective decisions, political decisions. But this is not how cultures have arrived where they are. Individuals have decided for themselves how much of the old they wished to retain, how much of the new they found useful in their own lives.

In this way, cultures have enriched each other in all the great civilizations of the world. In this way, great port cities and other crossroads of cultures have become centers of progress all across the planet. No culture has grown great in isolation—but a number of cultures have made historic and even astonishing advances when their isolation was ended, usually by events beyond their control.

Japan was a classic example in the nineteenth century, but a similar story could be told of Scotland in an earlier era, when a country where once even the nobility were illiterate became, within a short time as history is measured, a country that produced world pioneers in field after field: David Hume in philosophy, Adam Smith in economics, Joseph Black in chemistry, Robert Adam in architecture, and James Watt, whose steam engine revolutionized modern industry and transport. In the process, the Scots lost their language but gained world preeminence in many fields. Then a whole society moved to higher standards of living than anyone ever dreamed of in their poverty-stricken past.

There were higher standards in other ways as well. As late as the eighteenth century, it was considered noteworthy that pedestrians in Edinburgh no longer had to be on the alert for sewage being thrown out the windows of people's homes or apartments. The more considerate Scots yelled a warning, but they threw out the sewage anyway. Perhaps it was worth losing a little of the indigenous culture to be rid of that problem. Those who use the term "cultural diversity" to promote a multiplicity of segregated ethnic enclaves are doing an enormous harm to the people in those enclaves. However they live socially, the people in those enclaves are going to have to compete economically for a livelihood. Even if they were not disadvantaged before, they will be very disadvantaged if their competitors from the general population are free to tap the knowledge, skills, and analytical techniques Western civilization has drawn from all the other civilizations of the world, while those in the enclaves are restricted to what exists in the subculture immediately around them.

We need also to recognize that many great thinkers of the past—whether in medicine or philosophy, science or economics—labored not simply to advance whatever particular group they happened to have come from but to advance the human race. Their legacies, whether cures for deadly diseases or dramatic increases in crop yields to fight the scourge of hunger, belong to all people—and all people need to claim that legacy, not seal themselves off in a dead-end of tribalism or in an emotional orgy of cultural vanity.

DISCUSSION QUESTIONS

1. Most people have grown up with the United States leading the world in many areas, such as technology, medicine, education, and standard of living.
   a. Is it important that the United States always leads in these areas?
   b. How can diversity in the workforce help any country advance?
   c. Has the United States made good use of its social capital in the past? Why or why not?

2. It is well known that hundreds of languages have already become extinct and many more are nearly so.
   a. Per Sowell, what leads cultures to discard or to adopt various cultural practices?
   b. How would Sowell explain what happens to languages over time?

3. In America, the management of workers by "assimilation into the workforce" is being replaced by the "integration of diversity." How would the author explain this shift in approach?

4. Apply Sowell's basic premise about cultural transmission to the fact that the United States regularly exchanges scientists, business leaders, and technology with countries all over the world. Would the author think this is a good practice, or does this just help other countries get ahead of the United States in these areas?

5. The United States ranks 29th in the world in infant mortality; 22nd in adolescent science literacy, 20th in adolescent mathematics literacy, and 57th in education expenditures. What are the implications of these for
   a. work life?
   b. your children's work life?
   c. the future in the United States of healthcare, business, education, etc.?

6. Research the economic progress of the so-called BRICK countries. Which of these could you envision becoming the world leaders in business by 2050? In science and technology? In education? Explain the reasons for your predictions.

Writing Assignment

Ethnicity refers to a person's membership in a specific cultural group with a shared national origin or cultural heritage, such as being Greek or Vietnamese. To better understand how ethnic differences may affect a person's life experiences, conduct an interview with someone from an ethnic group different from your own.

1. As a minimum, ask the following questions to get a sense of his or her experiences. Your instructor may add additional questions and you may find it necessary to add appropriate follow-up questions based upon the interviewee's answers that may help you to understand how this person's life experiences as part of a particular ethnic group has or has not contributed to shaping who he or she is today.

2. Then, write a three-page paper that analyzes how the interviewee's ethnic group membership has differed from your own. Specifically, how could these differences impact workplace communication and understanding? Be careful not to simply list questions and answers.

Interview Questions

1. What ethnicity were your parents and grandparents? Were your parents or grandparents immigrants? If so, approximately when did they come to this country?

2. As a child, who lived in your household? Did anyone in your household speak a language besides English? If so, do you also speak this language?

3. What holidays are most important in your culture(s)? Specifically, how are these holidays celebrated in terms of food, traditions, customs, etc.? Do you still celebrate these holidays? Which of these practices did you or will you pass on to your children?

4. What are examples of respectful and disrespectful behaviors in your culture(s)?

5. How do the roles of males and females differ in your ethnic culture(s)?

6. Is age regarded differently in your ethnic culture than it is in mainstream American culture(s)?

7. Describe any discrimination you may have experienced because of your ethnic group memberships.

WE HAVE AN AFRICAN AMERICAN PRESIDENT: HOW COULD RACISM STILL BE A MAJOR PROBLEM?

Joyce McNickles
Worcester State University

GOALS

- To understand the difference between prejudice and institutional racism
- To increase student awareness of the prevalence of racism in the United States today

On November 3, 2008, Americans of all racial backgrounds stood in Chicago's Grant Park, celebrating Barack Obama's historic election as the first African American president of the United States. In his victory speech, Obama opened with the following statement: "If there is anyone out there who doubts that America is a place where anything is possible, who still wonders if the dream of our founders is alive in our time, who still questions the power of our democracy, tonight is your answer." Barack Obama won 28 states, received 375 of the Electoral College votes to John McCain's 173, won the popular vote by 9 million votes, and had a margin of victory of 7.27 percent (Todd, Gawiser, Arumi, & Witt, 2009). In fact, the only other Democrat to win by a higher percentage since 1964 was Bill Clinton in 1996 (Brownstein, 2009).

To some observers, Obama's victory may have been undeniable proof that the United States had become a post-racial society, i.e., a society in which race is no longer significant or important (Wingfield & Feagin, 2009). Their argument was that if race still mattered and influenced how Americans think, then Americans would not have voted for Barack Obama in such large numbers (Wise, 2010). Implicit in this argument is that the voting action of White Americans is sufficient evidence to claim that race no longer matters and the United States has become a post-racial society. The next progression would be to ask if race still mattered to African Americans and other people of color, such as Latinos, Asian Americans, and Native Americans.

An ABC News\Washington Post opinion poll conducted in January 2009, the month Obama was sworn into office, found from a survey of 1079 adults that 44 percent of African Americans viewed racism a "big problem" in the United States compared with 22 percent of Whites who identified it as problem (ABC News\Washington Post Poll, 2009). Three-quarters of the African American respondents in that poll reported they had experienced racial discrimination. "Shopping while Black" was the most common form of racial discrimination. Shopping While Black describes a scenario in which African Americans are viewed suspiciously by retail employees simply because they are Black. Thirty-seven percent reported "Driving while Black," which is related to police use of racial profiling. Thirty-five percent reported that they had been denied a job and twenty percent said they were denied housing because of their race.

Whites and African Americans held different views about racial discrimination in the workplace. Thirty-eight percent of African Americans believed that they had equal chances with Whites to get a job for which they were qualified. Eighty-three percent of White respondents believed that African Americans had equal chances for getting jobs for which they were qualified.

According to the survey, Whites and African Americans held different views about racial discrimination in the criminal justice system. Seventy-six percent of Whites believed that African Americans received equal treatment from the police, but just thirty-four percent of African Americans held that view.

Many White people may have found it puzzling that so many African Americans surveyed still saw racism as a big problem, considering the fact that the country had just elected a Black man as president. One plausible explanation for this is the *racial perception gap* (Lawson, 2009) that is the difference in perceptions that Whites and people of color have about race relations and racism. President Clinton's 1998 Initiative on Race found that while most people of color understood that the legacy of race continued to shape their experiences, many White Americans did not (Lawson, 2009). The authors stated:

> Americans—Whites, minorities, and people of color—hold differing views of race, seeing racial progress so differently that an outsider could easily believe that Whites and most minorities and people of color see the world through different lenses (p. 44).

Differences in the ways in which Blacks and Whites use and understand terminology may contribute to the perception gap. Tim Wise, a White anti-racism writer, activist, and national lecturer, argues that the perceptions differ because when Whites and African Americans talk about race and racism they may not be talking about the same thing. According to Wise, most Whites see racism in terms of negative individual and interpersonal behavior such as "the uttering of a prejudicial remark or bigoted slur" (Wise, 2006). For African Americans it includes much more. Racism, for many people of color, includes policies and practices, intentional and unintentional, in various social institutions which are racially discriminatory. Confronting institutionalized racial discrimination in the criminal justice system, the education system, the health care system, and the workplace have the potential for creating far more significant consequences than the personal prejudice of one individual.

A MATTER OF TERMINOLOGY

Prejudice and racism are not the same thing. An important distinction must be made between *racial prejudice* and *racism*. Allport (1954) defined **prejudice** as a feeling, favorable or unfavorable, toward a person that was not based on actual experience (p. 7). Prejudice based on race is referred to as **racial prejudice** (Andersen & Taylor, 2006, p. 243). Racial prejudice resides within the individual; racism resides within society's structures and institutions. It is true that individuals make up society's institutions, and that in order for racism to exist in any institution there has to be some individual racial prejudice. However, racism extends far beyond any individual and his or her personal prejudice. It results when one racial group has the social power to act on racial prejudice and negatively impact the lives of another racial group (Tatum, 1997). One example of this is the illegal practice of "steering" that happens when real estate agents steer African American homebuyers away from homes in White neighborhoods based on a desire to keep the makeup of that neighborhood White (Galster & Godfrey, 2005).

Racism can also be seen as a system of advantage based on race (Wellman, 1977). Beverly Tatum (1997) finds this definition of racism useful.

> It allows us to see that racism, like other forms of oppression, is not only a personal ideology of racial prejudice, but also a system involving cultural messages and institutional policies and practices as well as the belief of individuals. In the context of the United States, this system clearly operates to the advantage of Whites and to the disadvantage of people of color (p. 7).

Institutions may have policies, practices, and procedures that confer advantages to Whites and disadvantages to African Americans and other people of color. **Institutional racism** is another term that is often used to describe the system of advantage operating within various societal institutions such as the criminal justice system, the education system, the health care system, and the workplace (Andersen & Taylor, 2006, p. 245; Wijeyesinghe, Griffin, & Love, 1997). Sociologists who study the structural aspects of racism point out that even if every White person were able to lose all of his or her personal prejudice and did not participate in any discriminatory behavior, institutional racism would continue for some time (Andersen & Taylor, 2008).

Institutional racism becomes structured into society at all levels and cannot be attributed to one single individual. For example, much of the standard curriculum in U.S. public schools is centered on the contributions and culture of White Americans rather than that of African Americans. This gives White students a psychological advantage because they have many opportunities to see themselves and their racial group reflected in history, literature, the arts, and the sciences (Nieto, 2004). Conversely, this disadvantages African Americans because, aside from Black History Month programs, they rarely see themselves reflected in the curriculum. It is important to note that these policies, practices, and procedures may be unintentional or intentional, overt or covert.

Diller (2004) described racism as "the manipulation of social institutions to give preferences and advantages to whites and at the same time restrict the choices, rights, mobility and access of people of color" (p. 30). Feminist scholar Peggy McIntosh (1990) referred to the advantages Whites receive as "**White privilege**" and believes that these privileges are invisible to most Whites. African Americans and other people of color cannot count on these privileges.

Institutionalized racism promotes disparities and inequities between Whites and African Americans. The Agency for Healthcare, Research and Quality (AHRQ) defines **disparities** as any differences among populations that are statistically significant and differ from the reference group by at least 10 percent (National Healthcare Disparities Report, 2006).

Although this essay highlights the racial experiences of African Americans, this is not to suggest that other people of color such as Latinos, Asians, and Native Americans do not experience racism in the Unites States. Institutional racism also promotes disparities between Whites and other people of color.

RACIAL DISPARITIES AND INEQUITIES IN THE WORKPLACE

In recent years African Americans have certainly made gains in the workplace, but they are still underrepresented at the higher levels of management in just about every professional field. Despite affirmative action initiatives and federal employment laws against racial discrimination, racial disparities continue. Whites hold 83% of all the management level jobs in both the private and public sector, but they make up 68% of the country's population (U.S. Department of Labor, 2010). Research studies have suggested that White men in organizations are more likely to be promoted over African Americans with the same education (Dewitt, 1995; Zwerling & Silver, 1992).

One study found that in the advertising field, African Americans contend with racial discrimination that is 40% worse than in the national labor market (Helm, 2009; Bendick, Jr. & Egan, 2009). Furthermore, when African American college graduates enter the advertising field, they earn 20% less than White graduates with the same qualifications and they are half as likely as their White counterparts to be placed in management positions.

Another study commissioned by The Restaurant Opportunities Center found that in New York City restaurants, people of color were half as likely as Whites to get hired (Bendick, Jr., Rodriguez, & Jayaraman, 2009). The researchers sent White and Black applicants to apply for jobs at upscale restaurants. Both groups had equal qualifications, education, and language skills. The researchers found that the employers discussed the positions in greater detail with White applicants than they did with the applicants of color. White applicants were offered better hours and given longer interviews. The employers challenged the resumes of the applicants of color more than the White applicants. The conclusion was that discrimination occurred in one-third of the restaurants included in the study.

A Princeton University workplace study examined discrimination in hiring young minority males and male ex-offenders in entry-level low wage jobs (Pager & Western, 2005). The researchers sent African American, Latino, and White male applicants to over 1500 private employers in New York City during a nine-month period. The applicants were given fake résumés indicating equal educational and work experience. In several situations the résumés also indicated an 18-month prison term. The study showed that White males with a criminal record had a slightly better chance of getting a job than an African American male with no criminal record. Young White male high school graduates were twice as likely to receive a positive response (call back or interview) from the employers as equally qualified African American males.

For African American women in the workplace, racial disparities and discrimination are also issues. Catalyst (2004), a leading research organization working to advance women in business, conducted a survey of over 900 African American women working in Fortune 1000 companies. It found that African American women at various professional levels faced institutional barriers related to their race. Many women described these institutional barriers as a "concrete ceiling" (p. 3), highlighting how much more impenetrable they are than the barrier of the "glass ceiling" which many White women face. More than half of the women surveyed held graduate degrees yet reported racial stereotyping, scrutiny of their work, and repeated questioning of their authority and credibility. They also reported a lack of support from their organizations and exclusion from informal networks. Even though many women reported that their companies had diversity recruitment initiatives, many believed the initiatives did little to address institutional racism.

Research has also suggested that African American names may also make people the target of institutional racism. Researchers from the University of Chicago and Massachusetts Institute of Technology (Bertrand & Mullainathan, 2004) sent 5,000 fictitious résumés in response to 1,300 help wanted ads in the Boston and Chicago newspapers. They randomly assigned "White sounding" first names to half the résumés. Names such as Emily, Jill, Kristen, Allison, and Laurie were given to the female applicants; males were given names such as Brett, Todd, Neil, Greg, Brendan, Jay and Brad. The other half of the résumés were assigned "African American sounding" names such as Ebony, Lakisha, Tamika, Keisha, Latoya, and Kenya to female applicants and Jamal, Hakim, Leroy, Tyrone, Darnell, and Jermaine to male applicants. Aside from the difference in names, the résumés reflected the same experience, education, and skills for both groups. The study found that applicants with the "White sounding names" received 50% more callbacks for interviews than applicants with "African American sounding names." The disparities were consistent across occupation, industry, and company size. The researchers concluded that African Americans may be screened out of the hiring process in favor of White applicants before they even have a chance to be interviewed.

RACIAL DISPARITIES AND INEQUITIES IN HEALTH CARE

Research suggests that African Americans and other racial minorities tended to receive lower quality health care than Whites, even when they had the same insurance and income as Whites (Jha, 2005; Smedley, Stith, & Nelson, 2003; Sonel et al., 2005). In a major study conducted by the Institute of Medicine, researchers found in interviews with doctors that even though most doctors are well-intentioned, subconscious racial bias against African Americans influenced their medical decisions (Smedley et al., 2003; Stolberg, 2002).

The same Institute of Medicine study reviewed one hundred previous research studies and concluded that racial minorities were less likely to be given appropriate medication for heart disease and to undergo bypass surgery, less likely to receive kidney dialysis and transplants than Whites, but three times more likely to have lower limb amputations as a result of diabetes than Whites.

In terms of mental health, African Americans were more likely to be diagnosed as psychotic but less likely to be given anti-psychotic medication. They were more likely to be hospitalized involuntarily and placed in restraints compared to Whites (Smedley et al., 2003). In a study of Medicaid programs in four states, Blacks with depression and diabetes were less likely to be treated for their depression than Whites with the same conditions, and they were more likely to receive older tricyclic antidepressants which alter blood sugar levels, unlike the newer selective serotonin reuptake inhibitors (Sambamoorthi, Olfson, Wei, & Crystal, 2006).

In another study that involved 405 women who had been recently diagnosed with breast cancer, researchers found that in initial consultations oncologists communicated differently with the women based on their race (Siminoff, Graham, & Gordon, 2008). The researchers conducted interviews with the patients and physicians immediately after the consultations and found that the oncologists asked White women more questions and spent more time with them than with women of color. The impact of doctors communicating differently with women based on race may explain why Black women with breast cancer are less likely than White women to receive chemotherapy, immunotherapy, radiation therapy, and hormone therapy following their surgeries (Siminoff, Graham, & Gordon, 2008).

Another study addressed whether doctors' racial biases determined treatment options for patients (Green, Carney, Pallin, Ngo, Raymond, Lezzoni et al., 2007). Two hundred and twenty doctors, who were in training to become emergency services physicians, were asked to diagnose a hypothetical case in which two 50-year-old men, one White and one African American, both complaining of chest pain and with heart attack symptoms, came to them for treatment. The majority of the doctors prescribed clot-busting drugs for the White patient but not for the African American. After their evaluation of the patients, the doctors were given an "implicit association" test designed to reveal a person's unconscious views of Blacks and Whites. While most doctors' test scores did not reveal any explicit bias towards Whites or Blacks, but most showed some degree of implicit bias towards Whites or Blacks, but the researchers found a correlation between high implicit bias and the likelihood that doctors would provide the most effective heart attack treatment for Black patients.

RACIAL DISPARITIES IN EDUCATION

The 1954 U.S. Supreme Court case, Brown v. Board of Education, made racially segregated schools unconstitutional. The argument against segregated schools was that White children and Black children received different and unequal educational experiences in the public school system. Differences were found in school facilities, textbooks, curriculum, and teacher qualifications. In 2010, African American children in many large cities are attending racially segregated public schools despite that Supreme Court decision. For example, in the Chicago public schools 90% of the students are Black, Latino or Asian (Chicago Public Schools, 2010). Meanwhile, in 2007 the average White child attended a school that was 80% White, further proof of segregation. Urban private schools, both religious and secular, are also segregated and Catholic school systems are the most segregated (Yun & Reardon, 2005).

> Racially segregated schools produce unequal educational outcomes between African American children and White children. Urban schools with high minority populations are often in areas with high concentrations of poverty. In Chicago, for example, 86% of the public school children are from low income families (Chicago Public Schools, 2010).

In contrast, the average White student attends a school that is 80% white with no more than 30% of the school's population composed of low income families (Orfield, 2009). In 31 of 49 states, school districts with the highest minority enrollment receive fewer resources than school districts with the lowest minority enrollment (American Civil Liberies Union, 2007). The American Civil Liberties Union report to the United Nations Council on the Elimination of Racial Discrimination summarized the correlation between schools in high poverty areas and educational outcomes:

> Historically, schools with high concentrations of minority students have lacked the resources necessary to provide equal educational opportunity, demonstrated through inferior access to qualified and experienced teachers, higher turnover rates among staff, larger class size, fewer advanced placement courses, poorer infrastructure, and fewer basic educational supplies (p. 144).

Teachers with less experience are hired more often by racially segregated, lower income schools. In California, more than half of the teachers who lack appropriate credentials for the subject areas they teach work in schools with a majority-minority population. One recent research study found that teachers with a track record for raising student achievement leave their schools when the Black student population begins to increase (Jackson, 2009). Another example of racial disparities in the educational system is the use of *tracking*. This occurs when standardized tests are used to measure students' cognitive ability and then assigning them to academic tracks based on their scores (Andersen & Taylor, 2008). The assumption is that students will learn better when they are grouped with those of similar ability. The argument is that the teacher can teach more effectively because the curriculum is geared to a particular ability level.

Researchers have found that there are positive outcomes for the higher track students and negative ones for lower track students. The racial aspect of this institutional practice is revealed by studies that show African American students disproportionately assigned to lower ability tracks. Teachers have lower expectations for students placed in lower tracks. The results are that they are taught less, learn less, and read less. The higher track students are expected to perform better and are taught more. They receive more acknowledgements for their abilities. Sometimes students with the same test scores are placed in different tracks, suggesting that in addition to actual test performance, race is used as determining factor when grouping students by ability levels (Andersen & Taylor, 2008; Orfield, 2009).

RACIAL DISPARITIES AND INEQUITIES IN THE JUSTICE SYSTEM

Perhaps in no other institution are there more blatant examples of institutional racism than in law enforcement and the criminal justice system. Racial profiling is a major concern for African Americans. **Racial profiling** is the use of race alone as a criterion by police officers as a reason for stopping and detaining someone who appears suspicious of criminal activity. It has become so common that African Americans call it the crime of "DWB," short for "**Driving While Black**." Every year at least 90% of African Americans who are stopped by police are not arrested, which means that there's only a 10% probability that a Black driver in a car has actually committed a crime (Andersen & Taylor, 2006). Many police departments attempt to justify racial profiling by using statistics that point to a higher proportion of crimes committed by African Americans than Whites. A 2007 Department of Justice study reviewed data collected nation-wide and found that while White and Black drivers were stopped at about the same rate, Black drivers' cars were searched 10.2% of the time as opposed to White drivers who were searched only 3.5% of the time (Sentencing Project, 2009).

One frequently quoted study on profiling showed that eight out of ten automobile searches conducted by state troopers over a ten-year period on the New Jersey Turnpike were of cars driven by African Americans and Latinos. The vast majority of these searches found no evidence of crimes or illegal materials (Kocieniewski & Hanley, 2000). Another study based on data collected in a Midwestern city over a two-year period showed that of 13,566 officer-initiated traffic stops, minority drivers were stopped at a higher rate than Whites and were also searched for contraband at a higher rate than Whites. However, the police were no more likely to find contraband on the minority drivers than on the White ones (Leinfelt, 2006).

African Americans are often victims of **police brutality**, or the use of excessive force by police officers. Race is a factor in capital punishment. Blacks are disproportionately placed on death row. In 2003, blacks constituted just 12 percent of the total U.S population, yet made up 42 percent of the nearly 3500 prisoners on death row nationally (U.S. Bureau of Justice Statistics, 2004). Research shows that when Whites and African Americans commit the same crime against a White victim, the African American offender is more likely to receive the death penalty. African Americans who kill Whites get the death penalty at a 300 percent higher rate than if they killed another African American (Paternoster, Brame, Bacon, Ditchfield, et al., 2003). Race of the victim is a factor in federal death penalty cases. There is evidence showing that the U.S. Attorney General is more likely to seek a death sentence if the victim is White than in cases with victim is of color. For example, Attorney General Gonzales, under the Bush Administration, authorized the death penalty in 28 of the 67 cases when the victim was White, a seek rate of 42 percent, compared with 43 out of the 261 cases when the victim was not White, a seek rate of 16 percent. The difference in these seek rates is 25 percent (ACLU Persistent Disparities; Carolnew/racial_disparities_federal_deathpen.pdf). A 2007 Department of Justice report found that contact with the police yielded very different outcomes for Blacks and Whites (Sentencing Project, 2009). Blacks were 3 times as likely to be subjected to police threat or force during the contact. However, municipalities where African Americans are in charge of the police department reported a decline in police brutality charges, an increase in minority police recruitment, and in some cases, a decrease in crime.

Disparities in the criminal justice system continue after African Americans are arrested. They are faced with higher bails and are not as likely as Whites to be given the opportunity to plea bargain. After going to trial, they are found guilty more often than Whites and they are likely to get longer sentences, even when they come from the same economic background and have similar arrest records. They are not as likely as Whites to be released on probation (Andersen & Taylor, 2006).

Race is a factor in capital punishment. Blacks are disproportionately placed on death row. In 2003, blacks constituted just 12% of the total U.S. population, yet made up 42% of the nearly 3500 prisoners on death row nationally (U.S. Bureau of Justice Statistics, 2004). Research shows that when Whites and African Americans commit the same crime against a White victim, the African American offender is more likely to receive the death penalty. African Americans who kill Whites get the death penalty at a 300% higher rate than if they killed another African American (Paternoster, Brame, Bacon, Ditchfield, et al., 2003). Race of the victim is a factor in federal death penalty cases. There is evidence showing that the U.S. Attorney General is more likely to seek a death sentence if the victim is White than in cases with victims of color. For example, the attorney general in the Bush administration, Alberto Gonzales, authorized the death penalty in 28 of 67 cases when the victim was White, a seek rate of 42%, compared with 43 out of the 261 cases when the victim was not White, a seek rate of 16%. The difference in these seek rates is 25% (American Civil Liberties Union, 2007).

African American youths encounter racial disparities in the criminal justice system. A review of government data revealed that African American youths are serving life without possibility of release sentences at a rate that is ten times higher than White youths (de la Vega & Leighton, 2007). They are also more likely to be sentenced to adult prisons. One report found that 26 out of every 100,000 African American children were sentenced to adult prisons while for White children the rate is only 2.2 per 100,000 (de la Vega & Leighton, 2007).

The Sentencing Project study, using U.S. Justice Department statistics, reported that even though African Americans constituted just 13% of all monthly drug users, they represented 35% of arrests for drug possession, 55% of the convictions, and 74% of the prison sentences. (Sentencing Project, 2006a). Data from the U.S. Sentencing Commission found that crack cocaine sentences are the single most significant factor contributing to racial disparity in federal sentencing (Sentencing Project, 2006b). According to the Sentencing Project, more than 80 percent of the defendants prosecuted for crack are African-American, despite the fact that more than two-thirds of crack users are White or Latino (Sentencing Project, 2006b).

THE FUTURE

For some, the election of Barack Obama as the first African American president ended the social significance of race and racism. The proof offered was that in the national election the majority of White voters supported Obama instead of John McCain, a White senator with an accomplished political career. How could race and racism hold any significance in light of Obama's landslide victory? As discussed in this article however, race and racism continues to hold significance for the vast majority of African Americans and other people of color. Racism continues to plague society through its institutions and continues to create policies, intentional and unintentional, which have led to racial inequities for African Americans. No one could argue that the blatant racism against African Americans has not diminished over time. African Americans and White Americans have made steps toward understanding and accepting each other's differences. They work side-by-side in many American workplaces and live in racially mixed neighborhoods with each other. However, much work needs to be done to improve the experiences of African Americans as they enter American institutions. This can begin with Whites acknowledging that institutional racism still exists and that it puts African Americans as a racial group at a disadvantage. Until this acknowledgement happens, it will be very difficult for the two racial groups to have any meaningful dialogue to improve race relations.

DISCUSSION QUESTIONS

1. According to McNickles, what explains the perception gap that exists between whites and African Americans when it comes to matters of race and racism?

2. What is the difference between racial prejudice and racism?

3. In what societal institutions can institutional racism be found?

4. How do Arab Muslims suffer biases and prejudices similar to African Americans in a post 9/11 America?

5. How does the factual evidence presented in this article lend support to affirmative action programs and policies?

6. What must white people acknowledge for race relations to improve?

Writing Assignment

African Americans are not the only racial minority experiencing racism. Go to the Internet address below and take the test on Native Americans.

What was your score? Why do think you did or did not do well on this test? Which of the answers on the test surprised you the most? Why?

http://www.understandingprejudice.org/nativeiq/

Writing Assignment

The author argues that the election of Barack Obama suggested to some that race is no longer an issue for whites. The next progression would be to contemplate if race is no longer an issue for African Americans.

Go to http://www.diversityinc.com/ or search the general Internet. Conduct a search using any of the following words or combination of words:

a. African Americans or Blacks
b. Employment discrimination
c. Disparities
d. African American youth

e. Justice
f. Profiling
g. Health

What are some of the issues that result from being African American or Black?

Bibliography

ABC News/Washington Post Poll. (2009). Race relations fewer call racism a major problem though discrimination remains. Retrieved October 18, 2010, from http://abcnews.go.com/images/PollingUnit/1085a2RaceRelations.pdf.

Agency for Healthcare Research & Quality. (2006). National healthcare disparities report. Retrieved from ahrq.gov/qual/inhdr06/nhdr06report.pdf on May 2, 2011.

Allport, G. W. (1954). *The nature of prejudice.* Cambridge, MA: Addison-Wesley.

American Civil Liberties Union. (2007). Race and ethnicity in America: Turning a blind eye to injustice. Retrieved October 18, 2010, from http://www.aclu.org/files/pdfs/humanrights/cerd_full_report.pdf.

American Civil Liberties Union. (2007). The persistent problem of racial disparities in the federal death penalty. Retrieved October 18, 2010, from http://www.aclu.org/pdfs/capital/racial_disparities_federal_deathpen.pdf.

Andersen, M. L., & Taylor, H. F. (2006). *Sociology: The essentials* (4th ed.). Belmont, CA: Thomson/Wadsworth.

Andersen, M. L., & Taylor, H. F. (2008). *Sociology: The essentials* (5th ed.). Belmont, CA: Thomson/Wadsworth.

Bendick, Jr., M., & Egan, M. L. (2009). Research perspectives on race and employment in the advertising industry. Retrieved October 18, 2010, from http://www.bendickegan.com/pdf/2009/Bendick%20Egan%20Advertising%20Industry%20Report%20Jan%2009.pdf.

Bendick Jr, M., Rodriguez, R. E., & Jayaraman, S. (2009). *Employment discrimination in upscale restaurants: Evidence from matched pair testing.* Retrieved October 15, 2010 from http://www.bendickegan.com/pdf/2009/Testing_article_%20Feb_2009.pdf.

Bertrand, M., & Mullainathan, S. (2004). Are Emily and Greg more employable than Lakisha and Jamal? A field experiment on labor market discrimination. *American Economic Review, 94*(4), 991–1013.

Brownstein, R. (2009). For GOP, a southern exposure [Electronic Version]. *National Journal*, 15-15. Retrieved October 18, 2010 from http://www.nationaljournal.com/njmagazine/cs_20090523_2195.php.

Butterfield, F. (1995, October 5). More blacks in their 20's have trouble with the law. *The New York Times*, p. A8.

Carr-Ruffino, N. (2006). *Managing diversity: People skills for a multicultural workplace* (7th ed.). Boston, MA: Pearson.

Catalyst. (2004). Advancing African American women in the workplace: What managers need to know. New York: Catalyst. Retrieved November 12, 2010, from http://www.catalyst.org/file/10/advancing%20african-american%20women%20in%20workplace.pdf.

Chicago Public Schools Office of Performance. (2010). Chicago Public Schools Racial Ethnic Surveys. Retrieved from research.cps.k12.il.us/cps/accountweb/Reports/RSracial survey. Retrieved May 2, 2011.

Dewitt, K. (1995, April, 20). Blacks prone to job discrimination in organizations. *The New York Times*, p. A19.

de la Vega, C., & Leighton, M. (2007). Sentencing our children to die in prison: Global law and practice. Retrieved October 18, 2010, from http://www.ctjja.org/resources/pdf/reform-sentencingourchildren.pdf.

Diller, J. V. (2004). *Cultural diversity: A primer for the human services.* Belmont, CA: Wadsworth.

Gallup Organization. (2004). *Civil rights and race relations.* Princeton, NJ: The Gallup Organization. Retrieved November 12, 2010, from http://assets.aarp.org/rgcenter/general/civil_rights.pdf.

Galster, G., & Godfrey, E. (2005). By words and deeds: Racial steering by real estate agents in the U.S. in 2000. *American Planning Association. Journal of the American Planning Association, 71*(3), 251–268.

Gest, T. (1995, November 6). New war over crack. *U.S. News & World Report, 119,* 81.

Green, A. R., Carney, D. R., Pallin, D. J., Ngo, L. H., Raymond, K. L., Lezzoni, L. I., et al. (2007). Implicit bias among physicians and its prediction of thrombolysis decisions for black and white patients. *JGIM: Journal of General Internal Medicine, 22*(9), 1231–1238.

Jha, A. K. (2005). Racial trends in the use of major procedures among the elderly. *The New England Journal of Medicine, 353*(7), 683.

Helm, B. (2009). Madison avenue accused of racial bias [Electronic Version]. *BusinessWeek Online*, 25. Retrieved November 12, 2010 from http://www.businessweek.com/bwdaily/dnflash/content/jan2009/db2009018_161828.htm.

Jackson, C. K. (2009). Student demographics, teacher sorting, and teacher quality: Evidence from the end of school desegregation. *Journal of Labor Economics, 27*(2), 213–256.

Kocieniewski, D., & Hanley, R. (2000, November 28). Racial profiling was the routine, New Jersey finds. *The New York Times*, p. A1.

Lawson, S. F. (2009). One America in the 21st century: the report of President Bill Clinton's initiative on race. New Haven, CT: Yale University Press.

Leinfelt, F. H. (2006). Racial influences on the likelihood of police searches and search hits: A longitudinal analysis from an American midwestern city. *Police Journal, 79*(3): 238–257.

Males, M. & Macallair, D. (2000). *The color of justice: An analysis of juvenile adult court transfers in California*. Washington, DC: Justice Policy Institute. Retrieved November 12, 2010, from http://www.buildingblocksforyouth.org/colorofjustice/coj.html.

Mauer, M., & Huling, T. (1995). *Young black Americans and the criminal justice system*. Washington, DC: The Sentencing Project. Retrieved November 12, 2010, from http://www.sentencingproject.org/pdfs/rd_youngblack_5yrslater.pdf.

McIntosh, P. (1990). White privilege: Unpacking the invisible knapsack. *Independent School, 49* (2), 31.

Neuspiel, D. R. (1996). Racism and perinatal addiction. *Ethnicity & Disease, 6*(1–2), 47.

Nieto, S. (2004). *Affirming diversity: The sociopolitical context of multicultural education* (4th ed.). Boston, MA: Allyn and Bacon.

Orfield, G. (2009). Reviving the goal of an integrated society: A 21st century challenge. Retrieved October 18, 2010, from http://civilrightsproject.ucla.edu/research/k-12-education/integration-and-diversity/reviving-the-goal-of-an-integrated-society-a-21st-century-challenge/orfield-reviving-the-goal-mlk-2009.pdf.

Pager, D., & Western, B. (2005). *Discrimination in low wage labor markets: Evidence from New York City*. Paper presented at the Population Association of American Annual Meeting.

Retrieved November 12, 2010, from http://paa2005.princeton.edu/download.aspx?submissionId=50874.

Paternoster R., Brame, R., Bacon, S., Ditchfield, A., et al. (2003). *An empirical analysis of Maryland's death sentencing system with respect to the influence of race and legal jurisdiction*. University of Maryland, Department of Criminology. Retrieved January 1, 2007, from http://www.newsdesk.umd.edu/pdf/finalrep.pdf.

Sambamoorthi, U., Olfson, M., Wei, W., & Crystal, S. (2006). Diabetes and Depression Care among Medicaid Beneficiaries. *Journal of Health Care for the Poor and Underserved, 17*(1), 141–161.

Sentencing Project. (2006a). *Crack cocaine sentencing policy: Unjustified and unreasonable*. Washington, DC: The Sentencing Project. Retrieved November 12, 2010, from http://www.sentencingproject.org/doc/publications/dp_cc_sentencingpolicy.pdf.

Sentencing Project. (2006b). *Race and class penalties in crack cocaine sentencing*. Washington, DC: The Sentencing Project. Retrieved October 30, 2006, from http://www.sentencingproject.org/pdfs/5077.pdf.

Sentencing Project. (2009). Reducing racial disparity in the criminal justice system: A manual for practitioners and policymakers. Retrieved October 17, 2010, from http://www.sentencingproject.org/doc/publications/rd_reducingracialdisparity.pdf.

Siminoff, L. A., Graham, G. C., & Gordon, N. H. (2006). Cancer communication patterns and the influence of patient characteristics: Disparities in information-giving and affective behaviors. Patient Education and Counseling, 62(3), 355–360.

Smedley, B. D., Stith, A. Y., & Nelson, A. R. (2003). *Unequal treatment: Confronting racial and ethnic disparities in health care*. Washington, DC: National Academy Press.

Sonel, A. F., Good, C. B., Mulgund, J., Roe, M. T., Gibler, W. B., Smith, S. C., et al. (2005). Racial variations in treatment and outcomes of black and white patients with high-risk non-ST-elevation acute coronary syndromes: Insights from CRUSADE (can rapid risk stratification of unstable angina patients suppress adverse outcomes with early implementation of the ACC/AHA guidelines?). *Circulation, 111*(10), 1225–1232.

Stolberg, S. G. (2002). Race gap seen in health care of equally insured patients [Electronic Version]. New York Times, A1. Retrieved November 10, 2010 from http://query.nytimes.com/gst/fullpage.html?res=9901E2DD1138F932A15750C0A9649C8B63.

Tatum, B. D. (1997). *Why are all the Black kids sitting together in the cafeteria? and other conversations about race.* New York: Basic Books.

Todd, C., Gawiser, S. R., Arumi, A. M., & Witt, G. E. (2009). *How Barack Obama won: A state-by-state guide to the historic 2008 presidential election.* New York: Vintage Books.

United States Bureau of Justice Statistics. (2004). *Capital punishment, 2003.* Washington, DC: U.S. Department of Justice. Retrieved October 18, 2010, http://bjs.ojp.usdoj.gov/content/pub/pdf/cp03.pdf.

United States Bureau of Justice Statistics. (2005). Contacts between police and the public findings from the 2002 national survey. Retrieved October 18, 2010, from http://bjs.ojp.usdoj.gov/content/pub/pdf/cpp02.pdf.

United States Department of Health and Human Services, Agency for Healthcare Research and Quality. *2006 National Healthcare Disparities Report.* (2006). Retrieved October 15, 2010, from http://www.ahrq.gov/qual/nhdr06/nhdr06.htm.

United States Department of Labor, Bureau of Labor Statistics. *Labor Force Characteristics by Race and Ethnicity, 2009.* (2010). Retrieved October 15, 2010 from http://www.bls.gov/cps/cpsrace2009.pdf.

van Ryn, M., & Burke, J. (2000). The effect of patient race and socio-economic status on physicians' perceptions of patients. *Social Science & Medicine, 50*(6), 813.

Wellman, D. T. (1977). *Portraits of white racism.* New York: Cambridge University Press.

Wijeyesinghe, C., Griffin, P., & Love, B. (1997). Racism curriculum design. In M. Adams, L.A. Bell, & P. Griffin (Eds.), *Teaching for diversity and social justice: A sourcebook.* (pp. 82–110). New York: Routledge.

Wingfield, A. H., & Feagin, J. R. (2009). *Yes, we can?: White racial framing and the 2008 presidential campaign.* London: Routledge.

Wise, T. J. (2006). Ray Nagin, white rage and the manufacturing of "reverse" racism [Electronic Version]. *The Black Commentator.* Retrieved October 18, 2010, from http://www.blackcommentator.com/169/169_think_wise_ray_nagin.html.

Wise, T. J. (2010) *Colorblind: The rise of post-racial politics and the retreat from racial equity.* San Francisco: City Lights Books.

Yun, J. T., & Reardon, S. F. (2005) "Patterns of multiracial private school segregation." In Janelle Scott (Ed.), *School Choice and Diversity: What the Evidence Says.* New York: Teachers College Press.

Zwerling, C., & Silver, H. (1992). Race and job dismissals in a federal bureaucracy. *American Sociological Review, 57*(5), 651–660.

Diversity on the Web

Go to the African American site below. It features news, politics, culture, business, and lifestyles information. It is maintained by African Americans for African Americans. After reviewing the site, what new perspectives have you gained about the role of race in African American lives?

http://www.netnoir.com/

Joyce McNickles, EdD is a Professor at Worcester State University. Prior to teaching in higher education, she was program coordinator for the National Conference for Community and Justice.

TO BE ASIAN IN AMERICA

Angela Johnson Meadows

GOALS

- To provide an historic and cultural context for understanding Asian Americans
- To illustrate that Asian Americans are not a monolithic minority group
- To explain the myth of the "model majority" stereotype

C. N. Le barely remembers fleeing Vietnam for the United States when he was 5. Sketchy images of riding a cargo ship to Guam, having his documents processed and boarding a plane that would take him to Arkansas are all that remain of the life-altering experience.

But the reason for leaving his war-ravaged homeland is crystal clear. After military pressure from communist North Vietnam caused the South Vietnamese government to collapse in 1975, Le's family was in jeopardy.

"The U.S. government knew that those who worked for the U.S. military were going to be persecuted pretty harshly if they stayed back in Vietnam," says Le, whose parents both were U.S. military workers. "So [the U.S. government] made arrangements for their Vietnamese employees and their families to be evacuated."

Le and his family spent their initial days in the United States at Fort Chaffee, an Arkansas military base that served as a processing center for Vietnamese refugees.

"We had a little playground there that kids would play on, so in a lot of ways my experience was more of a typical kid's experience . . . than a refugee experience," recalls Le, a visiting assistant professor at the University of Massachusetts Amherst.

"Adults who had more of a recognition of what was going on would probably tell you, like my parents have said, it was a pretty traumatic experience for them, having to leave their country, leave everything behind and try to start life in a whole new country," Le says.

Le's status as a refugee is different from that of Chinese, Asian Indians, Japanese and some other Asians who have come to America, yet regardless of country of origin or mode or time of arrival, the majority of these immigrants share a common goal—a better life. For some, that means educational or professional opportunities they were denied in their homelands; for others, it's escaping political turmoil; and for others still, it's sacrificing the comforts of middle-class life to provide better chances for their children. It is the quintessential U.S. immigrant story.

There are nearly 12 million people of Asian heritage living in the United States. Asian Americans (a term used by *DiversityInc* to describe both immigrant and American-born Asians) represent East Asian nations such as China, Japan and Korea: South Asian countries including India, Pakistan and Nepal; and Southeast Asian nations such as Thailand, Vietnam and Malaysia.

Reprinted with explicit permission from *DiversityInc*, April 2005, pp. 29–47.

Still only 4.6 percent of the U.S. population, the Asian-American segment is experiencing astronomical growth. Between 2000 and 2050, the population is expected to surge 213 percent, according to the U.S. Census Bureau. The projected general-population growth during the same time? A paltry 49 percent.

But this growth isn't a 21st-century phenomenon. Historians have traced their presence in the land that evolved into the United States of America as far back as 1763, when Filipinos traveling aboard Spanish galleons jumped ship in New Orleans to escape imprisonment and fled into the Louisiana bayou to establish the first recorded Filipino settlement in America. Some argue their history in the United States dates back to the 1400s.

The Chinese were the first group of Asians to arrive in great numbers, appearing in the mid-1800s. The lure? The potential economic prosperity of the 1848 California Gold Rush and job opportunities associated with agriculture and the building of the intercontinental railroad.

Asian Americans were recruited as laborers—mostly men who were enticed by the opportunity to earn money to support their families or indentured servants who were sent to work off the debts of other Asians back home.

"These people were often deceived," says Gary Okihiro, director of the Center for the Study of Ethnicity and Race and a professor of international and public affairs at Columbia University. "Although these [work and payment] conditions were spelled out to them, they were oftentimes unfulfilled."

Many planned to return to their homelands when their contracted work period ended, but were prevented by U.S. immigration laws.

"They locked those that were here in the U.S.," says Okihiro. "Their remittances were crucial for the sustenance of their families back in Asia, so they were oftentimes trapped into remaining in the U.S."

Subsequent Asians came in waves, with the largest population arriving after the 1965 passage of the Immigration and Nationality Act. Immigrants and their offspring from China, the Philippines, India, Vietnam, Korea and Japan now account for the largest Asian populations in the country.

A BRAVE NEW WORLD

W.E.B. DuBois once described the African-American experience as one of a double-consciousness, rooted in the need to navigate between one's own culture and that of the mainstream. It is an experience that rings true for Asian immigrants and their descendants as well.

"When they arrive, they begin to realize that they're different," says John Kuo Wei Tchen, the founding director of the A/P/A Studies Program and Institute at New York University. "Identities get challenged and they have to deal with what it means to be American or resident alien."

Some Asian Americans relied on assimilation as a means of blending in with American society and as an attempt to escape anti-Asian sentiments that heightened during World War II. "This question about how much they wanted to or did assimilate is a question of how much they were permitted to assimilate," says Okihiro.

Today, ties to home remain strong for new Asian immigrants; however, many families experience acculturation—the process of assimilating new ideas into an existing cognitive structure—with U.S.-born generations.

"Parents would like to think their children are going to be very embracive and very welcoming of the parents'own culture," says Franklin Ng, a professor in the anthropology department at California State University–Fresno. "Parents may have these kinds of supportive mechanisms, encouraging them to go to a temple, or ethnic church, so their children will become familiar with their ethnic culture . . . [but] the youth are having their own trajectory."

Growing up in a Southern California suburb, Le struggled with his Vietnamese name. By the time he reached high school, racial and ethnic tensions had set in and Le decided to go by the name Sean. "At that age, you just want to fit in and be like everyone else," he says.

But a college course on race and ethnicity changed his thinking. "That's when I became more socially conscious . . . and really began to see that my identity . . . was a source of strength . . . rather than a source of embarrassment. I wanted to go back to my Vietnamese name. The name Sean didn't really fit my identity," says Le, who is also the founder of Asian-Nation.org, an online resource for Asian-American historical, demographic, political and cultural issues.

Today, Le uses his first and middle initials, a way to keep his Vietnamese name—Cuong Nguyen—without having to face the pronunciation problems of non-Asians.

This balancing act isn't limited to language issues. Many struggle with the expectations of both their family and mainstream society.

"We were raised in the family to be in a very consistent way with the traditional Chinese culture." says Lora Fong, a third-generation Chinese American. "We spoke Chinese in the home and ate Chinese food in the home. The home life was one thing, but going out into the regular world, you have to fit in; there is a certain amount of biculturalism."

When Fong's father died in 1984, her Chinese and American worlds collided. She was working at IBM at the time, a company that often assisted employees in making funeral arrangements for loved ones.

"I was a team leader, I was frequently running projects and giving assignments and keeping people on task," says Fong, now an attorney at Greenbaum, Rowe, Smith & Davis in Woodbridge, N.J. Fortunately, Fong had a Chinese-American supervisor who understood that her professional persona was in stark contrast to her status within her traditional Chinese family.

"He knew that I could not take on a role of being in charge [in my family]." Fong recalls. "He just said, 'She's the daughter. She's the youngest. She's not running things. The company does not have a role there, so just back off.' And that was really antithetical to the way the company took on a role in an employee's personal life. That was such a dichotomy."

STRIVING FOR SUCCESS

Despite viewing America as the proverbial land of opportunity, the path to a better life has not been without roadblocks, particularly for those who arrived prior to 1965. Chinese in the United States were denied citizenship in the late 1800s, while immigration of all Asians, except for Filipinos (whose residence in a U.S. territory gave them the status of nationals), was halted in 1924 through the National Origins Act. It wasn't until the Immigration and Nationality Act of 1965 that Asian Americans were accepted into the country in larger numbers. The gates to the United States were opened, particularly to those with expertise in the medical, science and technology fields, explaining in part the proliferation of Asian Americans in those disciplines today.

In the face of language barriers, cultural adjustments and government and societal oppression, Asian Americans as a whole appear to have done quite well in America. A look at demographic data shows that Asian Americans as a group surpass all other racial and ethnic groups in the country in median household income and education levels. And while many marketers are turned off by the small size and myriad languages of the population, the buying power of Asian Americans is projected to jump 347 percent between 1990 and 2009, compared with a modest 159-percent increase for the overall population.

For aspirational Asian Americans, social mobility is a priority and education often is viewed as the method of achievement. This focus contributes to the group's economic success.

"Researchers suggest that one legacy of Confucianism in many Asian countries (notably China, Korea, Japan and Vietnam) is the notion that human beings are perfectible if they work to improve themselves," write Yu Xie and Kimberly A. Goyette, authors of *Demographic Portrait of Asian Americans.* "Given this cultural heritage, some Asian Americans may be more likely than whites to believe that hard work in school will he rewarded."

"In China, you have a kind of high-stakes testing," adds Tchen, referring to the country's civil-service system. "The emperor constantly recruits the best to come to the capital or to work . . . It's not so odd for higher education to be seen as the modern variation of that practice."

Mia Tuan's mother and father encouraged higher learning. "Even though my parents knew nothing about the U.S. educational system . . . it was always assumed that I would go to college," says Tuan, an associate professor of sociology at the University of Oregon.

Tuan's mother wanted her daughter to be the next Connie Chung. "Connie opened that door and parents encouraged us to go through that same door," says Tuan.

"I chose to not be the next Connie Chung, but a whole cohort of Asian-American women did hear that call and answered that call . . . When I told them I was going into sociology, they didn't know what the hell that was, but it was a Ph.D., so that counted for something."

But educational attainment isn't a priority for all Asians in America.

"If you come from a rural society where schooling and education was not such a benefit to your ability to raise crops . . . your emphasis on education would be different," says Tchen. "That would be true for Hmong or Southeast Asians . . . They don't necessarily relate to higher education as a way to better themselves."

This is played out in the educational statistics of Asian Americans. For example. in 2000, 76 percent of Asian Indians and 67 percent of Chinese Americans between the ages of 25 and 34 had a college degree or higher, compared with 43 percent of Filipino Americans and 27 percent of Vietnamese Americans.

THE MODEL MINORITY AND OTHER MYTHS

While the myths of universal affluence and intelligence among Asian Americans are just that, it hasn't stopped society from pinning them with the "model minority" label. They are seen as smart, wealthy and successful, and on the surface, it appears to be a positive perception.

"My parents' generation? They liked the model minority stereotype," says Tuan. "In their mind, it has served us well . . . They saw it as the price you pay for being an outsider and it was a price they were willing to pay."

But a look behind the stereotype and its implications reveals a troubling story.

"A lot of these [income] statistics can be misleading," says Le. "Family median income is mainly inflated because Asian-American families tend to have more workers . . . They're more likely to live in urban areas where salaries are higher, but the cost of living is also higher."

Per capita income for Asian Americans in the 2000 census measured $20,719, compared with $21,587 for the overall population.

A look at Fortune 500 companies illustrates that an intense focus on education really doesn't guarantee professional success. Despite high education levels, Asian Americans represent less than 1 percent of senior-management ranks or corporate boards.

"Everybody cites the success of Asian Americans, yet if you compared the level of education and position with that of white people, they come below white people," says Okihiro. "Their investment in education does not pay off. There's a glass ceiling for them."

How They Score Class of 2003 SATs

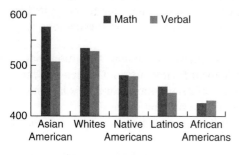

U.S. Asian Population

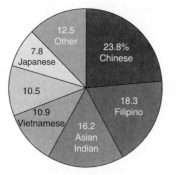

Educational Attainment
People 25 years and older, 2004

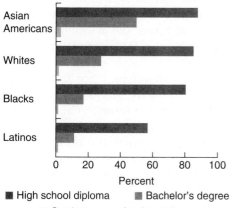

■ High school diploma   ■ Bachelor's degree
■ Graduate or professional degree

Median Family Incomes
In U.S. Population 25+

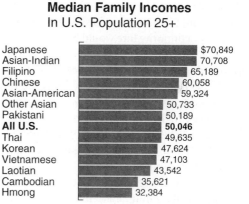

Japanese	$70,849
Asian-Indian	70,708
Filipino	65,189
Chinese	60,058
Asian-American	59,324
Other Asian	50,733
Pakistani	50,189
All U.S.	**50,046**
Thai	49,635
Korean	47,624
Vietnamese	47,103
Laotian	43,542
Cambodian	35,621
Hmong	32,384

Asian-American Buying Power
Projected rate of increase 1990–2009

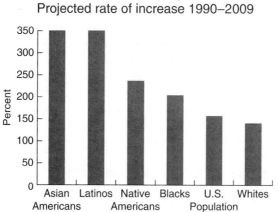

FIGURE 2-1

Tuan's father was a diplomat with the Taiwanese government; however, after the U.S. office closed, he found it wasn't easy to translate his skills. He ended up opening a pizza shop.

"They lost a lot of status," says Tuan of her parents, whose migration to the United States erased the prestige of their advanced degrees. "That put pressure on the next generation to make it worthwhile."

The belief that Asian Americans can succeed on their own dilutes the notion that some could benefit from programs ranging from Medicaid to affirmative action. Thirteen percent of all Asian Americans live in poverty. Twenty-three percent of Asians outside of the six largest groups are impoverished, rivaling the 24 percent of blacks of this economic status.

"With this spotlight on the talented tenth, there is neglect of those who may be in the lower tiers," says Ng.

Tuan recalls a meeting with faculty members and graduate students in her department.

"At one point [during the meeting] a graduate student said, 'We take issue with the fact that the department isn't hiring minorities,'" says Tuan, who was one of three recently hired Asian Americans in the department. "I was stunned when the student said that, and I said, 'So, do we not count?' And his answer was basically [that] we didn't, that Asians were this middle category . . . In his mind a minority hire would have been Latino, African American and Native American."

In addition to not being viewed as a traditional minority, Asian Americans also have an imposed identity as "eternal foreigners." Many American-born Asians have at least one story of being asked about their origins. A reply such as Fresno or Washington. D.C., is often met with the incredulous response of: "No, where are you *really* from?"

Even high-profile American-born Asians can't escape the stereotype. When Tara Lipinski defeated Michelle Kwan in the 1998 Winter Olympics figure-skating competition, MSNBC ran a headline that read: "American beats out Kwan." Kwan, who was born in Torrance, Calif., is just as American as Lipinski.

This misconception has some basis in truth, says Le. Approximately two-thirds of Asian Americans are immigrants. "But the social implications are that when someone is judged to be a foreigner, it is easier for that person to be treated as if they're not a real American . . . It becomes easier to deny them the same rights and privileges that are given to real Americans."

Asian Americans also face the perception that they are all the same. When Ng first settled in Fresno, Calif., he was taunted by a group of teenagers who ordered him to "Remember Pearl Harbor Day," an allusion to Japan's attack on the United States. As a child growing up in a Chicago suburb during the Korean War era, Tchen received the label of "gook," a disparaging term for Southeast Asians. Both Ng and Tchen are Chinese.

But perhaps the most notable misidentification occurred in 1982, when 27-year-old Vincent Chin visited a suburban Detroit strip club to celebrate his impending nuptials. While there, Chin encountered a couple of disgruntled autoworkers, one of whom had recently been laid off. The autoworkers hurled insults at Chin and blamed him for the demise of Detroit's auto industry. After Chin left the club, the two men met up with Chin in front of a fast-food restaurant and beat him with a baseball bat. Chin, who was Chinese—not Japanese, as his attackers had assumed—slipped into a coma and died five days later.

THE ASIAN-AMERICAN IDENTITY IN AMERICA

Asian Americans represent nearly 25 countries and speak at least as many languages: however, it is the challenges stemming from stereotypes, misconceptions, discrimination and exclusion that help this disparate group to unite under the umbrella term of "Asian American."

"The experience of being treated as foreigners, exotics, outsiders, hordes, dangerous, those kinds of images that are recycled in American media . . . perpetuate some kind of basis for people of different backgrounds to come together," says Tchen.

"A pan-Asian orientation is useful as sort of an instrument for coalition building for political advancement," adds Ng. "Asian Americans are ignored in the corridors of power, and collectively they can have more impact and can address issues that are more common."

Although Fong identifies first as a Chinese American, she's also concerned about broader Asian-American issues.

"We are all sharing a unique experience in terms of people's preconceived notion of who we are and what we should or shouldn't be doing in this society," says Fong, who is a past president of the Asian Pacific American Lawyers Association of New Jersey.

In addition to fighting shared struggles, Asian Americans have been able to collectively celebrate the accomplishments of Asian Americans of various backgrounds. Norman Mineta, U.S. Secretary of Transportation, and Elaine Chao, U.S. Secretary of Labor, are two of the highest-ranking Asian Americans in the Bush administration. Andrea Jung, chairman of the board and CEO of Avon Products, and Indira Nooyi, president and chief financial officer at PepsiCo, are just a few people who have broken what career consultant Jane Hyun describes as the "bamboo ceiling" of corporate America. And the presence of Asian Americans in sports and entertainment continues to flourish.

"When I was growing up . . . there was not exactly a wide range," says Tuan. "But if you were to ask—and I do ask these questions of the students—to name five prominent Asian-American public figures, they can come up with them now . . . I can only see that as being a good thing, because it shifts this notion of what's possible or who or what an Asian American is or what they're capable of. That's very powerful to me."

DISCUSSION QUESTIONS

1. In what ways have Asian Americans experienced "target" status?

2. Why are Asian Americans often not thought of as a minority group?

3. As a group, Asian Americans have the highest SAT scores and the highest college graduation rates. Then, how do you account for the fact that Asian Americans have found more success in small businesses than they have in Fortune 500 companies?

4. How does the educational success of Asian Americans contribute to popular prejudices about these groups?

Inventing Hispanics: A Diverse Minority Resists Being Labeled

Amitai Etzioni

GOALS

- To illustrate the complexity of Hispanic cultural identity in the United States
- To present some of the economic and political issues that affect America's largest "minority" group

Thirty years ago immigrants from Latin America who settled in the United States were perceived in terms of their home nation—as, for example, Cuban Americans or Mexican Americans, just as European newcomers were seen as Italian Americans or Polish Americans. Today the immigrant flow from Central and South America has grown substantially, and the newcomers are known as Hispanics.

Some observers have expressed concern that efforts to make Hispanics a single minority group—for purposes ranging from elections to education to the allocation of public funds—are further dividing American society along racial lines. But attempts, both incidental and ideological, to forge these American immigrants into a strongly defined minority are encountering an unanticipated problem. Hispanics by and large do not see themselves as a distinct minority group; they do see themselves as Americans.

HISPANICS AND AFRICAN AMERICANS

Hispanics are particularly important for understanding the future of diversity in American society. Already they have overtaken African Americans to become the nation's largest minority, and immigration patterns ensure that the number of Hispanics will continue to grow more rapidly than that of African Americans.

U.S. race relations have long been understood in terms of black and white. Until recently, many books on the subject did not even mention other races, or did so only as a brief afterthought. Now recognition is growing that Hispanics are replacing blacks as the primary minority. But whereas blacks have long been raising their political consciousness, Hispanics have only just begun to find their political legs.

Recent increases in minority populations and a decline in the white majority in the United States have driven several African-American leaders, including Jesse Jackson and former

New York City Mayor David Dinkins, along with a few Hispanics, such as Fernando Ferrer, a candidate for the 2002 mayoral election in New York City, and some on the white left (writing in *The American Prospect*) to champion a coalition of minorities to unseat the "white establishment" and become the power-holders and shapers of America's future. The coalition's leaders are systematically encouraging Hispanics (and Asian Americans) to see themselves as victims of discrimination and racism—and thus to share the grievances of many African Americans. Whether they will succeed depends much on how Hispanic Americans see themselves and are viewed by others.

HISPANICS AND THE CENSUS

For several decades now, the Census Bureau has been working to make Hispanics into a distinct group and—most recently—into a race. In 1970, a 5 percent sample of households was asked to indicate whether their origin was Mexican, Puerto Rican, Cuban, Central or South American, or other Spanish. But it was only in 1980, that "Hispanics" became a distinct statistical and social category in the census, as all households were asked whether they were of "Spanish/Hispanic origin or descent." Had no changes been made in 1980, we might well have continued to think of Hispanics as we do about other white Americans, as several ethnic groups, largely from Mexico and Cuba.

The next step was to take Hispanics, who were until recently multiple ethnic groups that were considered racially white, and make them into a unique, separate group whose members, according to the census, "can be members of any race." This unusual status has had several notable results. One is the flurry of headlines following the release of new census data in March 2001 announcing that "California Whites Are a Minority"—even though 59.5 percent of Californians, including many Hispanics, chose white as their race. The only way for whites to be proclaimed a minority in California is for no Hispanics to be counted as white—even those 40 percent, or more than four million people, who specifically marked white as their race on the census form. Another curious result is the awkward phrase "non-Hispanic whites," by which the media now refer to the majority of Americans.

Because of their evolving status in the census, Hispanics are now sometimes treated not as a separate ethnic group but as a distinct race. (Race marks sharper lines of division than ethnicity.) Often, for example, when national newspapers and magazines, such as the *Washington Post* and *U.S. News and World Report,* graphically depict racial breakdowns on various subjects, they list Hispanics as a fourth group, next to white, black, and Asian. Much less often, but with increasing frequency, Hispanics arc referred to as "brown" Americans, as in a *Newsweek* article that noted a "Brown Belt" across America. The result is to make the country seem more divided than it is.

Should one mind the way the census keeps its statistics? Granted, social scientists are especially sensitive to the social construction of categories. But one need not have an advanced degree to realize that the ways we divide people up—or combine them—have social consequences. One may care little how the census manipulates its data, but those data are what we use to paint a picture of the social composition of America. Moreover, the census categories have many other uses—for college admissions forms, health care, voting, and job profiles, government budget allocations, and research. And the media use the census for guidance. In short, the census greatly influences the way we see each other and ourselves, individually and as a community.

This is not to suggest that the Census Bureau has conspired to split up the nation. The recategorizations and redefinitions reflect, in part, changes in actual numbers (large increases in the nation's Hispanic population might arguably justify a separate category); in part, efforts to streamline statistics (collapsing half-a-dozen ethnic groups into one); and, in part, external pressures to which all government agencies are subjected. To be sure, the Census Bureau is a highly professional agency whose statistics are set by scientific considerations. But there is as yet no such thing as a government agency that has a budget set by Congress, that needs public cooperation for carrying out its mission, and that is fully apolitical. Likewise, the Office of Management and Budget, which sets the racial categories, is among the less political branches of the White House, yet still quite politically attuned.

HISPANICS IN THEIR OWN EYES

How do Hispanics see themselves? First of all, the vast majority prefer to be classified as a variety of ethnic groups rather than as one. The National Latino Political Survey, for example, found that three out of four respondents chose to be labeled by country of origin, rather than by "panethnic" terms such as "Hispanic" or "Latino." Hispanics are keenly aware of big differences among Hispanic groups, especially between Mexican Americans (the largest group) and Cuban Americans, the latter being regarded as more likely to be conservative, to vote Republican, to become American citizens, and so on.

America has, by and large, dropped the notion that it will tell you what your race is, either by deeply offensive blood tests or by examining your features and asking your neighbors (the way the census got its figures about race until 1950). We now allow people to indicate which race they consider themselves to be by marking a box on a census form. Many Hispanics resist being turned into a separate race or being moved out of the white category. In 1990, the census allowed people to buy out of racial divisions by checking "other" when asked about their racial affiliation. Nearly 10 million people—almost all of them Hispanics—did so.

When the Census Bureau introduced its "other" category, some African-American leaders objected because, as they correctly pointed out, the resulting diminution in minority figures both curtails numerous public allotments that take race into account and affects redistricting. So the 2000 census dropped "other" and instead allowed people to claim several races (but not to refuse to be racially boxed in). The long list of racial boxes to be checked ended with "some other race," with a space to indicate what that race was. Many of the 18 million people who chose this category, however, made no notation, leaving their race as they wanted it—undefined.

Of those who chose only "some other race," almost all (97 percent) were Hispanic. Among Hispanics, 42.2 percent chose "some other race," 47.9 percent chose white (alone) as their race, 6.3 percent chose two or more races, and 2 percent chose black (alone). In short, the overwhelming majority of Hispanics either chose white or refused racial categorization, clearly resisting the notion of being turned into a separate race.

A MAJORITY OF MINORITIES

As I have shown in considerable detail in my recent book, *The Monochrome Society,* the overwhelming majority of Americans of all backgrounds have the same dreams and aspirations as the white majority. Hispanic and Asian immigrants and their children (as well as most African Americans) support many of the same public policies (from reformed health insurance to better education, from less costly housing to better and more secure jobs). In fact, minorities often differ more among themselves than they do with the white majority. Differences among, say, Japanese Americans and Vietnamese Americans are considerable, as they are among those from Puerto Rico and Central America. (Because of the rapid rise of the African-American middle class, this group, too, is far from monolithic.)

Intermarriage has long been considered the ultimate test of relationships among various groups in American society. Working together and studying together are considered low indicators of intergroup integration; residing next to one another, a higher one; intermarriage—the highest. By that measure, too, more and more Hispanic (and Asian) Americans are marrying outside their ethnic group. And each generation is more inclined to marry outside than the previous ones.

In the mid-1990s, about 20 percent of first-generation Asian women were intermarried, as compared with slightly less than 30 percent of the second generation and slightly more than 40 percent of the third generation. Hispanic intermarriage shows a similar trend. More and more Americans, like Tiger Woods, have relatives all over the colorful ethnic-racial map, further binding America into one encompassing community, rather than dividing it along racial and ethnic lines.

In short, there is neither an ideological nor a social basis for a coalition along racial lines that would combine Hispanics, Asians, and African Americans against the white majority to fashion a radically different American society and creed.

DIVERSITY WITHIN UNITY

Immigrants to America have never been supra-homogenized. Assimilation has never required removing all traces of cultural difference between newcomers and their new homeland. The essence of the American design—diversity within unity—leaves considerable room for differences regarding to whom one prays and to which country one has an allegiance—as long as it does not conflict with an overarching loyalty to America. Differences in cultural items from music to cuisines are celebrated for making the nation, as a community of communities, richer.

Highly legitimate differences among the groups are contained by the shared commitments all are expected to honor: the Constitution and its Bill of Rights, the democratic way of government, peaceful resolution of conflict, and tolerance for differences. These shared bonds may change as new Americans join the U.S. community, but will do so in a largely gradual, continuous, and civil process rather than through rebellion and confrontation. I write "largely" because no country, the United States included, is completely free of troublesome transitions and we have had our share.

No one can be sure what the future holds. A prolonged downward turn in the economy (a centerpiece of most radical scenarios) would give efforts to enlist new immigrants into a majority-of-minorities coalition a better chance of succeeding. But unlike some early Americans who arrived here as slaves, most new immigrants come voluntarily. Many discover that hard work and education do allow them to move up the American economic and social ladders. That makes a radicalization of Hispanics (and Asian Americans) very unlikely. As far as one can project the recent past into the near future, Hispanics will continue to build and rebuild the American society as a community of communities rather than dividing it along racial lines.

DISCUSSION QUESTIONS

1. What values, which tend to be strong in Hispanic cultures, contribute to popular stereotypes about Hispanic workers? How could these values contribute to a perception that Hispanics lack the initiative and drive so valued in today's workplace?

2. What are the common stereotypes about Hispanics? How could these stereotypes affect career mobility for Hispanics?

3. What role has the popular media (television, newspapers, movies, music, etc.) played in the perpetuation of these stereotypes?

Immigration: Cultural Transmission Today

M. June Allard
Assumption College
Worcester State University, Professor Emerita

"Cultures enrich each other through communication—communication through travel, trade and migration and communication through print and electronic media."

GOALS

- To extend Sowell's historic depiction of cultural enrichment to the cultural enrichment occurring in today's world
- To examine the issues and impact of immigration in the United States today
- To examine the costs and benefits of illegal immigration today

DEMOGRAPHIC TRENDS

Large shifts in workforce demographics are predicted for the next decade. Such shifts mean changes in consumer markets, executive recruitment and workplace policies:

- expected retirement of the first wave of baby boomers with not enough younger people in the workforce to replace them.
- significant downsizing of the Northeast and Midwest populations
- doubling of the labor pool in the South and Southwest due to migration and growth of the Hispanic population (Hispanics leaving poor job markets where they have established networks for jobs in new locales.)
- plunging of labor-force growth to near zero between 2015 and 2020
- growing immigrant labor force

These trends and their accompanying demographic shifts result in significant cultural transfers and economic impact. In *A World View of Cultural Diversity*, Sowell paints a global picture of how the "entire history of the human race, the rise of man from the caves, has been marked by transfers of cultural advances from one group to another and from one civilization to another." While cultures are shaped by the particular skills and orientations of different peoples and by geographic considerations, these factors are only part of the story, for in Sowell's words they fail to explain "many very large differences in the economic and social performances of nations and civilizations."

Sowell traces the historic transfer of some of the concepts, information, products, and technologies passed from one culture to another to illustrate the sharing of cultural features that advances have come and that cultures are shaped. The transmission of cultural features allows people to adopt superior features of other cultures and relinquish less useful features of their own.

In today's world, new avenues of cultural transmission continue to evolve that even more transcend the boundaries of geography. "Since the 1950s, rapidly advancing technologies have removed the physical limitations once placed upon human activity by darkness and distance, thus diminishing the natural barriers to free-market exchange" (Whybrow, 2009). Cultural sharing and transfer now occur extensively through print and electronic media as well as through modern avenues of travel, international trade and migration. Cultural transfer through print and electronic media is examined in the *Media Messages* article found in this text while the discussion in the present article examines the transfer occurring through travel and migration.

TRAVEL AND TOURISM

Travel is an old and venerated medium of cultural contact and the in-person contacts it affords remain important today. It is especially important in high context cultures such as those in Asia and South America where it is the social situation that provides the "cues" to the meaning of the words and silences in communication. Today, travel to nearly all parts of the world constantly increases in the form of business trips, tourism, scientific and cultural exchanges, study abroad, and other short-term more transitory contacts.

Business and Personal Travel

In 2008, business and pleasure travel found 63,554,000 international tourists visiting the U.S. and 57,949,000 U.S. tourists visiting other countries. "Tourism is a global industry and represents one of the largest movements of goods, services and people outside of wartime" (Ward *et al.*, 2001). Business travel and tourism both tend to be avenues of cultural contact more or less restricted to the more "privileged, industrialized first-world subjects" (Nakamura, 2000).

Study Abroad

A growing avenue of culture is study abroad. Worldwide, an estimated three million students studied outside their home countries in 2009, a figure expected to reach more than eight million by 2025 (French, 2009). Competition among countries is keen today not only for attracting foreign scientists, but also for attracting foreign students. Undergraduate students take home some knowledge and understanding of their host counties. Graduate students are tomorrow's scientists and researchers and are especially valued as they may choose to remain in their host countries.

In 2007–08, 623,800 foreign students studied in the U.S. Most were Asians coming from India, China and South Korea (The Chronicle of Higher Education, 2009). In 2006–07, nearly 241,800 American students studied overseas (Open Doors, 2008). Most still study in Europe, but increasing numbers now go to Asia, Africa and South America. More than half study for a term or less, about 36% for a semester and the remainder for longer terms of a year or more (Open Doors, 2008). The Institute of International Education reports over three million students being educated outside their home countries in 2008–2009 and by 2025, that number is expected to exceed eight million (VOA News, 2009).

MIGRATION AND IMMIGRATION

Migration and immigration provide longer term, more sustained cross-national contact. Unlike short-term travel and tourism, migration occurs for people of all economic levels. The poor and those with restricted opportunities move in search of jobs and better opportunities. Rich and poor alike leave home countries in times of political turmoil. But for whatever reasons they leave one culture for another, immigrants bring with them their home cultures—customs, religions, languages and ways of looking at the world—and so begins cultural transfer.

Government, industry and academic leaders generally *seek* transfer of knowledge and products not only by promoting scientific, educational and cultural exchanges but also by crafting immigration laws to facilitate visitation and immigration of the talented and educated from other countries. Certainly the competition among the victorious WWII allies to secure the German rocket scientists bears witness to this. The scientists (at least their skills) were so valued that they were eagerly sought even before the war was over and their politics (they *were* the enemy) were ignored; they were "prizes of war." In many countries today however, politics does not always encourage such exchange; sometimes even acting to interfere. Fearing to admit terrorists or striving to preserve native culture, governments sometimes stem the flow of scientists and students. Past activities or suspected political connections can result in visas that never seem to arrive.

In the U.S., the native-educated and businesses alike lobby strongly that the scientific and technical expertise and innovativeness these talented visitors bring are very badly needed (Anderson, 2007; Viscarolasaga, 2007) contending further that foreign students we have already educated should be allowed to stay permanently. "Indeed, foreign science, engineering and medical students who stay in the U.S. after completing their education . . . are a major source of skilled immigrants" (Friedman & Tomaso, 1996). A report from the Kauffman Foundation makes an even stronger case when it reports that "most immigrants who founded technology and engineering companies in the United States received degrees from U.S. universities" (MHT, 2007). Special waivers and visas in the U.S. aid the highly skilled and educated in immigrating.

Although the "import" of technology and expertise through skilled immigrants may generally be encouraged, the "import" of their cultural baggage, language especially, is frequently not welcomed. "Anti-immigrant sentiment has greeted every wave of immigrants" (DeGroat, 2006). Anti-immigration rallies and headlines such as: "English Language Lost Under the Stampede of Immigration" are not uncommon. (Worcester Telegram and Gazette, June, 2007). Hate groups are activated and local communities enact ordinances to deter immigrants from settling. Hardly welcoming notes.

THE IMMIGRANTS

Before the attacks of 9/11 in 2001, U.S. immigration gates were open wide. In the decade of the 1990s, almost 10 million foreigners came to the U.S. (Borjas, 2000) and "in the last 30 years, the United States . . . absorbed the biggest wave of immigrants since the turn of the [last] century . . . By 2007, approximately 38 million Americans were foreign-born—about 14.5 percent of the population (U.S Census, 2009).

The past decade witnessed a U.S. labor force filled with foreign-born workers representing "diversity in every sense of the word—from skin color, nationality and ethnicity to culture, religion, language, age, orientation and ability" (Ortiz, 2006). In terms of skill and education, immigrants range from a top layer comprised of the educated elite to a bottom layer of those with little or no education. They vary greatly too, in economic status. Contrary to popular stereotypes, not all immigrants are poor. Many are wealthy—for example, the 12,000 Chinese technicians working in Silicon Valley computer firms and the large numbers of wealthy Iranians in Beverly Hills (Clark, 1977). There are those in the United States who would ban all immigration. The practicalities are however, that there are not enough new workers to replace retirements in the U.S. Large numbers of workers are unemployed because of the recession, but many will find that their old jobs no longer exist when the recession ends. The U.S. Department of Labor projects that even though new jobs are not growing as fast as in past, in the decade between 2008 and 2018, there will be an increase of 15.3 million jobs while the increase in civilian workers will number only 12.6 million (2009). Baby boomers are delaying retirement, but U.S. companies still face a worker shortage. The U.S. will need an estimated 270,000 new workers every year. It is not just a question of *numbers* of new workers needed; it is also a question of *skill sets* needed. Closing the gates is not an option. The options are who and how many to admit.

U.S. immigration patterns reflect U.S. immigration policy and its changes over time. At times it sought to restrict racial/ethnic groups as with the Asian exclusion laws of the late 19th century, while at other times encouraging groups such as the Hmong tribesmen from Laos, nurses from the Philippines and farm workers from Mexico. In 1965, racist/nationality preferences were eliminated. Immigration policy "now involves three different sets of rules: those for legal immigration, those for humanitarian admissions, and those that affect illegal entry. These three sets of rules have generated three distinct immigration themes" (Friedman & DiTomaso, 1996).

Documented *vs.* Undocumented

The turmoil over immigration today stems largely from a huge influx of *illegal* immigrants ("illegals" or "undocumenteds") at a time of high U.S. unemployment. Fueled by plentiful job opportunities, illegal immigration totals reached 11.6 million in 2008 comprising about 30% of the total foreign-born population in the U.S. (U.S. Census, 2009; Gardner, 2007). Estimates from census data indicate the recession and stronger law enforcement and deportation reduced that number to 10.8 million in 2009.

Approximately 60% of illegals enter from Mexico (Pew Hispanic Center Report, 2009). Not all illegals sneak in over U.S. borders, though. Some arrive on work or student visas mothers. The voracious demand for labor, changing immigration policies and a confusion of court rulings have produced a two-tier system of legal and illegal immigrants with unprecedented numbers of undocumented workers—workers who may serve the U.S. economy's needs, but who are often very badly served by this economy. The growing backlash against the undocumented workers "is the same reaction seen in this country each time a new immigrant group reaches critical mass" (Frankel, 2006).

THE TRANSITION PROCESS

Acceptance

Once through the gates, the process of assimilation of immigrants into the host culture begins—a process that throughout U.S. history has been fraught with hostility, scape-goating, stereotyping, prejudice and discrimination to the detriment of host and newcomer alike. More than 200 years ago, Benjamin Franklin pronounced judgment on recent arrivals from Germany as "The most stupid in the nation. Few of their children speak English, and through their indiscretion or ours, or both, great disorders may one day arise among us" (Masci, 2001). The discrimination suffered by every past immigrant stream into the U.S. is no different for today's immigrants.

Viewed from one perspective, immigrants fall into three broad categories: naturalized (legal) citizens, in-the-process immigrants and unauthorized immigrants. From a social perspective, all categories experience discrimination. Those who are legally in the long and expensive process of becoming citizens often find themselves treated no better than aliens. Some were even arrested in the raids on the illegals.

Transition into another culture is a slow process at best and one requiring adaptation by both parties. Newcomers are interlopers in an established social scene and when they seek the company of others like themselves, host country prejudices escalate with fears of loss of culture and employment. Backlash erupts when newcomer numbers reach critical mass and the perceived foreign cultural encroachment triggers smoldering resentment building into resistance and discrimination. Historically, "many immigrants faced discrimination in employment and housing by society at large and violence at the hands of hate groups" (Brown, 2006). History repeats itself. In 2005 more than 600 racist hate groups (groups such as the Minutemen, Neo-Nazis, white supremacists and militia-men) were active (Brown, 2006), a number that grew to over 800 by the next year (Ressner, 2006).

In the U.S. today the smoothest transitions are probably made by the educated and skilled elite. They are recognized as important additions to the nation's social capital, as vital to keeping the country competitive in the global marketplace and they come to the U.S. with the added ben-efit of education and skills gained at someone else's expense. Often they arrive with jobs waiting.

Their value was perhaps best symbolized at President Obama's inauguration when four world-renown U.S. musicians (three immigrant and one native-born) performed as a quartet: cellist Yo-Yo Ma (born in Paris of Chinese parents), violinist Itzhak Perlman (born in Tel Aviv, Israel), pianist Gabriella Montero (born in Caracas, Venezuela) and clarinetist Anthony McGill (born in Cincinnati, Ohio). Immigrants not only make world-class contributions to the arts, but also to other areas such as Olympians and professional sports team members and to science as U.S. Nobel laureates (one-quarter of all U.S. Nobel laureates were born in other countries.)

Even top layer immigrants and visitors do not necessarily find the transition road a smooth one, however. Scientific, artistic, technical or academic acceptance does not mean *social accept-ance* even in high-tech industry and university workplaces where skills are valued. Immigrants, especially those without home country support groups, are often "loners." Suro (2000) observes that some immigrants are better off economically than the average American while others are worse off and "as such, immigrants elicit both envy and distain."

Acceptance of newcomers varies by community, particularly so for the undocumented. *The New York Times* reports that the rising backlash against illegal immigrants reached fever pitch and led every state legislature to consider immigration issues in 2007. According to The National Conference of State Legislatures, "a total of 1,404 measures were considered with 41 states enact-ing a total of 170 (Preston, 2007a). The American Civil Liberties Union reports that dozens of local communities also passed immigration ordinances in 2007 (Bazar, 2007; Broder, 2007). These laws and proposed ordinances targeted employers hiring illegal immigrants and companies doing business with the government, landlords renting to illegals and even taco stands. Some proposed using highway patrol officers as immigration law enforcers. Some made it more diffi-cult for illegals to obtain state identification documents like driver's licenses while still others barred illegals from collecting unemployment and other public benefits and admission to public colleges (Preston, 2007; The Chronicle of Higher Education, 2010, October 22).

Amidst a storm of controversy, in April 2010, Arizona passed a law aimed at identifying, prosecuting and deporting illegal immigrants. Under this law, local and state law enforcement are required to question people about their immigration status "if there is any reason to suspect they are in the U.S. illegally" (Cooper and Davenport, 2010). Opponents, including the U.S. President, labeled the law "an invitation to discrimination and harassment" and the federal government filed suit in federal court to invalidate the law. A federal judge has barred implementation of most provisions until the case is settled. Arizona has appealed.

Some of the local discriminatory laws have been struck down by the courts (the federal government has jurisdiction over immigration) and some have produced ironic results. In

Colorado for example, strict documentation requirements led documented and undocumented workers alike to avoid the state thereby resulting in such a severe labor shortage on farms that officials were forced to turn to prison labor (Guillen, 2007).

Not all states and communities seek to exclude illegal immigrants, however. Some states enacted legislation to extend education and health care to immigrant children and 15 adopted laws to punish immigrant smugglers "especially if the victims were foreigners coerced into prostitution or other sexual commerce" (Preston, 2007). In 2001, Tennessee became the first state to permit non-citizens to apply for state driver's licenses and several states such as Utah provide a "driving privilege card" for applicants who do not have Social Security numbers (Cole, 2006). In late 2009, a Massachusetts proposal, the "Massachusetts New American Agenda" carried a recommendation that police departments be required "to record each traffic stop, including the name, age, race and reason for the stop *to curtail racial profiling."* (Monahan, 2009) The city of New Haven, Connecticut openly welcomes immigrants. Police there are prohibited from asking about immigration status and the city has a program to provide illegal aliens with ID cards "to help them open bank accounts and access many city services." Some companies too, have instituted programs such as English language classes, financial-literacy information and networking systems to aid foreign-born workers (Kim, 2006).

Treatment of illegal aliens remains shrouded in political controversy. The 2009 Massachusetts proposal contains controversial recommendations that undocumented aliens be accorded driver's licenses and in-state tuition rates at public institutions of higher education—something the state law makers rejected three years earlier. Ten states currently give in-state tuition rates to undocumented students; four states ban the practice (Contreras, 2009). Welcoming or rejecting, the reception accorded to all immigrants seems to depend in large part on whether they are perceived as assets or liabilities, i.e., competition to, or complementary to, the local economy.

The Workplace

The highly trained are sought by universities and industries. The untrained (both documented and undocumented) are sought by employers to provide cheap labor for factories, restaurants, agriculture, construction, hospitality and service industries. Approximately half of the current undocumented workers work in the informal sector as gardeners, day-laborers, domestic workers, nannies, dishwashers, and other service workers. "Others work for subcontractors who ply their wares in the garment trade and other manufacturing industries . . ." (Fine, 2004). Seasonal migratory workers traditionally cross the southern U.S. border to pick crops while Europeans, particularly Eastern Europeans, work in resorts each summer at jobs that Americans shun (AP, Worcester Sunday Telegram, 2007, July 1). Unskilled immigrants are more often found in dangerous and undesirable jobs than are natives of comparable skill.

Exploitation

The undocumenteds comprise about 5 percent of the U.S. total workforce (Moorefield, 2008). In the marketplace, normal business practices are altered when illegal aliens and low-skill documented immigrants are employed. Conditions often deteriorate into long hours, low pay, uncompensated workplace injuries, lack of health benefits, failure to be paid, union smashing and evasion of basic rights and labor laws. Undocumented immigrants in particular, are at the mercy of their employers. Although the "federal employment discrimination laws protect all employees in this country who work for an employer with 15 or more employees, including those who are not authorized to work" (EEOC, 1999), most undocumented workers are afraid to stand up for their basic rights for they find themselves blacklisted or fired if they do.

Points of Law

It is unlawful to threaten to report, or to report a worker to INS because a worker opposed unlawful discrimination or participated in a proceeding under the anti-discrimination laws . . . If an unauthorized worker is retaliated against, that worker is entitled to damages without regard to his or her work status."

(EEOC, 1999)
http://www.eeoc.gov/policy/docs/qanda-ndoc.html

The federal employment discrimination laws protect all employees in this country who work for an employer with fifteen or more employees, including those who are not authorized to work.

(EEOC, 1999, October 29; NELP, n.d.)

The most common protections denied to undocumented workers include:

a. The right to receive the promised wage and/or at least the minimum wage and overtime pay for work actually performed
b. The right to healthy and safe conditions on the job
c. The right to receive workers' compensation benefits for injuries on the job
d. The right to be free from discrimination based on sex, color, race, religion, and national origin, age and disabilities.

Workplace Fairness (2007)

Employer arguments that illegal workers take jobs that no native citizen will take are countered by those of displaced native workers saying that the presence of the illegals allows management to reduce working conditions and wages so low that native workers won't take the jobs if decent wages and working conditions are present. Employers contend that they must hire cheap immigrant labor to remain competitive and not hiring these workers means down-sizing or sending work overseas where labor is cheap.

Points of Law

. . . the Immigration Reform and Control Act of 1986 makes it illegal to employ illegal aliens and punishes employers who knowingly do so . . . with fines and even jail time for repeat offenders.

(Masci, 2001)

The Employ American Workers Act of February 2009 prohibits financial institutions receiving federal bailout money from hiring foreign workers if they have recently laid off American workers in similar jobs or plan to do so.

In May 2006, the INS (Immigration and Naturalization Service) began sweeping raids aimed at rounding up "fugitive aliens" for deportation. Families were separated, children were stranded, deportation hearings were slow, and the aliens were held at grossly overcrowded detention centers in conditions that frequently violated federal standards of health and safety. "Most [immigrants] had no criminal records and less than 20% had previous deportation orders."

Immigration and Customs Enforcement (ICE) sent out 104 fugitive operation teams to search for undocumented aliens and by mid 2009, an estimated 369,483 detainees were held in custody. (Texas Civil Rights Review, 2009). According to ICE reports, 380,000 illegal immigrants were deported in 2009 alone (Myers, 2010). The plan was to deport *all* illegals, the cost of which is estimated to be at least $94 billion according to ICE Chief Myers (Nizza, 2007).

The Immigration Reform and Control Act of 1986 not only makes it illegal to employ undocumented aliens, it also punishes employers who knowing do so . . . with fines and even jail time for repeat offenders. Until 2006 however, this was rarely enforced (Masci, 2001) and U.S. employers had long turned a blind eye to the legal or illegal status of their workers. That became risky in 2008–9, when ICE focus shifted from deporting alien residents to prosecuting non-compliant employers. In November 2009, Immigration officials reported serving notice on 1,000 businesses that their paperwork (I-9 forms) would be examined to ensure they don't employ illegals. These "audits" aim to promote a "culture of compliance" among employers. In one six month period in 2009, ICE planned to fine companies nearly $16 million for violations (Carroll, 2009).

The deportation of tens of thousands of illegal immigrants and the fines levied on those that hired them leave employers in limbo—they face laying off thousands of workers—especially in agriculture and low-wage industries, a situation that will likely discriminate against Hispanic workers who are heavily concentrated in these jobs (Preston, 2007).

IMPACT: WHAT DO THEY BRING AND WHAT DO THEY COST?

Computing the costs and contributions of the foreign-born is complicated. Measurement is not easy and immigrant groups vary considerably in the form of their impact. Arguments are made about their value from a number of different perspectives such as, the economy as a whole, entrepreneurship, employment/productivity, services and consumer products, taxes, social services, neighborhoods and assimilation.

The Economy

Opinion varies from one extreme to the other on how much immigrants cost or add to the U.S. economy. Some estimates claim they are a burden, e.g., "Most immigrants are low-skilled workers whose earning generate little in taxes to help pay for their perquisites . . . for every dollar they pay in taxes, they use $10 in government services" (Ruhl, 2009); with the INS estimating that illegal aliens cost the taxpayers $45 billion annually (Kim, 2006). A Migration Policy Institute report however, finds that undocumenteds have little or no impact (Hanson, 2009). Still others assess them as an asset and even as making enormous contributions to the economy (e.g., "billions each year not counting the contribution of immigrant-owned businesses or the impact of highly skilled immigrants on overall productivity" (Incognito, 2007) and the U.S. "gross domestic product has grown from the result of immigration, leading to billions of dollars in economic output" (Peri, 2006). According to the Urban Institute

> Immigrants (undocumented and documented) bring an estimated benefit of $330 billion back into the economy, a figure surmised by adding their yearly estimated earnings ($240 billion) and what they pay in taxes ($90 billion). (Kim, 2006)

Supporters point out that illegal aliens pay taxes and by their cheap labor, reduce the costs of services to consumers. Further, "in some places the local economy is largely supported by the labor of illegal aliens . . . one estimate: one out of every three businesses in Atlanta employs undocumented workers" (Masci, 2001). Ironically, "The ICE (Immigration and Customs Enforcement) reports that even the U.S. military employs illegal migrant labor" (Carlsen, 2007).

Entrepreneurship

"Immigrants are more likely to start businesses—from corner grocery stores to giant computer companies—than native-born Americans are" and ". . . one out of every four new businesses in Silicon Valley is founded by an entrepreneur of Indian or Chinese origin" (Masci, 2001). A Duke University study reports that "immigrants started 25 percent of the new U.S. technology and engineering companies over the past decade (Mass High Tech, 2007).

The benefit the immigrants bring to the economy increases when the estimated value of the immigrant-based companies is included: "As of 2005, . . . immigrant-founded companies generated $52 billion in annual sales and created 450,000 jobs nation-wide" (Williams, 2007; Incognito, 2007). "Twenty-six percent of the biotech companies founded in New England have at least one foreign-born founder . . . These companies generated 7.6 billion in sales and employed 4,300 workers across the region" (MHT, 2007).

Employment/Productivity

Detractors accuse immigrants of causing low wages (Incognito, 2007) and assert that mass hiring of less-skilled workers has harmed the economic opportunities of less-skilled natives whose jobs are now at risk (Borjas, 1996). Proponents of immigration, arguing that immigrants do not take away jobs from natives, point to a Pew study finding that "In parts of the country with few immigrants, 'low-wage jobs still get done, and by native-born people' "(Masci, 2001) and to a study released in late 2009 reporting that illegal-immigrant workers drain neither jobs nor tax dollars. "The fate of the U.S. economy does not rest on what we do on illegal immigration" (Hanson, 2009). Proponents argue further that "skilled native workers . . . have much to gain when less skilled workers enter the United States. Skilled workers can then "devote all their efforts to jobs that use their skills effectively while immigrants provide cheap labor for service jobs" (Borjas, 1996). In the words of Hanson,

> Because the U.S. has dramatically raised the education level of its adult population in the last 50 years, the native-born, low-skilled work force has shrunk, while employers continue to require low-skilled workers. This leaves room for illegal immigrants to take such jobs at low cost. (2009)

Service and Consumer Products

Advocates of immigration report that "Our work shows that cities with more diversity—more immigrants—in the work force exhibit higher productivity than the American-born employees" (Kim, 2006) and that "without immigrants working these lower-wage jobs, the service sector and consumer products would balloon in price" (Kim, 2006). They argue too, that immigrant labor does not automatically lower wage levels. In the trades, for example, immigrants have a higher percentage of union membership than U.S.-born workers (Incognito, 2007).

Taxes

"Immigrants pay between $90 billion and $140 billion a year in federal, state and local taxes, according to the National Immigration Forum and the Social Security Administration" (Kim, 2006). Undocumented immigrants often "use fake social security numbers and though they don't get any benefits, they still have income tax taken out of their pay checks" (Kim, 2006). "A New York Times story in 2005 reported that an "estimated 7 million or so illegal immigrant workers in the United States are now providing the Social Security system with a subsidy of as much as $7 billion a year" (Porter, 2005).

Social Services

Immigrants settle in specific areas of the U.S. and while the national economy may benefit from their arrival, it is these local economies that bear the costs of the social and educational services they need. According to Stephen Moore, ". . . in areas with high concentrations of low-skilled, low-paid immigrants they impose net costs on U.S.-born workers" (Suro, 2000). The burdens they place on courts, police, jails, health facilities, housing, schools, the administrative problems of dealing with a population of non-English speakers, and the economic dislocations that can be caused by a steady influx of new immigrant workers can be overwhelming to local economies (Suro, 2000). One community of 40,000 residents for example, reported that more than 30 languages are spoken by students in the school system (Worcester Telegram and Gazette, 2007). In Pennsylvania, the cost of illegal immigration has been estimated at "$660 million per year for educating children of illegal aliens, at $50 million for healthcare and 17.5 million to incarcerate undocumented criminals" (FAIR, 2009).

Health care costs create enormous controversy. It is estimated that half of the illegal immigrants lack health care insurance—and they flood hospital emergency rooms which legally cannot turn them away—thereby costing millions of dollars in services (Jordan, 2009). Severe budget problems in Massachusetts, a state that provides health care insurance to all residents, has forced the reduction in coverage for *legal* immigrants—those who have been U.S. residents less than five years and so are not yet citizens (Contreras, 2009). Concerns are not limited to illegal-immigrants, however. "Clearly, it is immigration, legal and illegal, that is driving our healthcare problems to crisis proportions" (Ruhl, 2009).

An often overlooked factor in immigration assessment and policy is the *age* of the immigrant population. Age figures strongly in projections of productivity and of costs to society (Suro, 2000). The U.S. today has a growing "mature immigrant population." The heavy influx of the 1990s means that many of those young immigrants are now at the age when they have families. Their children (and elderly relatives who may join them) are mostly non-producers who draw heavily upon community services. The situation is not quite the same for the illegal immigrants however, as they are denied access to social services in most communities.

Neighborhoods

The impact of high concentrations of immigrants in neighborhoods brings both blame and praise. In some case they are blamed for *blighted* properties and neighborhoods. They run afoul of local laws governing housing—in particular, laws that prohibit overcrowding. Small single family houses turn into rooming houses with whole families living in each bedroom and more people sleeping on mattresses in the basements. In other communities however, immigrants are praised for *revitalizing* decaying neighborhoods by creating businesses there and thus generating employment and income. The maturing immigrant population is expected to positively impact the sagging housing market itself. Immigrants "both legal and illegal—and their native-born children are forecast to provide the bulk of coming years' growth in home-buying demand, nudging the market back up and aiding the broader economy" (Jewell, 2007).

Neighborhood crime is another area of disagreement. Illegals are blamed for raising crime rates. They are accused of bringing gangs, drugs and crime to U.S. cities (Rubinkham, 2007). Other observers however, find that immigrants help to keep crime down (Dale, 2007, June 30) reporting that the vast majority tend to work very hard to better themselves and are not involved in crime. Finally, there is the complaint that "high immigration levels are overcrowding the United States, especially in urban areas" (Masci, 2001); the population is too large now—more immigrants means more overcrowding.

Assimilation

Arguments that immigration should slow down (or cease) to provide time to "Americanize" current immigrants and let schools and governing institutions catch up arise from an "'Us vs Them' mindset." "The way we're going now we won't turn these people into Americans, and without assimilation we will increasingly be beset by ethnic conflicts," says John O'Sullivan (Masci, 2001). The large numbers of immigrants in the "two-tier" system "impedes our country's ability to integrate documented and undocumented newcomers into our society" (Visconti & Peacock, 2006).

Opponents are quick to counter that people who migrate to the U.S. *want to be Americans* (Masci, 2001). Indeed, many Americans consider that it is the immigrant work ethic and motivation that "makes them cornerstones of America's economic prosperity" (Masci, 2001). Perhaps the most cogent response to charges that we need to "Americanize" our immigrants comes from Barbara Frankel (2006): Yet the very essence of American culture is its ability to change and grow and build on the heritages of both its established citizens and its newest occupants.

IMMIGRATION POLICY

Current immigration policy is described as a patchwork quilt much in need of major repair. Although no major federal legislation has yet been considered, U.S. immigration policy is quietly shifting under President Obama. The sweeping raids on factories and homes that jailed and deported undocumented aliens have largely been halted and replaced with vastly increased audits of companies suspected of hiring illegals. Additional changes include:

- Local police checks now concentrate on the immigration status of those who pose a threat to public safety rather than on those with minor violations, such as traffic tickets.
- Requirements that federal contractors use E-Verify (a federal on-line employment-verification program)
- Illegals seeking asylum from torture or persecution are no longer handcuffed and jailed, but live freely while their applications are being processed.

(Alden, 2010)

The exploration of immigration policy and reform is a volatile and complicated issue socially, politically and legally. The questions of how to deal with the aging (mature) immigrant population and with the huge population of undocumented immigrants now in the U.S. however, must be added to the basic questions of who and how many to admit.

LESSONS FROM HISTORY

What Might History Say about Immigration?

Sowell's eloquent account of cultural transfer would argue that immigration provides an excellent avenue of cultural transmission directly through the different concepts, information, products and technologies it introduces and indirectly through the enrichment of the host country's social capital—providing skills and knowledge resources for future advances. Former Intel Chairman Andrew S. Grove voices similar thoughts stating that immigration keeps this country attractive "without inclusion and diversity of new workers and people, the United States would stop moving forward as a progressive nation" (Kim, 2006). Peter Ortiz (2006) puts the case in even stronger terms . . . "What would happen to the economy of the United States if the immigrants, legal and not, stopped coming? It would fall apart" (Ortiz, 2006).

What might history say about the fear that floods of immigrants are overwhelming the U.S. and chipping away at American culture? Other than the American Indians, the U.S. *is a nation comprised completely of immigrants*—something that later generations tend to forget. The global scope of all the cultural advances Sowell outlines vividly portray how much of American culture has come from other cultures and further that cultures existing in isolation do not advance nearly so much as those with doors open to other cultures:

> . . . many great thinkers of the past . . . [labored] to advance the human race. Their legacies . . . belong to all people—and all people need to claim that legacy, not seal themselves off in a dead-end of tribalism or in an emotional orgy of cultural vanity.

[Cultures] are "living, changing ways of doing all the things that have to be done in life. . . . Every culture discards over time the things which do not do the job as well as things borrowed from other cultures . . ."

What might history say about immigration policies and state and local laws restricting immigration? Sowell contends that it is not possible for governments or laws to stop the infusion of new ideas and ways of doing things. Historically,

> Individuals have decided for themselves how much of the old they wished to retain, how much of the new they found useful in their own lives. . . . In this way, cultures have enriched each other in all the great civilizations of the world.

DISCUSSION QUESTIONS

1. Research either today's *legal* immigrants or today's *illegal* immigrants. a) From which countries do they originate? b) What are their educational and skill levels? c) Specifically, what jobs do they take? d) Where do they relocate geographically?

Legal Immigrants: starting sources

The Foreign-Born Population: 2000 (2003, December). *Census 2000 briefs*. http://www.census.gov/prod/2003pubs/c2kbr-34.pdf.

Suro, R. (1999). Watching America's door. The immigration backlash and the new policy debate. In Henry Tischler (Ed.) (2000). *Debating points: Race and ethnic relations*. Upper Saddle River, N. J.: Prentice Hall. Source: Occupations 2000 (2003, August). *Census 2000 briefs*. http://www.census.gov/prod/2003pubs/c2kbr-25.pdf.

MPI Data Hub. *Migration Facts, Stats, and Maps*. http://www.migrationinformation.org.

Illegal Immigrants: starting sources

Edwards, James, Jr. (2006, February). Two sides of the same coin. The connection between legal and illegal immigration. Backgrounder. *Center for Immigration Studies,* Washington, D.C. Web search: James Edwards Two sides of the same coin

Ohlemacher, S. (2007, August 17). Census wants no immigration raids for 2010. Worcester Telegram and Gazette. www.telegram.com.

Johnson, H. (2006). Illegal immigration. At issue. *Public Policy Institute of California*. Web search: H. Johnson Illegal immigration at issue

News Batch. (2007, July). Immigration policy issues. Web search: July 1, 2007 Immigration Policy Issues News Batch

2. Research current immigration laws as they pertain to the workplace. What rights do undocumented immigrants have?

Starting sources

Cole, D. (2003). Five myths about immigration: The new know-nothings. in Scott Plous (Ed.) *Understanding prejudice and discrimination*. McGraw-Hill: Boston.

EEOC. (1999). Questions & answers. Enforcement guidance on remedies available to undocumented workers under federal employment discrimination laws. Retrieved March 26, 2007 from http://www.eeoc.gov/policy/docs/qanda-undoc.html.

Gardner, A. (2007, March 13). Undocumented immigrants childbirth is top emergency Medicaid expense. *Washington Post*. Retrieved March 13, 2007 http://www.washingtonpost.com/wp-dyn/content/article/2007/03/13/AR2007031300555.html.

Incognito, L. (2007). The human being is illegal. *Peoples Weekly World* newspaper online. http://www.pww.org/index.php/article/articleview/10597/1/359.

National Immigration Law Center: http://www.nilc.org.

Workplace Fairness. (2007). Short-changed undocumented workers. http://www.workplacefairness.org/sc/undocumentedworkers.php.

3. The ability to communicate in English is important for many jobs and therefore some companies offer ESL (English as a Second Language) courses to their non-English-speaking employees. One alternative to requiring company-sponsored ESL instruction is to require that all potential employees meet an English language proficiency standard before they may be hired. Compare and contrast these two alternatives in terms of advantages and disadvantages to the company.

4. *Contributions of United States immigrants.* The United States leads the world in Nobel awards with 320 laureates. Examine the list of U.S. Nobel winners on the Web site below.

Source: en.wikipedia.org/wiki/list_of_nobel_laureates_by_country

The list is ordered by year. For each laureate on the list, it gives the subject of the award and the country of birth if the laureate was foreign-born.

Note. At the end of the list are links to the laureates by subject except for economics.

Economics link: http://en.wikipedia.org/wiki/nobel_prize_in_economics

---

   a. How many and what percentage of the United States laureates are foreign born?
   b. Select one of the six areas of Nobel awards and access its Web site. How many and what percent of the U.S. laureates in the subject you selected were foreign-born?

Chemistry	Literature	Physics
Economics	Peace	Physiology and Medicine

5. Considering the three types of immigration law—legal, humanitarian, and illegal—what kind of immigration policies do you think the United States should pursue in the future? Why?

STARTING SOURCES

University of Denver. (2009). Architect for Immigration Reform: Fitting the pieces of public policy. http://www.du.edu/issues/reports/ Site search: 2009 immigration report.

Denier, G & Nielsen, N. (2009, April 14). Change to win and AF-CIO unveil unified immigration reform framework. http://www.changetowin.org.

Center for Immigration Studies. (2005). Legal immigration. Web search: CIS 2005 legal immigration

News Batch (2007, July). Immigration policy issues. Web search: July 1, 2007 immigration policy issues News Batch

Bibliography

Alden, E. (2010). Obama quietly changes U.S. immigration policy. *Revista-amauta.* http://revista.org/archives/10621.

Anderson, C. (2007, July 20–26). A call for congress to act now on high-skills immigration reform. *MHT (Mass High Tech)*, p. 26.

Archibold, R. (2010, April 24). Strict immigration measure becomes law. *Worcester Telegram and Gazette.* p. A1.

Bartsch, K. (2009). The employment projections for 2008–2018. *U.S. Bureau of Labor Statistics, EPP Publications* http://www.bls.gov/emp#tables.

Bazar, E. (2007 July 11). States target illegal hiring. Immigration laws focus on bosses. *USA Today,* 1A.

Borjas, G. (2000). The new economics of immigration. Affluent Americans gain; poor Americans lose. *Debating Points.*

Broder, D.S. (2007, July 9). Congress has failed in its duty regarding immigration reform. *Worcester Telegram and Gazette*, A7.

Brown, C. (2006, April). The history of hate. *DiversityInc.* pp. 62–66.

Carlson, L. (2007, March 4). Migrants, globalization's junk mail. PressTV. Retrieved March 13,

2007, from http://www.presstv.ir/detail. aspx?id=1413&section id=3510303.

Carroll, S. (2009, November 19). ICE targeting 1,000 companies. *Houston Chronicle*. Web search: S. Carroll ICE targeting 1,000 companies Houston Chronicle

Christophersen, J. (2007, July 25). How Northeast cities chart diverging paths for illegals. *Worcester Telegram and Gazette*, p. A4. Clark, C. (1977, June 24). The new immigrants. *Annual Editions*, Article 10 pp. 51–71.

The Chronicle of Higher Education (2009, April 3, A14). Foreign graduates lose job offers in finance because of federal stimulus rules.

The Chronicle of Higher Education (2009, July 13). Foreign students still face hurdles. p. A31.

The Chronicle of Higher Education. (2009, August 28, p.20). Students international. Reprinted from the *Institute for International Education*.

The Chronicle of Higher Education. (2010, October 22). Georgia bars illegal immigrants from some public colleges. p. A3.

Clark, C. (1977, June 24). The new immigrants. *Annual Editions*, Article 10 pp. 51–71. Guildford, CT: McGraw-Hill/Dushkin.

Cole, D. (2003). Five myths about immigration: the new know-nothings in Plous, S. (Ed.) *Understanding prejudice and discrimination*. Boston: McGraw Hill.

Cole, Y. (2006, April). Creating wealth and strife in Tennessee. *DiversityInc*. pp. 36–43.

Contreras, R. (2009, November 16). College assistance for illegals sought. *Worcester Telegram and Gazette.*

Cooper, J. & Davenport, P. (2010, April 23). Arizona governor signs immigration law. Retrieved May 9, 2011 from: http://hispanicohio. northcoastnow.com/2010/04/23 arizona-governor-signs-immigration-law

Dale, M. (2007, June 30). Some say immigrants help keep crime down, higher immigration rates linked with less homicide, experts note. *Worcester Telegram and Gazette*. A11.

DeGroat, T.J. (2006, April). A nation of immigrants, a culture of nativism. *DiversityInc*. pp. 44–51.

EEOC. (1999, October 29). Questions and answers. Enforcement guidance on remedies available to undocumented workers under federal employment discrimination laws. Retrieved on July 28 from http://www.eeoc. gov/policy/docs/qanda-udoc.html.

FAIR (Federation for American Immigration) (2009, August 6). New study shows true cost of illegal immigration in Pennsylvania. Retrieved May 10, 2011 from www.fairus.org/site

Fine, J. (2004, January 11). Bush plan's 3 flaws. *Boston Globe*. Web search: Bush plan's 3 flaws Boston Globe January 11, 2004.

Frankel, B. (2006, April). Us vs them doesn't work. *DiversityInc Editor's letter*. p. 14.

French, C. (2009). Number of students studying abroad on rise globally. *VOA News*. Web search: C. French Number of students studying abroad VOA News

Friedman, J. & DiTomaso, H. (1996, summer) Myths about diversity: What managers need to know about changes in the U.S. labor force. *California Management Review. v. 38. no. 4.*

Gardner, A. (2007, March 13). Undocumented immigrants' childbirth is top emergency Medicaid expense. *Washington Post*. Web search: A. Gardner Undocumented immigrant's childbirth Washington Post 2007

Guillen, R. (2007, March 12). Replacing immigrants with convict slaves. *Texas Civil Rights Review.*

Hanson, G. (2009, December 3). Study: U.S. economy largely unaffected by illegal immigration. *Arizona Star*. Web search: G. Hanson Study: U.S. economy largely unaffected by illegal immigration Arizona Star 2009

Incognito, L. (2007, December 21). The human being is illegal. *The peoples world* newspaper online. Web search: Where's the humanity in immigrant enforcement?

Jewell, M. (2007, July 31). New country, new homes. *Worcester Telegram & Gazette*, p. D2.

Jordan, M. (2009, August 15). Illegal immigration enters the health-care debate. *The Wall Street Journal*. http://online.wsj.com

Kim, W. (2006, April). The rising value of immigration. *DiversityInc*. pp. 53–56.

Martin, J. (2009, July). The cost of immigration to Pennsylvania. *Federation for American Immigration Reform*. www.personalliberty.com

Masci, D. (2001). Debate over immigration. The issues. In Kromkowski, J. (Ed), *Race and ethnic relations,* 11th ed. 2001–2002. McGraw-Hill/Dushkin Guilford, CT.

McFarlane, C. (2007, August 15). Immigrants may hold security key. *Worcester Telegram and Gazette*, p. B1.

MHT. (2007, June 22-29). Immigrants come to study, leave to be entrepreneurs. *Mass High Tech, v. 25 issue 25.*

Monahan, J. (2009, number 18) 131 changes in immigrant report. *Worcester Telegram and Gazette.*

Moorefield, G. (2008, December 19). United States: Immigration issues: Contractor liability Peckar & Abramson PC. Retrieved May 9, 2011 from: http://www.mondaq.com/unitedstates/article.asp?/articleid=71856

Myers, A. (2010, August 13). Illegal immigrant deportations up, according to ICE. *WorcesterTelegram and Gazette.* A14.

Myers, D. (2007, October 1). Boardroom focus on immigration. *Directorship.* www.directorship.com/immigration-on-board-agenda

Nakamura, L. (2000). "Where do you want to go today?" Cybernetic tourism, the internet and transnationality. From Dines, G and Humez, J. eds. *Gender, Race and class in Media text reader Second* ed. Thousand Oaks, CA: Sage 2002 pp. 684–687.

NELP (n.d.). Immigrant worker project. Workplace rights. *National Employment Law Project.* www.nelp.org/iwp/rights/index.cfm

Nizza, M. (2007, September 13). Estimate for deporting illegal immigrants: $94 billion. *The Lede.* http://the lede.blos.nytimes.com/2007

Open Doors. (2008, November 17). U.S. study abroad up 8%, continuing decade-long growth. http://opendoors.iienetwork.org/?p=131592

Ortiz, P. (2006, April). Immigration: America's lifeline. *DiversityInc.* pp. 24–25.

Peri, P. quoted in Kim, W. (2006, April). The rising value of immigration. *DiversityInc.* pp. 53–55.

Pew Hispanic Center Report (2009, July 22). Cited in Solís, D. (2009, July 23). Recession, enforcement put damper on immigration from Mexico. *Dallas News.* www.dallasnews.com

Porter, E. (2005, April 5). Illegal immigrants are bolstering social security with billions. *The New York Times,* business and financial, section A, col. 1, p. 1. http://www.nytimes.com

Preston, J. (2007, August 6). Surge in immigration laws around U.S. Retrieved August 8, 2007 from *New York Times:* http://www.nytimes.com

Preston, J. (2007, August 8). Toughening stance. New rules aim at illegal employment. *Worcester Telegram & Gazette,* p. A2.

Reagan, M. (2006, August 28). English language lost under the stampede of immigration. *Worcester Telegram and Gazette* A7.

Ressner, J. (2006, June 5). Rousing the zealots. *Time.*

Ruhl, J. (2009, August 23). Illegal immigration is driving our health care problems. *Mansfield News Journal.* www.mansfieldnewsjoural.com

Suro, R. (2000). Watching America's door. The immigration backlash and the new policy debate. In Tischler, H. (Ed). *Debating Points: race and ethnic relations.* Upper Saddle River, N. J: Prentice Hall.

Texas Civil Rights Review (2009, December 4). *TRAC: U.S. immigration takes first place for numbers detained, transferred.* http://texas-civilrightsreview.org

The Associated Press (2007, July 1). Europeans fill Maine seasonal jobs. *Worcester Sunday Telegram and Gazette* A4.

U.S. Census. (2009). Table 40 Native and foreign-born population by state: 2007. www.census.gov

U.S. Census. (2009). Table 47. Estimated unauthorized immigrants by selected states and countries of birth: 2000–2008. http://www.census.gov

U.S. Department of Commerce (2009). Table 1232. International travel: 1990–2008. http://www.tinet.ita.doc.gov

University of Denver (2009). Architecture for immigration reform: fitting the pieces of public policy. www.du.edu/issues/reports Site search: 2009 immigration report

Viscarolasaga, E. (2007, August 3–9). Stunting growth. Fast-growing companies find it harder to fill key posts. *Mass High Tech.* pp. 1, 20.

Visconti, L. & Peacock, F. (2006, April). Learning from history: The business case for immigration. *DiversityInc. Publishers Letter.* p. 17.

VOA News. (2009, November 18). Number of students studying abroad on rise globally. http://www.voanews.com

Ward, C., Bochner, S., & Furnham, A. (2001). Quoted in Innocence abroad. A pocket guide to psychological research on tourism. (2005, September). *American Psychologist.* p. 594.

Williams, C. (2007, June 1–7). New England immigrants play a growing role in tech entrepreneurship. *Mass High Tech,* pp. 1, 28.

Worcester Telegram and Gazette. (2007, June 13). Marlboro immigrants upset over proposal. pp. A1, A6.

Workplace Fairness. (2007). Undocumented workers. Retrieved March 26, 2007 from www.workplacefairness.org/sc/undocumented-workers.php

Whybrow, P. (2009, March 13). Dangerously addictive. *The Chronicle Review.* p. B11.

Diversity on the Web

Visit the site below to learn about U.S. citizens traveling out of the country, and visitors and immigrants to the U.S. Research the four questions below.

http://tinet.ita.doc.gov/research

Travel
1. How many visitors came to the United States last year? What were their countries of origin? Where did they visit in the United States?
2. How many U.S. citizens traveled out of the United States? Where did they go?
3. There are 300 million U.S. citizens and over 32 million (legal and illegal) immigrants. Considering a) the number of U.S. citizens who traveled outside the United States last year (and their destinations) and b) the number and origin of foreign visitors traveling to the United States, what cultural changes might you predict by the year 2030?

Trade
4. Examine the amounts and patterns of world and U.S. trade figures. What does this say about the transmission of products among cultures?

Canadian Note: Web site above also contains Canadian information.

Diversity on the Web

The U.S. Citizenship and Immigration (USCIS) programs listed below grant special waivers and visas. These programs have been extended by Congress until September 30, 2012. Research these programs. What are the implications of these special programs for immigration and immigration policy?

- Conrad 30
- Specials immigrant visa category for Non-Minister religious workers
- Immigrant Investor Pilot Program

http://www.mdgreencard.com
http:/hatch.senate.gov

http://www.hackleyserrone.com

Program (EB-5)/EB-5-immigrant-visa program.html

Negotiating: The Top Ten Ways that Culture Can Effect Your Negotiation

Jeswald W. Salacuse

When Enron was still—and only—a pipeline company, it lost a major contract in India because local authorities felt that it was pushing negotiations too fast. In fact, the loss of the contract underlines the important role that cultural differences play in international negotiation. For one country's negotiators, time is money; for another's, the slower the negotiations, the better and more trust in the other side. This author's advice will help negotiators bridge the cultural differences in international negotiation.

International business deals not only cross borders, they also cross cultures. Culture profoundly influences how people think, communicate, and behave. It also affects the kinds of transactions they make and the way they negotiate them. Differences in culture between business executives—for example, between a Chinese public sector plant manager in Shanghai and a Canadian division head of a family company in Toronto—can create barriers that impede or completely stymie the negotiating process.

The great diversity of the world's cultures makes it impossible for any negotiator, no matter how skilled and experienced, to understand fully all the cultures that may be encountered. How then should an executive prepare to cope with culture in making deals in Singapore this week and Seoul the next? In researching my book *The Global Negotiator: Making, Managing, and Mending Deals Around the World in the Twenty-First Century* (Palgrave Macmillan, 2003), I found that ten particular elements consistently arise to complicate intercultural negotiations. These "top ten" elements of negotiating behavior constitute a basic framework for identifying cultural differences that may arise during the negotiation process. Applying this framework in your international business negotiations may enable you to understand your counterpart better and to anticipate possible misunderstandings. This article discusses this framework and how to apply it.

1. *Negotiating Goal: Contract or Relationship?*

Negotiators from different cultures may tend to view the purpose of a negotiation differently. For deal makers from some cultures, the goal of a business negotiation, first and foremost, is a signed contract between the parties. Other cultures tend to consider that the goal of a negotiation is not a signed contract but rather the creation of a relationship between the two sides. Although the written contact expresses the relationship, the essence of the deal is the relationship itself. For example in my survey of over 400 persons from twelve nationalities, reported fully in *The Global Negotiator*, I found that whereas 74 percent of the Spanish respondents claimed their goal in a negotiation was a contract, only 33 percent of the Indian executives had a similar view. The difference in approach may explain why certain Asian negotiators, whose negotiating goal is often the creation of a relationship, tend to give more time and effort to negotiation preliminaries, while North Americans often want to rush through this first phase of deal making. The preliminaries of negotiation, in which the parties seek to get to know one another thoroughly, are a crucial foundation for a good business relationship. They may seem less important when the goal is merely a contract.

It is therefore important to determine how your counterparts view the purpose of your negotiation. If relationship negotiators sit on the other side of the table, merely convincing them of your ability to deliver on a low-cost contract may not be enough to land you the deal. You may also have to persuade them, from the very first meeting, that your two organizations have the potential to build a rewarding relationship over the long term. On the other hand, if the other side is basically a contract deal maker, trying to build a relationship may be a waste of time and energy.

2. *Negotiating Attitude: Win-Lose or Win-Win?*

Because of differences in culture, personality, or both, business persons appear to approach deal making with one of two basic attitudes: that a negotiation is either a process in which both can gain (win-win) or a struggle in which, of necessity, one side wins and the other side loses (win-lose). Win-win negotiators see deal making as a collaborative, problem-solving process; win-lose negotiators view it as confrontational. As you enter negotiations, it is important to know which type of negotiator is sitting across the table from you. Here too, my survey revealed significant differences among cultures. For example, whereas 100 percent of the Japanese respondents claimed that they approached negotiations as a win-win process, only 33% of the Spanish executives took that view.

3. *Personal Style: Informal or Formal?*

Personal style concerns the way a negotiator talks to others, uses titles, dresses, speaks, and interacts with other persons. Culture strongly influences the personal style of negotiators. It has been observed, for example, that Germans have a more formal style than Americans. A negotiator with a formal style insists on addressing counterparts by their titles, avoids personal anecdotes, and refrains from questions touching on the private or family life of members of the other negotiating team. A negotiator with an informal style tries to start the discussion on a first-name basis, quickly seeks to develop a personal, friendly relationship with the other team, and may take off his jacket and roll up his sleeves when deal making begins in earnest. Each culture has its own formalities with their own special meanings. They are another means of communication among the persons sharing that culture, another form of adhesive that binds them together as a community. For an American, calling someone by the first name is an act of friendship and therefore a good thing. For a Japanese, the use of the first name at a first meeting is an act of disrespect and therefore bad.

Negotiators in foreign cultures must respect appropriate formalities. As a general rule, it is always safer to adopt a formal posture and move to an informal stance, if the situation warrants it, than to assume an informal style too quickly.

4. *Communication: Direct or Indirect?*

Methods of communication vary among cultures. Some emphasize direct and simple methods of communication; others rely heavily on indirect and complex methods. The latter may use circumlocutions, figurative forms of speech, facial expressions, gestures and other kinds of body language. In a culture that values directness, such as the American or the Israeli, you can expect to receive a clear and definite response to your proposals and questions. In cultures that rely on indirect communication, such as the Japanese, reaction to your proposals may be gained by interpreting seemingly vague comments, gestures, and other signs. What you will not receive at a first meeting is a definite commitment or rejection.

The confrontation of these styles of communication in the same negotiation can lead to friction. For example, the indirect ways Japanese negotiators express disapproval have often led foreign business executives to believe that their proposals were still under consideration when in fact the Japanese side had rejected them. In the Camp David negotiations that led to a peace treaty between Egypt and Israel, the Israeli preference for direct forms of communication and the Egyptian tendency to favor indirect forms sometimes exacerbated relations between the two sides. The Egyptians interpreted Israeli directness as aggressiveness and, therefore, an insult. The Israelis viewed Egyptian indirectness with impatience and suspected them of insincerity, of not saying what they meant.

5. *Sensitivity to Time: High or Low?*

Discussions of national negotiating styles invariably treat a particular culture's attitudes toward time. It is said that Germans are always punctual, Latins are habitually late, Japanese negotiate slowly, and Americans are quick to make a deal. Commentators sometimes claim that some cultures value time more than others, but this observation may not be an accurate characterization of the situation. Rather, negotiators may value differently the amount of time devoted to and measured against the goal pursued. For Americans, the deal is a signed contract and time is money, so they want to make a deal quickly. Americans therefore try to reduce formalities to a minimum and get down to business quickly. Japanese and other Asians, whose goal is to create a relationship rather than simply sign a contract, need to invest time in the negotiating process so that the parties can get to know one another well and determine whether they wish to embark on a long-term relationship. They may consider aggressive attempts to shorten the negotiating time as efforts to hide something For example, in one case that received significant media attention in the mid-1990s, a long-term electricity supply contract between an ENRON subsidiary, the Dabhol Power Company, and the Maharashtra state government in India, was subject to significant challenge and was ultimately cancelled on the grounds that it was concluded in "unseemly haste" and had been subject to "fast track procedures" that circumvented established practice for developing such projects in the past. Important segments of the Indian public automatically assumed that the government had failed to protect the public interest because the negotiations were so quick. In the company's defense, Rebecca Mark, chairman and CEO of Enron International, pointed out to the press: "We were extremely concerned with time, because time is money for us." (Enron's Rebecca Mark: 'You Have to be Pushy and Aggressive' *Business Week,* February 24, 1997, http://www.businessweek.com/1997/08/b351586.htm.)

This difference between the Indian and U.S. attitudes toward time was clearly revealed in my survey. Among the twelve nationalities surveyed, the Indians had the largest percentage of persons who considered themselves to have a low sensitivity to time.

6. *Emotionalism: High or Low?*

Accounts of negotiating behavior in other cultures almost always point to a particular group's tendency to act emotionally. According to the stereotype, Latin Americans show their emotions at the negotiating table, while the Japanese and many other Asians hide their feelings. Obviously, individual personality plays a role here. There are passive Latins and hot-headed Japanese. Nonetheless, various cultures have different rules as to the appropriateness and form of displaying emotions, and these rules are brought to the negotiating table as well. Deal makers should seek to learn them.

In the author's survey, Latin Americans and the Spanish were the cultural groups that ranked themselves highest with respect to emotionalism in a clearly statistically significant fashion. Among Europeans, the Germans and English ranked as least emotional, while among Asians the Japanese held that position, but to a lesser degree.

7. Form of Agreement: General or Specific?

Whether a negotiator's goal is a contract or a relationship, the negotiated transaction in almost all cases will be encapsulated in some sort of written agreement. Cultural factors influence the form of the written agreement that the parties make. Generally, Americans prefer very detailed contracts that attempt to anticipate all possible circumstances and eventualities, no matter how unlikely. Why? Because the deal is the contract itself, and one must refer to the contract to handle new situations that may arise. Other cultures, such as the Chinese, prefer a contract in the form of general principles rather than detailed rules. Why? Because, it is claimed, that the essence of the deal is the relationship between the parties. If unexpected circumstances arise, the parties should look primarily to their relationship, not the contract, to solve the problem. So, in some cases, a Chinese negotiator may interpret the American drive to stipulate all contingencies as evidence of a lack of confidence in the stability of the underlying relationship.

Among all respondents in my survey, 78 percent preferred specific agreements, while only 22 percent preferred general agreements. On the other hand, the degree of intensity of responses on the question varied considerably among cultural groups. While only 11 percent of the English favored general agreements, 45.5 percent of the Japanese and of the Germans claimed to do so. Some experienced executives argue that differences over the form of an agreement are caused more by unequal bargaining power between the parties than by culture. In a situation of unequal bargaining power, the stronger party always seeks a detailed agreement to "lock up the deal" in all its possible dimensions, while the weaker party prefers a general agreement to give it room to "wiggle out" of adverse circumstances that are bound to occur. According to this view, it is context, not culture that determines this negotiating trait.

8. Building an Agreement: Bottom Up or Top Down?

Related to the form of the agreement is the question of whether negotiating a business deal is an inductive or a deductive process. Does it start from an agreement on general principles and proceed to specific items, or does it begin with an agreement on specifics, such as price, delivery date, and product quality, the sum total of which becomes the contract? Different cultures tend to emphasize one approach over the other. Some observers believe that the French prefer to begin with agreement on general principles, while Americans tend to seek agreement first on specifics. For Americans, negotiating a deal is basically making a series of compromises and trade-offs on a long list of particulars. For the French, the essence is to agree on basic principles that will guide and indeed determine the negotiation process afterward. The agreed-upon general principles become the framework, the skeleton, upon which the contract is built.

My survey of negotiating styles found that the French, the Argentineans, and the Indians tended to view deal making as a top down (deductive process); while the Japanese, the Mexicans and the Brazilians tended to see it as a bottom up (inductive) process. A further difference in negotiating style is seen in the dichotomy between the "building-down" approach and the "building-up" approach." In the building down approach, the negotiator begins by presenting the maximum deal if the other side accepts all the stated conditions. In the building-up approach, one side begins by proposing a minimum deal that can be broadened and increased as the other party accepts additional conditions. According to many observers, Americans tend to favor the building-down approach, while the Japanese tend to prefer the building-up style of negotiating a contract.

9. Team Organization: One Leader or Group Consensus?

In any negotiation, it is important to know how the other side is organized, who has the authority to make commitments, and how decisions are made. Culture is one important factor that affects how executives organize themselves to negotiate a deal. Some cultures emphasize the individual while others stress the group. These values may influence the organization of each side in a negotiation.

One extreme is the negotiating team with a supreme leader who has complete authority to decide all matters. Many American teams tend to follow this approach. Other cultures, notably the Japanese and the Chinese, stress team negotiation and consensus decision making. When you negotiate with such a team, it may not be apparent who the leader is and who has the authority to commit the side. In the first type, the negotiating team is usually small; in the second it is often large. For example, in negotiations in China on a major deal, it would not be uncommon for the Americans to arrive at the table with three people and for the Chinese to show up with ten. Similarly, the one-leader team is usually prepared to make commitments more quickly than a negotiating team organized on the basis of consensus. As a result, the consensus type of organization usually takes more time to negotiate a deal.

Among all respondents in my survey, 59 percent tended to prefer one leader while 41 percent preferred a more consensual form of organization. On the other hand, the various cultural groups showed a wide variety of preferences on the question of team organization. The group with the strongest preference for consensus organization was the French. Many studies have noted French individualism. (Edward T. Hall and M. Reed Hall, *Understanding Cultural Difference*, Yarmouth, Maine: Intercultural Press, 1990.)

Perhaps a consensual arrangement in the individual French person's eyes is the best way to protect that individualism. Despite the Japanese reputation for consensus arrangements, only 45 percent of the Japanese respondents claimed to prefer a negotiating team based on consensus. The Brazilians, the Chinese, and the Mexicans to a far greater degree than any other groups preferred one-person leadership, a reflection perhaps of the political traditions of those countries.

10. Risk Taking: High or Low?

Research supports the conclusion that certain cultures are more risk averse than others. (Geert Hofstede, *Culture's Consequences: International Differences in Work-related Values.* Newbury Park, CA: Sage Publications, 1980)

In deal making, the negotiators' cultures can affect the willingness of one side to take risks—to divulge information, try new approaches, and tolerate uncertainties in a proposed course of action. The Japanese, with their emphasis on requiring large amount of information and their intricate group decision-making process, tend to be risk averse. Americans, by comparison, are risk takers.

Among all respondents in the author's survey, approximately 70 percent claimed a tendency toward risk taking while only 30 percent characterized themselves as low risk takers. Among cultures, the responses to this question showed significant variations. The Japanese are said to be highly risk averse in negotiations, and this tendency was affirmed by the survey which found Japanese respondents to be the most risk averse of the twelve cultures. Americans in the survey, by comparison, considered themselves to be risk takers, but an even higher percentage of the French, the British, and the Indians claimed to be risk takers.

Negotiating styles, like personalities, have a wide range of variation. The ten negotiating traits discussed above can be placed on a spectrum or continuum, as illustrated in the chart below. Its purpose is to identify specific negotiating traits affected by culture and to show the possible variation that each trait or factor may take. With this knowledge, you may be better able to understand the negotiating styles and approaches of counterparts from other cultures. Equally important, it may help you to determine how your own negotiating style appears to those same counterparts.

Faced with a risk-averse counterpart, how should a deal maker proceed? The following are a few steps to consider:

1. Don't rush the negotiating process. A negotiation that is moving too fast for one of the parties only heightens that person's perception of the risks in the proposed deal.
2. Devote attention to proposing rules and mechanisms that will reduce the apparent risks in the deal for the other side.
3. Make sure that your counterpart has sufficient information about you, your company, and the proposed deal.
4. Focus your efforts on building a relationship and fostering trust between the parties.
5. Consider restructuring the deal so that the deal proceeds step by step in a series of increments, rather than all at once.

The Impact of Culture on Negotiation

Negotiation Factors

Goal	Contract	←——→	Relationship
Attitudes	Win/Lose	←——→	Win/Win
Personal Styles	Informal	←——→	Formal
Communications	Direct	←——→	Indirect
Time Sensitivity	High	←——→	Low
Emotionalism	High	←——→	Low
Agreement Form	Specific	←——→	General
Agreement Building	Bottom Up	←——→	Top Down
Team Organization	One Leader	←——→	Consensus
Risk Taking	High	←——→	Low

DISCUSSION QUESTIONS

1. To conduct successful negotiations, why does Salacuse think that business people need to know more than the cultural tendencies of specific cultures?

2. If you are trying to negotiate a contract in another culture, why is it advantageous for you to understand how the other party may view your approach?

3. **a.** Write an original short business case that illustrates how a lack of knowledge of several of these dimensions could cause misunderstandings in a contract negotiation for leasing office space in another country.
   b. Then rewrite the case with the culture-appropriate dialogue. Compare the two cases. How did the second version improve the chances of a successful outcome for the negotiators?

GLOBAL CALL CENTER EXERCISE: LEARNING TO NEGOTIATE

Carol P. Harvey
Assumption College

GOALS

- To improve one's ability to communicate with people from another culture
- To apply the Salacuse framework in an interactive manner
- To practice mindful listening and negotiation skills

With today's focus on Customer Relationship Management (CRM), organizations are trying to reduce costs and provide better service through the increased use of technology. However, to save money, companies are increasingly outsourcing these functions to offshore call centers. So without even leaving home, we can find ourselves in the position of having to communicate by telephone with someone from an unknown culture to resolve our billing problems, order a product, fix our computers, etc. When we dial that toll free number, we frequently have no idea where the phone is going to be answered but most of the time it will be ringing in a global call center and answered by one of the world's 4.78 million customer service agents.

It is a human tendency to communicate through our own cultural lenses and in spite of his or her training, the person answering that phone is probably doing the same thing! Cultural differences and mismatched communication styles often complicate the conversation, misunderstandings often occur, conflict escalates and frustration builds. None of this usually results in a satisfied customer or good CRM.

One way to minimize these cultural miscommunications and to maximize understanding is to learn to communicate and negotiate from a culture general perspective. This means that one does not assume that the listener typifies the communication style and tendencies of a particular culture. Instead, listening carefully for the ten elements detailed in the Salacuse article and adapting your communication to the style elements that you hear should improve understanding and diminish miscommunication.

THE CALL CENTER ASSIGNMENT

Have you ever experienced a frustrating phone conversation while trying to negotiate for something with a global call center customer service representative? The following exercise will give you the opportunity to observe how these communications can create conflict through cultural miscommunication and illustrate how to obtain more satisfying results.

1. Your instructor will form teams of 4–5 students who may be required to meet outside of class to prepare this assignment. Students should divide the assignment among the team members into writing, presentation and class discussion responsibilities.

2. Each group will develop *two* scripts for one of the telephone conversation situations detailed below. The first role play should exemplify poor intercultural communication for any four of the ten elements discussed in the Salacuse article. The second one presented in step # 4, will demonstrate the conversation with these communication errors corrected. Each role play should last 3–5 minutes, feature no non-verbal cues (remember that this conversation is taking place on the telephone), and not identify the countries of origin of the sender or receivers of the communication.

3. After the group presents the first role play, they should involve the whole class by asking them to identify examples of particular elements from the Salacuse article that they heard in the conversation.

4. After the class identifies these connections, the group should demonstrate their second scenario's script where these elements have been handled using a more mindful intercultural conversation style.

5. After each group has presented, what conclusions can be drawn about the need to develop flexible non-culture specific intercultural communication skills?

Suggested Topics for the Intercultural Telephone Conversations between a North American Consumer and a Global call Center Somewhere in the World

> *Consumer originated phone call topics:* Asking questions about a technical problem, receiving an incorrect bill, trying to cancel some service, complaining about the quality of a product, not receiving a product that was ordered, etc.
>
> *Global call center originated phone call topics*: Selling a product, trying to upgrade a current customer, collect an overdue payment, telling you that you have overdrawn your checking account when you know that you have not, etc.

Diversity on the Web

To see a global call center and intercultural miscommunication in action, go to http://www.nbc.com. In the search box, write "jolly vindaloo day." Then, click on the 10-14-10 episode. This will give you a short clip from the television show Outsourced. Select and watch this video and provide specific examples of as many of the ten elements from the Salacuse article that you hear and see.

The Coca-Cola Company: Then and Now

Carol P. Harvey
Assumption College

GOALS

- To understand how a lack of attention to internal diversity issues resulted in a $192.5 million dollar discrimination lawsuit
- To illustrate how an organization can benefit from diversity when it uses diversity as a strategic business advantage
- To analyze the process of changing an organizational culture to adapt to a more diverse environment
- To recognize the importance of corporate leadership in effective diversity management

What happened at Coca-Cola illustrates the need for effective corporate diversity leadership. Although Coca-Cola is considered the world's most recognized brand name, is the world's #1 producer of sparkling beverages, and sells 1.6 billion drinks a day in over 200 countries (The Coca-Cola Company, 2009), the organization is also also known for losing the largest racial discrimination lawsuit) in United States history (*Ingram et al. v. The Coca-Cola Company*).

In less than ten years, with the guidance of an external task force, the corporation has transformed itself in terms of diversity management. Today, Coca Cola's workforce is 23% African American, 7% Hispanic and 5% Asian and is evenly divided in terms of gender. As of 2009, minorities comprise 34% of the exempt workforce (The Coca-Cola Company, 2009). The corporation is listed as one of FORTUNE magazine's 2010 Most Admired Companies and has consistently earned a place on DiversityInc.'s Top 50 Companies for Diversity list. When those in corporate leadership learn that diversity can be a competitive advantage in a global environment and provide the support and resources needed, the organizational culture can change from overt racism to one that is considered as a diversity leader.

Although Coca-Cola has a long history of external social responsibility in terms of financial contributions to organizations such as the Southern Christian Leadership Conference, the Historic Black Colleges, and the Rainbow Push Coalition, according to Foust (2000b),

> When it came to its own workforce, the story was quite different. . . . According to allegations filed in the discrimination lawsuit, former CEO Ivestor told a transferee stunned by the latent racist culture, at its headquarters that it would take "15 to 20 years before blacks would be fairly represented in the company" (p. 58).

The company's Southern bottlers taunted and terrorized Coke's first Black salesman. Privately, legendary Chief Executive, Robert S. The lawsuit was not the first time that racism at Coca-Cola was an issue. Woodruff questioned civil rights legislation in the 1960's. And if the worst excesses of the past are gone, according to internal Coke documents released as part of a current lawsuit, even today the median salary for black employees is 44% less than that for whites (Foust, 2000b, p. 58).

THE SOFT DRINK INDUSTRY

The soft-drink industry has its roots the United States when physicians in the 1800s began prescribing the bubbling waters discovered in New York as a cure for ailments ranging from arthritis to headaches and including everything in between. Later, the development of artificial carbonated water by laboratory scientists, the addition of flavors like lemon and root beer by pharmacists, and the growing popularity of the local pharmacy's soda fountain as a social gathering spot, led to increased demand for these products.

From its humble beginnings, the highly profitable soft-drink industry, which now includes soda tea/coffee, sports and juice drinks, enjoyed a phenomenal growth rate. In 2009 in the U.S. alone soft drink companies grossed over $57 million in sales. One in every four beverages consumed in the United States is a soft drink, which amounts to an annual consumption of 600 12oz servings or 150 quarts per person per year (everyday-wisdom.com, 2010).

Because the consumption of soda has declined while the demand for other bottled beverages has increased, the sales rate for soda drinks became stagnant in the United States. To increase profits, soft-drink producers, like The Coca-Cola Company, adopted two strategies: diversification through acquisition of other bottled beverage products like water, fruit juices, tea and sports drinks; and implementation of aggressive international marketing campaigns in countries where there is less potable water and more opportunities. For example, China is already Coca-Cola's third largest market. Today more than 70% of Coca-Cola's net revenues are generated from outside of the United States (Coca-Cola Company.org, 2010).

THE COCA-COLA COMPANY

The history of the Coca-Cola Corporation, the producer of two of the world's three most popular carbonated drinks, parallels the industry trends in terms of growth and product lines. Pioneering a sophisticated distribution system of local bottlers who purchase the coke syrup from the corporation and implementing an aggressive growth strategy, Coke is the world's largest producer and distributor of non-alcoholic beverages. In 2009, the corporation generated $31 billion in operating revenues and had a net income of $6.8 billion from its over400 brands sold in over 200 countries. (www.wikinvest.com, 2010).

However, the organization had humble beginnings when John S. Pemberton began a patent medicine business in Atlanta, Georgia, in 1886, where he invented such products as liver pills, hair dye, and the beverage known today as Coca-Cola. With caffeine and cocaine in his sugary syrup concentrate, the product was marketed as a cure-all remedy. In 1891 they sold the business and its secret formula for coke syrup for $2300 to Asa Candler. The new owner, a druggist, improved the original formula, removed the cocaine, and hired a sales force that blanketed the United States and beyond selling syrup concentrate to local bottlers.

During WWII, General Eisenhower requested that Coke be made available to American soldiers serving in North Africa and Europe. So the company set up multiple foreign bottling plants that paved the way for a global business presence after the war. During the 1950s the company expanded rapidly internationally and opened 15 to 20 plants per year. As early as the

1950s Coke recognized the potential of minority markets and included racial minorities in their advertisements (Pendergast, 2000).

Although Coca-Cola was primarily a one-product company until the 1960s, it quickly became synonymous with the American way of life with its growing success and in its promotional messages. The company's "advertising never reflected the problems of the world, only a good and happy life" (Derdak, 1988, p. 233).

For Coke the 1960s were a time of diversification, product development, and increased competition. Because Pepsi began to aggressively challenge Coke for market share, Coke bought Minute Maid and Belmont Springs Water and launched Tab, Sprite, and Fresca, making significant inroads into the diet soda market. During the 1970s Coca-Cola focused on foreign expansion, particularly into China and Russia. As a result, by 1984 Pepsi outsold Coke with a 22.8% market share compared to Coke's 21.6% (Derdak, 1988, p. 234). Although the introduction of Diet Coke, now the world's #1 diet beverage, pumped up sales, the introduction of a reformulated "New Coke" was a marketing and public relations disaster. "Coke's great (financial) returns in the 1990s were based on the notion that it could keep increasing earnings at 20% or more per year. It can't" (Sivy, 2000, p. 42). In 2000 Coca Cola's stock price had declined from $88 (1998) a share to $50 a share.

COCA-COLA THEN: CORPORATE CULTURE AND LEADERSHIP

Fueled by phenomenal marketing and financial successes, Coca-Cola was "run by bureaucrats and accountants focused more on getting the most out of what they had . . . than of thinking of new ideas" (New Doug, 1999, p. 55). Described as "insular" and "predominated by the 'good old' boys from the University of Georgia" (Foust, 2000a, p. 56), the organization was "a marketing machine that created desire for the Coke brand (at whatever price), rather than a sales company that gave consumers what they wanted" (Feldman, 2000, p. 33). In some parts of the world, Coca-Cola was seen as representing American imperialism. This attitude is exemplified by former CEO Roberto Goizueta's wish that one day Coke should replace tap water. In 1997 when Goizueta suddenly died, the board replaced him with his protégé, M. Douglas Ivestor. Refusing to appoint a chief operating officer, "Ivestor did what accountants do best, he put his head down and carried on with the old way of doing things" (New Doug, 1999, p. 55). Over the next two years, Ivestor, described as "arrogant and insecure" (Morris & Sellers, 2000 p. 15), inherited many problems, including a tainted Coke scare in Europe that resulted in the largest product recall in company history (Europe Shuns, 1999), a decline in earnings for two straight years, which generated the need to steeply increase the price for Coke syrup sales to bottlers in an attempt to bolster profits, and an organizational climate of racial tension.

THE LAWSUIT

In 1999, just when things seemed like they couldn't get worse for Ivestor, Coca-Cola was served with a lawsuit that accused the company of systemically discriminating against black employees in promotions, evaluations, terminations, and pay. "Publicity surrounding the case troubled Coke, whose U.S. customer base is disproportionately made up of African Americans and Latinos" (Mokhiber, 2000, p. 30).

Could this lawsuit have been prevented? Earlier when black employees shared their complaints with the Rev. Joseph Wheeler, president of the local NAACP, he brought these concerns to Coca-Cola officials. He was told that the company was under no obligation to talk to him because he was not a lawyer. Greg Clark, one of the plaintiffs, said, "that he would never have sued had he felt that his concerns were taken seriously: 'They ignored me, ignored me, ignored me, to the point where I felt that I had no other recourse'" (Harrington, 2000, p. 188).

In response to the lawsuit, Ivestor appointed Carl H. Ware, the highest-ranking black executive in the company, as the co-chair of the Diversity Advisory Council along with Senior Vice-President Jack Stahl. Ware, a Harvard graduate, joined the company in 1974 to work in the area of urban and government affairs. As vice-president of the Africa group, Ware focused on "cultivating African governments and bridging cultural hurdles so that the company can do business, often in partnerships, with local governments" (Holsendolph, 2000). He is credited with influencing Coca-Cola's decision to divest its South African assets in support of the antiapartheid cause. In 1994, Ware helped to organize Nelson Mandela's fund-raising tour in the United States which smoothed the way for Coke sales in post-apartheid South Africa (Foust, 2000b, p. 138).

Having worked 26 years at the company, Ware was known for his ability to defuse problems before they became full-blown crises. In 1981, Jesse Jackson, critical of Coke's hiring record and its weak support for black-owned businesses, was set to kick off a "Don't choke on Coke" boycott. Jackson called it off after Ware helped craft a $50 million program to help support black vendors (Foust, 2000b, p. 138).

As the lawsuit wound its way through the court system, the number of plaintiffs increased, and both sides turned up the pressure. What began with four current and ex-employees eventually became a major class-action suit with approximately 2,000 plaintiffs. The claim was that Coca-Cola had "systematically discriminated against African-Americans by paying them lower salaries, than whites for the same work, passing over them for promotions, and subjecting them to harassment" (Mokhiber, 2000, p. 30), since at least 1995. Coincidentally, 1995 was the same year that Carl Ware presented Ivestor, then Coke's COO with a report documenting racial disparities in pay, performance evaluations, and promotions for black employees. The plaintiffs asked both for monetary damages and a court order that required the company to change some of its employment practices. The lead co-counsel in the case was Cyrus Mehri, a 37-year-old lawyer, who had successfully won the $176 million Texaco racial discrimination lawsuit.

Coca-Cola denied the charges of discrimination, claiming that the plaintiffs' claims had nothing in common but their race. Carl Ware said, "I think we've made great strides in developing a gold standard for diversity management" (Foust, 1999, p. 2) and "I myself am a good example, a proof that glass walls do not exist at the Coca-Cola Company" (Holsendolph, 1999, p. 1). However, "the company's dithering continued even after the suit was filed. For starters, rather than pursue the almost inevitable settlement, Coke first engaged in a vigorous pre-trial defense" (Harrington, 2000, p. 188) and attempted to stop the class-action status of the lawsuit.

U.S. District Court Judge Richard Story instructed the company to add a disclaimer to company e-mails to employees about the case that read, "The foregoing represents Coca-Cola's opinion of the lawsuit. It is unlawful for Coca-Cola to retaliate against employees who choose to participate in this case" (Unger, 1999). The company did not add the statement.

In October 1999, while the case was pending, Ivestor effectively demoted Ware, the company's highest-ranking black executive, by having him report to a fellow senior vice-president. "In response, Ware announced that he would retire at the end of the year. The episode fueled questions about Coke's commitment to diversity" (Smith, 2000, p. 52).

Although Ivestor's tenure was fraught with financial problems, the demotion of Ware seemed to be one of the catalytic events/public relations problems that moved influential board members to strongly suggest to Ivestor that he was no longer the man to run Coke.

On December 5, 1999 reportedly with the intervention of board members Warren Buffett and Herbert Allen, Ivestor submitted his resignation at an emergency meeting called on a Sunday evening.

> Ivestor's sudden fall from one of the world's premier corporate jobs is more than just a tale of bad luck or plans gone wrong. It is a management story full of leadership lessons. It features colossal arrogance and insecurity. Its main character was blind to his own weaknesses and unwilling to take advice. . . . But the ultimate measure of a CEO is how he handles crises, and again and again, in the view of certain directors and the powerful bottling executives, Ivestor was a day late and a dollar short. . . . He took pride in being a substance-over-style guy but that translated into taking no heed of image and perception issues, which are merely all important to a company like Coke (Morris and Sellers, 2000 p. 78).

The board elected Douglas Daft, a 56-year-old Australian with 30 years experience at Coke, primarily in their Asian and Middle-Eastern markets, as president and CEO. In contrast to his predecessor, Daft was a delegator, who spoke of repositioning the company from three perspectives: building brand, thinking and acting locally in global business relations, and being seen as a model citizen. In a speech delivered to the Chief Executive's Club in Boston, he said,

> I want the Coca-Cola Company to be one of the most desired employers in the world. I have told our people that we are going to take our company to the head of the class when it comes to the diversity of our workforce and our business (Daft, 2000, p. 606).

He quickly mended fences with Carl Ware by naming him Vice-President for Global Public Affairs, reporting directly to him and adopted two of the suggestions from Ware's 1995 report: clear support for diversity from the top executives and tying compensation increases to the achievement of diversity goals. As a result, Ware rescinded his retirement plan.

In November 2000, as a result of a court-ordered mediation, Coca-Cola settled the lawsuit with almost all of the 2,200 plaintiffs for $192.5 million. Approximately 1% of the plaintiffs decided to "opt-out" of the settlement agreement. On June 7, 2002, the U.S. District Court for the Northern District of Georgia approved the Settlement Agreement in what is formally known as *Ingram et. al. v. The Coca-Cola Company*. The Agreement applied to all non-hourly U.S.-based employees of the company but not to employees of its bottlers. The terms of the Agreement called for back pay to current and former employees, future pay equity adjustments, linkage between senior managers' compensation and the company's EEO performance and the creation of an outside seven-member Task Force to provide independent oversight of Coca-Cola's compliance. The Task Force was responsible for preparing annual reports evaluating the implementation of these programs. Cyrus Mehri, head of the plaintiffs' legal team, summed up his opinion of the case.

> The biggest problems at Coke were their HR practices. They had almost as many job titles as they did jobs, there was no consistent form of job posting, and promotional practices were not consistently applied. This gave undue discretion to managers and prevented employees from having a fair chance to compete for these positions. Coke had cultivated an image of being extraordinarily progressive and generous in the African-American community. Unfortunately, Coke—like so many companies—got very arrogant and believed their own PR. They valued minorities as consumers, but not as employees (Wiscombe, 2003, p. 34).

When asked to comment on the case, Coca-Cola corporate media relations spokesperson Karyn Dest wrote

> Clearly, we learned a valuable lesson from the lawsuit. But, in addition to the learning around diversity, another great learning for us was that we had no documented proof when it came to the lawsuit of our efforts. We didn't measure the growth and development of minorities and women at the company (personal communication, November 5, 2003).

AFTER THE LAWSUIT

Alexis Herman, a former U.S. Secretary of Labor, chaired the Task Force that issued its first report in September 2002. Since the settlement, Coca-Cola implemented numerous systemic changes in its policies and procedures. (See Exhibit 1) with measurable results (see Exhibit 2). Although the report was generally positive, the Task Force cited key areas that needed additional work: identification of employees for senior management positions and improvement in the perceptions of minority employees that their career opportunities are comparable to those of white employees. Currently, "about a third of Coke's employees are minorities but most top employees are white. . . . All minorities, the report said are over represented in lower-paying support jobs" (Wyatt, 2002, p. 1).

EXHIBIT 1   Programs and Policies Implemented by Coca-Cola Since the Settlement Agreement was Accepted

- Established uniform processes for employee reviews
- Required that all job postings attract at least three candidates, one of whom must be a woman or minority
- Implemented mandatory diversity training for managers and employees
- Conducted human resources audits and adverse impact analyses
- Tied performance appraisals and compensation for managers to their effectiveness in performance management
- Implemented a uniform compensation system based on job-related measures, including a market-based salary structure, a common review date, and additional compensation training for managers
- Established a mentoring program
- Initiated executive briefings for senior management concerning diversity strategy
- Implemented a "Solutions" program that included an ombudsman and an hotline to resolve employee disputes

Based on the *First Annual Report of the Task Force* (Herman et al., 2002)

EXHIBIT 2   Key Findings from the First Annual Report of the Task Force

- Of the 6,864 non-hourly U.S. Coke employees, 30% are minorities, up 4% since 12/00. Two thirds of the minorities are African Americans.
- In the first 6 months of 2002, white men were promoted at the rate of 4.7%, women at 5%, and minorities at 5.7%; of the 301 new hires 29% were minorities, and 55% were women.
- Minorities make up only 20% of the workforce at the executive level and are overrepresented at 47% among the lowest paid support personnel.

The Task Force also chided the corporation for missing an opportunity to diversify the board of directors, which was then composed of nine white men, two white women, and one African-American man. In the spring of 2002, when the board membership was expanded from 12 to 14 members, two white men were selected. "The company's failure to consult with the task force with respect to the nominations undermined its diversity efforts and suggested a lack of sensitivity to diversity goals" (Bean, 2002b, p. 1).

Shortly after the report was published, CEO and Chairman Daft wrote a memo to employees that said, "There is still work to do. Our commitment to diversity is a journey not an endpoint. Diversity is not an initiative; it is a fundamental element of our business success" (Day, 2002, p. 3). At the 2002 annual shareholders meeting at Madison Square Garden, some African-American employees protested because they believed that blacks remain underrepresented in the top corporate ranks, get fired more often, and are still paid less than white employees. "Protesters handed out material claiming that 16% of the Coke workforce is black but that blacks have just 1.5% of the top jobs" (White, 2002, E03). In May of the same year, some employees in Texas accused Coca-Cola of repackaging nearly out-of-date soda, marking it down, and then reselling it in minority neighborhoods since 1993. Coca-Cola management denied the allegation.

On May 24, 2002, The Coca-Cola Company, in a conciliation agreement with the U.S. Department of Labor, agreed to pay $ 8.1 million in back pay to over 2,000 female employees. The agreement followed an audit by the Office of Federal Contract Compliance (OFCCP), which enforces federal rules against discrimination at companies holding government contracts. The audit revealed wage disparities between male and female employees between 1998 and 2000 (Bean, 2002a).

In 2003, Coca-Cola extended health benefits to same-sex domestic partners and named the first Hispanic female, Maria Elena Lagomasino, Chief Executive of J. P. Morgan, a private bank, to its board of directors and for the first time, appeared on the DiversityInc list of the Top 50 Companies for Diversity, ranked at #18.

E. Neville Isdell, replaced Daft as CEO in 2004. Isdell, who grew up in Northern Ireland, Zambia, and South Africa had experienced discrimination first hand and credited his parents for his values of fairness and justice. He was quick to grasp the extent of across the board employee dissatisfaction and made improving employee engagement a major focus of his tenure. Isdell said,

> As far as I am concerned, the prime thing that I had to do was restore the overall morale
> of the company . . . In tandem with the work we did against the it, I put in place a
> whole review of what became the "Manifesto for Growth" (Spruell, 2007, p. 29).

This document detailed strategic initiatives such as maximizing profit while making Coca-Cola a employer of choice. Knowing that organizational change is a slow process, in 2005 Isdell voluntarily asked the diversity task to continue for an additional 5th year.

COCA-COLA NOW: AS INCLUSIVE AS OUR BRANDS

In terms of diversity, much has changed at The Coca-Cola Company, where diversity now is listed as one their seven core corporate values. In its "As Inclusive as Our Brands" 2009 report Coca-Cola organizes its diversity efforts and assessment of success into a framework addressing four key areas: workplace, marketplace, suppliers and community. In terms of its workforce initiatives, the Global Diversity & Workplace Fairness team monitoring program tracks progress in terms of hiring, workplace demographics, performance management, merit pay, short and long-term incentives and pay equity.

Because understanding and meeting the needs of its increasingly diverse global marketplace is a driving force behind Coca-Cola's financial future, the Diversity Business Development Team (DBD), is working with the Multicultural Marketing team to identify and capitalize on product and promotional opportunities in growing multicultural markets especially targeting African American, Hispanic and Asian consumers.

Although Coca-Cola has had a Minority and Women Owned Business Enterprises (MWBEs) supplier program for more than thirty years, in 2000, the organization pledged to expand its efforts by purchasing $800 million worth of goods and services from MWBEs over the next five years and exceeded its goals over each of those years. In 2009, during a tough economy, the organization spent $459 million through supplier diversity programs. The Coca-Cola Company also participates in a MWBE mentoring program and sponsorships for minority and women business owners to attend executive management programs at large universities.

In terms of social responsibility, Coca-Cola's strategy is to provide support for multicultural consumers through three initiatives: establishing a leadership presence in diverse communities, aligning business and community strategies and a commitment to education (The Coca-Cola Company, 2009). As a result, the corporation contributes to Historically Black Colleges, sponsors Special Olympics and Altanta's Gay Pride Parade, and over the past 20 years donated over $93 million to scholarships and educational programs (The Coca-Cola Company, 2009).

Current CEO, Muhtar Kent, opened Coca-Cola's 2009 "Inclusive as Our Brand Report" with the following statement:

> At the Coca-Cola Company, one of our seven core values is diversity, which we define in a simple but powerful way: "As inclusive as our brands." Our great brand represents moments of refreshment and connection that transcend cultural differences and help tie our diverse world together. As a company we believe we must act accordingly by taking a leadership position in diversity, inclusion and fairness. (p. 3)

DISCUSSION QUESTIONS

1. The traditional change model consists of three steps: unfreezing, i.e., recognizing the need for change because of some event or threat, the actual change actions and refreezing, i.e., incorporating new ways of operating and thinking into the everyday operations of the organization. Apply this model to the situation at The Coca-Cola Company at the point when the lawsuit was served in 1999.

2. How would you describe the leadership styles of four of the CEOs mentioned in this case (Investor, Daft, Isdell, and Kent) in terms of their abilities to accomplish both strategic goals and to manage the people?

3. How does Parker's triangle, "The Emotional Connection of Distinguishing Differences and Conflict," help to explain a) why so many minority employees joined the class action lawsuit and b) how Coca-Cola failed to "manage diversity"?

4. Specifically, how does The Coca-Cola Company today exemplify the business case for diversity? Going forward, what threats could there be to the continuation of Coca-Cola's progress in terms of diversity management?

Writing Assignment

Research the details of any other major recent employment discrimination case. How is this case similar to or different from the Coca-Cola case? Applying Thomas and Ely's framework (See introduction to the text for Thomas and Ely material) to each of these organizations, what can be learned about managing diversity from applying their model?

Bibliography

Bean, L. (2002a, September 30). *Coca-Cola to pay $8 million to resolve salary discrimination.* Retrieved September, 30, 2003, from http://www.diversityinc.com/members/3034print.cfm

Bean, L. (2002b, September 30). *Coca-Cola rebuked for missed opportunity to diversify board.* Retrieved October 20, 2003, from http://www.diversityinc.com/members/3597print.cfm.

Cole, Y. (2002, September 12). *Baloney meter measures Coca-Cola's claims of supplier-diversity progress* (electronic version). Retrieved September 30, 2003, from http://www.diversityinc.com/members/351printcfm.

Coca-Cola Company.org. (2010). *The Coca-Cola Company 2009 Annual Report.* Retrieved October 15, 2010 from cocacolacompany.com.

Daft, D. (2000). Speech delivered to the Chief Executives Club of Boston, May 3, 2000. *Vital Speeches of the Day, 66*(19), 606–609.

Day, S. (2002, September 26). Anti-bias task force gives Coca-Cola good marks but says challenges remain. *The New York Times.* p. C3.

Derdak, T. (Ed). (1988). *International directory of company histories* (pp. 232–235). Chicago: St. James Press.

Europe shuns tainted Coke. (1999). *MacLean's, 112,* 26, p. 78.

Everyday-Wisdom. (2010). *Soft Drink Consumption: The Frightening Statistics and Associated Health Risks.* Retrieved October 15, 2010 from everyday-wisdom.com/soft-drink-consumption.html.

Feldman, A. (2000). The real thing. *Money,* 29, 33–36.

Foust, D. (2000a). Coke: Say goodbye to the good ol' boy culture. *Business Week, 3683*(55), 58.

Foust, D. (2000b). Will Coke go better with Carl Ware? *Business Week, 3665* (55), 138.

Foust, D. (1999). A different cola war. *Business Week, 3632*(54), 38–39.

Harrington, A. (2000). Prevention is the best defense. *Fortune, 142*(2), 188.

Herman, A., Burns, A., Casellas, G. F., Cooke, E. D., Jr., Knowles, M. F., Lee, B. L., Holsendolph, E. (1999, June 1). Once again, Carl Ware takes on an assignment, a big one. *The Atlanta Journal and Constitution.*

Holsendolph, E., (2000, January 20). Miami Times. Retrieved from http:www.highbeam.com/doc/1gi-54768736.html on May 2, 2011.

Mokhiber, R. (2000). Coke settles race suit. *Multinational Monitor, 21*(12), 30.

Morris, B., and Sellers, P. (2000). What really happened at Coke. *Fortune, 141*(1), 14–17.

New Doug, old tricks. (1999, December 9). *Economist, 353*(8149), 55.

National Soft Drink Association (NSDA), (2003). Growing Up Together: The Soft Drink Industry and America Retrieved from nsda.org/softdrinks/History/growup.html.

Pendergast, M. (2000). *For god, country and Coca-Cola the definitive history of the great American soft drink and the company that makes it.* New York: Basic Books.

The Coca Cola Corporation. (2003). *The Coca-Cola Company 2002 annual report.* Atlanta.

The Coca-Cola Corporation. (2009). As inclusive as our brands: 2009 U.S. diversity stewardship report. Retrieved on October 1, 2010 from coca-cola company.com/citizenship/pdf/2009.

Sivy, M. (2000). Why Coke still isn't it. *Money, 29*(2), 42.

Smith, V.E. (2000). Things are going better with Coke. *Newsweek, 135*(3), 52.

Spruell. S.K., (2007). Retrieved on May 2, 2011 from http://www.thecoca-colacompany.com/ourcompany/manifesto_for_growthhtml.

Unger, H. (1999a, May 12). Plaintiffs in suit against Coca-Cola to meet in court. *Knight Rider/Tribune Business News.*

White, B. (2002, April 12). Black Coca-Cola workers still angry: Despite 2000 legal settlement, protesters say little has changed. *The Washington Post*, p. E03.

Wikinvest.com. (2010). Coca-Cola Company. Retrieved October 15, 2010 from www.wikinvest.com/stock/Coca-Cola_Company_(KO).

Wiscombe, J. (2003). Corporate America's scariest opponent. *Workforce, 82*(4), 34–40.

Wyatt, K. (2002, September 25). Coke's diversity work gets approval. *Associated Press News Release*. Retrieved October 31, 2003, from http://www.ap.org.

Diversity on the Web

Now that you have read the Coca-Cola case, visit the Web site below where you will find the task force reports that were part of the legal settlement of the Coca-Cola discrimination case. Within each annual report, you will find an "executive summary" section.

Beginning with the 2002 report, read the summaries and develop a time line that tracks the yearly actions Coca-Cola took to remedy the issues that led to the lawsuit.

What were the problems with implementing the new programs and policies here? Go to http://www.thecocacolacompany.com Web site. Type in "diversity task force reports" in the search box. Scroll down and select each annual task force report, reading from the earliest to the last one.

BEING AN ONLY: A FIELD ASSIGNMENT

Carol P. Harvey
Assumption College

Given the demographic changes in today's workforce, it is important to understand what it feels like to be a visible minority. Sometimes, differential treatment is due to the context of the workplace situation rather than to discrimination. When an organization or a department has one or a few people who are different in terms of some visible social identity group membership, the majority may, often unconsciously, treat them differently. In turn, the minority employees may find that they react differently to their contextual situation than they would if there were more balanced numbers in the work situation. If one is a part of the majority, it may be difficult to recognize the impact of this phenomenon. One of the most effective ways to recreate this learning experience is to watch the award-wining video, "A Tale of O" (Goodmeasure) and to complete the following field assignment.

INSTRUCTIONS

1. Watch the film, "Tale of O," and take meaningful notes about the experiences of the O's (minority) and X's (majority).

2. Think creatively about how you could place yourself in a safe, alcohol free field situation where you would be a visible minority, i.e., be an "O." (Some examples include a female student going truck shopping at a local automotive dealer, a male student attending a Tupperware party, a student standing on a street corner soliciting money as a homeless person and then donating it to a shelter, a young student going to a water aerobics class with senior citizens, an able bodied student shopping in a mall in a wheelchair and others attending religious services of faiths very different from their own, etc.) Submit your idea to your professor for approval. (Note: Some experiences are inappropriate for this assignment. For example, attending an Alcoholics Anonymous meeting, going to a gay bar, or trying to recycle your study abroad semester, or any additional situations that your instructor considers inappropriate will not fulfill the requirements of the assignment. Also, sometimes, your may need to obtain permission from the person in charge of the organization, such as the minister, rabbi, etc.) to attend the activities of an organization.

3. Once your idea is approved, complete the field experience, keeping in mind the material from the video. Do not have a friend accompany you on the field experience.

4. Write a 3–4 page typed report that analyzes your field experience from the perspective of the consequences of being an "O." How does it feel? How did you act differently in this situation? How did people treat you differently? What did you learn about yourself and others? Try to relate your experiences closely to the information presented in the video.

Integrative Questions for Section 2

1. If Sowell is suggesting that someday the United States, like so many other countries in history may lose its dominant position in the world, wouldn't the United States be better off to impose immigration barriers now to prevent this from happening? Why or why not?

2. Think about the immigrant roots of your family. What has been the contribution of people from these countries to American culture?

3. In terms of change, what are the lessons from Sowell's article for organizations like the Coca-Cola Corporation?

4. Although China has experienced rapid economic change in the past thirty years, what aspects of Asian culture might be the most resistant to change and why?

5. What lessons does the Salacuse article provide in terms of successfully negotiating with clients from other cultures when you are not sure what countries/cultures they originated from?

6. When a person is the only one of his or her race in an office, how might he or she behave differently? Why?

7. In an office where everyone is white except one African American, Hispanic, or Asian, what can the white workers do to be more inclusive of their co-worker of color? What should they not do?

3

Understanding Primary Diversity: Gender, Sexual Orientation, Age, and Physical and Mental Challenges

In this section, students will

▪ Discover why so few women have advanced into leadership positions.

▪ Consider the negative aspects of masculinity.

▪ Examine the progress and backlash experienced by LGBTs (lesbians, gays, bisexuals, transgenders) in the workforce.

▪ Learn about the four generational age cohorts currently in the workplace.

▪ Contrast the case of a well-managed diversity program with an organization that failed to value the diversity of its workers.

Section III continues to explore the relationship between primary diversity characteristics and how these social identities influence people's experience in the workplace. It begins with an analysis of the workplace realities for women (Harvey and Larsen), men (Farough), and LGBTs (Hunt). Then, this section explores the dynamics of having four generations in the workforce (Holtzman, Kruger, and Srock), exploring prejudice about age (McKechnie), and participating in an exercise that allows you to actually experience physical challenge (Allard). The Best Buy case presents an example of an organization that demonstrates its strong commitment to diversity through its programs for physically and mentally challenged employees, customers, and community members (D. Harvey).

This section concludes with two examples of what can happen when diversity is not valued or managed well: the Cracker Barrel case (Howard) and an exercise on sexual harassment (Harvey).

Women in Leadership Positions: Why Aren't They There Yet?

Carol P. Harvey
Assumption College

Deborah L. Larsen
UniBank

GOALS

- To identify the complex issues that may be holding women back in corporate America
- To understand the differences in male and female leadership styles
- To examine the statistics on women's progress in the workplace
- To consider the how the multiple identities of race and gender complicate work-life for women of color

Although women have benefited more than any other social identity group from diversity initiatives, they still have far to go in terms of corporate, economic and government leadership. In the 1960s an employed married woman could not get a credit card in her own name or a loan without a male co-signer and help wanted ads were segregated into "Help wanted—female" and "Help wanted—male." While these blatant forms of discrimination are now illegal, it is still more difficult for women to achieve positions of power than it is for men. In 2010, only thirteen or 2.6% of the Fortune 500 companies had a female CEO and only 15% of their Board members were female—79% white and 21% women of color. (Catalyst, 2010) Despite being 51% of the population, women hold only 17.2% of the seats in the U.S. House of representatives and seventeen of the one hundred seats in the U.S. Senate (Emily's List.org, 2010).

Gender is a socially constructed characteristic consisting of behaviors and attitudes considered proper for males and females. Gender varies from one culture to another and serves as a significant way in which society privileges its members. Many societies set up barriers to provide unequal access to power, property, and prestige on the basis of sex. "Privilege exists when one group has something of value that is denied to others simply because of the groups they belong to, rather than because of anything they've done or failed to do" (Minas, 1993). An example of gender privilege is being able to assume that your gender, engagement ring, or status as a parent is not a factor in a hiring decision.

Many factors, some within the control of women and some that are not, account for women's lack of progress into more powerful positions. According to the 2000 census, 60% of all women are employed outside of the home but most work in the lower and middle levels of organizations. Because women tend to **horizontally segregate** themselves into occupations that are predominately female, approximately half of all working women are employed in industries (like education, healthcare, retailing, etc.) that are at least 78% female and traditionally pay less money. There is a perception that these "jobs require interpersonal skills, such as service roles or teachers and often these jobs are not as valued as highly as jobs requiring technical skills and consequently are not paid as well" (Dunn, 1997).

In terms of gender there is also **vertical segregation** in the workplace. This occurs when both genders work in the same industries but men are *perceived* as being more capable, skillful and qualified for the better paying and more upwardly mobile line positions (like sales, branch management, etc.), than women (Charles & Grusky, 2004).

> Vertical segregation reinforces the idea that women are suited for lower level roles with less responsibility rather than professional and managerial roles within the same occupational category because they possess certain innate characteristics (passivity, nurturance, emotional sensitivity, for example) or because they have less cognitive capability or fewer higher-level skills compared to men (Reeves, 2010, p. 18).

Consequently, over the last five years the gap between men's and women's wages has not changed much. Women still average seventy-seven cents for every dollar that a man makes. In terms of women of color, African American women make 68.7% of men's salaries, Asian American women 89.5% and for Latinas 59% (National Committee on Pay Equity, 2008).

GENDER DIFFERENCES IN LEADERSHIP AND COMMUNICATION STYLES

Researchers have documented that male and female leadership styles do differ but "there is little evidence to suggest that one sex or the other is more effective leading" (Powell, 2010, p. 142). Males tend to use a more **transactional**, i.e., goal directed leadership style in contrast to women's more **transformational**, i.e., relationship oriented leadership style. "In the business arena, the perception of women's communication style is one explanation for the lack of women CEO's: women's tendency to weigh feelings and the impact on people when making decisions may be taken for weakness" (Powell, 2010, p. 142 from Oakley, 2000). On the other hand, if a woman shows that she can be assertive and competitive, she may be described as being "cold" or a "bitch." If a woman changes her behavior to be more accepted by her male co-workers, her female co-workers may label her as a traitor.

Conversational style differences between genders also contribute to the perception of men as stronger leaders. Men tend to talk in a more assertive conversational style that includes tendencies to interrupt, question in an interrogating manner, and be more direct in their speech patterns. In contrast, women tend to favor a communication pattern where they speak in short bursts, add questions asking for support at the end of their statements, and be more indirect (Tannen, 1990).

Everyday communication can reinforce the devaluation of women and feminine traits. A baseball player making a poor throw might be told, "You threw that one like a girl." "It's a man's world" is an expression pointing to the male dominated character of society that places most power in the hands of men. It is still common to use masculine pronouns to refer to people in general, or to use *man* to name the entire species as in "mankind." The concept of "brotherhood" carries powerful meaning about human connection, as in the line from *America the Beautiful,* "And crown thy good with brotherhood from sea to shining sea" (Bates, 1893). It is an honor to be considered "one of the guys" but to reverse this would certainly be an issue.

A HISTORY OF PATRIARCHY

History provides some insights into how a society comes to value a more masculine style over a more feminine one. A society is patriarchal to the degree that it is male-dominated and identified with what are considered to be male values. Most political, economic, legal, religious, educational and military positions of authority are filled by men. Heads of state, CEOs, corporate board members, religious leaders, members of legislatures at all levels of government, senior law partners, generals, etc. tend to be mostly males under a patriarchal system. When women are in these positions, people tend to think of them as *exceptions*. Consequently, male dominance creates power differences between men and women and promotes the idea of male superiority. If men occupy more powerful positions, then viewing men as superior is not a stretch. If presidents, generals, legislators, and corporate CEO's are mostly men with a few women as exceptions to the rule, then men as a group become more identified with leadership and power.

In patriarchal societies core ideas about what is desirable or normal are associated more with men. The idea of a high-level career with its implicit 60+ hour work weeks assumes the worker has support at home to provide child care, cook, clean and do laundry.

> In the U.S. almost half of the women who have made it into the corporate ranks or who make over $100,000 have no children. The double standard is alive and well in the workplace. The presence of children signals stability and responsibility for men, who are assumed to be better workers because of their roles as breadwinners. The identical situation for women has the opposite effect (Cheung & Halpern, 2010, p. 183).

WOMEN'S LEGAL RIGHTS

In early U.S. society, the second-class status of women was taken for granted. A husband and wife were legally one person: him. Women could not serve on juries, vote, make legal contracts, or hold property in their own name. Because men tenaciously held onto their privileges and used social institutions to maintain their positions, basic rights for women came only through a prolonged struggle. In 1848 a group of women led by Elizabeth Cady Stanton used the Declaration of Independence as the framework for writing the "Declaration of Sentiments." Among the many inequalities it sought to correct were women not being allowed to vote, enter the professions, etc.

Women finally won the right to vote in 1920. In 1963 President Kennedy convened a commission on the status of Women, naming Eleanor Roosevelt as its chair. The report documented discrimination against women in virtually every area of American life. That same year Betty Friedan published *The Feminine Mystique*, a book that acknowledged the oppression that middle class educated women experienced because of their limited life options. In 1964 Title VII of the 1964 Civil Rights Act was passed. This legislation prohibited employment discrimination on the basis of sex as well as race, religion, ethnicity and national origin. With the inclusion of Title IX in the Education Codes of 1972, equal access to higher education, professional schools and high school and college sports teams became the law. The number of female doctors, lawyers, engineers, and other professionals grew substantially. Sports participation by women and girls also rose as a result of Title IX.

However, the Equal Rights Amendment to the U.S. constitution languished in Congress for almost fifty years, was finally passed in 1972 and sent to the states for ratification. The wording was simple: "Equality of rights under the law shall not be denied or abridged by the United States or any state on account of sex." When the deadline for ratification came in 1982, the ERA was three states short of the 38 needed to write it into the U.S. Constitution, but it was never passed. While many women today may be hesitant to be thought of as "feminist" for fear of being criticized, few would give up the personal freedoms and opportunities that women have won over the last 150 years.

INEQUALITIES IN THE EDUCATIONAL SYSTEM

Gender inequality in education often is not readily apparent. According to the U.S. Department of Education, women earn 57% of the bachelor's degrees, 60% of the master's degrees and 51% of the doctorates awarded in the U.S. (United States Department of Education, 2008). However, horizontal segregation is apparent here too. Men earn 83% of bachelor's degrees in the more "masculine" and better paying fields like engineering, while women received 88% of the bachelor's degrees in the "feminine" field of library science (Henslin, 2005).

In the summer of 2006, the U.S. Department of Education scheduled in-depth investigations of how colleges and universities treat women and men students and faculty in their science and mathematics departments. The current initiative to apply Title IX to academic departments stems in part from a July 2004 study by the Government Accountability Office that found Title IX compliance reviews in the sciences were largely neglected and that many math and science programs had polices that resulted in women feeling unwelcome in pursuing advanced degrees or tenured positions, according to Stephanie Monroe, Assistant Secretary for Civil Rights (Feminist Majority Foundation, 2006). The National Science Foundation is working with the U.S. Department of Education to create the review process, focusing in part on whether engineering and computer science departments offer as much support to women students as to men. The report found that women's lack of participation in science and technology fields in academia can be attributed to gender bias and barriers within hiring and promotion practices in research institutions.

GENDER INEQUALITIES IN SALARIES

Technically, equal pay has been the law since 1963 when President Kennedy signed the Equal Pay Act that prohibits discrimination based on sex resulting in unequal pay for equal work as an amendment to the Wages and Hours Act. More recently on January 29, 2009, President Obama signed The Fair Pay act that extends the statute of limitations for an employee to sue for pay discrimination to 180 days from the date of the last paycheck.

While many people believe that the earnings gap between men and women is disappearing, the statistics show that the gender pay gap has persisted over the past half century with little evidence of narrowing (U.S. Census Bureau, 2005). As of 2009, in the U.S. women earned seventy-seven cents for every dollar made by a man. Between 1994 and 2009 the pay gap for women has ranged from seventy-two to seventy five cents for each dollar that a man earned (AAUW, 2010).

Economists Rex Fuller and Richard Schoenberg studied the starting salaries of the business majors at the University of Wisconsin in 1991 where 47% of the graduates were women. They found that starting salaries for the women averaged 11% ($1,737) less than those of the men. Reviewing college records, the economists found that women had higher grades and more internship hours. Even with equal or better qualifications, women were offered lower salaries. Checking five years later, Fuller and Schoenberg found that instead of narrowing, the pay gap had grown even wider with women earning 14% ($3,615) less than men (Henslin, 2005).

Several factors may explain such differences. Women sometimes choose different and often lower paying careers than men. Through the seventies, women married and had children earlier than today's women. These choices usually moved them off the fast track while their husband kept advancing. When these women finally returned to work, they could not match the experience or the seniority of their male counterparts. While new mothers usually leave the workforce more often than new fathers do, women also often choose jobs with flexible hours or even part time positions that don't pay as well.

A study of the 1972–1975 University of Michigan Law School graduates found first year salaries to be similar, but fifteen years out of law school the story was different with men earning 40 percent more than women. In addition, only a little over half of the women graduating in the 1980s reach the level of partner after ten years of experience. Today only about 12 percent of law firm partners are women, and a much smaller number can be found in top management roles (Wood, Corcoran, & Courant, 1993).

Similar findings hold true in education with an often significant gap between male and female professors. In April of 1999 both MIT and the University of Texas released information confirming what many female professors suspected all along. MIT's report "documented a pattern of discrimination which grew more evident as women faculty members progressed through the university's hierarchy." The University of Texas report quoted Committee Co-chair Janet Staiger, a professor in UT's Department of Communications as saying, "All the efforts to take affirmative measures to get people into the upper echelons of teaching positions have been unsuccessful" (Barnett, 1999).

Former Harvard President, Larry Summers publicly remarked that innate differences between men and women might explain why men tend to dominate science and engineering. The furor that followed his remarks led many colleges to re-examine the standing of women in the sciences and eventually contributed to Mr. Summer's resignation.

> At a roundtable discussion on equal pay, Hillary Clinton cited a report issued by MIT stating that tenured women faculty in the School of Science were discriminated against in areas such as hiring, awards, promotions, committee assignments and the allocation of resources such as lab space and research dollars. "The report showed that even women who supposedly break through the glass ceiling and reach the highest echelons of their professions still find themselves bumping up against some gender discrimination" (The White House Office of the Press Secretary, April 1999).

THE GLASS CEILING/LABYRINTH

Traditionally, women's inability to advance into corporate level positions was described as "hitting a **glass ceiling**", i.e., having a career progression that went only so far, usually to mid-level management positions and then stopped. While there are personal and organizational factors that do limit women's careers, some women do make considerable progress but it is usually a more complicated process than it is for men. Eagly and Carli describe this type of career trajectory more accurately as a labyrinth, or indirect uneven path that requires women develop a leadership style that integrates assertiveness with nurturing for career progression. Additionally, women need to cultivate social capital by networking more with colleagues and finding mentors who can help them achieve success (2007). "Women can achieve leadership positions but only by carefully traversing complex paths as they confront issues associated with childcare needs, racism, sexism and discrimination on the basis of identity" (Sanchez-Hucles and Davis, 2010, p. 172). "There are still pervasive stereotypes that women don't want the top job, that women don't want to relocate, and that they don't want to travel" reports Paulette Gerkovich, Senior Director of Research at Catalyst (2004). Successful women business leaders differ from their male counterparts in another fundamental way. Throughout their careers, they had to operate with multiple levels of pressure: the pressure of the job itself, the pioneer pressure of breaking new ground on the job, and the strain of their family obligations that made their advancement more difficult because of care-giving and household responsibilities. A 2005 study by the Families and Work Institute found that working women still spend more time on household duties than men do.

While white women at least gain some benefit from the unearned privilege of being white, women of color have to deal with the additional difficulties of finding mentors interested in working with them and the intersection of racism and sexism. Latinas often do better than Latino men in the workforce but few are found on corporate boards or on the executive level (Floyd, 2003). Asian American women who exhibit the influences of Confucian values, such as humility and harmony, often do not fit the American business expectation of assertiveness and self-promotion (Eagly & Karau, 2001). In addition,

> African American women are too different from white women to benefit from their shared gender status and too different from Black men to benefit from their shared race. Hence, women of color who strive for leadership positions are different from those who are also different—white women and African American men (Sanchez-Hucles & Davis, 2010, p. 174).

From the many studies describing gender differences in leadership styles, a number of important themes emerge. Companies trying to promote women into leadership positions report the following:

- Overall, women are less prepared to enter the upper ranks based on time in the pipeline and years of experience.
- Women often have time constraints as a result of family obligations.
- Women tend to focus more on being good at what they do rather than on gaining a strong and broad circle of influence.
- Women's leadership styles often differ from men's. The consensus style of leadership observed in many women differs from those in senior management and consequently, prevents promotion.

WHAT'S HOLDING WOMEN BACK?

The percentage of high-powered women in the world remains diminutive compared to their male counterparts. Power as defined by Forbes magazine, requires influence in the global marketplace as well as economic and cultural clout. In its annual power rankings, Forbes compares individuals based on global visibility and economic impact as well as the size of the economic area over which they have influence. In 2010, Michelle Obama, wife of the U.S. president, leads Forbes' 2010 list of the Most Powerful Women in the World. Others in the top ten rankings include popular celebrities such as Lady Gaga and Oprah Winfrey but only one political leader, Angela Merkel, Chancellor of Germany and two corporate executives, Irene Rosenfeld of Kraft Foods and Indra Nooyi of PepsiCo. In comparison, the top ten rankings in Forbes' 2010 list of the Most Powerful People in the World includes only two women, both politicians and neither American: Angela Merkel of Germany and Sonia Ghandi, head of the Indian National Congress (forbes.com). Hillary Clinton, U.S. Secretary of State is listed at the 20th place and is the first American woman on the list.

In 2003, Catalyst surveyed Fortune 1000 CEO's and women executives at the vice presidential level and above. Asked about the challenges women face in advancing to the highest levels of corporate leadership, most agreed that the lack of line experience was the primary obstacle. CEO's consistently reported that when they sought successors for chairman and CEO slots, they looked for people with high level profit and loss experience. Since men still hold a large majority of these positions, they thereby dominate the long-term pool available for the next generation of business leaders. Some women may be discouraged from pursuing these roles by colleagues or superiors who still don't think that women can perform well at this level.

Women cited a number of other factors that may block their advancement including exclusion from informal networks, stereotyping, lack of mentoring, a shortage of role models, commitment to family responsibilities, and little accountability for top management to promote diversity.

The statistics make it clear that women do not have it all. The demands of ambitious careers, the lack of balance within male-female obligations at home, and the stereotypes that still persist may take a personal toll on women's decision whether they will pursue an ambitious career. This choice is a difficult one and may involve giving up some things that are more important to a woman. "Companies and the economy also pay a price as industry cannot really afford to have 25% of the female talent pool forced out of their jobs when they have children" (Hewlett, 2002). In order to avoid the waste of educated talent, business leaders and the federal government need to establish new policies to support working parents and assist in improved work-life balance. For professional women, it's unusual not to step off the career fast track at least once. With family demands, many women feel they have little choice but to give up their demanding careers.

CONCLUSION

There can be no denying that women have made progress over the last twenty-five years. Women now sit on the Supreme Court, run for president and fight in combat. Overt sexual behavior in the workplace is less tolerated and a small percentage of women have successfully entered corporate management. Concern exists however, that the publicity around these successes leads to an illusion that issues around inequality based on gender no longer exist.

While blatant cases of gender discrimination are becoming less prevalent, there is nothing to gain and a lot to lose, by keeping so many women out of positions of authority. That doesn't mean that gender inequity has vanished. It has just gone underground and become more subtle. Most organizations have been created by and for men and are based on more masculine values. Even though educated women entered the workforce by the thousands in the last twenty years and added great value to their organizations, the definition of what makes an effective leader is still associated more with male behaviors such as toughness, aggressiveness, and decisiveness and less with what are considered as the more female characteristics of teamwork and relationship building. Perhaps, the challenge is in convincing others in management to mentor women and to appreciate the positive elements of their different styles.

The challenge society faces is that gender discrimination has existed for thousands of years and is even more complicated for women of color. One of the greatest obstacles to change is that dominant groups hardly ever see the issues of the subordinate groups as theirs. Diversity is the engine that drives originality and creativeness and gender is part of that diversity. To be effective in today's global marketplace, business organizations must fully utilize their talent pool and commit to advancing all groups of employees.

DISCUSSION QUESTIONS

1. This article states "women tend to focus more on being good at what they do rather than on gaining a strong and broad circle of influence." If you were the manager of a talented female employee who does this, what could you do to mentor her in terms of career development?

2. If women face difficulty in climbing the corporate ladder in part due to a "serious lack of mentors for young professional women"
   a. what could the women themselves do to correct this situation?
   b. what role can organizations play to facilitate mentoring?

3. This article states that women as a group tend to have a more collaborative style of management and more indirect communication styles.
   a. What are the advantages and disadvantages of this management style for women in today's business world?
   b. What could happen when a woman who has a more "masculine" style of communication has a manager who has a "feminine" style?

4. If there were only one woman at the corporate level of an organization, how could her status as an "only" affect her interactions with her male co-workers?

Writing Assignment

Go to http://www.diversityinc.com and search for "Things Never to Say to Women Executives." After reading this article, write a two-page essay that explains how these statements undermine women as leaders in organizations.

Bibliography

AAUW. (2010). The simple truth about the gender pay gap. p. 3. Retrieved May 9, 2011 from http://www.aauw.org/learn/research/simpleTruth.cfm

Barnett, E. (May, 1999). Academic Angst. *The Austin Chronicle*. Retrieved February 24, 2007 from http://weeklywire.com/ww/05-03-99/austin_pols_feature1.html

Bartlett, K. (1997). *Women in the legal profession: the good news and the bad*. Durham, N.C.: Duke University. Retrieved February 22, 2007 from http://gos.sbc.edu/b/bartlett.html

Bates, K. (1893, 1904, 1913). *America the Beautiful*. Verses contributed by R. Fitzpatrick, the Falmouth Historical society. Retrieved February 22, 2007 from http://www.fuzzylu.com/falmouth/bates/america.html

Brainard, J. (2010). Undergraduate diversity: More minorities, more women. The *Chronicle of Higher Education*, September 24, p. B24.

Committee on Maximizing the Potential of Women in Academic Science and Engineering. (2006). Beyond bias and barriers: Fulfilling the potential of women in academic science and engineering. *National*

Academy of Sciences, National Academy of Engineering, and Institute of Medicine. Washington, DC: The National Academies Press.

Costco Gender Discrimination Class Action Lawsuit. (August 17, 2004). Retrieved February 22, 2007 from the Costco Class Website https:// genderclassactionagainstcostco.com

Catalyst. (2010, December 13). Latest Catalyst census shows women still not scaling corporate ladder in 2010; New study indicates clues to reversing trend. Retrieved on May 9, 2011 from http://www.catalyst.org/press-release/ 181/latest-catalyst-census-shows-women-still-not-scaling-the-corporate-ladder-in-2010-new-study-indicates-clue-to-reversing-trend.

Charles, M. & Grusky, D. (2004). *Occupational ghettos: The worldwide segregation of women and men.* Stanford, CA: Stanford University Press.

Cheung, F.M. & Halpern, D. (2010). Women at the top. *American Psychologist.* 65, 3, 182–193.

Dunn, D. (1997). Gender and earnings. In P. Dubeckand K. Borman (Eds.). *Women and work: a handbook.* (pp. 91–93). New Brunswick NJ: Rutgers.

Eagly, A.H. & Carli, L.L. (2007). *Through the labyrinth: the truth about how women become leaders.* Boston MA: Harvard Business School Press.

Eagly, A.H. & Karau, S.J. (2001). Role congruity theory of prejudice toward female leaders. *Psychological Review,* 109, 573–598.

Emily's List.org. (2010).

Explaining trends in the gender wage gap: a report by the council of economic advisors. (June 26, 1998). Washington, DC. Retrieved February 23, 2007 from http://clinton4.nara.gov/WH/EOP/ CEA/html/gendergap.html

Feminist Majority Foundation. Postsecondary Science and Math Programs Face Title IX Review. *Inside Higher Education March 27, 2006. Feminist Daily News Wire, April 3, 2006.* Retrieved February 22, 2007 from http:// www.womenandpolicing.org/article. asp?id=9596

Floyd, K. (2003). Women of color and the corporate boardroom: Breaking through the "cement ceiling." Retrieved on November 30, 2010 from Interfaith Center for Corporate

Responsibility at iccr.org/publications/ examiner_cementceiling.php

Fortune 500 (2006). Women CEOs for Fortune 500 companies. *Fortune,* 153 (7). Retrieved from money.cnn.com/magazines/fortune/ fortune500/womenceos.

Friedan, B. (1963). *The Feminine Mystique.* NY: Dell Publishing.

Galinsky, E. (2005). Overwork in America: When the way we work becomes too much. New York: Families and Work Institute.

Golden, D. (2003, Jan 15). Admissions preferences given to alumni children draw fire. (Jan. 15, 2003). *Wall Street Journal.* Retrieved February 22, 2007 from http://www.wsjonline.com/public/ resources/documents/golden3.htm

Henslin, J. (2005). *Essentials of sociology,* 5th ed. NY: Allyn & Bacon.

Hewlett, S. (2002). *Executive women and the myth of having it all.* Boston: Harvard Business Review. 80, p. 1.

Institute for Women's Policy Research. (2010). The gender wage gap by occupation, April. Retrieved on November 23, 2010 from http://bls.gov/bls/blswage.htm.

Kinsley, M. (2003). *How affirmative action helped George W.* quoted in Discriminations posted by John Rosenberg, Jan 20, 2003. *Kinsley's Invidious Ubiquitous Non Sequitur.* Retrieved February 22, 2007 from http://www. discriminations.us/2003/01/kinsleys_ invidious_ubiquitous.html

Merrill Lynch settles sex discrimination suit. (May 5, 1998). *Feminist organization news.* Retrieved February 22, 2007 from http:// www.msmagazine.com/news/uswirestory. asp?id=3610

Miller-Obrien. (2002). *Judge approves $31 million payment to women at Amex.* Retrieved February 22, 2007 from http://www.miller-obrien.com/amex.html

Minas, A. (1993). *Gender Basics: feminist perspectives on women and men.* Belmont, CA: Wadsworth.

National Committee on Pay Equity. (2008). Wage gap narrows only slightly. Retrieved from pay-equity.org on October 14, 2008.

Powell. G. (2010). *Women and men in management,* 4th edition, Los Angeles: Sage Publications.

Remarks of the president and first lady at roundtable on equal pay (April 7, 1999). The White

House Office of the Press Secretary. Retrieved February 22, 2007 from http://clinton3. nara.gov/WH/EOP/First_lady/html/ generalspeeches/1999

Sanchez-Hucles, J.V. & Davis, D.D. (2010). Women and women of color in leadership. *American Psychologist.* 65, 3, pp. 171–181.

Reeves, M.E. (2010). *Women in business.* New York: Routledge.

Tannen, D. (1990). *You just don't understand: Women and men in conversation.* New York: William Morrow and Co.

U.S. Census Bureau. (2005). Income, poverty, and health insurance coverage in the United States 2005. U.S. Government Printing Office, Washington, DC. Retrieved Dec. 20, 2006 from http://www.census.gov/prod/2006pubs/ p60-231.pdf

U.S. Bureau of Labor Statistics. Wellington, S., Kropt, M., & Gerkovich, P. (2003). What's holding women back? *Harvard Business Review.* 81 pp. 6, 19. Boston: Harvard Business School Publishing Corporation.

United States Department of Education. (2008). Digest of Educational Statistics, Table # 258. Retrieved on May 9, 2011 from http://www. nces.ed.gov/programs/digest/d07/tables/ dt07258.asp.

Wood, R., Corcoran, M., & Courant, P. (July 1993). *Pay differences among the highly paid: the male-female earnings gap in lawyers' salaries. Journal of Labor Economics, 11,* No. 3, pp. 417–441.

Diversity on the Web

Because of the issues facing women in organizations today, many women are choosing to start their own businesses. In 1972, women owned less than 5% of all U.S. businesses. Today there are 10.1 million female owned businesses that employ 13 million people and generate $1.9 trillion dollars in sales.

Visit the Web site of the Center for Women in Enterprise. Why was this organization founded and what does it do that relates to some of the issues explained in this article? http://www.cweonline.org

Deborah L. Larsen is a Senior Vice-President of Commercial Banking at Unibank. In this position she is a member of the senior management team and is responsible for the commercial loan division.

THE PARADOX OF MALE PRIVILEGE

Steven D. Farough
Assumption College

GOALS

- To explain why men both benefit and lose by investing in dominant masculinity
- To explain why men continue to maintain advantages in a society that is supposed to be open equally to both men and women
- To think about how men could change to better promote gender equality both in work and home life and still find a viable sense of manhood to construct a sense of masculinity

How can it be that men continue to have such economic success in an era where more women now graduate from college and have substantial achievements in the business world? How can men maintain their advantages at a time when women appear to be outpacing them, yet they ultimately lose from a system that has allowed them to win unparalleled wealth, power, and prestige? Despite their continued success, men wind up with a shorter life span and a higher rate of depression than women. In short, there is a *paradox of male privilege.* Paradoxes are confusing because they leave people baffled at the appearance of two seemingly irreconcilable trends. While "men are privileged; men are victims, too!" When one understands the underlying logic of this paradox however, it can lead to greater insight and to new ways of living our lives as men and women.

Being caught between advantages and disadvantages often leaves men unsure what to think. Although less pervasive than it once was, there still is some expectation that men should be the primary breadwinners for their families, make more money than their wives and climb the occupational ladder. On the other hand, women continue to succeed in high-powered jobs that challenge the belief that men should be the primary income earner. For some men, it may feel like the tables have finally tipped in favor of women. In the recent recession, men have been hit harder than women in the workplace, losing almost 75% of all jobs lost since 2007 (Cauchon, 2009).

This trend motivated Reihan Salam (2009) to call the economic downturn a "he-cession," and make the bold proclamation that we are now going through a shift in gender relations where men will no longer dominate the U.S. economy in the 21st century. As Salam (2009) points out, the greatest areas of job loss in the recession are in finance and home construction, two occupations where men have been dominant. However, characteristics such as risk and overconfidence are keys to driving the success and massive failure of Wall Street and the housing bubble—and these attributes are deeply embedded in the identity of masculinity. Risk and overconfidence have sent the economy into the worst recession since the Great Depression. Many now look back at the brazen use of sub-prime mortgages and seemingly endless leveraging by brokers and financiers with contempt. Have the implicit macho values of risk and overconfidence left men in the dust as our economy continues to trend toward a more feminized service economy and a more carefully regulated system? Sometimes, the answer is yes.

Women are just as capable as men of taking risks and being overconfident, but such practices are so strongly associated with masculinity that they create the impression that these are things that only men do. If both men and women can engage in such behaviors, then why are these behaviors so strongly linked to men in the work world? The answer to this question lies in how gender impacts our occupational structure.

DOMINANT MASCULINITY

Although in every culture there are a variety of ways one can be a man, some forms of manhood are perceived as more legitimate or "real" than others. Sociologists who study masculinity would argue that culturally legitimate forms of masculinity should be seen as **dominant masculinity**, a gender identity that allows those men who abide by its behaviors to have greater access to power and wealth. In the United States, dominant masculinity is defined by the ability to excel at competition and risk, be self-assured, withhold emotions, possess physical strength, have control over situations, be the breadwinners of families, and not act feminine or be gay (Kimmel, 2006; Messner, 1997; Connell, 1995). Embedded in all of these characteristics lies the expectation that in the U.S., masculinity needs to be consistently proven, which is rooted in the competitive, capitalist ethos and frontier mentality of the nation in the 18th and 19th centuries (Kimmel, 2006). Manhood was deemed successful in the U.S. when men could master tough terrain and accumulate wealth. Anything less than that left men grasping for this masculine ideal. Of course, the idealization of American masculinity in this nascent country was only for white men. African American men were either enslaved or oppressed through Jim Crow segregation; Native American men were killed or placed into reservations and many Mexican American and Asian American men were segregated into menial labor.

Particularly striking is how the history of a competitative, frontier-based masculinity persists even today. Indeed, it correlates strongly with some of the key strategies for success in American business: competition, risk, confidence, and withholding of emotions are all practices that are valued in the workplace. The outcome of this widespread use of masculinity results in the gendering of work, where the key jobs and strategies for success are deeply linked to manhood and male values (Hochshield, 2003; Pierce, 1995; U.S. Department of Labor, 2006). For instance, to achieve financial and professional success, lawyers are expected to be intimidating and aggressive (Pierce, 1995). Bill collectors are expected to deflate the status of truant clients through intimidation (Hochshield, 2003). Car salesmen are supposed to use their wits to get customers to purchase automobiles at higher prices. Stockbrokers' confident and assertive sales pitches are designed to hide the reality of substantial risk to clients. All of these are imbued with a culture of dominant masculinity that has provided untold wealth, power, and prestige for men as a group, and it is clearly woven into their identities. Men prove their masculinity by acting competitively and forcefully in the business world just as they did on the frontier and in times of industrial development.

In defining masculinity so strongly with work, this cultural norm creates an environment that is hostile to women entering the workplace. In the U.S., masculinity is defined in strict opposition to femininity. The growth of the industrial economy and the development of the frontier organized the ideal family structure in a new way. Prior to industrialization, the U.S. economy was largely agricultural, where both men and women were involved in economic production. As industrialization emerged, economic production left the family farm for the factory, and masculinity persisted. Men were expected to work outside the home while women were expected to work within it (Coontz, 1992). The net result is a cultural definition of manhood that links it to work, and views women's progress as an attack against masculinity itself. Although the anti-women attitude is changing and many individual men are not threatened by the progress made by women, this ideology of dominant American manhood creates a situation where men continue to receive both economic and psychological advantages. Dominant masculinity may be a stereotype, but it is a very powerful one perpetuated in the history of American manhood.

PRIVILEGES OF DOMINANT MASCULINITY

The recent success of women in education and the economy has not prevented men—particularly white men—from maintaining disproportionate access to power and resources. Men continue to earn more than women, whether they have a high school diploma or graduate degree (U.S. Department of Labor, 2007). Also, men are overrepresented in the decision-making processes of business and government. Men currently constitute over 75 percent of chief executives (CEOs), 70 percent of surgeons, and 73 percent of computer and math positions (U.S. Department of Labor, 2006). The same holds true with elected officials. In 2008, 84% of Congressmen were men and almost 77 percent of state legislators were men (Center for American Women and Politics, 2008). The data clearly demonstrate that men continue to be disproportionately represented in key positions of power. Still, these data tell us nothing about *why* men are overrepresented in high-ranking positions.

Upon closer examination of these generalized patterns, the data unequivocally demonstrate that men, especially white men, possess a whole set of advantages over equally qualified white women and people of color. Research shows that people envision successful mangers as men (Willemsen, 2002), men experience greater upward mobility than women (Glass Ceiling Commission, 1995), men have greater access to and control over networks for employment, and they also have better access to mentoring relationships (Lorber, 1994). Federal government data show that white men are the least likely to experience discrimination in the workplace (Reskin, 1998). Women now earn the majority of bachelor's degrees, yet men continue to earn more after graduation in part because of this continued discrimination.

The inequality in earnings of men and women also has to do with the structure of the American family and sex segregation in the workplace (Cohen, 2004; Cohen & Huffman, 2004; Rhode, 1997). Although changing, family gender roles continue to place men in positions as the primary income earners and women continue to be forced into work more compatible with family life (Cohen, 2004; Rhode, 1997). This gender role assignment contributes to gender segregation of the workforce. In more "family friendly" occupations such as elementary education, nursing, and secretarial work, women constitute over 80 percent of the workforce (U.S. Department of Labor, 2006). Men are clustered into high status jobs and women into lower status occupations.

Women have made significant inroads into the work world, but they still experience the glass ceiling. This results in greater difficulty in gaining access to higher paying jobs dominated by men (Glass Ceiling Commission, 1995). In male-dominated occupations, women are more apt to experience sexual harassment (Andersen, 2006). It is more difficult for women to move up into higher positions due to a lack of network contacts, and/or fewer mentoring relationships (Lorber, 1994; Pierce, 1995). Women can face the "**mommy track**," the practice of not hiring or promoting women during their childbearing years (Stone, 2007; Lorber, 1994). Even in women-dominated occupations such as teaching, social work, and library sciences, men often have the better paying administrative jobs (Williams, 2004).

In addition to the glass ceiling problem, women continue to be the primary caregivers of children, making it more difficult for women to move up the occupational ladder than men (Stone, 2007). With the passage of the 1993 Family and Medical Leave Act (see below), ironically, more men than women are capable of taking advantage of this legislation because they are more often in full-time positions. Still, only one to seven percent of eligible men take advantage of the legislation (Rhode, 1997).

Points of Law

The Family and Medical Leave Act of 1993 (FMLA) ensures anyone who works for private employers with fifty or more employees and any employee of a federal, state, or local agency be allotted twelve workweeks of unpaid leave for one or more of the following reasons:

- birth of a newborn child of the employee
- adoption of a child or foster care work by the employee
- care for a spouse, child, or parent with a serious health condition
- medical leave for a serious health condition
- situations arising out of the employee's spouse, child or parent who is on active military duty or in the National Guard or Reserves

To qualify for the FMLA, an employee must have worked for the employer twelve months and worked 1,250 hours. Upon completion of the twelve weeks of leave, an employee is also entitled to the same job or a job that is equivalent in pay, benefits and other conditions of employment.

http://www.dol.gov/whd/regs/compliance/whdfs28.pdf

Some might argue that men and women freely choose family roles and occupations. However, the choices men and women make are the *result* of gender inequality, not a *cause*. Despite the significant gains by women over the past thirty years, discriminatory practices and structural constraints limit their chances for upward mobility and occupational choice. Such data fly in the face of Affirmative Action critics who claim white men are the "new minority" and experience "reverse discrimination." Even though there is variation in terms of race, class, and sexuality, when it comes to access to power and resources, white men continue to do very well compared to women. They are not the "new minority" and experiences of reverse discrimination are extraordinarily rare, although highly publicized (Reskin, 1998).

The economic downturn has yet to alter the gendered patterns of the economy and family structure. In a world where masculinity is so strongly associated with work, one should not assume that men would want to give up these advantages. This is not because all men are power hungry; it is because masculine identity is so strongly connected to work and so opposite to femininity. Although the machismo of dominant masculinity clearly has its shortcomings, dominant masculinity is something familiar to men and has provided many a sense of connection to something larger than themselves. To break up this paradox that surrounds manhood, a case must be made for men stepping away from something that feels like a fundamental part of their identity and a viable alternative offered.

NEGATIVE CONSEQUENCES OF DOMINANT MASCULINITY

Some men might ask themselves why on earth they would want to give up such a wide range of advantages? These structural benefits are no doubt seductive to many men, but they come with a range of negative consequences. Public health data clearly show some of the problems. The average life span for men is 71.3 years, but for women it is 78.3 years (Sabo, 2004). Men are more likely to develop heart disease, have accidents, and be victims of violent crime and homicide than women (Sabo, 2004). There are multiple reasons for these differences, but one key factor is the investment in dominant masculinity. Men who buy into it must engage in elaborate techniques of withholding their feelings and engage in behavior that puts them at greater physical risk (Sabo, 2004). To be a "man" is to deny physical pain, which can result in a failure to notify doctors of potentially life-threatening ailments. If one desires to be a "real man," one should be prepared for an early death. Men who withhold their feelings suffer psychologically, experience higher rates of depression and suicide than women and have more emotionally shallow relationships with families and friends (Sabo, 2004).

Men who do not fit into dominant masculinity also suffer. Often denied access to living wages or control over their environment, working class men, men of color, and gay men may not fit fully into dominant masculinity, leaving them subject to critiques of their self-worth. Dominant masculinity works as the underlying rationale for men bullying other men who do not conform to this norm. Such harassment leaves significant numbers of men marginalized from, and scarred by, a dominant masculinity, that is often white, middle class, and straight. Dominant masculinity makes it more difficult to have a variety of legitimate masculinities in our society. Because dominant masculinity is defined as being superior to femininity (Connell, 1995), men who invest in it can suffer from being unable to have more egalitarian and emotionally open relationships with women. It also can result in creating discriminatory work environments.

Dominant masculinity can even undermine democracy. Because men receive unearned advantages for being men in the workplace and in political life, it is more difficult for equally qualified women and people of color to be rewarded for their hard work. Clearly, dominant masculinity has negative consequences, leaving men with shorter lives, higher rates of physical ailments, less emotionally fulfilling experiences, and contributes to the undermining of democratic principles. Greater access to power and resources may seem attractive, but when compared with the negative consequences, dominant masculinity becomes more problematic and less desirable.

TOWARD DEMOCRATIC MANHOOD

Although it might be intellectually rational for men to give up their privileges, it may not feel right on an emotional level. Dominant masculinity is not just an abstract concept and its privileges are not merely vague, structural advantages; masculinity is also personal because it gives many men a sense of self-worth and connects them to something larger than themselves. It provides men with a moral bearing and a sense of purpose. Without an alternative to dominant masculinity, change will continue to be met with resistance. However, the culturally viable options to dominant masculinity that exist in our culture lie somewhere between the nonexistent and clichés.

Casual analysis of the alternatives in American culture often leaves many men uncomfortable with what they see. Images of "sensitive New Age guys," "metrosexuals," and "girly men" are peppered across the mass media landscape. These images evoke silly men who are overly concerned with their appearance and themselves in general. Think of the 1990s men's movements and events such as Robert Bly's mythopoetic men, the Million Man March, or the Promise Keepers. In this these groups and movements, men headed to all-male retreats in the deep woods, marched on Washington, and filled football stadiums where they bonded, searched for some primal inner male essence, evoked essentialist gender differences, cried, and professed their commitment to becoming better men who are different from women (Messner, 1997). However, these groups were either too focused on finding some inner male essence or taking back "their" families in the context of patriarchal marriage. The combination of self-absorption and exclusive male bonding did little to realign men in a more democratic trajectory with women (Messner, 1997).

What is more, these images of men likely make many people think of men who are overly emotional, undesirable, self-absorbed, and effete. Whereas men were once too macho, they are now seen as too sensitive and self-involved. Although being in touch with feelings can be psychologically healthy, it does little to address the structural inequities that exist between men and women. It also does little to address some of the good parts of dominant masculinity, such as a public commitment to service and sacrifice. The alternative forms of manhood sent men inward to address their feelings instead of maintaining some kind of useful connection to the public sphere. Alternative manhood also did little to create an egalitarian space with women and those men marginalized by dominant masculinity. From a macho point of view, men like these "new men" are wimps, and from the point of view of feminism, these "new men" are reacting negatively to the gains of women.

Where do men find a gender identity if all that appears is polar opposites? A good starting point lies in democratic manhood. The perspective of **democratic manhood** envisions

> . . . Men who are secure enough in their convictions to recognize a mistake, courageous enough to be compassionate, fiercely egalitarian, powerful enough to empower others, strong enough to acknowledge that real strength comes from holding others up rather than pushing them down . . . (Kimmel, 2006, p. 55).

Democratic manhood addresses both the psychological and structural privileges of men and envisions men who are emotionally engaged and yet strong, who are self-reliant but still connected to the community, and who see women as equal partners. In this milieu, masculinity is something men have, but it is not defined in strict opposition to femininity and being gay. Nor does masculinity have to be constantly proven. Under democratic manhood, men are men, period.

In democratic manhood, men are partners who work with women to make the world a better place; which means being flexible about the roles and tasks men and women take in the world of work and family. In a sense, democratic manhood asks men to be more secure about being men. From this perspective, manhood is re-centered from rigid gender roles to a more flexible definition that clearly focuses itself both at work and at home.

This more flexible and democratic form of manhood will also help to resolve this paradoxical anxiety that some men feel in their gender order. Men who feel threatened by women's success in the labor market may see it as a threat to their manhood. From this perspective, men are hard-wired to be the breadwinners. However, when men look upon gender relations over the past forty years, they see clear gains by women. In the back of men's heads, they might privately wonder how women can be so successful in the work world when it is supposed to be only for men. This female success comes while there are clearly still notable disadvantages for women moving up the occupational ladder. If men believe that they are genetically suited for the business world, then they will be unable to resolve the contradictory reality that men are privileged as a group and yet women are gaining fast. Men will be unable to overcome the reality that the privileges of masculinity come at the expense of a fuller human experience.

Democratic manhood breaks through this impasse by realizing that masculinity and gender are largely social constructions, i.e., humanly-created cultural norms that are changeable. Manhood changes along with history and varies across cultures. If masculinity is not a fixed, immutable thing, but something that is changeable, then it can be altered for the greater good. Democratic manhood's foundation would be centered around egalitarianism and empowerment. The locus of manliness can move from aggression and control to aggressively working toward equality. Such a shift means focusing on strategies and social policy designed to eliminate the glass ceiling, concentrating on how unequal family obligations lead to gender inequality, and recognizing that occupations are unfairly sex segregated. Democratic manhood is outwardly public in its orientation, but it correlates well with traditional masculine virtues like strength, responsibility and taking care of one's family. Instead of following the logic of strict gender role differences and the belief that men are more suited for work than women, democratic manhood asks men to envision being strong, independent providers through the rubric of egalitarianism.

At work, men who embody democratic manhood would see women as colleagues who have the potential to make the workplace better. Men would not look at women as impediments to other men who want to provide for their families, but as partners who work not just to maximize profits but to create a better work climate where people get promoted for merit. Because manhood is not defined in strict opposition to anything feminine, democratic manhood would also free up men to feel comfortable with employment that allows men to be with their families more and even put work-life balance goals above career goals.

Despite all the rhetoric about male self-reliance under dominant masculinity, men rely heavily on women to take care of them. In marriage, men have and continue to expect their wives to cook, clean, take care of their children, and massage their egos. This reliance on women allows men to go out into the workforce unencumbered by the significant challenges that are required to take care of a family. In turn, the over-reliance on women to take care of families makes it more challenging for women. The egalitarian aspect of democratic manhood frees up men to take care of themselves and their families while still bringing home a paycheck. If men embrace the idea that families should be equal partnerships, it will free up both men and women to pursue their desired careers, lessen the stereotyping of working-women being a liability due to child-care commitments, and allow both men and women to share in both the joys and challenges of family life.

Clearly, the case for democratic manhood sketched out here only scratches the surface. The move toward democratic manhood is already happening; more men are wary of the downside of the traditional breadwinner role with long hours because they know it keeps them away from their families, and fathers today are far more involved with their children than in the past (Coltrane, 1996; Gersen, 2002). In order for there to be true equality in the workforce between men and women, a transformation of the relationship between work and family life must occur and this means that men must work against a social system that has benefited them for so long. Men do not need to give up sports or hanging out with the guys, but men do not have to define themselves in opposition to women either. They need to become real men who take pride in gender equity. Democratic manhood holds that promise. What kind of man do you want to be?

DISCUSSION QUESTIONS

1. How do the key characteristics of dominant masculinity privilege men? How do these characteristics hurt men?

2. What other characteristics could be included in dominant masculinity?

3. If dominant masculinity is defined through such characteristics as physical strength, competition, control, and emotional distance, what does this say about femininity?

4. How does democratic manhood encourage men and women to work together against sexism?

5. How viable is democratic manhood as a starting point in helping men and women work together to overcome sexism?

6. If the structure of the traditional family contributes to gender inequality, what can American businesses do so that women have the same chances for upward mobility as men?

7. How could democratic manhood be implemented in American businesses?

8. What can be done to reduce the glass ceiling in American business?

Writing Assignment

A research study conducted by the National Coalition to Protect Family Leave revealed that females are more than twice as likely (21%) to take a FMLA leave than male employees (10%). While some would say this is to be expected because women are still the primary care givers of children and the elderly, this article suggests additional factors may be operating within society and the workplace that discourage men from applying for these leaves.

1. How might dominant masculinity also be a factor in fewer men than women applying for FMLA leaves?

2. If more people and organizations were to think in terms of the feminist sociological perspective discussed in this article, what could be the personal benefits to taking FMLA leaves for men and their families?

3. Research family leave policies/laws in another country and compare and contrast the foreign plan with the FMLA.

4. What conclusion(s) can you draw from this research?

Bibliography

Andersen, M. (2006). *Thinking about women: Sociological perspectives on sex and gender.* 7th edition. Boston: Allyn & Bacon.

Cauchon, D. (2009). "Women gain in historic job shift." *USA Today.* September 3. p. 1A

Center for American Women and Politics (2008). *Women in elective office 2008.*

Cohen, Phillip N. 2004. "The gender division of abor: 'Keeping house' and occupational segregation in the United States." *Gender and Society* 18.2: 239–252.

Cohen, P., Huffman, M. 2004. "Occupational Segregation and the Gender Gap in Workplace Authority: National versus Local Labor Markets." *Sociological Fourm* 19.1: 121–147.

Coltrane, S. (1996). *Family man: fatherhood, housework, and gender equity.* New York: Oxford University Press.

Coontz, S. (1992). *The way we never were: American families and the nostalgia trap.* NY: Basic Books.

Connell, R.W. (1995). *Masculinities.* Berkeley: University of California Press.

Gersen, K. (2002). "Moral dilemmas, moral strategies and the transformation of gender: Lesson from two generations of work and family change." *Gender & Society.* 16 (February): 8–28.

Glass Ceiling Commission. (1995). *Good for business: Making full use of the nation's human capital.* Washington, D.C.: U.S. Government Printing Office.

Hochshield, A. (2003). *The managed heart: commercialization of human feelings.* 2nd edition. Berkeley: University of California Press.

Kimmel, M. (2006). *Manhood in America: A cultural history.* 2nd ed. New York: Oxford University Press.

Lorber, J. (1994). *The paradoxes of gender.* New Haven, CT: Yale University Press.

Marx, K. (1999/1852). "The eighteenth Brumaire of Louis Bonaparte," In Lemert, C. (Ed.) *Social theory: The multicultural & classic readings.* pp. 41–49. Westview Press.

Messner, M. (1997). *Politics of masculinities: Men in movements.* Thousand Oaks, CA: Sage Publications, Inc.

Pierce, J. (1995). *Gender trails.* Berkeley: University of California Press.

Reskin, B. (1998). *The realities of affirmative action.* Washington, D.C.: American Sociological Association.

Rhode, D. (1997). *Speaking of sex: The denial of gender inequality.* Cambridge, MA: Harvard University Press.

Sabo, D. (2004). "Masculinities and men's health: Moving toward post-superman era prevention." In Kimmel, M. (ed.) *The gendered society reader.* pp. 327–343. New York: Oxford University Press.

Salam, R. (2009). "The death of macho." *Foreign Policy.* (July/August).

Stone, P. 2007. *Opting out? Why women really quite careers and head home.* Berkeley: University of California Press.

U.S. Department of Labor. (2006). *Current population survey.* Table 10 & 11. pp. 25–34. Washington, D.C.: U.S. Department of Labor.

U.S. Department of Labor. (2007). "TED: The editor's desk." October 19, 2007. Washington, D.C.: U.S. Department of Labor.

Willemsen, T. (2002). "Gender typing of the successful manager: A stereotype reconsidered." *Sex Roles.* 46 (June): 385–391.

Williams, C. (2004). "The glass escalator: Hidden advantages for men in the 'female' professions" In Kimmel, M., & Messner, M. (Eds.) *Men's lives.* 6th edition. Boston: Allyn & Bacon.

Diversity on the Web

From the 1973 to today, there have been a variety of men's movements, some attempting to reaffirm traditional gender roles; others to overcome male privilege and sexism.

Using the links below, research the principles or worldview of Robert Bly's Mythopoetic Men's Movement, the Promise Keepers, and the National Organization for Men Against sexism.

Write a two to three page paper:

a. highlighting the core values of each group,
b. explaining why these groups were founded in the historical context of their time and
c. explaining which group or groups' beliefs would support democratic manhood.

Starting Sources

- http://boston.com/news/globe/ideas/aricles/2005/06/19/daddy_what_did_you_do_in_the_mensmove.html (Zakrewski, P. (2005, June 19) *The Boston Globe*
- http://www.menstuff.org/pov/povs/mensmove.html
- http://stason.org [click "search" on left column, type in "28.17"]

Robert Bly's Mythopoetic Men's Movement

- http://www.xyonline.net/conent/wildmen

The Promise Keepers

- http://www.promisekeepers.org/about
- http://www.now.org/issues/right/pk.html

National Organization for Men Against Sexism

- http://www.nomas.org

Historical Overview of Men's Movements

- http://www.australianhumanitiesreview.org/archive/Issue-Dec-1996/Connell.html

Steven D. Farough is Associate Professor of Sociology and a member of the Women's Studies program at Assumption College. His research focuses on race, gender, identity formation, privilege, and stay-at-home fathers.

Are We Equal Yet? Making Sense of Lesbian, Gay, Bisexual, and Transgender Issues in the Workplace

Gerald Hunt
Ryerson University, Toronto, Canada

GOALS

- To understand the legal, social, and political situation for lesbian, gay, bisexual, and transgender (LGBT) persons
- To explore the nature of opposition to LGBT equality in general, and in the workplace in particular
- To illustrate the initiatives employers take to accommodate LGBT minorities

Many American cities have an annual lesbian, gay, bisexual, transgender (LGBT) Pride event. St. Petersburg, Florida is no exception: "St. Pete Pride," as it is called, is held at the end of June, beginning with a parade down Central Avenue at 10 am, followed by a day-long street festival with food, music, and dancing in the street. At the 2009 Pride, the newspaper estimated a crowd of over 80,000, including thousands of heterosexuals, participated in the event. Noticeable by their presence were a number of people with banners proclaiming the alleged evils and dangers of the "homosexual lifestyle," along with several church delegations suggesting damnation for this minority was around the corner. Equally noticeable by his absence was the mayor the city. Even though Pride generated a much needed economic boost to the city, the mayor refused to endorse, recognize or attend the event, just as he had done in the past. Earlier in the year, controversy had erupted at the city hall about whether banners highlighting "gay pride week" would be allowed to adorn street lamps in the area, and a newspaper blog about the event unleashed a torrent of anti-gay anger.

The positive and negative exchanges that occurred in relation to St. Pete Pride illustrate some of the contradictions and mixed messages that continue to surround lesbians, gays, bisexuals, and the transgendered in America. St. Pete's has a significant LGBT population, including many retired people from other states. Overall, it tends to have a live-and-let-live attitude appropriate to its huge reliance on tourism. Its neighbor city, Tampa, has in the last few years marketed itself as a "gay" destination and some of this marketing also benefits St. Pete's since the best beaches are on its side of Tampa bay. At the same time, there is an easily exposed degree of hostility and anger towards LGBT people by some segments of the population that can be quite explosive and disturbing.

In its own way, St. Pete's is a microcosm of America. On one hand, throughout the country there are many signs of acceptance with important and supportive shifts in the legal and in public opinion sectors. LGBT characters have become a common and accepted part of mainstream television programs and Hollywood films. More and more Americans consider discrimination against this group in the same league as discrimination against any other minority. On December 22, 2010, President Obama signed the legislation ending the "don't ask, don't tell" policy for gays and lesbians in the United States military.

In a few jurisdictions, same-sex marriage is possible. More and more organizations fully embrace issues related to sexual and gender diversity, and have removed as many discriminatory policies and procedures as possible.

On the other hand, many institutions continue to discriminate openly and many individuals continue to hold extremely negative or hateful attitudes towards the LGBT minority population. It is still legally possible to discriminate based on sexual orientation in 29 states, and gender identity in 38 states. Throughout much of the country antigay bias remains in law, housing, and the media. Some churches and media pundits are very vocal in their opposition, declaring homosexuals to be "sick" and "perverse," and not worthy of support of any kind. The American Boy Scouts legally exclude gay men from their midst. Unfortunately, in some situations, discrimination and hate escalate to bashing and even murder. To the casual observer, it is confusing. Are LGBT minorities equal to other Americans? Are organizations legally and/or morally required to accommodate sexual and gender identity diversity? Is it still okay to discriminate against this minority group?

LGBT: WHO ARE THEY AND WHAT DO THEY WANT?

Lesbian and gay people are sexually and emotionally attracted to people of the same sex. Bisexuals are attracted to both sexes, but may function primarily as homosexuals or heterosexuals at different points in their life. Transgenderism is an umbrella term referring to a person who does not conform to traditional gender norms. It includes those who are inter-sexed (people whose biological sex does not conform to either male or female), and people who live substantial portions of lives as other than their birth gender. This minority often challenges gender roles related to dress codes, use of cosmetics, and "normal" gender appropriate behavior. Some people in this group feel so deeply drawn to the gender opposite to their birth sex that they undergo surgical procedures to change their status. Transgender issues are often grouped under the term "gender identity." LGBT people come from all racial, religious, class, and ethnic backgrounds. As a group, LGBT people can be thought of as "sexual minorities." Some LGBT use the term "queer," an appropriation of what historically has been a derogatory term. It would be inappropriate for those outside of the LGBT identity structure to use the term queer.

Estimates of the LGBT population vary. In the late 1940s, in his pioneering work on human sexuality, Kinsey (1948) found upwards of 10 percent of the American population to be engaged in homosexual activity. Recent studies report 5–6 percent of the population to be predominately homosexual, identifying exclusively as gay or lesbian. This percentage rises to as high as 13–15 percent when bisexuals and transgendered people are included (Bagley and Tremblay, 1998). These figures mean that the LGBT population may be larger than the number of Asian Americans (estimated at 3.6 percent) and greater than the number of Jewish people living in the United States (estimated at 3 percent).

Unlike most minority groups however, LGBT people are not always readily visible. Many have chosen to remain invisible, especially at work, because they fear the negative consequences that might result from revealing their identity. As the murder of Matthew Sheppard illustrated, being openly and visibly gay can still cost you your life. Matthew was an openly gay 21-year-old student at the University of Wyoming who was savagely murdered to make the point that homo-sexuals deserve to die. Throughout history there are many examples of organizations harassing and dismissing employees when they learned, or just suspected, that they were homosexual.

In recent years, more and more LGBT people have come-out (revealed their sexuality). They have done this in order to declare their right to be who they are publically, and to fight for equal rights. They find living in the closet too demeaning a price to pay for "protection" from dis-crimination. As a result, equality for LGBT people is now an issue of concern and an important rallying point for all people (straight and gay) who are concerned about equity in society gener-ally and at work in particular.

Spokespersons for this group offer a clear message: the gay, lesbian, bisexual, transgender community is discriminated against and treated inequitably at work. Change is demanded in human resources policies and practices concerned with recruiting, hiring, promotion, discipline, and benefits. Activists call for organizational leaders to foster and promote an environment that is positive and supportive of all human difference and diversity. These demands closely parallel those made by women and Afro-Americans, and reflect the fact that the LGBT movement has caught up with other human rights movements. All of these minority groups come together in desiring equal treatment, not special or exceptional treatment, and they want the social and insti-tutional barriers that prevent them from gaining full equality eradicated.

The overwhelming difference between sexual minorities and other minority groups is that for some people sexual diversity is more controversial. Homosexuality and gender nonconformity make some people extremely uncomfortable and/or angry. Some conservative thinkers portray the LGBT minority as immoral and degenerate. Others feel that homosexuality is a "private" issue and should not be exposed in the public domain, even though heterosexuality is never reduced to being merely a bedroom activity. Some, guided by Christian teachings, quote from the Bible to defend their views (Leviticus 18:22 states that homosexuality is an abomination). These people fail to note that Leviticus 10:10 also indicates that eating shellfish is an abomination and that Exodus 35:2 clearly states that a neighbor who insists on working on the Sabbath should be put to death.

The polarization around homosexuality creates some work situations characterized by a lack of consensus regarding the merit of appeals for equal treatment and justice made by the LGBT community. This results in a range of organizational responses. Some organizations make extensive efforts to ensure that policies and benefits are equal for everyone and value their LGBT employees equally with other workers. Other organizations show little if any accommodation with a few employers going so far as to dismiss these minorities if their identity becomes known.

SOCIAL, LEGAL AND ECONOMIC DEVELOPMENTS

In spite of controversies and differing perspectives, more and more LGBT people are open about their identities and vocal about their desire for change. This, when combined with a changing social, legal, and economic environment, has convinced more and more organizations to rethink and overhaul policies and practices in order to be inclusive of their LGBT employees.

Social Forces

Public opinion polls show a steadily increasing tolerance toward homosexuals in general, and their workplace rights in particular. Wilcox and Wolpert (2000), in a summary of polling data from throughout the 1990s, found attitudes moving in a positive direction since 1992. Yang (1999) reports that by 1998 a majority of Americans supported the idea of gays and lesbians having equal-ity in employment (84%), housing (81%), inheritance rights (62%), social security benefits (57%), and the military (66%). Since then, public opinion has shifted steadily toward increased acceptance. Gallup polls in 2008 and 2009 found that 89% of Americans believed gays and lesbians should have equal rights in job opportunities, 76% thought homosexuals should be allowed in the armed forces, and 62% believed they should be hired as high school teachers (Gallup, 2009). Public opinion data also point to a large generational divide, with younger people tending to be much more favorable toward gay rights than older Americans. In other words, while there may not be widespread public involvement in the fight for LGBT rights, and some people continue to be extremely vocal in their opposition, there is no basis for believing that the majority of citizens in the United States support either overt or covert discrimination in the workplace on the basis of sexual orientation.

Legal Change

The increased visibility of LGBT people, combined with more assertive demands for equal rights, generates considerable legal action. In recent years, federal, state, and municipal legislators debated changes in legislation affecting LGBT minorities in almost every aspect of their lives, including violence and harassment, employment and housing discrimination, adoption and child care, domestic partner benefits, and the freedom to marry. In some jurisdictions, the legal changes are wide-spread; in others there has been little or no change; and in other situations, progressive change has subsequently been overturned.

At one time, all states had laws regulating and criminalizing consensual sexual activity between adults of the same sex. The beginning of 2003 found "sodomy" laws still on the books in 13 states. However, in a landmark case in June 2003, the Supreme Court struck down the sodomy law in Texas, effectively eliminating discriminatory sodomy laws throughout the country.

Governments at all levels have now passed bills to include sexual orientation as a protected class, particularly in employment and housing. As of 2010, twenty-one states, along with the District of Columbia, prohibit discrimination based on sexual orientation (California, Colorado, Connecticut, Delaware, Hawaii, Illinois, Iowa, Maine, Maryland, Massachusetts, Minnesota, Nevada, New Hampshire, New Jersey, New Mexico, New York, Oregon, Rhode Island, Vermont, Washington, and Wisconsin). Of this group, twelve states and the District of Columbia *also* prohibit discrimination based on gender identity (California, Colorado, Illinois, Iowa, Maine, Minnesota, New Jersey, New Mexico, Oregon, Rhode Island, Vermont, and Washington). In addition, many cities such as Boulder, Atlanta, Dallas, and Houston prohibit employment discrimination based on gender identity (HRC, 2009a).

In December 1999, Vermont made history by becoming the first American jurisdiction to formalize same-sex, civil unions. As a result, for the first time in American history, lesbians and gays who entered civil unions automatically became eligible to receive the same protections and benefits that Vermont provided to heterosexual, married couples. Since then, a growing list of states offer same-sex couples the possibility of civil unions, and a few have marriage equality. As of 2010, six states issue marriage licenses to same-sex couples (Connecticut, Iowa, Maine, Massachusetts, New Hampshire, and Vermont). In addition, New York and D. C. recognize marriages by same-sex couples that occur in other jurisdictions. Five additional states, as well as D. C., legally provide the equivalent of state-level spousal rights to gay and lesbian couples.

Economic Forces

The LGBT community represents an important market segment and a group with considerable clout if it decides to boycott a product, service, or organization. Badgett (2000) argues that gays and lesbians are not as affluent as many believe, and on average earn no more than heterosexuals.

However, this is a group (especially gay men) that is less likely to have children, probably making discretionary income levels higher than average, and spending with more political sensitivity than most other groups. Buford (2000) points out that advertising for these so called "gay dollars" in the media generally and the "gay media" in particular, is big business. Like Badgett, he argues that what matters about this group from a marketing point of view, is not affluence, but slightly higher discretionary income, combined with more free time and desire to patronize and support LGBT-positive companies.

Activists can also affect the bottom line of anti-LGBT corporations in a variety of ways. They wage proxy contests against homophobic companies, urge public institutions to buy the shares of companies that prohibit antigay discrimination and to sell the shares of companies that do not. (See Cracker Barrel case.) In the early 1980s, the Coors organization went so far as to require lie detector tests to screen out prospective gay or lesbian employees. This prompted countrywide boycotts, leading to a significant reduction in the company's market share. Since then, Coors has taken steps to position itself as a more LGBT-positive company, even sponsoring gay Pride events.

Best Practices

Companies such as Starbucks and IKEA recognize the economic impact of sexual minorities in several ways. IKEA uses advertisements showing same-sex shoppers and runs ads in newspapers and magazines that appeal to LGBT audiences. Starbucks signals its support in the same way, and actively recruits from the LGBT talent pool. Many large cities hold an annual Pride Day, with events sponsored by high profile corporations, such as breweries and clothing manufacturers.

ORGANIZATIONAL RESPONSE

More and more organizations are responding positively to discrimination concerns raised by the LGBT community. State and local governments, colleges, and universities were among the first organizations to institute nondiscrimination policies and to offer benefits packages that include same-sex partners. In 1998, President Clinton signed an executive order banning discrimination based on sexual orientation throughout the federal civil service. Even though most of the federal government does not yet offer same-sex benefits, all cabinet-level departments and 24 independent agencies have non-discrimination policies. If the Employment Non-Discrimination Act currently before Congress moves forward, it will provide further protections against discrimination in the workplace based on sexual orientation and gender identity. Another bill currently before Congress, The Domestic Partnership Benefits and Obligations Act, would open the door to equal family benefit packages to all federal civilian employees, regardless of sexual orientation.

Increasing numbers of public and private organizations have adopted antidiscrimination policies and instituted domestic partner benefit packages inclusive of same-sex partners. According to one survey, fewer than 24 employers offered same-sex domestic partner benefits at the beginning of the 1990s, but this number rose to nearly 10,000 by the year 2007 and continues to grow (HRC, 2009a). One of the largest LGBT rights organizations (The Human Rights Campaign) reports that by 2009, 423 of the Fortune 500 companies had nondiscrimination policies that included sexual orientation and 176 also had anti-discrimination policies related to gender identity (HRC, 2009a). As a result, most of the well known brand names such as Ford, eBay, AT&T, Boeing, Home Depot, Walt Disney, McDonald's, Xerox, Gap, Nike, Verizon, and Starbucks, offer equal benefits to their LGBT and straight workforce.

CORPORATE EQUALITY INDEX

The Corporate Equality Index (CEI) is a set of standards and benchmarks established by the Human Rights Campaign Foundation Workplace Project to examine and evaluate corporate policies affecting LGBT employees throughout the country (HRC, 2009b). Among the items measured by the CEI are:

- Official recognition of a LGBT group
- Sexual orientation nondiscrimination policy
- Health and other benefits for domestic and same-sex partners
- Training aimed at increasing the understanding of sexual orientation and/or gender identity
- Coverage for domestic partner health insurance, transgender wellness benefits, and/or other domestic partner benefits, unrelated to health

Many companies now realize that a positive CEI score is a good idea. It often equates to a more inclusive work environment overall since it sends a strong message about valuing diversity in all its forms. The CEI is now in its seventh year, and in 2009, 260 businesses received the top rating of 100%, compared to 195 in 2008. This significant jump can be attributed to the double-digit increase of companies adhering to CEI criteria, and a domino effect, whereby an initial company institutes standards and others within the industry realize they need to catch up. Some of the well-known companies who scored 100% are Ford, Gap, Google, Shell, and US Airways (HRC, 2009b).

GENDER IDENTITY AND TRANSGENDER ISSUES

In recent years, workplace issues related to gender identity gained a much higher profile. The transgendered minority pose a number of unique issues in the workplace, ranging from restroom use to dress codes. The response to this minority and the issues they raise is often hostile, but some companies do go out of their way to accommodate. American Airlines, for example, was one the first organizations to expand its equal opportunities statement to include gender identity, with policies and guidelines specifically addressing transgendered issues. Employees must use restrooms appropriate to their current gender, but have the right to access different restrooms if they alter their gender identity. American's policy stipulates that that the attire of a transitioning employee should reflect the appropriate dress codes of the job they hold and the office where they work, underscoring that all employees are held to the same uniform appearance standards within their gender identity status. Recently, openly gay Congressman, Barney Frank, hired the first out transgender congressional aide.

BACKLASH: THE STING OF DISCRIMINATION CONTINUES

Not all people and organizations are committed to confronting sexual orientation discrimination. Some conservatives feel such gains have happened too quickly, gone too far, and represent a threat to their sense of identity and well being. The shifts in attitudes, policies, and legislation related to LGBT minorities, especially in relation to relationship recognition, have in fact become rallying points for uniting conservative thinkers. In 1996, Congress passed the "Defense of Marriage Act," which, among other things, defined marriage as between one man and one woman, and allowed states to refuse to honor same-sex marriages performed in another state. By 2009, twenty-nine jurisdictions had enacted constitutional amendments to define marriage as between a man and a woman, and eleven others had enacted statutory "defense of marriage" acts. Eleven states have laws that are amendments that go so far as to ban all forms of same-sex partner recognition, including marriage, civil unions, and domestic partnerships. Another interesting example of backlash happened in California, a state thought by many to be one of the most liberal in the union. In May 2008 the California Supreme Court struck down a ban on same-sex marriage. However, in a highly contested November 2008 referendum, voters overturned the ruling. As part of the publicity surrounding the events, people were reminded of the fact that it had taken a 1948 Supreme Court ruling to overturn a ban on interracial marriages in California, but in that case the ruling was allowed to stand.

A number of religious and conservative groups exist whose mission seems to be to defeat what they term "the gay agenda." The Web site of "Concerned Women for America," for instance, indicates the following: "many of the largest corporations in America have bought into the homosexual agenda. Americans should work to roll back these ill-advised policies" (reported in Knight, 2009). Other groups such as Focus on the Family, and the American Family Association, also launch major attacks on gains made by LGBT minorities in general, and in the workplace in particular, using vitriolic and often hateful language to cast aspersions on their radio and TV programs that attract audiences in the millions.

Some corporations steadfastly refuse to alter their human resources policies and practices to accommodate LGBT minorities with others even rescinding such protections and benefits after mergers and changes in ownership. ExxonMobil is a good example. Prior to the merger of Mobile Oil and Exxon, Mobile had a nondiscrimination policy and offered domestic partner benefits, whereas Exxon did not. After the merger, policy became one of allowing same-sex partners of former Mobile employees to continue receiving benefits, but excluding former employees of Exxon or new employees of ExxonMobile from the same perks. As a result, ExxonMobile has the odd distinction of being the only company on the Fortune 500 not to include sexual orientation in its nondiscrimination language.

Another organization fighting to retain homophobic policies is the Boy Scouts of America. After a prolonged court battle, the Supreme Court ruled in July 2000 that the Boy Scouts could maintain a policy excluding gay men from joining the organization. Several organizations, such as Levi Strauss and the United Way, discontinued contributions to the Boy Scouts as a form of protest, and several churches, such as the United Methodists, have condemned the policy, but the Boy Scouts remain adamant. In contrast, the Girl Scouts has reaffirmed its inclusive nondiscrimination policy.

Walmart, American's biggest employer with approximately 1.4 million workers, affords a glimpse into the contradictions and backlash surrounding LGBT discrimination. For years, Walmart refused to add protections for sexual minorities to its non-discrimination language, but in 2003 it finally added sexual orientation as a protected ground. Since 2006, Walmart has voluntarily participated in the Corporate Equality Index, although in 2009 it only scored 40% out of 100%. Walmart now has a LGBT pride group, and does comply with domestic partnership and civil union provisions in locations where these options exist. However, other than these small steps, few initiatives embrace sexual minorities. Walmart is one of only a few Fortune 500 companies not including gender identity in its non-discrimination language, even though it does offer some benefits to same-sex partners, these do not include highly valued items such as extended health care insurance. In 2007, Walmart announced it would discontinue its financial support to LGBT community-based organizations.

DEVELOPMENTS IN OTHER PARTS OF THE WORLD

The situation for LGBT people has undergone spectacular change in many other parts of the world. Canada, Belgium, Spain, the Netherlands, Norway, Sweden, and South Africa all allow same-sex marriage. Many other jurisdictions such as the United Kingdom and Denmark have civil union provisions that provide couples, regardless of sex, with the same protections and responsibilities. At the same time however, LGBT minorities continue to confront serious discrimination in some parts of the world with sexual acts between consenting adults of the same sex carrying the death penalty in five countries and prison terms in seventy-two.

Amongst the more progressive countries, Canada stands out. The charter of Rights and Freedoms, roughly equivalent to the American constitution, has been interpreted to include sexual orientation. All provinces and territories include sexual orientation in their provincial human rights codes as a protected ground and recognize same-sex relationships in family law, including the right to adopt children. These legislative changes followed initiatives already underway in many Canadian organizations. As early as the mid-1980s, labor union were fighting nondiscrimination policies and negotiating same-sex benefit packages in collective agreements and these changes soon became the norm in many unionized and non-unionized organizations (Hunt and Eaton, 2007). Even though Canada has been a leader in challenging sexual orientation bias, it continues to lag in relation to transgender discrimination. Transgendered people have many fewer protections in law, and most organizations have yet to enact policies or other provisions that would extend a more welcoming environment for this group of workers.

CONCLUSIONS

Of all the diversity challenges an organization faces, accommodation to sexuality differences remains the most contentious. Although there has been considerable accommodation to the LGBT minority in American organizations over the past two decades, this progress has produced a backlash by people and organizations that do not endorse or support change. As a result, there are contradictions and mixed messages in the response LGBT people receive to their demands for equity resulting in significant variation among states, local authorities, cities, and organizations.

On the one hand, significant change has occurred. The majority of Americans, particularly young Americans, support equal rights for LGBT minorities. A number of state and local governments prohibit employment discrimination and increasingly, organizations take steps to curb heterosexual bias in their human resource policies and practices. Some companies go out of their way to provide a welcoming environment for their LGBT workers and actively recruit within this community as part of their "finding-the-best-talent" human resource strategy. On the other hand, some people and organizations fight assertively to prevent or overturn LGBT positive measures. Many organizations passively comply with legal changes, but make no effort to create a safe and welcoming environment for LGBT minorities.

In many ways, accommodating sexual diversity in the workplace acts as a litmus test for an organization's general acceptance of diversity. An organization that recognizes and acknowledges its sexual minorities is almost certain to do the same for others. Benchmark organizations with a broad based commitment to diversity accept the challenges and opportunities associated with their LGBT employees. They discontinue discriminatory practices and alter human resource benefit polices to ensure that they are equal and fair for everyone by including sexual diversity in training programs and recruitment strategies. Progressive, pro-diversity organizations make clear through their disciplinary policies and cultural messages that anti-LGBT behavior will not be tolerated any more than sexist or racist behavior.

DISCUSSION QUESTIONS

1. What is meant by the term "gender identity"?

2. Provide an example of some type of event that you have witnessed in your life that illustrates the contradictions and mixed messages that surround LGBT people.

3. Develop five key criteria that could be used for evaluating how much an organization is "gay-friendly" versus "anti-gay."

4. Discuss the ways in which the challenges an organization faces in creating an inclusive environment for LGBT people differ from the challenges it might face in creating an inclusive environment for other diversity categories such as race and disability.

Bibliography

Badgett, L. (2000). *Money, myths, and change: The economic lives of lesbians and gay men.* Chicago: University of Chicago Press.

Bagley, C., and Tremblay, P. (1998). On the prevalence of homosexuality and bisexuality, in a a random community survey of 750 men aged 18–27. *Journal of Homosexuality,* Vol. 36(2).

Bowman, K., and Foster, A. (2006). *Attitudes about homosexuality and gay marriage.* Washington, D. C.: American Enterprise.

Buford, H. (2000). Understanding gay consumers. *The Gay and Lesbian Review,* Vol. VII(2), Spring.

Gallup (2009). Information obtained from http://www.gallup.com in August 2009.

HRC. (2006). *Corporate equity index 2006: A report card on gay, lesbian, bisexual and transgender equality in corporate America.* Washington, DC: Human Rights Campaign Foundation.

HRC. (2009a). Information obtained from http://www.hrc.org in August 2009.

HRC. (2009b). *Corporate equity index 2009: A report card on gay, lesbian, bisexual and transgender equality in corporate America.* Washington, DC: Human Rights Campaign Foundation.

Hunt, G., and Eaton, J. (2007). "We are Family: Labour Responds to Gay, Lesbian, Bisexual and Transgender Workers." In, Hunt, G., and Rayside, D. (eds.), *Equity, Diversity and Canadian Labour.* Toronto: University of Toronto Press.

Kinsey, A., et al. (1948). *Sexual Behavior in the Human Male.* New York: Saunders.

Knight, R. (2009). *The Corporate Curtain: How companies are using views on homosexuality to punish their Christian employees.* (Retrieved on-line September 9, 2009 from http://www.cwfa.org).

Wilcox, C., and Wolpert, R. (2000). *Gay rights in the public sphere: Public opinion on gay rights.* Chicago: The University of Chicago Press.

Yang, A. (1999). *From wrongs to rights, 1973–1999: Public opinion on gay and lesbian Americans moves toward equality.* Washington, D. C.: Policy Institute of the National Gay and Lesbian Task Force.

Diversity on the Web

1. Go to the YouTube site below. Why do you think IBM officially approved this YouTube program?
2. IBM is thought to be a very LGBT-positive company and has achieved 100% on the Corporate Equity Index (see http://www.HRC.org). Do you think all American organizations should be as LGBT positive as IBM? Why/Why not?

http://www.youtube.com/watch?v=al5Euju-rOg

Points of Law

- Managers should be aware of the laws in their state and city regarding same-sex marriages.
- Discrimination based on sexual orientation is illegal in at least twenty-one states and in the District of Columbia.
- Twelve or more of these twenty-one states also prohibit discrimination based on gender identity.
- Many cities also prohibit employment discrimination based on gender identity.
- Same-sex unions are now recognized in an increasing number of states "thereby giving same sex couples the same rights, benefits and protection as heterosexual, married couples."
- The federal "Defense of Marriage Act" allows states the right to refuse to honor same-sex marriages performed in other states.
- Many countries, including Canada, recognize same-sex marriages.

Dr. Gerald Hunt is a Professor of Organizational Behavior and Human resources Management at Ryerson University in Toronto, Canada. He publishes widely on topics related to diversity, including comparisons of American and Canadian response to gay, lesbian, bisexual, and transgender issues in the workplace.

GENERATIONAL DIVERSITY
IN THE WORKPLACE

Diane M. Holtzman
The Richard Stockton College of New Jersey

Evonne J. Kruger
The Richard Stockton College of New Jersey

Charles D. Srock
The Richard Stockton College of New Jersey

GOALS

- To gain a greater understanding of diversity among generations
- To describe how groups of individuals in a generational cohort may be influenced by social, historical, and cultural forces of their generational timeframes
- To analyze workplace cases and apply generational concepts in written and/or oral communications

For the first time in history, four distinctively diverse generations are employed in our workforce: Veterans, Baby Boomers, Gen Xers, and Millennials and soon to be entering our workforce are the 23+ million individuals in Generation Z (Schroer, 2010). Depending on the years used to define the Generation Z cohort, soon we may have five diverse generations in our workforce (King, 2010). These cohorts frequently collide in today's workplace, creating environments characterized by individual and generational enmity where attitudes of "Us" versus "Them" and "every man and woman for himself and herself" surface (Zemke, Raines, & Filipczak, 2000, p. 5). The adversarial atmosphere impedes the energies, productivity, teamwork, and collaborative problem solving required by complex and competitive global markets. To foster organizational environments that are positive and productive, employers must be aware of the strengths and assets that each generation as a group brings to their organizations, and become skilled in dealing with individuals from each generation as subordinates, supervisors and customers.

Each generation tends to have different attitudes about work ethics, career development, work/life balance, job expectations, communication styles, training, adaptation to and use of electronic technology, rewards and compensation (Center for Generational Studies, 2006). According to Lancaster and Stillman (2002),

> . . . different generations of employees won't become more alike with age. They will carry their "generational personalities" with them throughout their lives. In fact,

- The oldest workers, those 44.2 million born between 1922 and 1943 are termed "veterans," the "swing generation," or the "great generation" depending on the social observer. The term "greatest generation" was used by the journalist Tom Brokaw to describe the generation that grew up during the Great Depression and who fought in World War II (Brokaw, 2004).
- The baby boomer generation, approximately 77 million people, has been defined both as those born between 1943 and 1960 and those with births spanning the years 1946 through 1964.
- The 52.4 million generation Xers have been defined as being both born between 1965 and 1980, as well as between 1960 and 1980.
- The Generation Y cohort is termed the Millennials and Generation Nexters. At 77.6 million, they are now the largest generation. Some place their births between 1980 and 2000, others between 1981 and 1999 (Lancaster & Stillman, 2002; Zemke, Raines, & Filipczak, 2000).
- The generation that follows Gen Y is called "generation Z," the "digital generation," "generation 9/11" and the "iGeneration"; and includes those individuals born after 1994 but before 2004 (*Generation Z*, 2010). Others state that Generation Z includes those born after 2001 (*Working with Generation Y and Z*, 2010).
- Those born within a year or two of the start of a new generation are called "cuspers" because they "stand in the gap between the two sides . . . [and] become naturals at mediating, translating, and mentoring" (Lancaster & Stillman, 2002, p. 39).

when hard times hit, the generations are likely to entrench themselves even more deeply into the attitudes and behaviors that have been ingrained in them (p. 8).

Demographers agree about the overall profiles of the distinct cohorts in the workforce, but disagree on the years of birth and cohort names.

The workplace behaviors associated with this generation are still evolving but it is known that Generation Z individuals have grown up and been influenced by access to the newest communication tools such as the internet, cell phones, MP3 players, and IPods. This generation uses technology and is dependent upon it. Although Gen Zers are well connected, it is predicted that they will be weaker in terms of interpersonal skills and experience more unemployment and downsizing and may distrust corporations and have less loyalty to organizations than previous generations (*Generation Z*, 2010; *Generation Y and Z*, 2010).

As Generation Z individuals begin to enter the workplace, there will be employees from the Swing Generation and the Baby Boom Generation who continue to be in the work force. In an article in *Business Week*, Coy (2005) found that starting in the mid-1980's, older Americans chose to keep working which can be attributed to improved physical and mental health, the desire to stay useful and the need for organizations to hold on to experience. Even executives are making career switches rather than retiring because they become bored with retirement and miss a sense of productivity and intellectual challenge (San Jose Business Journal, Report, 2007). Others remain in the workforce longer because they are not financially prepared for retirement (Moore, 2010) especially with the recession that began in 2008.

Each generation has unique perspectives and values about work and the work environment. In traditional hierarchical organizations, generations tend to be more segregated as experienced individuals rise to higher positions with experience. In general, older employees tend to be in upper and upper-middle management, middle-aged employees in middle management and occasionally in upper management, and younger employees in lower to more central levels. However, as organizations flatten into more horizontal structures, a "mixing" of generations occurs that profoundly influences organizational processes. As teamwork increases, intergenerational differences spark interpersonal conflict, creating issues surrounding collaborative problem solving, motivation, communication, training, and supervision. Thus, because of its impact on organization effectiveness, generational diversity must be added to traditional discussions of diversity in the workplace. The nomenclature and the time frames for the cohorts that follow are those defined by Ron Zemke, Claire Raines, and Bob Filipczak (2000) and Raines (2002).

GENERATIONS IN THE WORKPLACE

The Profile for Veterans: Born between 1922 and 1943

The core values of Veterans include dedication, discipline, sacrifice, hard work, duty before pleasure, delayed rewards, conformity, consistency and uniformity, a sense of history, and an orientation toward the past; respect for authority, adherence to the rules, preference for hierarchy; patience; conservative spending, and a deep sense of personal organizational and national honor.

Veterans were influenced by world events that included the 1929 stock market crash, Dust Bowl, and Great Depression in the 1930s; Franklin Roosevelt's presidency—particularly his optimism and the New Deal which brought Social Security and other social programs; the rise of Hitler and fall of Europe; Pearl Harbor and the United States at war; victories in Europe and Japan; and the Korean War.

Assets of having Veterans in the workplace include their stability, orientation to detail, thoroughness, loyalty, and consistent hard work. Their *liabilities* include their difficulty coping with ambiguity and change, reluctance to buck the system, discomfort with conflict and reticence to disagree with those in positions of authority.

Messages that motivate Veterans include, "Your experience is respected here; it's valuable to the rest of us to hear what has, and hasn't, worked in the past." When communicating with Veterans, employers should use inclusive language, written or face-to-face communication, and more formal language.

In their leadership style, Veterans are directive, use command-and-control leadership, and use executive decision-making. They want to take charge, delegate and make the bulk of the decisions themselves (Aldisert, 2002, p. 25; Zemke, Raines, and Filipczak, 200, pp. 29–32).

The Profile for Baby Boomers: Born between 1943 and 1960

The core values of Baby Boomers include optimism, team orientation, personal gratification, health and wellness, personal growth, staying young, hard work, and involvement.

Boomers were influenced by: the McCarthy hearings in 1954; victories over polio and tuberculosis; the struggle for Civil Rights from Rosa Parks, through school integration; Martin Luther King, Jr.; the involvement of students in voter registration, bomb shelters, and nuclear power; easily accessible birth control; John F. Kennedy's presidency, including the establishment of the Peace Corps; the Cuban missile crisis; astronauts in space; the assassinations of JFK, Martin Luther King, and Robert Kennedy; the Vietnam War and student protests that culminated in the Kent State University shootings; founding of the National Organization for Women; and the disgrace of Richard M. Nixon.

Assets of having Boomers in the workplace include their service orientation, willingness to "go the extra mile," ability to establish and maintain good working relationships, desire to please, and their team spirit. *Liabilities* include frequent lack of budget orientation, discomfort with conflict to the point of conflict avoidance, reluctance to disagree with peers for fear of harming working relationships, comfort with process frequently overshadowing the need for goal attainment, being overly sensitive to feedback, being judgmental of those who see things differently, and self-centeredness.

Messages that motivate Boomers include, "You're valued here," "We need you," "I approve of you," and "Your contributions are unique and important." When communicating with Boomers employers should use an open, direct style; answer questions thoroughly; avoid controlling, manipulative language; use face-to-face or electronic communication; and convey flexibility.

In their leadership style, Boomers are collegial and consensual, but sometimes authoritarian. They are passionate and concerned about participation, spirit, humanity in the workplace, and creating a fair and level playing field for all. Because Boomers grew up with conservative parents and worked in their early careers for command-and-control supervisors, they often slip into that style when collegiality fails. Many Boomer managers lack sophisticated communication, motivation, supervision, and delegation skills (Aldisert, 20023, pp. 25–26; Zemke, Raines, Filipezak, 2000, pp. 63–91).

The Profile for the Gen Xers: Born between 1960 and 1980

The core values of the Gen Xers include appreciation of diversity, ability to think globally, the balance of work and home, technoliteracy, espousing the idea that work should be fun, having a casual approach to authority, self-reliance and independence, and pragmatism.

The Gen Xers were influenced by the following events: the struggle for women's liberation and gay rights, the Watergate scandal, the energy crisis, personal computers, the Three Mile Island meltdown, disenchantment with nuclear power, successive recessions accompanied by massive layoffs, the Iran hostages episode, erosion of America's world dominance and respect, the Challenger disaster, the Exxon Valdez oil spill, AIDS, Operation Desert Storm, and the fall of communism.

Assets of having Xers in the workplace include that they are adaptable, technoliterate, independent, not intimidated by authority, voracious learners, financially savvy, multitask oriented, experienced team members, and creative. *Liabilities* include that they are impatient, have poor people skills, are cynical, have low expectations about job security, are less willing to make personal sacrifices at work, and resist being micromanaged.

Messages that motive Gen Xers include, "Do it your way," "We've got the newest hardware and software," and "There are not a lot of rules around here." When communicating with Gen Xers, employers should use electronic communication as the primary tool, write in short sound bytes, present facts, ask for feedback, share information immediately, use an informal style, and listen.

In their leadership styles, Xers are uncomfortable with bureaucratic rules and procedures and traditional chain-of-command systems. They know that sophisticated and demanding customers expect their needs to be met immediately. The Gen X leader is skilled at supporting and developing a responsive, competent team that can change direction, or projects, quickly. They are egalitarian and not hierarchical in their thinking. In addition, they are adept at accessing information electronically (Aldisert, 2002, p. 26; Zemke, Raines, & Filipczak, 2000, pp. 92–126).

The Profile for the Millennials: Born between 1980 and 2000

The core values for the Millennials include a sense of civic duty, confidence, optimism, achievement, sociability, morality, collaboration, open-minded, street smarts, an appreciation of diversity, respect for community and authority, okay at staying connected to others and the world through communication technology.

The Millennials' sphere of seminal events and trends includes violence such as the terrorism of September 11th, the shootings at Columbine, and the Oklahoma City bombing; the increased use of technology; busy lives; the President Clinton and Monica Lewinsky scandal; and years of service learning throughout elementary and secondary school.

Assets of having Millennials in the workplace include their optimism, tenacity, heroic spirit, multitasking capabilities, technological know-how, collaborative skills, and their being goal oriented. *Liabilities* include their need for supervision, mentoring, and structure, inexperience in handing difficult interpersonal issues, need for constant feedback and praise, distaste for menial work, lack of skills for dealing with difficult people, impatience, and overconfidence.

Messages that motivate Millennials include, "You'll be working with other bright creative people," "You and your colleagues can help turn this company around," "Your boss is in his (or her) sixties," "Your schedule will be flexible." When communicating with Millennials, employers should use descriptive language and action verbs, not talk down, show respect, use electronic and visual communication to motivate, promote constant feedback, use humor, and be encouraging.

In their leadership style, Millennials combine the teamwork ethic of the Boomers with the can-do attitude of the Veterans and the technological savvy of the Xers. Resiliency is one of their strongest traits. They are very comfortable dealing with Boomers. Their learning preferences include teamwork, technology, structure, entertainment and excitement, and experiential activities. (Aldisert, 2002, pp. 27–29; Zemke, Raines, & Filipczak, 2000, pp. 127–150); Raines, 2002; Zust (nd)).

APPLYING GENERATIONAL DIVERSITY KNOWLEDGE TO THE WORKPLACE

The case that follows presents a situation in which there are generational differences in a work setting. Read the case and answer the discussion questions at the end of it. Keep in mind that general cohort differences are tendencies of a group and not all people in a cohort will behave in the same manner.

MANAGING DIVERSE GENERATIONS IN A RETAIL SETTING

Julia just graduated from Valley Community College with her associate degree in Business Administration. She is anxious to start her new position as an entry-level manager of the Electronics Department at Everything's Here Inc., a retailer that offers customers clothing, pharmaceuticals, food, automotive, house wares, electronics, small appliances, toys, etc.

Julia, who is 34, has worked for the retail giant as a sales associate and then assistant manager in the clothing department over the last 5 years while attending college part-time and raising her two young children. During each of the past 4 years she has received a store customer service award. She is techno-literate and can multitask. When Julia heard of a job opening for an entry-level manager in the Electronics Department of Everything's Here Inc., she applied and received the position—she had the associate's degree, assistant manager experience at the store, and excellent customer service skills.

The Electronics Department has a range of products including CDs, mobile phones, laptop computers, video games, MP3 players and flat-screen TVs. The department's 3 full-time sales associates, Ethel, Larry, and Rick and six part-time sales associates will report to Julia. The sales associates are responsible for aiding customers in purchase decisions, using the cash register for sales, and taking inventory. Julia relies on the full-time associates to help her meet the sales goals for the department. At Everything's Here Inc. there are no sales commissions for the employees.

Upon taking the position, Harold Lee, the store manager, told Julia that she needs to increase the department's sales and improve her employees' customer service skills. He said that he has received many complaints about the lack of attention given to customers in Electronics. Julia is expected to "turn the sales figures and the customer comments—positive" within the next six months.

Ethel, age 70, has worked at Everything's Here Inc. for 20 years, with 18 of those years in sales in the fabric and crafts department—a department that was closed at Everything's Here Inc. due to lack of revenue. Over the last two years, Ethel has been transferred from department to department. She has been in the Electronics Department now for one year and limits her work to assisting customers with CD and video selections. Many times Ethel is the only sales person on the floor and when asked a question about the other technological equipment in the department, she tells the customers to "come back when the younger people are working—they understand this stuff!" Ethel is pleasant with customers and hard working. She told the upper managers at Everything 's Here Inc. that she wants to work for a few more years because she receives health benefits that cover the secondary insurance under Medicare for herself and her husband, who is in an Alzheimer's unit in the local nursing home.

Ethel had great difficulty learning the new computer inventory control program that was recently installed in the store to check if items are in stock. She has tested the patience of several people, including the last manager, who tried to teach her how to use the program. She does like the personal attention, and tries hard, but has not been successful. At work, when Ethel watched the customer service training videos supplied by corporate training, she fell asleep. She cannot use e-mail to communicate with Julia from home since she doesn't have a computer or from work since she doesn't know how use email or instant messaging. When Ethel is at home, she shuts her phone off so her attention is not interrupted when watching television. "After all . . . I can't watch television and talk on the phone!"

Larry, age 20, has been working at Everything's Here Inc. for two years since graduating from high school. He was told by his parents "get out of the house, get a job and quit playing video games." On his job application, Larry stated that he was qualified to work in the Electronics Department because he was an avid "gamer" and "an expert at text messages." Mr. Lee thought that Larry was the ideal employee since "Larry is young and knows about computers." While at work, Larry gets so caught up in checking his messages and learning to use the newly arrived PDAs and video games, that he ignores customers needing assistance. He perceives that his activities are work related. After all, he must be an expert on the equipment/games in order to sell them.

Larry prefers helping young customers because he believes they are more "techno-saavy" and know what they are looking for in terms of games or technology. He doesn't have a lot of patience with customers, particularly those who need assistance understanding mobile phones and accessories. Larry is often seen using his mobile "smart" phone to send text messages to friends before ringing up a customer's sales. "This'll take only a minute" Larry says to the customers, and quickly enters a message before ringing up the sales. He does not see text messaging as intrusive or time consuming—"Heck! It's just like talking—it's quicker and less annoying!" Larry only wants to communicate with Julia through text messaging or emails since he is connected to email and social sites "almost 24/7." He has told her "Don't use the phone to contact me . . . I'm usually texting . . . that's the way I like to communicate."

Rick, age 51, took a job as sales associate at Everything's Here Inc. when the local appliance store where he worked for 20 years closed. He enjoyed working at the appliance store because he was selling kitchen and laundry appliances, TVs and stereos—equipment with which he was familiar. He liked spending time with customers and hearing their stories. In fact, many of his customers frequently return to make other purchases. Although he lacks experience with sophisticated communication technologies, Mr. Lee wanted to give Rick "a chance" in Electronics. Rick knows the basics of working a computer for word processing, emails, and surfing the net. Mr. Lee was heard saying "At Rick's age, he probably knows how to use technology—after all, everyone has a computer and smart phone today—even me and I'm 60!" Rick does well selling TVs, but not the other equipment in Electronics. He tends to stay near the TVs and does not rotate around the department.

When Rick is approached by a customer with a technical question, he goes out of his way to find Julia, Larry, or one of the younger part-time associates. He introduces them to customers as "my young knowledgeable colleagues." He will go online to find the answer or use the computerized "Frequently Asked Q & A" module developed by Julia for the Electronics Department staff only if no one else is around and the customer needs an answer to make a purchase decision.

After completing her first week working the various shifts with the 3 full time employees assigned to her, Julia realizes that there may be generational issues that are affecting customer service in her department.

An additional intergenerational diversity case can be found in the Instructor's Manual.

DISCUSSION QUESTIONS

1. What are the generational issues Julia faces with each employee? What cultural, historic, or societal issues may influence these generational issues?

2. How do these generational issues affect Julia's management of the department?

3. What can Julia do to improve customer service within the department?

4. What generalizations are made by upper management about the employees? In your opinion, are they right, or are they wrong? Be specific.

5. Have you faced similar or different exchanges in your retail shopping experience with employees of different generational cohorts? Give details to support your answer.

Diane M. Holtzman, EdD, is an assistant professor who teaches business studies at The Richard Stockton College of New Jersey. Her areas of specialization include management skills, public relations, international management, and marketing.

Evonne J. Kruger, PhD, is an associate professor at The Richard Stockton College of New Jersey. Her areas of expertise are strategic management, managerial decision making, and community engagement.

Charles Dwaine Srock, RN, MBA, ABD, is the Critical Care Educator at Florida Hospital Waterman. He continues to do consulting in management skills and specializes in organizational behavior and organizational development.

Writing Assignment
Generational Differences

To better understand generational differences, conduct an interview with someone from an age group different from your own. As a minimum, ask the questions below to get a sense of his or her experiences. Your instructor may add additional questions and you may find it necessary to add appropriate follow-up questions based upon the interviewee's answers to help you to understand how this person's life experiences as part of a particular generation may have contributed to shaping who he or she is today.

From the interview material, a) write a three-page paper that analyzes how these experiences have impacted that person's life. The emphasis here should be on learning if your subject had life experiences that may have shaped him or her in some significant ways as Holtzman, Kruger, and Srock suggest in this article; b) examine how these generational differences could impact workplace communication and understanding.

Be careful not to simply list questions and answers.

Questions

1. Besides family members, who were your role models when you were growing up?

2. As a child and a teenager, did you have any close friends who were of a different race or religion than you?

3. Describe your first job in terms of salary, benefits, work schedule, and responsibilities.

4. How long did you stay in this position?

5. Approximately how many organizations have you worked (in a full-time capacity) for in your lifetime?

6. What historic, political, and/or personal events were most significant during your childhood and young adulthood?

7. How did these make a difference in your life?

8. What inventions affected your life the most? Why?

9. How have health care, education, and the economy changed in your lifetime?

10. How have any of these affected how you have lived your life?

11. How has your gender impacted your life experiences?

12. What year were you born? What is your highest level of education?

Bibliography

Aldisert, L.M. (2002). *Valuing people: How human capital can be your strongest asset.* Chicago: Dearborn Trade Publishing.

Brokaw, T. (2004). *The Greatest Generation.* New York: Random House.

Center for Generational Studies. (2006). Frequently asked questions about generational differences. Retrieved from http://gentrends.com/faq.html

Coy, P. (2005, June 27). Old. Smart. Productive. Surprise! *Business Week,* 78–84.

Generation Z (2010). Retrieved from Babyboomercaretaker.com http://www.babyboomercaretaker.com/baby-boomer/generation-z/Generation-Z-Behaviour-Change.html

King, C.B. (2010). 5 Generations in the workplace. Retrieved from Ezine Articles http://ezinearticles.com/?5-Generations-in-the-Workplace&id=3878298

Lancaster, L.C. & Stillman, D. (2002). *When generations collide: Who they are. Why they clash. How to solve the generational puzzle at work.* New York: Harper Collins.

Moore, R. (2010). For many boomers retirement means still working. Retrieved from PLANSPONSOR.com http://www.plansponsor.com/For_Many_Boomers_Retirement_Means_Still_Working.aspx

Raines, C. (2002). Managing millennials. Retrieved from http://www.generationsatwork.com/articles/millenials.htm.

Report: Baby boomer execs are making late career switches (2007, March 29). *San Jose Business Journal.* Retrieved from http://sanjose.bizjournals.com/sanjose/stories/2007/03/26/daily58.html

Schroer, W.J. (2010). Generations X, Y, Z, and others. Retrieved from the social librarian http://www.socialmarketing.org/newsletter/features/generation1.htm

Working with generation Y and Z (2010). Retrieved from Kelly: Smart manager http://www.smartmanager.us/eprise/main/web/us/hr_manager/articles_sept07_generation

Zemke, R., Raines, C. & Filipczak, B. (2000). *Generations at work: Managing the clash of veterans, boomers, Xers, and nexters in your workplace.* New York: AmRickan Management Association.

Zust, C.W. (nd). Baby boomer leaders face challenges communicating across generations. *Emerging Leader.Com.* Retrieved from http://www.emergingleader.com/article16.shtml

Diversity on the Web

1. Go to the Web site below and read the report by Deloitte Consulting Group: *Gen Y-ers Baby Boomers & Technology: Worlds Apart? Technology Usage in the Global Workplace.* http://www.deloitte.com/ Search for "Gen Yers, Baby Boomers & Technology."

   Answer the following questions:

   a. What does the article reveal about the use of technology by Baby Boomers in the United States and the Baby Boomer generation in emerging nations? Give examples to support your answer.
   b. What impact did technological developments and culture have on the use of technology by American Baby Boomers compared to Baby Boomers from emerging nations?
   c. Read the Recommendations section of the report and apply two concepts presented to the workplace scenario involving the use of technology by the employees at Everything's Here.

2. Go to the Web site below and read the article on *Mixing and Managing Four Generations of Employees* by Greg Hammill (2005). In the article Hammill presents a chart of Workplace Characteristics for Veterans, Baby Boomers, Generation X, and Generation Y.

   http://www.fdu.edu/newspubs/magazine/05ws/generations.htm

   a. Analyze the information presented in the chart.
   b. Using the information from the chart, state how Julia should communicate with each member in the Everything's Here Inc. case. Give details to support your answer.
   c. Using the information from the chart, state how Julia could motivate each member of her department. Give details to support your answer.

HOW OLD SHOULD YOU BE TO DRIVE A BUS? EXPLORING AGEISM

Sharon P. McKechnie
Emmanuel College, Boston

GOALS

- To explore attitudes and opinions related to chronological ages
- To illustrate legal and cultural frameworks related to age that shape beliefs, expectations, and actions.
- To understand that ageism includes the young as well as the old although in the United States, only those over forty are legally protected under the Civil Rights Act of 1964.

INSTRUCTIONS

Write down the age you feel is appropriate for each event in the scale below and give a one to two sentence explanation of why you selected that age for that event.

How old should you be to ......

1. . . . . start formal schooling?
2. . . . . live alone?
3. . . . . serve in the armed forces?
4. . . . . drive a bus?
5. . . . . fly a commercial plane?
6. . . . . buy an alcoholic drink in a bar?
7. . . . . have a baby?
8. . . . . retire from work?
9. . . . . manage a department of 50 employees?
10. . . . . get married?
11. . . . . vote in state elections?
12. . . . . start your own business?
13. . . . .
14. . . . .

Sharon P. McKechnie is an Assistant Professor at Emmanuel College, Boston. She received her PhD in management from Boston College.

MUSICAL CHAIRS

M. June Allard
Assumption College
Worcester State University, Professor Emerita

GOALS

- To provide an experience in how it feels to be physically challenged
- To understand how it feels to be unable to communicate with people in the traditional way

INSTRUCTIONS

1. Form a group of four to six members and arrange your chairs in a circle.

2. Read the following passage to yourself:

> Fifty students reported for a class that had 35 student desk-chairs: 30 RH (Right Hand) and five LH (Left Hand). Fifteen RH students then volunteered to transfer to an honors section down the hall, thereby leaving everyone in the original class seated.
>
> After class, six RH students and one LH student reported their chairs were broken and needed replacing. Later that afternoon the honors instructor called saying that eight of the transfer students were not eligible for the honors class and were, therefore, returning to the original class.
>
> How many additional RH and LH desk-chairs did the original instructor need for his class?

3. **Working as a group,** come to a consensus on the answer to the question posed above.

4. Your instructor will provide further instructions on how your group will conduct the exercise.

Diversity on the Web

ACCOMMODATING CHALLENGES

Under the ADA (Americans with Disabilities Act), employers may not discriminate in the hiring of persons with disabilities. Further, employers are required to provide reasonable accommodations to enable individuals with disabilities to perform their jobs and communicate effectively.

Note that tax incentives are provided for "qualified architectural and transportation barrier removal expenses." The employer is not required, however, to provide accommodations primarily for personal use such as hearing aids and wheelchairs.

Directions

1. Search the Internet for jobs and select two postings for jobs. Make them as different as possible: different types of jobs, different levels, different industries.
2. Try to select jobs for which you have some familiarity.
3. Your instructor will assign a physical challenge for each of your jobs.
4. Assume that someone with the physical challenge assigned to each of your jobs is by far the best-qualified candidate for the job. Research those disabilities, noting how many Americans are afflicted.
5. Devise accommodations appropriate for the challenge.

Sources

> http://www.monster.com   http://www.careerbuilder.com
> http://www.usa.jobs.gov   http://www.hotjobs.yahoo.com

> option: *web search* employment opportunities

The Office of Disability Employment Policy, part of the U.S. Department of Labor, maintains JAN (Job Accommodation Network), a valuable resource on work site accommodations:

> http://www.jan.wvu.edu/soar/disabilities.html

The Best Buy Case: Committed to the Inclusion of People with Disabilities

David P. Harvey

University of Minnesota

Best Buy is committed to, "growth through a world of diversity and inclusion . . . One employee, customer, and community at a time."

GOALS

- To explore Best Buy's award-winning program for the inclusion of people with disabilities
- To understand the critical role of corporate values and executive support in Best Buy's program
- To provide evidence for the business case for employing workers with disabilities
- To present the basic legal obligations of businesses to employees and customers with disabilities

Best Buy has a long track record of success in the fast-paced retail technology industry. Best Buy's focus on constantly changing products amplifies the need for innovation and responsiveness in the marketplace. Throughout its history, Best Buy has grown by staying at the forefront of both general management and industry-specific trends. One area where Best Buy has led the pack is in diversity for people with physical and mental challenges. Best Buy's strong commitment to diversity and inclusion involves each of its "Three Pillars," i.e., employees, customers and the community.

Edgar Schein's framework for analyzing organizational culture is a valuable tool for gaining insight into the factors that influence a company's actions. Applying Schein's framework to Best Buy shows that diversity is deeply ingrained into the culture, from store associates to the executive level. Best Buy's leadership provides resources to build a diverse culture from the bottom up and the top down because it believes in the value of diversity from both the societal and business perspectives. Best Buy's business decisions are strongly rooted in the company's four corporate values: have fun while being the best, learn from challenge and change, show respect, humility and integrity and unleash the power of our people. It was from these values that Best Buy developed its corporate vision, "People. Technology and the pursuit of happiness (Best Buy Corporate Values and Vision, 2010)."

THE BUSINESS CASE FOR DIVERSITY—PEOPLE WITH DISABILITIES

According to a report published by the U.S. Census Bureau in 2008, 16.5% of Americans between the ages of 21 and 64 had a disability and only 45.6% of this group was employed. The employment rate was far lower, 30.7%, for people with a severe disability. By comparison, 75.2% of people with a non-severe disability and 83.5% of people with no disability were employed. These findings suggest that there are millions of Americans with disabilities who can and want to participate in the workforce. For example, 59.1% of people with hearing issues were employed compared to 40.8% of people with sight issues (Brault, 2008). Finally, disabilities reach across other dimensions of diversity including: age, gender, race, religion and sexual orientation.

While a great deal of literature and press is focused on hiring employees with existing disabilities, current employees also can incur disabilities. The cost of accommodating an existing employee is typically far lower than replacing that employee. According to the Job Accommodation Network (JAN), 56% of employers reported that accommodations cost nothing. Of the accommodations that did incur a cost, the average expenditure was $600 (Job Accommodation Network, 2010). Similarly, a study of 600 accommodations at Sears, Roebuck & Co. concluded that 75% of the accommodations cost nothing while only 2% cost more than $1,000 (Blanck, 1999). In contrast, it is generally accepted that the cost incurred for a single incidence of employee turnover is one to two times the employee's annual salary. So, the cost of accommodation is very likely to be more than offset by the direct benefits of retaining a qualified employee. A 2007 study conducted by researchers at DePaul University found that performance ratings of workers with disabilities were nearly identical to those of workers without disabilities (Disabilityworks, 2007).

The U.S. Census Bureau reported that individuals with disabilities and their families have over $1 trillion in annual income and $220 billion in discretionary spending power (McNeil, 2000). A 2005 survey indicated that 92% of Americans have a more favorable view of companies that hire people with disabilities than those that do not. Furthermore, 87% of the American public prefers to give their business to companies that hire individuals with disabilities (Siperstein et al., 2006).

Businesses that can create an inclusive environment for people with disabilities may have an advantage in attracting and retaining the most talented employees in the future. According to the Department of Education, there are over 2.1 million individuals with disabilities enrolled in post secondary education. Finally, the tax credits available to businesses that improve physical access for people with disabilities and hire new employees who have disabilities can exceed $20,000.

BEST BUY: CORPORATE PROFILE

Best Buy was founded in 1966 as the Sound of Music store and reached $1 million in annual revenues by 1970. In 1995 the company entered the Fortune 500 and in 2004 was named "Company of the Year" by Forbes magazine. Today, Best Buy operates 1,044 retail stores which account for 75% of its revenue. The remainder of their $45 billion in annual sales is generated by nine other divisions (Datamonitor, 2010). Best Buy has 155,000 employees at sites in the United States, Canada, Europe, China, and Mexico and a corporate headquarters in Richfield, Minnesota. Annually, Best Buy donates 1.5% of pre-tax profits to non-profit organizations. In 2009, this reinvestment in the community amounted to $33.4 million.

EXECUTIVE LEADERSHIP

Consultant and author Michael W. Wright states that "leaders are like eyes—a window into the soul of the corporation." The leaders at Best Buy provide a clear example of this concept. Best Buy has been led by only two individuals. Founder Richard Schulze was CEO until 2002 and still serves as Chairman of the Board. Current CEO Brian Dunn started in 1985 as a sales associate. When it comes to diversity, Dunn takes a hands-on approach. In a recent meeting with the executive sponsors of Best Buy's ten employee resource groups (ERGs), Dunn inquired about their efforts and reminded them that he would hold them accountable for the performance of their groups (Best Buy Conference Call, June 8, 2010). Dunn also met directly with the field leaders of these ERG groups that had the best executed business plans (Best Buy Conference Call, July 13, 2010). Dunn has publicly stated that, "every one of us has amazing gifts, talents and perspectives to offer. I'm committed to making sure we have the kind of environment where we respect and celebrate all individuals and their unique contributions" (Diversity at Best Buy, 2010).

DIVERSITY AT BEST BUY

Best Buy is committed to "growth through a world of diversity and inclusion . . . One employee, customer, and community at a time" (Best Buy EBN, 2010) and has a variety of programs focused on harnessing the power of inclusion in each of the "Three Pillars" of diversity: employees, customers and community. Best Buy currently provides transformational learning opportunities, employee resource groups, and many types of online and in-person diversity training. With clear values, consistent executive support and a wide array of resources available to all Best Buy employees, the company empowers employees at the local level to make decisions that support the inclusion of people with disabilities. Best Buy then builds support for existing and future initiatives by celebrating successes and disseminating diversity best practices throughout the organization. In addition to supporting new initiatives, the corporate Diversity and Inclusion Team at Best Buy is very responsive to the needs of the employees in the field. For example, in addition to being available by appointment, the Corporate D&I team has "Office Hours" when team members are available by phone and email. The D&I team also partnered with corporate PR to develop public relations training for EBN participants (Best Buy Conference Call, September 8, 2010) who often represent Best Buy at community events.

EMPLOYEE BUSINESS NETWORKS (EBNs)

Best Buy has ten employee resource groups (ERGs) which are called Employee Business Networks (EBNs). Best Buy defines an EBN as, "a group of employees who form a network based on interest in and support for a common dimension of diversity." In 2010, the ten networks, including one for people with disabilities, had a total of 117 chapters with over 2,000 members. (Best Buy Conference Call, August 10, 2010) The EBN program was initiated with a loosely defined structure. As the program grew, Best Buy added more structure, improved communication tools and developed mechanisms for feedback (EBN Express, 2010).

Each employee business network must submit an annual business case with specific business outcomes, complete a scorecard which tracks: membership and promotions of EBN members, and Tag Team service awards received (Best Buy Conference Call, June 8, 2010). Best Buy pays its employees for the time they spend working on EBNs and the groups are allowed use of company resources, including meeting space.

INCLUDE—THE DISABILITY EBN AT BEST BUY

Founded in 2006, *INCLUDE*'s mission is, "to foster an inclusive work environment where all employees feel a level of confidence, support and belonging that allows them to maximize their full potential by focusing on their abilities, not disabilities." In striving to "promote opportunities, supportive services and accommodations in a manner that ensures dignity for everyone— employees, customers, family and the community" (INCLUDE, 2010). *INCLUDE* has grown to

seven chapters that are invited to bi-monthly conference calls, to discuss challenges, best practices, available resources, upcoming events, recruiting new members, new initiatives, or to listen
to a guest speaker. (Best Buy Conference Call, August 10, 2010)

To clarify responsibilities and provide leadership opportunities for non-managers, the
INCLUDE group is organized around clearly defined roles such as Executive Sponsor, Co-chairs,
Finance, Communications, Community Outreach, Commitment & Recognition Chairs, and
Store Captains. For example, the Finance Chair is responsible for managing and tracking budget,
measuring ROI, seeking additional funding and tracking results to prove the business case. (Best
Buy Conference Call, January 28, 2010). Each new member of INCLUDE must complete a tem-
plate to formalize his or her commitment to the network. Beginning with a dictionary definition
of commitment, the document asks employees to provide their personal definition of commitment along with detailed examples of how this will be demonstrated. These documents are read
aloud to the group and two other members are asked to check the employee's progress towards
meeting these goals at the next meeting.

Armed with a specific mission and resources, INCLUDE members have developed the following strategy, "highlight disability as a customer-centric business case and using the influence
of its members and customer feedback to drive culture change" (INCLUDE, 2010). Drilling down
to the tactical level, *INCLUDE* groups around the United States are actively involved in a wide
range of activities engaging each of the Three Pillars. For example, volunteers from one
INCLUDE chapter worked with Geeksquad employees to identify products that assist people
with disabilities and to showcase these at a community health and wellness event (Best Buy
Conference Call, May 12, 2010). Recently, an *INCLUDE* team attended a Science, Technology,
Engineering, and Mathematics (STEM) Education Coalition conference to recruit new employees (Best Buy Conference Call, July 13, 2010). Another *INCLUDE* group reached out to the parents of a local school for children with special needs, developed an ongoing relationship with the
school and educated parents about technical assistance products.

INCLUDE also conducts many activities focused on the in-store experience. At the request
of INCLUDE members, the corporate team is creating a training program for employees about
Autism Spectrum disorders. The educational materials will focus on employee and customer
interactions. Another field chapter created an end cap with an iPad displaying a number of apps
that can benefit customers with disabilities (Best Buy Conference Call, July 13, 2010).

FOCUSED INVOLVEMENT NETWORKS (FINs)

To supplement its employee business network program, Best Buy launched *Focused Involvement
Networks* (FINs) in 2010. FINs are more targeted, less formal networks organized around "a common interest or shared passion that is not formally recognized as a primary dimension of diversity" (FIN page). One of two inaugural FIN groups is FACE, *Facing Autism in a Caring
Environment* (Best Buy Conference Call, January 28, 2010). Autism Spectrum Disorders (ASD)
are neurodevelopmental disorders characterized by widespread abnormalities of social interactions and communication. A recent report by the Centers for Disease Control suggest that as
many as 1 in 110 children are affected by ASDs, a six fold increase over the rate twenty years ago.
Researchers at Columbia University found that 26% of the rise in autism diagnoses could be
directly attributed to changes in diagnostic criteria. Increased awareness of autism and advanced
parental age explain some, but not all, of the remaining increase. The mission of The FACE network is to "to build a community of Best Buy employees that will promote awareness of Autism
Spectrum Disorders and support our families through networking, the sharing of resources and

providing encouragement." Best Buy recognizes that Autism will need to be addressed from the talent pool perspective as well as the customer perspective. Therefore, the company encourages "parents of ASD children, employees and customers to share their stories about how ASD has touched their lives" (Best Buy FACE, 2010).

OPERATIONALIZING DIVERSITY AT BEST BUY

Best Buy's willingness to make adjustments stems largely from its deeply-rooted value of "learning from challenge and change." Store managers believe that empowering these employees provides "a stronger teachable point of view for staff members that do not have a disability." Armed with increased knowledge and experience, employees without disabilities are better able to serve the other two pillars, customers and the community.

Best Practices at Best Buy

Best Buy's industry and its corporate values create an organizational bias toward action and encouraging new ideas. One example is the Kalamazoo, Michigan store that implemented a two-hour "Quiet Time" shopping period each weekday. Overhead music is turned off and sensory-sensitive customers have access to a "Relaxation Room" where they are welcomed to take a break from the simulation of shopping. In addition to serving its sensory-sensitive customers, such as those with autism spectrum disorders, this practice can benefit individuals with severe attention deficit hyperactivity or seizure disorders.

Managers at the Best Buy store in Lake Jackson, TX are grateful to have Ryan Hemphill on their sales team. Store manager Chris Banuelos said, "If I had one hundred Ryan's, it would be wonderful" (Ryan Hemphill, 2010). Ryan, who has the autism spectrum disorder, Asperger syndrome, is an Eagle Scout and works at Best Buy while attending college. Although he has difficulty processing social information such as facial expressions and body language, Ryan has had a lifelong interest in and knowledge of electronics which serves him well at Best Buy. During his employment, Ryan demonstrated that he had a strong grasp of what the customer experience should entail. Ryan is determined to succeed and ends each shift by asking managers what else he can do before he leaves. Ryan's experience at Best Buy has allowed him to flourish and provided an important step towards his independence.

Store 493 in Alexandria, Virginia has three team members with known disabilities. Two employees use wheelchairs and one associate is deaf. Jai Datt was 24 and a frequent customer when the manager asked him, "You are always in here, why aren't you working for me?" (APSE, 2008) Shortly thereafter, Jai began working by helping locate customers in the store who needed assistance. Jai, who uses a wheelchair, eventually moved to the Car Audio department and worked with Best Buy and a local government agency to develop a system that allows him to check stock for customers on his own. Robyn Schuler, who also uses a wheelchair, began working at the store in 2006 and earned a promotion to Customer Associate. Robyn told store managers that the store's aisles were not wide enough. Upon her return from rehab, the issue had been fixed. Robyn is grateful that the store manager "treats [her] like any other person" and "doesn't baby her"

(APSE, 2008). Geek Squad agent Lisa Goodwin is deaf. She communicates with customers using a computer and monitor equipped with two keyboards. Managers have data to support their belief in the contributions made by their employees with disabilities. Best Buy's Customer Service Index tool allows guests to provide feedback on interactions with employees and these three employees are consistently among the highest rated.

Not content to rest on past successes and acknowledging that there is more value to be gained from further inclusion, Best Buy continues to seek new opportunities for employees with disabilities. In 2010, a local non-profit and an Illinois government agency partnered in awarding Best Buy a two-year grant to develop Internal Disability Teams for its stores in the Chicago area. The teams will be self-sustaining and capable of providing training on accommodations, support for employees with disabilities and actively encouraging the recruiting, screening, training and promoting processes for employees with disabilities.

SOCIAL RESPONSIBILITY: PARTNERING WITH SCHOOLS FOR THE DEAF

Two Best Buy stores located near schools for the deaf have developed programs to better serve hearing impaired customers. Store 427 in Fredericksburg, MD created a video introducing its associates who are fluent in American Sign Language (ASL) and listing the departments in which each works. The video, which was distributed to the nearby Maryland School for the Deaf, also informed customers that they could communicate with employees while in the store using a computer and monitor with dual keyboards. In Riverside, CA, store #392, is near the California School for the Deaf, one of the largest K-12 institutions for the deaf in the country. So, management recruited six employees to serve as ASL interpreters both in-store and online, designed a web interface that allows consumers to browse the products on the website and discuss them with employees fluent in ASL via a window on the screen. Customers can also view the work schedules of these employees before going to the store.

INTERNSHIPS

Internships can provide a mutually beneficial opportunity for both the employer and the employee. While participating on the school's Business Advisory Board, Best Buy established a partnership with Minnesota Life College, which trains young adults with learning disabilities and is located near Best Buy's headquarters in Richfield, MN. INCLUDE member Michele Swiech went beyond hiring interns from the college when she encouraged two of Best Buy's corporate vendors, Bon Appetit and Pitney Bowes, to hire students from the program as well (Pershing, 2008).

AWARDS

In 2010, National Rehabilitation Association (NRA) recognized Best Buy for being a leader in recruiting, hiring and accommodating employees with disabilities. Best Buy was nominated for the award by Brendon Cunningham, the Virginia Territory Project Manager who was paralyzed from the waist down in a swimming accident. After the accident, Best Buy provided support to his family and retrofitted the store where he worked to meet his needs. Recounting her response to Cunningham's accident, Susan Williams, the territory HR director said, "I knew we would find a place for Brendon. And, I said that with certainty without talking to anyone." Williams' reaction indicates that the inclusion of people with disabilities may be deeply imbedded as what Schein would call an operational value in Best Buy's culture. As a Territory Project Manager, Brendon is responsible for the planning and implementation of growth initiatives in the field and leading complex rollouts while also sharpening their individual skills through continued involvement in management training programs. Providing anecdotal support for the business case for diversity, Cunningham said that he frequently receives emails and phone calls from customers reporting that they made purchases at Best Buy after learning about how well the company treated him (Cunningham, 2008).

Diversity Best Practices presented its 2010 Executive Sponsor award to Julie St. Marie, executive sponsor of INCLUDE and the mother of a child with a disability. She has developed new positions for *INCLUDE* members, implemented policy changes for accommodation programs and created consortiums with retail competitors. St. Marie's efforts were also rewarded by the Department of Labor's New Freedom Initiative Award in 2008 which is the highest honor in the U.S. for organizations and individuals demonstrating exemplary and innovative efforts to further the employment and workplace environment for people with disabilities.

Down Syndrome of Louisville (DSL) presented Best Buy's Geek Squad and its INCLUDE group the Employer of the Year award in 2010, recognizing their actions to, "improve the quality of life or promoted a positive image for individuals with Down Syndrome." Local Best Buy employees have shown a commitment to "hiring individuals with developmental delays in respectful and meaningful employment along with volunteer fundraising to build DSL's Lifelong Learning Center" (INCLUDE, 2010).

The Association for Persons in Supported Employment (APSE) presented Store 493, in Alexandria, VA which employs the three persons with disabilities with its 2008 award for Best Employment Practices. This award recognizes businesses that "hire persons with disabilities, fully integrates them into the workforce and encourages other organizations to do the same." A Best Buy customer, who owns an employment agency for individuals with disabilities, saw these employees in action and nominated the store for the award.

AMERICANS WITH DISABILITIES ACT (ADA, 1990)

This federal legislation is designed to "prevent discrimination and enable individuals with disabilities to participate fully in all aspects of society" (U.S. Department of Justice, 2000).

Points of Law

The ADA prohibits discrimination on the basis of disability in employment, state and local government, public accommodations, commercial facilities, transportation, and telecommunications (U.S. Department of Justice, 2005). To be protected by the ADA, one must have a disability or have a relationship or association with an individual with a disability.

An individual with a disability is defined by the ADA as a person who has a physical or mental impairment that substantially limits one or more major life activities, a person who has a history or record of such an impairment, or a person who is perceived by others as having such an impairment. The ADA does not specifically name all of the impairments that are covered (U.S. Department of Justice, 2005).

From an employment perspective, Title I applies to organizations with 15 or more employees and it prohibits discrimination in recruitment, hiring, promotions, training, pay, social activities, and other privileges of employment. The law requires that employers make reasonable accommodation to the known physical or mental limitations of otherwise qualified individuals with disabilities, unless it results in an "undue hardship" for the organization which means accommodations that would result in significant difficulty or expense (U.S. Department of Justice, 2005).

Examples of reasonable accommodations include: reducing clutter and distractions for an employee with a brain injury, providing specialized equipment such as a large-key keyboard for a data entry operator who has lost an arm, providing written instructions and information for an employee with hearing loss and allowing an employee to bring his or her service animal to work.

CONCLUSION

Over many years, Best Buy has carefully created a culture of diversity inclusion in its stores and at its corporate headquarters and has operationalized this into each of its three pillars: employees, customers and the community. Best Buy has gone beyond its espoused values to involve employees at all levels of the organization, provide resources that support action and celebrate its success. While Best Buy recognizes the value of including people with disabilities as corporate citizen, the company also understands the impact on the bottom line. As a 2010 company publication states, "by creating an inclusive environment . . . Best Buy can find and keep the best talent, become a trusted community partner and achieve profitable growth" (Diversity & Inclusion, 2010).

Bibliography

About Best Buy. Best Buy Co, Inc. http://www.bby.com/about/

All field employee business network conference call. Best Buy Co, Inc. records. January 28, 2010.

All field employee business network conference call. Best Buy Co, Inc. records. September 8, 2010.

All field employee business network conference call. Best Buy Co, Inc. records. June 8, 2010.

ASL Canyon Springs [Video file]. Best Buy Co, Inc. Retrieved from http://ourstories.iambestbuy.com/ASL_Canyon_Springs.html

Best Buy corporate values and vision. Best Buy Co, Inc. 2010. Retrieved from http://phx.corporate-ir.net/phoenix.zhtml?c=83192&p=irol-faq#4

Best Buy FACE—Facing autism in a caring environment. Retrieved from http://www.facebook.com/group.php?gid=110145238996618

Blanck, P.D. (1999). Empirical study of disability, employment policy, and the ADA. *Mental and Physical Disability Law Reporter, 23,* 275–284.

Brault, M.B. (2008). *Americans with disabilities: 2005.* Current population reports. United States

Census Bureau. December 2008, 70–117.

Cunningham, B. Brendon's story [Video file]. Retrieved from http://www.youtube.com/watch?v=IUGuNmvkJ2U. October 9, 2008.

Datamonitor company profile: Best Buy Co, Inc. (2010). London, UK: Datamonitor.

Disabilityworks. (2007). DePaul University study of costs and benefits of employing people with disabilities finds few risks to employers. Chicago, IL.

Diversity & inclusion brochure. (2010). Best Buy Co, Inc. Retrieved from http://www.canyoubeyou.com/CanUbeU_brochure_1.7MB.pdf

Diversity at Best Buy. (2010). Retrieved from http://www.canyoubeyou.com/home.html

Dunn, B. (2010, November 28). Brian's whiteboard. 26 and counting. Retrieved from http://www.bbycommunications.com/briandunn/index.php

EBN express newsletter. Best Buy Co, Inc. records. March 2010.

Employee business networks homepage. Best Buy Co, Inc. Retrieved from http://canyoubeyou.com/Employee_Business_Networks.html

Focusing on abilities [Video file]. Best Buy Co, Inc. Retrieved from http://ourstories.iambestbuy.com/Focusing_On_Abilities.html

For Best Buy workers, a racial orientation [Video file]. MSNBC. April 4, 2008. Retrieved from http://www.msnbc.msn.com/id/22425001/vp/23960059#23960059

Hiring the best . . . at Best Buy! (2008). The Advance. APSE: The Network on Employment, 19 (1), 4–7. Retrieved from http://www.apse.org/docs/Spring 2008 Final.pdf

INCLUDE employee business network homepage. (2010). Best Buy Co, Inc. Retrieved from http://canyoubeyou.com/INCLUDE.html

INCLUDE employee business network conference call. Best Buy Co, Inc. records. August 10, 2010.

INCLUDE employee business network conference call. Best Buy Co, Inc. records. July 13, 2010.

INCLUDE employee business network conference call. Best Buy Co, Inc. records. May 12, 2010.

INCLUDE employee business network conference call. Best Buy Co, Inc. records. February 17, 2010.

Job Accommodation Network. (2010). *Workplace accommodations: Low cost, high impact.* JAN Fact Sheet Series. Morgantown, WV.

King, M. and Bearman, P. (2009). Diagnostic change and increased prevalence of autism. *International Journal of Epidemiology*, 38, 1224–1234.

McNeil, J. Employment, earnings, and disability. (2000). *Data from the survey of income and program participation.* Prepared for the 75th Annual Conference of the Western Economic Association International. Vancouver, BC. Retrieved from http://www.census.gov/hhes/www/disability/emperndis.pdf

Number of disabled U.S. veterans rising. (2008). CBS News. May 11, 2008. Retrieved from http://www.cbsnews.com/stories/2008/05/11/national/main4086442.shtml?source=RSSattr=Health_4086442

Pershing, J. (2008). Application for 2008 New Freedom Initiative Award. Best Buy Co, Inc. records. May 30, 2008.

Rice, C. (2009). Prevalence of autism spectrum disorders, 2006. Autism and developmental disabilities monitoring network. *Morbidity and Mortality Weekly Report*, 58 (SS-10).

Riley, C.A. (2006). *Disability and business: Best practices and strategies for inclusion.* Lebanon, NH: University Press of New England.

Ryan Hemphill Best Buy story [Video file]. (2010). Retrieved from http://www.youtube.com/watch?v=6-sVj4Ja-tM

Schein, E.H. (2010). *Organizational culture and leadership.* New York, NY: John Wiley & Sons.

Siperstein, G.N., Romano, N., Mohler, A. and Parker, R. (2006). A national survey of consumer attitudes towards companies that hire people with disabilities. *Journal of Vocational Rehabilitation*, 24, 3–9.

Territory Business Manager job description. Best Buy Co, Inc records. November 28, 2010.

U.S. Department of Justice, Civil Rights Division, Disability Rights Section. (2000). *Americans with disabilities act: A guide for people with disabilities seeking employment.* ICN 951750.

U.S. Department of Justice, Civil Rights Division, Disability Rights Section. (2005). *Guide to disability rights laws.* Retrieved from http://www.ada.gov/cguide.pdf

U.S. Department of Justice, Civil Rights Division, Disability Rights Section. (2010). *Know your rights, returning service members with disabilities.* Retrieved from http://www.ada.gov/servicemembers_adainfo.pdf

U.S. Department of Education. Institute of Education Sciences. National Center for Education Statistics. Digest of Education Statistics. (2005). Table 210. *Number and percentage of students enrolled in postsecondary institutions, by level, disability status, and selected student characteristics: 2003–04.* Retrieved from http://nces.ed.gov/programs/digest/d05/tables/dt05_210.asp

Vogel, N.O. and Brown, C. (2009). *Dive in: Springboard into the profitability, productivity and potential of the special needs workforce.* Ithaca, NY: Paramount Market Publishing.

Wright, M.W. and Ferguson, W.J. (2005). *The new business normal: the peril and promise of new global realities.* Chaska, MN: Knowledge Management Press.

DISCUSSION QUESTIONS

1. Best Buy's flagship Transformational Learning Program is a three-day immersion experience in Memphis, Tennessee. In recent years, Best Buy has sent more than 1,300 workers to participate in the program, which includes a visit to the National Civil Rights Museum. Each participant develops a Diversity & Inclusion Action Plan aimed at creating an inclusive environment for employees and customers. This program is an example of a hands-on learning experience. How could Best Buy create a hands-on experience to train its employees on the inclusion of people with disabilities?

2. The INCLUDE group for persons with handicaps has three areas of focus: to utilize disability recruitment, resources and innovations to close gaps in the workforce and marketplace, to provide growth, profitability and a competitive advantage; to serve a diverse market by providing products and services expected by our customers; to communicate and educate information to the community that does not often get into the mainstream papers or news programs. Evaluate Best Buy's performance against the three focus areas for INCLUDE. How can Best Buy improve its performance in each area?

3. Best Buy offers financial support for local store employees to test new ways to reach out to customers with disabilities. Several specific examples are listed in the case above. List three additional examples of low-cost initiatives any retail store could develop to strengthen relationships with customers with any type of disability.

4. Explain why Best Buy's industry provides the company with incentives to create a strong culture of inclusion for people with disabilities.

Writing Assignment

In 2007, the Anderson School of Management at UCLA created a leadership development program for mid-level managers with disabilities. Go to http://www.anderson.ucla.edu and search for "Leadership Institute for Managers with Disabilities." Read about the program and write a one- to two-page memo to your boss justifying how both your company and the employee could benefit by sending one of your talented subordinates to this program.

Diversity on the Web

Go to http://ourstories.iambestbuy.com. Search for and watch the video "Focusing on Abilities." How does Best Buy's commitment to the inclusion of people with disabilities affect your perception of the company as a customer and as a potential employee?

David P. Harvey is a graduate student at the Carlson School of Management at the University of Minnesota. Prior to returning to graduate school, he held sales and finance positions at manufacturing and technology firms in Boston and Seattle.

Sexual Harassment—Who Is Right and Who Is Wrong?

Carol P. Harvey
Assumption College

INSTRUCTIONS

Given the legal guidelines in the Points of Law box below, which of the following incidents are examples of sexual harassment? Explain your reasons for your answers.

🏛 Points of Law

The Equal Employment Opportunity Commission's Guidelines defines sexual harassment as . . . Unwelcome sexual advances, requests for sexual favors, and other physical and verbal contact of a sexual nature when it affects the terms of employment under one or more of the following conditions: such an activity is a condition for employment; such as an activity is a condition of employment consequences such as promotion, dismissal, or salary increases; such an activity creates a hostile working environment.

---

1. While teaching Gary how to run the new spreadsheet program on the computer, Lois, his supervisor, puts her hand on his shoulder.

2. Julie, the new secretary to the vice president of manufacturing, frequently has to go out into the plant as part of her job. Several of the machinists have been whistling at her and shouting off-color remarks as she passes through the shop. One of the other women in the company found Julie crying in the ladies' room after such an incident.

3. Paul and Cynthia, two sales reps, are both married. However, it is well known that they are dating each other outside of the office.

4. Jeanne's boss, Tom, frequently asks her out for drinks after work. She goes because both are single and she enjoys his company. On one of these occasions, he asks her out to dinner for the following Saturday evening.

5. Steve's boss, Cathy, frequently makes suggestive comments to him and has even suggested that they meet outside of the office. Although at first he ignored these remarks, recently he made it clear to her that he had a steady girlfriend and was not available. When she gave him his performance appraisal, much to his surprise, she cited him for not being a team player.

6. Jackie received a call at work that her father died suddenly. When she went to tell her boss that she had to leave, she burst into tears. He put his arms around her and let her cry on his shoulder.

7. Marge's coworker, Jerry, frequently tells her that what she is wearing is very attractive.

8. While being hired as a secretary, Amanda is told that she may occasionally be expected to accompany managers on important overnight business trips to handle the clerical duties at these meetings.

9. Joe, an elderly maintenance man, often makes suggestive comments to the young females in the office. His behavior has been reported to his supervisor several times but it is dismissed as, "Don't be so sensitive, old Joe doesn't mean any harm."

10. Jennifer frequently wears revealing blouses to the office. Several times she has caught male employees staring at her.

THE CRACKER BARREL RESTAURANTS

John Howard
King's College London

GOALS

- To explore sexual orientation employment discrimination issues in the workforce
- To understand the implications of having only minimal legislation in the United States that protects LGBT employee rights
- To provide current information on workplace and customer discrimination conflicts at Cracker Barrel Restaurants

Discrimination against lesbians and gays is common in the workplace. Sole proprietors, managing partners, and corporate personnel officers can and often do make hiring, promoting, and firing decisions based on an individual's real or perceived sexual orientation. Lesbian and gay job applicants are turned down and lesbian and gay employees are passed over for promotion or even fired by employers who view homosexuality as somehow detrimental to job performance or harmful to the company's public profile. Such discrimination frequently results from the personal biases of individual decision makers. It is rarely written into company policy and thus is difficult to trace. However, in January 1991, Cracker Barrel Old Country Store, Inc., a chain of family restaurants, became the first and only major American corporation in recent memory to expressly prohibit the employment of lesbians and gays in its operating units. A nationally publicized boycott followed, with demonstrations in dozens of cities and towns. The controversy would not be resolved until a decade later. In the interim, Cracker Barrel would also face several charges of racism from both its employees and customers—suggesting that corporate bias against one cultural group may prove a useful predictor of bias against others.

THE COMPANY: A BRIEF HISTORY OF CRACKER BARREL

Dan Evins founded Cracker Barrel in 1969 in his hometown of Lebanon, Tennessee, 40 miles east of Nashville. Evins, a 34-year-old ex-Marine sergeant and oil jobber, decided to take advantage of the traffic on the nearby interstate highway and open a gas station with a restaurant and gift shop. Specializing in down-home cooking at low prices, the restaurant was immediately profitable.

Evins began building Cracker Barrel stores throughout the region, gradually phasing out gasoline sales. By 1974, he owned a dozen restaurants. Within five years of going public in 1981, Cracker Barrel doubled its number of stores and quadrupled its revenues: In 1986, there were 47 Cracker Barrel restaurants with net sales of $81 million. Continuing to expand aggressively, the chain again grew to twice its size and nearly quadrupled its revenues during the next 5 years.

By the end of the fiscal year, August 2, 1991, Cracker Barrel operated over 100 stores, almost all located along the interstate highways of the Southeast and, increasingly, the Midwest. Revenues exceeded $300 million. Employing roughly 10,000 nonunionized workers, Cracker Barrel ranked well behind such mammoth family chains as Denny's and Big Boy in total sales, but led all U.S. family chains in sales per operating unit for both 1990 and 1991.

As of 1991, Cracker Barrel was a well-recognized corporate success story, known for its effective, centralized, but authoritarian leadership. From its headquarters, Cracker Barrel maintained uniformity in its store designs, menu offerings, and operating procedures. Travelers and local customers dining at any Cracker Barrel restaurant knew to expect a spacious, homey atmosphere; an inexpensive, country-style meal; and a friendly, efficient staff. All were guaranteed by Dan Evins, who remained as president, chief executive officer, and chairman of the board.

THE POLICY: NO LESBIAN OR GAY EMPLOYEES

In early January 1991, managers in the roughly 100 Cracker Barrel operating units received a communiqué from the home office in Lebanon. The personnel policy memorandum from William Bridges, vice president of human resources, declared that Cracker Barrel was "founded upon a concept of traditional American values." As such, it was deemed "inconsistent with our concept and values and . . . with those of our customer base, to continue to employ individuals . . . whose sexual preferences fail to demonstrate normal heterosexual values which have been the foundation of families in our society."

Throughout the chain, individual store managers, acting on orders of corporate officials, began conducting brief, one-on-one interviews with their employees to see if any were in violation of the new policy. Cheryl Summerville, a cook in the Douglasville, Georgia, store for 3½ years, asked if she were a lesbian, knew she had to answer truthfully. She felt she owed that to her partner of 10 years. Despite a history of consistently high performance evaluations, Summerville was fired on the spot, without warning and without severance pay. Her official separation notice, filled out by the manager and filed with the state department of labor, clearly indicated the reason for her dismissal: "This employee is being terminated due to violation of company policy. The employee is gay."

Cracker Barrel fired as many as 16 other employees across several states in the following months. These workers, mostly waiters, were left without any legal recourse. Lesbian and gay antidiscrimination statutes were in effect in Massachusetts and Wisconsin and in roughly 80 U.S. cities and counties, but none of the firings occurred in those jurisdictions. Federal civil rights laws, the employees learned, did not cover discrimination based on sexual orientation.

Under pressure from a variety of groups, the company issued a statement in late February 1991. In it, Cracker Barrel management said, "We have re-visited our thinking on the subject and feel it only makes good business sense to continue to employ those folks who will provide the quality service our customers have come to expect." The recent personnel policy had been a "well-intentioned over-reaction." Cracker Barrel pledged to deal with any future disruptions in its units "on a store-by-store basis." Activists charged that the statement did not represent a retraction of the policy, as some company officials claimed. None of the fired employees had been rehired, activists noted, and none had been offered severance pay. Moreover, on February 27, just days after the statement, Dan Evins reiterated the company's antagonism toward nonheterosexual employees in a rare interview with a Nashville newspaper. Lesbians and gays, he said, would not be employed in more rural Cracker Barrel locations if their presence was viewed to cause problems in those communities.

THE BOYCOTT: QUEER NATIONALS VERSUS GOOD OL' BOYS

The next day, when news of Cracker Barrel employment policies appeared in *The Wall Street Journal, New York Times,* and *Los Angeles Times,* investment analysts expressed surprise. "I look on [Cracker Barrel executives] as pretty prudent business people," said one market watcher. "These guys are not fire-breathing good ol' boys." Unconvinced, lesbian and gay activists called for a nationwide boycott of Cracker Barrel restaurants and began a series of demonstrations that attracted extensive media coverage.

The protest movement was coordinated by the Atlanta chapter of Queer Nation, which Cheryl Summerville joined as co-chair with Lynn Cothren, an official with the Martin Luther King, Jr. Center for Non-Violent Social Change. Committed to nonviolent civil disobedience, lesbian and gay activists and supporters staged pickets and sit-ins at various Cracker Barrel locations, often occupying an entire restaurant during peak lunch hours, ordering only coffee.

Protesters were further angered and spurred on by news in June from Mobile, Alabama. A 16-year-old Cracker Barrel employee had been fired for effeminate mannerisms and subsequently was thrown out of his home by his father. Demonstrations continued throughout the summer of 1991, spreading from the Southeast to the Midwest stores. Arrests were made at demonstrations in the Detroit area; Cothren and Summerville were among several people arrested for criminal trespass at both the Lithonia and Union City, Georgia, stores. Reporters and politicians dubbed Summerville the "Rosa Parks of the movement," after the civil rights figure whose arrest sparked the Montgomery, Alabama Bus Boycott of 1955–1956.

Support for the Cracker Barrel boycott grew, as organizers further charged the company with racism and sexism. Restaurant gift shops, they pointed out, sold Confederate flags, black mammy dolls, and other offensive items. The Cracker Barrel board of directors, they said, was indeed a good ol' boy network, made up exclusively of middle-aged and older white men. In addition, there was only one female in the ranks of upper management. Among the numerous groups that joined in support of the protests were the National Organization for Women (NOW); Jobs with Justice, a coalition of labor unions; the National Rainbow Coalition, founded by Reverend Jesse Jackson; and the American Association of Public Health Workers. By early 1992, Summerville and Cothren had appeared on the television talk shows "Larry King Live" and "The Oprah Winfrey Show." The two were also featured in a segment on ABC's "20/20," after which Barbara Walters declared that she would refuse to eat at Cracker Barrel restaurants

THE RESOLUTION: NEW YORK ATTEMPTS TO FORCE CHANGE

Meanwhile, New York City comptroller, Elizabeth Holtzman, and finance commissioner, Carol O'Cleiracain, at the urging of the National Gay and Lesbian Task Force, wrote a letter to Dan Evins, dated March 12, 1991. As trustees of various city pension funds, which owned about $3 million in Cracker Barrel stock, they were "concerned about the potential negative impact on the company's sales and earnings which could result from adverse public reaction." They asked for a "clear statement" of the company's policy regarding employment and sexual orientation, as well as a description of "what remedial steps, if any, [had] been taken by the company respecting the employees dismissed."

Evins replied in a letter of March 19 that the policy had been rescinded and that there had been "no negative impact on the company's sales." Unsatisfied, the City of New York officials wrote back, again inquiring as to the status of the fired workers. They also asked that the company put forth a policy that "would provide unequivocally" that discrimination based on sexual orientation was prohibited. Evins never responded.

Shortly thereafter, Queer Nation launched a "buy one" campaign. Hoping to gain additional leverage in company decision making, activists became stockholders by purchasing single shares of Cracker Barrel common stock. At the least, they reasoned, the company would suffer from the relative expense of mailing and processing numerous one-cent quarterly dividend checks. More importantly, they could attend the annual stockholders meeting in Lebanon, Tennessee.

In November 1991, company officials successfully prevented the new shareholders from participating in the annual meeting, and they used a court injunction to block protests at the corporate complex. Nonetheless, demonstrators lined the street, while inside, a representative of the New York City comptroller's office announced the submission of a resolution "banning employment discrimination against gay and lesbian men and women," to be voted on at the next year's meeting. The resolution was endorsed by the Philadelphia Municipal Retirement System, another major stockholder. Cracker Barrel refused any further public comment on the issue.

THE EFFECT: NO DECLINE IN CORPORATE GROWTH

The impact of the boycott on the corporate bottom line was negligible. Trade magazines reiterated the company's claim that neither sales nor stock price had been negatively affected. Indeed, net sales remained strong, up 33% at fiscal year-end 1992 to $400 million, owing in good part to continued expansion: There were now 127 restaurants in the chain. Though the increase in same-store sales was not as great as the previous year, Cracker Barrel at least could boast growth, whereas other chains blamed flat sales on the recession. Cracker Barrel stock, trading on the NASDAQ exchange, appreciated 18% during the first month after news of the scandal broke, and the stock remained strong throughout the next fiscal year, splitting three-for-two in the third quarter.

Dan Evins had good reason to believe that the firings and the boycott had not adversely impacted profitability. One market analyst said that "the feedback they get from their customers might be in favor of not hiring homosexuals." Another even ventured that "it's plausible . . . the majority of Cracker Barrel's local users support an explicit discriminatory policy." Such speculation was bolstered by social science surveys indicating that respondents from the South and from rural areas in particular tended to be less tolerant of homosexuality than were other Americans.

Queer Nationals looked to other measures of success, claiming at least partial victory in the battle. Many customers they met at picket lines and inside restaurants vowed to eat elsewhere. Coalitions were formed with a variety of civil rights, women's, labor, and peace and justice organizations. Most importantly, the media attention greatly heightened national awareness of the lack of protections for lesbians and gays on the job. As the boycott continued, increasing numbers of states, counties, and municipalities passed legislation designed to prevent employment discrimination based on sexual orientation.

THE STANDOFF: OLD ANTAGONISMS, NEW ALLEGATIONS

As the November 1992 annual meeting approached, Cracker Barrel requested that the Securities and Exchange Commission make a ruling on the resolution offered by the New York pension fund administrators. The resolution, according to Cracker Barrel, amounted to shareholder intrusion into the company's ordinary business operations. As such, it should be excluded from consideration at the annual meeting and excluded from proxy ballots sent out before the meeting. The SEC agreed, despite previous rulings in which it had allowed stockholder resolutions regarding race- or gender-based employment bias.

Acknowledging that frivolous stockholder inquiries had to be curtailed, the dissenting SEC commissioner nonetheless expressed great dismay: "To claim that the shareholders, as owners of the corporation, do not have a legitimate interest in management-sanctioned discrimination against employees defies logic." A noted legal scholar warned of the dangerous precedent that had been set: "Ruling an entire area of corporate activity (here, employee relations) off limits to moral debate effectively disenfranchises shareholders."

Thus, the standoff continued. Queer Nation and its supporters persisted in the boycott. The Cracker Barrel board of directors and, with one exception, upper management remained all-white, all-male bastions. Lynn Cothren, Cheryl Summerville, and the other protesters arrested in Lithonia, Georgia, were acquitted on charges of criminal trespass. Jurors ruled that the protesters' legitimate reasons for peaceably demonstrating superseded the company's rights to deny access or refuse service. Charges stemming from the Union City, Georgia, demonstrations were subsequently dropped. Meanwhile, within weeks of the original policy against lesbian and gay employees, Cracker Barrel vice president for human resources, William Bridges, had left the company. Cracker Barrel declined comment on the reasons for his departure.

Lesbian and gay activists' charge of racism at Cracker Barrel seemed to be borne out over time. In the year 2000, a local human rights commission awarded $5,000 in damages to a black employee in Kentucky after she suffered racial and religious bias in the scheduling of shifts. Months later, the NAACP joined a group of employees and former employees in a class-action lawsuit against Cracker Barrel, alleging that the company repeatedly discriminated against African Americans in hiring, promotions, and firing practices. African-American workers further were said to have received less pay, to have been given inferior terms and conditions of employment, and to have been subjected to racial epithets and racist jokes, including one told by Dan Evins. In a second suit filed by the NAACP, along with 42 customers, and supported by over 400 witnesses, Cracker Barrel was accused of repeatedly offering better, faster, segregated seating to whites and inferior service to blacks. A similar case was filed by 23 African Americans in Little Rock a year later.

THE OUTCOME: POLICY REVERSALS

As of 2002, Cracker Barrel's annual net sales surpassed two billion dollars. The company still had not issued a complete retraction of its employment policy with regard to sexual orientation, and those employees fired back in 1991 had never been offered their old jobs back. In contrast, for a year's work, Chairman Dan Evins regularly pulled in over a million dollars in salary, bonus, awards, and stock options.

A total of 14 states and the District of Columbia offered protections for lesbians and gays on the job, both in the public and private sectors. With over 400 restaurants in 41 states, Cracker Barrel now operated in 11 of those jurisdictions with protections: California, Connecticut, Maryland, Massachusetts, Minnesota, New Hampshire, New Jersey, New Mexico, New York, Rhode Island, and Wisconsin. (The other states with antidiscrimination statutes were Hawaii, Nevada, and Vermont.) Expansion had taken the company into areas even less receptive to employment discrimination. As one business editor had correctly predicted, "Cracker Barrel [wa]sn't going to be in the South and Midwest forever. Eventually they w[ould] have to face the issue—like it or not."

In 1998, the SEC reversed itself, allowing the New York City Employees' Retirement System to again offer a shareholder resolution, which was defeated yet again and again. By 2002, however, the tide was turning. In its proxy statement sent out in advance of the annual meeting, the Cracker Barrel board of directors still recommended that stockholders vote against the proposal. "[A]ny attempt to name all possible examples of prohibited discrimination other than those . . . specifically prohibited by federal law," it said, "would result in a long list" that was neither "appropriate" nor "necessary."

But shareholders were ready to defy the board. After 58 percent voted in support of the proposal in an informal vote, the board members unanimously agreed to add the category of sexual orientation to its equal employment opportunities policy.

THE PROPOSAL: FEDERAL LEGISLATION

In 36 states it is perfectly legal to fire workers because they are gay—or straight. For example, a Florida bar owner decided to newly target a lesbian and gay clientele and so fired the entire heterosexual staff. Queer activists boycotted, and the bar eventually was forced out of business. Still, in most American jurisdictions, employment discrimination based on sexual orientation remains a constant threat.

The vast majority of Americans, 80%, tell pollsters that lesbians and gays should have equal rights in terms of job opportunities. In every region including the South, among both Democrats and Republicans, solid majorities support federal legislation to remedy the situation. Nonetheless, despite several close votes in Congress, the Employment Non-Discrimination Act, or ENDA, has yet to be passed into law.

Although there are no federal laws to prevent discrimination based on sexual orientation, protections do exist for workers on the basis of religion, gender, national origin, age, disability, and race. Still, as the NAACP and other lawsuits against Cracker Barrel demonstrate, federal legislation does not ensure corporate compliance. Aggrieved parties and their supporters often must invest years of their lives in protest and litigation simply to achieve the equal treatment ostensibly guaranteed in the American marketplace. Even after the terms *race* and *sexual orientation* have been added to policy statements, broader cultural transformations will be required before these added burdens are removed from the shoulders of workers already greatly disadvantaged in our society.

DISCUSSION QUESTIONS

1. Discuss the factors that make it more difficult to establish workplace discrimination based on sexual orientation than discrimination based on race??

2. Do chain restaurant operations, which prize uniformity—and thus reliability—in store design, products, and operating procedures, require uniformity of personnel policies? Were the regional variations that Dan Evins proposed on February 27, 1991, a viable corporate strategy? Why or why not?

3. How does the Cracker Barrel case support or challenge the notion that federal legislation is warranted to stop employment discrimination based on sexual orientation?

4. Why are particular retail products, for example, inanimate objects such as mammy dolls, perceived to be racist?

5. Which areas of corporate activity should be open to broader scrutiny through shareholder resolutions? How much stake in the company should a shareholder have in order to present a resolution?

6. If a controversial corporate policy is reversed only after a decade of defiance, how should the company's public relations officers present the change to the media?

Bibliography

Atlanta Journal-Constitution, 6, 11 July 1993; 2, 3 April 1992; 29 March 1992; 4, 18, 20 January 1992; 9 June 1991; 3, 4, 5 March 1991.

Carlino, B. (1991, December 16). Cracker Barrel profits surge despite recession. *Nation's Restaurant News*, 14.

———. (1991, April 1). Cracker Barrel stocks, sales weather gay-rights dispute. *Nation's Restaurant News*, 14.

CBRL Group, Inc. Annual Reports, 2002, 2001.

———. Notice of Annual Meeting of Shareholders to be held on Tuesday, November 26, 2002. 30 October 2002.

Cracker Barrel Old Country Store, Inc. Annual Reports, 1999, 1996, 1992, 1991, 1990.

———. Notice of Annual Meeting of Shareholders to be held on Tuesday, November 26, 1996. 25 October 1996.

———. Third Quarter Report, 30 April 1993.

———. Second Quarter Report, 29 January 1993.

———. First Quarter Report, 30 October 1992.

———. Securities and Exchange Commission Form 10-K, 1992.

———. Securities and Exchange Commission Form 10-K, 1991.

Cheney, K. (1992, July 22). Old-fashioned ideas fuel Cracker Barrel's out-of-sight sales growth and profit increases. *Restaurants & Institutions*, 108.

Chicago Tribune, 5 April 1991.

Cracker Barrel Hit by Anti-Bias Protests. (1992, April 13). *Nation's Restaurant News*, 2.

Cracker Barrel sued for rampant racial discrimination in employment. (1999, October 5). NAACP press release.

Cracker Barrel's emphasis on quality a hit with travelers. (1991, April 3). *Restaurants & Institutions*, 24.

Dahir, M.S. (1992, June). Coming out at the Barrel. *The Progressive*, 14.

Documented cases of job discrimination based on sexual orientation. (1995). Washington, DC: Human Rights Campaign.

Farkas, D. Kings of the road. (1991, August). *Restaurant Hospitality*, 118–22.

Galst, L. (1992, May 19). Southern activists rise up. *The Advocate*, 54–57.

Greenberg, D. (1988). *The construction of homosexuality*. Chicago: University of Chicago Press.

Gutner, T. (1993, April 27). Nostalgia sells. *Forbes*, 102–3.

Harding, R. (1991, July 16). Nashville NAACP head stung by backlash from boycott support. *The Advocate*, 27.

———. (1991, April 9). Activists still press Tennessee eatery firm on anti-gay job bias. *The Advocate*, 17.

Hayes, J. (1991, August 26). Cracker Barrel protesters don't shake loyal patrons. *Nation's Restaurant News*, 3, 57.

———. (1991, March 4). Cracker Barrel comes under fire for ousting gays. *Nation's Restaurant News*, 1, 79.

Investors protest Cracker Barrel proxy plan. (1992, November). *Nation's Restaurant News*, 2, 14.

Larry King Live. CNN television, aired 2 December 1991.

Lexington-Fayette Urban County Human Rights Commission. (2000, August 2). Press Release: Lexington woman awarded $5,000 in discrimination case against Cracker Barrel. Retrieved from http://www.lfuchrc.org/News/2000/Press%20Release%20080200.htm

Los Angeles Times, 28 February 1991.

New York Times, 25 June 1999; 11 November 1992; 22 October 1992; 9 April 1992; 20 March 1991; 28 February 1991.

Oprah Winfrey Show. Syndicated television, aired January 1992.

Queer Nation. (n.d.) Documents on the Cracker Barrel Boycott. N.p.

San Diego Union-Tribune, 30 July 2003.

SEC upholds proxy ruling. (1993, February 8), *Pensions & Investments*, 28.

Star, M.G. (1992, October 26). SEC policy reversal riles activist groups. *Pensions & Investments*, 33.

The (Nashville) *Tennessean*, 27 February 1991.

20/20. ABC television, aired 29 November 1991.

Walkup, C. (1991, August 5). Family chains beat recession blues with value, service. *Nation's Restaurant News*, 100, 104.

Wall Street Journal, 9 March 1993; 2 February 1993; 26 January 1993; 28 February 1991.

Washington Lawyers' Committee for Civil Rights and Urban Affairs. (2003, July 30). Press Release: 23 African American patrons file lawsuit against Cracker Barrel Restaurants for civil rights violations. Retrieved from http://www.washlaw.org/news/releases/073003.htm

Wildmoon, K.C. (1992, December 10). QN members allowed to attend Cracker Barrel stockholder's meeting. *Southern Voice*, 3.

———. (1992, October 22). Securities and Exchange Commission side with Cracker Barrel on employment discrimination. *Southern Voice*, 1.

———. (1992, July 9). DeKalb drops most charges against Queer Nation. *Southern Voice*, 3.

John Howard, PhD, is Professor of American Studies at King's College London. He is the author of *Concentration Camps on the Home Front* (2008) and *Men Like That* (1999), both from the University of Chicago Press.

CRACKER BARREL OLD COUNTRY STORES: POSTSCRIPT

Carol P. Harvey
Assumption College

Although Cracker Barrel Old Country Stores added sexual orientation to its anti-discrimination policies in 2002, and posts an Equal Opportunity Statement on its website, the restaurant chain has been sued for racial discrimination involving employees and customers, as well as sexual harassment and retaliation against an employee who lodged a formal complaint for a supervisor's derogatory racial remarks. Employees alleged disparate treatment because of race, such as inadequate wages and assigning African Americans primarily to dishwashing duties and/or waiting only on African American customers (Iwata, 2004). African American customers complained of excessive supervision while shopping; racial slurs; long waits while white patrons received tables; being segregated into smoking sections in the back of the restaurants, even when they requested the non-smoking section; and being served food from the trash.

Department of Justice interviews with current and former employees revealed that 80 out of 150 witnessed or experienced racial discrimination and that most complaints were not investigated.

As a result, the Department of Justice ordered Cracker Barrel to implement changes, such as hire an outside auditor to ensure civil rights compliance, employ mystery shoppers to test individual stores for discriminatory practices, institute employee diversity training programs, post signs indicating how to file a formal discrimination complaint, and develop and implement procedures for investigating all discrimination allegations. (Schmidt & Copeland, 2004). In September, 2004, Cracker Barrel agreed to pay $8.7 million to the plaintiffs, which included the NAACP, to settle the civil lawsuits (Iwata, 2004).

In 2009, Cracker Barrel paid $250,000 to settle two additional diversity related lawsuits. The first one alleged that male managers and employees made suggestive remarks and told dirty jokes to female employees. When the employees complained, no action was taken by management. The second lawsuit, which was part of a Supreme Court ruling protecting workers who file bias claims from retaliation, involved a Black employee who was fired when he complained about racially offensive comments made by his supervisor (*USA Today*, 4/9/2009 & Biskupic, 2008).

The Cracker Barrel Old Country Stores Corporation now has almost 600 stores in forty-one states. In addition, the organization continues to win awards such as the Consumers Choice in Chains "Best Family Dining Chain" which it has won for 19 consecutive years. Beginning in 2000, Cracker Barrel Old Country Store Inc. was listed in Fortune magazine's annual list of "America's Most Admired Companies" for nine consecutive years (Cracker Barrel.com).

Bibliography

Biskupic, J. (2010). Bias rulings protect workers, respect past. *USA Today*, May, 28. Retrieved July 25, 2010 from http://www.usatoday.com/cleanprint/?1280089603808.

Cracker Barrel.com. Cracker Barrel Old Country Store Inc., Recent Awards & Recognition. Retrieved July 22, 2010 from http://www.crackerbarrel.com/mediaroom-presskit.cfm?doc_id=1119.

Iwata, E. (2004). Restaurant to settle 7 lawsuits, pay $8.7 million. *USA Today*, September 9, p. B. 06

Schmidt, J. and Copeland, L. (2004). Cracker Barrel customer says bias was flagrant. *USA Today*, May 7, p. B. 01

USA Today. (2009). Cracker Barrel settles sexual harassment lawsuit. April 9. Retrieved on July 25, 2010 from http://www.usatoday.com/cleanprint/?1280089499396.

Diversity on the Web

Many of the Cracker Barrel restaurants are located in states with a significant African American population. Visit the Web sites below. These articles discuss popular misconceptions and stereotypes about the spending power of African American consumers. As the postscript indicates, Cracker Barrel has had ongoing legal issues with the Black community.

In terms of the business case for diversity, that is the business advantages of diversity in terms of profits, productivity, and recruitment of the most qualified employees, what can Cracker Barrel now do to repair its image with African American customers and potential employees?

a. http://www.multicultural.com. Under "multicultural experts," click on "African American Markets." Read "Maximizing Your Share of the African American Market."

b. http://www.frontpage.wiu.edu and search for "African Americans and Consumer Behavior."

Integrative Questions for Section 3

1. Provide examples of able bodied and age privileges.

2. For a young female employee, what are the advantages and disadvantages of having a mentor who is a member of the Baby Boomer generation?

3. Why are there no federal laws protecting LGBT workers from losing their jobs due to their sexual orientation?

4. Once after conducting the "Musical Chairs" exercise, an instructor asked the class how it felt. A student who spoke English as a second language responded by saying, "Wonderful. Now everybody has experienced what I feel every day." What could he have meant by that statement?

5. List the forces resisting change at Best Buy and Cracker Barrel. Then, apply Schein's organizational culture model to determine the underlying assumptions of these forces. Which of these are more apt to change and which are the most resistant?

6. How does the article on women as leaders help to explain why sexual harassment is still a workplace problem?

7. Since technology skills play a role in the differences among generations, what can organizations do to minimize these differences?

4

Understanding Secondary Aspects of Diversity: Social Class, Religion, Appearance/Weight, and Military Service

In this section, students will

▪ Learn that changes in one's secondary characteristics can impact one's work experiences.

▪ Explore the ramifications of social class privileges.

▪ Become more knowledgeable about the role of religion in U.S. society.

▪ Understand that one's weight, appearance, and military experience can make a difference in the workplace.

Aspects of one's social identity that are more changeable and less fixed are categorized as being secondary dimensions of diversity. We begin by examining the impact of social class on one's life experiences (Fahy; Harvey), then, continue to explore the role that religion (Fisher, McNett, and Sherer), weight and appearance (Allard), and military experience (Harvey) can play in the workplace.

This section concludes with an integrative exercise that illustrates the complexity of multiple aspects of diversity and team formation (Allard) and a case that demonstrates how subtle prejudice and multiple dimensions of social identity actually can prevent the most qualified candidate from being hired.

SOCIAL CLASS: THE FICTION OF AMERICAN MERITOCRACY

Colleen A. Fahy
Assumption College

GOALS

- To understand what "classism" means and its connection to views on America as a meritocracy
- To clarify the popular myths about social class mobility in the United States
- To understand the importance of social and cultural capital in the workplace
- To explore the connections between socioeconomic status, race, gender, access to education, and home ownership

INTRODUCTION

Oprah Winfrey, the nation's wealthiest African American, overcame impoverished beginnings in rural Mississippi to accumulate an estimated net worth of $2.7 billion.[1] High school friends Steve Jobs and Steve Wozniak founded the Apple Computer Company in Jobs' garage with $1300 in start-up money.[2] Sonia Sotomayor rose from a South Bronx housing project to become a U.S. Supreme Court justice. Such stories of self-made men and women help fuel the perception of America as the land of opportunity, a place where anyone can achieve almost anything with a combination of hard work, intelligence, and determination.

Do you believe that anyone, regardless of the family and community into which he or she was born, could be where you are today? If you are like most, your answer is yes. In a New York Times poll, 80 percent of Americans answered "yes" to the question, "Is it possible to start out poor, work hard, and become rich?"[3] A Chronicle of Higher Education poll found that 78.8 percent of college freshman agree that "through hard work, everybody can succeed in American society."[4]

The U.S. economic system is commonly viewed as a "**meritocracy**" where rewards are bestowed upon those who have earned them. If individuals face equality of opportunity, then one's social class position becomes a reflection of his or her personal qualities. Those who have achieved success must have earned it somehow, and those who have failed to climb the social ladder must simply have not tried hard enough. This common perception leads to the negative stereotyping and discrimination of individuals from lower social classes known as "classism."

Classism like many other "isms," results from prejudices based on false assumptions. Despite widely held perceptions, social class mobility in the United States is far from fluid. Those born with few resources face serious obstacles in their efforts to achieve higher economic and social status. Those born into privilege are given a head start in life with many extra boosts along the way. Once it is recognized that merit has only a small role in determining one's place on the social ladder, the foundation of classism crumbles.

SOCIAL CLASS MEASUREMENT

The most popular measures of social class are income and wealth. Persons, households or families can be ranked according to their income or wealth and then divided into groups. For example, in 2007, the highest 20 percent of U.S. households had an income exceeding $100,000—while the income of households in the lowest quintile fell below $20,300.[5] Because of its cumulative nature, wealth is unevenly distributed among the U.S. population, with the top 10 percent of families having an estimated median net worth of $1.4 million and the bottom 25 percent having a median net worth of $1700. The top 10 percent of families own an estimated 70 percent of the total net worth in the United States.[6]

Social class is also measured by educational achievement and occupational prestige. A National Opinion Research Center survey ranked 447 jobs in terms of their prestige level. Doctors came in first, accountants 35th, elementary school teachers 45th, retail salespersons 366th, and dishwashers 446th.[7] A housekeeper with an eighth grade education making $20,000 per year and holding $5000 in net worth is in the 16th percentile of total social class. A surgeon making $300,000 per year, with $1 million net worth is in the 99th percentile.[8]

CLASS IN THE WORKPLACE

The frequency of workplace interaction among persons of different social classes will vary by occupation and industry. For example, in occupations such as construction and education, workers are less likely to interact frequently with coworkers from significantly different social classes. In other settings, particularly when there is a hierarchical structure, individuals are more likely to work closely with those from other social classes. In hospitals, for example, doctors, nurses, CNAs (Certified Nursing Assistants), and maintenance workers come into frequent contact with one another (Scully & Blake-Beard, 2006, p. 442).

Defining class in the workplace is complicated by its multidimensional nature. While income, wealth, education, and occupation are undoubtedly correlated, associations are not always perfect. A carpenter may never have finished high school or he or she may be a college graduate. A retail salesperson may be a single mother working as the sole breadwinner for her family or a college-educated, married mother working for extra income.

In a meritocracy, those higher on the social ladder have done something to deserve their place and are therefore somehow considered "better" than those below them. The resulting sense of status can undoubtedly lead to friction in the workplace. According to Bullock (2004),

> In the United States, individualistic explanations for poverty (e.g., lack of thrift, laziness) and wealth (e.g., hard work, ability) tend to be favored over structural or societal attribution for poverty (e.g., failure of society to provide strong schools, discrimination) and wealth (e.g., inheritance, political influence, and "pull") (p. 232).

Bullock further argues that these beliefs lead to "classism" including negative stereotypes such as "lazy, uninterested in self-improvement, and lacking in initiative and intelligence" and discrimination that includes "behaviors that distance, avoid, and/or exclude poor and working class people" (p. 232).

Thus classism is rooted in the ultimate faith in America as a meritocracy, i.e., that economic and social outcomes are a function of merit because individuals face equal opportunity. Level playing fields promote social class mobility. Unfortunately, this is an idealistic view that fails to stand up under scrutiny. Social class mobility is very much constrained by existing economic and social systems. The movement of individuals from one social class to another is the exception, rather than the rule. Much of where you end up depends on where you begin.

SOCIAL MOBILITY IN THE UNITED STATES

In contrast to popular opinion, a number of studies have concluded that (1) social class is actually quite sticky, (2) class mobility has not increased in recent decades (and may even have decreased)[9] and (3) the United States has a relatively low level of social mobility compared with other developed nations. For example,

- 53.3 percent of the families who were in the lowest income quintile in 1988 were still there in 1998. Only 10.7 percent of these families made it into the top two quintiles (Bradbury and Katz, 2002).
- 53.2 percent of the families who were in the highest income quintile in 1988 were still there in 1998. Only 8.7 percent had fallen to the lowest two quintiles (Bradbury and Katz, 2002).
- One intergenerational study found that 6% of those born into the lowest income quintile end up in the highest while 42% stay in the bottom quintile (Isaacs, 2008a,b).
- An intergenerational study found that while 32.3 percent of white children born into the poorest income quintile were there as adults, this number jumps to 62.9 percent for blacks. (Hertz, 2006).
- The odds of reaching the top 5 percent of income earners is less than 2 percent for anyone starting out in the bottom 3 quintiles (Hertz, 2006).
- Parental income is highly correlated with the future income of children in the United States. A 10 percent change in parental earnings is predicted to have a 4.7 percent change in the expected future earning of the child (Hertz, 2006).
- In a 27 country survey, while only 19% of Americans agreed that "coming from a wealthy family is essential/very important to getting ahead," a comparison of nine high income countries found the United States to be second to last in terms of intergenerational mobility (Isaacs 2008a).

These studies paint a picture of a country where class mobility is significantly less fluid than most people would like to believe. The correlation between parent and child income and the low probability of moving up the income ladder seem to indicate that "making it" must not be as simple as setting a goal and working hard to achieve it. Of course, some parent–child correlation is expected. Sawhill and McLanahan (2006) write "the attributes that contribute to success in both generations—ability, motivation, and health—are at least partially inherited" (p. 5). However, such a high level of intergenerational correlation indicates that there is more than genetics at work.

If the playing field were truly level we would see significantly more movement between classes. Many more of those born into poverty would work their way up the ladder and many more of those born rich would find themselves sliding down.

EDUCATION

Equality of education is often cited as the key to social mobility. If our educational system ensured equal access and opportunities for all, regardless of social class, then the playing field would be significantly leveled. Unfortunately, socioeconomic status has a great deal of influence on what students bring to, as well as what they take from, the classroom. In summarizing sixteen recently published works on educational opportunity, McPherson and Schapiro (2006) conclude, "Educational opportunity in the United States is simply spectacularly unequal" (p. 6). Children's academic achievements are heavily dependent on the income, education, and race of their parents.

Elementary and Secondary Schools

Measures of math, reading, and social skills show significant differences among socioeconomic groups as early as kindergarten.[10] Possible explanations for this gap include differences in birth weight, health, parental skills, and the effect of stress on neurocognitive development.[11] While high quality preschool programs can offset some of the disadvantages faced by lower-income children, access to such programs is extremely limited (Barnett and Belfield, 2002).

The disadvantages that individual poor children face are compounded in the aggregate. The primary source of funds for public elementary and secondary schools is property taxes. Thus, wealthier communities with higher housing values have greater sources of revenue. In many states, this disparity is offset somewhat by additional state funds going to poorer communities. However, poorer districts tend to have higher costs due to a greater proportion of special education and higher need children, as well as higher wage costs. The same dollar simply doesn't go as far in a poorer neighborhood school.

Even if resources were equalized, children from poorer communities face additional obstacles. Academic expectations from parents, neighbors, and teachers may be lower for children from poorer backgrounds. There is a good deal of evidence from experimental studies that show students will achieve more if more is expected of them (Rouse and Barrow, 2006). Unfortunately, teachers are not impervious to stereotyping and discrimination. One study found that given children with equal academic abilities, teachers were more likely to recommend the children with "high status" names to a gifted and talented program (Figlio, 2005).

Post Secondary Education

A college education improves social class rank in many ways. Education level itself is a measure of social class, occupations that require a college education tend to be more prestigious and a college education usually leads to higher income. In 1979, college graduates made 75 percent more than high school graduates. In 2003 the income premium stood at 230 percent (Rouse and Barrow, 2006). This relationship between a college education and social class is amplified by the tendency of college graduates to marry one another. For example, a college-educated married couple each making the median income for his or her gender would have a household income of almost $108,000 (in 2007), while for a single, high school–educated woman, the median income is just over $27,000.[12]

While 91 percent of all 10th grade students aspire to a college education,[13] this dream is particularly difficult to achieve for students from low income families. While financial constraints are an obvious factor, other issues play an important role as well.

Knowledge.   The first hurdle faced by less privileged high school students is the general lack of knowledge about the "college education game." Selecting potential colleges, understanding and applying for financial aid, putting the right materials together, all of these are more difficult for families who are unfamiliar with the process. In fact only one-third of inner-city students take the SATs by October of their senior year, compared with 97 percent of suburban students (Haveman and Smeeding, 2006).

Preparedness.   Bowen (2006) argues that, in contrast to ability to pay, "more consequential factors include college preparedness in all of its dimensions such as health, attitudes at home, motivation, the availability of information, the quality of elementary and secondary education, out-of-school enrichment opportunities, and residential and social segregation" (p. 25). Quantifiable results support this argument. SAT scores are directly and positively correlated with family income. In 2008 students with a family income of less than $20,000 per year had an average combined SAT score of 1320, while those whose families made more than $200,000 had an average combined score of 1676.[14] Hill and Winston (2006) find that only 13 percent of the students from the bottom two income quintiles would qualify for admission to the nation's most selective colleges and universities.

Affordability.   There are three general categories of postsecondary education: a) state systems including community colleges, b) private four-year colleges, and c) elite colleges and universities. For generations, state schools have been a means for lower income students to gain access to higher education. Unfortunately, the recent trend has been for a decrease in state support for such institutions. In many states, public funding has decreased while tuition and fees have risen sharply.

A majority of private, four-year colleges have academic standards that are not out of reach for students of low income backgrounds. Unfortunately, these institutions tend to have lower endowments and are therefore heavily tuition dependent. There has been a growing tendency for such institutions to increase the emphasis on "merit" as a criterion for financial aid and to decrease the emphasis on "need" (McPherson & Schapiro, 2006). The source of this shift is a topic for debate, but many feel that it is driven by publications such as U.S. News and World Report, whose college rankings are determined, in part, by the academic credentials of students. This shift in emphasis toward merit and away from need is doubly hurtful to economically disadvantaged kids who don't have the cash for tuition or the high SAT scores the colleges want.

The final category of postsecondary education is the elite college or university. Such schools have plenty of endowment money and can afford to meet any economic need a family might face. The problem is a lack of qualified students. Of those students who score 1420 or better on the SAT, 3.7 percent of are from the lowest income quintile while 45.9 percent are from the highest income quintile (Hill & Winston, 2006).

A lack of information, academic preparedness, and financial means constitute a significant obstacle for poorer children in achieving a college education. In 2007, 58.4 percent of high school graduates from the lowest income quintile began college right away. For the highest income quintile this figure was 78.2 percent.[15] In 2005, 53 percent of children from the highest-income families attained college degrees while only 11% of those from the poorest families were able to achieve this goal (Haskins, 2008a).

The education of children begins at birth. The income and education of their parents; the quality of their neighborhood, peers, and school; and the opportunities for outside enrichment will all have an effect on the intellectual growth of children. Children born into privilege are read to more and taken to museums and libraries. Their parents attend more school functions. Their families have the time and money for extracurricular activities, enriching not only their educational experience, but their odds of gaining admittance to the college of their choice. In school, they are surrounded by high-achieving peers and teachers with high expectations. If trouble arises, tutors can be hired. A high quality college education is both achievable and affordable. While it is certainly not impossible for children from lower socioeconomic groups to achieve the goal of a college education, it is clearly a more daunting task.

SOCIAL AND CULTURAL CAPITAL

In their book *The Meritocracy Myth*, Stephen McNamee and Robert Miller, Jr., explain the importance of social and cultural capital in gaining access to quality educational and employment opportunities. They argue that social capital or "who you know" is critical in developing "academic aspirations" and is therefore directly related to a child's academic success. More directly, personal connections are very helpful in job placement and advancement. Those from lower socioeconomic groups are disadvantaged in terms of social capital as they "tend to be members in resource-poor networks that share a relatively restricted variety of information and influence" (p. 78).

Cultural capital or "fitting in" is also critical to upward mobility. Belonging to a group means knowing about the things they know. Cultural capital is accumulated from birth. The things a person knows about, the things he or she values, and the way he or she dresses and speaks will have much to do with the environment in which he or she is raised. McNamee and Miller argue that the accumulation of cultural capital is not perfectly correlated with socioeconomic status, as some lower income parents may emphasize cultural knowledge or young adults may seek it on their own. Because such knowledge is easier to pick up along the way than to consciously learn, there is a strong tendency for those born into a particular group to acquire the cultural capital necessary to "fit in" with that group.

Scully and Blake-Beard (2006) emphasize the importance of cultural capital in the identification of social class in the workplace. Dress, speech patterns, accents, manners, and reasoning styles are all used to distinguish those of different classes. The player must fit the part and "people from privileged backgrounds often enter organizations with this kind of style already in hand" (p. 441). In competition for jobs and promotions, the sheer number of equally qualified applicants can make personal style in all its forms, the "tie-breaker."

HOMEOWNERSHIP AND NEIGHBORHOOD EFFECTS

The probability of owning one's own home increases significantly with income and wealth. While 83 percent of those individuals from the highest income quintile own their own homes, only 40% of those from the lowest quintile do (Haskins, 2008b). This is important because home ownership itself is associated with numerous personal and social benefits. To begin with, a house is a primary source of wealth. This accumulation of wealth has an intergenerational effect, as home equity can be used to finance a child's education or can be passed down as an inheritance. Additionally, studies have found multiple positive effects on children whose families own their own home. Holding family characteristics constant, home ownership leads to improvements in home environment (physical condition of the house itself, the presence of educational materials, self esteem, mental and physical health). The improvement in educational outcomes may be due to the improvements in home environment, as well as an increased probability of remaining in the same school for a longer period of time (Haurin, 2003).

There are spillover effects of home ownership as well. Owners have a stake in the capital gains on their homes. They have a greater incentive to maintain their homes and push for better community resources, including safety and quality schools. Better public services increase property values and thus the wealth of the individuals living in the community.

While neighborhood quality is dependent on the values of the families residing therein, the reverse may also be true. We have seen that residents of affluent neighborhoods have access to higher quality schools and superior social and cultural capital. Incorporated into the concept of social capital is the broader notion of neighborhood effects. The general question is whether individuals are affected by the behavior of those around them. It seems intuitive that people are social and therefore not immune to the values of those with whom they associate. While it is generally accepted that families play the largest role, the role of the neighborhood is more controversial with some studies finding significant effects and others dismissing these effects as inseparable from the role of the family.

In any discussion of socioeconomic outcomes there is a difficulty in separating out the effect of race. Home ownership rates are much lower for minorities than for whites, with 75 percent of whites owning their own homes, as opposed to 46 percent of blacks and 48 percent of Hispanics (Ohlemacher, 2006). Much of this difference is simply due to the lower average income of minorities. In fact, one study found that, holding income and wealth constant, minorities were no less likely to own their homes than whites (Di & Liu, 2005).

However, in terms of neighborhoods, the United States is highly segregated by race. It has been estimated that 65 percent of blacks would need to relocate in order to achieve full geographical integration (Friedman, 2006). Some of this clustering is explained by economics, as minorities are more likely to be poor and neighborhoods tend to be homogenous in terms of income. However, McNamee and Miller (2004) argue that only 20–25 percent of black segregation is explained by economic factors. They go on to say that, in general, blacks do want integrated neighborhoods, but whites do not. It is estimated that more than 60 percent of blacks face housing discrimination. Samantha Friedman (2006) reports that blacks—regardless of whether they are urban or suburban—face poorer neighborhood conditions, including trash, abandoned buildings, bars on the windows, and more "social disorder."

Once again, we see the self-perpetuating nature of social class. Those born with less are less likely to live in their own homes. The result is a lower quality of life for parents and children alike. Educational quality suffers as children change schools more often. Families lose out on an important source of wealth, one that could be used as a source of financing for investments in their children's future. Residents of poor neighborhoods suffer from a lack of funding for public goods, including safety and education. Such neighborhoods lack quality social networks, peers, and role models. These problems are exacerbated for minorities, who face housing discrimination and neighborhood segregation.

RACE AND GENDER

Issues of race, gender, and class often intersect, making it difficult to isolate individual sources of stereotyping and discrimination. Minorities have lower average values for commonly used measures of social class status. While 18 percent of whites are in the lowest income quintile, the figure is 33 percent for blacks and 25 percent for Hispanics (See Note 4). While 30 percent of adult whites have at least a bachelor's degree, only 20 percent of blacks and 13 percent of Hispanics have achieved this level of education.[16] Finally, occupational prestige is significantly lower for blacks than whites, although the gap does appear to be shrinking (Kim & Tamborini, 2006).

Tom Hertz (2006) completed an extensive study of social mobility and found that among those born into the poorest income quartile, blacks are twice as likely as whites to remain poor and only one quarter as likely to move to the highest quartile. He also finds that a significant portion of the income gap between blacks and whites is due to factors other than parental attributes, such as education, occupation, attitudes, and behavior. Isaacs (2008b) finds a significant difference in downward mobility for black children: "A startling 45 percent of black children whose parents were solidly middle income end up falling to the bottom income quintile while only 16 percent of white children born to parents in the middle make this decent." (p. 76)

Gender and social class are also intrinsically linked. Women make approximately 75 cents on the dollar compared with men (Bergmann, 2005). While women have made significant headway in terms of education (according to the NCES, 57 percent of bachelor's degrees in 2007 were awarded to women), there is still significant segregation by occupation. Pay and prestige vary by occupation. For example, chemical engineers—86 percent of which are men—have a prestige ranking of 6th and an average annual income of approximately $85,000. Nursing, on the other hand is a predominantly female occupation (92 percent) and has a prestige rank of 31 and an average annual income of $62,000.[17]

Workers without a college degree are often segregated into blue collar and pink collar occupations. Again the prestige (given in parentheses) and pay vary by field. Women are a vast majority of the workers in such fields as secretarial (186), hairdressing (313), and child care workers (335). Men represent a strong majority in such fields as firefighting (111), electricians (135), and auto mechanics (278). An interesting example is teaching, where 98 percent of pre-school and kindergarten teachers are women and the occupational prestige ranking is 100. For secondary school teachers, women's representation falls to 57 percent and the prestige rank increases to 34.

The relationship between occupational pay/prestige and gender has a certain chicken-and-the-egg quality. Do women's occupations pay less because they are women's occupations or are women somehow steered into these occupations? Is prestige a function of gender representation or vice versa? Such questions are important, but whatever the cause, the result is the same. Many low-paying, low-prestige jobs are filled by women. Thirty-eight percent of women working full time in 2007 earned less than $30,000—while the figure for men was 26 percent.[18]

Because social class is intrinsically linked to gender and race, issues of classism, sexism, and racism are often intertwined. The disadvantages faced by poor black women are more than merely the sum of the disadvantages faced by each particular group. It is also wrong to assume that some "isms" are merely mistaken for others. While women and minorities are over-represented among the poor, it is incorrect to say that racism and sexism are simply classism in disguise or vice versa.

Social class diversity undoubtedly deserves its own seat at the table. As Jim Vander Putten (2001) argues, Bill Gates and an Appalachian coal miner are quite different, even though they are both white men. In fact, when a group of experts were asked which they would choose at birth if they could—race, class, or gender—the vast majority picked class (Sawhill & McLanahan, 2006). The relevance of social class should not, however, minimize the importance of race and gender as each "will have a great deal to do with the resources (social as well as financial) that are available to us as individuals, the reactions that we will face from other individuals and our self image" (Albelda, Drago, & Shulman, 2004, p. 129).

CLASS IN THE WORKPLACE REVISITED

Workplace attitudes toward social class are certainly a reflection of the attitudes of the greater society. An appreciation of the difficulties facing individuals from less privileged backgrounds is a good first step in diminishing biases held by those working within an organization. However, the categorization of social class as something determined outside of an organization can make things worse.

Scully and Blake-Beard argue that many organizations view social class identity as something that is determined before the employee walks through the door. What these businesses fail to see is that their own practices often reinforce preexisting social class stratification. One example of such a reinforcing policy is the rise in credentialism. The precise qualifications of a potential employee are often difficult to measure, especially when the application process is still in the paper stages. In order to efficiently rank applicants, employers often use educational achievement as a sorting mechanism. When the ability to do the job is not dependent on an academic degree, social class stratification becomes unjustly reinforced.

A MULTI-LAYERED APPROACH TO CHANGE

The social class structure within an organization both reflects and reinforces attitudes toward class held by society at large. Stereotypes justified by a meritocratic myth must be challenged at all levels, from national economic policies to business-specific diversity training. At all levels, the measurement of merit and existing institutional reward systems must be called into question.

At the national level, while the stickiness of social class has remained fairly constant over time, relative income positions have widened. This is due to a dramatic increase in income inequality in the United States. According to Bernstein (2006), "Since the late 1970s, the real after-tax income of those at the top of the income scale grew by 200 percent . . . and those at the bottom, 9 percent" (p. 84). The average American has been treading water for some time, while the rich have gotten significantly richer. Possible explanations for this change are many. However, one quick statistic is illuminating. In 2009 the federal minimum wage was $7.25 per hour. In real terms (inflation adjusted) the value of the minimum wage in 1968 was $9.27 per hour. As the range of incomes has spread, the difference between rich and poor has become more pronounced. A full-time minimum-wage worker earns $14,500 annually, while the average S&P 500 CEO pulls in $8.3 million (Simon, 2007). As this relative reward system changes, so does the implicit value of the work being done.

There are signs that Americans are becoming uncomfortable with the current obstacles facing the poor. A surge in support for higher minimum wages led to an increase in the federal rate by $2.10 between 2007 and 2009. There has also been an increased role for the federal government in education policy (No Child Left Behind) and a building momentum for some type of universal health care coverage. However, given the widespread belief in a meritocratic system, government policy will probably play only a small role in minimizing the benefits associated with class and in aiding the mobility of those at the bottom. Institutional changes are also needed.

A glaring example of the disconnect between rewards and merit is the unequal access to higher education. This is a particularly important issue because a college education is linked to higher income, wealth, and occupational prestige, as well as numerous positive effects on future children. Admissions policies that emphasize standardized test scores and ability to pay reward existing class privilege. SATs, which many argue are a relatively poor predictor of college success, are heavily weighted in admissions decisions and are highly correlated with economic resources. Fortunately, the trend toward SAT prep courses, admissions coaches, and merit-based aid is beginning to produce a backlash of sorts. A number of colleges are implementing plans to increase the number of students from economically disadvantaged backgrounds. Universities such as Princeton, Harvard, and Brown have replaced loans with grants for low-income students. The University of Virginia and the University of North Carolina have gone one step further in improving recruitment efforts from lower income groups (Tebbs & Turner, 2006). A growing number of colleges and universities are making SAT scores optional in the admissions process. Improved access to higher education by members of lower economic classes will carry many of the same benefits as greater representation of racial minorities. A diverse student body (in all aspects) promotes understanding of differing world views and helps to diminish negative stereotyping.

While many of the components of social class are determined outside of the workplace, it is a serious mistake to assume class is simply exogenous to an organization. Businesses themselves must realize that social class is reinforced within their own walls. Are qualified persons from all social classes considered for job openings? Is everyone given equal access to opportunities once employed, or are outward symbols of social class, such as dress and speech patterns, weighed in these decisions? Are academic credentials being used as appropriate placement tools or are they being used to unjustly eliminate people from consideration?

Businesses should also take a hard look at wages and benefits. Are only some employees given access to paid leave and educational opportunities? If so, are these differences justified? Are symbols of class apparent in the work environment, executive washrooms, and lunchrooms, for example? According to Bullock (2004), changes in workplace policies will meet with resistance, "Creating a more just workplace requires middle-class managers and others in positions of authority to examine the implications of 'business as usual' and take personal responsibility for the classist policies and practices within their own organization. For those who unquestioningly accept their class privilege as earned, this will likely be a difficult process" (p. 241).

Because social class is commonly viewed as something that is changeable, resulting inequities are often seen as deserved. But like racism and sexism, classism is based on false assumptions about underlying differences among groups. Structures and systems create a set of rewards that typically reinforce the status quo. Americans need to take a hard look at the way the system really works, how merit is measured and rewarded. Only then will conceptions of the personal qualities of those of lower status be questioned and discrimination reduced.

Notes

1. *Forbes* list of 400 richest Americans for 2008. Retrieved August 19, 2009 from http://www.forbes.com/lists/2008/54/400list08_search.html?Name=oprah+winfrey&Age=0-99&NetWorth=1.0-70.0&City=&Source=

2. Shiny Apple. (1979, November 5). *Time*. Retrieved July 30, 2007 from http://www.time.com/time/magazine/article/0,9171,912528,00.html

3. Class Matters: A Special Section. *New York Times*. Retrieved June 24, 2007 from http://www.nytimes.com/packages/html/national/20050515_CLASS_GRAPHIC/index_04.html?adxnnl=1&adxnnlx=1182864457-HIF4kzqfFaXW0qu7fLgACA

4. Chronicle of Higher Education (2008) This Year's Freshmen at 4-Year Colleges: a Statistical Profile. Retrieved August 17, 2009 from http://chronicle.com/premium/stats/freshmen/2008/data.htm#opinions

5. U.S. Census Bureau, Current Population Survey. (2008) *Annual Social and Economic Supplement*. Table HINC05. Retrieved August 17, 2009 from http://www.census.gov/hhes/www/macro/032008/hhinc/new05_000.

6. Net worth data is for 2004 and is taken from table 3 in Bucks, Kennickell, & Moore (2006).

7. As reported on the *New York Times* interactive site. (See Note 3 for web address).

8. See Note 3 for web address

9. Ever higher society, ever harder to ascend—Meritocracy in America. (2005, January *The Economist*), 374, p23. Retrieved July 30, 2007, from InfoTrac OneFile

10. See Denton & West (2002).

11. See *Future of Children* (2005) Vol 15(1) for a number of articles on these issues.

12. U.S. Census Bureau, Current Population Survey. (2008) Table PINC03. Retrieved August 17, 2009 from http://www.census.gov/hhes/www/macro/032008/perinc/new03_136.htm (for men) and http://www.census.gov/hhes/www/macro/032008/perinc/new03_262.htm (for women).

13. Author's calculation from the National Center for Education Statistics. (2005). *Youth Indicator* Table 18. Retrieved July 30, 2007, from http://nces.ed.gov/pubs2005/2005050.pdf

14. Author's calculation from the National Center for Education Statistics. (2008). *Digest of Education Statistics* Table 143. Retrieved August 17, 2009, from http://nces.ed.gov/programs/digest/d08/tables/dt08_143.asp?referrer=list

15. National Center for Education Statistics. (2009). *Condition of Education* Table A-21-1. Retrieved August 17, 2009, from http://nces.ed.gov/pubs2009/2009081.pdf

16. Author's calculations from U.S. Census Bureau. (2008). *Educational Attainment* Table 10. Retrieved August 17, 2009, from http://www.census.gov/population/www/socdemo/education/cps2008.html

17. The percentage in each occupation by gender is taken from table A1 of Bergmann (2005). The occupational prestige is taken from the *New York Times* web site, (see note 3). Data for wages is the mean for 2007 found in the Bureau of Labor Statistics. (2008). *Occupational Employment Survey by Occupation.* Table 1. Retrieved August 17, 2009, from http://www.bls.gov/news.release/archives/ocwage_05092008.pdf

18. Author's calculations from U.S. Census Bureau, Current Population Survey. (2008). *Annual Social and Economic Supplement.* Table PINC10. Retrieved August 19, 2009, from http://www.census.gov/hhes/www/macro/032008/perinc/new10_000.htm

DISCUSSION QUESTIONS

1. In your own success in achieving a college education, consider the four factors listed below. Rank these factors in terms of their importance in your own experience.

   a. your parents' attitude toward education,

   b. your parents' financial resources,

   c. the quality of your elementary and secondary schools, and

   d. your own hard work and determination.

2. Choose any three combinations of two factors listed in question 1 (for example, school quality and student work ethic) and explain why they are likely to be correlated.

3. Suppose a financial services company offered tuition reimbursement to employees who work as financial advisors, but not to administrative assistants. Why might a company do this? How do policies such as this reduce class mobility? Do you believe such policies are fair?

4. Do you agree with the statement: "through hard work, everybody can succeed in American society?" If so, try to counter the arguments given in the article. If not, what do you believe is the biggest obstacle? If you believe that change is needed, give an original example of a government or organizational policy that needs to be altered to help reduce classism.

Bibliography

Albelda, R., Drago, R.W., & Shulman, S. (2004). *Unlevel playing fields: understanding wage inequality and discrimination.* MA: Economic Affairs Bureau, Inc.

Barnett, W.S., & Belfield, C.R. (2002). Early childhood development and social mobility. *Future of Children, 16*(2), 73–98. Retrieved July 30, 2007, from http://www.futureofchildren.org/usr_doc/05_5563_barnett-belfield._pdf

Bergmann, B.R. (2005). *The economic emergence of women.* New York: Palgrave Macmillan

Bernstein, J. (2006) All Together Now: Common Sense for a Fair Economy. San Francisco: Berrett Koehler.

Bowen, W.G. (2006). Extending opportunity: What is to be done? In M.S. McPherson, & M.O. Schapiro (Eds.). *College access: opportunity or privilege?* (pp. 19–34). The College Board.

Bradbury, K., & Katz, J. (2002). Are lifetime incomes growing more unequal? Looking at the new evidence on family income mobility. *Regional Review, 12*(4), 3–5. Retrieved July 30, 2007, from http://www.bos.frb.org/_economic/nerr/rr2002/q4/issues.pdf

Bucks, B.K., Kennickell, A.B., & Moore, K.B. (2006, March 22). Recent changes in U.S. family finances: Evidence from the 2001 and 2004 survey of consumer finances. *Federal Reserve Bulletin.* Retrieved July 30, 2007, from http://www.federalreserve.gov/pubs/oss/oss2/2004/bull0206.pdf

Bullock, H.E. (2004). Class diversity in the workplace. In M.S. Stockdale & F.J. Crosby (Eds.), *The psychology and management of workplace diversity* (pp. 224–242). MA: Blackwell.

Denton, K., & West, J. (2002). Children's reading and mathematics achievements in kindergarten and first grade. *National Center for Education Statistics Report 2002125.* Retrieved July 30, 2007, from http://nces. ed.gov/pubs2002/2002125.pdf

Di, Z.X., & Liu, X. (2005). The importance of wealth and income in the transition to home-ownership. *Joint Center for Housing Studies, Harvard University Working Paper W05-6.* Retrieved July 30, 2007, from http://www.jchs.harvard.edu/publications/homeownership/w05-6.pdf

Figlio, D. (2005). Names, expectations and the black-white test score gap. *National Bureau of Economic Research Working Paper 11195.* Retrieved July 30, 2007, from http://www.nber.org/papers/w11195

Friedman, S. (2006). Not in my neighborhood: numbers show Americans still cluster in segregated communities. *Northeastern University Alumni Magazine, 32*(1), 24–25.

Haskins, R. (2008a). Education and Economic Mobility. Getting Ahead or Losing Ground: Economic Mobility in America. Retrieved August 17, 2009, from http://www.brookings.edu/reports/2008/02_economic_mobility_sawhill.aspx

Haskins, R. (2008b). Wealth and Economic Mobility. Getting Ahead or Losing Ground: Economic Mobility in America. Retrieved August 17, 2009, from http://www.brookings.edu/reports/2008/02_economic_mobility_sawhill.aspx

Haurin, D.R. (2003). *The private and social benefits of homeownership.* Transcript from Habitat for Humanity University Lecture Series, December 11, 2003. Retrieved June 24, 2007, from Habitat for Humanity Web site: http://elearning.hfhu.org/hfhu/documents/haurinshow.pdf

Haveman, R., & Smeeding, T. (2006). The role of higher education in social mobility. *Future of Children, 16*(2), 125–150. Retrieved July 30, 2007, from http://www.futureofchildren.org/usr_doc/07_5563_haveman-smeeding.pdf

Hertz, T. (2006). *Understanding mobility in America.* Retrieved June 24, 2007, from the Center for American Progress Web site: http://www.americanprogress.org/kf/hertz_mobility_analysis.pdf

Hill, C.B., & Winston, G.C. (2006) How scarce are high-ability, low-income students? In M.S. McPherson, & M.O. Schapiro (Eds.).*College access: opportunity or privilege?* (pp. 75–102) The College Board.

Isaacs, J.B. (2008a). International Comparisons of Economic Mobility. Getting Ahead or Losing Ground: Economic Mobility in America. Retrieved August 17, 2009, from http://www.brookings.edu/reports/2008/02_economic_mobility_sawhill.aspx

Isaacs, J.B. (2008b). Economic Mobility of Black and White Families. Getting Ahead or Losing Ground: Economic Mobility in America.

Retrieved August 17, 2009, from http://www.brookings.edu/reports/2008/02_economic_mobility_sawhill.aspx

Kane, T.J., Orszag, P.R., & Gunter, D.L. (2003). State fiscal constraints and higher education spending. *Urban-Brookings Tax Policy Center Discussion Paper No. 11.* Retrieved July 30, 2007, from http://www.urban.org/UploadedPDF/310787_TPC_DP11.pdf

Kim, C., & Tamborini, C. (2006). The continuing significance of race in the occupational attainment of whites and blacks: a segmented labor market analysis. *Sociological Inquiry, 76*(1), 23–51.

Mazumder, B. (2004). Sibling similarities, differences and economic inequality. *Federal Reserve Bank of Chicago Working Paper 2004–13.* Retrieved July 31, 2007, from http://www.chicagofed.org/publications/_working-papers/wp2004_13.pdf

McNamee, S.J., & Miller, R.K. Jr. (2004). *The meritocracy myth.* Lanham: Rowman & Littlefield.

McPherson, M.S., & Schapiro, M.O. (Eds.). (2006). *College access: opportunity or privilege?* The College Board.

Ohlemacher, S. (2006, November 14). Persistent race disparities found: Minorities still lag in income, education, census data show. *The Washington Post.* Retrieved July 31, 2007, http://www.washingtonpost.com/wp-dyn/content/article/2006/11/13/AR2006111301114.html?referrer=emailarticle

Rouse, C.E., & Barrow, L. (2006). U.S. elementary and secondary schools: equalizing opportunity or replicating the status quo? *Future of Children, 16*(2), 99–123. Retrieved July 31, 2007, from http://www.futureofchildren.org/usr_doc/05_5563_barnett-belfield.pdf

Sacks, P. (2007, January 12). How colleges perpetuate inequality. *The Chronicle of Higher Education, 53*(19), B9-B10.

Sawhill I., & McLanahan, S. (2006). Introducing the issue. *Future of Children, 16*(2), 3–17. Retrieved July 31, 2007, from http://www.futureofchildren.org/usr_doc/01_5563_intro.pdf

Scully, M.A., & Blake-Beard, S. (2006). Locating class in organizational diversity work: class as structure, style and process. In A.M. Konrad, P. Pushkala, & J.K. Pringle (Eds.), *Handbook of workplace diversity* (pp. 431–454). London: Sage.

Simon, E. (2007, June 11). Half of S&P 500 CEOs topped $8.3 million. *Washington Post.* Retrieved July 31, 2007, from http://www.washingtonpost.com/wp-dyn/content/article/2007/06/11/AR2007061100798.html

Tebbs, J., & Turner, S. (2006). The challenge of improving the representation of low-income students at flagship universities. In M.S. McPherson, & M.O. Schapiro (Eds.). *College access: opportunity or privilege?* (pp. 103–115). The College Board.

Vander Putten, J. (2001). Bringing social class to the diversity challenge. *About Campus, 6*(5), 14–19.

Colleen Fahy, PhD, is an Associate Professor of economics at Assumption College. Her research interests include local government structure and finance and equity issues associated with public education funding.

Writing Assignment

Choose one of the following impediments to social mobility:

1. Access to quality elementary and secondary education

2. Access to a college education

3. Ability to own a home in a good neighborhood

4. Access to social and cultural capital

Explain why the particular opportunity you have chosen differs among social classes (find evidence beyond what is given in this article) and discuss what can be done to improve access.

Diversity on the Web

Visit the Web site below to determine your social "class percentile."

Respond with answers that represent where you expect to be in 10 years. If you are currently employed full time, use your current information or estimate 10 years forward.

http://www.nytimes.com

In the search box, 'type': "Class Matters" and follow the link to the special section on class matters. Click on the link titled "Where Do You Fit In." Then, determine your social class percentile using answers that represent where you are today and where you expect to be in 10 years.

DOES SOCIAL CLASS MAKE A DIFFERENCE?

Carol P. Harvey
Assumption College

Social class may be less visible than other types of difference. However, in many countries like the U.S., where individualism is valued, it is common to believe that all people are created equal and that the same opportunities are available to everyone who has the innate talent and is willing to put in the effort. This position ignores the challenge of overcoming the social, educational, and networking resources of class origins. This exercise is designed to help you to understand how social class *could* affect a person's life experience due to differences in access and resources. Although social class in childhood does *not* necessarily determine status across one's life span, it may limit educational and career options that may make it more difficult for a person to achieve personal goals. Of course, individuals within a social class can have very different experiences due to a variety of factors.

DIRECTIONS

Complete the following two columns by thinking about what is apt to be the more common experience of a child growing up in Justin's or Clark's situation. Considering that Justin represents a child born into the lower socioeconomic class and Clark represents one born into the upper middle class, your answers should reflect what is likely to be the more common experiences for children born into these situations.

Justin was born to a 16-year-old single mother who lived with her family in an inner-city housing project. When he was born, she dropped out of high school to care for him. After he started school, she took a job cleaning rooms in a local hospital. She is currently studying nights to get her General Equivalency Diploma (GED).

Clark was born to a suburban couple in their mid-thirties. His mother has an MBA, and his father is a lawyer. Clark's mother quit her job when he was born. She returned to a managerial position when his younger sibling was in junior high.

	Justin	Clark
How might this child spend his time before he attends kindergarten?		
When he goes to kindergarten, he is diagnosed with a learning disability. What types of help is he most likely to receive?		
During grammar school, how is he likely to spend his school vacations?		
What types of after-school activities is he likely to participate in?		
What role may sports play in his life?		
He needs help with math in high school. What types of resources are most apt to be available to him?		
Where can he learn about technology?		
If his College Board scores aren't too high, what resources may be available to help him raise his scores?		
If he needs an internship in college, who can help him secure one?		
Given the differences of growing up in different social classes, what job-related life and career skills may he have that give him workplace advantages or disadvantages?		

DISCUSSION QUESTIONS

1. In terms of the workplace, how does social class matter?

2. Is social class *really* an invisible difference or are there ways that people often deduce other's social class origins? What can be the effect of this in job interviews, work-related social situations, etc.?

3. What role does the media play in perpetuating both positive and negative social class stereotypes? Support your answer with examples.

4. In this exercise, both people were male and no specific race was suggested. Which of your answers might have been different if the examples were female or nonwhite? Why?

Writing Assignment

1. There are many programs and organizations such as Head Start, the Nativity Schools, Big Brothers and Big Sisters, Boys and Girl's Clubs, Girls Inc., among others, that attempt to help individuals to overcome some of the effects of social class. Research and visit one of these organizations to better understand their mission and the roles that they play in providing access and opportunity. Specifically, how can these organizations change the life experiences and access to resources for children from lower classes?

2. Spend a day in a school that is the opposite from your own grammar or high school experience. If you attended a private school, arrange to visit a public school. If you attended a school that was predominately lower or working class, arrange to visit a private school. Analyze any differences that you observe in terms of the student body, how students dress, the academic experience, the faculty, the physical plant, and athletic and after-school activities. Try to interview students and faculty about their perceptions of the total educational experience at the school. How does what you learned from this visit relate to this exercise? How do these differences translate into "privileges" in the workplace?

RELIGION IN THE U.S. WORKPLACE

Kathleen M. Fisher
Assumption College

Jeanne M. McNett
Assumption College

Pamela D. Sherer
Providence College

GOALS

- To build awareness of the historic role of religion in the United States
- To examine potential contributions and challenges religion brings to the workplace
- To explore the best practices in involving religious diversity in the workplace

INTRODUCTION

What is the role of religion in the U.S. workplace and why does it matter? These questions are the central concern of this article. To place them in context, this article begins with a focus on the historical role of religion in the U.S. and a summary of the most common religions practiced. It next considers how the presence of religion in the workplace may play out, first with a brief view of the positive contributions religion can bring to the workplace; and then with an examination of the workplace challenges religious practice introduces. Finally, the best practices aimed at religious accommodation are considered, i.e., that is how employers and employees can assure that the diversity of religions helps add value to the organization's output.

THE HISTORICAL ROLE OF RELIGION IN THE UNITED STATES

The United States is often described as a "Judeo-Christian nation," a country founded on a combination of Jewish and Christian religious principles. This belief about the country's religious foundations has had a significant impact on the way U.S. business is conducted. The indigenous peoples of North America had their own ancient ancestral religions. Christianity first appeared in the late 1500s, when Queen Isabella of Spain sent Catholic missionaries to the Pueblos in modern-day New Mexico in an effort to convert them from their Native religious traditions. Through forceful evangelizing, many Pueblos eventually became Catholic. Later when the first immigrants arrived from England to settle Jamestown, Virginia in 1607, they brought with them a Protestant form of Christianity called "Anglicanism." So, the American colonies were founded, in part, on Christian principles, but Christianity was not the first religion in North America.

The desire for both profit and religious freedom did bring more settlers to America. The people we know as the Pilgrims were dissatisfied members of the Church of England who came to Massachusetts in the early 1600's seeking to practice a purified form of Anglicanism. Known as "Puritans," they demanded uniformity of belief and did not tolerate religious dissent. Consequently, critics of the religious leaders like Roger Williams and Anne Hutchinson were banished from the Massachusetts Bay Colony and would settle in or found colonies such as Rhode Island and Maryland. New European immigrants of the Dutch Reformed Church and Jews came to settle in New Netherlands and New Amsterdam (present-day New York). Later, during the slave trade of the 17th and 18th centuries, the people enslaved from West Africa brought new forms of worship that would eventually be melded with Christianity.

Though the Puritans came to America in search of religious liberty, their demand for strict adherence to the church's doctrines created a new kind of authoritarianism. So, in 1682 William Penn established his "holy experiment" in Pennsylvania where all faiths were made welcome, though only Protestants were granted the right to vote.

More than a century after the arrival of Puritanism, the ability of a group to impose its religion through force of law ended in America. In declaring independence from England, the Declaration of Independence of 1776 and the Constitution, ratified in 1787, asserted that citizens had God-given rights to "life, liberty and the pursuit of happiness." To ensure these rights would be protected, the Congress appended to the Constitution in 1791 the Bill of Rights with the provision that "Congress shall make no law respecting an establishment of religion, or prohibiting the free exercise thereof . . ."

When Americans discovered the open land of the western frontier, they saw it as an opportunity for greater political and religious freedom and individual fortune. A new, more fervent religious revival led to a mass westward migration where populist and utopian communities could take root. Though the formal authority of Puritan church leaders had been replaced by religious independence, the moral values of Puritanism, especially its work ethic, animated the desire for survival and success in the wilderness.

Ever since the Protestant Reformation in 16th century Europe, Protestant theology emphasized the moral value of work. To work was to serve both God and society. Individual and communal survival in the American frontier required hard work, responsibility and frugality. These moral values became American ideals and the path to prosperity. In the 19th century the American West and South were largely agricultural societies, while the North was becoming industrialized. The Protestant work ethic that had developed the West became the business principle of the new industries and, as the German sociologist Max Weber said in 1905, contributed to the "spirit of capitalism." Religion and business became partners; thrift and hard work would again bring national prosperity, this time through industrialization.

The financial success of industrialized work, however, was not shared by the workers. The desire for profit and the cost of buildings, machinery, supplies and labor required business owners to run their factories as many hours as possible. Working conditions favored the owner rather than the worker, and long hours, low wages and dangerous physical environments became common.

In the 1930's the Great Depression changed the fortunes of all Americans, workers and owners alike. Poverty overwhelmed the country as the economic gains of industry vanished in the Stock Market Crash of 1929. A "social gospel" that called for shared wealth and care for the poor replaced the earlier belief that prosperity was ordained by God. In the "Cold War" with the Soviet

Union, Christianity became the enemy of communism and the proof of one's patriotism (http://www.pbs.org/godinamerica).

THE FIVE MAIN U.S. RELIGIONS AT A GLANCE

Until well after World War II, Christian religions predominated in the U.S. religious landscape, and in the postwar years, the picture became gradually more complex, largely due to increased immigration. The Religious Landscape Survey conducted by the Pew Forum indicates that most Americans now identify with one of five major religions—Christianity, Judaism, Buddhism, Islam and Hinduism. Each of these religions has various forms and traditions within it and expresses its beliefs through particular kinds of worship and prayer, rituals, dietary rules, and modes of dress. What follows is a description of the main beliefs or principles that define each religion.

The majority of Americans identify themselves as **Christian** (see Table 1). **Christianity** has many denominations, but all of these share a belief that there is one God who is revealed through human history. Christians believe that Jesus was God's Son who came to earth as a man and he was killed about 30 C.E. by authorities of the Roman Empire, but came back to life and ascended to heaven. Christians claim that all who profess their belief in the Resurrection of Jesus will be received into heaven after death.

Judaism began about 1900 BCE in Israel, and shares the belief that God acts in human history, especially in times of struggle and oppression. The "Tanak," Judaism's Scripture, tells the story of how the Jews were repeatedly conquered and enslaved by foreign powers, but were freed by God's power acting through figures such as Abraham, Moses, and David. Jews believe that God made a "covenant" or promise to protect them as long as they continue to believe in and worship the one God.

Islam began in the 7th century CE and, like Christianity and Judaism, originated in the Middle East. From an Arabic word meaning "submitting," Islam also professes belief in one God, Allah. Muslims (those who practice Islam) focus on living their lives according to God's will, which is revealed through the "Qur'an" (the Scripture) and a long line of messengers. Mohammed is revered as the last and most important prophet of the religion and is said to have received the words of the Qur'an directly from God in a series of visions.

Buddhism was founded between the 6th and 4th centuries BCE in northeastern India. Based on the teachings of Siddhartha Gautama, a royal prince who became known as the Buddha (Enlightened One), it encompasses several schools of thought, established over the centuries by different teachers. In general, Buddhists believe that earthly life is a continuous cycle of birth and death that is the cause of human suffering. When we finally escape this cycle to achieve a state of being called "nirvana," we become, like the Buddha, enlightened.

Hinduism is the oldest of the major world religions and began in India around 2500 BCE. Hindus believe in one Supreme Reality, called Brahman, which takes many forms and names. Hindus seek to be in harmony with Brahman by living an ethically good life through self-discipline, the sharing of wealth and following the teachings of the Scriptures (Vedas). Like Buddhists, they believe in reincarnation (the cycle of re-birth) and seek to escape it to achieve union with God.

Table 1 lists the major religious traditions found in the U.S. as reported in the Pew Forum on Religion & Public Life (2008).

Table 1	Major Religious Traditions in the U.S.		
Christian	**78.4**	**Other Religions**	**4.7**
Protestant	51.3	Jewish	1.7
Catholic	23.9	Buddhist	0.7
Mormon	1.7	Muslim	0.6
Jehovah's Witness	0.7	Hindu	0.4
Orthodox	0.6	Other religions	<0.3
Other Christian	0.3		
		Unaffiliated	**16.1**
		Declined	**0.8**

RELIGION IN THE WORKPLACE

Many people who involve themselves seriously in their religion try to integrate their religious practice into all parts of their lives, including work. They want deeper satisfaction from their work, what we might think of as a spiritual involvement. For example, the Christian may think of the workplace as an important part of her life's work, a journey that leads toward the holy state of sanctification (Sire, 1990). Attempts at such faith integration that involve the workplace, who we are and who we are becoming as a person, how we think and feel, and what we do as a member of a specific religion, are increasing (Cafferky, 2011). David Miller, executive director of Yale University's Center for Faith and Culture, has observed that religion in the workplace is "a bona fide social movement" whose significance is growing (Fenner, 2007).

POSITIVE ASPECTS OF RELIGION IN THE WORKPLACE

Religion can make an important contribution to an organization's culture because it provides commonly held, shared values that connect people. An organization's culture is a shared understanding of what the organization is, how it ought to be, and how its members should behave, i.e., the shared collective beliefs, values and norms of its members. It emerges as a result of people working together and giving meaning to their shared environment. As a result, members are likely to readily pool their efforts in line with the organization's strategy and move forward with collaborative commitment. Because a strong organizational culture is difficult to build and nearly impossible to imitate, it can provide the organization with a valuable competitive advantage.

An inclusion of religion in the workplace can also contribute to the organization's ability to understand their diverse stakeholders, including customers. It creates another access point to cultural knowledge that is so important in a diverse marketplace.

The numbers of mainstream companies that involve religion as a part of their organizational culture are growing, and include Walt Disney, American Express, some Wal-Mart subsidiaries, Marriott, Amway and Chick-Fil-A. For example, Chick-Fil-A, whose CEO is an evangelical Christian, closes over 1,000 restaurants on Sunday in order to observe the

Sabbath. In addition to involvement at the top levels, voluntary prayer groups are encouraged in many organizations in the government, non-profit and for-profit sectors. There are also service companies such as Chaplains at Work that provide faith-based and nondenominational support services to corporations, with services ranging from crisis intervention to general clergy duties such as marital counseling and hospital visits (Religion in Business, n.d.).

This trend is in opposition to the traditional we have come to expect, rooted in Thomas Jefferson's concept of the separation of church and state, although it may be much closer to the practices of our earlier forebears. Now, though, the workforce is diversified, and, as it brings faith beliefs to work, members may encounter assumptions about being and doing in the world that are different from and possibly contradict their own. This can be unsettling, and in many organizations that have not addressed religion directly, it has become an uncomfortable subject. Melissa Dylan's recent on-line contribution to a discussion of religion in the workplace is an example. She pointed out that

> too much God-Talk (is) unprofessional . . . This week I opened an interdepartmental e-mail and found a line from scripture quoted as part of the signature line. When religion comes up in the workplace, it is difficult to know how to react. Arguments fly in both directions: inclusion of religion in the workplace can lead to camaraderie and bring a deeper sense of meaning to work. But choosing a deity to worship excludes those with different beliefs. Both arguments are valid, but they miss a very important point: *religion has nothing to do with it* (Dylan, 2006).

CHALLENGES THAT ACCOMPANY RELIGION IN THE WORKPLACE

Often conflict issues with religion in the workplace result from the desire for the religious practitioner to have a unified life and practice religion beyond the bounds of belief. The potential conflict areas include the way the employee self-presents, including demeanor, dress and hairstyle, their desire that others conform to their dress and modesty values. They might desire to proselytize and convert others to a belief system that has brought goodness to their lives. Diet might also be an area of conflict, as could observance practice, including holidays and prayer patterns.

The First Amendment of the U.S. Constitution guarantees citizens two rights: the right to be free of a government-imposed religion and the right to practice any religion. Those rights, along with the freedom of expression also guaranteed by the First Amendment, are joined by Title VII of the 1964 Civil Rights Act (see below) that prohibits disparate treatment, disparate impact and the creation of a hostile environment.

TITLE VII OF THE CIVIL RIGHTS ACT OF 1964 AND RELIGION

Title VII provides the basis for understanding and interpreting religion and its relationship to the work environment. The Equal Employment Opportunity Commission (EEOC), defines religion in terms of observance and practice as well as beliefs. Title VII includes not only traditional, organized religions, but also religious beliefs that are new, not part of a formal church or sect, or only subscribed to by a small number of people. Title VII protections also extend to those who are discriminated against or need accommodation because they profess no religious beliefs" (EEOC, 2010).

EXHIBIT 1   Title VII of the Civil Rights Act of 1964, Points of Law

Points of Law

Title VII of the Civil Rights Act of 1964

Title VII of the Civil Rights Act of 1964 **prohibits employers from discriminating against individuals because of their religion in hiring, firing, and other terms and conditions of employment.** Title VII covers employers with fifteen or more employees, including state and local governments, employment agencies and labor organizations, as well as to the federal government.

Under Title VII:

Employers may not treat employees or applicants more or less favorably because of their religious beliefs or practices—except to the extent a religious accommodation is warranted. For example, an employer may not refuse to hire individuals of a certain religion, may not impose stricter promotion requirements for persons of a certain religion, and may not impose more or different work requirements on an employee because of that employee's religious beliefs or practices.

Employees cannot be forced to participate—or not participate—in a religious activity as a condition of employment.

Employers must reasonably accommodate employees' sincerely held religious practices unless doing so would impose an undue hardship on the employer. A reasonable religious accommodation is any adjustment to the work environment that will allow the employee to practice his religion. An employer might accommodate an employee's religious beliefs or practices by allowing flexible scheduling, voluntary substitutions or swaps, job reassignments and lateral transfers, modification of grooming requirements and other workplace practices, policies and/or procedures.

An employer is not required to accommodate an employee's religious beliefs and practices if doing so would impose an undue hardship on the employers' legitimate business interests. An employer can show undue hardship if accommodating an employee's religious practices requires more than ordinary administrative costs, diminishes efficiency in other jobs, infringes on other employees' job rights or benefits, impairs workplace safety, causes co-workers to carry the accommodated employee's share of potentially hazardous or burdensome work, or if the proposed accommodation conflicts with another law or regulation.

Employers must permit employees to engage in religious expression, unless the religious expression would impose an undue hardship on the employer. Generally, an employer may not place more restrictions on religious expression than on other forms of expression that have a comparable effect on workplace efficiency.

Employers must take steps to prevent religious harassment of their employees. An employer can reduce the chance that employees will engage unlawful religious harassment by implementing an anti-harassment policy and having an effective procedure for reporting, investigating and correcting harassing conduct.

It is **also unlawful to retaliate** against an individual for opposing employment practices that discriminate based on religion or for filing a discrimination charge, testifying, or participating in any way in an investigation, proceeding, or litigation under Title VII.

(adapted from http:/www.eeoc.gov/types/religion.html)

Title VII establishes that every worker has a right to reasonable accommodation for religion. This accommodation might include days off for religious holidays and schedule adjustments for weekly observance; the right to wear clothing signifying religious membership, such as a scarf or turban; having a place to pray; having appropriate food and beverages available in the cafeteria or at company gatherings. Hindu, Muslim, Jewish and Buddhist colleagues may be vegetarian or vegan, or refrain from specific foods such as pork, and not drink alcohol. Modesty for women may be important and may include wearing a covering (*abaya, burqa* or *hijab*). Prayer during the day, fasting and pilgrimage may be part of the employee's regular practice. All religions follow a slightly different religious calendar, lunar in the case of Hinduism, Islam, Judaism, and Islam. Christians follow a year-long calendar, either the Gregorian or the Julian version, that commemorates the birth, life death and resurrection of Jesus Christ.

Reasonable accommodations are arrangements that eliminate the religious conflict for the employee and does not cause undue hardship on the employer. If the requested accommodation would cause the employer undue hardship, the employer must demonstrate that a good faith effort has been made to meet the employee's religious need and that the suggested accommodation would cause hardship. Undue hardship often is demonstrated by addressing the suggested accommodation's cost impact. Exhibit 2 contains examples of the application of reasonable accommodation.

Just as in sexual harassment, religious harassment is of two types, *quid pro quo* and hostile environment. *Quid pro quo* harassment occurs when the harasser seeks to influence the behavior and makes demands of a religious nature on the victim. Examples would include pressure to attend religious services, to participate in a prayer group or to convert. When the victim does not comply, the harasser retaliates. The second type of harassment, hostile environment, occurs when there is severe or pervasive conduct in the workplace directed towards an employee because of that employee's religion. The employer has a responsibility to take actions to stop this conduct. In hostile environment, the workplace must be "permeated with discriminatory intimidation, ridicule, and insult that is sufficiently severe or pervasive to alter the conditions of the victim's employment and create an abusive working environment" (*Harris v. Forklift Sys., Inc.*, 510 U.S. 17, 21, 1993). Title VII also protects the employee from the employer's retaliation for making a complaint or testifying against discrimination. It is in this area, retaliation, that EEOC has seen the fastest growth in complaints.

ADDRESSING RELIGIOUS DISCRIMINATION IN THE WORKPLACE

Just as religion provides personal strength, organizations realize that it can also contribute in positive ways to the workplace. Major organizations are finding ways to bring religion into the workplace and manage it. In order to tap into its strength, the diversity that accompanies the practice of religion in the workplace in the U.S. needs to be managed because unmanaged, it can move to discrimination. We now look at best practices and a religious diversity checklist. The best practices are modified from material developed by EEOC, and they address practices for employers. The focus areas are the challenging changes religion can bring to the workplace: religion itself, harassment, accommodation, undue hardship, schedule changes, job changes, workplace practices, the practice of prayer, and retaliation.

EXHIBIT 2 Reasonable Accommodation of Religion in the Workplace, Examples

The Issue	What Reasonable Accommodation Means: Title VII of the Civil Rights Act
A shipping company refused to hire a Jewish man as a driver because of his beard, which he wears for religious purposes. The company required him to either shave his beard or apply for an "inside," lower paying position with no public contact.	Employers must make reasonable accommodations to employees' and applicants' sincerely held religious beliefs as long as this does not pose an undue hardship. If the company cannot show why a beard is a hardship, it must hire the man as a driver. Notably, the company may not argue that its customers would prefer non-bearded drivers as "customer preference" is not a valid basis for a hardship.
A restaurant chain fired a server with a tattoo on his wrist. The tattoos are part of his sincerely held belief that his faith, the Kemetic religion, requires them. He explained his religion to management, but was fired. Management stated that the company has Christian values and that the company seeks out "clean-cut kids" as servers. Management held that its dress code, including prohibitions on tattoos, would detract from its wholesome image, an undue hardship.	Employers are required to support claims of undue hardship with more than hypothetical hardships based on unproven assumptions about image. Moreover, customer preference is not a legitimate reason for not accommodating a religious need.
An employer requires employees to read passages out loud from her preferred religious text at meetings, offers paid days off to attend religious gatherings, and helps to advance the careers of employees who adopt her faith.	An employee who refuses to participate in such activity must not be penalized. An employer is not permitted to treat acceptance of religion or participation in religious rituals as a condition of employment, including advancing the careers of adherents or providing benefits not open to non-adherents, such as paid days off.
A co-worker occasionally teases a Muslim employee about her *hijab* (headscarf). The employee is offended and tells her colleague to stop and does not report it because the company has no reporting process. A manager begins to criticize her for wearing the *hijab*, and moves her into a lower-paying back office position. In a fit of anger, he grabs at the *hijab* and tears it and knocks the employee down to the floor.	The company is probably not liable for a hostile work environment on the basis of the co-worker's actions. The harassment was neither severe nor pervasive and did not effect her terms and conditions of employment. The manager's actions probably give rise to a hostile work environment. The constant criticism plus the physical assault are both likely to meet the "severe or pervasive" test. Moreover, there was a clear adverse employment action (the move to the back office). The employer will not be able to avoid liability because there was an adverse employment action and there was no reporting mechanism.
A co-worker refuses to sign a workplace pledge concerning tolerance of differences because she believes homosexuals to be immoral and against God's word. Her manager orders her to sign it and she refuses. She is fired.	The employer has an obligation to determine whether her refusal to sign the pledge could be accommodated. By immediately firing her, the employer failed to determine if there was an accommodation available.

(Continued)

The Issue	What Reasonable Accommodation Means: Title VII of the Civil Rights Act
An employee has a religious belief that requires her to wear an anti-abortion button that shows a color photo of an fetus. The button causes disruptions and complaints. In response, the employer offers the employee three accommodations: (1) wear the button only in her cubicle; (2) cover the button at work, or (3) wear a different button with the same message but without the photograph. When she refused these accommodations, she was terminated.	Title VII does not require an employer to allow an employee to impose her religious views on others. The employer is only required to reasonably accommodate an employee's religious views. In light of the workplace disruption and complaints, and given that the proposed accommodations allowed her religious expression, she was offered a reasonable accommodation and her refusal to accept them justified her termination.

Adapted from www.adl.org/religious_freedom/resource_kit/religion_workplace.asp

---

EXHIBIT 3   Best Practices for Religious Diversity in the Workplace

Religion in the Workplace Best Practices

- Use written, objective criteria for evaluating candidates for hire or promotion and apply consistently to all candidates.
- In job interviews, ask the same questions of all applicants for a particular job.
- Record the accurate business reasons for disciplinary or performance-related actions, and share these reasons with the affected employees.
- Provide training to inexperienced managers and encourage them to consult with more experienced managers or human resources personnel when addressing difficult issues.
- If confronted with customer biases, consider engaging with and educating the customers regarding any misperceptions they may have and the EEOC laws.

Religious Harassment

- Anti-harassment policy that is well-publicized and consistently applied covers religious harassment; clearly explains what is prohibited; describes procedures for bringing harassment to management's attention; and assures that complainants will be protected against retaliation.
- Allow religious expression to the same extent that other types of personal expression are allowed.
- Once an employee objects to religious conduct that is directed at him or her, take steps to end the conduct. Even conduct that you regard as harmless can become sufficiently severe or pervasive to affect the conditions of employment if allowed to persist, given the objection.
- If harassment is by a non-employee assigned by a contractor, demand that it cease, that disciplinary action be taken if it continues, and/or that a new person be assigned.
- To prevent conflicts from escalating to the level of Title VII violation, immediately intervene when you become aware of objectively abusive or insulting conduct, even absent a complaint.
- Intervene proactively and discuss with subordinates whether particular religious expression is welcome if you think the expression might be construed as harassing to a reasonable person.
- Supervisors can engage in certain religious expression, yet should avoid expression that might reasonably be perceived by subordinates as coercive, even when not so intended.

Reasonable Accommodation

- Inform employees that you will make reasonable efforts to accommodate religious practices.
- Train managers and supervisors on how to recognize religious accommodation requests.

- Develop a process for religious accommodation requests.
- Assess each request individually and avoid assumptions or stereotypes about what constitutes a religious belief or practice or what type of accommodation is appropriate.
- Confer fully and promptly to the extent needed to share any necessary information about the religious needs and the available accommodation options.
- Consider the employee's proposed method of accommodation and, if that plan is denied, explain the reasoning to the employee.
- Train managers to consider alternative available accommodations if the particular accommodation requested would pose undue hardship.
- If the accommodation cannot be implemented promptly, consider offering alternative methods of accommodation temporarily.

Undue Hardship

- The undue hardship standard refers to the legal requirement. Be flexible in evaluating whether an accommodation is feasible.
- Don't assume that an accommodation will conflict with a seniority system. Check for exceptions for religious accommodation to allow accommodation consistent with seniority.
- Don't reject a request for religious accommodation automatically because the accommodation will interfere with the existing seniority system or terms of a collective bargaining agreement (CBA). Voluntary modification to a CBA may accommodate employee religious needs.
- Train managers to be aware that, if the requested accommodation would violate the CBA or seniority system, they should confer with employee to determine alternatives.
- Ensure that managers know reasonable accommodation may require making exceptions to policies or procedures that are not part of a CBA or seniority system, where it would not infringe on other employees' legitimate expectations.

Schedule Changes, Voluntary Substitutes and Swaps

- Work with employees to adjust a work schedule to accommodate religious practices.
- Consider adopting flexible leave and scheduling policies that will allow employees to meet their religious and other personal needs.
- Encourage voluntary substitutions and swaps with employees of similar qualifications by publicizing policy, promoting atmosphere in which substitutes are favorably regarded, and providing a central file, bulletin board, group e-mail to facilitate this process.

Change of Job Assignments and Lateral Transfers

- Consider a lateral transfer when no accommodation that would keep the employee in the position is possible without undue hardship.
- If no lateral transfer is available that would permit the employee to remain in a current or equivalent position, offer an available lower position as an accommodation and permit the employee to decide.

Modifying Workplace Practices, Policies, and Procedures

- Make efforts to accommodate an employee's desire to wear a yarmulke, hijab, or other religious garb.
- Train managers to avoid stereotyping based on religious dress and grooming practices and to not assume that atypical dress creates undue hardship.
- Encourage flexibility and creativity with work schedules, duties, selection procedures as practicable.
- Avoid pressuring or coercing employees to attend social gatherings after the employees have indicated a religious objection to attending.

Permitting Prayer, Proselytizing, and Other Forms of Religious Expression

- Train managers to gauge the actual disruption posed by religious expression in the workplace, rather than to speculate that disruption may result.
- Discuss religious expression and the need for all employees to be sensitive to beliefs of others.

Retaliation

- Reduce the risk of retaliation claims by training managers and supervisors to be aware of their anti-retaliation obligations under Title VII, including specific actions that may constitute retaliation.
- Reduce the risk of retaliation claims by carefully and timely recording the accurate business reasons for disciplinary or performance related actions and sharing these reasons with the employee.

Source: adapted from http://eeoc.gov/policy/docs/best_practices_religion.html

---

EXHIBIT 4   Religious Diversity Checklist

Policies

Does your diversity policy include religious diversity and is there a method to communicate this policy to employees? What do you know about the religions of your employees?

Holidays/Time Off

Is there a clearly articulated policy regarding religious holiday leave (paid or unpaid) and is this policy clearly explained to employees? Is there a way for employees and managers to address scheduling conflicts resulting from religion and to find coworkers who can cover shifts? Do you take into account employees' religious holidays when planning meetings, workshops, trips, dinners and special events?

Dress

Does your company have a dress code that is communicated to all employees? If an employee's religious practice conflicts with the code, do you have policies in place regarding attire?

Food

Does your company provide food for employees that accommodates their religious needs (kosher, halal, vegetarian)?

Employee Networks

Does your company allow the formation of on-site religion-based, employee networks and does your company clearly communicate the policies for these groups and their relationship to the company as a whole?

Office Space

Does your company have a policy regarding personal workspace that includes religious decoration and is this policy clearly explained to employees? Does your company allow holiday decoration of office space and do these accommodate the needs of religiously and culturally diverse employees?

Religious Practice

Does your company allow religious practice in the workplace (prayer, meditation) and how do you communicate the policies regarding religious practice to the employees and how do employees communicate their religious practice needs to management?

Excerpted from: www.tanenbaum.org/resources/workplace-tools/religious-diversity-checklist

RELIGIOUS DIVERSITY CHECKLIST

This checklist is a good way for you to determine where an organization stands now in terms of addressing issues related to religious diversity. Its is adapted from a model presented by the Tanenbaum Center for Interreligious Understanding.

SUMMARY

This article focused on the role that religion plays a role in the U.S. workplace today. Given the diversity of religious practice, there is a growing trend in the U.S. toward an integration of faith and work life, a trend that brings both benefits and challenges to the workplace. As a part of an organization's culture, religious beliefs can give meaning to shared goals and environments, and lead people to support the company's mission and one another. The diversity of religious practices today presents an increased potential for conflict between religious values and business expectations. Balancing the needs of an organization with the rights of employees requires a clear understanding of the legal protections provided for religion by the U.S. Constitution and Title VII of the 1964 Civil Rights Act with careful management, an organization can tap into the strengths and benefits of a diverse religious environment to add value to the organization members' quality of life and output.

DISCUSSION QUESTIONS

1. Comment on the general involvement of religion in U.S. public life, and particularly in the workplace. If a Puritan religious leader were suddenly to show up at your most recent job site, how might you explain the issues related to religion there to him?

2. You are an entrepreneur beginning your first start-up company, and you have ample seed money. How might you intentionally involve religion in the new business culture you are about to build?

3. Using the Religious Diversity Checklist in Exhibit 4, conduct an audit of an organization to which you have belonged. Once you answer the questions, analyze the answers and generalize from them to offer the organization advice on its treatment of religion in the workplace. How would you rate the organization on its performance on a scale of 1 to 10 (with 10 being excellent)?

4. Discuss the contributions religion might make to an organization for which you have worked. Then, discuss the challenges that the introduction on religious diversity there might create.

Writing Assignment

You manage a department of twenty-three employees, many of whom are Christian. Write a policy that clearly articulates how the organization accommodates requests for religious holiday leave. Include an explanation of how employees and management will communicate and resolve scheduling conflicts that may arise as a result of multiple requests for leave. Explain how you will communicate this policy to your employees.

Diversity on the Web

Select a religion that you are unfamiliar with from Table 1 and, using some of the resources listed below, answer the following questions:

a. What are some of the basic beliefs and practices of the religion you chose?

b. Are there any specific past or current workplace issues that have been raised with respect to this religion and/or its practices?

c. In general, what strategies can organizations use to educate employees about religious diversity? Comment on challenges organizations may face when addressing the discussion of religious diversity.

The following Internet resources will be helpful in beginning your research.

BBC Religion	http://www.bbc.co.uk/religion/
The Pew Forum on Religion and Public Life	http://pewforum.org/
The Pluralism Project at Harvard University	http://www.pluralism.org/resources/ links/index.php
Krista Tippett on Being	http://being.publicradio.org/
Virtual Religion Index	http://virtualreligion.net/vri/
Wabash Center for Teaching and Learning in Theology and Religion Internet Guide to Religion	http://www.wabashcenter.wabash.edu/ resources/guide_headings.aspx

Bibliography

Anti Defamation League. (2010). *Religious freedom resources.* Retrieved October 28, 2010, from www.adl.org/religious_freedom/resource_kit/religion_workplace.asp

BBC Religion. http://www.bbc.co.uk/religion/

Cafferky, M. (2011). Principles of management. Manuscript submitted for publication.

De Grazia, S. (1992). *Of Time, Work and Leisure.* New York: Vintage Books.

Dylan, M. *Religion in the workplace: Too much God-talk unprofessional.* (2006). Retrieved November 1, 2010, from www.suite101.com/content/religion-in-the-workplace-a4672/

Fenner, L. (2007) Religion in the Workplace is Diversity issue for U.S. Companies, 28 Nov., 2007, America.gov. Accessed 4 Nov., 2010.

"God in America" http://www.pbs.org/godinamerica

Lunden, R. (1988). *Business and Religion in the American 1920s.* New York: Greenwood Press, p. 153.

Pew Forum on Religion & Public Life. (2007). The U.S. religious landscapes survey. Retrieved November 12, 2010, from http://religions.pewforum.org/

Pew Forum on Religion & Public Life. (2008). *Report Two: Religious beliefs and practices.* Retrieved November 16, 2010, from http://religions.pewforum.org/reports/

Religion in business: Is it faith or suicide? (n.d.). Retrieved October 25, 2010, from www.buzzle.com/articles/religion-in-business-is-it-faith-or-suicide.html/

Sire, J.W. (1990). *Discipleship of the mind: Learning to love God in the ways we think.* Downers Grove, IL: InterVarsity Press. pp. 97–98, 106.

Society for Human Resource Management. (2008). *Religion and corporate culture: Accommodating religious diversity in the workplace survey report.* http://www.shrm.org/Research/SurveyFindings/Articles/

Pages/ReligionandCorporateCulture.
aspx

The Tanenbaum Center for Interreligious
Understanding. (n.d.). https://www.
tanenbaum.org/

The U.S. Equal Employment Opportunity
Commission. (2008). *What is religion under
Title VII?* Retrieved November 3, 2010, from
http://eeoc.gov/policy/docs/qanda_religion.
html

The U.S. Equal Employment Opportunity
Commission. (2009). *Resources on religious
discrimination.* Retrieved November 8, 20010,
from http://www.eeoc.gov/ laws/types/
religion.cfm

The U.S. Equal Employment Opportunity
Commission. (n.d.). *Title VII of the Civil
Rights Act of 1964.* Retrieved on October 20,
2010, from http://eeoc.gov/policy/vii.
html

U.S. Supreme Court. (1993). *Harris v. Forklift Sys.,
Inc.,* 510 U.S. 17, 21. Retrieved November 21,
2010, from http://supreme.justia.com/us/
510/17/

Virtual Religion Index. http://virtualreligion.
net/vri/

Wabash Center for Teaching and Learning in
Theology and Religion Internet Guide to
Religion http://www.wabashcenter.
wabash.edu/resources/guide_headings.aspx

Kathleen M. Fisher, PhD, is an associate professor of theology at Assumption College. Her focus areas are medieval history and religion with research interests in Irish Christianity, monastic life, and the place of contemplative practice in teaching and learning.

Jeanne M. McNett, PhD, is a professor of management at Assumption College. Her focus areas include the crossing of cultural boundaries building value and with the intersection of business with the liberal arts in higher education.

Pamela D. Sherer, PhD, is professor of management at Providence College, where she teaches courses in managing workplace diversity, comparative management, and organizational theory. Her research interests include diversity issues, faculty development practices, collaborative learning, and pedagogy and technology.

APPEARANCE AND WEIGHT INCLUSION ISSUES IN THE WORKPLACE

M. June Allard

Assumption College

Worcester State University, Professor Emerita

GOALS

- To foster understanding of the effects of appearance and weight discrimination
- To examine the law regarding appearance and weight discrimination
- To examine the relationships among weight, gender, race, and age dimensions of diversity

President Lincoln used his homeliness as humor. When accused of being two-faced, he replied "Do you think I would wear this face if I had another one? Appearance counts. Attractive people are often seen as having more desirable personality characteristics and skills than less attractive people. Good looking people are judged to be happy, successful, kind, smart, honest, sociable, and popular. Beauty carries a "halo effect" that psychologists refer to a "physical attractiveness stereotype," that implies good-looking people also possess many other positive characteristics.

Every culture has standards of physical beauty and these standards are "relatively constant across time and to some extent across culture, race and ethnicity" (Bell and McLoughlin, 2006, p. 456). In collectivist cultures, beauty equates with cultural good (Wheeler & Kim, 1997). The halo effect surrounding good looking people works to disadvantage less attractive women and those with visible physical disabilities who may experience prejudice and discrimination in the social and business arenas.

Workplace

Physical attractiveness and pleasing body image have long been known to have marketplace advantages. In the workplace, good looks are generally an asset in hiring, performance ratings, securing plum assignments, promotion and long term salary growth (Bell & McLoughlin, 2006, p. 457). ". . . [F]avoritism toward good looks and prejudice against homeliness is pervasive in most jobs" and within most occupations (Carr-Ruffino, 2003, p. 483).

Attractive people earn about 5 percent more than those with average looks (*Harvard Law Review* 2035, 1987) while homely workers make about 7 percent less than those with average looks. The most aesthetically-challenged members of our society face severe discrimination. In the words of Hamermesh and Biddle, there is a "salary premium for physical attractiveness and a salary penalty for 'plainness'" (Bell & McLaughlin, 2006, p. 457).

Height bias, for example, can affect salaries. Research suggests that tall males (6 feet and over) earn, on the average, nearly $166,000 more over 30 years than men who are 5 feet 5 and under even when gender, age and weight are considered (Dittman, 2004, p. 14). These findings are especially strong in sales and management positions, but occur in other positions as well.

There are other gender differences in the impact of good looks on the job. "Attractive women are advantaged in lower level jobs and in jobs held predominately by women but not at higher levels, in professional jobs or those perceived as men's jobs" (Bell & McLaughlin, 2006). Attractive women face discrimination in obtaining "masculine" jobs such as mechanical engineer, director of finance and construction supervisor (Headapohl, 2010). The impact good looks has in the workplace depends in part on many additional factors such as gender, credentials, position, ethnicity, etc.

APPEARANCE STANDARDS

At the beginning of its 2005–2006 season, the National Basketball Association (NBA) made headline news when it announced that it had decided to impose an off-the-court dress code on its players (King, Winchester & Sherwyn, 2006).

Businesses are increasingly rejecting casual dress (Armour, 2006). Colleges such as Morehouse and Savanah State University are imposing dress codes (Bartlett, 2009). Even the U.S. White House imposes dress standards for tourists. Organizations set appearance standards for their employees not only to project a particular corporate image, but also to create a favorable working environment and/or to "limit distractions caused by outrageous, provocative or inappropriate dress." Such standards generally take the form of requirements such as uniforms or of restrictions on dress, grooming, personal hygiene, hair styles, beards, mustaches, tattoos, make-up, face piercing, tongue metals, jewelry, "overwhelmingly bare midriffs" and weight. Penalties for violation of these standards are often serious and can even result in termination (Personnel Policy Services, n.d.). Noncompliant or penalized employees in return are increasingly filing lawsuits. Consider these examples of standards and their consequences:

- *Harrah's Operating Company, Inc.* fired a long-term employee who refused to comply with a new policy requiring female employees to wear facial make-up.
- *L'Oreal* terminated an employee who refused to fire a sales associate who was "not sufficiently attractive."
- *Harvard* was charged by a librarian with refusing to promote her because she didn't fit the librarian image she felt that she was seen as "just a pretty girl" who wore "sexy outfits."
- *Costco Wholesale Corporation* was sued by an employee, a member of the Church of Body Modification, who defied company policy prohibiting facial jewelry (except earrings) by refusing to remove eyebrow rings. The employee sued on the grounds of religious discrimination.

APPEARANCE LAW

How legal are appearance standards? In general, "requirements for professional appearance may be legitimate and job related or illegitimate and discriminatory" (Bell & McLaughlin, 2006, p. 458). Generally, under federal law, it *is legal* for employers to discriminate on the basis of appearance except for those characteristics such as sex and age that are protected under the anti discrimination laws or when appearance standards conflict with religious beliefs or negatively affect women or racial/ethnic minorities. The exception is a **BFOQ** (bonafide occupational qualification).

Courts have occasionally recognized that sex and age and other protected characteristics *can* be relevant to some jobs. Under BFOQ, employers *can sometimes* legally discriminate in terms of certain protected characteristics *if* the characteristics are "reasonably necessary to the normal operation of that particular business." Southwest Airlines for example, was allowed to limit its hiring to females for ticket agent and flight attendant positions in order to project its "love in the air" image and Hooters was permitted to continue hiring only girls as "Hooter girls" (Corbett, n.d., p. 10, 11, 16). Businesses such as airlines, fashion stores, restaurants, beauty salons and real estate agencies often want to hire attractive people in the belief that they engage customers and increase sales.

Although federal law may not prohibit appearance policies, employers are cautioned that a) creative attorneys often tie appearance codes to religious discrimination or to race or to sex stereotyping or discrimination, b) states and localities may have laws barring appearance-based hiring and c) union contracts may prohibit or regulate dress codes. There is no single model for dress code or appearance policy. Employers creating or reviewing existing policies might do well to consult an attorney.

WEIGHT

Weight counts. The visibility of excess weight, like other aspects of physical appearance, lends itself to stereotyping. Even though Americans are becoming increasingly heavy, there are severe social sanctions against obesity. Research by Hebl and Mannix (2003) suggests that biases even exist against people who merely associate with overweight people.

Overweight people live with negative stereotypes that include being lazy, undesirable, stupid, slow, lacking self control, out of shape, depressed, uneducated, slobbish, greedy, glutinous and having low energy levels. They are stigmatized and find themselves ridiculed, the butt of jokes and the recipients of hostility and tasteless and cruel comments. Discrimination occurs in education, health care, daily life, housing, public accommodations, employment and other areas.

"Discrimination may also exist for obese tenants seeking apartment rentals and in places such as fitness clubs and clothing stores" (Rudd Center, *b,* n.d.). Appropriate workplace clothing can be difficult to find and usually costs more than clothing for people of normal size. The Rudd Center (*b,* n.d.) further reports that ". . . obese people can experience problems in public settings such as restaurants, theaters, airplanes, buses and trains because of inadequate seat or seatbelt sizes." Being excessively overweight is likely to lead to higher medical expenses, difficulty in obtaining health insurance and life insurance premiums that are two to four times higher as those of their average size peers (Darlin, 2006).

Discrimination extends to the workplace where "the magnitude of bias against fat people far exceeds that for age or race or any other measure" (Smith, 2001).

> A stellar career path, a solid resume and a call from a headhunter may be the ticket to a better job. But if you're overweight, there's a good chance you won't be selected as a finalist for an executive position (Voros, 2007, March 11).

Obesity bias weighs against job seekers. "They are not hired as often as those of average size, are not promoted as often, have a harder time securing choice assignments, are more often assigned to non-visible jobs, receive more disciplinary actions, are paid less than their thinner counterparts, may be charged more for employee insurance coverage and are sometimes fired because of their weight." (Fact Sheet, n.d.; Goldberg, 2003; Darlin, 2006). In the words of one worker, "Our culture thinks heavier people are not qualified to be picked for the job."

One large study "found that among those 50% or more above their ideal weight, 26% indicated that they were denied benefits such as health insurance because of their weight, and 17% reported being fired or pressured to resign because of their weight" (Puhl & Brownell, n.d., p 6).

WEIGHT STANDARDS

Employer weight standards are especially resented and extremely contentious as they are often based on stereotypes about the control of weight and presumed characteristics of the overweight individual. Some of the standards and their effect on workplace experience are:

- *Weight Loss Centers, Inc.* a company specializing in weight loss plans, refused to hire a 350-pound man as a sales associate (Corbett, n.d., p. 8).
- *Jazzercise* (a company with 5,300 franchises in 38 countries) turned down a 240-pound job applicant because "Applicants must have a higher muscle-to-fat ratio and look leaner than the public" (Corbett, n.d., p. 8).
- *Korn/Ferry* an international executive search firm, reports the case of a very qualified 300-pound manager who was refused a job interview at a telecommunications company because "he wouldn't fit in" (Voros, n.d.).
- *Xerox Corporation* refused to hire an overweight applicant for a computer programming position because her obesity made her "medically unsuitable for the job" (Puhl & Brownell, 2001).
- *Rivier College* removed a morbidly obese woman from her teaching position because of her weight (Puhl & Brownell, 2001).
- *Agency Rent-a-Car Systems* fired an office manager because of his obesity in spite of his excellent employment record and excellent commendations (Puhl & Brownell, 2001).
- *Southwest Airlines* terminated a flight attendant and denied his reinstatement because his weight exceeded airline requirements (Puhl & Brownell, 2001).
- *Commonwealth of Virginia State Police* demoted a 9-year state trooper to dispatcher for failing a weight-loss program (Puhl & Brownell, 2001, pp. 6,7,23).

IS FAT ALBERT OVERWEIGHT OR OBESE?

Obesity is increasing world-wide. "Of the 6.5 billion people in the world, more than one billion are overweight and at least 300 million are obese" (Bell, 2007, p. 424). In the U.S., the National Center for Health Statistics reports that American population weight has been increasing since the 1980's" (NCHS, n.d.). On the average, Americans gained 10 pounds during the 1990s (Warren, 2004). Approximately 65% of U.S. adults are overweight or obese and almost 10 million (approximately 3 percent) are morbidly obese (Bell, 2007, p. 464; Darlin, 2006, p. 2; Smith, 2001, Dec. 8).

Weight Categories

How heavy is "overweight"? "Obese"? "Morbidly obese"? Weight is defined both by culture and by the field of medicine.

Cultural Standards: " . . . media and advertising play roles in the perceptions of obesity, from the choices consumers make, to body images they strive for" (Rudd Center *a*, n.d., p. 1). The message is: fat is bad; thin is in. American culture creates the ideal of slim beauty and condemns excess weight on one hand and on the other, encourages junk food diets and super-sized food portions.

Medical Standards: Medicine has created its own standards for weight judgments. The Body Mass Index (BMI) used by the medical profession is the accepted standard for distinguishing excess weight from obesity in adult men and women. Calculation of the BMI is shown below.

Body Mass Index		
BMI Formula	**Divide your weight in pounds by the square of your height in inches. Multiply the answer by 703.**	
Web Calculator	**www.nhlbisupport.com/bmi/ or http://www.halls.md/ideal-weight/body.htm**	
BMI Diagnosis	Underweight:	18.4 or less
	Normal:	18.5 – 24.9
	Overweight:	25 – 29.9
	Obese:	30 – 39.9
	[1]Morbidly Obese:	40 and over

[1]Facing serious health problems

The BMI Index is considered to be a reliable measure of body fat, but the National Institutes of Health warns that it does have limitations:

- "It may overestimate body fat in athletes and others who have a muscular build."
- "It may underestimate body fat in older persons and others who have lost muscle mass."

http://www.nhlbisupport.com/bmi/

The correlation between the Body Mass Index and fat varies by sex, race, and age. For children and teens, calculation of the BMI is the same as for adults, but interpretation of the resulting index number differs.

WEIGHT LAW

As with other appearance characteristics, there are no federal laws prohibiting discrimination against obese individuals (Rudd Center a, n.d.). A few places such as Michigan, the District of Columbia, Madison, Wisconsin and San Francisco and Santa Cruz, California provide legal protection (Puhl & Brownell, n.d.; Fyer & Kirby, 2005; Bell & McLaughlin, 2006).

"Overweight plaintiffs usually must prove that acts of bias against them are covered by federal laws prohibiting discrimination against disabled people" (ABCNEWS, 2004). Except for New Jersey, courts generally consider weight as under the control of the individual and therefore, not a disability (Puhl & Brownell, 2001). In New Jersey, obesity is defined as a disability and therefore is protected from workplace discrimination.

Being *moderately fat* is *not* a disability unless it is accompanied by another impairment. Under EEOC guidelines *obesity* is *not* a disability unless the weight is related to a physiological disorder or if the weight is extreme as in cases of morbid obesity. *Morbid obesity* can meet disability requirements (Puhl & Brownell, 2001).

The Social Security Administration does not consider obesity an impairment for purposes of determining eligibility for disability payments. This policy doubles the impact on obese people because they are then also denied opportunities for medical coverage afforded most people receiving social security disability benefits for two years or more (Puhl & Brownell, 2001).

When obesity is not a disability, there is no federal legal protection against discrimination. *When obesity is an impairment,* there is legal protection. When Xerox denied an obese computer programming applicant a job due to obesity that made her "medically unsuitable for the job" according to the company physician, she was protected (Puhl & Brownell, 2001, p. 23). The disability claim of the office manager fired by Agency Rent-a-Car System was upheld in court because he had sought "medical treatment for his condition" (Puhl & Brownell, 2001).

"Being overweight isn't just a health issue, however. It's also a political issue, one tied up with body image, sexism, discrimination, and self esteem" (Schwartzapfel, n.d.).

WEIGHT TIES TO WAGES, GENDER, RACE AND AGE

An interrelated set of factors both blurs and compounds the effects of weight on wages. Weight and wages are related to each other and both are tied to gender, race, age and social class. "Here since fat is more prevalent in certain racial and ethnic populations, more common in women than in men, and more common in older people than young. . ." (Goldberg, 2003, p. 97), weight discrimination is closely allied with discrimination of these protected characteristics. Among the relationships:

Weight and Age
- Weight gain often comes with age (Goldberg, 2003).

Weight and Gender
- "Fat women experience more negative outcomes than fat men" (Bell, 2007, p. 406).
- "Only 9% of top male executives are overweight" (Voros, n.d.).
- "Overweight women earn less than slim women" (Pagan & Davila, 1997).
- ". . . overweight men pay a salary penalty of $1,000 per year per pound if they're overweight" (Voros, n.d.)

Weight and Social Class
- ". . . poor women [in the U.S] tend to be heavier than more affluent women making class issues yet another factor to be considered" (Bell & McLaughlin, 2006, p. 468).

Weight, Wages, and Gender
- Overweight women get paid less for the same work than thinner women (Puhl & Brownell, 2001, p. 25).
- ". . . a weight increase of 64 pounds above the average for white women was associated with 9 percent lower wages" (Dalin, 2006, p. 5).
- "Men do not experience wage penalties until their weight exceeds standard weight by over 100 pounds" (Maranto & Stenoien, 2004, p. 2).

Weight, Gender, and Race
- "Women of color tend to be heavier than white women" (Bell & McLaughlin, 2006, p. 412).

Weight, Wages, Gender, and Race

- White women who are mildly obese (20% over standard weight) "experience greater wage penalties than do black men who are 100% over standard weight" (Maranto & Stenoien, 2004, p. 2).
- "Overweight men sort themselves into lower-level jobs."

Weight, Wages, Gender, and Social Class

- Overweight and obese women have lower incomes ($6,700 a year less) and higher rates of poverty (10% higher) than their non-obese peers" (NOW Foundation, n.d.).

Weight clearly is intertwined with other diversity characteristics. It is one of a person's multiple group memberships and the impact of excess weight has to be considered in conjunction with multiple social identities. If someone is old and obese and female—is this three strikes against the person, or do one or two factors outweigh all others in the behavior of the individual and in the way the individual is treated in the workplace?

DISCUSSION QUESTIONS

1. What are the pros and cons of an airline implementing a policy that heavier customers need to buy a second seat?

2. What can organizations do to counteract the high costs of employees who are obese?

3. Should television networks and stations set appearance and weight standards for news reporters, newscasters, weather forecasters, etc.? Why or why not? Should these standards be different for male and females?

Writing Assignment

Hiring obese employees does increase organizational costs. Investigate these costs and write a report that details how much obesity increases certain costs.

Minerd, J. (2007, April 24). Obese employees weigh heavily on bottom line. *Medpage Today.* Retrieved July 22, 2007 from http://www.medpagetoday.com/Pediataics/obesity/tb/5490

Leopold, R. (2004, August 2). Reining in the rising cost of obesity. *Managed Healthcare Executive.* Retrieved July 29, 2007 from http://www.managedhealthcareesecutive.com

Bibliography

ABCNEWS. *Fat activists see diet industry draining: Tyranny of the slender?* (2004, August 2). Retrieved July 15, 2007 from http://www.spinwatch.org/content/view/402/9/

Armour, S. (2006, October 25). Dress codes gussy up. *USA Today.* Retrieved July 24, 2007 from http://www.usatoday.com/money/workplace/2005-10-25-dress-code-usat_x.htm

Bartlett, T. (2009, November 13). Black colleges react to low point in fashion. *The chronicle of higher education.* pp. a1, 20.

Bellizi, J. (2000). Does successful work experience mitigate weight and gender-based employment discrimination in face-to-face industrial selling? *Journal of Industrial Marketing. 15 (6).*

Bell, M. & McLaughlin M. (2006). Outcomes of appearance and obesity in organizations. In (Eds) Konrad, A. Prasad, P & Pringle J. *Handbook of workplace diversity.* (pp. 455–474). Thousand Oaks, CA: Sage.

Bell, M. (2007). *Diversity in organizations.* Mason, OH: Thomson South-Western.

Bodypositive Forum. (n.d.). Retrieved September 5, 2007 from http://www.bodypositive.com/forum1.htm

Carr-Ruffino, N. (2003). *Managing diversity: People skills for a multicultural workplace, 6th ed.* Boston: Pearson Custom Publishing.

Corbett, W. (n.d.). The ugly truth about appearance discrimination and the beauty of our employment discrimination law. *Duke Journal of Gender, Law and Policy.* Retrieved July 15, 2007 from http://www.law.duke.edu/journals/djglp/articles/gen14p153.htm

Darlin, D. (2006, Dec 2). *Extra weight, higher costs.* Retrieved July 10, 2007 from http://www.nytimes.com [*click:* December 2, 2006, *then* Business, *then* Darlin, Damon]

Dittman, M. (2004, July). Standing tall pays off, study finds. Retrieved on May 4, 20111 from http://www. apa.org/monitor/julaugo4/standing.aspx

Fyer, B. & Kirby, J. (2005, May). Fat chance. *Harvard Business Review.* Reprint RO505A.

Goldberg, C. (2003). Citing intolerance, obese people take steps to press course. In Plous, S.

(2007). *Understanding prejudice and discrimination.* (McGraw-Hill) Retrieved July 27, 2007 from www.understandingprejudice.org/anth.htm

Headapohl, J. (2010, August 12). Attractive women are often passed over for "masculine" jobs www.MLive.com

Hebl, M. & Mannix, L. (2003). The weight of obesity in evaluative others: A mere proximity effect. *Personality and Social Psychology Bulletin, 29,* 28–38.

http://www.ppspublishers.com. Click on appearance of employees. Then, click on personal appearances of employees-dress code. Then click appearance and grooming standards. Retrieved May 5, 2011.

King, G.R., Winchester, J. & Sherwyn, D. (2006). You (don't) look marvelous. Considerations for employers regulating employee appearance. *Cornell Hotel & Restaurant Administration Quarterly 47, 4.* pp. 359–368.

Leopold, R. (2004, August 2). Reining in the rising cost of obesity. *Managed healthcare Executive.* Retrieved July 28, 2007 from http://www.managedhealthcareexecutive.com/MHE/articleDetail.jsp?id=134273

Maranto, C. & Stenoien, A. (2004, October 31). Weight discrimination: a multidisciplinary analysis. *Employee responsibilities and rights journal.* Retrieved July15, 2007 from http://www.springerlink.com/content/q7nhu072466g0136

McAdams, T., Moussavi, F. & Klassen, M. (2005, April 6). Employee appearance and the Americans with disabilities act: An emerging issue? Employee responsibilities and rights journal. Netherlands: Springer

National Center for Health Statistics. http://www.cdc.gov. Retrieved on May 5, 2011.

NIH National Heart, Lung and Blood Institute. (n.d). What are the health risks of overweight and obesity? Retrieved July 29, 2007 from http://www.nim.nih.gov/medlineplus/healthstatistics.html

NOW Foundation. (n.d.). Fact sheet: Size discrimination. *National Organization for Women.*

Retrieved July 15, 2005 from http://loveyour-bodynowfoundation.org/factsheet4.html

Pagan, J. & Davila, A. (1997). Obesity, occupational attainment, and earnings. *Social Science Quarterly, 78,* 756–770.

Panaro, G. (n.d). Is hiring on the basis of appearance illegal? *H.R. Corner.* Retrieved July 29, 2007 from http://www.bankersonline.com/operations/gp_appearance.html

Personal appearance of employees—dress code (n.d). Retrieved July 15, 2007 from http://www.hrpolicyanswers.com/preview/dresscode.pdf

Puhl, R. & Brownell, K. (n.d.). *Bias, discrimination, and obesity.* Retrieved July 15, 2007 from http://www.obesityresearch.org/cgi/content/full/9/12/788

Rouen, E. (2004, February 16). *A heavy burden: fighting for fat acceptance.* Retrieved July 15, 2007 from http://www.jrn. columbia.edu/studentwork/cns/2004-02-16/358.asp

Rudd Center (*a*). (n.d.) *Advertizing and the media.* Retrieved July 17 from http://www.yaleruddcenter.org/default.aspx?id=21

Rudd Center (*b*). (n.d.) *Other domains of weight bias.* Retrieved July 17 from http://www.yaleruddcenter.org/default.aspx?id=82

Schwartzapfel, B. (n.d.). The fat of the land. Retrieved July 21, 2007 from http://www.providencephoenix.com/features/

other_stories/multi_1/documents/05207016.asp

Schweitzer, T. (2007, May 22). Obese employees cost companies more. *Inc.com.* Retrieved July 10, 2007 from http://www.inc.com/news/articles/200705/obesity.html

Smith, E. (2001 May 21). Obesity bias weighs against job seekers. Retrieved July 15, 2007 from www.magellanassist.com/mem/library/default.asp?TopicId=122&CategoryId=08&ArticleId=51 http://www.associated content.com/article/95247/should_overweight_consumers_pay_extra.htm

The Harvard Law Review. (1987, June). Facial discrimination: Extending handicap law to employment discrimination on the basis of physical appearance. 100, Harvard Law Review 2035, The Harvard Law Review Association.

Voros, S. (n.d.) *Weight discrimination runs rampant in hiring.* Retrieved July 15, 2007 from http://www.careerjournal.com/myc/climbing/20000905-voros.html

Warren, M. (2004, November 6). Cost of fat air passengers takes off. *The daily telegraph, London. News,* p. 1.

Wheeler, L. & Kim, Y. (1997) What is beautiful is culturally good: The physical attractiveness stereotype has different content in collectivist cultures. *Personality and Social Psychology Bulletin, 23,* 795–800.

Points of Law

When obesity is not a disability, there is no federal legal protection against discrimination. Under ADA law, obesity is an impairment and employees who qualify as morbidly obese are allowed to request reasonable accommodation from their employers which accommodation may include (but is not limited to) making facilities readily accessible, job restructuring, modifying work schedules, reassignment to a vacant position.

Diversity on the Web

When business discriminates against "customers of size," there are costs to good will for the business as well as costs to the customers themselves.

1. Research the crash of US Airways Express 5481 on Jan 8, 2003 shortly after take off from the Charlotte-Douglas International Airport, in North Carolina. Note: notice the youth of the pilot (age = 25) as well as the weight issue.

   Wald, M. (May 13, 2003, Section A, column 1). Weight estimates on air passengers will be increased. http://www.nytimes.com
   New flight risk: Obesity? (January 30, 2003, News, p. 12A)
   http://www.usatoday.com

2. Research the implications of a policy that people have to declare their weight before boarding a plane.

   Warren, M. (2004, November 6, News, p.1). Cost of fat air passengers takes off. *The Daily Telegraph,* London. Retrieved September 5, 2007 from http://www. telegraph.co.uk/news/ index.jhtml
   Southwest Airlines forces larger passengers to buy two tickets
   http://www.cswd. org/docs/airlineseating.html
   Southwest Airlines' policy concerning overweight travelers
   http://www.everything2. com/index.pl?node_id=1343085
   Smith, A. (2006, December 8). Should overweight consumers pay extra for services from Southwest Airlines & other businesses?
   http://www.associatedcontent. com/article/ 95247/should_overweight_consumers_pay_extra.htm

Military Veterans

Carol P. Harvey
Assumption College

GOALS

- To understand the obstacles military veterans may face in today's workplace
- To present hiring and training programs that utilize the skills and talents learned through military service
- To learn about the laws governing the employment of military veterans

Military service experience is considered as a secondary dimension of diversity. Currently, there are more than twenty-two million veterans in the United States but these numbers are expected to increase significantly because of the Gulf War era II veterans, those returning from conflicts since 2001 (U.S. Bureau of Labor Statistics, 2010). The U.S. government discharges between 270,000–325,000 military personnel a year (Bergeron, 2008). Transitioning former military into or in the case of reservists and National Guard members, back to the workplace, presents unique, opportunities, challenges and legal issues.

Despite the popular belief that the U. S. military has always been an equal opportunity employer, diversity in the military has not come easily for racial minorities, women or LGBTs. Until 1948, when President Truman signed Executive Order #9981, military units were segregated by race. "Black and white soldiers did not fight side by side, dine in the same mess halls or sleep in the same barracks until 1951 during the Korean War" (DiversityInc, 2010a,). During World War II, females in the military were limited primarily to positions as nurses and secretaries and most were dismissed after the war ended. In contrast, during the Gulf War II era, 18% of the veterans are women.

In 1981 the Department of Defense passed Directive 1332.14 that required the dismissal of gay and lesbian personnel. "Between 1941 and 1996, the military discharged about 100,000 gays and lesbians, an average of roughly 2,000 a year" (DiversityInc, 2010a,b). Since 1992, the armed forces have followed the "don't ask, don't tell" policy which prohibits gay, lesbian or bisexual military personnel from revealing their sexual orientation or speaking about their personal relationships, while serving in the U.S. military. The Navy ended its ban on females serving on submarines in 2010 but even today, females, Latinos and Asians are still proportionally underrepresented within the officer rank in the armed services.

Military service can provide leadership, personal, and team skills as well as the technical expertise needed in today's workforce. A 2001 report from the Army Training and Leadership Development Panel revealed that the two most important qualities for leadership in an uncertain world today are self-awareness and adaptability which contrast with the specialization and top down control styles that worked well managing pervious conflicts. General David Petraeus, currently the Commander of the U.S. forces in Afghanistan said, "Tell me anywhere in the business world where a 22 or a 23 year old is responsible for 35 or 40 other individuals on missions that involve life and death" (O' Keefe, Birger, & Burke, 2009).

Many organizations such as CSX transportation, where one out of every five employees is a vet (CSX.com) recognize the business benefits of hiring ex-military personnel. Experiences and skills that translate directly to the business world include: dealing with cultural and racial diversity and decision making (Gilbert, 2010), leadership training, teamwork, discipline and integrity (O'Keefe, Birger, Burke, 2010), and crisis management and technical skills (DiversityInc.com, 7/14/2010).

Best Practices

AFL-CIO—When the AFL-CIO Building and Construction Trades unions realized that one-third of its members would retire in the next 10–15 years, they joined with nine construction companies to found H2H (Helmets to Hardhats). This program links veterans with career training and job opportunities in building and construction industry. H2H recruits at military job fairs and through Monster.com and even offers a placement program for disabled vets called The Wounded Warrior Program (helmetstohardhats.org).

Home Depot—Since 2004, Home Depot, the retail home improvement chain has worked with the U.S. Department of Defense to offer special employment programs designed for returning veterans, National Guard, Reservists both on leaving and returning from active duty, and for military spouses. As a result, Home Depot hired over 60,000 veterans. In addition, Home Depot supports Project Homefront, a national program to help families with home repairs while a military family member serves on active duty. (careers.homedepot.com).

WORKPLACE DISCRIMINATION AGAINST VETERANS

While military training and experience can be assets, veterans often experience difficulties and discrimination when transitioning back into the workplace. Those returning from the Gulf Wars experienced unemployment rates of 10.2% in 2009 and younger male veterans, ages 18–24 had a much higher unemployment rate of 21.6%. Post military employment transitions can be complicated by lack of social and professional networks due to frequent relocations (Gunn, 2005), failure to take advantage of the transition assistance workshops provided by the military (Military & Veterans Benefits, 2002) and a lack of effective job search skills (Clemens and Milsom, 2008). A survey conducted by Career Builder.com revealed that it took over six months after leaving active duty for 17% of returning military personnel to find a job and that the biggest challenge was "employers' inability to understand how military skills can fulfill civilian qualifications" (*Journal of Accountancy*, 2009 p. 23).

Points of Law

Veterans and the Law

Each year over 300,000 service members, many of them activated members of the National Guard or reserves, return to the civilian workforce. In the past, the primary employment legislation for veterans was the **Vietnam Era Veterans Readjustment Act** (1974) that required federal contractors to increase their employment of veterans through Affirmative Action policies.

Today, returning military personnel often reservists or National Guard members, are protected under the **Uniform Services Employment & Reemployment Act of 1994 (USERRA)** in terms of discrimination in hiring, reemployment, and promotions. In addition, veterans may also be members of a protected class that falls under other federal legislation, such as females, (Civil Rights Act of 1964) workers over forty, (Age Discrimination in Employment Act, 1967 & 1974) or survivors with serious physical and/or mental challenges (Americans with Disabilities Act, 1994).

The Uniform Services Employment & Reemployment Act of 1994 (USERRA) requires that employers rehire returning veterans (prior employees) who have served on active duty for no more than five years, and received either an honorable or dishonorable discharge, providing that the employee returns to the job within specified time limits after terminating military service. In addition, this law preserves some benefits while on military leave. Whenever possible, the employee must give the employer notice that he/she will be leaving. This statute applies to both large and small businesses unless the organization can prove that rehiring the veteran will cause the company an undue hardship (Tully, 2010; Aspen, 2010).

Although 13% of all veterans report a service connected disability, the number rises to 21% for Gulf Era II veterans who receive more advanced medical care and often survive what might previously have been fatal injuries (U.S. Bureau of Labor Statistics, 2010). In addition, a 2008 Rand Corporation study revealed that 19% of those returning from duty in Iraq and Afghanistan suffered from TBI (traumatic brain injuries) and one out of five (approximately 300,000) suffered from depression or PSTD (post-traumatic stress disorder) (Disabled American Veterans.org, 2009).

While it is clear that military experience can bring valuable skills and training to the workplace, this group may require assistance in transitioning back to civilian positions.

DISCUSSION QUESTIONS

1. Why do military veterans sometimes face discrimination in the workplace?

2. How could some of the misperceptions about military veterans in the workplace be changed?

3. What is the business case for employing veterans?

4. What provision(s) is/are in the URESSA Act that might unintentionally discourage an employer, particularly a small business owner, from hiring military veterans?

5. Do you think that female military veterans face additional discrimination because of their gender? Why or why not?

Writing Assignment

Interview someone who has served in the active duty military about his/her post military work experience. Possible questions could include: What branch of the service was he/she in and how long did he/she serve? Was he/she ever asked about his/her military service in a job interview? Did the military offer any workforce transition program when he/she was discharged? What skills does he/she think he/she gained from his/her service time that might be useful in the workplace? How does he/she think that his/her military experience changed him/her? What does he/she know about any workforce laws that benefit veterans?

Write a one- to two-page report that analyzes the information that you obtained from this interview that relates to this veteran and the workplace.

Bibliography

Anonymous. (2009). Vets face tough time finding work. *Journal of Accountancy*, 207, p. 23. Retrieved from Business Source Premier, July 23, 2010.

Anonymous. (2010). Treating returning veteran as a new employee violated USERRA. *Fair Employment Practice Guidelines*. Aspen Publishers, 659, 1–4.

Bergeron, A. (2008). Five years of Iraq war impact union program that turns military vets into craft workers. *Engineering News Record*, 260, #17, 141–2.

http://www.careers.homedepot.com.edgesuite.net/ our-culture/military-commitment.html Retrieved May 5, 2011.

Clemens, E.V. and Milsomn, A.S. (2008). Enlisted service members' transition into the civilian world of work: a cognitive information processing approach. *The Career Development Quarterly*, 56, 246–256. Retrieved from Business Source Premier, July 23, 2010.

CSZ. (2010). Retrieved July 25, from CSX.com.

Disabled American Veterans. (March 24, 2009). March is national brain injury awareness month. retrieved on July 29, 2010 from dav.org/news/NewsArticle.aspx?ID=111.

DiversityInc. (2010a). Diversity in the military. Retrieved July 23, 2010 from diversityinc.com.

DiversityInc. (2010b). How you and your company can help vets. Retrieved July 24, 2010 from diversityinc.com.

Gilbert, H. (2010). Soldiering on as civilians. *Personnel Today*, 14–16. Retrieved from Ebscohost on July 23, 2010.

Gunn, E.P. (2005). Why networking is still the best way to job hunt. *The Wall Street Journal Career Journal.com*. Retrieved July 23, 2010 from career-journal.com/jobhunting/ networking/20040511-gunn.html. http:// www.helmetstohardhats.org

Military and Veterans' benefits: Observations on the Transitions Assistance Program: Hearings Before the Subcommittee of the House Committee on Veterans' Affairs, 106th Congress (2002)(testimony of Cynthia Bascetta).

O' Keefe, B., Birger, J., & Burke, D. (2009). Battle tested. *Fortune*, 161, #4, pp. 108–118.

Tully, M.B. (2010). Veterans in the workplace. *Employee Benefit Plan Review*, 64, #12, 5–6.

U.S. Bureau of Labor Statistics, Retrieved May 5, 2011 from http://www.bls.gov/news.release/ vet.nrO.htm.

Diversity on the Web

Any student using an .edu email address can register for free diversity information at http://www.diversityinc.com. Once you are registered, go to this Web site and search for "6 Things NEVER to Say to a Veteran Coworker." After reading this article, what are your reactions? What did you learn?

CHOOSING THE BOARD

M. June Allard
Assumption College
Worcester State University, Professor Emerita

Heritage Medical Center is a moderately sized suburban hospital currently plagued with financial and management problems so severe they are reaching the crisis stage. The hospital is governed by a 12 member Board of Trustees. There are four open seats on the board. The eight remaining members are fiscally conservative, well-to-do industrialists who have known each other for years and who frequently see each other socially at the country club, a very exclusive yacht club and at community affairs. Board members are expected to contribute their expertise and to donate generously to the hospital fundraising campaigns.

There is friction among these Board members who are very concerned about the future of the hospital, but who cannot agree on what course of action to take in the face of its mounting problems.

You serve on the Board Development Committee which must now fill the four empty seats from eight nominees. Read the biographies provided here and select the best candidates.

1. Which four of the nominees would be your choices? Please list them in order of preference and indicate why you chose them.

2. Replacing one-third of the board members all at once will mean a radial change for this board. This is a source of concern for the board members and a serious concern of the hospital CEO who deals frequently with the board. What will you do to ease the transition for the board members and for the CEO?

NOMINEES

Drake Covington II is a very bright 23 year old computer systems analyst. He marches to a different drummer and is considered "far out." He is the nephew of an influential board member and owes his nomination to his uncle.

Layla Amini is a successful 27 year old financial analyst. She is very quiet and very conservative; a traditionalist with a solid reputation. She was nominated by her cousin, a state senator.

Carmen Diaz is a 33 year old highly respected medical doctor. She is very innovative and a self starter who has already set up a clinic. She has never met anyone on the board, but does know the hospital CEO. She was nominated by a group of doctors practicing at the hospital.

Charles Wong is a 35 year old management systems analyst. He lives near the hospital and works out of his home. He is reputed to be a team player and supportive person. He was nominated by the union representing the hospital staff.

Peter Skylar is a 46 year old CEO of an Health Maintenance Organization (HMO) who by nature of his position is very familiar with hospital operations. He is brilliant, a loner, and connected to the state regulatory agency. He is considered to be in the "out-group" by those members of the board that he knows.

Sue Novenski is a 42 year old social worker who works in a battered women's shelter. She works well with groups, is low key and extremely collaborative. She knows no one on the board; she was nominated by the hospital's Patients Advisory Committee.

Katherine Dobbs Courtney is a 55 year old widow of a very wealthy industrialist who served on the board. She has served on community boards. She is an idea person, an individualist and is outspoken. She plays golf with the mayor who nominated her.

Lamar Leroy Woods is a 56 year old retired owner of a profitable manufacturing company. He is very wealthy and has donated large sums of money to the hospital. He is conservative, easy-going, intelligent and comfortable to be with. He was nominated by the hospital CEO.

Fairfax Metropolitan Hospital: The Candidate

M. June Allard
Assumption College
Worcester State University, Professor Emerita

GOALS

- To examine the issues of weight discrimination and youth discrimination
- To illustrate legal and social issues in hiring decisions
- To consider personnel decisions such as selection from multiple perspectives: management, Boards of Directors, human resources, candidates, staff, patients

Fairfax Metropolitan Hospital is a moderately sized teaching hospital committed to quality care from a qualified staff. The hospital currently suffers from a lack of diversity among its staff, however—a glaring fault in nearly every unit at the hospital and one pointed out by several accrediting agencies. The hospital now seeks to develop a more diversified staff which they define as one representing the diversity of their community. There is also an urgent need to modernize the nursing department as its outdated procedures and inefficient practices also concern accreditors. Compounding the hospital's concerns is the recent retirement of the Director of Nursing—just as another nursing accreditation visit looms on the horizon.

THE INTERVIEW

HR Director Jorge Hansen listens as the Search Committee discusses a candidate, Dr. Saryn Soysa, who they have just interviewed for the Director of Nursing position. She is, a heavyset, pleasant young woman who looks even younger than her 32 years. Originally from Sri Lanka, she has been educated in U.S. universities and is now a U.S. citizen. Dr. Soysa's credentials are truly outstanding. She took advanced exams, graduated early from college *summa cum laude* and completed advanced graduate work by studying full time on national and international fellowships. With a doctorate from a prestigious U.S. university, this articulate young woman has already won several research grants as well as a number of awards and honors. Her work experience is appropriate for this position and her references laud not only her skills, but also her personality and sense of responsibility. Her credentials are superb and by far the best of all the candidates under consideration.

As the HR Manager listens, themes emerge from the Committee's discussion of Dr. Soysa. Typical of the comments he hears are:

"I am concerned about her health, given that she is so overweight."
"Did you notice how much she ate at lunch!!"
"It's important that we present a good public appearance . . ."
"This job involves a lot of public relations; the director has a lot of public exposure."

247

"Too bad our benefits don't include fitness clubs or Weight Watchers!"

"I just don't know about her . . ."

"She is qualified, but . . ."

"And she is so much younger than the other directors! Do you think she is too young to fit with them?

"Experienced nurses might not accept her . . ."

"I just don't know if she would fit well with our organization."

Someone suggests that maybe they should select one of the male candidates since there are few male nurses in the unit and the hospital has never had a male in the Nursing Director's position. Someone else tentatively suggests that maybe the search should be reopened.

As the committee continues its discussion, the HR Director is aware that no one is arguing for any other candidate in particular. There seems to be implicit acceptance that Saryn Soysa is by far the best qualified; easily head and shoulders above all the other candidates.

Their conversation however, reflects reservations tinged with some prejudices. Jorge knows that the search team is conscious of its charge to diversify the nursing unit and he thinks that their comments reflect underlying disapproval of Saryn's *weight and youth*. He is aware that his supervisor, the hospital CEO, is on shaky ground with the Board of Directors and he suspects that she may think it is too risky to hire someone so young for such an important post. The Board might well question her judgment in approving such a hire.

In summary, while there is universal agreement that Dr. Soysa is exceptionally qualified and the hospital really needs her expertise to modernize the Nursing Department, the Search Committee is clearly uncomfortable with her weight and youth although they avoid making many direct references to either. The CEO could likely be leery of her weight as well as her youth.

THE HR MANAGER'S ETHICAL DILEMMA

Jorge ponders the situation; the final decision is his. Should he yield to the committee's reservations by hiring a less qualified candidate? Would the CEO be happy with this decision? Should he consider reopening the search even though it is extremely unlikely to yield someone so well qualified? Would either of these alternatives be the best *ethical* and/or the best *business* decision for the hospital?

Or, should Jorge ignore committee reservations and hire Saryn Soysa? If he does, how should he explain his decision to the committee and to his boss, the CEO?

DISCUSSION QUESTIONS

1. Generate a list of possible actions the HR manager might take.

2. Which action(s) would you suggest as the most appropriate for the HR manager? Why?

3. Are there legal issues here? Explain. (See the article "Appearance and Weight Inclusion Issues in the Workforce" in this text.)

4. If Jorge hires Saryn, what message is he sending to the hospital staff? If he doesn't hire her, what message is he sending?

5. If Jorg hires Saryn, what problems is she likely to face? What problems will Jorge likely face?

6. What resources does Saryn have for dealing with the problems? What resources does Jorge have for dealing with the problems?

Diversity on the Web

Social Costs

There are considerable social costs including stigma, prejudice, and discrimination for those who are obese.

1. Research these costs, noting the interrelationships of obesity, gender, age, race, and social class.
2. How do those factors impact Saryn right now?
   If she is hired, how might they impact her in the future?
   http://www.obesityresearch.org [2001, v.9, p.788]
   http://www.nytimes.com [click: a) December 2, 2006 b) Business c) Darlin, Damon]
3. This case primarily involves the factors of weight and youth. Go to the Web site below and take the IAT test for weight ("Fat-Thin"). Also take the IAT test for Age (Young-Old) and compare the two results.
4. There are those who feel that the bias against weight is stronger than the bias against race. Take the IAT test for race and the one for skin-tone and compare these results against those from your tests for weight and age.

https://implicit.harvard.edu/implicit

Integrative Questions for Section 2

1. Social class can have a pervasive effect on one's life. How could one's social class impact someone's military service experience?

2. For many reasons, one group of people who still experience a lot of religious discrimination is Muslims. How could an organization minimize this discrimination for its Muslim employees?

3. The decisions made in the "Choosing the Board" exercise may result in a more diverse group. What types of positive and negative conflicts could result? How could these be reduced by effective diversity leadership?

4. Assume that you are a mentor to an employee who came from a lower class background. She is bright and has career potential. However, some elements of her socialization such as the way she speaks, her manners, and her communication patterns will prevent her from advancing to the next level. How could you help her?

5. The Fairfax case is very unique because it illustrates how younger workers, who are not legally protected from age discrimination, can experience negative stereotypes. What can they do on their jobs to try to offset the negative perceptions that some people have about young workers?

6. What changes have taken place in society that may make it more difficult than ever to move out of the lower social classes? What may make it easier?

7. Today many military veterans are female. What prejudices could they experience when returning to the workplace that their male counterparts may not?

5

Managing Diversity: Ethical, Legal, Communication, and Marketing Issues

In this section, students will

- Learn about the ethical and legal implications of diversity management.
- Examine the differences between Canadian and U.S. diversity laws.
- Explore communication issues in today's diverse workplace.
- Analyze the impact of diversity on consumer behavior.

This is the first of two sections on the organizational implications of managing diversity and the changes that need to be made because of the increasing diversity of today's stakeholders. In Section V, diversity is viewed from three perspectives: the ethical, legal, and economic. First, we present a theoretical discussion, that is, diversity as the "right thing to do" (McNett). Second, we consider the legal perspective, that is, what organizations are required by law to do in the United States (Allard) and in Canada (Mentzer). Third, we begin to consider the implications of the business case, that is, diversity from the economic perspective in terms of understanding and improving communication with a more diverse workforce (Colavecchio and Harvey) and the need to change marketing strategies (Allard) and media messages (Allard).

This section closes with a capstone exercise (Allard) that reviews the Legal Points of Law presented throughout the text and a case that illustrates both the legal consequences and missed marketing opportunities when diversity is poorly managed (DeWitt).

THE ETHICS OF WORKPLACE DIVERSITY

Jeanne McNett
Assumption College

GOALS

- To examine diversity as an ethnical process
- To explain and apply ethical theories to diversity

Spike Lee's suggestion in his 1989 classic film *Do the Right Thing* that we "do the right thing" on the issue of diversity seems a reasonable one to most people, on the face of it. But when we ask, "Why?" in a business environment, we are likely to hear that we should do the right thing because such actions are good for business results. That may be fine, but is it enough? Is there more than a pragmatic justification for diversity in the workplace? Is there an ethical justification for valuing diversity (the right thing) in the workplace?

We begin with a review of the pragmatic business arguments that are used to suggest that diversity is desirable in business. These arguments are not, though, based on an ethical analysis, but rather, on an economic one. We then explore what ethical theories tell us about valuing diversity in the workplace. Our conclusion then moves to an attempt to bridge between the practical (business) and the good (ethics).

By valuing *diversity* we mean valuing, respecting and appreciating the differences (such as age, culture, education, ethnicity, experience, gender, race, religion, sexual orientation, among others) that make people unique. Note that our definition has to do with *valuing* differences, so it is a frame of mind, a way of thinking, rather than a result. This is an important distinction because if we were to think of diversity as only a result and not a way of thinking, such an approach might lead to false conclusions. For example, we might observe that a workforce is diverse and then be tempted to infer that a valuing of diversity has led to the workforce composition. Yet we all recognize that a diverse workforce could be explained by many other factors, such as, poor work conditions, and business location. This workforce could be connected to diversity only by coincidence.

ECONOMIC ARGUMENTS FOR DIVERSITY

Most of the economic arguments for the desirability of a diverse workforce are based on a connection made between diversity and desired business outcomes. Most compelling is the connection made between a workforce that brings valuable and different perspectives and abilities to connect with a wide spectrum of customers. This market-driven argument for diversity becomes increasingly important because globalization has strengthened the role that relationships play in business transactions. Globalization has led managers to realize that business is all about relationships. The more diverse the workforce, the wider and deeper is the ability to communicate across cultures, and the greater the potential for deep, long-lasting relationships. An additional economic argument for diversity is that when the firm is recruiting from a larger, more diverse labor pool, the likelihood of hiring capable managers increases (Schraeder, Blackburn, and Iles, 1997).

There is also the argument that a diverse workforce is nontraditional, and therefore likely to be more creative and more capable of instituting and accepting change because diverse workgroups tend to be more accepting of ambiguity (Rosener 1995). Research suggests that the Western assumption that innovation comes from the center of the firm (which traditionally is the less diverse part) may be seen as a dying vestige of essentially an imperialist way of thinking. Prahalad and Lieberthal conclude that "over time . . . as multinationals develop products better suited to the emerging markets, they are finding that those markets are becoming an important source of innovation." That is a good explanation of how diversity may increase the potential for creativity (Prahalad 1998).

These arguments for diversity rest on a way of thinking about business known as the resource-based theory of the firm (Barney 1991). According to this theory, the firm is conceptualized as a bundle of resources that are poised, ready to take advantage of opportunities in the external environment. The more distinctive these resources are, the more difficult would be their imitation by a competitor. A diverse workforce with established customer relationships is an example of such a difficult-to-imitate resource. Lord Browne, former Group Chief Executive (CEO) of British Petroleum, offers an example of this economic rationale for diversity and its primacy over an ethical justification in his comments to the Women in Leadership Conference (2002, Berlin, Germany).

> For BP the issue is no longer about whether diversity is a good thing . . . the issue is how to deliver strategy. How to take immediate, real actions . . . We're competing for resources . . . And we're competing for markets . . . And therefore we're competing for talent. If we can get a disproportionate share of the most talented people in the world, we have a chance of holding a competitive edge. That is the simple strategic logic behind our commitment to diversity and to the inclusion of individuals—men and women regardless of background, religion, ethnic origin, nationality or sexual orientation. We want to employ the best people, everywhere, on the single criterion of merit. And the importance of that goal as a part of our overall business strategy has grown as competition has intensified.

BP is an energy company that needs to establish relationships that will allow it to extract oil and gas in Mexico, Indonesia, West Africa and Russia, while it competes for markets in America, China, South Africa and Europe. BP's approach to diversity, based on market economic arguments, makes a lot of sense. The rationale is not ethics, but rather, the strategic outcomes BP seeks. Such motivations, regardless of their impact on diversity, go to an assertion that the purpose of business is to increase profits, not to do good. The fundamental argument of this understanding is best articulated by the economist Milton Friedman in his oft cited essay, "The Social Responsibility of Business is to Increase Its Profits."

> There is one and only one social responsibility of business—to use its resources and engage in activities designed to increase its profits so long as it stays within the rules of the game, which is to say, engages in open and free competition without deception or fraud. (http://ca.geocities.com/busa2100/miltonfriedman.htm/)

In contrast, an ethical approach would consider judgments about right and wrong, good and bad, what ought to be in our world, definition criteria suggested by Laura Hartman (2002).

Another difference between a pragmatic, economic justification for diversity and an ethical one has to do with the judgment criteria. In economic business arguments, the criteria go to the business results. Making a decision about diversity is, at a superficial level, pretty easy: we look at the economic business results of a decision. In contrast, ethically-based decisions are judged sometimes by the reasoning that leads to the decision, not the decision's outcomes. The ethical dimension of a decision may not always be obvious from a surface consideration of that decision or an examination of the decision's outcomes.

CATEGORIES OF ETHICAL THEORIES

So what might an ethical justification for valuing diversity be? In order to move toward that question's answer, let's first look at the three categories that are often used to describe Western ethical theory. First is the set of theories that looks at the process or the means of a decision; that is, how do we arrive at the decision? Second are the theories that address what is good and bad by looking at likely outcomes or consequences of a decision. Third is a set of theories that looks at the caring aspects of decisions. These three categories remind us that the assumptions upon which ethical claims can be made may vary widely.

F. Neil Brady developed a matrix for these distinctive categories of ethical theories that offers a helpful summary (Brady 1996). Exhibit 1 is a modification of Brady's chart. His correlation of these approaches with the three virtues of faith, hope and charity is an added benefit as we think about the possible ethical bases for workplace diversity. The three columns on the right describe the three main theoretical bases for ethical judgment, with Brady's suggested equivalents in parentheses. We discuss each of them and their likely application to a diversity claim: that a valuing of differences—our definition of diversity—is good or produces the quality of goodness either by process (deontological) or outcomes (teleological), or through caring for others. We also consider whether the theory is universal in nature, for all times and all places, or particular, depending on the context.

The reason to consider universal or particular applications of an ethical theory has to do with culture. The cultural context in which a diversity decision is made may well affect the shared understanding of what *ethical* actually means. A short example of the results of different

EXHIBIT 1   Three Categories of Ethical Theories

	Deontology (Faith)	Teleology (Hope)	Caring (Charity)
Universal Application (all times, all places)	Universal duty: universal principles, The Way	Universal ends: Character ethic, utilitarianism, other -isms	Universal care: love for humanity
Particular Application (depends on context)	Particular duties: situation ethic, case by case approach	Particular ends: self-actualization	Particular care: personal relationships

(adapted from F. Neil Brady) With kind permission of Springer Science+Business Media assumptions about what is ethical may be found in the consideration of the quality of difference in Japan. The Japanese culture is homogeneous, and the introduction of difference is generally not seen as good. In fact, families and the individual's company will conduct a background investigation of an engaged employee's potential spouse to make certain he or she is pure Japanese and not from an outcast group such as the *borakumin*. Such activity is seen as fulfilling an ethical responsibility. In North America, especially on the part of the employer, such an investigation would likely be regarded not as a moral duty but as an immoral action, on the grounds of both privacy and what we in North America would consider racial prejudice.

Brady's categorization describes various ethical theories based on the claims that their application makes: is the theory universally applicable (*the* rule, built on understood similarities) or does it claim a situational focus (it all depends, built on differences)? This distinction is helpful as we consider the ethical bases for diversity because it incorporates the idea of the decision's context. This distinction also corresponds in interesting ways to the Universalism-Particularism dimension used to describe culture differences by Fons Trompenaars (Hampden-Turner and Trompenaars 2000). In cultures that measure high on the universalism dimension, such as the U.S., Switzerland, Australia, and Canada, rules are seen to apply to all equally. In particularist cultures such as China, Japan, Venezuela, Greece, and India, rules are seen as more variable, depending on the context and the actors.

The implications of these assumptions in the area of diversity are significant, especially if we consider the effects of a diverse workgroup on an organization's ethics. For example, Chinese assumptions about ethical decisions tend to be particularist and relationship-based. Awareness that American business ethics decisions, in contrast, tend to be universalistic and rule-based would help an international partner from a particularist culture such as China understand the assumptions that underpin Title VII of the Civil Rights Act of 1964. This act as amended prohibits "discrimination in hiring, promotion, discharge, pay, fringe benefits, job training, classification, referral, and other aspects of employment on the basis of race, color, religion, sex or national origin."

We now look at how each of these ethical theories might be applied to diversity in the workplace. The ethical argument would be that these differences are good or produce the quality of goodness either by process (deontological, faith) or outcomes (teleological, hope), or by caring for others (care, love, charity).

DEONTOLOGICAL CATEGORY OF ETHICAL THEORIES

The first category of ethical theories in our framework is deontological, and it stems from duties and moral obligations (the Greek *deont* means duty). Probably the most well-known deontological theory is Emmanuel Kant's categorical imperative, which dictates that one has a duty to "act only on that maxim by which you can at the same time will that it should become a universal law" (Kant 1785). We all know the popular paraphrase of Kant's categorical imperative, "Do unto others as you would have them do unto you." Deontological theories are based on duties, rules, and obligations that lie outside the person. Religious practice tends to rest on a deontological approach to ethics. For example, we can think of the Ten Commandments as a series of duties. Brady uses the term *faith* to capture this characteristic.

DEONTOLOGICAL ETHICAL SYSTEMS AND DIVERSITY

Can a claim that workplace diversity rests on duty be made in a convincing way? Such a claim would establish that we have a duty to at least tolerate differences. This tolerance would be not because of the *results* of these differences, but simply because, for some reason, having differences is a duty that is a good in itself.

To explore our sense of duty in this regard, let us go to an example of which we all are a part, the U.S. housing market. We all live somewhere. Consideration of the nature of the U.S. housing market, segregated as it is by race and economic class, might suggest that there is no widely accepted duty to incorporate or tolerate difference, at least in this narrow but universally inhabited sector, despite federal law prohibiting discrimination. At the particularist level though, we can recognize that we might have specific duties we hold to one another with regard to diversity, depending on the context. For example, when we find ourselves part of a public group, say, a search committee, we may well accept that there is a duty to diversify the committee membership, simply for the sake of diversity and not for a pragmatic reason. Of course, we may well want to diversify for reasons other than duty, for example, to meet legal obligations, ensure compliance with the choice by including various constituencies or stakeholders and their varied points of view in the search process, and so on. Yet we can see that in some situations, diversity may be understood to be a duty, a good in and of itself. On balance though, deontological approaches to diversity are probably few in the work situation.

This observation is in accord with sociologist William Julius Wilson's application of Blalock's theory of social power, which suggests that when majority or minority members change their beliefs about minority or majority members, these changes are initially a result of power shifts (in this case, Civil Rights legislation), and only secondarily, value shifts. Diversity in our workplaces developed initially as a response to a power shift, federal legislation (for example, Title VII of the Civil Rights Act of 1964, the Americans with Disabilities Act of 1990, the Equal Pay Act of 1963, the Age Discrimination in Employment Act of 1967) rather than as a response to a changed belief system about what is right.

In our discussion of deontological approaches, we have considered individuals as the location of ethical decisions. This approach is justified because decisions are made in the minds of individual managers. Yet we may think of organizations themselves as having a limited kind of personhood, at least in a legal sense. Considered from the perspective of an organization capable of ethical decision-making, we find another example of deontological ethics in the workplace when we consider the ethics codes of these organizations. Ethical codes are rule-based and suggest that the corporate citizen is bound by duty to follow the rules, some of which may address respect for diversity.

TELEOLOGICAL CATEGORY OF ETHICAL THEORIES

The second category of ethical approaches is teleological, addressing the good that comes from a focus on the ends achieved by a contemplated action (Greek *telos*, end). The teleological approach holds that decisions are right or good if they produce a desired goodness and bad if they produce some undesirable state (badness or pain). So teleological approaches are action-based, connected with implementation, while the deontological approaches concern the process (Hopkins, 1997). Utilitarianism, the greatest good for the greatest number, illustrates such an action-based, results-oriented approach. A business example is found in cost-benefit analysis, through which the benefit is weighed against its cost. The decision is then made to follow the path that provides the greatest overall gain for the least cost. In fact, research suggests that many American managers hold to utilitarian principles in their decision-making (Fritzsche, 1984). For example, a manager might structure a lay-off list with the least trained and newest members of the organization as the first to face cuts, on the basis that keeping people with seniority will lead to the retention of higher levels of knowledge, which in turn may lead to better results for a larger number of people.

Distributive justice, concerned with fair and equitable outcomes, is another ethical theory within the teleological category. Distributive justice suggests that ethical decisions are those that lead to a fair distribution of goods. John Rawls has developed a test for distributive justice: is the decision the one that we would make if we were cloaked in a *veil of ignorance*? (Rawls, 1971). This veil of ignorance would not allow us to know our status and position, so it protects us from our own self-interest's playing a role in decisions on distribution of goods. Laura Hartman describes how Rawls sees the veil of ignorance working and the ends it would achieve (2002). First of all, we would make decisions unaware of their immediate consequences to ourselves. We would develop a cooperative system in which the benefits would be distributed unequally only when doing so would benefit all, especially those who were least advantaged. Ethical justice would be measured by the capacity of the decision to enhance cooperation among all, by its fairness. Because these theories rely on outcomes that depend on actions, but we don't know the outcomes of an action often until well after it is completed, Brady connects these approaches to *hope*.

TELEOLOGICAL ETHICAL SYSTEMS AND DIVERSITY

Utilitarianism, in its assertion that a good or ethical decision is one that produces the greatest good for the greatest number, seems on first examination to be business-friendly. As a justification for diversity, a utilitarian approach might argue that valuing differences would lead to behaviors which themselves would be likely to lead to better results for the company's stakeholders, through a diverse workforce that is, perhaps, better at decision-making, that possesses increased creativity, better knowledge of markets, and increased communication abilities. Such a work team would be likely to produce better results for a broader array of people, the various stakeholders. We would expect utilitarian approaches to the valuing of diversity in the workplace to be frequent since both the management environment and utilitarianism share a focus on results. Note, though, that for an ethical decision, results have to show greater good, not simply bottom line good.

An example of the distributive justice theory applied to diversity is found in human resource processes that rest on principles of fairness and justice: all employees regardless of level and type of contract (part time / temporary) would receive medical and other benefits, profit sharing, retirement contributions and bonuses. Selection, compensation and promotion systems might also offer examples of distributive justice in the area of diversity. The ethical rationale would be that we take this decision because it is the right thing to do in order to produce equity, not that we take this decision because it will be good for business. These are all examples of universal application.

Teleological theories in a particularist context would be theories that apply to differences among people and also consider the ends or outcomes in order to judge the ethical nature of a decision. Self-actualization might be considered to be an example here, that we have a moral duty to fully develop our skills and talents, and that organizational decisions that lead in that direction (support for education, training programs, mentoring systems) are ethical ones. This approach, on a case-by-case basis, would have powerful application to diversity, since it would support individual learning and development within the company. Note that the increased learning could be thought to lead to improved results for the company, too, and this would be a utilitarian justification. Another application of distributive justice theories in a particularist context can be found in the justification (or failure of justification) of Affirmative Action legislation. The desired outcome (an increase in social equity universally) was thought to outweigh what some understood to be unfair processes (individual, particular decisions).

CARING ETHICAL THEORIES

The final category of our ethical framework addresses caring, which is, unlike deontology and teleology, a non-rational, emotional claim. These are the theories that come, not from a reasoned sense of duty nor from desired outcomes, but, because they are psychological and emotional in nature, "from an interpersonal connectedness"—an ethic of *charity*, as Brady suggests. On the universal side of this theory, examples drawn from religious situations and philanthropy come to mind readily: belief systems that value a love for humanity, for example, and a love for individuals because they are a part of that humanity. On the particular side, someone who joins the Peace Corps to do volunteer work in a specific setting or who does community volunteer work in a specific effort might offer us examples of particularized caring ethics. The layoff situation we discussed as an example of teleological ethics (the greatest good is achieved by keeping those who have the most seniority and knowledge) may also rest on an ethics of caring (the manager keeps the people about whom he/she cares most, those with the most seniority).

CARING THEORIES AND DIVERSITY

We can find a caring ethics basis for diversity in the workplace in Pope John Paul's belief that "the evil of our times consists in the first place in a kind of degradation, indeed in a pulverization, of the fundamental uniqueness of each person." He argues that the "fundamental error of socialism is anthropological." It tries to reduce humans to something less than they are, as did the Nazis (racial makeup) and the Marxists (class status) (Brooks, 2003). Pope John Paul's argument is caring-based. David Brooks points out that when Pope John Paul told his audiences in Poland and Cuba, "You are not what they say you are," the result was a revolution. The Pope's claim is that our human diversity is good and that we are fundamentally unique in our personhoods. This uniqueness should be recognized. Such ethical arguments for diversity would be strong in the workplace because they would offer the individual liberation from the crushing anonymity of a cubicle existence, for example. The ethics of caring leads to powerful emotional connections among people. Although we may not find it often at an official, articulated level (How does a CEO convincingly claim to care about 25,000 employees personally?), it may be more common, unarticulated, yet in the minds of organization members, than we realize. The college at which I teach is infused with the ethics of caring, caring about each other and about our students. Yet, as is frequently the case with ethics of caring, we don't know how to talk about it. When students come on campus, they feel this emotional connection and are often drawn to the school for this reason.

The diversity claim offered by ethics of caring might be stated as follows: we value diversity in our organization because we value every individual and his/her dignity and right to contribute and be a part of our organization. This particularist approach in a business setting seems more likely than does its universal aspect: we value individual, diverse members of our organizational community because we have come to respect, care for and perhaps love them.

BUSINESS PRAGMATISM AND AN ETHICAL APPROACH

The economic business arguments for diversity with whose review we began our exploration are each premised on the resource-based view of the firm and are all *pragmatic* in that they are concerned with *what works best* to meet business objectives. The American William James

(1842–1910), whose work bridges psychology and philosophy, captured pragmatism's essence in slightly different words:

> Pragmatism asks its usual question. Grant an idea or belief to be true, it says, "what concrete difference will its being true make in anyone's actual life? How will the truth be realized? What experiences will be different from those which would obtain if the belief were false? What, in short, is the truth's cash-value in experiential terms?" (James, 1911)

We examine pragmatism here because it may offer us a way to better understand and pin down the ethical claims for workplace diversity. Such an approach to decision-making, including that about diversity, is the cornerstone of business practice: *if it works, do it*, or as James suggested, if it works, it is true. The question that now faces us is, how do these pragmatic approaches square with the ethical options we have just reviewed? In order to summarize this issue, we use a four-cell grid with the horizontal axis representing Ethics (highly ethical to unethical), and the vertical axis representing the level of pragmatism, (fully pragmatic to non-pragmatic). We now have a way to categorize our theoretical justifications of workplace diversity that makes sense and is useful because it considers the practical aspect, "the cash value." We will see if any of our ethical theories can offer what is good and good for business at the same time.

This matrix is a useful way to think about the possible relationships between pragmatism and ethical choices (Henderson, 1982; Lane, DiStephano, & Maznevski, 2000). Quadrant I is where most business people would like to be, pragmatic (good numbers) and ethical (good results).

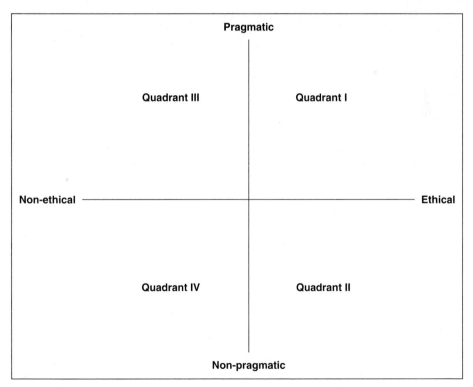

FIGURE 5-1   The Pragmatic and the Ethical with Regard to Diversity

Quadrant I is also where the teleological ethical theories we have reviewed would be, utilitarianism and distributive justice. They are judged by outcomes and the good that constitutes those outcomes. What we see by considering Quadrant I is that an argument for diversity in the workplace can be pragmatic (good for business) and also ethical. Such an argument might be, for example, that diversity is good, the right way to select personnel, because when we have a diverse team, we communicate better with diverse markets and are more innovative within the organization because we are always trying to question our unarticulated assumptions. Such an environment is good for its participants and for business results.

The argument for a diverse workplace because it is simply beneficial for business (the bottom line) is an example of a pragmatic and non-ethical argument, which is where the economic arguments for diversity that we reviewed earlier are located, Quadrant IV. Such an argument would be non-ethical often because it does not consider the treatment of humans in ethical terms; humans are inputs, parallel to semi conductors and motherboards. This brings to mind that horrible phrase, *Human Resources*.

Note that the arguments in Quadrant I (teleological) and IV (pragmatic without an ethical base) are close, and yet a world apart. The danger of the pragmatic non-ethical approach is that it might due harm to people. One can imagine a woman engineer being assigned to a project in the mainly male profession of construction engineering because the company wants to qualify to compete on projects that require a diverse workforce. In such a case, the woman engineer is there on the project for the business ends, almost as a token, but the company does nothing to support her integration into the work team. The hostile work environment that might result from the company's unconsidered approach to building a diverse workforce would be a harm.

In passing, we note that Quadrant III is where we would locate non-pragmatic, non-ethical efforts, a combination difficult about which to think. Perhaps some business decisions with regard to diversity are the result of personal prejudice or blindness that considers neither the practical aspects of the market nor the decision's ethical content. Consider a family consumer business in a geographic area that attracts many gays and a decision-maker who has unexamined homophobic values in the personnel selection process. Such an example would be non-pragmatic and non-ethical.

Quadrant II represents ethical, non-pragmatic approaches. Because for-profit business has to take care of the bottom line, has to show that outputs have added value over inputs, such approaches to ethics would be unusual, but they exist. Ben and Jerry's Ice Cream sources ingredients for their product from worker collaboratives in impoverished areas in the U.S., Africa and Latin America. This commitment to the support of businesses owned by minority groups may increase the production costs, but it appears to be a cost the consumer is willing to pay. The consumer subsidizes the ethical non-pragmatic approach Ben and Jerry's takes. One could argue that Ben and Jerry's has changed the nature of the product; it is not premium ice cream that the consumer purchases, but premium ice cream *and* a contribution to greater good in the world. In contrast to the for-profit sector, in the non-profit sector, ethical non-pragmatic approaches would be abundant. Think of the local art museum, symphony, opera and other community efforts that by their very natures are non-pragmatic.

Our analysis illustrates that Quadrant I is where most of the ethical arguments for diversity in the workplace are likely to be located. These teleological ethical arguments, because they focus on outcomes, are similar on the surface to the pragmatic economic justifications for diversity. They add an important dimension, though, an ethical consideration that is missing in the economic approach. It does seem that with some ethical analysis in the decision-making stage, business can do well and do good.

DOING WELL AND DOING GOOD

As a final step as we move towards our conclusion, we need to consider how the process of workplace decision-making about diversity might maintain a practical focus and at the same time, be encouraged to incorporate an ethical one. One key point we can draw from our earlier discussion is that if there is an ethical consideration present in a diversity-related decision, it is usually tacit, unarticulated, in the decision-maker's private thoughts. Laura Nash calls for discussion-based ethical analysis to become part of any organizational decision (Nash, 1981) and she offers a process to encourage discussion around these usually tacit elements. This review would be especially revealing of hidden assumptions in diversity-related decisions. The twelve questions to open such a discussion are:

1. *Have you defined the problem accurately?* A moral decision cannot be built on blind or convenient ignorance. Convenient ignorance is frequently a part of diversity-related issues.
2. *How would you define the problem if you were to stand on the other side of the fence?* There is a power in self-examination that may lead both to an awareness of the role of self-interest in a decision and to a tendency to dampen the expedient over the responsible action.
3. *How did this situation occur in the first place?* This course of questioning helps to distinguish the symptoms from the disease and helps to work against the tendency to ignore problems until they become crises.
4. *To whom and what do you give your loyalties as a person and as a member of the corporation?* The area of divided loyalties is a difficult one in the diversity area. The first steps to addressing such issues are to articulate them and then examine them.
   A. *What is your intention in making this decision?*
   B. *How does this intention compare with the likely results?* Intentions do matter. They can have effects on attitudes inside and outside the organization. Thus, their communication is important.
   C. *Whom could your decision or action injure?* This question helps to discover whether any resulting injury would be intentional.
   D. *Can you engage the affected parties in a discussion of the problem before you make your decision?* Participation of all or many stakeholders insures that affected parties can discuss what among the action alternatives may be in their best interests. At the same time, they learn of possible decisions that may cause them difficulties, and have the opportunity to see these issues in a larger context.
   E. *Are you confident that your position will be as valid over a long period of time as it seems now?* Articulation of values should anticipate good and bad times. A difference in time frame can make a huge impact on the problem's meaning.
   F. *Could you disclose without a qualm your decision or action to your boss, your CEO, the board of directors, your family, or society as a whole?* This test, referred to by some as the billboard test, helps to uncover conscience and loyalties.
   G. *What is the symbolic intention of your action if understood? If misunderstood?* How the symbol is perceived or misperceived is what matters. Getting intent out there early (see 5 and 6) helps to frame how the symbolic aspect of an action is understood.
   H. *Under what conditions would you allow exceptions to your stand?* It is important to discuss under what conditions the rules of the game may be changed.

Now we can begin to do the right thing as we implement diversity in the workplace, to make good and pragmatic business decisions.

DISCUSSION QUESTIONS

1. Describe an approach to a business diversity program that would be pragmatic and ethical.

2. What are some possible explanations for the hesitancy to discuss ethics in the workplace?

3. This discussion's definition of diversity rests on a valuing of differences across many groups of people. Explain why valuing (the process) is what should serve as the foundation for diversity and not the results.

4. Which of the final 12 discussion areas would be most difficult for you as a manager to discuss in the organization with your colleagues? Why?

Bibliography

Barney, J. (1991). Firm Resources and Sustained Competitive Advantage. *J. of Management* 17(1) 99–120.

Brady, F. N. (1996). Introduction: a Typology of Ethical Theories. *Ethical Universals in International Business*, p. 6. Berlin: Springer.

Brooks, D. (2003). Bigger Than Nobel. *The New York Times*, October 11. http://www.nytimes.com/2003/10/11/opinion/11BROO.html/

Fritzsche, D. & Becker, H. (1984). Linking Management Behavior to Ethical Philosophy: An Empirical Investigation. *Academy of Management Journal* 27(1) 166–176.

Goleman, D., Kaufman, P. & Rae, M. (1992). *The Creative Spirit*. New York: Dutton.

Hampden-Turner, C. & Trompenaars, F. (2000). *Building Cross-cultural Competence*. New Haven: Yale University Press.

Hartman, L. P. (2002). *Perspectives in business ethics*, 2nd ed. Burr Ridge, IL: McGraw-Hill Irwin.

Henderson, V. (1982). The Ethical Side of Enterprise. *Sloan Management Review* 23: 1982, 37–47. Henderson's matrix categorizes ethical and legal behaviors.

Hopkins, W. (1997). *Ethical Dimensions of Diversity*. Thousand Oaks CA: Sage.

James, W. (1911). The Meaning of Truth. New York:Longman Green & Co., ivx

Kant, I. (1785). *The Foundations of the Metaphysics of Morals*, section one.

Lane, H., DiStephano, J. & Maznevski, M. (2000). *International Management Behavior*, 4th edit. Malden, MA: Blackwell Publishers. This matrix is an adaptation of Henderson's.

Nash, L. (1981). Ethics without the sermon. *Harvard Business Review* 56(6) 79–90. The questions and the slight commentary are summarized from the author's more extensive and richer discussion, with applications to diversity added.

Prahalad, C. & Lieberthal, K. (1998). The End of Corporate Imperialism. *Harvard Business Review* 76(4) 68–79.

Rawls, J. (1971). A Theory of Justice. Cambridge, MA: Harvard University Press.

Rosener, J. (1995). *America's Competitive Secret: Utilizing Women as a Management Strategy*. New York, NY: Oxford University Press. Quoted in Schraeder (1997).

Schraeder, C., Blackburn, V. & Iles, P. (1997). Women in management and firm financial performance: An exploratory study. *Journal of Management Issues*, 9(3), 355–372.

Diversity on the Web

1. Investigate the inclusion (or lack of inclusion) of diversity/discrimination in the ethical codes of businesses. You can begin by searching for the words "diversity" or "discrimination" in the codes, but note that diversity concerns may be covered by words other than these, for example, "respecting the rights and privileges of all workers regardless of race, gender . . ."

2. Compare the codes of ethics for businesses with those of another type of organization such as a non-profit or a government agency in terms of inclusion of diversity or non-discrimination policies.

3. Compare and contrast the codes of two competing companies within the same industry, e.g., the Marriott and the Hilton hotels in the hospitality industry.

Sample Codes of Business Ethics

The site below, compiled by The Center for the Study of Ethics in the Professions at the Illinois Institute of Technology, contains hundreds of codes of ethics from corporations, professional societies, academic institutions, and government. The codes are organized into 25 professional categories such as arts, business, communications, etc. The codes can be searched for key words.

http://ethics.iit.edu/codes/coe.html

The Your Code of Ethics site, created by Irwin Berent, is a clearinghouse for "codes of ethics, oaths, pledges and other forms of verbal commitment, statements of purpose, or declared standards of conduct." This site is organized into categories including three categories of business association codes: General, Management and Sales or Selling as well as "Companies' (US) codes."

http://www.yourcodeofethics.com

The Business Ethics site by Sharon Stoerger lists business codes of ethics alphabetically by company name.

http://www.web-miner.com/busethics.htm

ETHICS AND DIVERSITY:
LEGAL APPLICATIONS IN THE WORKPLACE

M. June Allard
Assumption College
Worcester State University, Professor Emerita

GOALS

- To examine actual cases and situations in terms of how they may be judged ethically as well as legally
- To examine the ethical implications of actions that may be viewed as beneficial from one perspective but not from another
- To examine backlash and reverse discrimination

The managers of today have gone far beyond consideration of workers in terms of single diversity dimensions. Managers deal daily with multiple social identities: a worker who is not just old, but who is old and female and black or a male who is Latino with a visual disability. The judicial system however, still deals in single dimensions. Discrimination charges and lawsuits are not filed in terms of composites; they are filed in terms of age or gender or race or religion or disability or any other **single** dimension of diversity.

CASES AND SITUATIONS

1. For each case or situation, consider the ethical implications from your perspective. What do you personally think should be the outcome or resolution?
2. How would McNett characterize each situation in terms of the ethics involved? (Use the three categories of ethical theories found in Exhibit 1 of "The Ethics of Workplace Diversity" article in this text).
3. Investigate the resolution or current status of each case or situation. What was the rationale; why was this outcome reached?

Legal Commentary

A key to the analysis of almost any discrimination case is whether an employer's given reason for taking action against an employee is the real reason, or a lie that covers up intentional discrimination in the decision. This is known as a pretext analysis. . . .

Michels, L. (2006, July 6). The truth and nothing but. *Suits in the Workplace.*
http://suitsintheworkplace.com/blogs

CASES AND SITUATIONS

1. Mammone *v* President & Fellows of Harvard College

Diversity Issue: Mental Illness

Michael Mammone was a museum receptionist at Harvard with bi-polar disorder. He worked for seven years with no problem, but then his behavior changed in August of 2002. He began singing and dancing in the reception area, had loud conversations and phone calls and established a website denouncing the low pay at Harvard. Later he began wearing East Indian dress with necklaces, rings and bracelets and refused to stop using his personal laptop. He refused to meet with his supervisor to whom he used "abusive, threatening and sexually derogatory language" and refused police instructions to leave the premises. After receiving disability benefits from Harvard for six months, he was terminated. Mammone charged Harvard with disability discrimination.

> Weintraub, B. (2006, May 15). University Wins Anti-Discrimination Suit. *The Harvard Crimson.* http://www.thecrimson.com/article.aspx?ref=513483

Legal Commentary

Employers should be especially vigilant in defining and articulating essential job functions, and documenting the risks associated with an employee's failure to perform such functions.

> Satterwhite, R. (2007, March 9). Thin Line Between Misconduct and Disability. *Suits in the Workplace.* http://suitsintheworkplace.com/blogs/

2. Minnesota & Muslim Cabbies

Diversity Issue: Religion

In 2000, over 600 Minneapolis-St. Paul Airport Somali Muslim cabbies (approximately ¾ of the fleet) began refusing to pick up passengers carrying duty-free liquor stating that Islamic law forbids them from doing so. By 2007, over 5,000 passengers had been refused. The Muslim American Society tried using a different top light on cabs refusing to transport liquor but public reaction was overwhelmingly negative.

> Van Biema, D. (2007, January 19). Minnesota's Teetotal Taxis. *Time.* http://www.time.com/time/printout/0,8816,1580390,00.html

3. Brown *v* City of Salem

Diversity Issue: Sleep Apnea Disability

Brown, a 911 emergency dispatcher for almost 25 years, was diagnosed with sleep apnea (involuntary short sleeps) 10 years ago. The city excused him from night duty and gave him a fan in accordance with his doctor's recommendation. In 2003 he was terminated at least in part because he still fell asleep while on duty. Brown sued.

> Satterwhite, R. (2007, March 9). Thin Line Between Misconduct and Disability. *Suits in the Workplace.* http://suitsintheworkplace.com/blogs/

4. Walgreens Drug Stores *v* State of Illinois

Diversity Issue: Religion

Walgreens policy allowed pharmacists to decline to dispense birth control prescriptions as long as there was another pharmacist in the store or nearby to do so. In April 2005, Illinois passed a law requiring all pharmacists to fill all prescriptions. A follow-up letter from the governor indicated that pharmacists refusing to comply would subject their employers to heavy penalties. In September 2005, disciplinary actions against the pharmacies, including Walgreens, began. Walgreens suspended non-complying pharmacists, offering to help those in southern Illinois to get licensed in Missouri. The pharmacists declined to relocate to Missouri. Suspended Illinois pharmacists and Walgreens both sued the state.

> Michels, L. (2006, Sept. 25). Conflict Over Contraception. *Suits in the Workplace.* http://suitsintheworkplace.com/blogs/archive/2006/09.aspx

5. Football Referee

Diversity Issue: Visual Disability

When a Big Ten football official lost an eye, he informed the head of the Big Ten officiating and was told to continue working. He officiated games for six years including two Orange Bowl games until the Commissioner of the Big Ten learned about his vision. He was then terminated. He sued for violation of the Americans with Disabilities Act.

> Michels, L. (2006, July 20). Let's Hope the Judge Isn't a Michigan Fan. *Suits in the Workplace.* http://suitsintheworkplace.com/blogs/archive/2006/09.aspx

---

Removing Expensive Labor: Forced Retirement and Outsourcing

Case 6 examines the practice of removing expensive labor costs from the payroll by forced retirement. **Case 7** examines a different practice intended to accomplish the same end—forcing payroll labor into contract labor. There are both positive and negative effects of these practices.

"Full time jobs become contract work without benefits, and then vanish overseas."

> Reingold, J. (2004, April). Into Thin Air. *Fast Company.* http://www.fastcompany.com/magazine/81/offshore.html

"In the absence of a public policy that tells me what to do . . . I have no choice as corporate manager, nor do my colleagues . . . [but to make decisions] that very often involve moves of jobs into other countries."

> Andrew Grove (former Intel CEO) quoted in Reingold, J. (2004, April) Into Thin Air. *Fast Company.* http://www.fastcompany.com/magazine/81/offshore.html

---

6. Sidley Austin Brown & Wood *v* EEOC

Diversity Issue: Age—Forced Retirement

Sidley, a giant Chicago-based international law firm with 1500 lawyers practicing on three continents, has used a mandatory retirement policy to involuntarily retire partners since 1978. Further, in 1999, it demoted 31 partners thereby also forcing them out of the firm. The EEOC filed a class action suit charging that Sidley selected partners for expulsion from the firm on the basis of their age. "The New York Bar Association recently criticized mandatory retirement programs for older attorneys saying that the requirements effectively cheat the public out of competent counselors with a wide body of experience."

Michels, L. (2007, January 27). Sidley Update. *Suits in the Workplace.* http://suitsintheworkplace.com/blog

7. Allstate Insurance

Diversity Issue: Age—Demotion to Contract Work

In 1999 Allstate fired 6,400 home and auto insurance agents of which 90% were over age 40. Allstate offered to rehire them as independent contractors with slightly higher pay but without their expensive health and pension benefits—providing they waived their rights to sue Allstate for age or any other discrimination. Allstate also imposed a one-year freeze on rehiring former sales agents in other positions. This situation has now been repeated with 650 life insurance agents, 80% of whom are over 40. A class-action suit was filed by employees who were joined by EEOC. Allstate counter sued for fraud.

Sachs, S. (2002, May 22). Not in Good Hands. *The Harvard Crimson.* http://www.thecrimson.com/article.aspx?ref=214776.

Appelson, G. (2007, May 14). Baby Boomers Battle Bias. *Houston Chronicle.* http://www.chron.com/disp/story.mpl/business/4798277.html

LEGAL BACKLASH

Academia and Reverse Discrimination

The changing landscape of state laws first required colleges to increase diversity among students and staff but now requires them to undo the very procedures they put in place to comply with the original diversity mandate. Cases 8 and 9 exemplify the legal backlash that resulted.

---

8. Admissions Policies

Diversity Issue: Race

University admissions policies *favoring* minorities are increasingly under attack. Attempting to provide greater minority access to primarily white campuses, universities employed practices such as the awarding of extra points for minority status and separate applicant pools with separate standards for whites and minorities. Legal challenges to policies such as these have been mounted at major institutions including the universities of Michigan, Texas, Washington, Georgia, California, Maryland, Oklahoma State Regents (University of Tulsa) and the Commonwealth of Virginia Universities.

Reverse discrimination lawsuits have also been filed by white students denied access to federally-funded academic programs such as the National Science Foundation Minority Graduate Research Fellowships and summer science programs conducted on university campuses.

9. Faculty Hiring

Diversity Issue: Race

An example of reverse discrimination is that of the white female applicant who was a finalist for a position in the sociology department at the University of Nevada at Reno. The university hired an African-American male instead, paying him more than the posted salary range. One year later, the white female applicant was offered a position at $7,000 less than the black male at his hiring the year before. The female sued, arguing violations of the Equal Pay Act and the Civil Rights Act. The university argued that since only one (1) per cent of its faculty members were black, it followed a "minority bonus program" whereby a department could hire an additional faculty member if it first hired a minority faculty member.

> AAUP. (2005). University and Affirmative Action Update. *AAUP.*
> http://www.aaup.org/AAUP/protectrights/legal/topics/aff-
> ac-update.htm

Many of the following cases and charges have just begun litigation or have reached settlements outside of court.
Consider each of the cases and situations, in terms of Michael's legal commentary on pretext analysis and indicate if you think "the employer's given reason for taking action against an employee is the real reason or a lie that covers up intentional discrimination."

10. New York and New Jersey *v* Arbitron

Diversity Issue: Portable People Meters Diversity

New York and New Jersey sued Arbitron for civil rights violations with its new Portable People Meters (PPMs). PPMs measure radio station program ratings. The states filed the lawsuits because they believed the PPMs were not being distributed to people from traditionally underrepresented groups who heavily populate these areas.

11. National Federation of the Blind *v* Penn State University

Diversity Issue: Visual Disability

The complaint charges that Penn's technology such as course management software, library catalog, website for its Office for Disability Services, etc. are not usable to those who are blind and further that technology allowing professors to connect their laptops to a podium and display content on a screen cannot be operated by blind faculty without assistance from a sighted person, etc.

12. Creed *v* Family Express

Diversity Issue: Transgender

Christopher applied for a job as a male presenting a masculine appearance, although he had already begun a gender change transition. After employment he continued with the transition, changing to feminine attire including nail polish, mascara, eyebrow trimming, longer hair and finally using the name Amber, but continuing to wear the company mandated unisex uniform of polo shirt and slacks. After more than 50 customer complaints, the employer demanded that Amber come to work dressed as a man and finally fired her. She alleged gender discrimination.

13. EOC *v* Sears Roebuck

Diversity Issue: Disability Accommodation

A former Sears service technician was injured on the job resulting in a permanent disability. Sears did not provide him with an accommodation so he could return to work although he asked many times to return. Sears fired him when his disability leave expired. EEOC discovered that Sears had failed to provide accommodations for hundreds of employees when their compensation leave expired.

14. Bhatt *v* The University of Vermont

Diversity Issue: Mental Disability

Rajan Bhatt falsified an evaluation for a surgery rotation and at the hearing, claimed it was an isolated incident. It was learned that he falsified other evaluations as well as falsifying a diploma. At the next hearing dealing with these other forgeries, he claimed they were due to Tourette's syndrome and a related obsessive-behavior disorder.

The university dismissed him. He sought treatment and later requested that his medical condition be re-evaluated by the university. His application was denied and he sued the university under the ADA charging the university had not accommodated his disability.

15. Pickler and Ford Dealership

Diversity Issue: Pregnancy

Marilyn Pickler was working for auto dealership Berge Ford. A week after she told a manager that she was pregnant, she was fired because "it would not be safe for her to drive" (a part of her job).

16. The Diabetic Employee and the City of Bethlehem

Diversity Issues: Gender and Disability

A diabetic employee from the City of Bethlehem called in sick for two days when she was actually in Las Vegas having her lips and eyebrows permanently tattooed. She was reported and when questioned, she lied, saying that she wasn't in Las Vegas, but had been in her sick bed at her boyfriend's home. She was terminated for dishonesty and an investigation proved she had lied.

She sued stating she was terminated because of her gender and diabetes and that she was retaliated against for seeking an accommodation under ADA.

17. Schroer and the Library of Congress

Diversity Issue: Transgender

Diane Schroer applied for and was offered a job at the Library of Congress as David Schroer. At his first meeting with his soon-to-be boss, Schroer told her he was transgendering to become a female before starting the job. The job offer was rescinded the next day.

The legal question: Do the federal statutes against sex discrimination apply to transgendered people or only to males and females?

18. Lawless *v* L.P.G.A. and Two Sponsors

Diversity Issue: Transgender

Lana Lawless was a 52 year old retired male police officer who had gender reassignment surgery in 2005 and won the Long Drivers of America (golf) championship in 2008. She was ruled ineligible to compete in 2010, however, when the Long Drivers of America changed its rules to match those of the LPGA that requires competitors to be born as females.

She reported that the reassignment surgery resulted in hormones and muscle strength in line with someone who is genetically female. Losing the opportunity to compete resulted in losing the sponsorship from Bang Golf which sells golf drivers.

19. TV Networks and Talent Agencies *v* TV Writers

Diversity Issue: Age Discrimination

Seventeen television networks and seven talent agencies were sued by 165 television writers in the California Superior Court in Los Angeles in a case lasting 10 years. The writers, who are 50 years and older, claimed conspiracy to shut out older writers, via a "gray-list."

The studios' position: "they don't know how to write for younger people." (This was said to one former Emmy winner.) The writers' position: "Shakespeare wasn't 15 when he wrote Romeo and Juliet. Writers get better with age."

20. Texas Job Applicant and the Texas Alcohol and Beverage Commission

Diversity Issue: Gender Discrimination Backlash

A Midland Texas white man filed a lawsuit against the Texas Alcohol and Beverage Commission claiming he was unfairly passed over for employment because of his race. He claimed that the Commission used "a rigid and discriminatory system of 'workforce diversity points'" that awards white males the minimum allowable diversity points. Points are awarded for being black, Hispanic and being a woman. The Texas man claimed that he scored "better than most" in every other aspect of the Commission's pre-employment testing process.

Some 10 percent of a job applicant's employment eligibility grade depends on workforce diversity points. The lawsuit claims that the Commission's tables clearly show that the man would have made the hiring cut-off if the workforce diversity criteria had not been used.

Writing Assignment

Two landmark cases severely erode the rights of workers to sue employers who engage in gender discrimination (Lilly Ledbetter) and age discrimination (Jack Gross).

Ledbetter *v* Goodyear Tire and Rubber

Lilly Ledbetter was the only woman among the sixteen supervisors at the same management level. She worked at Goodyear over nineteen years and learned late in her tenure there that all the males made more than she did, even those with less seniority and that her salary was as much as 40% lower than the salaries of the male supervisors.

Gross *v* FBL Financial Services

In June 2003, Farm Bureau Financial Group merged with Kansas Farm Bureau and offered all employees who were over age 50 and had a certain number of years of employment a buyout. In Iowa, virtually every claims supervisor over 50 was demoted.

Jack Gross, aged 54 with thirteen consecutive years of top performance reviews was demoted. The company claimed it was a "reorganization," not a demotion.

Research these cases. Write a paper that explains:

1. The court rulings in each case,
2. Any subsequent legal actions, and
3. Implications for workers.

HOW CANADA PROMOTES WORKPLACE DIVERSITY

Marc S. Mentzer

University of Saskatchewan

GOALS

- To examine the differences between U.S. and Canadian employment laws
- To introduce the policies toward workplace diversity in Canada, a nation similar to the United States and yet having a very distinct history and a different approach to workplace diversity
- To present the concept of employment equity and employer policies leading to attainment of employment equity

It is easy to fall into the trap of treating Canada as merely a colder version of the United States. Although outwardly similar to the United States, Canada has its own unique history and traditions. The differences between Canada and the United States are deep, yet not immediately visible to the visitor.

To appreciate the differences between the two countries, one must go back to the time of the American Revolution. The American revolutionaries expected that present-day Canada would join them in the fight against the English king, but the area that makes up present-day Canada stayed loyal to the king and continued under British rule until Canada became independent in 1867. As a result, Canadians have a faith in government that is very different than the usual skepticism and suspicion toward government that one sees in the United States.

Another key difference is that the Canadian federal government has less power than the U.S. government, especially where employment regulation is concerned. On employment issues, laws of the Canadian federal government affect only those industries that are federally regulated according to the Canadian constitution: broadcasting, telecommunications, banking, railroads, airlines, shipping, other transport across provincial boundaries, uranium mining, and crown corporations. (A crown corporation is a company in which the government owns all the stock, such as the Canadian Broadcasting Corporation.)

All other businesses are beyond the jurisdiction of the Canadian government, and are affected only by the laws of the province in which they operate. As an example, consider Sears, the department store chain. In the United States, Sears must obey U.S. federal law regarding nondiscrimination, minimum wage, and so on. Each state has its own laws, but with some exceptions, a company like Sears can ignore the state laws because state laws are overridden by U.S. federal law.

In Canada, Sears also has stores throughout the country, but retailing is not federally regulated under the Canadian constitution. Therefore, Sears in Canada must obey the laws of each

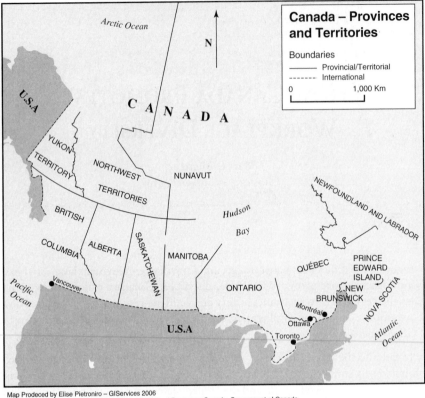

Map Prodeced by Elise Pietroniro – GIServices 2006
Base map data source: National Atlas of Canada, Natural Resources Canada, Government of Canada
Map projection: Lambert Conformal Conic – Cenrtral Meridian: 96˚ W; Standard Parallel 1:50˚ N; Standard Parallel 2:70˚ N;
Latitude of Origin; 40˚ N; Datum NAD 1983

FIGURE 5-2   Map of Canada

province in which it operates. A Sears store in Ontario must obey Ontario laws; a store in Quebec must obey Quebec laws, and so on, which complicates the work of Sears executives in Canada.

THE CANADIAN HUMAN RIGHTS ACT

In 1977, Parliament passed the Canadian Human Rights Act, which forbids discrimination by federally regulated employers on the basis of race, gender, and certain other grounds. This act prohibits systemic (indirect) discrimination, such as when an employer asks an applicant about her childbearing plans or engages in sexual harassment, as well as direct discrimination, such as when an employer says women applicants will not be considered. Instead of complaints being heard in court, as in the United States, discrimination complaints are typically made to the Canadian Human Rights Commission if the employer is federally regulated, or to its provincial counterpart if it is provincially regulated. By relying on commissions and tribunals to hear cases instead of courts, the Canadian approach allows victims to have a hearing without having to hire a lawyer, although monetary damages tend to be much lower than they would be in a U.S. court.

Another feature of the Canadian Human Rights Act is that it requires comparable worth in compensation, which in Canada is known as pay equity. Every covered employer must ensure that predominantly female occupations are paid the same as predominantly male occupations of equal importance or difficulty in the same organization. For example, secretaries working for a railroad might claim that their job is of equal importance or difficulty as that of a track maintenance worker, and thus could demand that their pay be the same. Pay equity or comparable worth is a type of law that does not exist in the United States at the federal level, because it is seen as interfering with market forces, but it is a fact of life for organizations under the jurisdiction of the Canadian federal government. At the provincial level, Ontario and Quebec also have pay equity laws that cover both public- and private-sector employers. Some other provinces have pay equity laws limited to public-sector organizations, such as universities and hospitals. A few provinces have no pay equity legislation at all, although pay *equality* legislation exists in every jurisdiction of Canada, meaning men and women doing the same job must be paid equally.

EMPLOYMENT EQUITY LEGISLATION

Initially it was hoped that the Canadian Human Rights Act would be sufficient to break down the barriers that prevent the economic progress of women and minorities. However, it became apparent that simply forbidding discrimination was not enough. In 1984 a parliamentary commission recommended legislation that would push employers to take proactive or aggressive measures to increase the numbers of women and minority employees (Canada, 1984). This commission noted that in the United States, affirmative action has been divisive because it pits men against women and whites against minorities. Thus, to avoid the ill will surrounding the term affirmative action, a new term, employment equity, was created to cover such proactive measures as targeted recruiting, providing child care facilities, accommodating the needs of people with disabilities, and so on.

The resulting legislation, the Canadian Employment Equity Act of 1986, was mainly symbolic, relying on persuasion and embarrassment so that employers would be more serious about creating workplaces that value diversity. Covered employers submit their data to the federal government, which then assigns grades (A, B, etc.) to each employer, which are made public. A later version of the law, the Canadian Employment Equity Act of 1995, put in place modest fines up to $50,000 for not meeting their targets. In practice, these fines are rarely imposed (Agocs, 2002). Some criticize these provisions for being too weak (Lum, 2008), but on the other hand, there was an underlying intent to rely on gentle persuasion on employers to maintain a constructive atmosphere and avoid ill will.

THE FOUR PROTECTED GROUPS

In the United States, the main thrust of civil rights legislation was initially to end discrimination against Blacks. However, in Canada, Blacks comprise only 3 percent of the population versus 13 percent in the United States. Although Black Canadians have been victims of racism, the difference in numbers means that discrimination against Black Canadians has never been the predominant issue that it has been in the United States. Similarly, Hispanics constitute only 1 percent of the Canadian population, compared with 15 percent in the United States. On the other hand, Canadians of Asian ancestry form a large portion of the Canadian population.

Therefore, when Canada introduced employment equity legislation, questions arose about which groups should be chosen for special protection. In the end, the government designated four groups to be the target of proactive measures in the spirit of affirmative action:

Points of Law

1. **Women**   As in the United States, Canadian women lag behind men in income and representation in high-paying jobs.

2. **Aboriginal Peoples**   This group includes Indians, Inuit (the Aboriginal people of the Arctic regions), and Métis (pronounced *may-TEE*), who are those of mixed French-Indian ancestry in western Canada. Aboriginal people constitute 4% of the Canadian population, compared with 1% in the United States. The low Canadian percentage is deceptive, because there are large regions of Canada where Aboriginal people are the majority.

3. **People with Disabilities**   Both Canada and the United States define disabilities to include psychological conditions as well as physical conditions.

4. **Visible Minorities**   This is the most interesting and most controversial protected group under Canadian law and it has no exact equivalent in U.S. law. "Visible minorities" refers to those of Black, Asian, Arab, Pacific Islander, or Latin American ancestry. The visible minority category includes some groups, such as Japanese Canadians, who have very high income levels today, but had historically been targets of discrimination. "Visible minorities" includes other groups, such as Pacific Islander Canadians or Southeast Asian Canadians, who are relatively recent arrivals in Canada and have on average high unemployment rates and very low incomes. The category of visible minorities, comprising 16 percent of the Canadian population, is an assortment of ethnic groups that have little in common with one another (Hum & Simpson, 2000).

Other minorities sought to be included under the Employment Equity Act, but were excluded, although it is still illegal to discriminate against them because of the Canadian Human Rights Act and similar legislation in the provinces. For example, note that lesbians and gays are not a protected group nor are French-speaking people in predominantly English-speaking areas. One fourth of the Canadian population speaks French as their first language, and in some areas they feel they are at a disadvantage in an English-language-dominated society. Because the Canadian Human Rights Act (and its provincial counterparts) cover these minority groups, it is still illegal to discriminate against people on the basis of their sexual orientation or whether they learned French before English. However, employers are not required to engage in proactive or aggressive actions to increase their representation in the workforce.

There have been some glitches in the implementation of employment equity (Mentzer, 2002). An employee cannot be counted as a member of a minority group unless he or she identifies as such on a questionnaire administered by the employer. If some minority employees don't complete the questionnaire due to a desire to blend in and not draw attention, then the employer cannot count them in employment equity statistics (Lum, 2008). Another dilemma is that people of Arab or West Asian (for example, Turkish or Iranian) descent often don't realize that the

---

🏛 **Points of Law**

Summary of key diversity legislation in the federal jurisdiction

Charter of Rights and Freedoms: This is part of the Canadian constitution and is roughly analogous to the U.S. Bill of Rights.

Canadian Human Rights Act: This forbids direct or indirect discrimination on the basis of race, gender, sexual orientation, and certain other grounds.

Canadian Employment Equity Act: This requires employers to engage in proactive measures to increase the representation of four specific groups: women, Aboriginal people, people with disabilities, and members of visible minorities.

---

government defines them as being in the visible minority category, so the resulting statistics are likely to undercount visible minority employees.

In the United States, some white individuals have won lawsuits claiming reverse discrimination, causing the unraveling of some of the U.S. affirmative action initiatives. A claim of reverse discrimination cannot be made in the Canadian legal system. Section 15 of the Charter of Rights and Freedoms, which is part of the Canadian constitution, states that discrimination is illegal. It then goes on to state that policies that improve the situation of disadvantaged groups are an allowable exception to the antidiscrimination clause. This key difference between the U.S. and Canadian constitutions has far-ranging implications for affirmative action and employment equity policies.

EMPLOYMENT EQUITY IN ACTION

Employment equity, when properly implemented, should go beyond increasing the number of women and minority employees, although this is important. The focus of employment equity should be to encourage flexibility and create a workplace in which people of all backgrounds feel comfortable and included.

For example, WestJet, a Canadian airline, has contracted with a nationwide chain of day care centers so that WestJet employees will receive reduced rates and their children will get priority instead of being put on a waiting list. In this way, WestJet is making its workplace more family-friendly for those balancing work with child care. Also, it has focused recruiting efforts on recent immigrants and people with disabilities, especially for cleaning crews where it is possible to be flexible in hiring criteria (WestJet, 2007). Because the majority of immigrants are from ethnic groups designated as visible minorities, any program that attracts immigrant applicants will strengthen the company's employment equity record.

Another success story is Telus, a telephone company based in Vancouver on Canada's west coast. Among its employment equity initiatives, Telus has created a program to encourage telecommuting in as many jobs as possible, if it is desired by the employee (Telus, 2009). Not only does this have environmental benefits, but the option of telecommuting helps employees to balance family and work responsibilities.

Employers often look for creative ways to increase the number of applicants from the four protected groups. For example, recruitment ads can be run in publications directed toward visible minority groups, such as Chinese Canadian newspapers. Job fairs can be conducted in predominantly Aboriginal communities. One creative example of recruiting is by Pelmorex, a company which operates The Weather Network on Canadian TV systems. Pelmorex identifies jobs that can be done by people who are blind, and works with the Canadian National Institute of the Blind to increase the number of employees with vision-related disabilities (Pelmorex, 2009).

Notice that all of these examples are industries that are federally regulated in Canada—airlines, telecommunications, broadcasting, and so on—because only federally-regulated industries are covered by the Employment Equity Act. These examples show how Canadian employers creatively reach out to those in the four protected groups. When properly implemented, employment equity changes an organization's internal culture to one that welcomes diversity in all its forms, and where all employees can reach their full potential.

CANADA'S PROVINCES AND TERRITORIES

Canada is divided into ten provinces and three territories, which, generally speaking, have more power than U.S. state governments. Each of the ten provinces and three territories has its own human rights laws forbidding discrimination. While every province and territory forbids discrimination, none of them, generally speaking, have laws requiring proactive measures in the spirit of employment equity or affirmative action.

The result is that only those employers in federally regulated industries are required by legislation to have employment equity programs. Such household names as Wal-Mart, McDonald's, or General Motors are not in federally regulated industries, and therefore are not covered by the Canadian Employment Equity Act, although they may create *voluntary* employment equity plans if they wish. However, such companies must obey the antidiscrimination laws of the provinces and territories in which they operate.

Lastly, provincially regulated companies that sell goods or services to the federal government are required to have employment equity programs or else risk losing their federal contracts.

Executives of companies operating in both the United States and Canada face a special challenge, because they must be knowledgeable about the laws of two countries, and in many instances the laws of Canada's ten provinces and three territories as well. Frequently, a human resource policy that is legal in the United States will be illegal in Canada, or vice versa, and such companies have to obey the laws of the jurisdiction in which they operate. Two countries, similar in so many ways, have entirely different legal structures to address the issue of increasing diversity in the workplace.

DISCUSSION QUESTIONS

1. How does the power of the Canadian federal government in relation to the provinces, differ from the power of the United States federal government in relation to the states?

2. If a U.S.-based retail chain has stores throughout Canada, which laws apply—those of the United States, those of the Canadian federal government, or those of each province?

3. What is the difference between employment equity and pay equity?

4. How does the Canadian constitution affect affirmative action-type programs?

5. a. Make an argument that it is easier for employers to comply with diversity legislation in Canada than it is in the United States.
   b. Make an argument that it is *not* easier for employers to comply with diversity legislation in Canada than in the United States.

Writing Assignment

Challenges Facing Canada's Aboriginal People

Among the Web sites listed at the end of the article, three relate to the three Aboriginal groups: Assembly of First Nations, Métis National Council, and Inuit Tapiriit Kanatami. Using the material on these Web sites, compare and contrast two of these three groups. For the two groups you chose, what challenges and needs are similar? What challenges and needs are different?

British Columbia	http://www.bchrt.bc.ca
Newfoundand and Labrador	http://www.justice.gov.nl.ca/hrc
Ontario	http://www.ohrc.on.ca
Quebec (clickable link converts Web page into English)	http://www.cdpdj.qc.ca
Saskatchewan	http://www.shrc.gov.sk.ca
Yukon	http://www.yhrc.yk.ca

Bibliography

Agocs, C. (2002). Canada's employment equity legislation and policy, 1987–2000. *International Journal of Manpower, 23*, 256–276.

Canada. Minister of Supply and Services (1984). *Report of the Commission on Equality in Employment.* Judge Rosalie Silberman Abella, Commissioner. Ottawa, Canada.

Hum, D., & Simpson, W. (2000). Not all visible minorities face labour market discrimination. *Policy Options/Options Politiques, 21*(10), 45–48.

Lum, J. M. (2008). The federal Employment Equity Act: Goals vs. implementation. *Canadian Public Administration/Administration Publique du Canada, 38*(1), 45–76.

Mentzer, M. S. (2002) The Canadian experience with employment equity legislation.

International Journal of Value-Based Management, 15, 35–50.

Pelmorex (2009). The Weather Network: Careers: Diversity. Retrieved August 2009 from http://www.theweathernetwork.com/careers/our_diversity

Telus Communications Company (2009). Work Styles. Retrieved August 2009 from http://csr.telus.com/csr_report/discussion_and_analysis/team_members/work_styles/

WestJet Airlines Ltd. (2007). 2007 Employment Equity Narrative Report, Human Resources and Skill Development Canada (HRSDC). Retrieved August 2009 from http://www.hrsdc.gc.ca/eng/lp/lo/lswe/we/ee_tools/software/employer_data/index-we.shtml

Note

U.S. statistics are from the 2005–2007 American community survey 3-year estimates, as reported by the U.S. census bureau. Retrieved august 2009 from http://factfinder.census.gov and the

Canadian statistics are from the 2006 census, as reported by Statistics Canada. Retrieved August 2009 from http://www.statcan.ca

---

Diversity on the Web

1. Choose a Canadian bank, and look at its Web site for information regarding employment equity or diversity. Next, choose a U.S. bank and look at what its Web site says regarding diversity. To what extent do differences between the two Web sites relate to differences between Canada and the United States? Note that in some cases, it will be necessary to do a Web search within the bank's Web site for the keywords "diversity" or "employment equity."
   Starting Web sites for Canadian banks:

   http://rbc.com   http://td.com
   http://cibc.com   http://nbc.ca
   http://scotiabank.com   http://bmo.com

2. Choose one province or territory, look up the Web site of its human rights commission or tribunal, and discuss what sort of cases or complaints dominate the work of that organization. (In some instances, there will be a section of the Web site labeled "Decisions.") Are the issues addressed by your chosen organization different than one would expect from a similar enforcement agency in the U.S recommended Web sites:

British Columbia	http://www.bchrt.bc.ca
Newfoundand and Labrador	http://www.justice.gov.nl.ca/hrc
Ontario	http://www.ohrc.on.ca
Quebec (clickable link converts Web page into English)	http://www.cdpdj.qc.ca
Saskatchewan	http://www.shrc.gov.sk.ca
Yukon	http://www.yhrc.yk.ca

Marc S. Mentzer, PhD is an associate professor of Industrial Relations and Organizational Behavior at the University of Saskatchewan. His research has appeared in Canadian Journal of Administrative Sciences, Canadian Review of Sociology & Anthropology, Organization Studies, and Ethnic Groups.

MEDIA MESSAGES: THE SHAPING OF CULTURE

M. June Allard
Assumption College
Worcester State University, Professor Emerita

GOALS

- To examine how media both foster and reflect cultural stereotypes and values
- To examine discrimination patterns in the media

Sowell states ". . . cultures have enriched each other in all the great civilizations of the world . . . No culture has grown great in isolation" (1991 p.43). He makes a compelling case for the importance of contact among cultures and one that modern cultures have been quick to appreciate. The last decade bought exponential expansion of communication with modern technological and electronic advances that transcend geographic barriers to provide limitless opportunities for cultural interaction and advancement.

Thus today, cultures enrich each other through expanded communication—communication through print and electronic media as well as through the traditional avenues of travel, trade and migration. The present article examines transmission occurring through media.

How do newspapers, magazines, books, TV, radio, Internet, e-mail, text messaging, etc. function to influence and enrich cultures? The answer is complex for the media serve multiple functions. As agents of transmission and cultural maintenance, media passes culture down to new generations and conveys it to newcomers. Media become shapers of a culture by informing and incorporating ideas and practices from other cultures. Finally, media serves to separate cultural groups from each other and from the mainstream.

The complexity of its roles can be seen in the case of immigrants in the U.S. where mainstream media (newspapers, radio and television) teach immigrants about the larger U.S. culture at the same time teaching the larger culture about them. While the larger culture dominates mainstream media, local ethnic, cultural and religious news and events appear as special features.

At the same time however, e-mail, telephone and electronic communication allow newcomers to maintain their ethnic and social class identities by providing easy contact with their home cultures and with fellow immigrants in the U.S. In recent years language programs on radio, television and the Internet as well as newspapers and magazines targeted to specific cultural groups further serve to maintain cultures of origin at the same time infusing into them elements of the larger culture.

THE MEDIA

Electronic Media

In developed countries, TV, like radio, is universal. By 2010, more than half (55%) of all U.S. households owned three or more television sets (Nielsen Wire, 2010).

The advent of Internet, e-mail, cell phones and text messaging provide additional means of cultural contact. Although these electronic advances are widespread in developed countries, they are the media of the more privileged in many countries and even within the U.S., the "digital divide" can still deny the less affluent these avenues of cultural exchange.

The rise of video-conferencing is especially important for business communication; e-mail and online chatting are important to social and business interchanges. Social media are multiplying—Twitter, Facebook, Foursquare, RSS, YouTube, Myspace, to name a few. "The popularity of these communication channels however, impacts the role of traditional media channels:

The meteoric rise of social media and the growing consumer power associated with it have been compounded by the proliferation of niche media channels and the diminishing impact of traditional broadcast and general interest media (Schakenbach, 2010).

Print and Entertainment Media

Print media play an especially important role in transmitting culture in low context cultures such as the U.S. where meaning and messages are derived mostly from the words themselves and much less from the situation in which they occur.

Newspapers and magazines, although not as widely read as before the advent of television and electronic media, are still very influential. Millions of U.S. adults read national circulation newspapers with substantial percentages of all cultural groups reading magazines. Even the entertainment media, most particularly films and videos, are far-reaching conveyers of culture as are other cultural products such as art, music, books, video games, toys and the knowledge and products of science and technology.

THE MEDIA AND WHO IT REACHES

The interaction of the media with various segments of society is not uniform. Just as international travel and electronic media are readily accessible to only part of society, other media forms are accessed in differing degrees by different segments of society. All groups do not "tune in" to TV to the same extent nor do they all read newspapers and magazines to the same extent, much less the same papers and magazines.

T.V. and Radio

In 2009–2010, some 114 million U.S. households owned televisions with Americans averaging more than 151 hours per month viewing time (Gardossy, 2009; Nielsen, 2009). In 2010, children between the ages of 2 and 5, spent almost 33 hours a week on screen (television, videos, video games) each week (World Ark, 2010).

The TV digital divide is disappearing, especially among the younger generation. Cable access is similar across the three major ethnic/racial groups with (83 percent to 87 percent) compared to the total U.S. with 89 percent. Estefa reports that Arabic Americans are "more densely equipped with satellite receivers than the majority population in the U.S." (2004).

Electronic Media

While it is the younger, better educated and more affluent in all cultures that use most electronic media. Technology is not just for the young. More than a third (37.6 percent) of Americans over age 62 used the World Wide Web in 2008. These "Connected Matures" (numbering nearly 750 million) averaged 44 minutes daily surfing the net (AARP, 2008).

The mushrooming social media impace the business world with usage not only among organizations and customers, but within organizations as well. The Burston-Marsteller study of the 100 largest Fortune 500 companies reports that 79 percent of them use Twitter, Facebook, YouTube or corporate blogs to communicate with customers or other stakeholders and supplies evidence that customers "like to engage with companies via social media" (Mashable, 2010).

Newspapers and Magazines

Americans also spend countless hours reading newspapers and magazines. In 2009, a total of 911 U.S. newspapers reported a combined circulation of 46,164,000 (Nielsen, 2009). In 2006, more than 59 million people, well over one-third of all active internet users, visited newspaper web sites for a total of 7.2 billion minutes in 1.4 billion visits (Sigmund, 2007).

Minority Media

There are historical as well as cultural reasons for the rise of minority media. Over the last decades of the 20th century, growing diversity in the U.S. led some media to avoid dealing with people of color as they moved into cities and trying instead to build audiences based on specific marketing niches such as age, education, income, or gender. Minority concerns were frequently ignored. Thus mass media developed into a segmented media—selective in *who* it transmits to and in *what* it transmits. Advertisers, the driving force behind the audiences targeted by newspapers, wanted predominantly affluent Anglo readers. In practical terms this means selectivity in terms of which stories are printed or aired and which are not. In some places, stories about African-, Latino and Asian-Americans still continue to be ignored.

As a result of this selectivity, the media *maximized* racial and ethnic division. As diversity numbers in the U.S. grew however, this exclusion from mainstream media provided an opportunity for newspapers and TV channels specifically targeting the excluded minorities. Today "there is not one ethnic media but more than a dozen in the United States. Some sectors . . . are big business. Others are more political and less commercial" (Butod, 2009). With an estimated 10.9 million Hispanic American television households in the U.S., Spanish-language TV channels are now common in urban areas (ASNE, 2001) and by 2010 have become major networks. In September of 2003, large mainstream English-language newspapers launched several Spanish-language daily newspapers (*Hoy, Diario La Estrella, Al Dia*) to complement the small Spanish-language weeklies.

In addition to Spanish-language TV channels, satellite dishes now bring in stations from Mexico and Colombia, CNN (in Spanish) and Fox Sports (in Spanish). Cable operators serve geographically-defined markets with programming geared to those areas. Smaller ethnic and cultural groups that are more diffused geographically such as the Arabic, Russian and Korean language groups are serviced by satellite television.

The ethnic media poll of 2005 reports that "Ethnic media now reaches 57 million African Americans, Hispanics and Asian Americans on a regular basis. . . . (New America Media, 2009). Ethnic-targeted media focus on culture-specific entertainment and news.

A New Media America study reports that "Forty-five percent of all African American, Hispanic, Asian American, Native American and Arab American adults prefer ethnic television, radio or newspapers to their mainstream counterparts" (Butod, 2009).

THE MEDIA AND WHAT IT TRANSMITS

Stereotypes

All forms of media engage in the transmission of cultural stereotypes. Traditional type-casting of African Americans and Native Americans by advertisers has decreased markedly in broadcast and print media. Unfortunately, other forms of stereotyping are alive and well, often in the character roles portrayed in TV dramatizations. Many studies have examined the stereotypes fostered by media. A sample of the stereotypes emerging from Nielson research and other studies include:

Businessmen.   Compared to characters in other occupations, this group is portrayed twice as often in a negative as a positive way. They commit 40% of the murders and other crimes, three times as often as characters in other occupations.

Public Officials.   This group has the worst negative image of any occupational group (civil servants were a close second). They commit crimes twice as often as other characters, take bribes, or do the bidding of special interest groups. Most political and legal institutions are portrayed as corrupt. Noteworthy exceptions: law enforcement officials and public school teachers who have positive images, but are rarely portrayed as government representatives.

Arab-Americans.   Positive images are hard to find. People of Arabic descent are presented as "billionaires or bombers" and rarely as victims or as ordinary people doing ordinary things.

Italian-Americans.   Far more male than female roles are found. Portrayals are more negative than those of other groups with one in six engaged in criminal activity (e.g., The Sopranos) or with most holding low status jobs and not speaking proper English.

Latino-Americans.   Latinos are portrayed as living in poverty and as criminals—"a dysfunctional underclass that exists on the fringes of mainstream U.S society." Some 66% of all network stories about Latinos last year involved "crime, terrorism and illegal immigration" (Méndez-Méndez & Alveiro, 2003).

Gender.   Sunday comic strips feature more males than females with males more likely to be central characters, authority figures, and non-emotional in nature. Both genders engage in stereotypical occupations such as the comic strip's Dagwood in an office and Blondie in a catering business. Video game heroes are primarily white males (over 80%) with females often depicted as sexy and seductive and as secondary or irrelevant characters (Berkeley Daily Planet, 2002).

Female models on television and in magazines are often unreasonably skinny and posed in demeaning and over-sexualized fashion.

Weight.   Obesity is linked to gender. On prime time TV, 3% of the females are obese and 33% are underweight (compared to real U.S. population figures of 25% and 5%, respectively). TV males are one-third as likely to be obese as real life males and male TV characters are six times more likely to be underweight as real life males (White, 2001).

Social Class.   Research on social class in television programming or in audience research is sparse. A few studies focused on drama programming often using occupation as an indicator of class of the television characters (Butsch, n.d.).

Minority Media Usage

Asian Americans	Asian ethnic TV has increased markedly since 2005
	Great increase in Chinese, Vietnamese, Korean and Filipino programming
	Asian-American radio reaches only about one fourth of all adults
	Chinese and Korean newspapers now reach 70% and 64% of those populations
	Telecom usage is high: Asians spent more on long distance and international calls than any other group or Caucasians
	Internet usage matches that of Caucasians
	Heavy cell phone usage; rely on laptops and Wi-Fi for cyber connection
	Web site owners and bloggers; 20% report blogging
Black/African Americans	Number of African-American-oriented channels is small; but majority of this group watches BET (Black Entertainment Television) regularly
	African American–oriented radio now reaches 2/3 of adults in this group
	African American papers have increased circulation
	African Americans spend a lot on local calls
	Internet usage less for African Americans than other groups
	Own cell phones, but don't use them as much as other groups for web and text messaging
	Heavy users of digital and video cameras especially when these come on cell phones
Hispanic/Latino Americans	Univision and Telemundo (TV networks) are almost universal
	Spanish-language radio stations have increased
	Spanish newspapers now reach about one-third of all Hispanic adults
	Hispanics spend a lot on local calls
	"Enthusiastic" web site owners and bloggers; more than 35% own a web site
	English-speaking Latino Internet usage matches that of Caucasians; less usage for Spanish-speakers
	Rely on cell phones to surf the Web, text message, download music, watch videos
	Heavy users of digital and video cameras especially when these come on cell phones

(Matsuda, 2009; New America Media, 2009, June 9)

The Poor.   Mantsios reports that very little coverage occurs of the *poor* and poverty. The messages sent: They are faceless, undeserving (e.g., welfare cheats, drug addicts, greedy panhandlers), an eyesore (e.g., homeless shelters and panhandlers are problems for the community), do not exist (the 40 million poor get scant press coverage), are down on their luck (soup kitchens and charity by the rich get coverage), have only themselves to blame implying the poor to be urban unemployed blacks and minorities entrapped by attitudes and culture.

The working class is coded by gender with gender status reversed, i.e., working class males are lovable and bumbling (sometimes buffoons), while females are more intelligent than males often acting like mothers to their husbands (Butsch, n.d.).

The *middle class* is generally portrayed as the universal class and as a victim of the lower class (the middle class pays their welfare costs and are the victims of their crimes). The middle class receives positive treatment—almost as the American ideal with "exaggerated displays of affluence and upward mobility" (Butsch, n.d).

The *wealthy* are seen as fascinating (celebrities, superstars, society stars and corporate empire builders appear in stories and gossip columns) and benevolent with an occasional bad apple. Newspapers and TV cater to this group far in excess of their numbers.

Gays.   Once non existent, gays are now a presence on TV, having emerged from the shadows in the last decade. Critics charge however, that gay portrayals are stereotypical: "Gays are often presented in extreme circumstances on television . . . They're either perpetually giddy and flamboyant . . . or traumatized by AIDS and social and emotional hardship" (Boone, 2003).

Religion.   Positive and negative portrayals are evenly balanced (35% and 34%, respectively). In 2003–2004, religion came up 2,314 times dropping to 1,425 in 2005–2006 (Learmonth, 2006). The bashing of Muslims in television shows by syndicated talk show hosts continues with name calling such as "rag heads," "goat humping weasels," etc. (Akbar, 2007).

People with disabilities   complain that the media often glorify disability or try to turn it into an 'inspiration of some kind' . . . "We are either the 'incompetent victim-child ... or the "brave super-warriors." (Yahoo Best Answers, 2008)

Nonwhites.   Non-whites are under-represented in TV dramatizations and when present, are often in roles that reinforce stereotypes.

Lack of Coverage

Positive images of youth are largely absent. Youth are stereotyped by exclusion from mass media suggesting their lack of importance. In local news they are often portrayed in the context of crime and other at-risk behaviors. A considerable gender imbalance in youth stories occurs with most stories about males. Racial imbalance occurs with 35% of the news about white youth involved in crime compared to 52% for nonwhite youth.

> Nowhere is the effect of discrimination more apparent than in the disparate coverage of missing persons. "If a missing person is white, female, young, attractive and has an upper-middle-class background, media coverage of her case will be far more thorough than coverage of missing men, minorities or the elderly" according to Roy Clark, vice president at the Poynter Institute (Santos, 2007).

THE MEDIA AND ITS PRODUCERS

Stereotypes and other cultural messages transmitted by media are products in part of "who" within the media decides on the messages to be transmitted. Ownership and control of the mass media (television, movies music, radio, cable, publishing and the Internet) have dwindled from the 50 two decades ago, to "less than two dozen with power concentrated in 10 huge conglomerates" (Forum on Media Diversity, 2010). Unfortunately, mass media has long been charged with a lack of diversity within its ranks. The Forum on Media Diversity reports that in 2010, "Journalists of color represent only 12.6 percent of newsroom management positions in the 151 television stations owned by the 10 big stations (July 29). In 2007, of the 35 hosts and co-hosts of cable-news primetime news, 35 were white and 29 of the 35 were male. Guests were primarily white and Latinos noticeably infrequent (Media Matters, 2007). Ron Smith of the Milwaukee Journal Sentinel writes that "Diversity is a word journalists often hear. In fact you can't go to a conference without hearing about it. But you can walk into just about any newsroom in the country and never see it" (2003).

Madison Avenue advertising agencies have long been known for gender discrimination. In 2009, however, . . . a decades-long pattern of racial discrimination in these agencies came to light. For example, "100 percent of the creative directors responsible for the advertising spots at the Super Bowl were white and 94 percent were men" (Ali, 2010). Thus, serious diversity imbalance among the producers of mass media messages has serious consequences for what is aired for everyone.

"On both sitcoms and dramas, exclusion is pervasive. Black, Latino and Asian performers have a hard time landing recurring roles" (Seitz, 2002) and behind the scenes—writers, directors, producers and crewmembers are mostly Caucasian.

Interestingly, ". . . African Americans, Asians, Hispanics and Middle Easterners tend to trust English-language media outlets more than native-language ones" (Journalism, 2007).

SUMMARY

Media are transmission and change agents of culture. Media messages foster stereotypes as well as the ideals of cultures as they reflect and reinforce cultural values. Virtually all forms of media now have extensive penetration in the U.S. Unfortunately, mainstream media's selective and stereo-typic coverage and woefully lacking diversity employment patterns still reflect extensive discrim-ination. The meteoric rise of ethnic media in all forms works to strength ethnic cultural ties.

Media Exercises

To examine media messages, select one of the following media to investigate. **Note.** *Your instructor will provide the recording forms from the Instructor's Manual to aid you in recording your observations.*

1. ***Electronic Media: Prime Time TV***   Watch prime time television, selecting option a) or option b) below. Record the information (role, gender, ethnicity, social group and behaviors) about the principal and secondary characters on the Recording Form. You will need several copies of the Recording Form for each program. Be sure to use separate forms for each program.
   Option a) Watch two hours of prime time TV drama (6–11 p.m.) or
   Option b) Watch three different prime time crime dramas. (6–11 p.m.)

   After you have made your observations, answer the questions below.

   i. What audience do you think each program targets? Why?
   ii. What stereotype and cultural messages do you think the programs send? Explain.
   iii. What audience do you think the commercials target? Why?
   iv. What stereotype and cultural messages do you think the commercials send? Explain.

2. ***Print Media: Magazines***   Visit a library or book store. Select three magazines, one from each column below. Use the Recording Form for your observations of the ethnicity, gender and social class and the tone of the commentary. You will need several copies of the Recording Form for each magazine.

Cosmopolitan	*Brides*	*BusinessWeek*
Good Housekeeping	*Maxim*	*Bicycling*
Instyle	*Money*	*Jet*
Marie Claire	*Seventeen*	*Real Simple*
Martha Stewart Living	*Sports Illustrated*	*Time*
Shape	*Travel & Leisure*	*Vanity Fair*

After you have recorded your observations, analyze the media messages and answer the following questions for each magazine:

a. What group(s) (gender, class, race/ethnicity, age, etc.) does each magazine seem to target? Explain. Give examples.

b. What messages (cultural value, stereotypes, etc.) does each magazine seem to convey? Explain. Give examples.

c. What group(s) (gender, class, race/ethnicity, age, etc.) do the advertisements in each magazine seem to target? Give examples.

d. What messages (cultural value, stereotypes, etc.) do the advertisements in each magazine seem to convey? Explain. Give examples.

3. ***Print Media: Mass Circulation Newspapers*** Examine a single issue of a mass circulation daily or Sunday newspaper and record your observations of the ethnicity, gender, social class and tone (i.e., positive, negative, neutral) of the commentary in option a) the stories or option b) features below on the Recording Form. You will need several copies of the form.

Option a) Newspaper stories.

Option b) Features including wedding, engagement, anniversary and death notices, financial reporting, clothing, travel articles, etc.

After you have recorded your observations, answer the following questions:

i. Are groups treated in proportion to their numbers in the population? Explain.

ii. Do you think groups are treated equally in tone (i.e., positive, negative, neutral)? Explain.

iii. What audience do you think these publications may target? Explain.

iv. What stereotypes do you think they may foster? Explain.

Bibliography

AARP magazine. (2008, September & October). We rule the net. www.aarp.org

Akbar, M.T. (2007). We are not done with racism—yet. Media Monitors Network. Retrieved December 6, 2010 from http://usa.mediamonitors.net

Ali, S. (2010, May 10). New study: super bowl ads created by white men. *DiversityInc* https://diversityinc.com

American Society of Newspaper Editors. (2001, April 3). *2001 ASNE census finds newsrooms less diverse: increased hiring of minorities blunted by departure rate.* Retrieved on December 6, 2010 from http://www.asne.org

Barnes, K. & DeBell, C. (1995). *The portrayal of men and women workers in Sunday Comics: no laughing matter.* Paper presented at the American Psychological Association Convention, New York, August 1995.

Berkeley Daily Planet (2002, December 11), Video Games Lack Diversity. Retrieved May 4, 2011 from http://www. berkleydailyplanet.com.

Boone, M. (2003). Television's gay characters aim to add diversity, but unintentionally reinforce negative stereotypes. *The Daily Orange.* Retrieved on September 7, 2007 from http://www.dailyorange.com

Butsch, R. (n.d.). Social class and television. The Museum of Broadcast Communications. Retrieved September 4, 2007 from http://www.museum.tv/archives/etv/S/htmlS/socialclass/socialclass.htm

Butod, M. (2009). The growth of ethnic Chinese media. *Ethnic media in the U.S.* http://ivythesis.,typed.com/term_paper_topics/2009/06/

Estefa, A. (2004). Satellite television viewing among Arabs in the U.S. Retrieved September 12, 2007 from http://www.allacademic.com/meta/p113211_index.html

Forum on media diversity. (2010, July 30). Forum report. www.mediadiversityforum.lsu.edu Search: race and media

Gardossy, T. (2009, February 24). TV viewing at "all-time high" Nielsen says http://article.cnn.com

Government goes down the tube: images of government in TV entertainment. Executive summary. Retrieved on December 6, 2010 from http://www.cmpa.com

Huang, T.T. (2003, November 17). Poynteronline. The battle for inclusiveness. Retrieved on December 6, 2010 from http://www.poynter.org

Italian-American characters in television entertainment. Executive summary. Retrieved on November 18, 2003 from http://www.cmpa.com

Journalism. (2007). Ethnic media audience trends 2007. www.journalism.org/node/2565.

Lichter, S. R. & Amundson, D. Distorted reality: Hispanic characters in TV Entertainment *1955–1992. Executive Summary.* Retrieved on November 18, 2003 from http://www.cmpa.com

Lichter, S. R., Lichter, L., Rothman, S. *Video Villains: the TV businessman 1955–1986 .*

Executive summary. Retrieved on November 17, 2003 from http://www.cmpa.com

Mantsios, G. (1998). *Media magic. Making class invisible.* From Paula Rothenberg (ed.), Race, Class and Gender in the United States: An Integrated Study. 4th ed. NY: St. Martin's Press, 1998.

Marketing Charts. (2010). Top 10 consumer trends for 2010. www.marketingcharts.com/interactive/top-10-consumer-trends-for-2010–11579

Mashable the social media guide. (2010). Social media trends at fortune 100 companies [stats]. http://mashable,.com/2010/02/23

Matsuda, C. (2009, July 7). Among ethnic groups, the digital divide narrows. *Knight Digital media center.* www.knightdigitalmediacenter.org

Media matters. (2007, May 7). Locked out: The lack of gender and ethnic diversity on cable news continues. http://mediamatters.org/print/reports/200705070003

Media Monitor. (2002, September/October). *What's the matter with kids today? Images of teenagers on local and national TV news.* Retrieved on December 6, 2010 from http://www.cmpa.com

Méndez-Méndez, S. & Alveiro, D. (2003). *Network Brownout 2003: The portrayal of Latinos in network television news, 2002.* National Association of Hispanic Journals (Access: Google senior author).

New America media. (2009, June 9). Ethnic media usage poll release at NAM national ethnic media expo & awards. http://news.newamericamedia.org/

Newspaper Association of America. (n.d.) www.naa.org

Nielsen (2009, March). Ethnic trends in media.

Nielsen Wire. (2010, April 28). U.S. homes add even more TV sets in 2010. http://blog.nielsen.com

Online NewsHour. (1999, August 23). *Diversity in the newsroom.* Retrieved on November 27, 2003 from http://www.pbs.org/newshour

Readership Institute. (1999). *Newspaper staffing, diversity and turnover.* Retrieved on November 27, 2003 from http://www.readership.org

Santos, M. (2007). Part 1: Missing people face disparity in media coverage. MSN Lifestyle. Retrieved September 4, 200 from http://www.lifestyle.msn.com

Schakenbach, J. (2010, July 7). Marketing heads for the data mine. *Mass High Tech* www.masshightech.com

Seitz, M. Z. (2002, July 16). Despite some progress, minorities remain an unseen presence. *Star Ledger* p. 28.

Shaheen, J.G. (1989) TV Arabs. From New Worlds of Literature, Jerome Beatty and J. Paul Hunter, eds. In Rothenberg, *Race, Class and*

Gender in the United States. An Integrated Study. Sixth ed. N.Y.: Worth 2004 p. 356–357.

Sigmund, J. (2007). NAA launches next phase of industry trade campaign. Newspaper Association of America. Retrieved September 3, 2007 from http://www.naa.org/sitecore/content/Global/PressCenter/2007

Smith, Ron. (2003, October 24). *Copy editing for diversity.* Poynteronline. Retrieved on November 18, 2003 from http://www.poynter.org

Sowell, T. (1991). A world view of cultural diversity. *Society.* vol. 29, no. 1, pp. 37–44.

The Insight Research Corporation. (n.d.). Telecom and ethnic groups: Uses of local, long distance, and wireless services in ethnic communities. www.insight-corp.com/reports/ethnic2.asp

White, R. (2001). TV portrayals of obese people perpetuate stereotypes. Retrieved September 4, 2007 from http://cas.msu.edu

Wilson C.C. II, Gutierrez, F., Chao, L. (2003). Racism, sexism and the media. The rise class communication in multicultural America. 3rd ed., Thousand Oaks, Sage 2003, pp. 25–34.

World Ark (2010, Spring). 32 hours 50 minutes. www.heifer.org spring 2010, p. 5

Yahoo Best Answers. (2008, December 2). Type in Search Engine: "yahoo answers best answers," then click: "Yahoo Answers - Best Answer"?—Yahoo Answers; then type in Search Y Answers box: "Do you think that they media stereotypes people with disabilities?"; then click "Search Y! Answers"

IMPROVING INTERPERSONAL COMMUNICATION IN TODAY'S DIVERSE WORKPLACE

Gina Colavecchio
Children's Hospital Boston

Carol P. Harvey
Assumption College

GOALS

- To understand how the elements of the communication process can be affected by cultural differences
- To develop a culture general approach to mindful interpersonal communication that recognizes communication patterns in the major cultural subgroups in the United States
- To identify the preferred communication tendencies of coworkers, customers, vendors, and supervisors in today's diverse workplace
- To understand and identify elements of communication styles such as differences in power distances, degree of tolerance of uncertainty, non-verbal communication, tendencies towards directness, and differences in time orientation

When dealing with intercultural communication on a global basis, people are more apt to anticipate having some communication issues. However, it is no longer realistic to ignore cultural communication differences *within* the U. S. workplace. Research indicates that communication between culturally diverse sub-group members are increasingly dissimilar rather than homogeneous (Searight and Gafford, 2005). With the workforce being more diverse, immigration increasing and technology rapidly advancing in terms of e-commerce, Skype, video conferencing, global call centers, and webcasting, nearly everyone participates in intercultural communication even if they never leave the United States. However, we tend to be less mindful of the differences in styles when communicating with coworkers, supervisor, suppliers and customers whose communication styles may differ considerably from our own.

THE COMMUNICATION MODEL

While all communication follows a basic model, cultural differences can complicate the process and contribute to misunderstandings in the workplace. All communication, verbal and non-verbal, involves a sender who encodes a message that he transmits over some channel to a receiver who decodes the message and provides feedback. This transmission happens within a context of "noise," i.e., all of the factors that can reduce the clarity of understanding the message (See Figure 1).

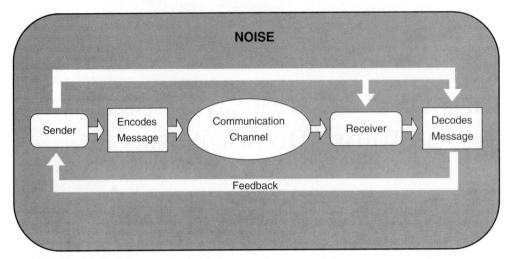

FIGURE 5-3   The Basic Communication Process

Certainly, when individuals exhibit communication styles that are based on different norms and values, i.e., create noise, the possibility of miscommunication increases significantly.

GROWTH AND FLEXIBILITY

Effective communication in the workplace can be both confusing and challenging. It requires not only significant knowledge of many different cultural frameworks, but also the willingness to attain personal growth and flexibility throughout the process. First, one needs to accept that the communication style that we are most familiar with often becomes the unconscious norm against which we judge others' communication styles.

For example, if you were socialized to believe that making eye contact indicates that a person is telling the truth, you may have an unconscious tendency to judge people who consider *not* making eye contact as a sign of respect as untrustworthy.

Second, in communication exchanges, there is a tendency to "categorize" individuals as being representative of their entire culture. So, when you start to communicate with a person, his appearance, clothing, accent or name may lead you to inaccurate interpretations conclusions and judgments about his message. However, such generalizations do not leave one open to an individual's life experiences and socialization.

> While generalizations may be accurate about groups, they're never going to be wholly true of individuals . . . This doesn't mean that we have gotten the facts wrong but only that in any culture you will always find a broad range of behaviors vis-à-vis particular characteristics (Storti, 1994, pp. 7–8).

So, in dealing with a customer from a Hispanic culture, or with a Hispanic name, it is easy to assume that he will typify all Hispanics when in fact his life experiences, could include many non-Hispanic influences.

Third, people have many social identities and some more salient or important influences on their patterns of communication than others. So, an African American woman may develop a communication style more influenced by her status as a woman, i.e. gender, or her generational cohort, i.e., as a baby boomer than her race.

Flexible communicators avoid using a **culture specific** approach which assumes that all members of a subgroup communicate in the same way. For example, if a person is working with a client from a group that tends to be sensitive to time, direct and not emotional, it does not mean that this particular person will respond well to communications that stress those elements. For many reasons, these parameters may not be strong in her personal communication framework. A better approach is to be *mindful*, i.e., more observant and tuned into her communication style, and listening for cues to determine if she seems to value this communication approach or not. Jandt (2004) proposes that by nature, people of all cultural backgrounds are inherently the same, and it is their exposure over time to their society and its values (i.e., socialization) that shapes the communication style of the culture and each individual has a unique life experience.

Being able to communicate effectively with people of diverse cultural backgrounds is a skill that can provide a competitive advantage in the marketplace and capitalizes on one of the positive aspects of having diversity in an organization. Employees who understand and appreciate differences, such as greetings, meeting formalities, scheduling, negotiations, and presentation skills will have a better chance of doing business effectively than those who continue to overlook the importance of developing more mindful and flexible intercultural communication skills or who assume that all members of a particular culture communicate with the same style. The key is to develop one's self-awareness to improve understanding.

THE NEW WORKFORCE: FACTS, FIGURES, EDUCATION AND LANGUAGE

Based on current trend analysis in the United States, by 2050 white Euro-Americans will compose 46% of the population, a decline of 20%, with approximately half of the country made up of ethnic minorities (Berry, 2009). The implications for the American workplace are remarkably similar: 1 out of 2 new workers in the US will be an ethnic minority (Morse, 2004). In contrast, as recently as 1999, white Americans made up approximately 72% of the United States population. As of 2006, according to the U.S. Census Bureau, the minority population in the U.S. reached 100.7 million of the 300 million people in the country. The 44.3 million Hispanics are the largest minority group (14.8% of the population), Blacks comprise 40.2 million, Asians 14.9 million and American Indian and Alaska Natives 4.5 million.

A recent CareerBuilder.com and America Online survey found that at least 50 percent of new hires in 2006 were Hispanics and one-third of hiring managers expect diverse candidates to make up a quarter of their new hires in the coming years (Barger, 2006). California has a minority population of 20.7 million—22% of the nation's total and Texas 12.2 million or 12% of the U.S. total. Over the past 40 years, 65% of the immigrant population has located in one of six states; New York, California, Texas, Florida, New Jersey and Illinoi (Shrestha, 2006).

EXHIBIT 2 Changing Composition of the U.S. Work Force		
Race/Ethnicity	**1999**	**2050**
Whites	72%	24.4%
Blacks	12%	15%
Hispanics	11%	50.1%
Asians	5%	8%
Other	0%	14.6%

EDUCATION AND SOCIO-ECONOMIC CONSIDERATIONS IN COMMUNICATION IN STYLES

Differences in education and socio-economic levels may also account for some of the communication differences that are often attributed to one's culture. A 2000 U.S. Census identified that there were more than 1.5 million Asians enrolled in colleges and universities in the United States. So, as might be expected, Asian Americans as a group earn more money than any other ethnic group and almost half are employed in managerial or professional careers. Comparatively, about 10% of Hispanics work in white collar or professional careers and Hispanic women attain higher educational levels than Hispanic men.

EXHIBIT 3 Employment Levels of Asians & Hispanics		
Race/Ethnicity	**White Collar**	**Blue Collar**
Asian	48%	52%
Hispanic	10%	90%

Although, the unemployment rate among Hispanics is still high and their earnings are lower compared to Euro-Americans, as the percentage of Hispanics in the population grows, the group as a whole will experience increased political and economic power.

This growing talent pool of workers includes 80% of Black Americans who have completed high school, 44% who have some college education and 25% who have a college degree (compared to 90%, 56%, and 38% respectively for white Americans). The difference in attainment percentages between White and Black Americans may relate to socioeconomic, access issues as a significantly larger percentage of Black Americans are living below the poverty level in the United States.

EXHIBIT 4 Educational Levels of the U.S. Workforce		
Educational Level	**Black Americans**	**White Americans**
High School	80%	90%
Some College	44%	56%
College Degree	25%	38%

LANGUAGES

Of 132 million workers in the United States, 77 percent speak fluent English, indicating that almost one-fourth of the U.S. workforce does not communicate in English very well (Peden, Mandell, & Moore, 2007). In a recent Gallup survey, 96% of Americans believed it was either crucial or very important for members of the U.S. workforce to speak English. However, approximately a quarter of the U.S. workforce can hold a conversation in a language other than their primary language, 55% of which is in Spanish (Fry, 2005). In the Hispanic community, 47% of Spanish youth are bilingual in Spanish and English. However, younger Hispanics often speak English as their primary language. With the median age of Hispanics in the United States at 27.4 years of age, compared to the median age of Euro-Americans at 36.4 years of age, the opportunity for this cultural group to utilize their English and bilingual communication skills to advance in business organizations is unprecedented.

Language is inherently problematic because it can be indefinite, vague, and unclear. As communicators, we are constantly subjectively interpreting everything we observe and hear, a concept described by Shramm and Osgood's circular theory that defines communication as an endless process with information constantly being received and redirected between sender and receiver. It is an art that is based on personal life experiences, cultures, stereotypes, and assumptions that leads differing degrees of ambiguity, difference, and inferences.

COMMUNICATION STYLES AND AMERICAN SUB-CULTURES

In communicating, each person participating in the conversation must understand their own experiences, culture, stereotypes, and assumptions, as well as put forth an effort to understand the experiences, culture, stereotypes, and realized and unrealized assumptions of the other participants. Stereotypes can be based on a variety of different experiences, including family beliefs, religion, previous interactions with people of that cultural background, travel, education, or having done business with someone from a particular country. These stereotypes are primarily subjective generalizations and are not necessarily an accurate way to describe the communication styles of each member of an entire culture. To think that everybody will communicate the same is of course a generalization and referred to as a culture specific approach. However, this often happens as an unconscious process. So, rather than assuming that *all* Asians will value and need time to establish a relationship before reaching an business agreement, it is preferable to observe the communication cues and behaviors of your Asian American client to determine *if* this seems to be important for him.

In Asian cultures, indirectness is often considered polite, but a common stereotype is that Asians are sneaky or hard to figure out, undoubtedly a result of their indirect communication style. This has led many to distrust Asians in the workplace. Some people may even feel that Asians are deceptive or hiding pertinent information while in fact they may have been socialized to communicate in a less directive style to demonstrate respect.

Another example is the stereotype that Black Americans are more violent and aggressive than whites. Black Americans as a group tend to have a more direct communication style than many White Americans or Asians. Black Americans consider it admirable to express feelings, and emotions and value members of society who do so. Early communications research by Foeman and Pressley (1987) identified five Black-American cultural values that, if leveraged appropriately, can be beneficial in an organizational environment and communication: assertiveness, directness, morality, receptiveness, and cohesion.

COMMUNICATION STYLES

Different styles of speech and language can cause anxiety in interpreting directions and verbal and non-verbal cues, especially when there are differences in the way words are articulated. It is assumed that people will contribute to an interaction in a greater capacity when they are comfortable and have similarities with their counterparts, including common economic, social, and cultural backgrounds (McComb, 2001).

While sociologists view different dialects as all being correct ways of speaking, others perceive some dialects, such as British English, as more prestigious (Langmia & Durham, 2007). In contrast, in Black American culture, language is individualistic and complicated, as described by Gudykunst and Ting-Toomey and uses vivid descriptive words, images and metaphors (Taylor, 1990). The language is a combination of the English vocabulary and complex Black structure that sometimes results in differences in the way that Black Americans use verb tenses. Black Americans sometimes talk in a more rhythmic speech than white Americans. So, conversations and presentations may appear more boastful and animated. Because of the percentage of Black Americans who live in poverty and their historically lower levels of academic achievement as a group, this speech style is sometimes unconsciously less respected than other styles.

Asian influenced communication styles tend to differ from Euro-American communication patterns in that Asians can be more indirect in providing information and data prior to making their main point. So, some may view this as a way to provide a complete rationale for the ultimate decision or strategy. However, this can leave other people searching for the substance at the beginning of a communication, lead to difficulty in identifying the main points and result in poor listening and a loss of interest. In contrast, many Euro-Americans tend to lead with the main point or decision (i.e., have more direct style), and then follow-up with supporting data and rationale. Asians listening to a presentation or reading this in an email could view this style as aggressive or forward.

Differences in communication styles often are unrecognized or denied because people are unsure of how to cope with these differences. For example, Asians have a tendency to shield others from knowing negative information and expect others to do the same (Searight, 2005). In contrast, African Americans can come across as blunt or too-straightforward because of their tendency to use a more direct style of communication (Gudykunst &Ting-Toomey, 1996).

MAINTAINING HARMONY AND EMOTIONALISM

People from different cultures may deal with conflict quite differently. For valid reasons, African Americans sometimes distrust the established ways of doings things, and challenge the norms and expectations within an organization. While Asians are more apt to conform to established processes, roles and hierarchies within an organization, while repressing public feelings and emotions (Searight, 2005).

For example, in terms of negotiation, Asians are often more willing to apologize as a way to continue moving forward especially when things become awkward. Asians are typically expected to apologize whenever there is tension or awkwardness but Euro-Americans and Black Americans often are less willing to take any blame and only offer an apology as warranted, if at all. Americans are also more likely to provide an explanation with an apology, while Asians tend to internalize the blame, acting in a more submissive manner, without necessarily providing any rationale (Carr-Ruffino, 2006).

Common stereotypes about Native Americans have led to generalizations that they have little education and tend to work in low-level jobs at casinos, or making and selling crafts. People sometimes even refer to Native Americans in the past tense, in a way that suggests the culture no longer exists, even though today there are more than 800,000 Native Americans living in the United States. Since some are soft spoken or quiet, this can create an expectation that they will not participate in conversations, or in contrast, the assumption that they are overly aggressive when they do speak up (Hernandez, 2007).

In Native American cultures, oral tradition is important and this may result in a less talk and more listening than most Americans expect. Because it is considered shameful in Native American culture to make mistakes in public, this may be another reason why some Native Americans tend to participate verbally in the workplace.

DECISION MAKING AND LEADERSHIP

From the values of Asian cultures, it is often more acceptable and normal to have greater respect for people in authority, i.e., employees maintain significant power distances between themselves and management. Centralization of organizational structures is a direct result of this power distance, as is the ability to eliminate uncertainty and risks, through the rigidity of hierarchical roles. If you work a subsidiary of an Asian company or for an individual who is strongly influences by Asian culture, there may be an expectation that you will have great respect for those in authority and feel comfortable with decisions being made top down.

In Hispanic cultures, major decisions, such as choosing career paths and arranging living situations, are often made as a family or a group and it's not uncommon to consult with siblings, parents and even grandparents. Because this culture is typically masculine and highly authoritarian, leaders and managers are considered all-knowing and are greatly respected, but in return are expected to provide for employees.

INDIVIDUAL AND GROUP COMMUNICATION

America as a whole is considered to be low context, highly individualistic culture where directness is valued and people are responsible for their own success. However, much of the U.S. population growth both through immigration and birthrate is more in the high context collectivist subcultures such as Asians, Africans, Native Americans and Middle-Easterners where the group is more important and indirect communication is more common (Lingley, 2006). Since these cultures are less direct, listening is more important and silence indicates understanding. Many Euro-Americans prefer a more direct communication style and rush to fill silences (McDowell, 2003).

In some cultures, there is a strong emphasis on group cohesiveness and belonging, i.e., collectivism. The group, which can span from anything as narrow as immediate family, to as broad as colleagues and acquaintances, is of utmost importance to members of these cultures, and they value conformity and commitment to the group (i.e., relationships), as well as compliance to maintain harmony, above even honesty, within the group.

This is in sharp contrast to the United States, where individualism and independence are critical to one's self value. In American culture, maintaining self-respect and one's image is extremely important and people will act more aggressively to preserve their self image in negotiations and conflict. In other cultures, such as Asian cultures, it is the group that matters more than any one individual. So, people may avoid conflict to not upset the collective group's image (McDowell, 2003).

In American Indian and Asian cultures, the individual is expected to remain modest and humble. Advancing or promotion of oneself and accomplishments or taking oneself too seriously violates this value (LeBaron, 2003). For example, a very talented American Indian student may hide academic competence to avoid seeming superior, which is considered inappropriate arrogance in that culture. To ensure harmony, American Indians may be less aggressively competitive and work best cooperatively (Deyhle & Swisher, 1997).

Frequently, people from these collectivist societies belong to a small number of very intimate groups to which they are extremely loyal over the entire course of their lives and this tendency has implications for teamwork and management. Reward systems benefit the group as a whole rather than any one individual and hard work is rewarded intrinsically. In contrast, low context cultures like the U.S., are more assertive, talkative, and direct in communication and often devalue the attentive listening and silences so common in high context communication.

When low context communicators actively question a speaker, it can make people in high context cultures uneasy because it can produce tension or disrupt harmony (Berry, 2009).

In contrast, in the United States an individual's personal needs are often placed above the needs of the group with minimal commitment or loyalty to the group.

GROWTH AND FLEXIBILITY

Intercultural communication in the global workplace can be both confusing and challenging. It requires not only significant knowledge of many different cultural attributes, but also the willingness to cultivate self-awareness and to attain personal growth and flexibility throughout the process. Accepting that everyone has some biases in regards to different cultures is essential to beginning to improve intercultural communication. As an increasingly vital component to the American workforce, the ability to communicate with people of diverse backgrounds and cultures can provide competitive advantages to those who support and embrace the concept. Employees who understand and appreciate different expectations, such as greetings, meeting formalities, scheduling, negotiating, and presentation skills will have a better chance of doing business effectively than a company whose employees continue to deal with disconnects or miscommunications.

In low context cultures, communication between people of different cultures can create additional uncertainty, which can diminish with extended exposure. Often, people are able to adapt their communication styles, over time, to successfully interact with those from difference cultures. In high context cultures, exposure to people from different cultures does not diminish the level of uncertainty, and can instead increase tension over time. In Asian cultures, extreme formality is expected in business communications and transactions, regardless of the level of intimacy between those engaged with adherence to strict rules and guidelines to ensure ambiguity is avoided.

Risk-takers, frequently financially successful in individualistic cultures, are more comfortable with risk and use risk to their advantage because they are willing to accept the possibility of loss, if the opportunity for gains is significant. Other cultural groups may value risk-avoidance, strict rules and adherence to set principles to minimize risk.

UNCERTAINTY REDUCTION THEORY

The **Uncertainty Reduction Theory** proposed by Charles Berger and Richard Calabrese, predicts and explains relationship progress during an initial reaction. This theory holds that during an interaction, people take certain steps to minimize uncertainty and enhance the comfort level of the interaction (Neuliep, 2003). Employees who are empathetic, and those who can identify *similarities* between themselves and others, are more likely to overcome the uncertainty of engaging with people from different cultures. For example, a doctor often meets patients in a tense setting. By sharing a conversation, common interest about a sport, etc., the doctor may be able to establish a more comfortable relationship with the patient, who will in turn be more forthright, responsive, and trusting. Think about the complications that inter-cultural communication differences could bring to this conversation.

NON-VERBAL COMMUNICATION

Many people utilize nonverbal cues to better understand communication when they are not certain they understand what the other person is trying to convey. Most cultures use different non-verbal cues, based on their own assumptions and values, making the combination of interpreting verbal and non-verbal cues particularly complex. For example,

> In the United States, eye contact, pleasantness of vocal expressions, affirmative head nods, head and arm gestures per minute, and closer physical distance between interactants are considered affiliative. In other cultures, these same behaviors may instead increase uncertainty and anxiety (Neuliep, 2003).

In Black American cultures, listeners may avert their eyes to indicate respect and attention, while speakers are expected to look at listeners directly in the eye. If one member of the interaction is unaware of this culturally accepted communication style, it could unknowingly create tension.

In North America there is far less emphasis placed on nonverbal communication than in high context countries. Non-verbal communication can also be challenging in terms of electronic communications because with little to no opportunity to view mannerisms or hear tones, the communication can likely be judged as too direct and can seem harsh and impolite (Sanders & Wiseman, 1993).

TIME ORIENTATION AND DECISION MAKING

The way that members of a culture perceive time is an element that affects both home and work life. In North America and most of Northern Europe, there is a short-term, highly scheduled orientation. Other cultures have an entirely different perception of time. In some cultures time is cyclical with little to no need for agendas, calendars or timelines. Tasks are guided by interactions between people. For example, many Hispanics do not adhere strictly to set times and schedules (Neuliep, 2003). In contrast, Asian cultures have a tendency to have a long-term outlook and value decision making based on resolve and determination in overcoming long-term obstacles regardless of available opportunities in the short-term. These tendencies can create communication conflicts in a work environment, where Euro-Americans are driven by deadlines and meetings and expect appointments to be punctual and decisions to be made rapidly. Workers from highly scheduled cultures can view those with a looser sense of time orientation as being unmotivated and lazy.

There is an expectation that older members of the culture will be consulted before finalizing any plans, as they are respected for their years and wisdom. Traditions are extremely important and Asian cultures sometimes leave decisions to fate, following the natural progression, with any changes expected to be introduced slowly to allow adaptation (LeBaron, 2003) Without understanding the psychological underpinnings of each person's perception of time management and decision making, working together can be extremely difficult (Neuliep, 2003).

BENEFITS OF INTERCULTURAL COMMUNICATION

Frequently, even leaders who understand the need for intercultural communication and the complexities of diverse organizations become tentative about the extent that they should assert themselves to encourage intercultural communication within an organization, questioning exactly how much change should be expected and what metrics will best measure success. It can be disruptive to promote intercultural understanding and communication without first observing and analyzing the organizational culture, individual attitudes, and potential buy-in. Then there is a need to develop a strategy to gain acceptance.

While all cultures have some strong beliefs and assumptions, others seem to have sharp contrasts with a wide range of values, beliefs, and assumptions. As a whole, one tendency will typically dominate another tendency and therefore be more influential, but not necessarily apply to every member of the culture equally.

Competency in intercultural communication creates a healthier, more productive workplace with an increased number of contributing perspectives and a better opportunity for creativity. Businesses, both domestically and internationally, have begun to focus on the idea that capitalizing on intercultural communication knowledge and development can provide diverse perspectives and competitive advantages. In essence, the overall goal of successful communications in business is increased commerce, decreased conflict, better understanding, more personal growth through tolerance and less uncertainty, anxiety and fear of difference (Neuliep, 2003).

DISCUSSION QUESTIONS

1. What makes it difficult for people to understand how differences in communication styles can cause serious misunderstandings?

2. Why is it so important not to think that all members of a cultural group exhibit the same cultural values in their communication styles?

3. Conversely, why is it important to understand some general cultural tendencies?

4. Briefly describe an example of an intercultural miscommunication exchange that you have either participated in or observed in the workplace, at college, or in a public place. How did the communicators exhibit some of the dimensions described in this article? In retrospect what could have been done differently to improve the communication in terms of the sender and the receiver?

5. Develop an original example of an intercultural communication misinterpretation in a job interview situation that could cause incorrect assumptions to be made about an applicant's potential suitability for a position.

Writing Assignment

Go to http://www.gmi.org and search for "The Ten Commandments of American Culture." This list presents ten sayings that represent commonly accepted American cultural values. Think about how these "American" values may not be as relevant to African Americans, Hispanic Americans, or Asian Americans as they are to Euro-Americans. Write a two- to three-page essay that analyzes how these could lead to lack of motivation, poor productivity, and conflict in the workplace.

Bibliography

Altwaijri, A.O. (1998). *The Arab Culture and other Cultures*, Morocco: The Islamic Educational, Scientific and Cultural Organization (ISESCO).

Barger, T.S. (2006). *Hispanics in the Workplace: Building Meaningful Diversity*, New York: The Conference Board Executive action series.

Berry, John. (2009). *Federal Equal Opportunity Recruitment Program Annual Report to Congress*, Washington, DC: US Office of Personnel Management.

Carr-Ruffino, N., PhD. (2006). *Managing Diversity: People skills for a multicultural workplace; 7th edition*, Boston: Pearson Custom Publishing.

Deyhle, D., & Swisher, K. (1997). *Research in American Indian and Alaska Native education: From assimilation to self-determination*, Washington, DC: American Educational Research Association.

Foeman, A. K., and Pressley G. (1987). Ethnic culture and corporate culture: Using black styles in organizations. Communication Quarterly, 35 (4) 293–307. doi:10.1080/01463378709369695.

Fry, R. & Lowell-Pew, B.L. (2005). *The Characteristics of Bilingual and Monolingual U.S. Workers*, Somerville, MA: Cascadilla Publishing.

Gudykunst, W.B., & Ting-Toomey, S. (1996). *Communication in personal relationships across cultures*, Thousand Oaks, CA: Sage Publications, Inc.

Hernandez, C. (2007). *Old and New Stereotypes of Hispanics*, Washington, DC: The Washington Post Company.

Jandt, F.E. (2004). *Intercultural Communication: A Global Reader*, Thousand Oaks, CA: Sage Publications, Inc.

Langmia, K., & Durham, E. (2007). *Bridging the Gap*, Bowie, MD: Sage Publication, Inc.

LeBaron, M. (2003). *Cross Cultural Communication*, Boulder, CO: University of Colorado, Boulder.

Lingley, D. (2006). *Apologies Across Cultures: An analysis of intercultural communication problems raised in the Ehime Maru incident*, Japan: Kochi University.

McComb. Chris. (2001). About One in Four Americans Can Hold a Conversation in a Second Language. *Gallup*. http://www.gallup.com/poll/1825/about-one-four-americans-can-hold-conversation-second-language.aspx.

McDowell, M.J. (2003). *Native American Literatures: High Context & Low Context*, Portland, OR: Portland Community College.

Morse, A. (2004). *A Quick Look at U.S. Immigrants: Demographics, Workforce, and Asset-Building*, Washington, DC: http://www.ncsl.org/programs/immig/National Conference of State Legislatures.

Neuliep, J.W. (2003). *Intercultural Communication: A Contextual Approach. 2nd Edition*, Boston: Houghton Mifflin Company.

Peden, J., Mandell, A., & Moore, D.R. (2007). *Council on Interracial Books for Children*, New York, NY: Department of Teaching and Learning Technologies at the University of Nevada, Reno.

Rojjanaprapayon, R., Chiemprapha, P., & Kanchanakul, A. (2004). *Conflict Management in Thai Organizations*, Thousand Oaks, CA: Sage Publications.

Sanders, J.A., & Wiseman, R.L. (1993) *Intercultural Communication Studies III: Uncertainty Reduction Among Ethnicities in the United States*, CA: California State Polytechnic University.

Scollon, R., & Scollon, S.W. (2001). *Intercultural Communication: A Discourse Approach. 2nd Edition*, Malden, MA: Blackwell Publishers, Inc.

Searight, H. Russell, PhD, MPH, & Gafford, J., PhD. (2005). *Cultural Diversity at the End of Life: Issues and Guidelines for Family Physicians*, St. Louis, MO: Forest Park Hospital Family Medicine Residency Program.

Shrestha, L.B. (2006). *CRS Report for Congress: The Changing Demographic Profile of the United States*, Washington, DC: The Library of Congress.

Storti, C. (1994). Cross-Cultural Dialogues. Yarmouth Maine: Intercultural Press.

Taylor, Orlando L., Ph.D. *Cross-Cultural Communication-Culture; Communication and Language*, Bethesda, MD: The Mid-Atlantic - Equity Consortium.

Diversity on the Web

Go to http://www.diversityinc.com and search for "Things Never to Say to American Indian Coworkers" (Article # 3621). After reading this list and the blog that follows it, what have you learned about communicating with Native Americans and about workplace communication? You will have to register to use this Web site, but if you use your ".edu" address. There is no charge and this is a very helpful workplace diversity Web site.

Gina Colavecchio is currently the Web Project Manager for Children's Hospital Boston, managing the hospital's external Web site, search engine marketing, and social media strategies and projects.

Changing Consumer Markets: The Business Case for Diversity

M. June Allard

Assumption College
Worcester State University, Professor Emerita

GOALS

- To increase awareness of the effects of population and demographic changes
- To present an overview of the marketplace of the future
- To explore the nature and trends of major minority markets

Changes in the population composition and demographics increasingly impact the need for businesses to market to growing diverse consumer markets. Forecasters predict that in less than 10 years, "The emerging marketplace [2020] will be very different than today, and filled with wide-ranging challenges" (Anderson in Nielsen, 2009).

THE MINORITY CONSUMER MARKET

As early as 1995, Bennett noted that minority market niches were "of sufficient size to be profitable while at the same time are of less interest to the major competitors" (p. 189). Today these minority niches are rapidly becoming major markets as their buying power (after-tax, disposable personal income) expands and their share of the U.S. market increases. Businesses need to understand these groups if they are to market to them effectively. The purchasing power of U.S. minority racial and ethnic groups is growing rapidly in dollar value and in market share. "As multicultural and female owned businesses gain more buying power and their lifestyles become more affluent, multicultural markets are growing in economic muscle" (DiversityBusiness.com, 2007).

Total U.S. buying power	$ 7.2 trillion	$ 13.1 trillion
Racial & ethnic buying power	$ 1.4 trillion	$ 3.4 trillion
U.S. Market Share	20.1%	26.0%
Year	**2000**	**2014** ....

Humphreys, J. (2009, July). The multicultural economy 2009.
Georgia Business and Economic Conditions, v. 64 no 3 Terry College of Business

The expanding multi-ethnic consumer pool combined with an "aging population, a declining birth rate, and growing ethnic diversity will change the face and the spending behavior of consumers in the U.S." To gain "share among population groups that most marketers do not reach today—older and ethnic consumers—will require shifts in focus, tactics, and products." (Anderson in Nielsen, 2009)

ASIAN AMERICANS

I am becoming convinced the Asian market in America is reaching the point of critical mass, where their economic clout in a number of urban markets is going to create great opportunities for businesses to pay attention to their needs (Humphreys in Dodson, 2007).

Asian Americans and Pacific Islanders (AAPI) comprise an astonishingly diverse workforce, representing more than a dozen and a half countries. "Their indigenous lands reach from the Himalayas to Hawaii and from the deserts of the Middle East to the tropics of the South Pacific. . . . encompassing "a vast array of cultural, religious, social and institutional entities." (The EEOC, 2008, Dec. 21).

Asian Americans originate from three broad regions:

Northeast Asians originate from countries such as China, Taiwan, Japan, Korea and Vietnam with linguistic and religious similarities. The Hmongs originate in the mountainous regions of southern China and adjacent areas of Vietnam, Laos and Thailand.

Southeast Asians come from countries such as the Philippines, Malaysia, Indonesia and Cambodia sharing a strong influence from the Portuguese, Spanish and/or French.

South Asians arrive from countries such as India, Pakistan and Bangladesh and are either Hindu or Muslim but share a strong British influence.

MAGAZINE PUBLISHERS OF AMERICA, 2008a

There is tremendous diversity within each region. For example, the ". . . Chinese represent only a little over a fourth of all Asian Americans and they share neither a common language nor culture with most of the other groups" (Hawkins and Mothersbaugh, 2010 p. 172). Although the nationality groups are distinct, many share the common values of hard work, education, collective effort and advancement (ibid. p. 174). Too, since so many are immigrants, they share the experiences of being physically distinct in a new culture. Most refer to themselves solely by their country of origin, such as Korean or Vietnamese; only the Japanese use a compound name, i.e., Japanese American (Tharp, 2000).

Asian American Profile

- Nearly two-thirds of Asian Americans are immigrants; only 36 percent were born in the U.S. (Asian-American Market Profile, n.d.).
- The majority of Japanese-Americans and Chinese Americans are U.S. born however, and many are third or fourth generation (Asian-American Market Profile, n.d.).
- Today the largest numbers of Asian Americans arrive from India (Asian-American Market Profile, n.d.)
- They are younger than the general U.S. population with a median age of 31.6 years; 28% are under age 18 (U.S. Census Bureau, 2007a).

- Asian Americans bring more languages to the United States than any other group, but they "often speak a fair degree of English before moving to the United States and adopt English at a rapid pace." Some 80 percent report they speak 'English very well'" (Asian-American Market Profile, n.d.).
- They have the highest income and the highest level of education of the minority markets (Hawkins and Mothersbaugh, 2010, p. 172).
- In 2003, 50 percent had a bachelor's degree or higher; the U.S. population averages 27 percent (Asian-American Market Profile, n.d.).
- Their yearly household income is higher than the U.S. average (nearly $9,000 higher), although their families tend to be larger (Asian-American Market Profile, n.d.).
- "Asian Americans are highly tech savvy and heavy users of the Internet." (DiversityBusiness.com, 2007).
- In 2008, 31 percent of Asian American consumers made five or more online purchases a year (Magazine Publishers of America, 2008a).

Asian Americans from India

- Asian-Americans from India number approximately 2.25 million, a population increasing rapidly through immigration (Hawkins & Mothersbough, 2010, p. 177).
- Indians are the fastest growing Asian segment. Large numbers live in New York, California, New Jersey, Illinois and Texas.
- They are affluent, well educated and fluent in English, but maintain cultural ties to their Indian heritage. They represent dozens of languages and subcultures.
- They value education, are concerned with financial security and save at a much higher rate than the average American (Hawkins and Mothersbaugh, 2010, p. 178).
- "They do not have a throw-away mentality. They shop for value and look for quality and durability" (Hawkins and Mothersbaugh, 2010, p. 178).
- They are tuned into mass media and the Internet.
- Christmas isn't a big holiday for them, but Diwali (in late October) is.

Asian American Market Segments

The **Traditionalists** are older, tend to strongly identify with their original culture, use their native language as their primary language and show little concern with status.

The **Established** are older, conservative, well-educated professionals with substantial incomes, relatively weak identification with their native culture, less need or desire for native-language programming and will pay premium prices for high quality.

The **Living for the Moment** are younger with moderate identification with native culture, tending to be bilingual, spontaneous, materialistic, given to impulse shopping and concerned with status and quality.

(Market Segment Research, 1993)

There is an influx of Mandarin-speaking Chinese causing a gradual shift from Cantonese to Mandarin in Chinese communications (Hawkins and Mothersbaugh, 2010). Geographic concentration and preferences of at least some segments means they can be reached through native-language media. "One estimate is that 80 percent of Asian Americans can be reached with 'in-language' promotions. The percentage who prefer to use 'in-language' is high" (Hawkins & Mothersbough, 2010, p. 172).

Asian American Consumer Market

It is estimated that the entire U.S. Asian population will number 12,635,000 adults in 2014 and will grow to 41 million in 2050, nearly tripling in size. The nation's white non-Hispanic population is expected to only grow only seven percent in this time (Gonzales, 2006).

Projections of future Asian-American buying power vary. There is limited market research on Asian Americans, especially by country of origin (Asian-American Market Profile, n.d.). Although the Asian share of the market is small, it is expected to more than double in just four years. Asian buying power has the second fastest rate of growth, behind Hispanic buying power" (Dodson, 2007).

Asian buying power	$ 268.7 billion	$ 696.5 billion
Market Share	3.7%	5.3%
Year	2000	2014...............

Humphreys, J. (2009) The multicultural economy 2009. Georgia Business and Economic Conditions, v. 64 no 3 Terry College of Business

Asian American Trends

- "The Asian population, and therefore its spending, is more concentrated geographically than other racial markets." Heaviest concentrations are in California, New York, New Jersey, Texas and Hawaii (Dodson, 2007). California alone accounts for over one-third of the Asian American population (Asian-American Market Profile, n.d.). The trend toward concentration in these geographic areas is increasing (Hawkins & Mothersbough, 2010).
- English-language media with Asian American content targets the second generation Asians who blend language and culture (Hawkins & Mothersbough, 2010).
- They are more likely to buy a new car rather than a used one and more likely to own a luxury car rather than a non-luxury one (Asian-American Market Profile, n.d.).
- Compared to the general U.S. population, they spend a significant amount per month on apparel (Asian-American Market Profile, n.d.).

BLACK/AFRICAN AMERICANS

The U.S. Census Bureau uses "black" and "African American" interchangeably. They consider the U.S. African-American population to include

> U.S.-born people whose families have been [in the U.S.] for more than 300 years, persons of Caribbean descent and recent immigrants from Africa. This includes "persons who indicate their race as 'black' or report themselves as African-American, Afro-American, Black Puerto Rican, Jamaican, Nigerian, West Indian or Haitian" on the U.S. Census (SIFMA, n.d.).

Note that "People of color" defines a broader group than either "African-American" or "Black," referring to anyone who is not Caucasian. (Magazine Publishers of America, 2008b).

Studies indicate that most Black/African-Americans "want to be viewed as heterogeneous rather than homogeneous, both culturally and racially." Two thirds say that ethnic identity is more important than national identity; they are "Black" first and "American" second (Magazine Publishers of America, 2008b).

Black/African American Profile

- "Overall median household income is increasing 60 percent faster than that of white households" (African American Readership Magazine, 2002).
- In 1997 there were 259,000 African American households with $100,000+ incomes" (African American Readership Magazine, 2002).
- Geographically, African Americans are not as concentrated as are the Asians, but they "drive the market in many U.S. cities." Forty percent live in 10 U.S. cities. Regionally, they are still in Northern urban centers and in the South (Magazine Publishers of America, 2008b).
- Their internet usage has grown tremendously. An estimated 62 percent of adults are online and for college graduates the figure rises to 93 percent. They have heavy media consumption, especially TV and magazine usage. (African American Readership Magazine, 2002; Magazine Publishers of America, 2008b).
- "Education, income and purchasing power have risen dramatically over the past several decades, trends that are expected to continue (Burns, 2005).

Black/African American Market Segments

The **Contented** are "mature and content with life, followers, not leaders, not status-conscious."

The **Upwardly Mobile** are "active, status-conscious professionals, financially secure, optimistic about the future."

The **Living for the Moment** are "young, socially active, carefree, and image conscious."

The **Living Day To Day** have low education and income, are price conscious and pessimistic about the future.

(Minority Segment Research, 1993)

Black/African American Consumer Market

In 2014, the U.S. Black African American population is projected to be 30,655,000 adults. African-Americans continue to increase their spending in proportion to their rising incomes and although "the African-American population isn't as large as the U.S. Hispanic market, . . . the disposable personal income of both groups is projected to increase at similar rates" (Progressive Grocer, 2010).

Black buying power	$ 590.2 billion	$ 1,136.8 billion
Market share	8.2%	8.7%
Year	2000	2014 ....

Humphries, J. (2009 July). The multicultural economy 2009.
Georgia Business and Economic Conditions, v. 64 no 3 Terry College of Business

In fact, more than 60 percent say this [whether companies show their understanding and respect for the Black/African American culture in their communications, marketing programs and sponsorships] will influence their choice when selecting companies with which to do business. (African American Readership Magazines, 2002)

Black/African American Trends

- "African Americans . . . are outpacing the general market by over 300 percent, in four critical measures of success: mortgage originations, median household income, small business ownership and obtaining degrees in higher education."
- "Building relationships within the African-American community is important not only to generate business, but to maintain loyalty. Relationship-building channels include event marketing and community-based programs. Successful companies . . . clearly show their understanding and respect for this community. . . ." (African American Readership Magazine, 2002).
- "This segment is fiercely loyal once a service provider is selected, and they remain loyal. . . ." (African American Readership Magazine, 2002).
- **Market leaders** tend to be brand loyal and not price sensitive. They see brands as communicating their style (Hawkins & Mothersbough, 2010, p. 161).
- **Market followers** tend to follow trends rather than lead the way. They often have "financial constraints that make them more conservative, more price sensitive and less brand loyal" (Hawkins & Mothersbough, 2010, p. 161).
- They make great use of mass media and report more influence by mass media than do whites (Hawkins & Mothersbough, 2010, p. 162). They prefer mass media specifically targeted to black culture.
- "African American consumers want to see themselves in advertisements. They want to know they are being invited to select a product or service" (African American Readership Magazine, 2002).
- They use shopping as a form of recreation more than whites (Floyd & Shinew, 1999; Packaged Facts, 2008). They are drawn to stores that employ black people, treat all people well and carry ethnic products.
- Research shows that considerably more African Americans than Caucasians will pay more for the best (African American Readership Magazine, 2002).
- African Americans now have greater reliance on banks, real estate and whole-life insurance. "Diversity within the company that manages their investments is of paramount importance to this population" (African American Readership Magazine, 2002).

HISPANIC/LATINO AMERICANS

> We are literally the economic backbone of this country . . . If you want your company to grow, you better market to Latinos or you're missing the boat (Cartagena, 2008).

Hispanics are categorized by the U.S. Census as an *ethnic* (rather than racial) minority. "The Bureau of the Census defines Hispanic as a person of Cuban, Mexican, Puerto Rican, South or Central American, of other Spanish culture or origin regardless of race." (Hawkins and Mothersbaugh, 2010, p. 165). In 2010, they constituted the largest and fastest growing minority group in the United States.

As might be expected, most U.S. Hispanics originate from Mexico, Central and South America, Puerto Rico, Cuba, and Domenica. Like the other ethnic groups, they are diverse. Most can be categorized into three distinct subcultures: Mexican Americans, Puerto Ricans and other Latinos mainly from Central and South America. Each group tends to live in distinct regions of the U.S., speaks a slightly different version of Spanish and has somewhat different values:

Mexican Americans comprise about 64 percent of this population. They are found primarily in the southwest and in California.

Puerto Ricans make up about 10 percent of this group. They are Mainly found in New York and New Jersey.

Cubans, together with the other Latinos are about 26 percent of Hispanic/Latino Americans. The Cubans are concentrated in Florida.

The remaining Latinos are found in California, in New York & Florida.

(U.S. CENSUS BUREAU, 2007b, p. 2)

Hispanic/Latino American Profile

- Hispanics of Cuban descent tend to have higher incomes than those of Mexican or Puerto Rican descent (Hawkins and Mothersbaugh, 2010, p. 165).
- With over 40 percent of the growth of this population due to immigration, **acculturation** ("degree to which an immigrant has adapted to his or her new culture") is very important (Ortiz, 2005; Penaloza, 1994, pp. 32–54).
- Most adults identify with the Hispanic culture (Berman, 2002).
- Hispanic teens are bicultural. This group is expanding faster than other U.S. teen groups. (*Nuesto Futuro*, 2006).
- The Hispanic/Latino culture is a masculine one (Webster, 1994)
- Sports are important, especially boxing, baseball and soccer (Hawkins and Mothersbaugh, 2010, p. 167).
- The Spanish language is very important with 69 percent of the households speaking primarily Spanish at home.
- They are young with 33 percent under 18 years and 50 percent under 34 years.
- They are slower than the general population to use the Internet—that is changing—especially for more acculturated English-language Hispanics (Latinos Online, 2007).

Hispanic/Latino American Market Segments

The **First-generation Adults**, 63 percent of this group, were born outside U.S. They have the lowest income and education. They are family-oriented and maintain extended family ties. Most often they speak Spanish as their primary language and they are most likely to possess traditional values.

The **Second-generation Adults**, 19 percent of the group, were born in U.S. of immigrant parents. They have higher incomes and education than the first-generation and are more likely to identify as American. They are equally split between bilingualism and English as their primary language. They are less likely to ascribe to traditional values than the previous generation.

The **Third-generation Adults**, 17 percent of this population, were born in U.S. to U.S-born parents. They have the highest education and income. They are the most likely to identify as American (57 percent) and most likely to have English as their primary language.

PEW HISPANIC CENTER/KAISER FAMILY FOUNDATION (2004)

Hispanic/Latino American Consumer Market

In 2010, the Hispanic/Latino population in the U.S. numbered over 50 million, a figure expected to rise to over 102 million by 2050 (U.S. Census Bureau, 2007). In 2014, the U.S. Hispanic/Latino population is projected to exceed 37,246,000 adults.

Hispanics control more disposable personal income than any other U.S. minority group. In 2007, the Hispanic market in the United States, like the African American market, is about the same size as Mexico's entire economy (Dodson, 2007).

Hispanic/Latino buying power	$ 489.4 billion	$ 1.3 trillion
Market Share	6.8%	10.2%
Year ....2000............................. 2014..................

Humphreys, J., (2009, July). The multicultural economy 2009
Georgia Business and Economic Conditions, v. 4 no. 2 Terry College of Business

Hispanic/Latino Trends

- Hispanics/Latinos often prefer Spanish media and most respond best to Spanish advertising (Hawkins & Mothersbough, 2010, pp 167, 169).
- A youth trend is emerging that spends more time using English-language media (*Nuesto Futuro*, 2006).
- "Price is important, but so too is the availability of high-quality national brands. Hispanics tend to be less receptive than the general market to store brands" (Packaged Facts, 2003).
- They tend to be highly brand-loyal, particularly to products adapted to their culture and needs (ibid.)
- Marketing messages must take into account this culture's unique appeals and symbols (just translation doesn't work).
- More and more specialty products are being developed for this market (Hawkins & Mothersbough, 2010, p. 171).
- Hispanics will "make up 40 percent of new home buyers over the next 20 years, opening business and marketing opportunities for banks, home furnishing stores and other companies catering to home ownership" (McLoone, 2008).
- "While Hispanic communities in the United States have traditionally been located in ... California, New York and Texas, there is explosive growth in Raleigh and Greensboro, N.C. and Atlanta, Georgia. Virginia and Delaware are also high-growth states" (McLoone, 2008).

NATIVE AMERICANS

"There are approximately 550 native American tribes, each with its own language and traditions." The tribes are regionally concentrated. Native Americans ". . . generally have limited incomes, but this varies widely by tribe." Larger tribes have their own newspapers and radio stations. Native Americans take increasing pride in their heritage and "are less tolerant of inaccurate stereotypes."

Native American Consumer Market and Trends

Estimates of this population range from 2.8 to 4.1 million depending upon whether individuals belong to only one tribe or are multicultural. The overall buying power of this group is estimated at $391 billion in 2000 (0.5 percent of the market) and is expected to grow to $82.7 billion (0.6 percent of the market) in 2014. (Humphries, 2009)

MATURE AMERICANS

"This is not a market that businesses should turn away from their doors" (U. S. Department of Justice Civil Rights Division, 2006).

Age crosses all ethnic, cultural, gender, sexual orientation, social class, religion, political and economic categories. By 2014, U.S. seniors are expected to number 83,345,000 adults over age 55 (Toosi, 2005) and by 2050, the population 65 years and older will more than double, rising . . . to 89 million" (U.S. Census, 2008).

Mature American Profile

- "Age carries with it culturally-defined behavioral and attitudinal norms" (Alreck, 2000; Henry, 2000).
- ". . . age influences the consumption of products ranging from beer to toilet paper to vacations" (ibid.).
- Age shapes the media that people use, where they shop, how they use products and how they think and feel about marketing activities (ibid.).
- Seniors are better educated than is popularly believed. Thirty-one percent of Americans who are 65 years and older, hold a bachelor's degree or higher (U.S. Bureau of Labor Statistics, 2008).
- "They are more careful about who they do business with, and they want to know more about you before doing business with you" (Seniormag.com, 2010).
- Seniors 55 years and older households are the fastest growing internet user market segment, spending $7 billion online annually (ibid.).
- An average retired senior who is online, spends more time online than an average teen-ager (ibid.).
- The graying of the workforce is expected to continue (U.S. Bureau of Labor Statistics, 2008).

Mature American Market Segments

Four segments have been described within the senior market. Surprisingly, age itself is not the major distinguishing factor among the segments.

The **Healthy Indulgers** are the most common and "will be increasingly composed of baby boomers as they age." This segment likes "activities, convenience, personal services and high-tech home appliances." They also like cruises and group travel.

The **Ailing Outgoers** are those with health problems. They are a key market for retirement communities and assisted-living housing. "Value-pricing and discounts are viewed positively as are ease and convenience."

The **Healthy Hermits** are healthy, but withdrawn. They "prefer clothing styles that are popular with other seniors." They "will pay a premium for well-known brands" and constitute an "important part of the do-it-yourself market."

The **Frail Recluses** tend to stay at home. They are a market for home and lawn care services and a major market for health-care products, home exercise and health testing equipment and emergency response systems.

(HAWKINS & MOTHERSBOUGH, 2010, pp. 126–127).

Mature American Consumer Market

This is a market to watch; the senior population is growing. Mature Americans make up a larger market than African-Americans and Hispanic markets combined and "control more than 70% of the disposable income. . . . One-third of the nation controls two-thirds of the spending capital (seniormag.com). Seniors have per capita incomes 25 percent higher than the national average (ibid.). "Seniors usually need and want the same things [as younger groups], just in different quantities and with different priorities. The most important difference is the message and the venue" (ibid.).

Mature American Trends

- "Proper age positioning is critical for many products" (Hawkins & Mothersbough, 2010, p. 122).
- Seniors are the most brand loyal age group (seniormag.com).
- Seniors account for 80 percent of all luxury travel and 74 percent of all prescription drugs (ibid.).

LGBT AMERICANS (THE GAY MARKET)

The self-identified LGBT (lesbian, gay, bisexual and transgender) adult population, 18 years and older, was estimated to be between 15 and 16 million in 2008. This community is comprised of many sub-groups identified by names such as the leather community, the bear community, the chubby community, the lesbian community, the bisexual community, the transgendered community, the drag community, the rave community and so on (http://lgbt.wikia.com/wiki/community).

LGBT American Profile

- This community varies in ethnicity, occupation, age and geographic region. These factors are often more important in the consumption process than sexual orientation (Greenspan 2003, July 30).
- They tend to be more tech-savvy and on-line than the general population and to spend more hours online (Chaplin, 1999).
- A large number of gay print media exists and numerous gay web sites have emerged (Hawkins & Mothersbough, 2010 p. 99).
- "It has been estimated that roughly half of the gay community rarely or never reads gay-oriented publications and spends considerable time using standard media" (Packaged Facts, 2007).

LGBT Consumer Market

The "size of gay market is estimated to be about 7 percent of the adult U.S. population, or 15.3 million people over the age of 18" (Brier, 2004).

LGBT buying power	$732 billion	$743 billion	$835 billion	$1 trillion
Year..........................	2009................	2010................	2011...............	2012................

(Packaged Facts and Witeck-Combs, 2010)

LGBT American Trends

- "A recent survey found that 82 percent of gay consumers are more likely to buy from companies they know are gay-friendly (Vence, 2004). (The CEI Index measures the gay-friendliness of companies and is discussed in "The Diversity Awards, What Do They Mean?" article in this text.)
- Gay consumers are extremely loyal to brands. "We're very, very loyal to LGBT-friendly brands and companies, because of the discrimination our community has faced." "We actively seek out those companies that cater to us" (Gricel Ocasio, quoted in J. Stevenson, 2007).
- Most products don't need modification for this market niche (Packaged Facts, 2007).
- Some of the areas that do need modification are TV content, bridal registries and financial services such as estate planning (ibid.).
- ". . . in addition to advertising in gay media, support of gay community events such as Gay Pride week is another important avenue firms use in approaching this market" (Hawkins & Mothersbough, 2010, p. 101).
- TV content (news, concerns, programs and movies) of specific interest to LGBT audiences is increasing (Hawkins & Mothersbough, 2010, p. 99).
- Firms are creating more and more ads targeting the gay market (Gay Press Report, 2004).
- Seventy percent of gay men and women report switching products or service providers when they learned the company had engaged in actions perceived as harmful to the gay and lesbian community. Over one-third had done so in the last two years (Packaged Facts, 2007).

AMERICANS WITH DISABILITIES

According to the Bureau of Labor Statistics,

> A person with a disability has at least one of the following conditions: is deaf or has serious difficulty hearing; is blind or has serious difficulty seeing even when wearing glasses; has serious difficulty concentrating, remembering or making decisions because of a physical, mental or emotional condition; has serious difficulty walking or climbing stairs; has difficulty dressing or bathing; or has difficulty doing errands alone such as visiting a doctor's office or shopping because of a physical, mental, or emotional condition." Americans with disability come from all backgrounds, cultures and ages [ethnicity, race, gender, age]. (2010, March)

	Adults with Disabilities	Adults without Disabilities
Workforce	5,930,000	147,936.000
Participation rate, May 2010	22.3%	70.1%

Americans with Disabilities: Profile

- "Of the nearly 70 million families in the United States, more than 20 million families (28.6 percent) have at least one member with a disability." (Cheng, 2002).
- Approximately "8.3% of U.S. children and teenagers—5.2 million, have a physical or mental disability. This reflects a sharp growth in the population of young Americans with disabilities over the past decade" (Witeck & Combs, n.d.).
- The top five cities where people with disabilities live are Detroit, Baltimore, Miami, Newark and Buffalo (Solutions Marketing Group, 2010).

Americans with Disabilities: Consumer Market

The aggregate income of people with disabilities tops $1 trillion. People with disabilities have $220 billion in discretionary spending power" (Blum, 2007). "The disability market controls more than twice the discretionary spending of the estimated $67 billion teen market," but receives far less attention (Blum, 2007).

In the ODEP's newsletter, Business Sense, of May 2009, the *A positive strategy for expanding market share* article states that people with disabilities, their families, friends and loved ones spend up to U.S. $1 trillion each year.

> http://www.accessibilitynet.nz/blog/disabilities-and-purchasing-power
> disabilities and purchasing power May 13, 2009

Americans with Disabilities: Trends

- "Individuals with disabilities exhibit strong brand loyalty toward products affiliated with disability-related causes. In order to tap into this brand loyalty, there must be a logical relationship between the company, its values, customer, community, employees and the cause" (Witeck & Combs, n.d.).
- People with disabilities travel. In 1995, they spent $81.7 billion on travel and this did not include the travel of family, friends and escorts (Solutions Marketing Group, 2010).
- ". . . implementing the access provision of the ADA has increased revenues in the hotel and hospitality industry by 12 percent" (ibid.).
- "Of the 54 million people limited in their activities due to long-term disability . . . 58% own their own homes and 48% are principal shoppers" (ibid.).
- Four out of 10 people with disabilities now conduct business and personal activities online, spending an average of 20 hours per week logged on to the Internet (ibid.).

AMERICAN WOMEN

Women currently comprise 51.4 percent of the U.S. population. They span all races, all ages, all cultures, all socioeconomic levels, and all backgrounds. By 2014, the female adult population is forecast to number 127,232,000. At that time, 59.7% will participate in the workforce (Toosi, 2005).

"When African-American Michelle Obama became the First Lady and Latina Sonia Sotomayer became a U.S. Supreme Court Justice in 2009, they became icons for an 'emerging wave of increasingly empowered multicultural women'" (Global Information, Ind, 2009). "Multicultural women comprise nearly a third of the women's population in 2010 and will be in the majority in "a little more than 30 years."

American Women: Profile

- Gender roles have undergone radical changes and are still evolving (Hawkins & Mothersbough, 2010, p. 107).
- There is less masculine orientation than in the past (ibid.).
- "One out of every 11 American women owns a business" and they are starting their own businesses at twice the rate of men" (Girlpower, n.d.).
- Women work more hours outside of home than in the past (Hawkins & Mothersbough, 2010, p. 107).
- Women feel pressured for time (ibid.).

American Women: Market Segments

The **Traditional Housewife** is generally married and is home and family-centered. "She seeks satisfaction from household and family maintenance as well as volunteers activities." She is generally satisfied.

The **Trapped Housewife** is generally married, but does not enjoy household chores. She would prefer to work, but stays at home because of young children, family pressure or lack of outside opportunities.

The **Trapped Working Woman** may be either married or single. She "works because of economic necessity or social or family pressure," but takes no satisfaction from employment. She is likely to enjoy household activities. She is frustrated by lack of time.

The **Career Working Woman** may be married or single. She prefers to work and derives satisfaction from employment. She is generally content; but feels pressed for time.

Women have a variety of role options and a range of attitudes concerning their gender roles. Note that women do not necessarily remain in any one segment; they may change segments several times.

(HAWKINS & MOTHERSBOUGH, 2010, pp. 103–104, 107)

American Women: Consumer Markets

"American women spend about $5 trillion annually . . . over half the GNP" (Girlpower, n.d.; PME Enterprises, n.d.). Women control more then 60 percent of all personal wealth in the U.S. and "account for 85 percent of all consumer purchases including everything from autos to healthcare" and they represent the majority of the online market (ibid.).

Black, Hispanic, Asian-American and other multicultural women already wield buying power in excess of one $1 trillion and are the primary decision-makers in the vast majority of their homes." (Global Information, Ind, 2009)

American Women: Trends

- Genders "respond differently to various communication elements For example, women respond to 'help others', while men respond to 'self-help'" (Brunel and Nelson, 2000).
- "Women do not respond to a marketing campaign that has simply been feminized with clichéd colors and topics (Girlpower, n.d.).
- Genders are similar in "readership of news magazines, but their top magazine category preferences vary dramatically" (Hawkins & Mothersbough, 2010, p. 105).
- About half of all business travelers are women.
- Some products are losing traditional gender stereotyping as women are increasingly shopping for traditionally masculine products such as lawn mowers, power tools, guns, cars, computer games and equipment (Hawkins & Mothersbough, 2010, pp. 104, 106).
- More and more time-saving products are recommended for the women's market (ibid.).
- Women and men alike, place high value on environment, i.e., on green marketing (Hawkins & Mothersbough, 2010).
- "Minority communities represent the most potent potential market force in the American economy" (Harrington & Yago, n.d.).

- To market to these communities requires effective communication and "effective communication is more than simply translating ad copy. It also requires adopting and infusing ads with cultural symbols and meanings relevant" to each diverse segment. (Hawkins & Mothersbough, 2010)

DISCUSSION QUESTIONS

1. Which of the diverse consumer markets mentioned in this article has the best future potential for sales of: a) sports cars, b) new technology c) energy drinks? Why?

2. Make a business case for diversity argument for translating your company's Web site into a foreign language if you are selling a) life insurance b) designer shoes c) computer technology services. In your answer be sure to select a specific language that matches the consumer demand for each product.

3. How could individualism and collectivism impact consumer buying decisions?

4. What marketing opportunities do consumers in the baby boomer age cohort present?

5. Besides income, how does social class impact buying decisions for products and services?

6. How might ignorance and stereotypes about Hispanic/Latino Americans impact marketing efforts targeted to this population?

Bibliography

African American readership magazine. (2002). The African-American market. www.sifma.org/services/hrdiversity/pdf/African.pdf (Type entire address in search box, rather than on url line).

Alreck, P (2000, October). Consumer age role norms. *Psychology and marketing.* pp. 891–909.

Anderson, D. (2009) quoted in Nielsen. *Below the topline: The United States in 2020, a very different place.* http://en-us.nielsen.com/main/insights/consumer_insight/July_2009

Asian-American market profile. www.magazine.org/content/files/market_profile-asian.pdf

Bennett, P. (1995). *Dictionary of marketing terms.* 2nd ed. American Marketing Association and Lincolnwood, IL: NTC Books.

Berman, G. (2002) Portrait of the new America. *Market segment group.* Coral Gables, FL. p. 21.

Blum, S. (2007, June/July). Overlooked opportunities: people with disabilities. Retrieved May 4, 2011 from http://www.dynamicgraphics.com/dgm/article/28791

Brier, N. (2004 November). Coming of age. *American demographics.* pp. 16–19.

Brunel, F. & Nelson, M. (2000, Fall). Explaining gender responses to "help-self" and "help-others" charity ad appeals. *J. Advertising.* pp. 15–28.

Burns, E. (2005, October 10). African American online population is growing. *The ClickZ Network*. www.clickz.com and AOL: Some 80 percent of African Americans online. *MarketingVOX* (2005, October 17). www.marketingvox.com (2008, June 7).

Cartagena, C. (2008). Quoted in McLoone, S. (2008).

Chaplin, D. (1999, April). The truth hurts. *American demographics.* pp. 68–69.

Cheng, K. (2002, April 18). What marketers should know about people with disabilities. *Solutions marketing group.* http://www.disability.marketing/com/newsroom/diversityInc.php4

DiversityBusiness.com (2007, March 7). Annual Asian American consumer behavior study reveals key findings in retail, automobile, insurance and telecom industries. www.diversitybusiness.com

Dodson, D. (2007, July 31). Minority groups' share of $10 trillion U.S. consumer market is growing steadily, according to annual buying power study from Terry College's Selig Center for Economic Growth. Retrieved on May 6, 2011 from http://www.terry.uga.edu/news/releases/2007/minority_buying_power_report.html

Floyd, M. & Shinew, K. Convergence in leisure styles and whites and African Americans. *J. leisure research* 3, no 4 pp. 359–384. See also, *Packaged Facts.* (2008). The African-American market in the U.S.

Gay Press Report. (2004).

Girlpower. (n.d.). www.girlpowermarketing.com

Global Information, Ind. (2009). U.S. market for multi-cultural women: New African-American, Latino and Asian-American women are driving change in the American consumer economy. 2nd ed.

Gonzales, O. (2006, first quarter). Capturing ethnic markets in the U.S. *CIPS Network, National Association of Realtors®*

Greenspan, R. (2003, July 30) Advertisers may find gay dollars online www.clickz.com

Harrington, M. & Yago, G. (n.d.). Mainstreaming minority business: Financing domestic emerging markets. www.milkeninstitute.org/pdf/mainstreaming.pdf

Hawkins, D. & Mothersbough, D. (2010). *Consumer behavior, building strategy.* McGraw-Hill/*Irwin.* New York.

Henry, P. (2000, May). Modes of thought that vary systematically with both social class and age. *Psychology and Marketing* pp. 421–440.

Humphries, J. (2009, July). The multicultural economy 2009. www.terry.uga.edu/selig. Click on Publications; then click on the multicultural economy; then click on Executive Summary.

Pew internet & American Life Project. (2007, March 14). Latinos online. Wash, DC. www.pewinternet.org search: Latinos Online, 2007; click March 14 report.

Magazine Publishers of America. (2008a). Asian-American market profile. www.magazine.org/content/files/market_profile_asian.pdf

Magazine Publishers of America. (2008b). African-American/Black Market Profile. www.magazine.org

Market segment research. (1993). The 1993 minority market report. Coral Gables, FL.

Marketing to Seniors retrieved on May 6, 2011 from http://www.seniormag.com/business/marketing toseniors.htm

McLoone, S. (2008, June 27). Booming Hispanic market opens business opportunities. Type entire title of article in search engine and click on https://bx.businessweek.com

Nuesto Futuro. (2006). Cheske N. Redwood Shores, CA p. 24.

Minority Segment Research. Minority market report (1993, April 21). Retrieved May 5, 2011 from http://www.highbeam.com/doc/1G1-13141371.html

Ortiz, W. (2005, May 9). Answering the language question. *Cable television advertising bureau,* press release. www.onetvworld.org

Packaged Facts. (2010, July 1). The gay and lesbian market in the U.S.: Trends and opportunities in the LGBT community, 6th ed. www.packagedfacts.com Search: The gay and lesbian market.

Packaged Facts. (2007, February). The gay and lesbian market in the U.S. 4th ed. www.packagedfacts.com Search: The gay and lesbian market

Packaged Facts (2003, October). The U.S. Hispanic market. 6th ed. New York. www.packaged-facts.com Search: The U.S. Hispanic market

Pew Hispanic Center/Kaiser Family Foundation. (2004, March). Generation differences. Wash. DC www.pewhispanic.org

PME Enterprises LLC, 216 Main Street, Hartford, CT).

Penaloza, L. (1994, June). *Atravesando fronteras*/Border crossings. *J. Consumer Research,* pp. 32–54.

Progressive Grocer. (2010). www.progressivegrocer.com

SeniorJournal.com. (2009, June 24). Senior citizen population on brink of explosion in world and in United States: Census Bureau. www.seniorjournal.com. Search: "June 24, 2009 senior citizen population on brink"

SIFMA. (n.d.). The African-American market. www.sifma.org/services/hrdiversity/pdf/African.pdf (Type entire address in search box, rather than on url line).

Solutions Marketing Group. (2010, March 2) *Disability facts* http://www.disability-marketing.com/facts

Stevenson, J. (2007, July 9). Equal shares. As business owners and consumers, the LGBT community gains strength. *Business west Online.* www.businesswest.com. Search: Jaclyn Stevenson Equal Shares.

Target Market News (2010, November 26). Power of Black America.

Tharp, M. (2000). Marketing and consumer identity in multicultural America. Sage: Thousand Oaks, CA p. 259.

Toosi, M. (2005). Retrieved on May 5, 2011 from usgovinfo.about.com/b/2007/0105growth-of-us-labor-force-just-keeps-dropping.htm (search growth of labor force 2005).

U.S. Bureau of Labor Statistics. (July, 2008). www.bls.gov/spotlight/2008/older_workers. www.seniorjournal.com

U.S. Census Bureau. (2007a). Annual estimates of the resident population by race, age and sex for the United States: April 1, 2000 to July l, 2006. Wash. DC.

U.S. Census Bureau. (2007b). The American Community—Hispanics, 2004. Wash. DC.

U. S. Census (2008). Retrieved May 5, 2011 from http://quickfacts.census.gov/qfd/states/0000. html (click on U.S.A.) (no www in this URL)

U.S EEOC. (2008, December 21). Asian American and Pacific Islander work group report to the chair of the equal employment commission. p. 14. http://www.eeoc.gov/federal/reportsaapi.html

Vence, D. (2004, September l). Pride power. *Marketing news.* pp. 1, 13.

Webster, C. (1994) The effects of Hispanic identification on marital roles in the purchase decision process. *J. Consensus research.* pp. 319–331.

Witeck, B. Combs, W. (n.d.) Disability Factoids. Retrieved on May 6, 2011 from http://www.diversityinc/content/1757/article/4536/? Disability_Factoids

Diversity on the Web

In June 2010, The Coca-Cola Company launched a "first-ever, fully-integrated marketing campaign created exclusively for U.S. Hispanic consumer(s)" called POWERADE Latino. This Spanish-language advertising campaign was timed to coincide with the 2010 World Cup in South Africa. Visit the Web sites below and evaluate this campaign in terms of what you now know about this Hispanic/Latino community.

Sources:

http://www.us.powerade.com
http://www.arrobanews.com/powerade
Witeck & Combs Communications. (n.d). http://www.witeckcombs.com
http://www.terry.uga.edu/selig click on Publications; then click on the Multicultural Economy; then click on Executive Summary

Points of Law: The Bar Exam

M. June Allard
Assumption College
Worcester State University, Professor Emerita

GOALS

- To assess knowledge of basic discrimination laws and regulations
- To promote discussion and application of discrimination laws and regulations

There is an enormous amount of litigation arising from diversity issues. It is a complex area as there are federal, state and local laws pertaining to discrimination as well as case law. It is important for managers to have some knowledge of the areas to which these laws apply and to understand that the laws themselves frequently change and are subject to (court) interpretation.

THE BAR EXAM QUESTIONS

1. You are the manager in a Canadian branch of an American company. What employment discrimination laws must you follow?

2. You are an employer or manager in a small company of 60 employees. When employees adopt children, do you have to provide adoption leave?

3. As a manager in a retail store, you are concerned about the appearance of employees who meet customers. Can you impose a dress/appearance code, i.e., require that employees not wear nose rings, not have visible tattoos, etc.?

4. Are you required to provide benefits such as health insurance for same-sex partners of your employees?

5. Faced with a bad economy, you are forced to lay off a substantial number of workers. To avoid being accused of age discrimination, what must you ensure?

6. Your local labor pool contains a large number of immigrants. If you hire people living in the U.S. illegally, what may happen?

7. As part of your company's health program, you would like to have the name of each employee's doctor and a list of medications taken in case of a personal or workplace emergency. Can you require employees to provide this information?

8. Your Vice President is pregnant. Are you required to provide maternity leave and benefits for her?

9. You want to hire some teenagers to work at your company. Is there a limit on how many hours they can work?

10. You are the manager of a non profit organization employing 100 people. After demoting one of your 55 year old employees for excessive absences, she files a claim citing age bias. What do you have to prove and what does she have to prove?

11. Your employee of five years began exhibiting bizarre behavior on the job last year. It was discovered that he was using drugs illegally. At that time he claimed he would stop using them and his behavior returned to normal until a few weeks ago when he began acting strangely again. Can you insist he be tested for drugs?

12. Your employee in the previous question insists that he has a disability and the drugs are a necessary accommodation under the Americans with Disability Act. Must you agree to allow this, i.e., is this employee protected under ADA?

13. If your employee is an alcoholic, is she considered to be a person with a disability and therefore protected by the ADA?

14. A woman applying for a job requiring foreign language translation skills has a qualifying disability. Another applicant without a disability has better foreign language skills, however. Must you hire the woman with the disability?

15. An applicant has a child with a disability. Your company is extremely busy and you are convinced that the applicant will need to take much time off caring for this child. Can you refuse to hire this person for this reason?

16. If you do hire the parent in question 15, is this parent entitled to a reasonable accommodation?

17. In two weeks there will be an election and many of your employees expect to vote, does the law allow employees time off to vote?

18. If your employees do take time off to vote during work hours, must you pay them for this time?

THE UBS DIVERSITY CASE

Arlene O. DeWitt
Assumption College

GOALS

- To examine the relationship between corporate culture and gender discrimination
- To illustrate the costs of inadequate diversity management
- To demonstrate opportunities for marketing to diverse markets

Look out, Wall Street. The professional women of high finance are fighting back and attacking the entrenched male-dominated culture and glass ceilings that have long characterized this industry. Female professionals are going after the very thing that their financial firms value most—money—by winning sexual discrimination lawsuits. While many financial firms realized the marketing advantages of matching culturally diverse employees with global customers of similar ethnicities, these same firms failed to capitalize on the advantages that a well-managed and motivated professional female workforce offers to the marketplace.

A case in point was the lawsuit of Zubulake v. UBS Warburg LLC, the financial, investment and banking services company which resulted from the merger of the United Bank of Switzerland and Swiss Bank Corporation in 1998. In 2005, Laura Zubulake, a top-ranked equities trader sued UBS AG for gender discrimination, failure to promote her and for retaliation while working at her firm's offices in Stamford, CT and Manhattan from 1999 to 2000. She won this case and was awarded $29.27 million in damages: $2,241.90 million in back pay, $6,863 million in front pay and $20,169 million in punitive damages (LexisNexis, 2007, 9). This was one of the largest awards to a single plaintiff in a discrimination lawsuit.

> This sends a message not just to Wall Street, but to everybody. The message is that all senior women on Wall Street are not afraid to stand up and speak out when they feel they are being treated differently," says Ms. Zubulake (Porter, 2005). "It's not a culture that changes overnight," Zubulake continues. "It's going to take time. I'm sure there are lots of other firms out there saying, 'This can't happen to us. . . . You're going to see more and more of these cases'" (Zambito, 2006).

UBS HISTORY AND ORGANIZATIONAL CULTURE

UBS AG was formed from the 1998 merger of the Union Bank of Switzerland and the Swiss Bank Corporation (SBC). The resulting financial giant became the second largest bank in Europe, after Deutsche Bank AG, and one of the tenth largest financial institutions in the world. In 2000, UBS acquired the U.S. Paine Webber Group Inc. to become the world's largest wealth management

EXHIBIT 1   Gender Distribution by Employee Category[1]

	Male		Female		
	Number	Percent	Number	Percent	Total
Officers	25,590	77.9	7,241	22.1	**32,831**
Non-Officers	19,944	50.2	19,760	49.8	**39,704**
Total	45,534	62.8	27,001	37.2	**72,535**

[1]Calculated on the basis that a person (working full-time or part-time) is considered one headcount in this table only. This accounts for the total UBS end-2005 employee number of 72,535 in this table. Normally, UBS expresses employee numbers in terms of full-time equivalents (FTEs), which is measured as a percentage of the standard hours normally worked by permanent full-time staff. When calculated according to FTEs, the end-2005 total is 69,569 (UBS Workforce, 2010).

firm. Headquartered in Switzerland, the organization employs approximately 64,000 people in over 50 countries with 37% of its employees in the Americas, 37% in Switzerland, 16% in Europe and 10% in Asia Pacific (UBS, Who, 2010). UBS has a major presence in the U.S. located in New York City, Weehawken, NJ, and Stamford, Ct. The corporation is divided into three business units: Wealth Management, Global Asset Management and Investment Banking (UBS, 2010). The UBS brand of wealth and asset management and investment banking is valued at $4.4 billion, making it the 72nd most valuable brand in the world.

Current gender distribution by employee category is heavily male dominated, especially at its upper management levels, as shown in Exhibit 1.

It is significant to note that Simmons Associates, a highly respected international consulting firm focused on issues related to global diversity leadership and inclusion management, targets German executives for diversity and inclusion training because of this country's having a history of leading a homogeneous workforce while having a diverse external customer base. Simmons Associates states on their website:

> Companies whose focus in on the higher-end consumer, who is often older, white and male, face less pressure to diversify. Success comes from treating it like a business issue and holding people accountable. Companies focusing on the higher-end investor don't always have as strong a business case to push it because of the demographics (Diversity, 2010).

Tanya Hinton, president and chief executive officer of Diversified Search Services of Chicago, states: "You want to see people who look like you" (Trends, 2010).

DEMOGRAPHICS OF PROFESSIONAL WOMEN IN FINANCE DRIVE GENDER DIVERSITY LAWSUITS

Women held 37% of the jobs in the securities workforce in 2003 and racial minorities made up 18.3% of the securities industry workforce in 2003, according to *the Security Industry Association's (SIA) Report on Diversity Strategy, Development and Demographics.* Approximately 27% of the securities industry's executive management positions were held by women or minorities in 2003 and 15% of branch managers were either women or minorities. The proportion of women or minority managing directors rose from 17% to 20% (Trends, 2010).

Lance LaVergne, Vice President of Human Capital Management at Goldman Sachs and manager of the firm's U.S. diversity efforts, says:

> The focus on many diversity efforts is on gender, mainly because women are both a larger demographic and more evolved politically and organizationally than Blacks and Hispanics. There are more women in the organization than any other minority group. They have critical mass (Trends, 2010).

"A lot of different things are coming together," says Attorney Wayne N. Outten of Outten and Golden who represented female plaintiffs in sexual discrimination cases. "There's a large number of women going to business schools who are running into the glass ceiling. There will be others—more and more women are saying—I don't have to put up with this" (Porter, 2005).

A 2005 *Harvard Business Review* article reported that in a survey of 2,443 women, nearly four in ten highly qualified women left work voluntarily at some point in their careers; i.e., they were not forced out for any other reasons by their firms (Trends, 2010).

The financial industry is still and dominated by white males who fill the bulk of the most powerful and highest-paying jobs in the industry. EEOC data shows that: men make-up more than two-thirds of the officials and managers in the securities industry; white men fill four out of five executive management positions and comprise more than 70% of investment bankers, traders and brokers (McGeehan, 2004).

A 2010 study conducted by Catalyst Inc, a non-profit focused on workplace diversity, found that women occupy only 16.8% of executive officer positions and only 2.5% of chief executive officers position in financial companies. This is especially significant because the number of women who joined the industry in the 1970's and 80's and are now older (over age 55) has grown by 56% since 1999, outpacing a 34% increase in similar-aged men.

It is evident that longevity does not necessarily equate to advancement (Stock, 2010). Quite the contrary is true as seen in the class-action lawsuit filed in 2010 by five former managing directors and analysts who were laid off from Citigroup in November 2008. The women charge Citigroup with "recessionary discrimination" in denying women employees equal terms and conditions of employment that it provides to similarly situated and sometimes less qualified male employees, in their cut back of a tenth of their workforce in 2008 (Ali, 2010).

Since 2000, the number of young women between the ages of 20–35 working in the financial industry has dropped by 16.5% or 315,000, while the number of men in that age range increased by 7.3% or 93,000. Analysts suggest a variety of reasons for this decline: women bore the brunt of layoffs in the late 90's and recessions, technology and computers have replaced entry level and junior positions, more men are being hired for entry level and junior positions and women, in general, are not as attracted to jobs in the finance industry given recent volatility in the markets and scrutiny on compensation (Stock, 2010).

THE ZUBULAKE v. UBS WARBURG LLC CASE, 2005

Laura Zubulake was a top-ranked equities trader who sold Asian equities to institutional investors and earned about $650,000 per year. In her complaint against UBS, she said she was passed over for the job of manager of the Asian Equities Sales Desk in the U.S. and that the position was given to Matthew Chapin (Porter, 2005).

Ms. Zubulake, who was 40, said Mr. Chapin proceeded to undermine her by belittling her and ridiculing her in front of her co-workers, excluding her from some outings, making sexist remarks and denying her important accounts. She alleged that her boss singled her out for public verbal abuse about her age and looks and said that she was not attractive or young enough to handle her accounts. Zubulake's case was bolstered by a former UBS sales assistant's testimony that she heard Chapin call Zubulake "old and ugly" and that he made sexual insinuations about women at work (White, 2005).

Ms. Zubulake also alleged that her department, on two occasions, took her clients to adult entertainment clubs and excluded her from the outings (Boyd, 2005). She said her mistreatment extended to the repositioning of her desk in the Manhattan office across the aisle from the rest of her colleagues into the area of lower-level desk assistants (Porter, 2005).

A year later, in August 2001, Ms. Zubulake filed a complaint with the Equal Employment Opportunity Commission, and in October of that year, Mr. Chapin sent her a letter stating her employment was terminated. Ms. Zubulake then sued UBS for gender discrimination, failure to promote and retaliation (Porter, 2005).

Her lawyer, James Hubbard of Liddle and Robinson, said the three-year lawsuit was a routine gender-discrimination case with a lot of he-said, she-said and circumstantial evidence to prove Ms. Zubulake's claims. Evidence of co-workers' trips with clients to strip clubs was admitted into court proceedings because women might not want to attend such outings and Ms. Zubulake alleged discriminatory treatment that included purposeful exclusion from client outings (LexisNexis, 2009).

In addition, plaintiff Zubulake was allowed to introduce evidence of alleged acts of discrimination directed at a sales associate, Peggy Yeh, by Mr. Chapin. These acts included: (1) use of the expressions "chicks" and "yellow fever" when referring to Asian women; (2) asking whether Yeh planned to wear a one-piece or two-piece bathing suit on vacation; (3) asking whether Yeh had any "weekend exploits"; (4) stating his beliefs that extramarital affairs between consenting adults are acceptable and (5) suggesting that Yeh use her feminine charms to improve client relationships (LexisNexis, 2005).

At trial, UBS said Ms. Zubulake herself was the problem, not gender discrimination. Officials testified during the three-week trial that Zubulake undermined colleagues, had problems getting along with associates and was insubordinate to Mr. Chapin. UBS argued that the two types of discrimination were different: (1) the sexual harassment experienced by Yeh was because of Chapin's attraction to her; and (2) the alleged treatment of Ms. Zubulake by Chapin was because she is a woman. But the court ruled that there was a common thread—both resulted from Mr. Chapin's reaction to individuals based on their gender and degraded individuals because of their sex in different ways (LexisNexis, 2005).

When the court ordered UBS to re-construct e-mails from its backup computer system, it proved that relevant e-mails were deleted and even falsified. Mr. Chapin claimed that Ms. Zubulake's colleagues and co-workers sent him e-memos and e-complaints about her. The back-up tapes proved that in at least one case, Mr. Chapin took an e-mail and falsified the language and then sent it to his superiors. Other e-mails from Mr. Chapin to Ms. Zubulake proved her retaliation claim (White, 2005).

At the conclusion of the trial, Zubulake's lawyer, James Hubbard, said, "The jury saw what her life would be like after this and gave her a real head start on starting over." He also conceded that Wall Street traditionally shuns those who litigate against it. "There's a lot of history and tradition in the way" (Boyd, 2005).

Barbara Gatfield, an executive recruiter at Gatfield-Greenwich, agrees:

> Firms often hire perspective employees who have had private arbitrations over salary disputes with former employers, but would draw the line on someone involved in public litigation. Anything that draws attention to how they make their money is going to be a big problem (Boyd, 2005).

In resounding dispute, the official UBS reply to the Zubulake case was:

> We are disappointed with the verdict rendered by the jury. We regard the amount as excessive and will now move to set aside the verdict. UBS is committed to its diversity efforts and will continue to ensure that it has an open and diverse work environment (Porter, 2005).

THE TREND: OTHER SEXUAL DISCRIMINATION LAWSUITS AGAINST WALL STREET

During the same period as the Zabulake v. UBS lawsuit, a series of class action sexual discrimination cases were brought by female professionals against other Wall Street houses and financial firms. In 2004, Morgan Stanley agreed to pay $54 million to settle a sexual discrimination lawsuit brought by former bond seller Allison Schieffelin on behalf of herself and approximately 300 other female employees (Porter, 2005). The women claimed discriminatory promotion practices, being subjected to breast-shaped cakes, hearing lewd comments and being invited to events that featured strippers. Morgan Stanley denied any wrong doing in the case, but it later fired a research analyst and three salesmen for taking a client to an Arizona strip club after a company-sponsored conference (Boyd, 2005).

Smith Barney, a brokerage unit of Citigroup, Inc, was ordered to pay $3.2 million to four current and former female employees who sued the company for sex discrimination in the U.S. District Court in San Francisco, CA. The women sought class-action status for 5,000 female brokers alleging that male branch managers routinely passed over female brokers when assigning the most lucrative accounts and gave them poorer offices, less training and sales support. Citigroup tried to dismiss the allegations as being "entirely without merit" (Facts, 2005).

Despite the success of these sexual discrimination lawsuits, "complaints—even salacious suits—continue to occur up and down the Street, from trading operations to investment banking." says Theodore Eppenstein, a securities lawyer for Eppenstein & Eppenstein, NY. He asserts that he gets the same amount of calls from people with discrimination claims as he did five years ago. "Just recently, I had a woman call saying she was fired from a major firm because she wouldn't have sex with her boss. I don't see any change and these claims are pretty consistent" (Touryakai, 2006).

David Thomas, a Harvard professor, sums it up by saying, "If you look at any of the top 20 brokerage houses, they have a pretty poor record in diversity. This portion of the financial services lags about 20 years behind the rest of corporate America" (Touryakai, 2006).

Linda Friedman, a partner at Stowell & Friedman in Chicago, backs up Thomas' claim:

> The industry has failed . . . Ten years ago I would have said Wall Street is behind 30 years. Today I say it is 10 years behind. Some might call that progress, but it's not fast enough . . . Firms are much more cooperative about resolving claims than ever before, and they realize they are just as vulnerable as the rest of corporate America to discrimination suits. They used to stick their fingers in our faces and tell us there was no problem with the way things are. They had the support of the NASD and NYSE, and knew getting a jury to hear our cases was a long shot. If there was no fear back then, there is certainly fear today (Touryakai, 2006).

WHAT DRIVES UBS' DIVERSITY STRATEGY AND LEADERSHIP?

"Diversity is one of our core values," states Robert Wolf, president and chief operating officer of UBS Investment Bank.

In order to maintain our position as a leading global financial services firm, we constantly strive to ensure our workforce represents the diverse clients we serve. Having employees from a broad mix of cultures, all working together as a team, helps us to identify and develop new market opportunities and strengthen relationships with clients (UBS Investment, 2010).

Examining UBS' recent and current diversity management strategies, there are examples of cultural diversity based on geographic/ethnic customer bases. For example, when UBS took control of Beijing Securities in China in 2006, it was the first foreign investment firm to run a Chinese securities company and the first foreign business with a license to trade shares and manage assets and wealth on China's mainland. What is even more impressive in this venture is that UBS only held a 20% minority share, and yet secured the right to manage the new company. So, how did UBS manage and grow their new company? They played "the shell game" (Wei, 2006).

> Shell Game: 1) a swindling game in which a small ball is placed under one of three nutshells or cones, the spectators being challenged to place a bet on the location of the ball, and being deceived by the sleight of hand of the operator 2) any game or scheme in which the customers are victimized. (Webster, 1983)

UBS sold 21 of their 27 Beijing Securities branches to another company (Merchants Securities) and even persuaded their customers to use these offices. "At first we couldn't understand why UBS wanted to turn clients away," explained Li Kai, a staff member at Beijing Securities. "Those were good quality clients who can bring a good return. Later we realized that those operating branches would serve as a 'shell' for UBS—a platform to develop high-end customers (Wei, 2006).

Another example of a market-driven diversity strategy was shown in July 2010 when UBS appointed Joseph Yam, a prominent former Hong Kong banker, to its board in "a move reflecting the growing importance of the Swiss bank's Asian business that analysts said also may help to deepen trust in the bank's top echelon." UBS Chairman Kaspar Villigar announced Yam's appointment by saying, "Joseph's presence will significantly expand the geographic diversity of the board and provide powerful additional impetus to the growth of our already market-leading investment-bank and wealth-management businesses in Asia Pacific" (Mijuk, 2010).

UBS CULTURAL DIVERSITY Vs GENDER DIVERSITY STRATEGIES

If UBS' corporate "diversity" strategy is solely based on a profit motive to secure culturally diverse customers around the globe, why does its strategy not include gender diversity—or the profit potential of targeting wealthy women as investors?

Women are becoming an increasingly powerful and formidable force in owning and managing wealth. Boston Consulting Group (BCG) valued female global wealth at $20 trillion in 2010 (Wilkinson, 2010) and estimates women's share of wealth in financial management will increase at a compound annual growth rate of 8 percent through 2014, to $29 trillion. Women in the U.S. and Canada controlled 33 percent of wealth in 2009, or about $9 trillion and BCG estimates it will grow to $11.7 trillion by 2014. BCG states the reasons for women's wealth growth are: a growing presence of women in the workforce; their greater involvement in managing family finances and the greater incidence of inherited wealth due to women's longevity (Gleason, 2010)

The global distribution of women's wealth reveals trends on which UBS could capitalize. Forty-six percent of the UK's millionaires are female and this is predicted to rise by 53% in 2020 according to BCG. These women include author JK Rowling and Christina Green, wife of Topshop founder (Wilkinson, 2010). Female investors at Forex, a UK subsidiary of Gain Capital foreign exchange services, increased by 50 percent in 2009 in a predominantly white-male client base (Foley, 2010).

Women in the Middle East controlled 22 percent, or $500 billion, of the region's total assets under management in 2009. Women in Saudi Arabia, the world's largest exporter of crude oil, are estimated to be sitting on $11.9 billion in cash. The World Bank estimated in 2007 that one-third of women-owned businesses in the United Arab Emirates generated over $100,000 a year compared to 12 percent of American women-owned companies (Reuters, 2010).

THE UBS STRATEGIC DIVERSITY RESPONSE

Mona Lau, Global Head of Diversity for UBS, sees two trends in the industry: "For diversity to take, business leaders have to be involved. It's a key to success." She refers to this concept as having "a champion in the senior executive suite." Secondly, she sees diversity and multiculturalism taking hold as global concepts and acknowledges that

At higher levels, executives say, diversity is spreading more slowly because of a relatively shallow pool of women and minority staff members to draw from. So, while companies are actively seeking recent minority graduates for the entry levels, they're also trying to strengthen their retention efforts through employee networks, surveys to measure real (and perceived) progress, and mentoring programs designed to help employees navigate the organization and achieve the visibility often necessary for advancement (Trends, 2010).

Ms. Lau's comment on the "shallow pool" of women and minorities begs the question. Or, could there be a male-dominated, macho culture at UBS? Their bottom line is the profit motive which is funded and secured by their "culturally diverse" customers around the globe. It's called the "diversity dividend" or the ability of organizations to capture and "capitalize on diversity and extract the value to the business that can be gained from . . . developing business opportunities that arise from this difference" (Diversity, 2010).

Beyond the necessity for UBS, a foreign company operating in the U.S., to comply with legal requirements, diversity at financial institutions has emerged as a practical business opportunity that enhances the bottom line in a world in which the ownership of wealth is increasingly diverse. However, in their strategic diversity planning, UBS has not yet focused on the profit potential of the rising global wealth of women to the same extent that they have focused on the wealth of culturally diverse investors. Their first strategic step would be to redefine their organizational culture and promotional practices to assure equity for women.

🏛 Points of Law

Foreign companies, employing workers within the United States, are subject to Title VII of the Civil Rights Act of 1964 that prohibits discrimination based on race, color, religion, sex, or national origin.

Title VII applies to a foreign employer when it discriminates within the United States. See, e.g., Ward v. W & R Voortman, 685 F. Supp. 231, 233 (M.D. Ala. 1988) (any company, foreign or domestic, that elects to do business in this country falls within Title VII's reach).

By employing individuals within the United States, a foreign employer invokes the benefits and protections of U.S. law. As a result, the employer should reasonably anticipate being subjected to the Title VII enforcement process should any charge of discrimination arise directly from the business the employer does in the United States. Commission Decision No. 84-2, supra.

DISCUSSION QUESTIONS

1. What socio/economic changes over the past twenty-five years may indicate that women as investors might be an untapped target market?

2. How could a women's network or affinity group (ERG) have been utilized at UBS to prevent these gender discrimination lawsuits?

3. Given the fact that there are not a lot of women in upper management positions at UBS, what are the issues with implementing an effective mentoring program?

4. Analyze the UBS organizational culture using Edgar Schein's model of levels of culture: artifacts, espoused and operational values, and basic underlying assumptions.

5. What are some workplace situations in this case that could demonstrate valid sexual harassment claims?

Diversity on the Web

Visit the following Web site, http://www.corporateleavers.org, "The Cost of Employee Turnover due to Failed Diversity Initiatives in the Workplace: The Corporate Leavers Survey 2007," Korn/Ferry International. Analyze this report for key findings and structural requirements of diversity programs, and then compare/contrast "this" with UBS' new diversity model and make recommendations.

Bibliography

Ali, Sam. (2010, October 15) Citigroup accused of gender bias. Retrieved October 16, 2010, from http://www.diversityinc.com/article/8078/Citigroup-Accused-of-Gender-Bias

Boyd, Roderick (2005, April 19) Woman who sued UBS aims to get back on wall street, *The New York Sun*, Retrieved August 1, 2010 from http://www.nysun.com/business/woman-who-sued-ubs-aims-to-get-back-on-the-street

Civil Rights; News in Brief (2005, May 5) Facts on File World News Digest, 311D2.

Diversity and inclusion training for Germany, cross cultural and global skills from Simmons Associates, Retrieved August 1, 2010 from http://www.simmonsassoc.com/html/germanyleadership2020print.html

Diversity working—about, Retrieved August 1, 2010 from http://www.diversityworking.com/employerZone/diversity Management EEOC, Retrieved October 15, 2010 from http://www.eeoc.gov/policy/docs/extraterritorial-vii-ada.html.

Foley, Jane. (2010, March 8) Women on course to control larger proportion of wealth Retrieved October 30, 2010 from http://blogs.reuters.com/great-debate-uk/2010/02/03/women-on-course-to-control-larger

Gleason, Jerry. (2010, August 25) Women investors want more from advisors, report finds Retrieved October 30, 1010 from http://registeredrep.com/newsletters/wealthmanagement/women_want_more_from-advisors

LexisNexis, Freddie H. Cook, Sylvester L. Fleming, JR. and Timothy J. Gandy, on behalf of themselves and all other similarly situated persons, Plaintiffs—against—UBS Financial Services, Inc, Defendant, March 21, 2006, 1–6.

LexisNexis, Zabulake v.UBS Warburg LLC, Case in Brief, LexisNexis, Reed Elsevier Inc, 2007, 1–23.

LexisNexis, Zabulake v.UBS Warburg LLC, Case text, LexisNexis, Reed Elsevier Inc, 2007, 1–9.

McGeehan, Patrick (2004, July 4) MARKET PLACE; Discrimination on Wall Street? The numbers tell the story, *The New York Times*. Retrieved August 1, 2010 from http://www.nytimes.com/2004/07/14/business/market-placediscriminiation-on-the-street-the-numbers-tell-the-story

Mijuk, Goran. (2010, July 24) UBS turns to Hong Kong's Yam, *The Wall Street Journal*, B3.

Ng, Grace. (2008, March 17) Making career comeback easier for former execs; UBS-SMU course lets them update knowledge and strategies before re-entering workforce, *The Straits Times*, Singapore.

Pederson, Jay P. (2003) International Directory of Company Histories, St. James Press: Thomas/Gale, 52, 352–359.

Porter, Eduardio. (2005, April 7) UBS ordered to pay $29 million in sex bias lawsuit, *The New York Times*, 4.

Reuters. (2010, October 27) Mideast banks funds seek to tap women's wealth. Retrieved October 30, 2010 from http://www.aawsat.com/english/news.asp?section=6&id=22819

Solis, Diane. (2005, June 14) Diversity slowly seeps into corporate American, *The Dallas Morning News*, Business and Financial News Section.

Stock, Kyle. (2010, Sept 20) Women on Wall Street declining, *Wall Street Journal*, C1, C3.

Trends in diversity: industry chases same minority talent, Retrieved August 1, 2010 from http://news.efinancialcareers.com/NEWS_ITEM/newsltemld-5780

Touryakai, Halan. (2006, March 1) Our diversity problem, registered red: the source for professionals, Retrieved August 1, 2010 from http://registeredrep.com/mag/finance_diversity_problem

UBS Investment Bank, Leadership in Diversity and Inclusion, Retrieved August 1, 2010 from UBS Who we are, Retrieved July 15, 2010, from http://ubs.com/1/e/about/our profile.html

UBS The UBS workforce, Retrieved July 15, 2010 from http://ubs.com/1/e/investors/annual_reporting 2005/handbook/0012/0014.html

Webster, Noah. 1983. Webster's New Universal Unabridged Dictionary, Second Ed, New York: New World Dictionaries/Simon and Schuster, 1672.

Wei, Tang. (2006, December 19) UBS takeover a serious makeover, *Beijing Review.com.cn*

White, Natalie. (2005, May 21) Wall Street firm hit with $29 million discrimination award, *St Louis Daily & St. Louis Countian*.

Wilkinson, Tara Loader. (2010, October 25) Women on the rise at wealth managers, *Financial News*. Retrieved October 30, 2010, from http://www.efinancialnews.com/story/2010-10-25/women-on-the-rise-at-wealth-managers

Zambito, Thomas. (2006, January 15) Wall St. women fight back, *Daily News*, 30.

Arlene O. DeWitt is an Assistant Professor of Organizational Communication and Marketing at Assumption College, Worcester, MA.

Integrative Questions for Section 5

1. In December of 2010, the United States Congress approved the repeal of the "Don't ask, don't tell" policy for gay and lesbian military personnel. What will the military need to do to prevent conflict as this policy is implemented?

2. Do you think that this repeal will lead the way for the United States to include LGBT employees under civil rights legislation? Why or why not?

3. Comparing Canadian diversity legislation with that of the United States, which appears more progressive and why?

4. Do Canadian and American laws fit into one of the theoretical ethical perspectives presented in the McNett article? Justify your answer.

5. Given the high growth rate of the young Hispanic population, what might your college or university do to improve its recruiting of Hispanic students?

6. Considering both the communication differences and media preferences of diverse consumers, what are the future implications for advertising?

7. Keeping in mind the communication, media messages, and marketing articles in this section, analyze and evaluate the Web site of your college or university for all of the following groups that your institution markets to: a) Day college students, b) Evening college students, c) Graduate students. Provide a grade from A to F and justify your answer in terms of how well the Web site addresses its message to meet the needs of these distinct populations.

6

Managing Organizational Change and Diversity

In this final section, students will

- Examine strategies for building a more inclusive workplace.
- Explore the challenges of effective corporate leadership, employee resource groups, diversity training, and corporate social responsibility initiatives.
- Understand the need for more flexible work programs for parents, caregivers, and older workers.
- Evaluate the value of diversity award programs.
- Assess a real organization in terms of its diversity policies and practices.

The material in Section VI is intended to close the change loop by examining what organizations can do to effectively manage diversity and evaluate their progress.

These readings provide current material on corporate diversity leadership initiatives, effective utilization of employee resource groups, well-designed community philanthropy programs, the need for a more flexible workplace (Harvey), and an analysis of the frameworks underlying diversity training (DeRosa). Having this background, the student is now ready to evaluate diversity implementation by considering the criteria for diversity awards (Allard) and actually audit an existing business (Harvey). The text ends with an integrative case, the Air Force Academy (Diodati) that provides students with an opportunity for learning about the need and complexity of implementing effective organizational change.

Leadership, Employee Resource Groups, and Social Responsibility: What Organizations Can Do To Manage Diversity

Carol P. Harvey
Assumption College

GOALS

- To examine corporate diversity leadership
- To consider the role of employee resource groups as organizational assets
- To understand the importance of supplier diversity programs
- To analyze corporate social responsibility and philanthropy initiatives

Well-managed diversity programs can benefit an organization in terms of the business case for diversity and the stakeholders in terms of the involvement of employees, suppliers and the community. John Robinson, Director of the Office of Civil Rights for the U.S. Department of State, lists five requirements for effective diversity leadership as: making diversity visible, being specific about what needs to be done, requiring evaluation for results, providing constant reinforcement, and making change intentional (diversityinc.com, n.d.). Consequently, direction needs to come from the top of an organization where the CEO and Board provide the necessary vision and support. Without sufficient resources and leadership it is difficult for organizations to operationalize mission-critical diversity initiatives such as recruiting a diverse Board, appointing a Chief Diversity Officer, forming effective employee resource groups, developing successful supplier diversity programs and contributing meaningfully to corporate philanthropy.

GOVERNANCE AND DIVERSITY: CORPORATE BOARDS AND CHIEF DIVERSITY OFFICERS

To understand the importance of diversity leadership, think back to the Pitney Bowes case where the three CEOs championed diversity and made it an operational value. Once diversity has a highly ranked champion, two ways to strengthen governance in terms of support for diversity initiatives are to have diversity on the Board of Directors (or Board of Trustees in the case of a non-profit organization) and to appoint a **Chief Diversity Officer** (CDO), "a designated corporate executive at the VP level or above, responsible for building, managing and maintaining corporate diversity initiatives" (Virtcom, 2009, 16).

Board Leadership

Corporate boards are expected to provide expert financial, legal, management, and strategic advice from an external perspective. Since one of the advantages to having diversity is to add unique viewpoints, appointing diverse directors to a board should improve decision making by minimizing groupthink and challenging the status quo. Kim Goodwin, a director at Akami Technologies Inc. said, "When everyone is the same whether it is race, gender, nationality, or sexual orientation—you create a fraternity like organization where conformity and fitting in become the norm . . . For corporations, that's death" (Carrns & Johnson, 2010, p. 12).

However, board membership in the U.S. tends to be homogeneous and second, adding diverse members, if not managed well, may result in more conflict and gridlock (Manzoni, Strebel and Barsoux, 2010). Statistics on board diversity are limited to gender and race/ethnicity and usually do not reveal other social identities. Currently, women (51% of the United States population) hold 17% of the board seats at the Fortune 100 companies, Blacks 10% (14% of the U.S. population), Hispanics 4% (15% of the U.S. population) and Asians 2% (5% of the U.S. population). Only 17 of the Fortune 100 companies have a board that is considered to be "highly diverse" with 40% of the directors being female or people of color (Virtcom, 2009).

There are reasons for this lack of diversity at the board level. First, diverse directors may be harder to find. Membership is by the invitation of the nominating committee, which is made of current board members. Ramirez (2004) contends that the homogeneity of corporate boards is largely a result of women and racial minorities not having the same access to networks and the social capital that white men do. Board members, like most people, tend to know and associate with people like themselves. Consequently, these are the ones that they nominate for board membership. Second, corporate boards require a range of specific skill sets such as experience at the executive level, in global markets and knowledge of law, finance, accounting, etc. Diverse individuals with these qualifications may be harder to find. However, when diverse voices are valued in the boardroom, companies manage to overcome these obstacles. Women, African Americans, Asians and Hispanics comprise 50% of the board at Alcoa, 46% of the boards at PepsiCo, Aetna, Dow Chemical, and IBM, and 43% of the boards at CitiGroup, Well Point, Wal-Mart, and Wells Fargo (Virtcom, 2009).

As with any group, just adding diverse individuals to the mix is not enough to ensure that an organization will benefit from diversity. Diverse directors may be reluctant to speak freely or to take a devil's advocate position because they fear being in the "O" or only position. Diversity brings a range of differences in communication styles, such as directness vs. indirectness and culturally acceptable behaviors such as respectfully waiting for an opportunity to break into the conversation vs. interrupting others. Board diversity, like employee diversity, must be well managed by selecting new members carefully, helping newcomers to adjust, not dismissing dissenting opinions too quickly, and sharing the role of devil's advocate, etc. (Manzoni, Strebel, Barsoux, 2010).

There is a growing body of research that relates but *not* yet correlates financial performance to board diversity. For example, in 2007, a Catalyst study of Fortune 500 companies revealed that "companies with higher representation of women on their corporate boards outperformed on three key financial measures (Return on Equity, Return on Sales and Return on Invested Capital) compared to companies with lower representations of women" (Catalyst, 2008, p. 2). A similar study in Finland, where the law that requires board composition to be 33–50% members of each gender, showed an adjusted return on assets 14.7% higher in companies with a majority of female directors compared to those with a male majority (Kotiranta, Kovalainen and Rouvinen, 2007). So, there are many good reasons to strive for board diversity.

Chief Diversity Officers

Today, many organizations are moving the internal management of diversity away from Human Resources where it was treated as a legal compliance matter to the executive level where it can be treated as a strategic business issue by creating a new position called **chief diversity officer** (CDO). "While the position did not exist a few decades ago, a study last year of Fortune 500 companies by executive search firm Heidrick & Struggles found that of 490 companies, 307 had an executive dedicated to diversity" (Lobb, 2010, p. 8). In contrast, in 2005 approximately 20% of these same corporations had someone responsible for diversity at the senior level (Picture, 2005).

The primary responsibilities of the CDO position are to provide strategic leadership for an organization's diversity agendas and to assure that the corporation's culture values diversity as a business imperative, i.e., linking diversity to the bottom line. CDOs function as change agents coordinating and integrating diversity as a strategic opportunity for talent recruitment, product development, penetration of global markets and community involvement. While this role will vary based on an organization's mission, a 2010 study of 170 United States CDOs by *Diversity Officer Magazine* revealed that about 65% are at the vice-presidential level and 75% report to the board on a regular basis. Recently, The Nielson Company, the global media measurement corporation, appointed Susan Whiting, currently vice-chair, as its CDO. She will report directly to the CEO, David Calhoun. She defines her role as focusing "on improving the diversity of The Nielsen Company's leadership ranks, global workforce of more than 35,000 as well as increasing purchasing from diverse suppliers" (Grimes, 2010). The movement towards having a CDO is a positive step in the diversity management process.

AFFINITY GROUPS/EMPLOYEE RESOURCE GROUPS (ERGs)

In theory, having a diverse workforce should be an asset to an organization in terms of multicultural marketing, creativity and innovative decision-making. However, membership in a non-dominant race, ethnicity, gender group, etc. may lead to feelings of isolation, miscommunication and a lack of mentoring. If employees don't feel included and/or free to speak openly, organizations risk minimizing the advantages of having a diverse workforce.

> Affinity groups not only promote diversity within firms, but also act as the catalyst for an inclusive culture. They act as advocates, connectors, and communicators. They can transform the corporate culture from a loose collection of competing interests to a community that draws on the diverse strengths of its members to ensure that no one is left out or left behind in the common journey toward success
>
> (Douglas, 2008, p. 17).

Today, many companies are responding to their diverse employees' needs for inclusion and the corporate need to stay competitive in a diverse marketplace by sponsoring affinity or Employee Resource Groups (ERGs). While some use these terms interchangeably, technically **Affinity groups**, as the name implies, are "communities within a corporation that are organized around employees' similar circumstances and common goals" (Douglas, 2008, 12). Affinity groups often have a more social and mentoring focus. Although **Employee Resource Groups** (EGRs) usually provide similar support for diverse employees, these are also tied more closely to the mission of the organization and utilizing diverse employees as a business resource. For example, ERGs can offer promotional advice for products targeted to diverse populations, assist in linking the company with diverse communities for employee recruitment and in product development.

The origins of these groups goes back to the 1960s, when corporations such as Digital Equipment, and Xerox pioneered efforts to diversify their workforces in response to Title VII of the 1964 Civil Rights Act. Management soon learned that just hiring women and employees of color was often problematic. These new recruits often felt isolated, unwelcome and misunderstood in organizations long dominated by white males. Additionally, many of these employees experienced backlash and were unjustly stereotyped as "tokens," i.e. unqualified people just hired to comply with EEO/AA laws, or to meet a government quota, even if they were fully qualified for their positions.

In the turbulent 1960s the Black employees at Xerox Corporation formed regional caucus groups to secure fairer treatment for Black employees. In the process, these groups became a mentoring resource for newer minority employees and a network for the recruitment of additional minorities. Because both employees and management benefited, Xerox soon established caucus groups for its female and Asian employees.[1]

Changing over time there are broader more inclusive categories for group memberships. For example, Microsoft has ERGs for parents, GLBTs, and Employees with Disabilities, etc. In addition, membership now is usually open to any employee with an interest in that topic. So, someone who is able-bodied but who has a blind parent might have an interest in participating in the group that focuses on people with disabilities and is usually allowed to do so.

Since ERG members can provide diversity related expertise in terms of reviewing promotional materials for offensive content, contributing ideas for product development that meet the needs of diverse markets, linking the company to diverse communities for employee recruitment, and outreach and promoting cultural awareness the members can operationalize diversity as a competitive advantage.

ELI LILY & FORD MOTOR COMPANY BEST PRACTICES

Because the Latino population is expected to reach 132 million by 2050 and the proportion of Latinos in clinical trials traditionally is quite low, the Latino ERG at Eli Lily pharmaceuticals worked with medical staff and the community to develop more effective recruitment techniques for this population. Hopefully, this will enable Eli Lily "to gain more information on medicine safety and effectiveness within this population" (Hartley, 2010, p. 39).

At the Ford Motor Company, the "Employees Dealing with Disabilities Group" has offered input into vehicles designed for people with physical challenges, and the "Parenting Network" reviewed minivan designs.

---

[1]Note. For a complete history of these pioneering groups see: Mary Gentile. (1960). The Black Caucus Groups at Xerox Corporation (A) Case. *Managing Excellence Through Diversity*, Waveland Press.

EXHIBIT 1	Individual & Organizational Benefits of Affinity & Employee Resources Groups

Employee Benefits	Organizational Benefits
Opportunity to be mentored	Improved communication with diverse consumer markets
Safe place to discuss diversity issues	Assistance with recruiting diverse employees
Networking opportunities	Outreach to diverse communities
Professional development	Product development for diverse markets
Increase feeling of inclusion	Increase global business opportunities

Recent research indicates that an important business outcome of these groups can be increasing employee satisfaction and motivation. Each year Aetna Insurance conducts a yearly employee engagement survey of 34,000 employees. "Among the respondents to its 2009 survey, ERG members consistently scored higher (8%) than those who did not join ERGs (Zappo, 2010, September–October, p. 35).

The most successful employee resource groups have direct communication and/or a sponsor on the corporate level, capitalize on the idea that diverse employees can be a competitive advantage and tie to the business case for diversity. (See Exhibit 1).

Unfortunately a 2005 Society for Human Resources Survey of diversity practices indicated that "only 29% of the companies surveyed support employee network groups" (Arnold, 2006, 145).

To prevent future legal liabilities involving affinity groups or ERGs, organizations need to proceed carefully to minimize the appearance of favoritism towards specific groups. First, there should be clear written guidelines and policies that specify where and when the group can meet (on company property or not, on paid or unpaid time, etc.), and which organizational resources they can or cannot use (email, intranet, copiers, office supplies, etc.). Second, membership in all groups must be open to all employees, even those who do not share the social identity characteristic that is the focus of the group. For example, if the adoptive father of an Asian child wants to join the Asian employees group, he should be allowed to do so. Third, ERGs or affinity groups cannot negotiate terms of employment with management or they will be in violation of the National Labor Relations Act. Fourth, all employees must be treated alike.

In 2005, General Motors won a court ruling related to employee groups from the 7th U.S. Court of Appeals (Moranski vs. General Motors Corp.). Mr. Moranski, a GM employee, claimed religious discrimination under Title VII of the Civil Rights Act because the corporation refused his request to form a Christian Employee Network at GM. Fortunately for GM, they had a written policy that no affinity groups could have a religious or political focus. The court reasoned that all religious groups were being treated the same and therefore, there was no religious discrimination.

SUPPLIER DIVERSITY PROGRAMS

Initially, many of these procurement programs were driven by government mandates to organizations that benefitted from federal contracts. While some would argue that there is no longer a need to nurture the development of women and minority owned businesses, the data do not support that position. "Women own between 25% and 33% of private businesses globally . . . but

AT&T & SUPPLIER DIVERSITY BEST PRACTICES

AT&T established its first supplier diversity program in 1968 by purchasing $175,000 in goods and services from nine women and minority owned businesses. Today, AT&T considers supplier diversity as a "critical component of their quality processes and standards" and has spent over $43 billion doing business with women, minority and disabled veteran owned businesses. In addition, AT&T: has a staff of sixteen employees dedicated to supplier diversity programs, requires all suppliers with $500,000 in AT&T contracts (Tier I) to also develop their own supplier diversity programs (Tier II); partners with colleges and universities to provide graduate level business training to these suppliers; and educates diverse suppliers by offering e-commerce workshops on web-based procurement (AT&T.com).

receive less than 1% of contracting opportunities, a barrier to their growth" (Zappo, 2010). "Currently, minorities represent 28% of the United States population but minority businesses represent only 15% of the total businesses, 3% of gross receipts and 4% of the total corporate purchases" (Minority Development Council, 2010).

Supplier diversity programs can be divided into two levels: **Tier I suppliers** are direct contractors. However, many corporations that have supplier diversity programs also require that their Tier I suppliers purchase from organizations that are owned by non-dominant groups. This is called a **Tier II** supplier program and "consists of payments made to small, minority, non-ethnic women, veteran or service-disabled veteran-owned businesses for the purchase of goods and services, used directly or indirectly, from the prime suppliers" (hp.com, 2010). These programs are intended to add mutual benefits to the purchasing organizations and to the suppliers. Well run programs can provide buyers with competitive advantages through innovative ideas, inroads into multicultural communities, better understanding of emerging markets, (diversity-inc.com, July 23, 2010), and even lower costs. For the suppliers, the advantages are business development opportunities, educational/training opportunities such as the Johnson & Johnson scholarships to Kellogg & Tuck Business Executive programs offered to women and minority small business owners (jnj.com).

The best managed supplier diversity programs share several common features: a requirement that the business is certified by independent agencies such as the National Minority Development Council and the Women's Business Enterprise National Council as at least 51% woman, minority or disabled veteran owned; commitment from the leadership of the purchasing organization; and ongoing assessment of policies and procedures.

CORPORATE SOCIAL RESPONSIBILITY AND PHILANTHROPY

The National Philanthropic Trust estimates that corporate foundations donated total of $4.2 billion to charity in 2006 with the most significant contributions coming from Bank of America ($188.2 million), Sanofi-Aventis Patient Assistance Foundation ($177.4 million), and Wal-Mart

---

McDONALD'S BEST PRACTICES

McDonald's Hispanic ERG provides an example of how these groups can be linked to community philanthropy. Their "Hispanic Employee Business Network has an internal mission of developing talented Latino employees to move up in the organization and an external mission that includes promoting the largest Latino scholarship program (Hispanic American Commitment to Educational Resources) in the United States" (Gilmore, 2010).

Foundation ($110.9 million). The largest private foundations in terms of assets all have their roots in business: the Bill & Melinda Gates Foundation ($38.9 Billion), The Ford Foundation ($11 billion), and the J. Paul Getty Trust ($10.8 billion) (nptrust.com, 2010). Currently, Warren Buffet and Bill and Melinda Gates are successfully soliciting pledges from some of the rich capitalists to leave at least 50% of their wealth to charity.

A significant number of organizations target their charitable giving and/or employee volunteer programs to diverse populations. For example, in 2007, the Aetna Inc. Foundation donated $24.5 million to support college scholarships to educate future Hispanic leaders, Habit for Humanity to build homes for the disabled, and a grant for the construction of the Martin Luther King memorial in Washington, D.C. (Aetna, 2010). Bank of America has a company sponsored Volunteer Network which allows employees paid time to volunteer in their communities to tutor and mentor youth, restore homes for the elderly, raise money for AIDS charities, etc. (Bank of America, 2010).

Because funding derives from the profits of a business, corporations often link their contributions to social causes that are related to their core values, missions, and stakeholders. For example, Tyco, the manufacturer of safety and security products, supports a program to reduce home-based injuries, in particular burns and domestic violence. The Wal-Mart Foundation's mission statement specifies that its financial support is targeted to the charitable causes that are important to customers and associates in their own neighborhoods. In 2010, Wal-Mart donated $1.5 million to Share Our Strength nutrition education and $2 million for an affordable loan program both for low income families. In addition, the foundation contributed 3.9 million to help students reading below their grade levels (Walmart.com). Cox Communication, the third largest cable company in the U.S., contributes over $100 million annually to organizations such as The Latin American Association, the National Urban League and the United Negro College Fund. Cox also provides free television advertising to the Boys and Girls Clubs of America, and Cable in the Classroom, a commercial free programming and online resource to teachers (cox.com, 2010).

While corporate philanthropy benefits both internal and external stakeholders, it also provides advantages to the organization. In addition to tax breaks, "consumers respond favorably to companies that exhibit good corporate citizenship. Publically embracing diversity helps companies recruit and retain diverse staff. Both practices can also improve the image of companies within increasingly diverse markets." (Shaw, jointaffinitygroups.org, 2010).

Writing Assignment

Find an individual who serves on a Board of Directors or a Board of Trustees (a non-profit) and interview this person about board membership. Try to learn the answers to the following questions:

1. How he or she was selected?
2. Did he or she know someone on the board?
3. Does he or she have a particular expertise that the Board needed (lawyer, accountant, civil engineer, etc.)
4. Does he or she know how future Board members are selected?
5. How are members of this Board, diverse or not diverse?
6. **If this is a for-profit corporation,**
   What is his or she compensation for serving as a Board member?
   If this is a non-profit Board,
   What are the expectations for financial contributions?
7. Has recruiting diverse members to the Board been an initiative?
8. What types of diversity did the Board seek? If so, how was this done and was it successful? Why or Why not?
9. If there are diverse members, do they participate fully in Board discussions?

Remembering that this is only one individual's perception and that his or her position may have some bias,

a. Analyze the material from this interview and write a two- to three-page essay that evaluates this Board from the perspective of diversity.
b. Answer one of the following questions: If the Board is diverse now, how does the board diversity link to the organization's mission and the business case for diversity? Or, if this Board is not diverse, how could a more diverse board potentially improve the link between the company's mission and the business case for diversity?

DISCUSSION QUESTIONS

1. Why is corporate and Board involvement so crucial to the business case for diversity?

2. Besides the legal considerations, why does locating the responsibility for diversity initiatives in Human Resources limit the effectiveness of diversity initiatives in an organization?

3. How can corporate boards, which want more diverse members, recruit good candidates?

4. How can an organization minimize backlash and conflict about ERG membership?

5. How can an effective supplier diversity programs support the business case for diversity?

6. Thinking as a consumer, does an organization's social responsibility and corporate philanthropy make a difference in your buying decisions? Why or why not?

Bibliography

Anonymous. (2010). AT&T launches "operation hand salute" in an effort to help disabled-veteran businesses improve their operations and contracting opportunities, May 13. Retrieved July, 28, 2010 from att.com/gen/press-room.

Anonymous. Diversity professional profiles. Chief Diversity Officer Magazine. Retrieved on October 25, 2010 from diversityofficer-magazine.com/diversity-professional-profiles.

Anonymous. History. National Minority Development Council. Retrieved from nmsdc.org on July 30, 2010.

Arnold, J.T. (2006). Employee networks. HR Magazine, vol. 51, 6, 145–49.

Bank of America. (2010). Retrieved on December 4, 2010, from bankofamerica.com.teambook/index.cfm?template=Tb_voinetwork.

Carrns, A. & Johnson, C. (2010). Wider horizons: companies work to make boards more inclusive. The Boston Globe: Diversity Boston, summer, p. 12.

Catalyst. (2008, June). 2007 Catalyst census of women board directors of the fp 500; Voices from the boardroom, p. 2. Retrieved December 11, 2010, from catalyst.org.

Chao, J. and Branch, R.B. Eds. (2009). Diversity in action: strategies with impact. Retrieved from rockpa.org/ideas_and_perspectives/publications on August 6, 2010.

Cox Communications. (2010). Diversity within Cox's Communities. Retrieved from ww2.cox.com/aboutus/diverisity/communities.cox on August 4, 2010.

Diversityinc.com. (n.d.). Diversity leadership. Retrieved November 21, 2010 from diversityinc.com/department/52/Leadership-Profiles,

Diversityinc.com. (July 23, 2010). Walmart donates $1.5 million to Help Share Our Strength. Retrieved from diversityinc.com on August 3, 2010.

DiversityInc.com. (April 26, 2010). Ways to Work receives $2 million from the Walmart Foundation to expand affordable loan program for low income families. Retrieved from diversityinc.com on August 3, 2010.

DiversityInc.com. (May 21, 2010). Walmart foundation gives 3.9 million to help increase middle school student reading levels. May 21, retrieved from diversityinc.com on August 3, 2010.

Douglas, P.H. (2008). Affinity groups: catalyst for inclusive organizations. Employment Relations Today, 34, (4) 11–18.

Gilmore, A., (2010). McDonald's Hispanic employee business network. Diversity Executive, vol. 3, 5, p. 398.

Grimes, M. (2010). Nielsen vice-chair Susan Whiting adds chief diversity officer responsibilities. Business Wire. Retrieved from ProQuest on October 19, 2010 at proquest.umi.com/pqdweb?index=3&sid=1&srchmode=2&vins.

Hartley, D. (2010). Eli Lilly & Co's OLA Lilly. Diversity Executive, vol. 3, 5, P. 398.

hp.com. (2010). HP global citizenship report: Supplier diversity. Retrieved from hp.com on December 20, 2010.

Institute for Supply Management. Welcome & introduction. Retrieved from ismsupplierdiversity.com on July 26, 2010.

Johnson & Johnson. Programs and activities. Retrieved from jnj.com/connect/about-jnj/diversity programs on August 3, 2010.

Joy, L., Carter, N. Wagner, H., & Narayanan, S. (2007). Corporate Performance and women's representation on boards. Catalyst:New York. Retrieved on October 30, 2010 from catalyst.org/file/139/bottom%20line%202.pd

Kotiranta, A., Kovalainen, A. & Rouvinen, P. (2007). Female leadership and firm profitability. EVA: Finnish Business & Policy Forum. Retrieved on October 30, 2010 from europeanpwn.net/files/eva_analysis_english.pdf.

Lobb, A. (2010). Changes at the top., The Boston Globe: Diversity Boston, summer, pp. 26–27.

Manzoni, J., Strebel, P., and Barsoux, J. (2010). Why diversity can backfire on company boards. The Wall Street Journal. January 25th. Retrieved on October 25th 2010 from online.wsj.com.

McGlothlen, C. (2006). Inclusive, exclusive or outlawed? HRMagazine, July, 2006, vol. 51,7, Retrieved from Proquest on October 19, 2010 proquest.umi.com/pqdweb?index+13&si9d=4&srchmode=1&vins

National Philanthropic Trust. Philanthropy statistics. Retrieved from nptrust.org on August 4, 2010.

Picture, B. (2005). Are diversity officers changing the face of corporate America? Asian Week (blog), November 26th.

Ramirez, S. A. (2004). Games CEO's play and interest convergence theory: why diversity lags in America's boardrooms and what to do about it. Washington and Lee Law Review, Fall, 61, 4. Retrieved from ABI/Inform on October 18, 2010.

Shaw, A. (2010). Corporate philanthropy: the business of diversity. Retrieved from jointaffinitygroups.org on August 4, 2010, 121–134.

Tyco. Corporate philanthropy. Retrieved from tyco.com on August 4, 2010.

Virtcom. (2009). Board diversification strategy: realizing competitive advantage and shareholder value. Retrieved from cii.org/Boarddiversity on October 28, 2010.

Zappo, G. (May 16, 2010). Think globally: Marriott's new supplier-diversity model. Retrieved from Diversityinc.com. on March 16, 2010.

Zappo, G. (June 24, 2010). WBENC: helping women-owned business connect and grow. Retrieved Diversityinc.com on July 23, 2010.

Zappo, G. (2010). ERG members have higher engagement rates. DiversityInc, September/October, 34–35.

Diversity on the Web

For examples of supplier diversity programs benefiting business owners, the local communities in terms of job creation and the organizations for which they provide services, go to http://makingittv.com. Click on "Tweets with Business Tips & Featured Entrepreneurs with Free Streaming Video." Then, click on "entrepreneur success stories." Select "The Power of Partnerships" episode # 512 which features Linda Stone, an Asian American female entrepreneur and "Frontier Electronics Systems," episode #511 which presents the story of Peggy Shreve, a female Native American business owner who is a supplier to Boeing Aircraft.

WORK-LIFE BALANCE ISSUES: CHANGING WHEN AND HOW THE WORK GETS DONE

Carol P. Harvey
Assumption College

GOALS

- To understand how the changing composition and values of today's workforce impact traditional work schedules
- To present a business case for a more flexible workplace
- To illustrate successful business models for work-life balance issues for parents, caregivers, and mature workers

Because the 21st century labor force includes more working women, more fathers who want to be involved in their children's lives, more single parents, and more people who are responsible for caring for an elderly relative or person with a handicap, and more older workers, there is an increasing interest in more flexible work schedules. Ninety percent of the companies interviewed in a 2009 Hewitt Associates survey cite work-life balance issues as the leading reason that their workers wanted more flexible work arrangements such as job-sharing, temporary leaves, compressed work weeks, telecommuting, phased retirement, on and off ramps and part-time employment.

Many countries have more progressive work-life laws and organizational policies than the United States where the only federal legislation is the Family Medical Leave Act that grants *unpaid* leave. Globally, particularly in the European Union, longer vacations, paid maternity/paternity leaves, subsidized child care, etc., are more common. "While U.S. companies generally offer work-life programs as a competitive advantage the EU mandates them as a function of social responsibility" (Joshi, et al., 2002, p. 16).

THE BUSINESS CASE FOR WORK-LIFE BALANCE

Offering workplace flexibility relates directly to the business case for diversity because such policies attract a larger and better pool of potential applicants, decrease stress, burnout, absenteeism and turnover, salary expenses and increase employee satisfaction, customer service, organizational commitment, and motivation. For example, Deloitte & Touche, the global accounting firm, saved $41.5 million in employee turnover costs by retaining employees through their flexible work programs (Corporate Voices, 2005). A 2000 study by the Center for Work & Family "found that 70% of managers and 87% of employees reported that working a flexible work arrangement had a positive or very positive impact on productivity" (2000).

When work-life balance issues are *not* addressed there can be organizational costs. A survey by Work-Life Benefits Consultants found that more than 25% of all employee absences were caused by family issues. "For every $1 an employer spends in helping employees balance their home and work lives, the company will get a return investment of $3 to $4 in work hours saved, insurance costs, sick leave, decreased absenteeism and fewer on-the-job injuries" (Ortiz, 2006).

Although there has been an increase in the number of organizations that offer flexible working arrangements, actual implementation and usage are not always easy to achieve due to the "implementation gap" i.e., the resistance of organizational cultures to change. "When the culture is not supportive of these initiatives, they rarely succeed" (Van Deusen, James, Gill & McKechnie, 2008, p. 5). The 2008 Workplace Flexibility study from the Boston College Center for Work & Family found that flexible work arrangements are highly dependent on management's perceptions about the worker's ability to continue to meet the needs of the job and are often available only after a worker has gained her manager's trust and successfully negotiated the working arrangements. A Catalyst study revealed that 91% of women and 94% of men surveyed, said that flexible work options were available to them for family emergencies or personal matters. However, only 15% of the women and 20% of the men felt that they could use these options without jeopardizing their careers

Additional objections to flexible work arrangements include resentment from employees who may not be eligible for such schedules, supervision concerns, difficulties in scheduling meetings, and staffing-level issues during peak times (Carlson, 2004). The 2007 Work-life Evolution Study concluded that "Work-life and flexibility still face skepticism in terms of their impact on the bottom line" (p. 20). Additionally, even many of the organizations that do have flexible work policies indirectly discourage their use for male employees and/or fail to promote those who take advantage of such options (Frankel, 2007).

WORK-LIFE BALANCE: PARENTAL ROLES AND CARE GIVING

Work-life as a diversity issue results from changing gender roles, new family structures, differences between generational values that conflict with traditional work schedules and older employees financially unable or personally unwilling to retire. Women, who now receive 57% of the bachelor's degrees and 60% of the master's degrees awarded each year, comprise 50% of the U.S. workforce (Harrington, Deusen & Ladge, 2010). Both parents work in over 70% of two-parent households and only 20% of U. S. families with children still have a working father and a stay at home mother (Boushey & O'Leary, 2009). "The traditional family structure has been replaced mainly by dual-career couples and single heads of household (20%) where the single parent is employed" (Boston College Center for Work & Family, 2008).

However, because so many women with children are now working, "work-life integration is no longer just a women's issue: it's a workforce issue" (Sally Helgesen in Prokopeak, 2010). A study conducted by the Boston College Center for Work & Family, revealed that today's fathers want more involvement in raising their children but that there is less organizational support for men than women to take on childrearing responsibilities (Harrington, Van Deusen & Ladge, 2010). U. S. organizations

> Have yet to come to terms with what it means to live in a nation where both men and women typically work outside of the home and what we need to do to make this new reality workable for families who have child care and eldercare responsibilities throughout most of their working lives (Boushey, 2009, p. 31).

Even when the childbearing years are over, there may still be a need to balance work responsibilities with the care of elderly relatives or those with a handicap. Currently, forty-four million people or over 21% of all U.S. households provide care for an older family member or one with a handicap. A 2006 study conducted by MetLife and the National Alliance for Caregiving estimated that the annual lost productivity costs to U. S. employers is $17.1 billion due to turnover, absenteeism, workday interruptions and medical crises involved with care giving responsibilities. For an organization, the estimated total cost to replace a worker usually ranges from one to one and half times his annual salary.

Even those without current family or caregiver responsibilities may value the option of a more flexible work schedule. A survey by the Center for Work-Life Policy found that "87% of baby boomers and 89% of Generation Y workers said that flextime was important to them and a key motivating factor" (Hewitt Associates LLC, 2010).

WORK-LIFE BALANCE: FLEXIBLE WORK MODELS

Some organizations have developed innovative and productive models that address work-life balance issues and provide increased schedule flexibility for their employees who have parental and care giving responsibilities. For example,

WORK-LIFE BALANCE: FLEXIBLE WORK FOR MATURE WORKERS

Today, many mature workers are also interested in continued employment past their traditional retirement age but they seek a more flexible work schedule that allows more time for travel, grandchildren, hobbies and volunteer work. Due to the prevalence of Baby Boomers, in 2010

Best Practices

- At **Accenture**, the outsourcing, and consulting company, employees can take advantage of the "Future Leave" program. This is a self-funded sabbatical program that allows workers to defer their earnings and to draw on those funds while not working (Jewell, 2008).
- **Continental Airlines** reservation department has an annual turnover rate of 5% while the industry rate is 40%. Continental's 600 agents can work from home and also take advantage of an Expanded Shift Program that allows 25% of the staff to have three or more days off on a rotating basis (Galinsky, Elby, & Peer, 2008).
- At the **Raytheon Company**, a defense, security and aerospace supplier, employees have the option of working 80 hours over nine days and taking every other Friday off from work (Raytheon, 2010).
- **AstraZeneca Pharmaceutical** offers its sales reps the options of job sharing and part-time schedules. Productivity metrics such as number of calls, presentations and sales yields indicated that these workers compared favorably with the full time sales force (Corporate Voices, 2005).
- **1-800CONTACTS** has reduced employee turnover by implementing a phone system that allows its call center workers to take sales and customer service calls from home (Galinsky, Elby, & Peer, 2008).

there were 26.6 million workers over age fifty-five in the U.S. While this age group is healthier and more active, than previous generations, most are not eligible for traditional pension plans and experienced declining retirement portfolios and home values in the recent recession. As a result, by 2012 nearly 20% of the U.S. workforce is expected to be 55 or older and 50% of those 65 and older will be working or are actively seeking employment. "By the year 2020, there will be 27.7 individuals aged 65 and older for every 100 working adults: this ratio will represent a 28% increase in just two decades" (Challenger, 2005). With more people living longer, 79–83 years for men and 83–86 years for women but fewer workers contributing to the Social Security and Medicaid programs, these demographics could place an enormous economic strain both on the federal budget and the growth of American business.

According to the American Association of Retired Persons (AARP) 68% of the of workers age fifty to seventy plan to either continue working past their traditional retirement age or to continue to work in some different capacity than their current job. However, only 17% wanted to work full time, the remainder wanted more flexible scheduling (2007).

While it would seem advantageous in terms of the economy and the business case for diversity to develop more programs to keep older workers employed and contributing to Social Security longer, several factors account for the failure of many businesses to capitalize on the talents of this segment of the workforce. In a survey of middle to large sized employers, the Watson Wyatt consulting firm, found that only 16% of the organizations surveyed had some type of flexible program for older workers and 70% had simply not seen the need for such programs (Watson Wyatt Worldwide, 2004). In addition, negative perceptions and stereotypes about older workers such as their being inflexible, less productive, hard to manage, more costly and lacking and/or unwilling to learn new technology still prevail. Other employers may try to avoid hiring older employees because of a fear of age discrimination lawsuits. In addition, current federal regulations regarding pension benefits and contributions under ERISA legislation (Employment Retirement Income Security Act) and the IRS are outdated and may complicate adopting these innovative programs.

WORK-LIFE BALANCE: REDEFINING "RETIREMENT"

Traditionally, retirement used to mean leaving one's job completely and relying on defined benefit pension plans and Social Security for support. Soaring health costs, increased longevity, more reliance on self-managed defined contribution retirement plans instead of guaranteed income streams, low savings rates, and a desire to try a new occupation or self-employment has changed this concept for older workers. Today, retirement in stages, called "working retirement," is gaining in popularity (Cahill, Giandrea, & Quinn, 2006). In a recent survey, the American Association of Retired Persons (AARP) found that 70% of workers over forty-five plan to seek part-time work or flexible schedules or to never retire at all (AARP, 2007). A survey commissioned by MetLife revealed that the primary reasons for older workers to continue employment are that they either need the money (60%), or want to stay active (45%). However, motivators and needs varied among older workers depending upon their life stages. While workers 60–65 year-old value job design and flexible work schedules, workers 66–70 are more interested in meeting their needs for social interaction and mental stimulation (DeLong & Associates, 2006).

Some organizations offer **Phased retirement** programs which is a workplace plan that allows workers of a specified age to gradually reduce the hours that they work for their *current* employer. Such programs allow employers to maintain a trained workforce while employees can have more free time and a gradual transition to full retirement. Phased retirement works best when it ties to an organization's mission and objectives. For example, meeting the specific labor force needs for increased staffing during seasonal peaks, or to complete project-based work, etc. is a win-win situation in terms of the business case for diversity and for older workers. The company gets knowledgeable trained workers who already know the culture and procedures of the organization and the older workers are able to work fewer hours.

WORK-LIFE BALANCE: MATURE WORKERS

The following organizations provide some win-win examples of organizations that offer flexible workplace options that also benefit the company while presenting support for the business case for employing older workers.

Best Practices

- **Mercy Health System**—Since skilled employees in the healthcare industry, particularly nurses, are in short supply and 50% of all nurses in the U.S. will reach the traditional retirement age by 2015, Mercy Health System, located in Janesville, Wisconsin, provides an example of an organization that has linked its mission and needs to the flexible utilization of mature workers. They offer such innovative schedules as a Weekender Program—work only weekend shifts and a Traveler Option—work on a 6–13 week assignment (AARP, 2006).
- **The Vita Needle Company** is located in a former theater in Needham, MA where this 4th generation family business manufactures high quality reusable needles and fabricated stainless steel products. Most of Vita Needle's employees are part-time senior citizens averaging 74 years of age. Employing seniors who already have Medicare coverage saves on health benefits. The workers' hard work ethic and a commitment to quality production has allowed Vita Needle to compete successfully with global manufacturing competition by keeping quality high and manufacturing costs low. President Fred Hartman credits "the company's success to "this dedicated low-tech workforce that is behind Vita Needle's high-tech success" (Employees inject vitality, n.d). What makes Vita Needle unique is that the management has structured the work around the employees' needs and lifestyles, which Hartman describes as the "ultimate flex-time." Each worker has a key to the building and can come and leave according to their needs as long as the work gets done.
- **CVS/Caremark**—the pharmacy giant employs over 107,000 people and 18% are older workers. This organization offers a unique "Snowbirds" program that allows workers to transfer from a cold northern climate to a store in the South and Southwest during the winter months and then transfer back to their original store in the spring. Not only does this help CVS to retain employees who want to winter in warmer climates but it also staffs these stores with the extra already trained employees needed to accommodate increased consumer demand from these yearly population shifts (Gardner, 2006).

(continued)

- **L.L. Bean**—This Freeport, Maine based clothing and sports equipment retailer, encourages its 861 retirees to return to work when seasonal orders peak (AARP, 2006).
- **Monsanto**—Since 1991, Monsanto has maintained a database of retired workers who want to work part-time, full time or on special assignments. Currently, 66%, (200) of them have work assignments (Fetterman, 2005).
- **The Aerospace Corporation** located in El Segundo CA conducts federally funded defense and aerospace research for the government. Because of the complexity of their projects, retention of scientists and engineers with security clearances is vital. "We don't manufacture anything. Our greatest asset is the technical expertise of our people" (The Aerospace Corporation, 2007). Approximately one half of Aerospace's 3500 workers are over fifty. Consequently, the organization offers four options for retaining their highly skilled workforce past traditional retirement ages: phased retirement, pre-retirement leaves of absence, part-time status in preparation for retirement, and post retirement employment on a "casual" basis, i.e. recalling employees with particular skills during times of peak demand for particular skills (aero.org).

INNOVATIVE IDEAS: 10 TIL 2—PART-TIME

A Denver, Colorado placement firm, 10 til 2, bases its business model on matching college-educated parents and older workers needing flexible work schedules, with organizations that will hire on a part-time long-term basis. Started by four stay-at-home mothers, 10 til 2 considers its business model "win, win, win, win." Workers get flexibility and organizations get access to an experienced, college-educated talent pool. Job listings on the website include a range of positions such as a graphic artist, event planner, and customer service. Recently, 10 til 2 expanded by selling franchises on a national basis and now has offices in eleven states.

CONCLUSION

It is important to remember that the organizations mentioned in this article have made workplace flexibility succeed both for their employees and for their organizations but these companies tend to be the exceptions not the norm. Today's workforce is different in terms of its lifestyle and values. One way to capitalize on these differences is to think creatively about the way work gets done. Innovations that meet the needs of the individuals as well as those of the organization can create win-win solutions. "Current trends seem to suggest that the desire for work-life balance will continue to be a driving force for labor in America regardless of generation" (Beckman, 2010).

Points of Law

The Age Discrimination in Employment Act of 1967 was an expansion of Title VII of the Civil Rights Act. The provisions apply to federal, state, and local governments and organizations with twenty or more employees. In addition, this law protects job applicants and employees over forty years of age from employment discrimination based on age in terms of hiring, firing, promotion, layoffs, benefits, compensation, job assignments and or training. The ADEA forbids retaliation against those who file charges, testify, or participate in investigations, proceedings, and litigation under the ADAE.

http://www.eeoc.gov/types/age.html

DISCUSSION QUESTIONS

1. Analyze the need for work–life balance in terms of the forces promoting and the forces resisting these types of programs.

2. It is mentioned in the reading that even when organizations offer work–life balance plans, some workers, especially men, often do not feel that they can use them. Why might men feel this way more than women?

3. What might the presence *or* absence of flexible work programs suggest to you about the corporate culture and values of an organization?

4. Apply the concept of the business case for diversity to offering more flexible work arrangements for caregivers.

5. In spite of people living longer and healthier lives, stereotypes about older workers being hard to manage and slow to adapt to new technologies still persist. How do the media contribute to and reinforce these perceptions?

6. The organizations profiled in this article are quite different and represent a range from small businesses to huge corporations. What might they all have in common that has enabled them to be innovative about their programs for older workers?

Bibliography

AARP. (2006). Winning strategies, 2006. Retrieved on June 24, from http://www.aarp.org/money/careers/employerresourcecenter/bestemployers/winners/mercy_health_system.html.

AARP. (2006). Winning strategies 2006. Retrieved on June 21, 2007 from http://www.aarp.org/money/careers/employerresourcecenter/bestemployers/winners/ll_bean.html.

AARP. (2007).Workforce trends. Retrieved from http://www.aarp.org/money/careers/employerresourcecenter/trends/a2004-04-20-older-workers.html on June 20, 2007.

Aero.org. (2007). The Aerospace Corporation named one of AARP's best employers for workers over 50. Retrieved on November 15, 2010 from aero.org/news/newsitems/aarp8-12-05.html.

Beckman, G. (2010). Private correspondence. 10 til 2. November 2, 2010.

Boston College Center for Work & Family. (2008). Top 10 takeaways from the Kanter award finalists. *Work and Occupations*, vol.33, 2, May, p. 2–3.

Boushey, H & O'Leary, A. (2009). The Shriver report: a woman's nation changes everything. *Center for American Progress*. Retrieved on November 3, 2010, from americanprogress. org/issues/2009/10/womens_nation.html

Cahill, K., Quinn, J. and Giandrea, M. (2007). Down shifting: the role of bridge jobs after career employment. *The Boston College Center for Aging & Work*: Chestnut Hill, MA.

Carlson, L. (2004). Flextime elevated to national issue. *Employee Benefit News,* September, 8, (12), 1–2.

Catalyst. (2004). Women and men in U.S. corporate leadership: same workplace, different realities? Retrieved May 17, 2007 from http://www.catalyst.org/files/fact/2005%20 COTE%20-20Fact%20sheet.pdf

Challenger, J. (2005). 24 trends reshaping the workplace (part I). *Managing Diversity*, March, 2005, 14, #6, pp. 1, 6 & 8.

Corporate Voices (2005). Business impact of flexibility: an imperative for expansion. (November, 2005). Retrieved on November 10, 2010 from cvwf.org.

Deloitte & Touche. (2010). Redesigning the workplace: fitting life into work and work into life. Retrieved on November 8, 2010 from deloitte. com/view/en_US/us/About/Womens-Initiative/ Redesigning-the-Workplace/index.htm.

DeLong D. & Associates. (2006). Findings from a national survey of aging workers who remain in-or return to-the workplace, how they fare and why.

MetLife Mature Market Institute. Retrieved on June 20, 2007 from http://www.metlife.com/ WPSAssets/11091110421147725122V1FLiving Longer.pdf.

Employees inject vitality into needle production [Electronic version]. (n.d.). *Thomas Register's Trendletter,* 108, 1–2.

Fetterman, M. (2005, June, 8). Retirees back at work with flexibility. From USA Today, 6–8. Retrieved on May 16, 2011, from usatoday. com/money/perfi/retirement/2005-06—8- retiree-main_xhtm.

Frankel, B. (2007). Who really benefits from work/life? *DiversityInc*. March 6, (2), 22.

Galinsky E., Eby, S. & Peer, S. (2008). 2008 guide to bold new ideas for making work work. *Families and Work Institute*. Retrieved on November 8, 2010 from familiesandwork. org/3w/boldideas.pdf.

Gardner, M. (2006). Snowbirds work where it's warm. *The Christian Science Monitor*. February 8, Retrieved on November 15, 2010 from csmonitor.com/2006/0208/ p13s02-lifp.html.

Harrington, B. (2007). The work-life evolution study. *Boston College Center for Work & Family.*

Harrington, B, Van Deusen, F. and Ladge, J. (2010). The new dad: exploring fatherhood within a career context. *Boston College Center for Work and Family*. Retrieved on November 2, 2010 from http://www.bc.edu/centers/cwf/news. html.

Hewitt Associates, LLC. Timely topics survey. Retrieved on November 8, 2010 from, http://www.worklifebalance.com/assets/pdfs/ casestudy.pdf

Jewell, RE. (2008). Corporate Voices for Working Families. Retrieved on November 8, 2010 from http://corporatevoices.wordpress. com/2008/11/19/accentures-future-leave- program-in-wsj-column/

Joshi, S., Leichne, J., Melanson, K., Pruna, C. Sager, N. Slay, C & Williams, K.(2002). Work-life balance . . . a case of social responsibility or competitive advantage? *Georgia Institute of Technology*. Retrieved on November 8, 2010 from http://www.worklifebalance.com/ assets/pdfs/casestudy.pdf

MetLife Mature Market Institute and the National Alliance for Caregiving. (July, 2006). The MetLife caregiving cost study: productivity losses to U. S. businesses. *MetLife Mature Market Institute*. Retrieved October 13, 2010, from http://www.caregiving.org/data/ Caregiver%20Cost%20Study.pdf.

Ortiz, P. (2006) Employee resource groups: the hidden assets. *DiversityInc,* special issue, fall, 75–78.

Prokopeak, M. (2010). Women, wages and work-life balance. *Talent Management Perspectives*. Retrieved on November 3, 2010 from talent- mgt.com/includes/printcontent.php?aid= 1370.

Pruhno, R., Litchfield, L. & Fried, M. (2000). Measuring the Impact of workplace flexibility: findings from the national life measurement project, *Boston College Center for Work & Family*. Retrieved on November 10, 2010 from http://www.bc.edu/centers/cwf/research/publications/meta-elements/pdf/BCCWF_Flex_Impact_Final_Report.pdf.

Raytheon. (2010). Raytheon.com.

Van Deusen, F.R., James. J.B., Gill, N., & McKechnie, S.P. (2008). Overcoming the implementation gap: how leading companies are making flexibility work. *Boston College Center for Work & Family*.

Watson Wyatt Worldwide. (2004. Phased retirement: aligning employer programs with worker preferences. Washington, D.C: Watson Wyatt.

Work-Life Benefits. Retrieved May 13, 2007 from http://www.wlb.com

Writing Assignment

Go to the Web site below and read the "Measuring the Impact of Workplace Flexibility" study. Then, write a two-page memo to a past or present employer that presents a suggestion for implementing some flexible work arrangement for parents, caregivers, older workers, etc. currently not offered by that organization. Adapting ideas from this report, develop a "business case" that stresses the measurable benefits that this particular organization could derive from this new flexible work arrangement that you are proposing. Your answer should take into consideration the demographics of your local area and the size, mission, and resources of this organization.

http://bc.edu/cwf. Click on "publications." Then, click on "Flexibility Work" 2008.

Diversity on the Web

Go to http://cvwf.org (Corporate Voices for Working Families). Click on "publications" and then click on the report, "Business Impacts of Flexibility: An Imperative for Expansion" (November, 2005).

This report details many arguments for increasing flexibility in terms of the way that work is done. Select one company mentioned in this report as having a flexible way of scheduling work. Go to that company's Web site and attempt to find additional information on this plan. You may have to be creative in trying to find this material but be persistent. What does what you found or didn't find indicate about the implementation of this plan?

DIVERSITY TRAINING: IDEOLOGICAL FRAMEWORKS AND SOCIAL JUSTICE IMPLICATIONS

Patti DeRosa
ChangeWorks Consulting

GOALS

- To become familiar with six common approaches to diversity training
- To identify the ideological framework underlying each approach, and the likely outcomes of training designed from this perspective
- To understand strengths and limitations in each framework, and implications for social change

Diversity training is an increasingly common approach that organizations use to address the realities and challenges of a diverse workforce and society and it is estimated to be multi-billion dollar industry. With so much money being spent, and so many companies offering diversity training, it is important to determine exactly what is meant by this term, yet a shared definition remains evasive. Sometimes the term diversity is used so broadly to include such a wide variety of personal human differences that it seems that nothing is exempt from its banner. Being tall or short, a computer technician or an accountant, an ice cream fanatic or a frozen yogurt lover—the talk is just about differences pure and simple. At other times, "diversity" is used as a euphemism for discussing racism and people of color. Most often, "diversity" is used to discuss a de-politicized kind of cultural pluralism that avoids naming and addressing the more difficult topics of racism and oppression directly.*

There are many names, approaches, philosophies, and methodologies that claim the title of "diversity training." Most profess the ultimate goal of establishing a workplace or community of respect, dignity, and inclusion for all people. But do they all envision this in the same way, and will these approaches lead to substantive social transformation?

In over twenty-five years of experience, I have identified six basic ideological frameworks that shape diversity training. They are: (1) Intercultural (IC), (2) Legal Compliance (LC); (3) Managing Diversity & Inclusion (MDI), (4) Prejudice Reduction (PR), and (5) Valuing Differences (VDF); and (6) Anti-racism/Anti-oppression (AR/AO). In this article, each model is presented in its "purest" form in order to provide some generalizations about the ideological

---

framework of each approach. The reader is urged to remember that the models are not quite as rigid, nor are they as mutually exclusive, as an initial review of this discussion might imply. There is often much overlap between them, and practitioners borrow extensively from each of them, especially in technique and methodologies. The actual strategies that each approach uses may also vary to better suit the needs of the particular organization where the training takes place, such as schools, businesses, social services, health care institutions, or community groups.

Each training approach has strengths that should be recognized and encouraged. There are also limitations involved in each that are related to their underlying philosophical systems. The focus of this discussion will be specifically on the ideological grounding diversity training approaches used in workplace settings. It will not directly address diversity planning strategies, multicultural organizational development theory, cultural competency, or multicultural education (although this discussion has application for each of these). The models are arranged alphabetically, except for Anti-Racism/Anti-Oppression, which I have placed at the end for reasons that will become evident later.

1. THE INTERCULTURAL APPROACH (IC)

The primary focus of the Intercultural Approach is the development of cross-cultural understanding and communication between people and nations. It examines the ways in which human beings speak, reason, gesture, act, think, and believe. It tries to help people develop sensitivity to the cultural roots of one's own behavior, as well as an awareness of the richness and variety of values and assumptions of peoples of other cultures. When you hear terms like "worldviews," "cultural relativism," "mores," "value orientation," "verbal/non-verbal communication," and "foreign," you are likely to be dealing with the IC approach.

In the IC approach, ignorance, cultural misunderstanding, and value clashes are seen as the problem, and increased cultural awareness, knowledge, and tolerance are the solution. Cultural identity and ethnicity are the focus, while racial identity is not often explicitly examined. Gender and sexual orientation is explored within the context of culture and tradition, but not often critiqued within the framework of power and oppression.

Cultural simulation games, that attempt to provide participants with the feeling of encountering a different culture, are an IC a staple, as are activities that explore the similarities and differences of culturally specific worldviews and values. IC training is most commonly used to prepare people for working abroad and for helping new immigrants adjust to life in their new country.

Unlike some approaches, IC has a well-developed body of literature and professional organizations. A great deal of IC work takes place in international business settings, foreign student exchanges, and places where people of different nationalities come together.

2. THE LEGAL COMPLIANCE APPROACH (LC)

The classic Legal Compliance training approach is based in legal theory and civil rights law and is primarily concerned with compliance with anti-discrimination law and the subsequent monitoring of recruitment, hiring, and promotional procedures affecting women and people of color to increase their representation in the organization. A main driver is often the avoidance of costly discrimination lawsuits so LC trainings tend to focus on the recitation of laws and policies. In training terms, this can lead to a "teach 'em the law, and fix the 'bad' manager/employee" approach, rather than understanding and changing discriminatory systemic patterns of behavior and organizational culture that go beyond the parameters of the law. Participants may be told the legal do's and don'ts, but given little else to understand the historical context and the cultural changes that are necessary in their work environment.

The LC approach can sometimes lead to misguided enforcement that actually reinforces, rather than challenges, "isms." For example, managers may comply with a quota or goal for hiring women and people of color, but not search for the best candidate—and then when their chosen candidate does not succeed, they claim they "complied" with the law, and blame the poor outcome on Affirmative Action, rather than on their own limited and biased efforts. When implemented this way, existing stereotypes can be reinforced, increasing resistance to legitimate AA/EEO efforts.

A strictly legal compliance perspective can also reinforce the notion of "colorblindness," which says that "people are just people" and differences should not be taken into account. For some, to even acknowledge our obvious differences may be interpreted as evidence of prejudice, and in recent years, there have been increasing legal challenges to civil rights laws based on this assumption. As a basic assumption and as a desired outcome, colorblindness presents a serious contradiction. By definition, Affirmative Action requires organizations to notice information about people relative to their race, ethnicity, and gender and needs to be an explicitly color-conscious policy to combat centuries of color-conscious discrimination. Diversity, by definition, is about seeing and valuing differences, but a traditional LC approach downplays the recognition of differences. In reality, it is not our differences that are the problem and they cannot, and should not, be ignored. The real problem is the negative values that are socially assigned to those differences and the resulting unequal distribution of resources, access, power, and respect on the basis of those differences.

In the LC approach, diverse representation ("parity") and ultimate assimilation to the dominant culture may be seen as the ultimate goal of diversity efforts. This perspective inadvertently reinforces the dominant group's worldview, with the standards of whiteness and maleness as the norm. If the goal is the creation of "multi-colored" organizations, but not truly multicultural ones that reflect the values, histories, and approaches of a wide diversity of people at all levels, full equity and inclusion will remain evasive goals, even if all laws are complied with.

Legal Compliance training usually consists of presentations, lectures, and case studies more often than experiential activities. The legal emphasis of this model also places great limitations on what is covered in training programs. Issues of diversity that are not covered by the federal or state law, such as sexual orientation, may be seen as being outside of the jurisdiction of the program, and therefore omitted.

As a training strategy, the Legal Compliance approach can be regulatory and punitive, rather than transformative, and has limited effectiveness in complex organizational change. It needs to be stressed however, that as a legal strategy, the power and necessity of civil rights law, class-action suits, and other litigation are essential, and are recognized as being one of the most effective tools for intervention and change, especially at the state and federal level.

3. THE MANAGING DIVERSITY AND INCLUSION APPROACH (MDI)

Managing Diversity and Inclusion (MDI) has a very strong presence in the business world, and a large body of publications and research have developed regarding it. The driving force in MDI is that the demographics of the U.S. are rapidly changing, as documented by the U.S. Census which estimates that by 2050, White people will no longer be the majority in the United States. MDI asserts that to survive and thrive in the 21st Century, this diverse labor pool and customer base must be leveraged to enhance business performance. In this approach, one hears phrases like "getting the competitive edge" and "the changing demographics." However, the term "managing diversity and inclusion" seems to imply that if diversity and inclusion aren't "managed," they will somehow get out of control, begging the question of just who is supposed to be managing whom, and why. The word "inclusion" can also have multiple meanings—do we mean inclusion as colonization, where "others" are included into an existing organization as participants to serve that structure but not as full partners, or do we mean inclusion as equity and justice, where power and decision-making is fully shared in a new transformed organization?

While experiential activities are included in MDI training, examination of personal attitudes and behavior may be limited to how they impact the business context, and how stereotypes and prejudice affect hiring and promotional decisions, undermine team effectiveness, productivity, and ultimately profitability. Conflict resolution techniques may also be included, as may strategies for overcoming obstacles to individual professional development. Racism, sexism, and other "isms" are identified as problems to be addressed only inasmuch as they affect the bottom line, and direct terms like "racism" are often consciously avoided.

Much emphasis is placed on seeing diversity and inclusion as a "business issue," rather than as a legal, political, or moral one. There certainly is a legitimate business case to be made for diversity and inclusion. Yet, if a company addresses diversity and inclusion solely for financial gain, what happens if the company sees a way to increase profits by continuing or expanding racist and sexist policies? In some cases, corporations thrive because of the very power inequalities diversity and inclusion initiatives claim to seek to address. Diversity and inclusion training will be nothing more than window-dressing if corporations are unwilling to address and change destructive corporate practices, and political alliances, that foster and maintain inequality and injustice at home and abroad. Dangerous products, environmental racism, multinational expansion and globalization, unemployment, the school-to-prison pipeline and the mass incarceration of people of color, lack of access to quality affordable education and health care, political affiliations and lobbying—these are all "diversity and inclusion issues" that need to be addressed, and that big business has deep financial stakes in.

4. THE PREJUDICE REDUCTION APPROACH (PR)

The Prejudice Reduction (PR) model has its roots in the Reevaluation Counseling (RC) movement. RC theory asserts that all human beings are born with tremendous intellectual and emotional potential but that these qualities become blocked and obscured as we grow older from "distress experiences"—fear, hurt, loss, pain, anger, etc. The RC approach teaches people to help free one another from the effects of these past hurts. As a diversity training model, PR applies the RC framework of exploring and healing past hurts caused by prejudice and bigotry. Common PR phrases include "guilt is the glue that holds prejudice together," "healing past hurts," and "emotional healing."

PR trainings rely heavily on activities that promote emotional release. Sharing personal stories about how you were hurt by prejudice, exchanging painful lessons about stereotyping, hand holding, and crying are likely to be part of a PR workshop. PR techniques can help get at the emotional core of prejudice, setting the stage for change and activism. However, the focus on personal hurt rather than institutional racism may obscure the very real differences in power and experience of dominant group members and oppressed people. The focus on the personal can be frustrating for some. A participant in this kind of workshop once told me, "We need to stop holding hands and start putting our hands to work."

5. THE VALUING DIFFERENCES APPROACH (VDF)

The term "Valuing Differences" is sometimes interchanged with "managing diversity and inclusion," but though similar, they are not the same. Cultural pluralism and the "salad bowl" vision (rather than the "melting pot") are core beliefs of the VDF approach. Rather than ignoring human differences, VDF recognizes and celebrates them as the fuel of creativity and innovation. VDF sees conflict as the result of an inability to recognize and value human differences, implying that the solution lies in learning about, and valuing, ourselves and one another. The core value of VDF is the recognition of individual uniqueness while also acknowledging different group identities.

VDF shares some aspects with other models. VDF builds relationships across lines of difference, recognizing the importance of this in a diverse work team and talks about capitalizing on our differences to help organizations reach their fullest potential. VDF also explores stereotypes and cultural differences, and all kinds of human differences may be addressed. Race and gender are often used as examples, but sexual orientation, language, physical abilities, age, and other personal differences are also included. Recognizing the variety of differences can help create a space for deeper evaluation and learning. Everyone can see ways they are "different" in a VDF program, and that connection is often the hook that leads people to consider the experiences of others.

The VDF approach also has its limitations. VDF training tends to be apolitical. Since all human differences are up for discussion, the unique, and critical, histories and experiences of specific groups that have experienced systemic oppression may be obscured or minimized. Issues of the privilege and entitlement of dominant groups may not be named or examined. In it's effort to be all-inclusive, oppression can be reduced to a "50/50 analysis," equalizing the impacts of mistreatment, and making the false assumption that all groups have equal power to impose their prejudices on others. In fact, from a VDF perspective, introducing the power vs. non-power paradigm may be seen as divisive and reinforcing of an "us vs. them" mentality.

The semantic challenges of MDI and PR are also found in VDF. Terms such as "people with differences" or "diverse people" are common, which begs the question, "Different from whom? Who is the standard?"—implying a hidden referent whiteness and maleness. Seeing the dominant group as somehow "neutral" fails to recognize how the lives of all people are distorted and impacted in societies stratified by race, gender, and other identities.

6. THE ANTI-RACISM APPROACH (AR)

Anti-Racism is at the heart of the "diversity movement," for without it, the other approaches would not exist (although many try to distance themselves from this connection). It is activist in focus and firmly rooted in the civil and human rights struggles in the U.S. and internationally. Based on an understanding of the history of racism and oppression, this expressly political approach emphasizes distinctions between personal prejudice and institutional racism. The goals are not limited to improved interpersonal relations between people of different races, but include an analysis of privilege, and a total restructuring of power relations. Terms such as power, oppression, privilege, and activism are common in this approach. The use of the word "racism" itself may indicate this approach, as followers of other models tend to purposely avoid it.

"Old School" Anti-Racism Training

AR training developed in the 1960s, although it's predecessors include the "race relations" training movement of the 1940s and 1950s, as well as the many, often anonymous, efforts throughout history that brought people of color and white people together to challenge racism. In what I call here "Old School AR," training tended to focus on educating White people, and was often confrontational. The bold, "in-your-face" activities sounded an alarm that motivated some to anti-racist action, but left others feeling blamed, guilty, angry, and powerless.

"Old School AR" could be dramatic and self-righteous, and though the analysis was on-target, attention to the personal, emotional level was sometimes lost in the rhetoric. "Old School AR" focused almost exclusively on black/white issues. The struggles of Latinos, Asians, and Native Americans were not fully included, and there was a reluctance to explore sexism, heterosexism, classism, and other isms as interlocking systems of oppression. In reflecting back, we can now see that while multiracial groups did incredibly powerful community organizing and civil disobedience that fundamentally changed our society for the better, they often unintentionally recreated internally the same hierarchical power dynamics or race, gender, class, etc. that they were struggling against externally.

Anti-Racism/Anti-Oppression Training Today (AR/AO)

Anti-racism training and education has grown and evolved over the years. It goes by many names, but is now sometimes called "Liberation Theory" or "Anti-Oppression work" to expand the focus beyond race, and acknowledge the interconnection with other forms of oppression. I am convinced that, combined with techniques and strategies from the other models, it can help us build authentic social change. The problem with "Old School AR" was not the analysis of power or the goal of total societal restructuring; it was in the process used to achieve that ends. The importance of making space for the personal part of this work was not fully recognized, nor had we yet developed the skills to facilitate change effectively.

Contemporary AR/AO draws from the best of the other approaches. It takes a knowledge of cultural dynamics from the Interculturalists and an understanding of the need for legal supports from the Legal-Compliance approach. From the Managing Diversity and Inclusion model, it takes the recognition of the impact of diversity and inclusion on organizational effectiveness. Like Prejudice Reduction, it is committed to emotional exploration and healing, and like Valuing Differences, it focuses on a wide spectrum of human differences.

Contemporary AR/AO takes all this and adds an analysis of power and oppression and a commitment to activism and social change. Approaches that define the core problem only as one of "exclusion," and promote access to and inclusion in the existing dominant culture, without critiquing and transforming the essence of that dominant culture, ultimately reinforce existing hierarchies. The underlying ideologies and structures of domination and subordination remain, even if the players and the trappings change. AR/AO holds that while the core cultural and institutional structures must fundamentally change, transformation of our personal attitudes are also essential. It examines the parallels, intersections, and distinctions between all forms of oppression, although the focus remains on racism and white supremacy. Bringing in concepts of dominant group privilege and of internalized oppression, AR/AO addresses both dominant and oppressed group members, and makes connections to other forms of oppression.

At its best, Anti-racism/Anti-Oppression training links the micro and the macro analysis, the personal and the political. It requires deep self-examination and requires action in our personal, professional, and political lives. It is inclusive and transformative, and not additive, reformist, or assimilationist.

CONCLUSION

As this article has documented, the label "diversity training" harbors many underlying ideologies and approaches, and it is critical to understand these models. I am concerned that the trend toward the professionalization and commercialization of the "diversity industry" will further remove the work from its activist roots. I often struggle with the contradictions implicit in doing this kind of work "for a living" and am mindful of the potential for my own complicity in the very practices and assumptions I raise here for examination. My observations and ideas are offered in a spirit of critical discourse that challenges all of us engaged in these efforts to carefully examine the profound implications of the work that we do. Ultimately, we must remember that "what we want is a new transformed society, not equal opportunity in a dehumanized one" (Harding, 1983).

DISCUSSION QUESTIONS

1. This article identified six approaches to diversity training. For each of the approaches:
    a. How is the problem defined?
    b. What is the desired outcome or goal?
    c. What kinds of training techniques are likely to be used?
    d. What impact will it have for social justice?

2. Why are the concepts of racism and oppression avoided or minimized in many approaches to diversity training? What could be the results of omitting this perspective?

3. The author takes the position that an Anti-Racism/Anti-Oppression analysis is essential for authentic social change to occur. Why?

4. Have you ever experienced diversity training? If so, which of the six frameworks was your training based on? Justify your answer with examples from the training session.

5. If you have attended diversity training, describe your own personal experiences as a participant:
    a. What approaches or techniques have helped you learn? Why?
    b. What approaches or techniques have blocked your learning? Why?
    c. What concepts made the greatest impact on you?
    d. What concepts were difficult for you? Why?

6. Think of some company that you have worked for. How could it have benefited from providing diversity training to employees? Which of the frameworks would you recommend to the company's management and why?

Reference

Harding, V., *There Is a River: The Black Struggle for Freedom in America,* Vintage Books, 1983.

Patti DeRosa is a consultant, educator, and activitst and President of ChangeWorks Consulting in Randoloph, MA. She has been on the faculty of Simmons College, Boston University, and Lesley University and has a Master of Social Work (MSW) and Master of African American Studies (MA), both from Boston University.

The Diversity Awards: What Do They Mean?

M. June Allard
Assumption College
Worcester State University, Professor Emerita

GOALS

- To explore the various types of diversity awards
- To examine the meaning of diversity awards
- To determine the criteria for selecting diversity winners
- To critically examine selection processes in choosing organizations to honor

Recognition of the diversity achievements in organizations comes in many forms: placing on high profile lists such as "Top companies for . . .," diversity awards, report cards, ratings or profiles.

Diversity awards span a broad spectrum of industries, organizations, functional units and special interest groups. There are international, national, regional, state, county and local awards; corporate, for profit, nonprofit, government and "unrestricted" awards; small-, medium- and large-size workforce, media, marketing, supplier and recruitment & retention awards, and the list goes on.

While there are awards restricted to specific types of organizations, there are also awards that *exclude* specific types of organizations. Some acknowledge diversity practices and programs pertinent to specific minority groups, some honor *innovative* diversity practices and some that consider diversity innovation as merely one of several requirements for corporate social responsibility or philanthropy. Finally, while many awards are designed to recognize diversity practices *per se*, there are others that view diversity as simply one component of good corporate citizenship.

SECTION I. JUDGING THE AWARDS

To understand what these awards mean requires knowing how the award winners are selected.

> . . . the human resources executives who are in charge of [applying for] the lists must examine the underlying methodology to make sure its credible. . . . It's important to look at the nature of the questions asked, the scoring methodology, and the reputation of the publication that's sponsoring the list before proceeding. Silver, L. quoted in Cleaver (2003)

Diversity awards are based on an organization's performance during the previous year, so awards presented in 2011 celebrate the achievements of 2010. The selection process rests upon the sponsor's purpose for creating the award. Sponsors publish clearly stated purposes for making awards that are usually very general and broad in scope such as advancing the working conditions of a particular group; seeking to recognize original diversity practices; informing minority consumers of companies with positive programs for minorities; and promoting minority suppliers. The following are important considerations in deciding what an award really means.

Selection . . . Criteria and Their Weights

All criteria are not created equal. Some may be more important than others with the data relating to these criteria weighted (counting more) than data for other criteria. Nowhere is this more apparent than in the CEI (Corporate Equality Index) ratings where some criteria are worth more points than others. Although some awards sponsors may indicate that certain criteria count more than others, it is rare than they reveal *how much more.*

Selection . . . Collecting the Data

Type of Information   Generally, most awards examine objective or numeric data. For example, organizations respond to questions about how much money they spent on minority vendors, number of workforce members registered in employee affiliation or resource groups, whether or not they have a diversity council, etc. In an effort to provide objectivity, awards may make a point of indicating that *only* quantitative and objective data are considered and that subjective, ancillary and supplementary data are not.

Other awards, most notably those for innovation and media, rest on subjective or qualitative data as they require descriptions of innovative and media programs. However, these are likely to require "hard data" (objective) data to document the effectiveness of their programs.

Finally, a few awards accept both types of data—objective data primarily with additional subjective data to explain and elaborate the objective responses.

Gathering the Information   Nearly all major national awards gather their survey data using online surveys (usually accessible only to registered applicants). Notable exceptions are "The Div 50" award that uses on-line voting and at the other extreme, Catalyst, that engages heavily in telephone and onsite interviews and focus groups.

Information Sources   The majority of the awards to be discussed here rest on extensive applications completed by senior management because central offices have the best overview of company-wide diversity initiatives, particularly in large organizations with global offices. This leaves open the possibility however, that workforce members may have very different views about implementation—views not reflected in the application sent to the awards sponsor. Some awards require a "reality check" through site visits and interviews with members of the workforce or surveys of random samples that include workforce employees to gain a broader perspective on the effectiveness of diversity efforts and the climate of inclusion. For example, an effective diversity-recruiting program in one plant may not be so effective in another plant or location.

Selection . . . The Applicant Pool

Becoming a Contender   How does an organization become a contender for a diversity award? Each award is different. Some send invitations to organizations; some *require* that organizations self-nominate; others do both. The national awards reviewed here that solicit applications tend to do so from the Fortune 500, 1,000 or similar lists. When organizations choose to become applicants, the decision is generally initiated at the corporate level. It is not feasible (or perhaps even possible) in most cases for members of an organization's workforce to initiate a nomination or application for most awards.

How many contenders?   A basic question in evaluating any award is . . . "How many applicants were in the pool?" This is especially important in awards naming "The Top 10 . . ." or "The Best X . . ." Placing in the top 10 is impressive when there are 200 organizations in the pool; much less so if there are 20.

Selection . . . The Judging Process

Blindfolds vs. Open-Eyes   Blind reviews are those in which the judges do not know the names of the organizations whose applications they review. Blind review goes a long way toward eliminating reviewer bias. It may not be totally effective however, when the applications are judged separately for each industry by judges who are drawn from and known in that industry.

When interviews and focus groups are used, blind review, at least in the data collection phase, is not possible. One way to help remove this reviewer bias is for a separate independent panel to make the final award choices without knowledge of applicant identity and without contact with the interviewer panel. Few sponsors indicate use of this practice, however.

Transparency   The greatest difficulty in determining what any award actually means is due to *lack of transparency*, i.e., the openness of the entire process that ranges from nearly completely open (for example, CEI, Corporate Equality Index) to "translucent" (either the survey or interview questions or the selection process is considered proprietary and therefore not public) to almost completely shuttered with little public detail about any part of the award determination. Most awards consider the *number* of applicants to be proprietary, thereby clouding interpretation of what it means to be in the top X of the organizations. The trend recently has been toward greater openness. NAACP, for example, announced procedural changes for greater openness for its 2011 awards. To date, few awards come close to matching CEI or NAACP in transparency.

Final Determination.   The most objective or systematic processes use some sort of preset scoring or point system. Even the more subjective data such as that arising from interviews, can be converted into point systems. It is generally accepted that the best (most objective) judgments are made by panels of judges rather than by a single individual. The names of the judges are not usually made public, presumably to prevent biasing pressures on the judges. It is rarely clear from published information for most awards if a minimum or cut-off score is employed in naming awardees. Cut-off scores, (i.e., no organization scoring below a specified point is given an award), have the advantage of ensuring that the award guarantees a minimum level of diversity program quality.

Results and Outcomes

Interpretation   Even when point systems are used, it is not always easy to interpret the meaning of some awards. Titles such as "Top Companies . . .," "The Best . . ." don't really convey just *how good* the organizations are if no scores are disclosed or more importantly, no minimum performance/score required. Without a minimum of some kind, being "one of the best" could mean anything, e.g., "the best of the mediocre." Without point systems, there is no way to know how good or bad a diversity program is nor is there any way to know the range of quality among programs.

Note that a ***rating*** indicates how well a standard or criterion is met (also called criterion-referenced evaluation). A ***ranking*** is a comparison with other applicants; it is competitive, but does not imply any standard is involved.

The Prize   Organizations get publicity from their own marketing and outreach and publicity from the award sponsor. Beyond publicity, many awards provide performance assessments to applicants. Report cards can "grade" performance by criterion and/or can compare an organization to all other applicants or just to the winners. Usually this feedback is free, but in some cases, applicants must purchase any feedback.

Best Practices   Many of the sponsors compile a list of the best practices they find in the applications they process. Some publish these practices; others offer them for sale. Published lists of winners often indicate why the winners were selected. While the "reasons" may not be explained in much detail, they do give other organizations ideas for improving their own diversity initiatives.

The Awards   To bring some order to the confusing array of awards, they are grouped here into broad categories based upon their principal focus. Each category is represented by descriptions of a few national awards drawn from public information.

- Section II. *Comprehensive Diversity Awards*
  These awards
  a. first specify the ***type of organization(s)*** that are eligible and then
  b. focus on the characteristics and quality of the corporate culture and the diversity efforts of these organizations.

- Section III. *Diversity Innovation Awards*
  These awards focus on the ***innovative character*** of diversity programs and practices, often ignoring the type of organization.

- Section IV. *Special Interest Awards: Race and Ethnicity*
  These awards
  a. first define ***the group(s) that the diversity initiativesserve*** and then
  b. focus on the characteristics and quality of the programs or practices.

SECTION II. COMPREHENSIVE DIVERSITY AWARDS

Comprehensive awards consider diversity programs and practices in general and are inclusive of all racial, ethnic and other minority groups.

Comprehensive Diversity Award		
Award	**Sponsor**	**Eligibility**
1. Top 50 Companies for Diversity®	DiversityInc	Minimum 1,000 employees

1. **Top 50 Companies for Diversity**® (DiversityInc)

   This major national general diversity award is restricted to organizations with large workforces that provide domestic partner benefits. It reflects "standardized measurements made of diversity-management practices and outcomes." From its applications in 2010, DiversityInc also created 12 "special interest" award lists. (DiversityInc, 2010, June, p. 2, 19) (http://www.diversityinc.com Click on: Diversity Top 50 Companies for Diversity; then click on: Methodology)

Criteria   include "demonstrated consistent strength in: 1) CEO commitment to diversity (most heavily weighted area), 2) human capital, 3) corporate and organizational communications, and 4) supplier diversity." Greater criteria detail appears on the web site. Diversity programs must have existed for a minimum of three months. *(ibid)*

Selection Method.   The 2010 awardees were selected from a pool of 449 surveys containing more than 200 proprietary "empirical" questions with predetermined weightings. Evaluation is based on ratios such as work force demographics compared with new-hire demographics and on practices such as refusal to do business in countries that "have values [the companies] perceive as oppressive." *(ibid)*

In the last stage of selection, reviewers do not know the names of the companies they review. Companies are evaluated "within the context of their industries" and a "company must score above 'the average in all four areas.'" *(ibid)*

Results.   Every company that applies receives a free report card.

SECTION III. DIVERSITY INNOVATION AWARDS

The Innovation Awards exhibit includes two awards specifically designed to acknowledge innovative programs and one special interest award for which innovation is one of several criteria. Innovation means different things in different awards. For some awards, innovation means *originality*. For others it means the introduction of programs and practices that are *new to the organization*, but not necessarily original.

Diversity Innovation Awards		
Award	**Sponsor**	**Eligibility**
2. Leading Lights Diversity Awards (general)	NMCI (National Multicultural Institute)	Nonprofit, for-profit, government
3. International Innovation in Diversity Awards (general)	*Profiles in Diversity® Journal*	Organizations and Institutions
4. Applause Awards (women)*	Women's Business Enterprise Council	Public and private organizations

*innovation is one of several criteria for this award

2. Leading Lights Diversity Awards (National MultiCultural Institute)

NMCI awards "celebrate exemplary nonprofit, government, and for-profit organizations which lead with courage, innovation, and commitment, lighting a pathway to a more inclusive society." (http://www.nmci.org Click on: Leading Lights Diversity Awards)

Criteria.   The criteria include: a) innovation of design and implementation, b) senior-level commitment and organizational participation, c) "genuine engagement with, and service to, multicultural communities, not as consumers, but as citizens," d) "transformational impact of diversity and inclusion within the organization/community served" and e) sustainability and replicability of initiative. (*ibid*)

Selection Method. The application is open-ended requiring statements of: a) the initiative including its origin, implementation, goals, objectives and uniqueness, b) organizational support and involvement, c) engagement and contributions to the multicultural communities served; d) evaluation methods including measurable outcomes, testimonials and demonstration of long-term sustainability and e) one successful and one unsuccessful diversity action and way(s) in which initiative could serve as a model. A listing of the Board of Directors and an Annual Report are also required. Applications are reviewed separately by sector by a panel. The application is published online.

3. **International Innovation in Diversity Awards** (*Profiles in Diversity*® *Journal*)

These awards aim to "encourage and share best-practice innovation in diversity; inspire organizations and institutions to take innovative approaches to diversity management; and recognize and reward innovations in industry." Innovations can be new ideas, methods, services or processes. In 2010, *Diversity Journal* published its seventh annual list announcing 21 awards. (http://www.diversityjournal.com.)

Criteria. "Selection criteria include ease of implementation and effectiveness in meeting the program's stated objective, as evidenced by positive outcomes produced by the initiative." The innovation 1) must have been launched within the previous two years, 2) delivered a positive outcome on diversity management, staff recruitment and/or toward inclusiveness and 3) improved equity in the workplace.

"Nominations must be in the form of a concise Executive Summary not to exceed 500 words in length." Two photos may be added; PowerPoint presentations, charts, videos and other files are not used. The application fee is $250.

Presentation of the innovation must include: a) the particularly novel or noteworthy aspect about the innovation, b) the purpose or goal, c) resources employed to implement it (e.g., management support, funding, staffing, communication tools), d) benefits and positive changes achieved, and e) evidence of effectiveness. (http:/www.worlddiversitynetwork.com/news_grdc_0403innovation_awards.aspx)

4. **Applause Awards** (WBE: Women's Business Enterprise Council)

In 2010, the Women's Business Enterprise Council presented its 11th annual awards "honoring corporations with world-class programs that create level playing fields for women's business enterprises . . . which compete for corporate contracts." (http://www.wbenc.org/default.asp?id=341)

Criteria. Initiatives include "impact on the growth of WBEs, creation of policies, procedures or initiatives that increase opportunities for WBEs; and innovative and inspirational leadership on behalf of women business owners and their companies." (http://www.wbenc.org/default.asp?id=342)

Selection Method. No formal application process is used; recommendations by e-mail are accepted. Review and selection of the applications are made by an internal panel from the WBE National Council with "selected WBE and corporate representatives." (*ibid*)

SECTION IV. SPECIAL INTEREST AWARDS: RACE AND ETHNICITY

Awards in this category tend to be sponsored either by organizations representing a specific minority constituency such as AARP awards given for diversity initiatives benefiting older workers or they are "segment" lists derived from larger data bases such as DiversityInc's Top 10 Companies for People with Disabilities. The first set of special interest awards focuses on race and ethnicity.

5. **Best Companies Awards** (Asia Society)

   The result of a landmark 2010 survey designed to strengthen Asian and American relations, the Asia Society presented four awards: Overall Best Company for Asian Pacific Americans to Work For; Best Company for Asian Pacific Americans to Develop Workforce Skills, Asian American Community Award, and Best Company in Promoting Asian Pacific Americans into Senior Leadership Positions. (http://sites.asiasociety.org/diversityforum/awards)

   Criteria. Specific criteria were not listed on the web site.

   Selection Method. An electronic survey, designed and analyzed by an independent company, was distributed to Asian Pacific American (APA) employees (Part I). Corporate chief diversity officers "described the program, policies and activities . . . that support APA employees" (Part II).(http://www.asiasociety.org/files/pdf/APA_Abidged_Report_final.pdf)

6. **40 Best Companies for Diversity** (*Black Enterprise* Magazine)

   Black Enterprise magazine awards focus on activities related to the participation of African Americans and to some extent, members of other ethnic minority groups in their companies. In 2010, the sixth annual listing was published. (http://www.blackenterprise.com/diversity/diversity-list-2009 See R column and click on: View 2009 lists)

Special Interest Awards: Race and Ethnicity		
Award	Sponsor	Eligibility
5. Best Companies Awards (4)	Asia Society	Fortune 500 Employers
6. 40 Best Companies for Diversity	*Black Enterprise* Magazine	Top 1,000 publicly-traded companies and 100 leading global companies
7. Consumer Choice	NAACP	Selected top firms in five Guide (*ratings*) selected industries
8. 50 Best Companies of the Year	*Latina Style Magazine*	None specified

*DiversityInc also publishes separate lists for Asian Americans, Blacks/African Americans and Latinos from its Top 50 Companies for Diversity® database.

Criteria. The survey measures the percentage of African Americans and members of other ethnic minority groups in the company's a) total workforce, b) board of directors and c) senior management as well as d) supplier diversity: the percentage of total procurement dollars spent with companies owned by African Americans and other ethnic minorities. Weights assigned to the four categories differ in different years. "All companies were surveyed on a secondary category—marketing and outreach. This includes advertising, promotions, community outreach and scholarships."

Selection Method. The 2010 survey was sent to the "top 1,000 publicly traded companies as well as the 100 leading global companies with strong U.S. operations." A total score for each company was derived from "quantitative assessment performed in each survey category." ". . . a heavier weighting was applied to scores in the senior management and supplier diversity categories."

7. **Consumer Choice Guide** (NAACP)

As part of its Economic Reciprocity Initiative, NAACP produces this Guide to provide "African American consumers with empowerment tools that enable them to make informed choices when purchasing products and services from the surveyed companies." In 2008, the 12th edition was released. (http://www.docstoc.com/docs/34328584/ NAACP-Consumer-Choice-Guide) (*see p. 5*)

Criteria. The Guide is derived from a survey covering five areas:

1) employment (workforce diversity, recruitment efforts, and employment benefits); 2) marketing/communications expenditures 3) supplier diversity; 4) charitable giving/ philanthropic activity and 5) community reinvestment.

Selection Method. Surveys comprised of quantifiable questions are sent to companies considered to be the leaders of the five industries under review (lodging, financial services, telecommunications, general merchandising, and automotive) that meet revenue or size criteria. In the 2008 survey of 51 companies, subjective and supplemental data were not used. ". . . the scores for supplier diversity were weighted more heavily in the calculation of final grades." Numeric scores ranging from.00 to 4.00 are translated into letter (A to F) grades. "Those companies that refuse to participate . . . receive a grade of F." (*ibid*)

Results. Each industry was graded, as was each corporation on each of the five areas. A summary grade is also given. All grades are published on the Internet.

8. **50 Best Companies of the Year** (*Latina Style* Magazine)

In 2010, Latina *Style* announced its 12th evaluation of "corporations that are providing the best career opportunities for Latinas in the U.S." (http://latina50.latinastyle.com/press.php)

Criteria. Principal areas of evaluation include: number of Latina executives, mentoring programs, Latina board members, educational opportunities, alternative work policies, dependent/child care support, employee benefits, women's issues, job retraining, affinity groups and Hispanic relations. Criteria are weighted, but the weights are not published. (http:/latina50latinastyle.com click: About LS50)

Selection Method. A multi-step selection process begins with a survey sent to the Fortune 1000 companies. In 2007, over 800 companies responded. "Each survey category (employee statistics, employee benefits, recruitment and procurement, career advancement opportunities, diversity initiatives/strategies, and additional programs and policies) is evaluated separately, and then in its entirety. Each company is compared to its own previous performance and also to similar companies. Hispanic community involvement and philanthropic efforts are considered as are data pertaining to Hispanic women. Each company is ranked on a point scale ranging from 0 to 15 for each criterion. The final list is reviewed and approved by an external committee comprised of senior officials from the U.S. Department of Labor and the U.S. Equal Employment Opportunity Commission. (http:/latina50.latinastyle.com click: LS50 special report)

Results.   Large charts reporting on multiple criteria for each company are published on the web (http:/www.latinastyle.com Click on "LS 50 special report").

SECTION V. SPECIAL INTEREST AWARDS: AGE, DISABILITY, SEXUAL ORIENTATION AND GENDER

A second set of Special Interest awards crosses all racial and ethnic lines. These awards recognize organizations with programs or practices that benefit minority groups based on characteristics such as age or sexual orientation.

Special Interest Awards: Age, Disability, Sexual Orientation & Gender		
Seniors Awards	**Sponsor**	**Eligibility**
9. Best Employers for Workers Over 50	AARP (American Ass'n of Retired Persons)	Any U.S.-based employer: minimum 50 employees
Disabilities Awards		
10. Top 10 Companies for People with Disabilities*	Diversity employees*	Inc Minimum 1,000
Sexual Orientation Awards**		
11. Corporate Equality Index for Workplace Equality Innovation	Human Rights Campaign Found.	"Large private-sector U.S. businesses"
Women's Awards**		
12. Working Mother 100 Best Companies work/life or child care firms	*Working Mother* Magazine (NAFE)	Public and private firms No government agencies,
13. Catalyst (women)	Catalyst	No restrictions

* Selected from DiversityInc's Top 50 Companies for Diversity® database.
**DiversityInc also publishes separate lists for Sexual Orientation (LGBT) and Executive Women from its Top 50 Companies for Diversity® database.

9. **Best Employers for Workers Over 50** (AARP)

   AARP recognizes "companies and organizations whose best practices and policies for addressing the issues affecting our aging labor force create roadmaps for the workplaces of tomorrow." This list first appeared in 2001. (http:/www.aarp.org/work/employee-benefits Search keyword: Best Employers)

   Criteria.   Award considerations include: 1) recruiting patterns, 2) opportunities for training, education, and career development, 3) workplace accommodations, 4) alternative work options, such as flexible scheduling, job-sharing, and phased retirement, 5) employee health and pension benefits and 6) benefits for retirees.

   Selection Method.   Applications are evaluated by an independent survey firm and submitted to an independent panel of judges of private sector, nonprofit, and government labor experts. Judge's names and professional associations are posted on the AARP web site. The survey form can be downloaded by registered organizations.

   Results.   All applicants receive feedback comparing their organizations to other applicants.

10. **Top 10 Companies for People with Disabilities** (DiversityInc)

    This annual list is drawn from the pool of applicants for DiversityInc's Top 50 Companies for Diversity®.

    Criteria.   DiversityInc examines "recruiting programs for people with disabilities; work/life and other accommodation benefits; diversity-awareness training that addresses people with disabilities; employee-resource groups for people with disabilities and/or care-givers; and communications, such as web sites and other materials that feature employees with disabilities. DiversityInc also holds discussions with disability organizations for supplemental information." (http://diversityinc.com Click on: DiversityInc Top 50 Companies for Diversity®; then click on: 2010 DiversityInc Lists)

    Selection Method.   The survey and procedures are the same as those of the DiversityInc Top 50 Companies for Diversity®.

    Results.   In 2010, nine of the 10 honorees were also in the DiversityInc Top 50 list. The remaining firm was included in DiversityInc's 25 Noteworthy Companies, i.e., companies that senior editorial staff believe have the potential to make the next year's DiversityInc Top 50 list.

11. **Corporate Equality Index (CEI) for Workplace Equality Innovation (CEI Index)** (Human Rights Campaign Foundation)

    The Human Rights Campaign Foundation does not give awards *per se*, but rather creates an index that "measures how equitably large, private sector businesses in the United States treat their lesbian, gay, bisexual and transgender employees, consumers and investors . . ." The CEI began in 2002. (www.hrc.org/cei)

    Criteria.   Main criteria: 1) non-discrimination policy, diversity training on sexual orientation, 2) non-discrimination policy, diversity training and benefits on gender identity or expression, 3) domestic partner benefits, 4) LGBT employee resource group/diversity council or (half credit) support if employees express interest, 5) appropriate and respectful advertising and marketing or sponsoring LGBT community events or organizations and 6) responsible behavior toward the LGBT community. Subcategories are weighted. Points awarded for each subcategory are published. Total points equal 100. Ratings are criterion-based rather than competition-based. *(ibid)*

Selection Method.   Invitations are sent to the "largest and most successful U.S. employers including the *Fortune* magazine's 1,000 and the American Lawyer's Top 200 Revenue-grossing Law Firms." Additionally, "any private-sector employer with 500 or more full-time U.S. employees can request to participate . . ." In 2010, five hundred ninety firms were rated. The survey is published on-line and available to the public. "A team of researchers investigates and cross-checks the policies and practices of the rated businesses . . ." *(ibid)*

Results.   Findings are published for each company, criterion, industry, globally and in terms of a) nondiscrimination policies and diversity, b) benefits, c) employee groups and diversity councils and d) external engagement. (http://www.hrc.org/documents/HRC_Corporate_Equality_Index_2010.pdf)

12. **Working Mother 100 Best Companies** (National Association for Female Executives, *Working Mother Magazine*)

    2010 marked the 25th year that [*Working Mother* magazine's] 100 Best "raised awareness and encouraged development of new programs to help working moms balance work and family." *Working Mother* also publishes other specialty lists. (http:/www.working mother.com Click on: Best Companies Categories)

    Criteria.   1) workforce profile, 2) benefits, 3) women's issues and advancement, 4) child care, 5) flexible work, 6) paid time off and leave, 7) company culture and 8) work-life programs. Criteria are weighted, but weights are not disclosed.

    Selection Method.   Organizations self-nominate and complete an online survey (available only to registered applicants) of "500 questions on workforce, compensation, child care, flexibility programs, leave policies and more . . . including usage, availability and tracking of programs as well as the accountability of managers who oversee them." An essay "regarding best practices to support working mothers is also evaluated." "Involvement in sex discrimination cases and how the law suits are handled by the organization, are also taken into consideration." *(ibid)*

    Results.   "All applicants receive feedback showing how they compare to other applicants" in terms of usage, availability and tracking of programs and accountability of managers who oversee them. (http://workingmother.com Click on: 2010 Working Mother 100 Best Companies)

13. **Catalyst** (Catalyst)

    "Annually honors innovative approaches with proven results taken by organizations to address the recruitment, development and advancement of all managerial women including women of color." Catalyst began giving awards for diversity initiatives within organizations in 1987. (http://www.catalyst.org/ Click on: Catalyst Award)

    Criteria   ". . . include business rationale, senior leadership support, accountability, communication, replicability, originality, measurable results." Details about each criterion are on the web site. There is an application fee of $2,500 and the requirement that the CEO or Managing Partners/Directors attend the award ceremony. (http://www.catalyst.org/ Click: Catalyst Award; click: Apply for the Catalyst Award)

Selection Method.   The application contains primarily qualitative questions with change outcomes requiring numeric data. Selection processes include telephone interviews and "intensive on-site visits with interviews and focus groups with executive management, high-level women, human resources professional and other employees at various levels." The application questions are public and appear on the web. *(ibid)*

Judges are aware of the identity of the organizations they review. A committee review is made from three perspectives: a) numeric data (minimum of three years of documented evidence of impact (change outcomes) required with data showing improvement), b) the pool of current nominations and c) against previous award winners. Finalists receive over 500 hours of assessment.

Results.   Finalist organizations that do not win have the opportunity to receive a feedback session.

SECTION VI. SUPPLIER AND MEDIA DIVERSITY

The third set of special interest awards has a more external focus and honors diversity business activities such as media content and promotional messages and purchases from multicultural suppliers.

Special Interest Awards: Supplier and Media Diversity		
Award	**Sponsor**	**Eligibility**
Supplier Diversity Award		
14. "The DIV 50" Top 50 Organizations for Multi-Cultural Business Opportunities-	DiversityBusiness.com	Fortune 500 companies and government agencies)
Media Diversity Award		
15. EMMA (Excellence in Multi-Cultural Business Opportunities	NAMIC	Membership in NAMIC) (Nat'l Ass'n. for Multi-Ethnicity in Communication)

*DiversityInc also publishes a separate list for Supplier diversity from its Top 50 Companies for Diversity® data base

14. Top 50 Organizations for Multicultural Business Opportunities

In 2010, DiversityBusiness.com announced its 10th annual list of "companies in the U.S. that truly differentiate themselves in the market place . . . The 'Div 50' list has . . . become the consumer guide for women and minority consumers." An annual list of the top government agencies for multicultural business opportunities is also published. (http://www. DiversityBusiness.com) . . . awarding the top buyers of multicultural products and services is becoming a natural part of the new socio-economic food chain. (http://diversitybusiness.com/news/supplierdiversity/45200906.asp)

Criteria. Selection is based on volume, consistency and quality of business opportunities granted to women and minority-owned companies.

Selection Method. Winners are selected via on-line voting, based on 10 questions about diversity. Each question is answered by selecting a company from a preset list. There is an optional "Comments" section. After selection of the awardees, the survey is published on-line and open to the public. Presumably the companies recording the highest votes make the DIV 50 list.

15. **EMMA** (NAMIC)

NAMIC's diversity awards reflect its mission to "educate, advocate and empower for multi-ethnic diversity in the communications industry." EMMA awards are made in two divisions: a) cable companies and b) networks and industry suppliers. (http://www.namic.com)

Criteria. Two (2) categories are available to both the (a) cable companies and (b) networks and industry suppliers divisions:

Category 1. "*Case Studies/Campaigns* awards recognize efforts ... to acquire and retain culturally diverse customers through marketing, operational community and public relations and/or diversity awareness."

Entrants complete an outline. Entries are evaluated on "strategy development, implementation and analysis of results." No weighting is mentioned.

Category 2. "*Marketing Tactics* awards recognize excellence in developing individual tactics for ethnic-targeted marketing . . . in direct mail, diversity awareness, grassroots, internet/new media, out of home, print, radio, television, and all other media." Entrants must include a brief strategy statement. Entries are judged on "sound or innovative strategy, strength of creative execution against the strategy, and results and how they can be duplicated and/or scaled." (http://emmacompetition.com Click on: enter)

One or more cultural segments must be included in both categories. Outline and strategy topics appear on the web site open to the public. The application fee is $200 per submission.

Selection. Judging is done by a "panel of independent industry experts chosen by NAMIC." (http://emmacompetition.com Click on: Rules and Guidelines)

SECTION VII. THE DECISION TO APPLY

Costs and Risks Most national awards are given by magazines or by industry associations and most do not charge an application fee. Applying for a national award is costly however, even without an application fee because of the need to compile all the application information.

In addition to costs, there are some risks in applying. An organization's affairs are opened to scrutiny by outsiders, thereby risking disclosure of company secrets. For those who do make the winner's list, sometimes winning can incur negative consequences. In 2005 for example, anti-gay groups targeted Kraft for its sponsorship of the 2006 Gay Games (DiversityInc, 2005) and for nine years, The American Family Association boycotted Disney for gay activities such as providing domestic partner benefits and hosting "Gay Day" at theme parks (HRC, 2005).

Additional negative consequences for winners may result from failing to win or receiving lower ratings in succeeding years—an embarrassment for managers, shareholders and the board of directors. Winning a place on the list creates internal and external pressures to *stay* on the list. *Winning* raises employee expectations . . . "If we're so good, why don't we have . . ." Organizations wishing to stay on a list must show constant improvement—a stated criterion for some awards. In the words of Cleaver, ". . . unless you improve the programs you offer, you won't stay on" (2003, p. 2). Winning gets harder each year as more companies compete and other winners improve their programs.

Benefits to the Organization   Given the costs and the risks, why do organizations apply? What might they gain and are the potential benefits really worth it?

Business Case for Diversity Unfortunately, the financial impact of winning is both complex and costly to measure. Because it is difficult to separate diversity from overall good management, impact studies are few, but have focused on measuring differing outcomes:

> ***Shareholder return.***   DiversityInc analyzed the stock market performance of publicly traded companies and "documented a significant and long-term connection between superior diversity management and share-holder return" (Visconti & Peacock, 2005).

> ***Productivity.***   In 2005, the National Urban League's large investigation of productivity found effective diversity programs "collectively generating 18 percent greater productivity than the American economy overall." (NUL, 2005)

Revenue & growth McKinsey et al report: "companies that leverage the diversity of their people . . . see an increase in revenue, more rapid growth, increased stock price and market valuation, and improved net-incomes" (USEEOC, 2008, p. 15).

Even though the findings of financial impact are only correlational rather than causal, i.e., diversity efforts are *associated* with financial gain, but don't necessarily *cause* this gain, organizations are increasingly convinced that diversity efforts do indeed affect the bottom line.

Human Capital Benefits National awards are viewed as badges of quality. Being on a list is a sure source of corporate pride, and a low-cost marketing and recruitment too." (Silver, 2003). ". . . we saw that rankings—with that third-party endorsement—would be powerful as a recruiting tool." (Heying, M. quoted in Cleaver, J. 2003)—an especially valuable asset in light of the McKinsey study finding that the most important resource for companies over the next 20 years will be the diversity among its employees (USEEOC, 2008).

National recognition cannot only impact recruiting, but also workforce retention and consumer loyalty (*DiversityInc* 2007, July/August p. 45). Thus, forward-thinking organizations now focus on the new demographics: the minority workforce and the global and minority consumer markets.

The Pressures of Changing Demographics

The Minority Workforce   The minority workforce will increase greatly in both size and in percentage of the total workforce and by mid-century will comprise more than half of the U.S. workforce. "Nearly one in five Americans (19 percent) will be an immigrant in 2050 compared with one in eight (12 percent) in 2005" thus underscoring the arguments that diversity recruitment and retention efforts will become even more critical as the war to gain talent escalates (Pew Research Center 2008, February 11)

The Minority Consumer Force   The purchasing power of U.S. minority racial and ethnic groups is growing rapidly in dollar value and in market share. "As multicultural and female owned businesses gain more buying power and their lifestyles become more affluent, multicultural markets are growing in economic muscle" (DiversityBusiness.com, 2010).

The dramatically-expanding, multi-ethnic consumer markets are expected to reach $43,400 billion by 2014, some 26 percent of the total U.S. buying power and these projections do not include other minorities such as older consumers, people with handicaps and LGBTs (Humphreys, 2009).

The composition of the workforce directly links to consumer markets. In the words of Greg Smith, "We *have* to have employees who look like and understand the nuances and buying practices of the diverse communities we want to serve" (Trebilcock, 2007). This becomes very important in light of the growing movement among minorities to buy from companies that support their own groups (e.g., support such as worker inclusion, supplier purchasing and community event support). "We're very, very loyal to LGBT-friendly brands and companies . . ." (G. Ocasio quoted in Stevenson, 2007)

SECTION VIII. THE AWARDS IN PERSPECTIVE

The Criteria

Overview of the Common Criteria   Exhibit 1 provides a general overview of the criteria for selecting winners of the comprehensive award and the racial and ethnic awards. The chart is intended only as a generalization—as some sponsors have very vague or very general statements of criteria while others are extremely detailed. For example, a criterion of "communication" may refer to activities within the organization, to media and marketing in the community or to both. Since most survey questions are kept confidential, it is frequently not possible to determine the measurement or meaning of many criteria from the published description of the selection method. Conversely, some sponsors break criteria down into very specific units such as multiple detailed health benefits.

Criteria for Innovation, Supplier and Media diversity awards are presented in Exhibit II. The criteria and corresponding data collection differ from those of the other awards. Here the focus shifts away from the work situation to external and far narrower concerns.

EXHIBIT I Overview of General Criteria for Selecting Diversity Award Winners

Criteria	Comp.	Asian	Black		Hispanic	Age	LGBT	Women
Award No:	1	5	6	7	8	9	11	12
Staffing								
Workforce diversity	*		*	*	*			*
Management diversity	*		*		*		*	
CEO/commitment	*							
Career Advancement						*		
Mentoring	*				*			
Affiliation/resource groups	*				*		*	
Fast track/leadership train.					*			*
Promotions	*							
Diversity training								
Training/educ'l opportunities					*	*		
Benefits/Incentives			*		*		*	*
Health					*	*		
Pension						*		
Company culture/inclusion								*
Alternative work schedules					*	*	*	
Communication	*		*					
External Relations					*			
Community involvement			*	*			*	
Philanthropy	*		*	*				
Vendor/supplier diversity	*		*	*				*
Marketing	*				*	*	*	
Recruitment	*			*	*	*		
Web site diversity	*							
Innovation/Initiative								
Impact/Results								
Replicability								
Implementation/Ease or								
Creativity								
Sustainability								
Business Opportunities for Women and Minority-Owned Companies								
Volume								
Consistency								
Quality								

Award

1 Top 50 Companies for Diversity
5 Best Companies *(not available)*
6 40 Best Companies for Diversity
7 Consumer Choice Guide

8 50 Best Companies of the Year
9 Best Employers for Workers Over 50
11 Corporate Equality Index (CEI)
12 100 Best Companies for Working Mothers

EXHIBIT II Overview of General Criteria for Selecting Diversity Award Winners

	...Innovation....				Supplier	Media
Award	2	3	4	13	14	15
Criteria Staffing						
Workforce diversity						
Management diversity						
CEO/commitment	*	*		*		
Career Advancement						
Mentoring						
Affiliation/resource groups						
Fast track/leadership train.						
Promotions						
Diversity training						
Training/educ'l opportunities						
Benefits/Incentives						
Health						
Pension						
Company culture/inclusion	*	*				
Alternative work schedules						
Communication	*	*				*
External Relations						
Community involvement	*					*
Philanthropy						
Vendor/supplier diversity					*	
Marketing						
Recruitment						*
Web site diversity						*
Innovation/Initiative						
Impact/Results	*	*	*			
Replicability	*		*			
Implementation/Ease or Creativity		*				
Sustainability		*				
Business Opportunities for Women and Minority-Owned Companies						
Volume		*			*	
Consistency		*			*	
Quality		*			*	

Key 2 Leading Lights Diversity Awards   13 Catalyst   15 EMMA Cable
    3 International Innovation in   14 "The DIV 50"   Companies and
      Diversity   Networks & Industry
    4 Applause Awards   Supplier Awards

QUALITY CONTROLS . . . NOTEWORTHY SELECTION PRACTICES

What have *sponsors* learned about making awards? Examination of award criteria and selection practices suggests that a number of quality controls have been developed. Some examples are:

- Programs and practices must be in existence for a specified length of time to be considered initiatives created shortly before the application are too new to demonstrate sustained effectiveness and those created too far in the past do not qualify as innovative.
- Programs and practices must have demonstrated (documented) consistent strength. Some programs start well, but have implementation problems.
- Companies are compared to others in their industries and employee skill sets . . . an engineering company is likely to have a small pool of women compared to a retail company.
- Evaluation criteria have preset weightings to avoid after-the-fact bias.
- The minimum required workforce numbers are only for **full-time** employees. Seasonal employees can temporarily swell diversity percentages.
- The minimum required workforce numbers are for U.S.-based employees. Global employees distort diversity numbers.
- The percentages of minority members holding line rather than staff jobs asks organizations to figure out which managers at every level are responsible for their units' bottom lines and what percentage of those managers are women.
- Companies must report the usage and availability of programs because it's not enough to have a great program if no one is using it."
- Companies must report the number of minorities in each workforce level.
- Supplier diversity companies are audited and must have third party certification.
- Diversity improvements must be documented with objective data.
- Distribution of diverse workforce groups must ensure they are not isolated at specific work sites or departments of the organization.
- Class action lawsuits and the organization's response to them are considered.

Considerations

"People don't know the components of the weighting . . . People assume that the lists are credible." (M. Weiner quoted in Cleaver, 2003). Given the lack of information readily available about how many awardees are chosen, caution is urged in attaching too much credence to them. Bear in mind that awards made to large national organizations are not necessarily reflective of their offices in all locations.

QUESTIONS TO CONSIDER . . . AS A POTENTIAL EMPLOYEE . . . AS A POTENTIAL CONSUMER

1. Is the award criterion-based or competitive, that is, are organizations judged against pre-set standards or only judged against other companies?
2. What are the specific criteria for the award?
3. What is the selection process? Does the sponsor divulge the details of how the selections are actually made? Who does the judging?
4. Are the data subjective? objective? both?
5. How large is the applicant pool?
6. Does the process use blind review?
7. Who within the organization actually completed the application? Who had a voice in it?
8. Is the organizational workforce comprised only of full timer employees or are part-timers also included (potentially adding to diversity ranks)?
9. Are contenders judged by industry?
10. What are the performance indicators, i.e., how is the "success" of the organization's diversity program measured?

DISCUSSION QUESTIONS

1. DiversityInc's list of Top 10 Companies for LGBT Employees requires that any company named to this list must have a Corporate Equality Index (CEI) rating of 100 percent, thus linking this list to the Human Rights Campaign Foundation corporate ratings. Do you think this is a good practice? Explain.

2. The Civil Rights Act of 1964 protects people from discrimination based on race, color, sex, national origin, and religion. Employee affinity and resource groups are common for all of these (except for religion) in organizations winning diversity awards. For example, only 10 percent of the 401 companies in the 2009 DiversityInc Top 50 Companies® competition have religious resource groups. Why do you think this is the case?

3. The hospitality and travel industries target a diverse consumer market. If you were to create a diversity award for one of these industries,
   a. What would be your mission?
   b. What criteria might you consider in making this award and why might you select these criteria?

4. In some companies, the human resources director selects the minority workers who respond to the employee survey from the award sponsor. Evaluate this practice.

5. If you were a potential employee such as a working mother or Asian man and saw an award for your group on a company's web site,

   a. Prior to a job interview at that company what would you ask a friend of yours who works at the company and why?

   b. What questions could you then ask in a job interview concerning whether this company actually implements the policies?

   c. Why should these questions differ from each other?

Writing Assignment

Select a diversity category (other than supplier diversity) and design an original diversity award for organizations in your category. Specify:

   a. Name of the award and type (list, profile, award, etc.)
   b. Purpose of the award
   c. Eligible organizations
   d. Criteria (clearly relate to the purpose of the award)
   e. Selection process

Starting Sources:
   • Section I. Judging the Awards (from the text article)
   • CEI methods/sources for checking the self-reports of the organizations it rates
   • Considerations and Quality Controls (from the text article)

Bibliography

Cleaver, J. (2003, May). Lust for lists. *Workforce Magazine*, pp. 44–48.

Diversity Business.com® (2010). 10th annual national business awards. http://www.diversitybusiness.com/businessawards

DiversityInc (2007 July/August) Partner with GLBT-advocacy organizations. p. 45.

DiversityInc. (2005, May 25). Anti-gay AFA targets top 50 company. downloaded 4/17/2006 from http://www.diversityinc.com/pblic/14574.cfm

DiversityInc. (2010, June 2). Top 50 companies for diversity. Retrieved May 15, 2011, from diverityinc.com. Click on diversity top 50 companies for diversity: then click on methodology. p. 18.

HRC (2005, May 25). American family association backs off Disney boycott. http://www.hrc/issues/parenting/2246.htm

Humphreys, J. (2009). *Georgia business and economic conditions.* The multicultural economy 2009. v 64 no. 3.

National Multi-Cultural Institute (http://www.nmci.org click: Leading Lights Diversity Award).

NUL (2005). Diversity practices that work: The American worker speaks. http://www.NUL.org Type in search engine: Diversity practices that work.

Pew Research center. (2008, February 11). U.S. population projections: 2005–2050. http://www.pewhispanic.org/files/reports/85.pdf

Silver, L. (2003, May). Quoted in Cleaver, J. Lust for lists. Retrieved on May 15, 2011, from http://www.workforce.com/section/recruiting-staffing/feature/lust-lists/index.html, p. 44.

Stevenson, J. (2007). As business owners and consumers, the LGBT community gains strength. http://www.businesswest.com Type in search box: As business owners and consumers.

Trebilcock, B. (2007). *DiversityInc.*, July-August). Diversity in the travel & hospitality Industry.

USEEOC. (2008, December 21). Asian American and Pacific Islander work group report to the chair of the equal employment opportunity commission. p. 14. http://www.eeoc.gov/federal/reports/aapi.html

Visconti, L & Peacock, F. (2005, June). Publishers' Letter. *DiversityInc.* p. 12.

Diversity on the Web

The NAACP is revising its procedures for evaluating large corporations in 2010 (for 2011 Consumer Choice Guide Ratings) "the processes associated with these report cards will be transparent."

Visit the Web site below to view the current methodology and the proposed changes. http://www.naacp.org/pages/naacp-corporate-fairness-scorecard

Compare and contrast the new selection procedures with the old ones.

1. In what way(s) will the new method be more transparent?
2. Can you think of ways that it might be made even more transparent?
3. Can you think of other ways the evaluation process might be improved?

Evaluating Diversity Management: Conducting a Diversity Audit

Carol P. Harvey
Assumption College

GOALS

- To provide a capstone learning experience for students that enables them to learn how the theories and cases studied during the semester apply in the real world
- To allow students to improve their critical thinking skills by developing and applying criteria to the evaluation of an organization's diversity initiative
- To provide students with the opportunity to compare and assess the relative levels of commitment that organizations have or do not have to implementing and managing diversity programs
- To help students to learn about the dynamics of working on a team
- To showcase the unique ways that some organizations are working to manage diversity and to illustrate that some organizations may be ignoring the business case for diversity and limiting their efforts to legal compliance

With the current emphasis on the business case for diversity and the goal of an inclusive workplace the diversity audit is designed to be a capstone assignment that measures where an organization is in terms of its change efforts. **Diversity audits** are evaluations based on qualitative and quantitative information about the status of diversity within the organization. Today, many organizations conduct audits to assess their progress in determining the effectiveness of diversity recruiting and retention efforts, measuring the value of diversity training, surveying workers about the success of diversity initiatives, such as supplier programs, employee resource groups and diversity councils. These audits reveal whether a gap exists between what is being done and what the organization should do in terms of diversity and are used as a basis for action planning.

Although this assignment is not as involved as a real corporate internal diversity audit, the *content* is designed to provide students with an opportunity to visit a real organization and to gather enough information to evaluate its progress in terms of its diversity initiatives. While the team should make recommendations for improving diversity at this organization in the paper and presentation, because of possible legal ramifications, it is *not* their role to act as actual consultants.

Dividing up the work equitably and preparing the criteria and questions for the interview are part of the assignment. Do not expect your instructor to do this for the group.

INSTRUCTIONS

After your instructor forms groups of 4 to 5 students, it is important to follow the sequence as numbered below.

1. **Find an organization** that is willing to work with your group. The group should meet early in the semester to brainstorm possible organizations that might be willing to participate in this project. As always, it may be easier to gain access if a group member already has an established relationship with an organization such as an internship placement, a job there, or a family member who is employed there. Notice how these connections illustrate an example of privilege.

   Groups should always have an alternative organization in mind just in case their first choice does not work out. Some companies may refuse because they are afraid of what students may find, or are currently involved in a lawsuit, etc.

   If a group selects a major corporation whose headquarters is not local, it may be necessary to visit more than one site to get a more accurate sense of the organization's diversity efforts. Very early in the semester, make contact with someone in the organization. Explain the assignment for what it is: an opportunity for students to learn firsthand how a real organization deals with diversity issues on a daily basis.

   The group needs to be realistic about this field assignment. Sometimes small companies of less than 300 employees are more difficult to audit because their size limits the financial and human resources available for diversity efforts. In contrast, in large *Fortune* 500 companies it may be more difficult to find the right contacts. Even organizations that are willing to cooperate may find it difficult to schedule meeting times that work for students. So, it is imperative that the team line up both a first choice and at least one backup choice for this project and begin the process early in the semester in case the group encounters difficulties.

2. **Conduct secondary research** which involves materials gathered for another reason. Internal examples include annual reports (a good source of mission and value statements), press releases, employee handbooks, and any other materials that the organization can provide. Explain to your contact person that the group would like to be as knowledgeable as possible about the organization to maximize the time on the visit. Today much of this information also can be found on the internet. While this is a good place to start, be aware that information on an organization's website is subjective and prepared by the public relations staff, whose job it is to present the organization in a favorable light.

   Any material that the group can find or the organization can provide should be read by each group member *before* preparing the questions for the visit. Students should also conduct thorough *external* secondary research on their organization for additional material. Utilizing various library databases, students may discover very useful information. For example, some companies are often the subjects of articles that can be found in newspaper and periodical databases. Many companies with strong diversity programs also have been involved in discrimination lawsuits that are detailed in legal databases. Since students are not apt to be told about these on site visits, it is important to thoroughly research your organization.

3. **Preparing to visit the organization** involves making an appointment to interview at least three company representatives, managers and/or employees. If you can interview people from different functions, areas and levels (CDO, human resources, training, managers, members of ERGs, and hourly employees), it will provide different perspectives and richer data. Although all team

members do not need to go on the interview, at least two or three should participate to minimize bias. Because many organizations are reluctant to let students record interviews, it is more realistic to be prepared to take notes. Of course, multiple visits would probably provide richer data, and some organizations will give students the time for this, but many will not.

When making an appointment, it is helpful to arrange for a tour of the organization because this is how the groups may discover interesting observations that contrast with the information that they will be given. For example, one student group visiting a medium-sized manufacturing plant observed that the entire manufacturing workforce was composed of Asian American women. They later learned that one of the top managers believed that Asian women had small hands that made assembling electrical components easier. So, he instructed his supervisors to hire only Asian women in the assembly area. Job applications from all others were immediately discarded. At another site, students were proudly shown a "Mother's Room" for the pumping of breast milk. When they asked about the usage of this facility, they were told that it was installed at the insistence of one female manager years ago and it is never actually used by anyone but her. Another group discovered a non-denominational chapel inside a major corporation.

NOTE: *To clarify steps four through eight, which are based on the critical thinking process, the same element, diversity training, will be used here as the example for each item. Before visiting the organization, the whole group should meet to work on three items:*

4. **Establish criteria** (i.e., standards) for a diverse organization. These could include easily measurable items such as the number of women and people of color on the Board, the presence or absence of ERGs, supplier diversity programs, funds spent on diverse community causes, etc. Remember that the group's criteria for what would make an inclusive diverse workplace must be tailored to the mission, size, resources, location, etc., of the organization selected. For example, a non-profit hospital located in a very diverse community will be very different from a Fortune 500 company with a headquarters in New York City and branches located in many countries. Other items like training may be harder to measure and this is why criteria are so important.

   Example: The group may be told that an organization has a diversity training program. Without items (i.e. criteria) that you can evaluate this program against, it is difficult to decide if this is an effective program or not. On an audit visit, one student group found out that the diversity training program consisted of requiring all new employees to watch a DVD. Their criteria for effective training included having employees involved in interactive learning, ongoing training efforts and training for all levels of the organization. Clearly, this methodology did not meet their criteria established for effective diversity training.

5. **Prepare a list of thoughtful questions** about this organization's diversity efforts that the group will explore on the visit(s). Avoid yes or no questions that will provide less information. Try to ask more open ended questions, basing these on what the group already knows about the organization through its secondary research. Always, start with the easier more general questions and progress to the more probing ones.

   Example: By questioning employees, based on the previously established criteria, the group found out that nobody supervised this "training," there was no follow up discussion or debriefing and that some new employees actually fell asleep in the darkened room!

6. **Visit the organization/conduct primary research.** Make an appointment that is convenient for your contact. Dress professionally; be on time, polite, and respectful of your contact's time constraints and send a follow up thanking the contacts for their time. If the group is

thoroughly prepared and is knowledgeable about the organization, it will show. Occasionally, student teams are asked that the name of the company be kept confidential. The teacher will have to know the true identity of the organization to assess the team's work. However, a fictitious name can be used for the paper and class presentation. Try to gather additional information through observation. Be sure to pay attention to "subtle" cues of inclusion or lack of inclusion. Is there evidence that they really do what they say they intend to do?

Example: On the visit, the students asked if they could watch the diversity training DVD. When they watched it together, the group was amazed at how simplistic and boring it was and this information was an additional negative factor to consider in determining the organization's level of commitment to change and inclusion.

7. **Review, connect and relate** what the group now knows from secondary and primary research the semester's readings to understand these theories may apply to this organization. This discussion which is the most critical part of the process, should only take place after the visit(s). Groups that do the best on this assignment, usually take ample time to do this stage well. The entire group should meet and debrief. In terms of diversity: What did they really see on the visit? What does it mean in terms of the organizational culture? What did they learn? How did the visit support or refute what they had learned through their secondary research? What seems contradictory? What evidence is there of true inclusion? How can the theory learned during the semester, help to explain what they know about the organization?

Example: What level of the Thomas & Ely framework does the training system seem to address? The group found that this national retailer, well known for its diversity hiring practices, focused all its diversity training such that is was, only on customer interactions (the access and legitimacy paradigm) and nothing on working in a diverse environment with people unlike themselves.

   After thoroughly discussing the data, the group should evaluate their organization *against their established criteria for a diverse organization*. At this point, the group may find that they omitted some factors and may need to add additional criteria.

Example: This same student group saw a coffee mug labeled "DIVERSITY the XYZ Company" on the visit. Obviously, they had no way to know about this in advance. In their post-visit discussions they decided that this mug was merely an artifact in Schein's levels of organizational culture. Their conclusion was that this company *espoused* diversity as a value only in a superficial way not to offend diverse customers and to avoid lawsuits not to operationalize diversity in terms of organizational change or inclusion. After watching the training video, each participant had to sign a paper attesting that they were present for the screening. These were kept on file in case of legal action. The mug was in fact given to each person who sat (or in some actual cases slept) through the training DVD!

8. **Prepare written report** *(NOTE: Your instructor may assign different length and additional content requirements)* approximately 12 to 14 pages in length that explains the findings in detail. The paper should be free from spelling and grammatical errors, cite all sources and interviews in a bibliography, and contain any additional helpful material in an exhibit section (copies of organizational value statements, relevant press releases, company newsletters, etc.).

   The report should detail the strengths and weaknesses of the organization's diversity initiatives and be organized as follows:
   - A one-paragraph executive summary
   - One page company background (history, size, industry, organizational structure, etc.)
   - One to two pages explaining the group's criteria for a diverse organization

- One to two pages describing what the group learned on the visit(s).
- The remainder of the paper should focus on evaluating the organization's efforts in terms of the diversity concepts covered in this course, by connecting course concepts to the organization's diversity programs. For example, how does this organization tie diversity to its mission and values, what inclusion strategies does this company implement, is there evidence of a business case for diversity in this organization, etc.?
- The paper should conclude with the team's recommendations for change and a team "grade" grade (A, A-, B+, B, B-, etc.) for this organization's diversity and inclusion efforts.
- Bibliography, exhibits, etc.

9. **A presentation** to the class will allow the groups to learn from each other. It is particularly interesting to see the different approaches and contrasts of the organizations. Each team of students should make a class presentation that details the results of their diversity audit. As a minimum, the presentation should include a short company background, a list of the group's criteria for a diverse organization, anything particularly interesting learned from the visit(s), and an explanation of the group's evaluation of their organization, linked to the textual theory, in terms of how it attempts to manage diversity and inclusion.

It is expected that the group will use visual material (PowerPoint slides, handouts, material supplied by the organization, etc.), rehearse their presentations so that individual speakers do not repeat each other's material, not exceed the time limits set by the instructor, not read their presentations, dress appropriately, and be prepared to answer questions from the class.

At the conclusion of the talk, the group, *without revealing the grade that they assigned to the organization*, should ask for a show of hands from the class members as to what letter grade from A–F should be assigned to this organization. Then, they can reveal what grade the group gave the company for their diversity efforts and the rationale behind the decision.

Writing Assignment

Assessing Group Diversity, Process, and Conflict Resolution

During the completion of this group project, you have had the opportunity to interact with students who may be different from you in their work habits and styles. In addition to visible social identity group differences, such as race, and gender, often differences in terms of personality, time management, leadership styles, values, etc. can cause conflict in terms of the quality, satisfaction, and completion of group projects both in classes and in the workplace. Since you are finishing a course on "diversity" management, this is a good time to assess the issues of productivity, individual difference, and conflict resolution in terms learning from this group experience.

Write a four- to five-page paper that analyzes the group performance in terms of the group process, i.e. how effectively this group worked together. In your paper be sure to answer the following questions but do NOT use any actual names of group members:

- What were the primary differences in terms of working style that helped or hindered this group from accomplishing their objectives for this project?
- How did the group effectively or ineffectively deal with these differences?
- Did someone assume a leadership role? Was the leadership style effective or ineffective? Why?

- If there were conflicts or conflict avoidance in this group, apply Parker's article, "The Emotional Connection of Distinguishing Differences and Conflict" to evaluate the resolution or lack of resolution of the conflicts.
- In retrospect what could the group have done differently to produce a more effective project? What could the group have done differently to do it more efficiently?
- From this analysis, what have you learned about this experience about diversity that can also be applied to productively managing the differences that can be "invisible" in the workplace?

Diversity on the Web

EVALUATING ORGANIZATIONAL COMMITMENT TO DIVERSITY: AUDITING WEB SITES

In the twenty-first century, Web sites are an important channel of communication between organizations and their external stakeholders. If an organization is serious about its commitment to diversity, one would expect that this would be reflected in the design, content, and graphics of the Web site. Potential employees, customers, suppliers, etc., often turn first to a Web site before initiating interaction with an organization. If diversity is really integral to the mission and values of an organization, information on diversity should be easily accessible, informative, and well integrated into the Web site.

Your instructor will select an industry such as healthcare, hospitality, manufacturing government, education, sports, etc. or specific Web sites that members of the class will use for this assignment. Then, prepare a report on the following:

1. Evaluate how *accessible* diversity-related material is on this Web site. Is there a direct link from the home page? What type of results does entering the term "diversity" in a search box yield? Or, do you have to explore on your own? Sometimes searching under "careers" or "press releases" may produce some diversity-related results. On some Web sites, students will have to explore deeply into Web pages to find material related to diversity. What does this say about the organization's commitment to diversity?
2. Evaluate the *usefulness* of the diversity information to potential employees, customers, and suppliers. Is the diversity material related to the organization's business case for diversity, core values, mission, etc. the way that the organization does business? How current is the diversity-related material? For a good example explore Hewlett Packard's Web site at http://www.hp.com/hpinfo/abouthp/diversity/
3. Evaluate the appropriateness of the photographs and graphic material that relates to diversity. Some Web sites will feature photographs of diverse employees and customers, yet not link this material to the verbal content. Some reuse the same pictures on different pages, etc. On the Hewlett Packard Web site, notice the photos they use and the diversity value chain graphic available at http://www.hp.com/hpinfo/abouthp/diversity/value.html

(continued)

4. Using the Web site that you were assigned for this assignment, assume that you are a) a potential employee, b) a potential customer and c) a potential supplier or subcontractor. What perceptions might you have about this organization's commitment to diversity based solely on the Web site? Looking at this Web site, do you think that it encourages or discourages diverse employees to apply for jobs in this organization? Why or why not?

5. What internal management issues can affect the prominence that diversity gets or doesn't get on an organization's Web site?

6. Are there any diversity awards listed on the Web site? If so, review the criteria and selection process as presented in the Allard article on awards or if the award is not mentioned in that article. Evaluate the value of the award through the sponsoring organization's Web site.

7. If students report their findings to the class, they can briefly demonstrate the best and worst features of the Web sites and the following question may then be used for class discussion:
Assume that you are a (female, over 55, racial minority, person with a physical challenge, gay or lesbian, etc.) job applicant and you have read ads for job openings for which you are fully qualified in all of the companies presented in class. What perceptions might you have of each company before you even walk in the door? Would you still apply? Why or why not?

8. Evaluate the appropriateness of the photographs and graphic material that relates to diversity. Some Web sites will feature photographs of diverse employees and customers, yet not link this material to the verbal content. Some reuse the same pictures on different pages, etc. On the Hewlett Packard Web site, notice the photos they use and the diversity value chain graphic available at http://www.hp.com/hpinfo/abouthp/diversity/value.html

9. Using the Web site that you were assigned for this assignment, assume that you are a) a potential employee, b) a potential customer, and c) a potential supplier or subcontractor. What perceptions might you have about this organization's commitment to diversity based solely on the Web site? Looking at this Web site, do you think that it encourages or discourages diverse employees to apply for jobs in this organization? Why or why not?

10. What internal management issues can affect the prominence that diversity gets or doesn't get on an organization's Web site?

11. Are there any diversity awards listed on the Web site? If so, review the criteria and selection process as presented in the Allard article on awards or if the award is not mentioned in that article. Evaluate the value of the award through the sponsoring organization's Web site.

12. If students report their findings to the class, they can briefly demonstrate the best and worst features of the Web sites and the following question may then be used for class discussion:
Assume that you are a (female, over 55, racial minority, person with a physical challenge, gay or lesbian, etc.) job applicant and you have read ads for job openings for which you are fully qualified in all of the companies presented in class. What perceptions might you have of each company before you even walk in the door? Would you still apply? Why or why not?

THE U.S. AIR FORCE ACADEMY CASE

Egidio A. Diodati
Assumption College

GOALS

- To give students an appreciation of the cultural forces within an organization that may drive member relationships and resulting actions
- To help students to understand the differences between organizational cultures and how these differences require a greater range of tolerance in working within such a culture
- To help students to understand the complexity and longer time frames sometimes required to affect meaningful cultural/organization change

OVERVIEW

This case provides an introduction to the diversity-related incidents occurring at the U.S. Air Force Academy in Colorado Springs, Colorado. The information in the case has been updated to reflect current statistical trends, and actions by the Department of Defense (DOD). Because of the strong military culture of this organization, change efforts, as well as gender and religious tolerance issues, present unique challenges to effective management.

BACKGROUND OF THE ORGANIZATION

The United States Air Force, originally known as the Army Air Corps, was part of the Department of the Army until after World War II. Because the educational requirements unique to Air Force officers could not be met by the other service academies, this new branch of the armed services established an Air Force Academy. The first U.S. Air Force Academy class entered in July of 1955 at a temporary location, Lowry Air Force Base, Denver, Colorado, and moved to Colorado Springs in 1958. Women, called the "eighties ladies," first entered the academy in July of 1976, as part of the class of 1980. (United States Air Force Academy Public Affairs Office, June, 2005, p. 3)

The core curriculum at the Academy includes courses in science, engineering, social sciences, and humanities. Additional courses must be completed in the cadet's major area of concentration. (United States Air Force Academy, Curriculum Handbook 2009–2010, pp. 81–96.)

Women currently represent 20.7 percent of the total 5,320 cadets. This is a fairly consistent number with the percentage of women at the academy ranging from 20.2 percent for the class of 2010, to 20.7 percent for the class of 2013. Female representation at the academy parallels that of the Air Force in general. Carl Builder of the RAND organization reports that, "due to the large numbers of support personnel needed to run . . . the Air Force, this service has gone farther than any other service in integrating women into its ranks" (Ziegler & Gunderson, 2005, p. 8). For the classes of 2010 through 2013, acceptance rates for women are roughly two percent lower than for males. The attrition rate for women seems to be fairly consistent with that of men, varying 0.1 percent to 4.3 percent. (United States Air Force Academy, Public Affairs Office, June, 2005, p. 1).

When looking at the Scholastic Aptitude Test average scores for the student population at the academy several trends come through. Women accepted to the academy generally (with the exception of the class of 2010) score better than their male counterparts on Verbal Aptitude with the opposite true on Math Aptitude:

	Class of 2010	Class of 2011	Class of 2012	Class of 2013
Verbal Aptitude				
Men	620	627	636	634
Women	616	635	643	640
Math Aptitude				
Men	656	662	668	669
Women	637	641	644	648

(Descriptive Characteristics and Comparisons for the Class of 2013, Headquarters United States Air Force Academy Directorate of Plans and Programs, Institutional Research Division, October, 2009)

Examination of high school class rankings for the cadets indicates that women tend to have higher class ranks than men. Data from the top ten percent of the high school classes indicates higher class rankings for women:

	Class of 2010	Class of 2011	Class of 2012	Class of 2013
Men	49.6%	48.9%	50.1%	49.7%
Women	55.7%	59.7%	62.7%	63.3%

(Descriptive Characteristics and Comparisons for the Class of 2013, Headquarters United States Air Force Academy Directorate of Plans and Programs, Institutional Research Division, October, 2009)

MILITARY CULTURE

Military culture has been described as "the prevailing values, philosophies, customs, traditions, and structures that collectively, over time, have created shared individual expectations with the institution about appropriate attitudes, personal beliefs, and behaviors" (Ziegler & Gunderson, 2005, p. 8).

The relative importance of personnel concerns is perhaps best expressed by Carl Builder, a RAND analyst and expert on military culture, who suggests that the Air Force worships at the altar of technology . . . and would gladly sacrifice personnel to have the budget strength to stay on the cutting edge of technology (Ziegler & Gunderson, 2005, p. 9).

Research shows that most bureaucracies, including the military, are not only resistant to change, but also are designed not to change because of the nature of the job that the armed forces perform. From their perception, change could increase risk of death. These organizations will innovate only when they fail, when pressured from the outside, and when they seek to expand (Ziegler & Gunderson, 2005, p. 7).

Geerte Hofstede's work on international cultural differences produces a framework that might also be used to understand this organizational culture. The five dimensions identified by Hofstede are:

Power Distance, the extent to which members of organizations accept and expect that power is distributed equally or unequally, is endorsed by the followers as much as by the leaders and is fundamental to the organization with all acting in accordance with high or low power distance relationships.

Individualism/Collectivism is the degree to which people are influenced or not by their group memberships. On the individualistic side, organizational ties between individuals are loose: everyone is expected to look primarily after himself and his immediate family. On the collectivistic side, people are integrated into strong, cohesive organizational groups that continue protecting them in exchange for unquestioned loyalty.

Masculinity/Femininity The dominant culture values assertiveness and competition as compared to cultures that value caring for others, nurturing behavior and the quality of life.
Long-Term vs. Short-Term contrasts a perception that values persistence in achieving long-term goals with one that focuses on living for the present. (http://feweb.utv.ns/center/hofstede/page3.html)

Although Hofstede's five dimensions were developed for analyses of national cultures, adapting these dimensions as a framework to militaristic cultures indicate that militaristic cultures tend to:

- Accept greater power distances between leaders and followers
- Reinforce collectivistic behaviors
- Value the masculine traits of assertiveness and competitiveness more that the feminine traits of nurturing and collaboration
- Avoid uncertainty, generally showing more discomfort in unstructured situations
- Espouse the long-term values of respect for tradition, fulfillment of social obligations, and protecting one's image

THE FIRST OF THE MAJOR ACADEMY PROBLEMS: SEXUAL ASSAULT (1993 AND 2003)

In early 1993, the first set of rape allegations by women cadets and graduates surfaced. In response to these allegations, and in an attempt to prevent further problems, the Air Force Academy embarked upon a number of new policies and initiatives. They set up a Center for Character Development to promote ethical conduct, established a twenty-four hour rape hotline, and issued a policy to "ensure [that] a climate exists that is free of discrimination, harassment, intimidation, and assault of any kind" (www.usafa.af.mil/commandant/cwc).

Ten years after the first set of allegations, on January 2, 2003, the Secretary of the Air Force, Chief-of-Staff of the Air Force, several U.S. senators and representatives, and major media outlets received an anonymous email asserting that "there was a significant sexual assault problem at the U.S. Air Force Academy and that it had been ignored by the Academy's leadership." One of the recipients, Senator Wayne Allard, told the *Washington Post*, "It seems like when a woman reports a rape case that the wheels get set in motion that she gets forced out of the Academy. And not always is there a similar thing happening to a man" (Cooperman, 2005). The 2003 investigation by the Air Force revealed that nearly all the women who came forward in 2003 to say that they were assaulted by fellow cadets in the previous decade alleged that they were punished, ignored, and/or ostracized by the commander when they spoke out.

> This subculture manifested itself through a disregard for regulations and the law, including the prohibitions regarding alcohol consumption, sexual harassment, and assault, which resulted in cadet order and discipline significantly below the level expected at a premier military institution funded at taxpayer expense.
>
> (AIR FORCE PRINT NEWS, SEPTEMBER 15, 2005).

Twelve percent of the women who graduated from the Air Force Academy in 2003 reported that they were victims of rape or attempted rape while at the Academy. Sexual predation was directed mainly toward freshmen and sophomore women who were under 21 and who were blackmailed after accepting alcohol from upper class cadets. Women who complained were generally pushed out of the Academy, ostensibly for alcohol abuse and fraternization—which allegedly led to the situation in which the rapes occurred (Air Force Print News, 2005).

Beginning in spring semester of 2003, new leadership at the Academy began making "sweeping changes" to the culture and environment to correct these problems. The commandant of cadets was quoted as saying, "If there is the perception of a problem in the wing, we've tried to take that head on. I will not tolerate retribution against a victim" (USAF Office of Special Investigations, 2004). These reported changes included new sexual assault reporting procedures instituted as part of an "Agenda for Change" program. Victims of sexual assault could have confidential counseling and medical care without triggering the disciplinary process and military commanders would receive notice of a request for help, *but* not know the identity of the victim (Report of the Panel to Review Sexual Misconduct Allegations at the U.S. Air Force Academy, 2003).

A March 26, 2005 memo to the then Secretary of the Air Force, Peter B. Teets, recommended that the commanders at the Academy at the time of the alleged incidents, who were found responsible by the Air Force Inspector General's investigation and a parallel congressional investigation, not be prosecuted. This recommendation was justified with the words, they had acted in good faith and were not intentionally or willfully derelict in their duties in dealing with the sexual assault issue.

> Moreover, any mistakes or misjudgments that some of them may have made are mitigated by the complexity of the issues they faced, the necessity of policy tradeoffs and compromises, and the difficulty of measuring program effectiveness. Their record of missed warning signs is disturbing, but these officers acted in good faith to discharge their responsibilities . . . by taking bold steps to deter sexual assaults and implement effective reporting procedures.
>
> (WIKIPEDIA: AIR FORCE ACADEMY SEXUAL ASSAULT SCANDAL, 2005, p. 2)

The memo went to Congress over the Easter weekend when they were in recess. Several members did register belated dismay over the document. The Miles Foundation, a group representing victim's rights, expressed concern over the inadequacy of the government's response.

THE SECOND OF THE MAJOR ACADEMY PROBLEMS: RELIGIOUS INTOLERANCE

On April 28, 2003, the executive director of Americans United for Separation of Church and State sent a fourteen-page report to the then Secretary of Defense Donald Rumsfeld that severely criticized the Air Force Academy for "instances of religious discrimination and the promotion of evangelical Christianity" at the school. The first paragraph of the report addressed the overall severity of the problem, as they saw it.

> We have investigated these complaints and come to the conclusion that the policies and practices constitute egregious, systematic, and legally actionable violations of the Establishment Clause of the First Amendment to the United States Constitution. (April 28, 2005, p. 1).

This document claims to be based upon reports from current and former cadets with some confirmation from Academy faculty and administration, that members of the chaplain's office and others frequently pressure cadets to attend chapel and to take religious instruction (April 28, 2005, p. 1).

The fourteen-page report was broken down into sections that addressed *Coerced Religious Practices, Pervasiveness of the Problem, Official Discrimination against Non-Christians and Nonreligious Cadets, Inadequate Remedial Measures, and Effect on Religious Discrimination at the U.S. Air Force Academy.* Each area of the report went into very specific detail to amplify the nature and scope of the problem.

Under *Coerced Religious Practices*, a number of critical incidents were detailed. In the first of these, a Protestant chaplain reportedly exhorted cadets attending chapel one Sunday to return to their housing and proselytize to cadets who had not attended the service with the penalty for failure being to "burn in the fires of hell" (p. 9). Outside observers confirmed reports that chaplains regularly encouraged cadets to convert other cadets to evangelical Christianity (p. 2). Another complaint was that there were numerous instances in which prayer was part of mandatory official events at the Academy. A mandatory meeting of all cadets during basic training was opened with a prayer, as were regular meals in the dining room, awards ceremonies, and mandatory military-event training dinners.

Other forms of coercion in the report included a number of faculty members who introduced themselves to their classes as born-again Christians and who encouraged their students to become born again during the semester. In one instance, an instructor reportedly ordered students to pray before they were permitted to begin the final examination for the course. In another example, the Academy newspaper published 2003 Christmas greetings with three hundred names listed from various academic departments. These individuals declared their joint "belief that Jesus Christ is the one real hope for the world—there is salvation in no one else" (p. 4). The names included six tenured academic department heads, nine permanent professors, the then-dean of the faculty, the current dean of the faculty, the vice-dean of the faculty, the Academy's director of athletics, the Academy's head football coach, and the other members of the faculty and staff.

In another example, the office of cadet chaplains sponsored a Christian-themed program related to *The Passion of the Christ* by placing a sign on each plate in the cadet dining hall indicating that "This is an officially sponsored U.S. Air Force Academy event." There were numerous reports of non-Christian cadets being subjected to harassment by upper class cadets, who often used religious epithets.

Under Pervasiveness of the Problem, it *was noted that "Violations . . . were not merely aberrant acts by a few rogue individuals, but instead are reflections of systematic and pervasive religious bias and intolerance at the highest levels of the command structure" (p. 7). In the report, these general allegations were followed by specific examples including:*

- A number of incidents in which the Commandant of Cadets officially endorsed evangelical Christianity—his own faith—and on one occasion, wrote that cadets "are first accountable to God" (p. 7);

- The Commandant of Cadets instructing cadets that whenever he used the phrase "Airpower," they should respond with "Rock, Sir!"—invoking the parable from Matthew 7:24–29 (p. 6).
- That faculty and staff also contributed through such widespread practices as faculty proselytizing in the classroom and directives from Academy chaplains to proselytize to other cadets (p. 7); and
- The conduct of the Head Football Coach, which included the placing of a large banner in the locker room that read "I am a Christian first and last. I am a member of team Jesus Christ!" (p. 8).

Other than one minor counseling session, the coach has never been disciplined.

Under Official Discrimination Against Non-Christian and Nonreligious Cadets, the report detailed a number of problem areas. First, it mentioned the situation where Christian cadets were given "non-chargeable" passes to attend religious services or religious study sessions. These passes were not counted against the cadet's leave time. However cadets who celebrate the Sabbath on other days of the week were not able to obtain such passes. There were reports of Saturday Sabbath worshipers who were denied such passes due to mandatory attendance at football games, parades, etc. The Academy makes it a practice never to schedule events on Sunday due to potential conflict with Christian worship services (p. 9).

Moreover, the report states that the Academy officials have discriminated against nonreligious students by denying them privileges that are routinely available to religious cadets. One example specifically mentioned was the Academy Commandant authorizing cadets to hang crosses and other religious symbols in their rooms, while Academy regulations specifically prohibit such a display (p. 9). When one atheist cadet complained to the Academy's MEO office (similar to EEO office in other organizations), the officer in charge first denied the complaint and then attempted to convince him to become a Catholic (p. 10).

THE AIR FORCE RESPONSE

The response from the Air Force was seemingly of substance. First, the acting Secretary of the Air Force directed the establishment of a cross-functional team to examine the issue of the religious climate at the Air Force Academy. Included in the composition of the team were Rabbi Arnold Resnicoff (only recently appointed as special assistant to the Secretary of the Air Force for Values and Vision to Air Force Leadership) and Ms. Shirley A. Martinez, deputy assistant Secretary of the Air Force for Equal Opportunity.

The Executive Summary section of the final report, states

> The HQ USAF team found a religious climate that does not involve overt religious discrimination, but a failure to fully accommodate all members' needs and a lack of awareness over where the line should be drawn between permissible and impermissible expressions of belief.

In an attempt to describe just how limited the problem was, the Air Force report attempted to minimize the fifty-five complaints from the earlier report by the Americans United for Separation of Church and State, with the statement that they were "in reality a collection of observations and events reported by about thirteen people, and purported to have taken place over a four-year period" (U.S. Air Force News Service Press Release, May 4, 2005).

The official Air Force investigation produced nine findings, which it documented with examples based on interviews and surveys from constituencies at the Academy.

Finding #1   ". . . there was a perception of religious intolerance among some at the Academy." This was identified through surveys of cadets, faculty, and administrators.

Finding #2   Although there are standing DOD, Air Force, and Academy policies regarding religious accommodation, religious discriminations, and members' rights of expression, there, "is no guidance indicating the specific appropriate parameters for either the free exercise or establishment of religion." It goes on to say, "... there are no relevant materials on culture and religion in the curriculum for new Air Force Commanders."

Finding #3   Although the Academy initiated a new program to enhance the climate of respect for individuals or different belief systems, the program is "not adequate, by itself, to address the issue of religious respect for the Academy community."

Finding #4   Cadets, faculty, and staff expressed concern about inappropriate bias toward a predominant religion and a perception of intolerance of other views. These concerns were focused in the following six examples:

- Senior faculty and staff regularly made public expressions of faith that others believed to be "inappropriately influential or coercive." As a result, some (cadets, faculty, and staff) expressed concern about the impact of religious affiliation on their career advancement. These included mandatory prayers at official functions and in sports locker rooms. A number of faculty members and coaches considered it their duty to profess their faith and to discuss it in their classrooms "in furtherance of developing cadet's spirituality" (p. 36).
- Cadets used printed fliers and the cafeteria public announcement system to advertise "religious events."
- Some cadets experienced religious slurs and disparaging remarks from other cadets.
- Some faculty and staff paid for their names to be included in a holiday announcement in the campus newspaper with an overtly Christian message.
- The commandant of cadets, at a voluntary Christian retreat, led cadets in a "challenge and response cheer" regarding Jesus. He later led a group of mixed-faith cadets in the same cheer. Some found it to be offensive.
- The head football coach at the Academy placed a banner on the wall of the team locker with an overtly Christian message. Some cadets, faculty, and staff found this to be inappropriate.

Finding #5   Internal control mechanisms to address cadet and staff complaints and assess trends were functioning, but not thoroughly integrated into Academy life. Cadets seemed unclear on when or how to use them.

Finding #6   The Academy "does not give appropriate consideration to the diverse religious practices of cadets of minority faiths." This heightens the perception that "individuals not of the Christian faith are not being treated fairly."

Finding #7   The process of granting religious accommodation requests to cadets is not standardized across the Academy.

Finding #8   Kosher meals are not always available to Jewish cadets as part of their religious observance.

Finding #9   The Academy's chaplain's office sponsors programs for religious education for eighteen groups that meet on Monday evenings. Many of these are conducted by outsiders who are given security badges to get on base. Some cadets, faculty, and staff expressed concern that this unlimited access to cadets "could be perceived as an institutional bias towards religious groups" (Headquarters, U.S. Air Force, 2005).

RECOMMENDATIONS FOR CHANGE

The official Air Force report recommended the following as remedies to the religious intolerance allegations and findings:

---

1. A policy should be developed regarding religious expression. It should provide specific guidelines to those who must exercise judgment in the area of religious expression.
2. The organization should "reemphasize policy . . . regarding appropriate endorsement and advertising of . . . groups which Air Force members may be a part."
3. The organization should "reemphasize policy . . . regarding oversight of unofficial groups that operate on Air Force bases and have access to Air Force personnel."
4. The organization will "reemphasize the requirement . . . to address issues of religious accommodation . . . when planning, scheduling, and preparing for operations."
5. The organization will develop a policy "that integrates cultural awareness and respect . . . to . . . operating Air Force units at home or deployed."
6. The organization will "expand its character development program that promotes increased awareness of and respect for diverse cultures and beliefs" throughout the Academy's curriculum.
7. The organization must ensure a single point of contact "for determining what statutorily established complaint mechanism is appropriate for complaints of this nature.
8. The organization will continue its use of "internal controls to assess climate and implement corrective action."
9. The organization will "create opportunities for cadets to discuss and learn about issues of religion and spirituality."

RECENT DEPARTMENT OF DEFENSE PROGRAMS

The DOD and its incorporated service elements (Army, Marine Corps, Navy, Air Force, and Coast Guard), as a result of the recommendations of the Task Force Report on Care for Victims of Sexual Assault as well as the requirements set forth in Public Law 108-375, established a sexual assault policy as of January 1, 2005. In the Air Force, this was represented by the establishment of the United States Air Force Sexual Assault Prevention and Response Program (SAPR).

This policy defined sexual assault as "intentional sexual conduct, characterized by use of force, threats, intimidation, abuse of authority, or when the victim does not or cannot consent. Sexual assault includes rape, forcible sodomy and other unwanted sexual contact that is unwanted, aggravated, abusive, or wrongful, or attempts to commit these acts.

The DOD and the various service elements established specific programs and, along with specific unit-level training and implementation, it set up web sites for public information and regular training, that "allow victims to report incidents without fear of organizational reprisal."

The organizations publish regular reports on sexual assaults. In 2009, the DOD reported that there were a total of 3,230 complaints of sexual assaults involving military service members. This is reported to be an increase of 11% from 2008.

The SAPR program has been implemented down to the unit level and claims to focus on:

- Preventing sexual assault
- Improving victim's access to service
- Increasing the frequency and quality of information provided to the victim regarding all aspects of his or her case
- Expediting the proper handling and resolution of a sexual assault case

CONCLUSION

This case presents, via a chronology of events at the U.S. Air Force Academy problems that have been reported in the media. The factual presentation is a function of research exploring a number of sources, including media reports, press statements, reports from private organizations, and official U.S. government reports. In addition, the case contains an appropriate amount of topical cultural organizational development research that is pertinent to this and many organizations being analyzed.

This case was updated in 2010 to reflect current research on the demographics at the U.S. Air Force Academy and to present recent programs established by the Department of Defense for the prevention reporting and monitoring of problems like sexual harassment and sexual assault.

DISCUSSION QUESTIONS

1. Describe the organizational culture of the Air Force Academy as presented in this case in terms of its similarity and differences to a typical college or university.

2. List the management and organizational forces that contribute to resistance to change at the Air Force Academy.

3. Are the two major problems in this case, the 1993 and 2003 sexual assaults, and the 2005 religious intolerance, related in any way? If so, how?

4. Evaluate the effectiveness of the changes that the Academy made after the 1993 and 2003 sexual assault scandals. Explain the reasons for your evaluation.

5. Evaluate the effectiveness of the changes made after the 2005 religious intolerance complaints. Explain the reasons for your evaluation.

6. Given the unique military culture of this organization, what recommendations would you suggest at this point in time?

7. What impact do you think that the DOD's new Sexual Assault Prevention and Response (SAPR) program will have on the culture and the historic problems of sexual assault/harassment and religious intolerance at the U.S. Air Force Academy?

Writing Assignment

Identify an organization with which you have some experience.

1. Research the culture of that organization from talking to employees, managers, researching HR policies, etc. What are the organizational values, mission, etc.?

2. Does the organizational mission address the issues of tolerance, diversity, etc.? If so, how effectively is it done?

3. For this organization, attempt to apply Hofstede's five cultural dimensions and evaluate where you would judge the organization is on each.

4. Could this organization and its relative positions on the various Hofstede dimensions have any relation to the propensity of the organization to have problems with sexual harassment/assault or intolerance of religious minorities? Discuss your reasons.

Bibliography

Air Force Print News (September 15, 2005). Officials release academy sexual-assault I.G. reports (www.af.mil/news/story-print.asp?ID=1230009362)

Americans for the Separation of Church and State. (April, 2005). *Report of Americans for Separation of Church and State on Religious Coercion and Endorsement of Religion in the United States Air Force Academy.*

Baldwin, C.C.(April 29, 2005). *A Rich Heritage of Religious Freedom and Respect.* Washington: Air Force Print News.

Cooperman, A. (May 4, 2005). *Air Force Announces Task Force.* Washington Post: p. A03.

Department of Defense's Sexual Assault Prevention and Response Program (June, 2010) (http://www.sapr.mil).

DOD Press Release. (April 28, 2005). *Watchdog Group Asks Rumsfeld, Air Force Officials, to Correct Problems.* Washington.

Dominquez, M. (June 22, 2005). *U.S. Air Force Report on the Religious Climate at the U.S. Air Force Academy.* (www.defenselink.mil/transcripts/2005/tr20050622-3104.html)

Executive Summary, United States Air Force Academy Institutional Self-Study Report, Prepared for the Higher Learning Commission of the North Central Association of Colleges and Schools (Spring 2009)

Feldman, N. (2005). *Divided by God: America's Church-State Problem—And What We Should Do About It.* New York, NY: Farrar, Straus, & Giroux.

Gentile, M. (April 29, 2005), *Air Force Focuses on Religious Respect.* Washington: Air Force Print News.

Headquarters, United States Air Force. (June, 2005). *The Report of the Headquarters Review Group Concerning the Religious Climate at the U.S. Air Force Academy.* Washington.

Headquarters United States Air Force Academy, Directorate of Plans & Programs, Institutional Research Division. (October, 2009) *Descriptive Characteristics and Comparisons for the Class of 2013.*

Hofstede, G. (n.d.). A summary about my ideas about national culture differences. (http://feweb.uvt.nl/center/hofstede/page3.htm).

Lopez, C.T. (June 8, 2005). *Air Force Appoints Task Force to Address Religious Climate At the United States Air Force Academy.* Washington: Air Force Print News.

Lopez, C.T. (June 22, 2005). *Report: Academy Grapples with Religion in the Public Forum.* Washington: Air Force Print News.

Lopez, C.T. (June 27, 2005). Air Force Advisor Chosen for Values, Vision. Washington: Air Force Print News.

Lumpkin, J.J. (June 23, 2005). *Intolerance at the Air Force Academy*. Boston, Boston Globe Newspaper.

Mount, M. (May 5, 2005). *Air Force Probes Religious Bias Charges at Academy*. Washington: CNN Washington Bureau.

Office of the Secretary of Defense, Sexual Assault and Prevention Office (2009), *Fiscal Year 2009 Annual Report on Sexual Assault in the Military*.

Report of the Panel to Review Sexual Misconduct Allegations at the U.S. Air Force Academy. (September 23, 2003). (Fowler Report) (http://www.defenselink.mil/news/sep2003/d 20030922usafareport.pdf)

United States Air Force Academy, Curriculum Handbook. (2009–2010). U.S. Air Force Academy, Colorado Springs, CO. pp. 81–96.

United States Air Force Academy Public Affairs Office. (2005, June). U.S. Air Force Academy, Colorado Springs, CO, p. 3.

United States Air Force Office of Special Investigations. (September, 2004). *Report on Sexual Assault Allegations*. Washington.

U.S. Air Force News Service Press Release. (April 4, 2005). *Air Force Appoints Task Force to Address Religious Climate at the United States Air Force Academy*, Washington.

Wikipedia Article. (June, 2005). *Air Force Academy Sexual Assault Scandal*. (http://en.wikipedia.org/wiki/united_states_air-force_academy).

Ziegler, S. & Gunderson, G. (2005). Moving beyond g.i. jane, *Women and the U.S. Military*. Lanham, MD: University Press of America.

Diversity on the Web

Visit the Web sites of at least five major organizations and examine their mission statements that address diversity. These may be for-profit, not-for-profit, or governmental/military organizations. Search other sources for additional information on these organizations.

1. Do the other sources confirm that the organizations actually implement their diversity mission statements?
2. Which of these organizations do you think seem to be doing the more effective job of providing environments free of harassment and hostility?

Egidio A. Diodati is an associate professor Management at Assumption College. Professor Diodati provides consulting services to corporations in the areas of network communications, market research, marketing, and management.

Integrative Questions for Section 6

1. How can one worker or one supervisor actually promote organizational change in terms of diversity? Consider this course as you answer.

2. In terms of the change model, what forces resist each of the following initiatives: appointing a chief diversity officer, requiring all employees to participate in an ongoing diversity training program, and offering a telecommuting option to parents.

3. Review the leadership styles and the performance of any of the CEOs from a major case in this text. On a scale of A–F, how would you grade this person now as a diversity change agent. Justify your answer.

4. What changes might you expect at the Air Force Academy as a result of the recent repeal of the "Don't ask, Don't tell" policy and how should these changes be implemented?

5. Select one of the diversity awards from the Allard article. Write new criteria for that particular award that improves the validity and value of receiving this honor.

6. What did you learn about organizational diversity from doing the audit assignment that might be helpful to you personally in the workplace?

7. Thinking about what effective Employee Resource Groups have done for businesses, how could your college or university benefit from forming similar groups?

INDEX